Houghton Mifflin
English

Houghton Mifflin Company · Boston
Atlanta   Dallas   Geneva, Illinois   Palo Alto   Princeton   Toronto

Authors

Ann Cole Brown is Director of Admissions and a teacher of English at The Tatnall School in Wilmington, Delaware. She was formerly Lecturer in English composition and literature at Northern Virginia Community College in Alexandria, Virginia.

Joyce Kinkead is Associate Professor of English and Director of Composition at Utah State University, in Logan, Utah. She is co-editor of the university's *Writing Center Journal*, and she has published journal articles on teaching composition and literature.

Nancy C. Millett is Professor of Secondary Education / English Language Arts at Wichita State University in Wichita, Kansas, and a co-author of *Houghton Mifflin English*, *Levels K-8*. She has taught English at the high school and college levels, and she has written textbook materials and professional articles on the subjects of literature, composition, and teacher education.

Sarah J. Morgan is Associate Professor of English and Director of Writing at Park College in Parkville, Missouri. She is a former Fellow of the Greater Kansas City Writing Project and serves as a teacher-consultant for the Project in the Kansas City area.

Michael J. Vivion is Professor of English at the University of Missouri at Kansas City and Director of Region 6 of the National Writing Project. He is also Language Arts Coordinator for the Center School District in Kansas City. He has published numerous journal articles in the United States and Canada on the teaching of literature and composition.

Richard A. Weldon is Assistant Principal, Associate Dean of Studies, and a teacher of English at Christian Brothers High School in Sacramento, California. Mr. Weldon is active professionally in workshops and in-service sessions for junior high and high school English teachers.

Editorial Adviser

Gabriele L. Rico is Professor of English and Creative Arts at San Jose State University in San Jose, California. Dr. Rico has served as a consultant to the Bay Area Writing Project, and she has been instrumental in developing an interdisciplinary writing program for students at San Jose State. She has written and lectured widely on the application of brain research to the creative process of writing. Dr. Rico received her degree from Stanford University, where she did her pioneering work on clustering. This research resulted in her publication of *Writing the Natural Way*, a work which has become a major influence on the teaching of the writing process. Dr. Rico holds a trademark on a clustering diagram related to her professional work.

Special Multicultural Adviser

Bartley L. McSwine is Coordinator of Secondary Education Programs in the College of Arts and Sciences at Chicago State University, where he also holds the position of Associate Professor in the Department of Curriculum and Instruction. He formerly served as Professor of Multicultural Methods at the University of North Texas.

Acknowledgments

The Publisher gratefully acknowledges the assistance of the students whose writing appears in this program as well as the cooperation of their teachers and the many other teachers from across the country who made their students' writing available for the Publisher's review. (Acknowledgments continue on page 806.)

Printed in U.S.A.   ISBN: 0-395-58425-6   ABCDEFGHIJ-VH-987654321

Contents

Exploring the Writing Process

Proofreading

Publishing

Applying the Writing Process

1 Writing with a Descriptive Focus 116

6 *Writing About Literature* 322

Theme: *Time*—how it evokes personal meaning and affects the world at large

7 Writing a Research Paper 372

Theme: *Science and technology*—past, present, and future developments

CELEBRATING **DIVERSITY** *A Brief History of Time* by Stephen W. Hawking G1

Related Skills

Grammar, Usage, and Mechanics

17 *Mechanics* 702

Theme: *Colleges and universities*—the opportunities and challenges they offer

Exploring *the* Writing Process

CONTENTS

THEME: CONNECTIONS

Investing in Your Writing

Think of something that you have read recently that you found effective: a lively magazine article, a compelling editorial, or a persuasive advertisement. Could you tell what made the writer so effective? By re-examining the piece of writing, you might point out a key feature that the writer used to make it effective: a wealth of detail, a strong line of reasoning, powerful word choices, and so on. In an overall sense, though, what makes writers effective may not be visible to their readers at all but may instead stem from their attitudes and from the way they approach the process of writing.

Do you ever consider yourself as a writer? You write every day, and it's probably safe to assume that you produce at least one significant piece of writing every week or so. It is possible, however, that you don't think about your effectiveness as a writer, and you may even try to avoid writing tasks. Now think of an essay that you've written recently—or a story or a term paper—and consider its effectiveness. Think about how you approached the piece of writing and how you felt about it when it was finished. Perhaps you had mixed feelings about it, satisfied that it was finished but aware that it was less than entirely effective.

Imagine what you could accomplish if nearly every piece of writing you produced were effective—if every time you wrote, you could count on your effectiveness as a writer. Of course, not even the most effective writers can be sure of success every time, but their chances of success are high because of their attitudes and techniques. You can improve your chances of being an effective writer by developing similar attitudes and by learning useful techniques.

Now read the essay on the next two pages. It was written by Karin Omlin, a twelfth-grade student, for an assignment given in her English class. Do you regard this essay as the work of an effective writer?

Are We Having Fun Yet?

Who's responsible for the myth that senior year is a time for taking it easy and enjoying yourself? After four months, I'm still awaiting the "laid-back" days of Grade 12--and so are most of the other seniors I know. Between keeping up with studies and school activities, pulling your load at home, maintaining some kind of social life, and trying to get a line on what you'll be doing for the next half-century, the average senior is more frantic than mellow. My personal senior nightmare has assumed the shape of a six-page form called COLLEGE APPLICATION. So far I've managed to fill out three of these bulky documents, but a pile of them remains on my desk. I truly want to attend college next year, but frankly, these applications are looking more and more like a monster devouring my time and sanity.

I understand that it's necessary for colleges to obtain information about potential students. However, little did I realize that providing this information would require answering 148 1/2 questions about myself. Tell me, if you will, why a college admissions committee needs to know the color of my eyes or the date of my last vaccination. Is the committee really interested in <u>all</u> my activities over the last four years? Who dreams up these questions, anyway? Believe it or not, one university inquired whether I have ever been involved in the Special Forces of the United States. I was tempted to write in the margin, "Sorry--that's Classified Information."

What I want to know is, given modern technology, why don't the colleges collaborate in designing a universal application? This would definitely lift a load from the weary shoulders of the average senior. Applicants could then focus their time and effort on one application, providing the best document possible about themselves. There's probably something wrong with that very simple suggestion, but then I haven't had the benefit yet of a college education.

Of course, the head of the college application monster, as every applicant knows, is the dreaded ESSAY. Yes, this is the item in which you get the chance to outshine the five million other applicants. Most colleges want you to describe your "special qualities" (i.e., what makes you stand out from the herd). Well, the sad truth is that aside from my

DNA code and fingerprints, I really don't know what makes me unique. Other colleges want you to explain just what you intend to do with your education once you've received it. Besides the obvious answer ("Pay for it!"), you need a crystal ball or a time machine to respond accurately to this issue.

I'm probably overreacting a bit here, but getting by on five hours of sleep the last few nights is starting to make me irrational. There's no way to complete these forms during the day. My schedule is crammed with six solid classes, student council, cheerleading practice, Big-sister tutoring, driving, house chores, and homework. (Is it my imagination, or are the teachers laying it on extra thick this year?) Lately I have found myself postponing class assignments, canceling plans with friends, and sitting isolated late at night in my room with a black pen and these tedious applications.

What bothers me most, I think, is the haunting suspicion that none of the college admissions committees will ever actually <u>read</u> my applications. Well--they'd <u>better</u> read them; otherwise they're going to learn the hard way just what I did in the Special Forces!

Like most of us, you probably judged "Are We Having Fun Yet?" to be an effective piece of writing. Most of us have at one time or another experienced similar time pressures. We appreciate the way Karin puts into words what many of us have felt. We also enjoy the irony and the occasional hyperbole in her expressions. Our attention never strays from Karin's essay, nor are we ever confused about what she is saying. We find reading her essay easy.

What we wonder about is how Karin Omlin, a seventeen-year-old high school student, produced such an effective essay. The most obvious answer would be that Karin's effectiveness results from natural talent. It would be easy to assume that she must be unusually bright and observant or that she has an extensive vocabulary and strong technical skills. Judging from what we read here, all of these possibilities seem likely. There is another explanation, though, one that probably outweighs the others: *Karin works hard to write well.*

Because we find "Are We Having Fun Yet?" easy and pleasant to read, we could assume that the essay was easy for Karin to write. On the contrary, she devoted several hours to the writing process: freewriting, outlining, drafting, revising, redrafting, and proofreading. When we read "Are We Having Fun Yet?" all we see is the final product of this writer's work—a lively and effective essay. What we don't see are the steps leading up to that product and the time, the effort, and the care that Karin invested in her writing. Study the next two pages to get a glimpse of her writing processes.

Karin's reactions to the pressure of senior activities gave her the idea for a piece of writing. **Freewriting** in her writer's notebook, she started with the idea that the "laid-back" senior year is a myth and simply wrote down whatever ideas came to her. Because she was **prewriting,** she didn't concern herself with word choice, sentence structure, or even paragraphing. She just wrote until she ran out of ideas.

What major should I choose... should I apply to? How am I going... the essay they want? Questions like the... designed to rattle the mind of most pe... trying to get into college... Who was it that said senior year is a... you kicking back? Well when does the... begin?

Look at all the pages in these applica... Admission committees want to know... thing—height, weight, eye color, acti... the way back to frosh year. I can... remember what I did last week... they need all this information? I... I don't know yet what major to ch... of the catalogs list 99 options to c... and they're different for each coll... fantastic. Close my eyes and pick a... Another decision to make and a... I still have three pages to go. W... homework due tomorrow? Life... to revolve around these applica... goodbye to friends, job, normal l... it's time to apply to college... essay is the hardest part... s they give you, like wh... special we should take yo... e's my DNA code and fin... t's about it.

opic – (general) pressure on time, energy of
  seniors (specific) frustration of trying
  to complete college application forms
udience – the general public (but aimed
  indirectly at college admissions
  committees)
urpose – to convey feeling of pressure,
  frustration, etc. about college
  application process and hopefully
  get colleges thinking about ways to
  simplify matters

troduction: Senior "relaxation" is a
  myth, especially if you've
  decided to apply to colleges.
Body: A. College applications ask
  for unnecessary information.
  1. seems like each applica-
     tion has hundreds of ques-
     tions
  2. what's the importance of
     infor...

Karin's freewriting provided her with plenty of ideas and supporting information for an essay. She then wrote down her **limited topic** for her essay, decided on an **audience,** and settled on her **purpose.** Having made these decisions, she was now able to draft a **preliminary thesis statement.** Finally, she made an **informal outline** of the points that she wanted to make and the order in which she planned to make them.

5

Having completed her planning notes and her outline, Karin wrote her **first draft.** Knowing that she would be spending time on revision later, she drafted her essay quickly, without stopping to polish her sentences or word choices. She concentrated on turning her freewriting notes into sentences and paragraphs. Once she had finished the first draft, Karin read it through. Then she noted on the draft the **revisions** that she wanted to make to the content of her essay.

Next, Karin typed her **second draft,** making the changes that she had noted during her revision. She evaluated the essay carefully, making additional **revisions** in organization, tone, and style. Then she returned to the typewriter, created her **final draft,** and did a careful **proofreading** to catch any errors in grammar, usage, spelling, and mechanics. Her final copy—the one that she considered ready to **publish,** or share with her readers —is the essay that you have read on pages 3–4.

6

This is starting to get ridiculous! Just when I think I c down my pen and call it a night, my eye falls on yet another s college application. It seems that my life these days revolves these bulky admissions documents. Is there no end to this proce
I wonder who started the myth
thought that senior year was supposed to be a time for taking th easy and enjoying yourself, but after four months I for one don'
days I've heard so much about.
I'm still waiting for those
the least bit "laid back". *My personal senior nightmare has assumed the*
six-page brochure called the COLLEGE APPLICATION... Whatever the college admissions commi might think, I do have a life of my own (or at least I used to). Frankly, college applications are starting to look more a monster devouring my time and

College Applications are Not Fun! — *change*

Who's responsible for
I wonder who started the myth that senior year in high schoo

time for taking things easy and enjoying yourself. After four m
a   *of Grade 12*
I'm still waiting for those "laid-back" days I've heard so much

and so are most of the other seniors I know. Between keeping up

studies and school activities, pulling your load at home, mainta
" get a live on "
some kind of social life, and trying to figure out what you'll b
half-century
doing for the next fifty years of your life, the average senior
than   *senior*
frantic, not mellow. My personal nightmare this year has assume

form of a six-page form called COLLEGE APPLICATION. So far I've

aged to fill out three of these rather bulky documents, but ther
remains   *and truly*
still a pile of them on my desk. I really do want to attend col

next year, but frankly, these applications are looking more and

like a monster devouring my time and sanity.
I understand
I'll be the first to acknowledge that it's necessary for col
about
to obtain vital information concerning potential students. Howe

little did I realize when I started this process that providing
148½
information would require that I answer [one hundred forty-eight

half] questions about myself. Tell me, if you will, why it's imp

We can see from examining this material that even a talented student like Karin Omlin must *work* to produce effective writing. Looking at the evidence of Karin's writing processes, you have seen how she developed a single idea into an entertaining and effective essay. You have seen the results of the thinking, planning, organizing, experimenting, changing, and polishing that Karin did— processes that she engaged in so that she could produce the outcome she wanted. Most important, you know that Karin made a substantial investment of her time, energy, thought, and care. She did so willingly, knowing that it would pay off. Karin knew that her own satisfaction and the benefit to her readers would compensate her for the time and effort she spent writing and publishing her essay.

We can conclude, then, that the most important factor in becoming an effective writer is attitude, rather than talent. Good writers *care* about the quality of their ideas and their writing, and they willingly invest their time and effort to achieve that quality.

In this textbook, you will encounter a wide variety of methods for developing your own writing processes. As you practice these techniques, look for the ones that work best for you, so that you can produce writing that is not only effective but uniquely your own. If you're ready to invest your own thoughtfulness and effort, if you use the techniques taught here and really care about the quality of your writing, then you, too, can earn a substantial return on your investment. You, too, can have the satisfaction of knowing that you are an effective writer.

Commencement Program

Marshall Madison High
Cumberland Center,

Processional
"Pomp and Circums
by Sir Edward William Elg

Salute to the F

National Anth

Address of Wel
Nathaniel Dav
Class Presi

Honor Essa
Vanessa Ja
Troy David Sullivan

Presentation of Class
Sharon O'Casey, Principal

Meet the Student Writer

A native of Sacramento, California, Karin Omlin is active in school and volunteer activities. Because Karin is drawn to helping others, she is considering a career in nursing. Karin offered this comment on investing in writing: "To me, writing is worth the effort because it is a great means of personal expression—a chance to convey my deepest feelings and concerns and my most important thoughts. When I write, I *volunteer* my ideas; no one forces me to give them."

Prewriting

Just about any process or task that you undertake begins with an idea. Whether you're planting a garden, deciding what you'll do after high school, or writing an essay, you need to discover what is possible within a wide range of choices.

In one sense, prewriting is everything that you do, learn, feel, or dream about up to the moment of drafting. This stage of the writing process allows you to comb your personal history to find ideas to write about. Prewriting provides a structure for making meaning out of random thoughts. It also provides a technique to use during other stages of the writing process when you need fresh ideas or new connections between thoughts. Prewriting encourages your curiosity and exploration of interesting subjects and approaches.

Prewriting

Getting Ideas

"Good" ideas or "perfect" subjects almost never pop into writers' heads automatically, but everyone has a storehouse of unique writing possibilities. If you've been *anywhere* or done *anything*, you can describe the place or explain the procedure to readers. If you've ever been entertained, annoyed, or embarrassed, you can share your experiences. Get ideas from your own plans, aspirations, and concerns. What are your hopes for changing the world in the future?

In these pages you'll learn several ways to extract ideas from your life and thoughts. As you practice prewriting techniques, you'll discover the ones that are the most effective for you.

Writer's Notebook or Journal

To assemble an ongoing source of ideas for writing, keep a writer's notebook or a journal. Jot down your perceptions in whatever order they occur, using single words, phrases, or sentences. Each of your entries should contain enough information to refresh your memory when you return to it.

When you record your experiences in your writer's notebook or your journal, capture their shapes, sounds, smells, and textures. Close observation will help you to see that all experience, no matter how trivial, is grist for the writer's imagination. In addition, remember that it's not only what you observe that counts. Consider the hows and the whys of the things that you see, hear, and think. Look for the patterns and connections among seemingly unrelated thoughts and activities.

Use these strategies for starting a writer's notebook or a journal:

▶ Strategies

1. *Jot down observations, thoughts, and activities that you want to remember.* Include facts as well as reactions, causes, and outcomes.

2. *Record problems or issues that concern or interest you.* These might be personal, school-related, local, national, or even international considerations.

3. *Take notes on what you read.* Keep track of fascinating facts as well as subjects that you'd like to learn more about. Include your opinions about what you read.

4. *Copy quotations, lines of poetry, song lyrics, and short prose passages that appeal to you.*

5. *Record your significant viewing and listening experiences.* Radio and TV shows, movies, exhibits, performances, and snippets of everyday conversation are potential sources of writing ideas.

6. *Save pictures, cartoons, articles, and advertisements* — anything that evokes your response, be it laughter, concern, or annoyance.

7. **Interpret** *what you read, see, and hear.* Go beyond the events, words, and sounds to understand them in a way that was not immediately obvious. From your new understanding, you may find ideas for writing. Ask questions that push you to interpret. Is the work (the cartoon, song, and so on) meant to entertain, persuade, or inform? Does the author (or painter, musician, and so on) seem to have a particular point of view about an issue? How do the ideas presented relate to your experience? What trends in current events or thinking does this work illustrate?

Critical Thinking:
Interpreting

8. *Create sentence completion exercises and trade them with another writer.* Completing such stems can engage your imagination by prompting you to make choices. For example, these stems will elicit ideas about connections.

I feel more connected to __?__ than to anyone else.
__?__ can connect us with the past.
__?__ and __?__ should be connected but aren't.

In your writer's notebook, keep the freewriting, interest inventories, brainstorming lists, and clustering that you will try. You'll soon have a rich supplement to your memory that will provide a variety of writing ideas.

Assignment 1 | Making Close Observations

Choose at least three of the following activities, and record your observations and reactions in your writer's notebook. Use words or phrases to capture specific details.

1. Visit a place with particularly strong odors, such as a bakery, a fish market, or a perfume counter. Describe the specific smells that you can separate and the overall effect of the combination of odors.
2. What sounds trigger memories for you? For example, describe how the creak of the stairs reminds you of your grandparents' attic.
3. What objects provide a feeling of comfort and relaxation? For example, you might describe what a strand of hair feels like as you twist it around your finger.
4. Buy something completely new at a grocery store or order a new dish at a restaurant. Describe the experience of eating it, emphasizing your reactions as well as the flavor, texture, and smell of the food.
5. Describe a familiar object from memory. Then look at the object closely and add any specific details that you might have missed.

Assignment 2 | Using Information

? Critical Thinking:

Interpreting
How do these ideas relate to my experience?

Read the passage that follows. On your paper, write your responses to the questions in Strategy 7 on page 9. Then list at least three possible writing subjects that you think of as you work.

Some kids just never grow up. Deep inside their mature bodies, many adults are still children at heart. Increasing numbers of men and women are playing with and collecting stuffed animals, toy soldiers, and model trains — whatever tickles their fancies and their happy childhood memories. Some collect old toys; others buy new ones. None are embarrassed about their seemingly juvenile tendencies.

Although some collectors are motivated by the increasing rarity and monetary value of old playthings, this isn't the only reason grown-ups crave toys. Unlike stamp collections or fine art, toys don't just sit around appreciating in value or decorating shelves. They also serve a practical purpose. Toys can offer a real, therapeutic tension release. A cancer specialist, for example, presents patients with a wind-up doll that, no matter how hard it is thrown off balance, always lands on its feet. A labor negotiator soothes tempers and breaks stalled conversations by setting a wind-up toy parade marching down the bargaining table.

Whether the attraction is financial, nostalgic, practical, or inspirational, toys are not just for tots. Those who collect them believe that youth has nothing to do with age.

Assignment 3 Sentence Completions

Step 1: In your writer's notebook, copy the following sentence stems and complete them with examples from your experience or your imagination. *Step 2:* Select three of the sentence completions and write a brief explanation of each.

1. I wonder what it would be like to live in __?__.
2. One hundred years from now, I predict that __?__.
3. If __?__ were alive today, he or she would probably be amazed by __?__.
4. __?__ is an invention that would make life better.
5. It would be interesting to live one day the way __?__ lives.
6. If I ever got to be on television, I would like to appear on the __?__ show.
7. __?__ is a ceremony that marks a passage from one stage of life to another.
8. The best gift I ever received was __?__.
9. Being punctual is __?__.
10. Speaking in front of a group is __?__.

Freewriting

As the word implies, the point of freewriting is to record whatever thoughts come into your mind — without pausing to evaluate either the content or the style of your writing. Begin with a word, a memory, a quotation, or a feeling, and write as quickly as you can. Don't worry about organization, sentence structure, grammar, mechanics, or word choice. Just get your ideas down on paper.

Because freewriting allows you to pursue mental connections, or **associations,** you may stray from your original stimulus or center your writing on only one detail. Either approach can produce interesting results. Once you've filled a page or so, read what you've written, and underline any surprising ideas. These may be the kernels of future writing topics.

Although each example of freewriting is highly individual, the passage on the following page shows what freewriting might look like. The writer begins with a single word.

Community. Plant and animal communities are ecosystems. Names of animal communities descriptive and captivating — exaltation of larks, knot of toads, parliament of owls. Ecosystem and community are the same — locality, similar conditions, common interests, certain interdependence. Even my apartment building is a community, particularly interdependent. Will never forget first time I volunteered to carry Mrs. Dvorak's groceries when the elevator broke. She was frightened, thinking that I was going to steal her food. Now she feeds our cats when we visit our grandparents, lets me run errands for her when it's too nasty for her to go out.

You'll find that freewriting is also a useful extension of other prewriting techniques, such as sentence completions *(page 9)*, an interest inventory *(pages 12–13)*, brainstorming *(pages 13–14)*, and clustering *(pages 14–15)*. By filling a page or so with freewriting after one of these activities, you can clarify your thoughts and bring them full circle. Freewriting can also give you a head start in developing your idea into a writing topic.

Assignment 4   Freewriting

Choose one of the following and an idea of your own as starting points for two pieces of freewriting. In your writer's notebook, write without stopping until you have filled a page for each idea. Read both freewriting passages, and underline words and phrases that might represent future writing ideas.

1. "The entire ocean is affected by a pebble." — Blaise Pascal
2. How does "an apple a day keep the doctor away"?
3. Soup and sandwich
4. Best-seller list
5. Contests and prizes

Interest Inventories

Take stock of the things in your life that can serve as writing ideas. By keeping an ongoing list of your talents, preferences, and goals in your writer's notebook, you'll always have a current source of inspiration. Read through your inventory occasionally, looking for patterns, similarities, and differences. Add or change categories of information as your feelings, tastes, and interests change. The things that you feel most strongly about will undoubtedly yield many possible subjects for writing.

Your interest inventory might include categories like these.

Categories for an Interest Inventory

Favorite subjects:	Greatest lesson learned:
Favorite place:	Biggest accomplishment:
Favorite music:	Most unusual interest:
Favorite people:	Most interesting career choice:
Favorite season:	Most difficult decision:
Favorite food:	Most important goal:
Favorite possession:	Most courageous act:
Strongest quality:	Most important influence:
Most important lesson:	A turning point in your life:

Assignment 5 Making an Interest Inventory

Step 1: In your writer's notebook, copy the categories for an interest inventory from the preceding chart. *Step 2:* Add at least three categories of your own choice. *Step 3:* Respond to each category as fully as you can. *Step 4:* Choose two of your responses and freewrite about them, explaining why you completed the categories as you did.

Brainstorming

Brainstorming is similar to freewriting in that it encourages your mind to play spontaneously and freely with ideas and their associations. Begin by writing any word or phrase at the top of a piece of paper, and then list any ideas, images, or details that come to mind. Try to respond instantly, without pausing to evaluate or reflect. Don't ignore odd notions — they may turn out to be among your most creative ideas. When you run out of immediate responses to the first word, choose another from your list and spread a new set of associations across your paper.

Once you've exhausted the possibilities, read over your list. Circle anything that strikes you as unexpected and draw arrows to connect items that relate to each other.

 ? **Critical Thinking:** Determining relationships

The list at the top of the following page stems from the word *neighborhood.* Notice how quickly the writer abandons the original topic, how many twists and turns her thoughts take, and how she returns, in one sense, to her original idea.

NEIGHBORHOOD
basketball hoops   pesticides
back fences   pollution
garden   immunity
smells   measles
roses   eyes
propagation   compresses
red   darkened room
pink   salami sandwiches
yellow   magazine articles
bumblebees   Norman Rockwell illustrations
catching butterflies   homey realism
Japanese beetle containers people next door

Critical Thinking:

Determining relationships
What ideas are related to my subject?

Critical Thinking:

Determining relationships

Assignment 6 Brainstorming

Choose two of the following ideas and one that you have thought of independently. In your writer's notebook, brainstorm on each subject. Then read through your brainstorming lists, circling items that surprise you and drawing arrows to connect related ideas.

1. Reunions
2. Friendship
3. Ancestors
4. Ally
5. Clique
6. Propaganda
7. The food chain
8. Balance of power
9. Camouflage

Clustering

Like brainstorming, clustering encourages you to capitalize on your mind's ability to produce ideas in relation to one another. Instead of creating a list as you did with brainstorming, however, clustering allows you to diagram your thoughts, showing their connections and relationships. For example, the cluster at the top of the following page shows one writer's associations with the word *connections*.

When you cluster, start with any word or phrase, write it in the center of a piece of paper, and circle it. Then, as you think about this idea, record your thoughts quickly in other circles that you connect to the original circle. Use arrows to indicate the direction of your thoughts. As you continue to cluster, you'll branch out, connecting ideas to later circles. As with brainstorming, don't evaluate and don't be afraid to include odd notions. Once you've exhausted the possibilities, look over your cluster and consider how the circled areas in one part relate to ideas on different branches. You'll surely discover any number of ideas that you can use as subjects for writing.

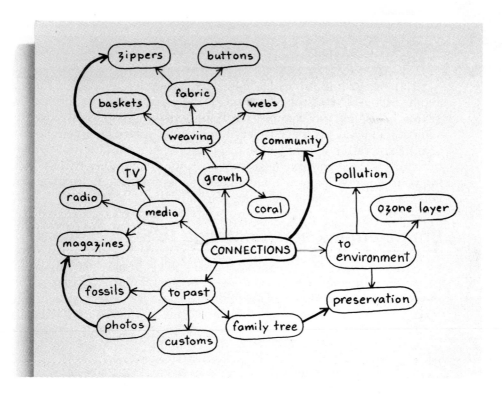

Assignment 7   Clustering

Choose two items from the following list and one that you have thought of independently as the centers of three clusters. In your writer's notebook, develop the three clusters.

1. Photograph album
2. Twins
3. Charity
4. Reunion
5. Allergies
6. Roots
7. Heredity
8. Vacation
9. Orchestra
10. Romeo and Juliet
11. Computers
12. Job
13. Patriotism
14. Festivals

? Critical Thinking:

Determining relationships
What ideas are related to my subject?

Continuing Assignment   Find Ideas for Writing

Select several possible writing ideas that you would consider developing in the series of Continuing Assignments that begins here. Look through your writer's notebook, choosing among your sentence completions, your interest inventory, your freewriting, your brainstorming, and your clustering. You may also choose ideas that have occurred to you independently. Write each idea on a separate sheet of paper and save your papers.

For writing a **paragraph** or an **essay**

Exploring Ideas

Exploring an idea enables you to assemble rich and varied material about a subject. By probing a thought that surfaced during freewriting or brainstorming, for example, you'll find out what you know about a subject and what you need to learn in order to give a complete account of it. Exploration allows you to inspect an idea from different perspectives, uncovering patterns in seemingly random material. By approaching your ideas with an open and questioning mind, you'll discover what you want to write about and what you want to say.

Brainstorming and Clustering to Explore Ideas

? Critical Thinking:

Determining relationships

Brainstorming and clustering, which you've already used to get ideas for writing *(pages 13–15)*, are also valuable for exploring ideas. Rather than allowing your mind to roam freely as you did before, stay close to your subject this time, exploring all that you know about it. Try to make all of your associations relate directly to the word that you place at the top of your paper or to the word or phrase that you circle in the center of your paper.

In this example, an idea from the cluster on page 15 is explored with a new cluster. Notice the specific details.

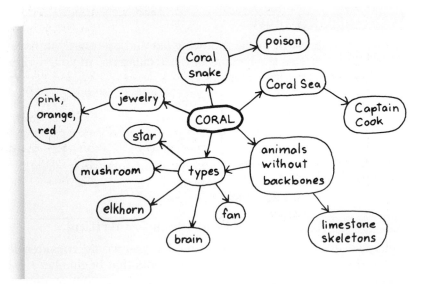

When you use brainstorming or clustering to explore an idea, save evaluation until the end of the process. Once you have exhausted ideas, images, and details that come to mind, read over your list or your cluster, circling unexpected associations and connecting related ideas.

Choose two of the following subjects to explore. *Step 1:* Write one of the subjects at the top of your paper and brainstorm, listing everything you know, think, or feel about it. *Step 2:* Write the second subject in the center of another sheet of paper and create a cluster of associations, staying as close to the subject as you can.

Critical Thinking:

Determining relationships
What ideas are related to my subject?

1. Reflexes
2. Rhythm
3. Tides

4. Anthill
5. Perfume
6. Traditions

7. Opera
8. Cooking
9. Dictionary

Charting

Charting, like clustering, is a visual method of exploring ideas. By dividing a subject into its logical parts, you can **analyze** its characteristics and their relationships. New ideas can spring from the variety of information that you uncover in your chart. This writer uses a chart to explore various tools used to connect Earth and the heavens.

Critical Thinking:

Analyzing

Tools for Watching the Night Sky	Binoculars	3-inch telescope	12-inch telescope
The moon	Can see lunar seas, some craters	Can see hundreds of craters in good detail	Can see details of lunar surface only 1 mile across
The planets	Can see satellites of Jupiter	Saturn's rings barely visible	Can see surface features of Mars, Jupiter, Saturn
Stars and deep-sky objects	Can see double stars, clusters, nebulae, and galaxies	Detail of deep-sky objects visible	Can see faint and little-known deep-sky objects

Using your own experience and a reference book if necessary, complete the following chart, including at least two details under each category.

? Critical Thinking:

Analyzing
What categories will help me to explore my idea?

	How I contribute	How I am affected	What I can do to prevent
Air pollution			
Water pollution			
Noise pollution			
Litter			

Asking Questions: The Five *W*'s and *How*

Ask the questions *Who, What, When, Where, Why,* and *How* in ways that apply to your subject. Asking and answering these questions will generate information and help to refine your thinking because the questions can't be answered with a simple *yes* or *no*. In addition to drawing out specific detail, the questioning process can help you to find a new perspective or a unique approach.

Don't limit your questions and answers to those based only on your own knowledge, memory, or experience. Do research: observe, read, or talk to someone who is an expert on your subject. Your answer to a question or your investigation of an answer may suggest other questions. This continuing questioning process will help you to develop your subject.

The following list of general questions will help you to explore many aspects of your subject. Not all of these questions will be useful for every subject; use only those that apply and that will produce useful information.

Questions for Exploring Ideas

- What are the characteristics of my subject?
- When was it formed or discovered? How did it happen or begin?
- Where does it exist or occur?
- Who is associated with my subject?
- Why is my subject valuable or destructive?
- How can it be compared or contrasted with something else?
- How can my subject be contrasted with something else?
- What controversies, issues, or problems are involved?
- What processes are involved?
- What definitions are necessary to understand my subject?
- How does my subject affect people?
- What are some examples of my subject?
- What personal experiences have I had with my subject?
- Where can I find more information about my subject?

Choose one of the following subjects and one of your own. For each subject write on your paper five questions that begin with *Who*, *What*, *When*, *Where*, *Why*, and *How*. Then answer the questions from your personal experience, or use a reference book if necessary.

1. Immigration
2. Buttons
3. Architecture
4. Wilderness areas
5. Stereo equipment
6. Maps

Cubing

When you can't get going on a subject because you're locked into a single way of looking at it, try cubing. Cubing allows you to **analyze** a subject, or examine all sides of it, in order to understand it better.

When you cube, record your responses in words, phrases, or sentences, exploring whatever ideas arise from a particular point of view. Use the following steps to explore a subject with cubing.

? Critical Thinking:
Analyzing

▶ **Procedure**

1. *Describe it.* What is it? What do you know about its name, shape, size, color, and other features?
2. *Compare it.* What is it like? How is your subject or the features of your subject like something else?
3. *Associate it.* What does it remind you of?
4. *Analyze it.* What are its parts? How does it work?
5. *Apply it.* What can you do with it? How could it be used?
6. *Argue for or against it.* What is it good for? Do we need it or should we get rid of it? Should we honor or protect it? Oppose or destroy it?

Here's the beginning of an exploration by cubing on crocuses.

> *Describe it.* Crocus: 6 in. stemless plant, grass-like leaves arising from bulb; cup-shaped white, yellow, purple, striped flowers; most grow in spring, though some appear in fall or winter. Dutch have developed many hybrids
> *Compare it.* Like other spring flowers that grow from bulbs; petals collect moisture like buttercup.
> *Associate it.* Like robin, foreshadows spring just when it seems as though it will never arrive.

If your response to a particular cubing task suggests other questions or subjects, continue cubing your idea. Remember that your purpose in exploring is to discover whether you have a good idea for writing. Cubing will help you to think about any subject in a number of different ways.

? Critical Thinking:

Analyzing
What different ways can I see my subject?

Assignment 4 | Cubing

Choose two of the following subjects and one that you have thought of independently. Write them on your paper. Then, for each subject, write responses to the cubing tasks that apply to your choices.

1. Islands
2. Constellations
3. Cotton

4. Pets
5. Leather
6. Hobbies

7. The telephone
8. Stamps
9. Paper clips

Changing Viewpoints

Whereas cubing enables you to examine your subject from the inside, changing viewpoints allows you to see it from a variety of external perspectives. Changing viewpoints may even provide you with the unique angle that you want, the one that will turn an ordinary idea into a fresh and lively writing topic.

A city skyline, for example, would look different from various vantage points. If you view the skyline from a highway several miles from the city, you won't see sharp detail, but you will observe differences in size, architecture, and building materials. If you're at the window of one of the skyscrapers, perhaps you'll see only the smooth sides and faceless windows of the other buildings and the city spread out below. On the other hand, your window might be close enough to several others that you can describe their activities in sharp focus.

In addition to varying your physical perspective, experiment with changing viewpoints in time, situation, or circumstance. For example, you might explore the subject of skyscrapers from the perspective of a city resident watching the construction of the very first tall building, a newcomer to the city, or an architect or a historian imagining the skyline of the future. New angles on your subject can unleash a rush of new details and give your exploration — and the writing that follows — an individual and spirited flavor.

Assignment 5 | Changing Viewpoints

Choose two of the following subjects. On your paper, list at least two details for each of the viewpoints given.

SAMPLE   A family photo album
 a. three-year-old granddaughter
 b. ninety-year-old grandfather
 c. antique-photograph collector

ANSWER **a.** Photos black-and-white — why? No familiar faces
b. Make me remember good times long ago
Seems like just yesterday this photo was taken
c. Some photos badly faded and cracked — worthless
Black leather album in good shape

1. A poodle
   a. Biologist   **b.** Veterinarian   **c.** 6-year-old boy
2. A sports car
   a. Teen-age purchaser   **b.** Salesperson   **c.** Accident victim
3. Snow
   a. Motorist   **b.** Skier   **c.** Weather forecaster
4. A monkey
   a. Another monkey   **b.** A trainer   **c.** Someone afraid of animals

Making a Time Line

To explore a subject that has developed, changed, or occurred over a span of time, try making a time line. Begin with a line divided into segments that are appropriate to your subject: hours, days, months, years, or even spans of years. Then use points to show relevant events or brackets to show periods of time, as in this example.

1966	NOW founded
1968	
	1ST accredited women's studies course: Cornell U.
1970	50,000 march NYC: 50TH anniversary of women's suffrage
1972	Shirley Chisholm runs for President
1974	Little League admits girls
1976	
1978	
1980	
	Sandra Day O'Connor — 1ST female on Supreme Court
1982	
	Sally Ride — 1ST female astronaut in space
1984	Geraldine Ferraro runs for Vice-President

Making a time line can help you to recognize patterns, but it doesn't lock you into writing about a development or a series of events in chronological order *(page 36)*. It's merely another technique for exploring a subject. Of course, if you do choose to focus on a process or a history, your time line will give you a head start on organization.

Assignment 6 | Making a Time Line

Choose two of the following subjects. For each, make a time line by drawing a line on your paper and dividing it into the appropriate segments. Fill in as much information as possible. Do any research that may be necessary.

1. Your "typical" Monday
2. Birth years of your relatives since 1900
3. Winners of Super Bowls since 1966
4. The films of Fred Astaire and Ginger Rogers
5. The development of labor unions in the United States
6. The life of one of your favorite writers

Continuing Assignment | Explore an Idea

For writing a **paragraph** or an **essay**

From the several ideas that you chose in the Continuing Assignment on page 15, select two subjects that interest you and that you think you may want to share with an audience. Use at least three of the following techniques to explore each subject: brainstorming, clustering, changing viewpoints, charting, and making a time line. Use a separate piece of paper for each technique. Keep these papers in your writer's notebook.

Prewriting

Focusing Ideas

Exploring involves a lot of jotting and scribbling. When you feel as though you've exhausted your imagination, put down your pencil or turn away from your keyboard. Focusing involves very little writing but a good deal of thinking — analyzing and making connections. Step back and review your notes, clusters, and lists, for you now have important decisions to make.

Your prewriting is raw material for your paragraph or essay. From it, you will choose certain ideas and eliminate others. As you read your notes, look for patterns, natural groupings of information, and ideas that spark your interest. It's not enough to have chosen a subject; you also need to articulate a **focus**, an idea that draws certain details together and gives your writing — and eventually your reader — some direction. Your focusing idea will answer the question "What specific aspect of your topic will your piece of writing cover?"

Use these questions to discover a suitable focusing idea.

Focusing Your Subject

- When you read your prewriting notes, what picture do you see in your mind's eye? What is in the foreground of this mental picture?
- As you think about your subject, what idea, word, phrase, or image keeps surfacing in your mind?
- As you read your details, which ones seem difficult or impossible to omit?
- For what part of your subject did you list the greatest number of details? What do these details have in common?
- What part of your subject interests you the most? What part do you care about the most?

Once you begin to focus your ideas, several other questions will naturally follow. Is your topic too large or too small? What is your purpose? Who is your audience? What voice will you use? Picture these decisions as threads in a fine piece of woven cloth, intertwined and mutually dependent. They are treated individually for clarity in the following pages. In reality, though, these decisions are inseparable.

Limiting Your Topic

If you set out to write a paragraph or an essay about friendship, computers, or rock climbing, you'll be frustrated, flailing in an ocean of possible details and approaches. Subjects like these are simply too broad to cover in even a long essay. Consequently, you need to limit your subject to smaller proportions. For a paragraph, closely limited topics will force you to be specific and concrete. An essay topic, of course, can be somewhat broader. For all of your writing, pull a tight rein on your topic, and your organization later will be much easier.

To limit a broad topic, use one or more of the following strategies.

▶ **Strategies**

1. *Select an example or a person that represents your subject.*

        SUBJECT Farming

    LIMITED TOPICS Cyrus McCormick, inventor of the reaper [person]
                    Irrigation methods [example]
                    Baling hay with my uncle [example, person]

2. *Limit your subject to a specific time or place.*

SUBJECT   Bridges

LIMITED TOPICS   Roman bridges in Italy [time and place]
Fishing off the Oldtown Bridge when I was six years old [place and time]
Famous bridges of World War II [time]

3. *Limit your subject to a specific event.*

SUBJECT   Medicine

LIMITED TOPICS   The bubonic plague, 1348–1350
Madame Curie's discovery of radium in 1898
Getting my tonsils removed

4. *Limit your subject to a specific condition or purpose.*

SUBJECT   Telephones

LIMITED TOPICS   What happens when you place a telephone call [purpose]
The advantages of digital transmission [condition]
How talking on the phone is a good way to relax [condition]

Assignment 1 **Limiting Topics**

The following subjects are too broad for paragraphs or essays. Choose three subjects that interest you. On your paper, limit each subject in at least three different ways, using the strategies on pages 23–24. Then underline the limited topic that is most interesting to you.

SAMPLE   Tapestry
ANSWER   Egyptian tapestries from the seventh century; "Unicorn in Captivity" from Brussels, sixteenth century; How to operate a loom

1. Weddings
2. Space flight
3. Supermarkets
4. Karate
5. Hieroglyphics
6. Handshakes
7. The Panama Canal
8. The nervous system
9. Silverware

Factors That Influence Your Writing

After you've limited your topic, you'll face three choices that become crucial threads in your writing tapestry. You need to decide how you want to approach your limited topic (purpose), whom you will write for (audience), and what position you will take as writer (voice). As you consider these three decisions, analyze their effects on your limited topic.

Critical Thinking:
Analyzing

Identifying Your Purpose

All good writing has some direction, some purpose, some objective to achieve. For example, you may approach the limited topic of a common connector, the zipper, with one of several purposes.

To inform or explain how zippers work
To describe a photograph of a zipper magnified 10,000 times
To persuade your readers that zippers are impractical fasteners for infants' and toddlers' clothing
To narrate the story of a friend getting his tie stuck in his coat zipper minutes before speaking in front of his entire school

A piece of writing, especially an essay, may combine purposes. For example, narration often includes passages that describe characters or the setting in detail; facts and statistics are included to strengthen persuasive writing. For any piece of writing, however, you should be able to articulate your primary, overall purpose.

Identifying Your Audience

Don't write to the walls of your room; relate what you write to a live reader or readers, your audience. Your audience may be one person, such as yourself (if you are writing in a diary or in a journal), or the recipient of a letter. Your readers may be limited and familiar — your classmates or your school community. On the other hand, your readers may be widespread and unknown if you are publishing in a magazine or if you are writing a book.

Identify your readers by asking yourself the following questions.

Identifying Your Audience

- Is your audience older, younger, or the same age as you?
- Are the members of your audience predominantly male or female?
- How much does your audience already know about your subject?
- Does your audience already have strong opinions about your subject?
- What do you want your audience to know, do, think, or feel after reading your piece of writing?
- What will interest your audience most?
- What purpose or combination of purposes will best suit the audience that you have identified?

Identifying your audience does *not* imply that you should change your opinions to conform to theirs or cater solely to their tastes or preferences. It *does* mean that you should speak a language that they will understand and take their experience and expertise into account.

On your paper, copy the following ten topics. For each topic, write an appropriate purpose and audience from the choices listed.

Purposes:

To inform or to explain   To persuade or to express an opinion
To narrate   To describe

Audiences:

A close friend   The editor of your local newspaper
Your student council   A college admissions representative
A state senator   Readers of a health club newsletter

SAMPLE   A guide to the most common vitamins
ANSWER   To inform readers of a health club newsletter

1. Preparing Thanksgiving dinner at your great-grandmother's house
2. Why swimming is the best exercise
3. Why sixteen-year-olds should be given the right to vote
4. The pros and cons of being a twin
5. The disadvantages of daylight-saving time
6. How to pass a driving test
7. The difficulties in choosing a career
8. Memories of your first day of school
9. Calories burned in various physical activities
10. Why high schools should require community service for graduation

Identifying Yourself as the Writer

Behind every piece of writing, there is a human voice. It may or may not be the writer's own. This voice expresses an attitude about the subject through its words and sentences. You need to decide what voice you will use by making four important decisions: persona, point of view, tense, and tone.

(pər-sō' nə)

Persona   Have you ever wanted to be someone else? When you take on the personality, feelings, expressions, and reasoning of another person in a piece of writing, you are using a **persona.** Free yourself from the boundaries of time, place, experience, gender, and age. You can be a grandfather or a toddler, Richard III or Richard Nixon, a matador or a mouse. Your only limit is your own imagination.

To create a believable persona, choose a person or a character with whom you have some direct experience — a relative, a friend, a person whom you have studied or admired, or a character from a piece of literature that you have read. Experimenting with persona can expand your imagination and give your writing a unique and personal touch.

Point of View   Writers can stand very close to their subjects or they can stand at some distance. This distance is partially expressed by pronouns. First-person pronouns (*I* and *we*) create an intimate and subjective feeling. The second-person *you* is casual and useful for "how to" writing. Third-person pronouns (*he, she, it, they*) create a more distant and objective feeling. Make sure that the point of view you choose is suited to your limited topic, your purpose, your audience, and your persona. In any piece of writing, use only one persona and one point of view; skipping around will confuse your readers.

Reference Point: *pages 536–539*

Tense   Like pronouns, tense can create intimacy or distance. The present tense conveys a sense of immediacy, a feeling of "being there." Also use it to state general truths or when writing about literature ("Thoreau writes in *Walden* that . . ."). The past tense emphasizes objectivity and reason. The future tense can create anticipation. Unless you have a specific reason for changing tenses, choose one and stick to it throughout a piece of writing.

Reference Point: *pages 623–630*

Tone   Once you've determined the persona that you will use, you can begin to identify the tone of your writing, the attitude expressed toward your topic. Tone is expressed through word choices and sentence structure. It is also expressed between the lines; enthusiasm, excitement, fear, depression, and humor are conveyed in many subtle ways. Prose that informs or explains may seem to be completely objective or toneless, but remember that most words carry **connotations** and, thereby, some feelings and associations. Compare the tones expressed in these two passages that describe a family photo album.

Reference Point: *page 481*

> The photos were faded and cracked. They were part of a forgotten time. The glue was hard and useless; they either fell from their pages or hung askew. No one could identify these people. No one even cared to try.
>
> The photographs were soft and wrinkled like a grandmother's face. The glue held them tenuously to their pages, just as the unfamiliar faces were a fading link to a mysterious past.

The tone of the first passage might be described as indifferent or even cynical. The tone in the second passage is caring or even reverent. What words in these passages convey these tones? How do the structures of the sentences contribute to the tones?

Inappropriate tone can ruin a piece of writing. For example, a letter of application written in a flippant tone could lose a job. Choose a tone that fits your audience and your purpose.

Assignment 3 **Identifying the Writer's Voice**

Each of the following passages is written in a different voice. On your paper, describe each voice by identifying the persona, the point of view, the tense, and the tone.

1.

*M*y grandmother began school teaching quite young, at a time when it was still somewhat unusual for a girl to teach school. When my grandfather, who was also a teacher, came home from the Civil War, he married my grandmother and they went to college together. They also graduated together. She gave a graduation address in the morning and my grandfather, who gave one in the afternoon, was introduced as the husband of Mrs. Mead who spoke this morning.

My grandfather was a school superintendent who was such a vigorous innovator that exhausted school boards used to request him to leave after a one-year term — with the highest credentials — to undertake the reform of some other school. . . . He died when my father was six. Two days later the principal took his place and my grandmother took the principal's place.

Margaret Mead *(1901–1978)*
from *Blackberry Winter*

2.   I've given up cooking. I have boiled vegetables until they were shriveled and hard, stuck to the bottom of a saucepan. Once I fried an expensive filet of fish instead of baking it, and it fell apart in crusty, greasy chunks. Another time I tried to make whole-wheat bread, but I forgot to put in the yeast. Last week when I baked my sister's birthday cake, I forgot the sugar and used baking soda instead of baking powder — we used it as a doorstop. This morning my instant oatmeal turned out gloppy, dry, and cold. Consequently, I'm giving up cooking, which probably means that I will have to eat what my roommate cooks or what they serve in the cafeteria. It's probably safer, however, than eating my own cooking!

3.   The summer cabin stood abandoned and forlorn, leaning to one side, covered in vines. Glass from the shattered windows littered the ground and the stone chimney was crumbling. A padlock covered in layers of rust hung on the door uselessly. An old, wooden rocker stood on the porch, covered with a dusty, grimy sheet. The flower bed remained empty except for a few dried weeds. A raccoon waddled out the front door and a noisy blue jay darted in one window and out another. The bench on the front lawn was tipped over and the birdbath was filled with green, slimy water. Behind the cabin, half hidden by a fallen tree, lay a rusty, beat-up convertible Ford.

Choose one of the following topics and three of the personae listed below. For each, freewrite *(page 11)* to "try on" the persona. Observe how the persona affects what you write.

Topics:

Classical music	A credit card	A snake
A basketball game	Hugging	Watching TV

Personae:

A six-year-old girl	Someone your age of the opposite sex
One of your teachers	A parent or a close relative
A homeless man	A character from a book you've read

Continuing Assignment Focus Your Ideas

With one of the ideas that you selected in the Continuing Assignment on page 15, consider your audience, your purpose, and your role as writer. After focusing your idea, try two or three combinations of limited topic, purpose, audience, and voice, and keep a record of the possibilities. Also make some notes about the persona, point of view, tense, and tone you could use in the various options. Save your notes.

*For writing a **paragraph** or an **essay***

Prewriting

Kinds of Support or Elaboration

No general statement, universal idea, or abstract plan will stand on its own without concrete and specific details to support it. These supporting details can take one of several forms: example, illustration, comparison, contrast, analogy, cause and effect, definition, classification, or a combination of these. As you read your prewriting notes with your limited topic, purpose, and audience in mind, choose an appropriate kind of support to elaborate upon your main idea.

Example and Illustration

If someone wrote, "Women make superb Presidents of the United States," no reader would take the claim seriously because there are no relevant **examples** to prove it. Drawn from history, from literature, and from personal experience, examples are specific cases or instances that clarify or prove a broad assertion. An **illustration** is an extended example that also includes specific details. Examples and illustrations show that what you are suggesting is true.

This paragraph describes connections between common customs and their practical origins. Notice the use of examples.

Customs often have roots that extend for centuries. For example, Puritan parents began the custom of bedtime stories by reading religious stories to their youngsters; later, during the 1800s, parents chose "classics" designed to educate their children. The tradition of a bride wearing "something borrowed" dates back to the eighteenth century; it symbolizes the idea that the couple's community participates in and approves of the wedding. The ritual of knocking on wood for luck goes back hundreds of years to Britain, where people idolized trees, especially oak and ash. Now, people often knock on anything made of wood to avoid bad fortune. Who knows what customs of the future are being generated today?

In a paragraph three to five examples are usually convincing. Find the right combination; don't over-illustrate, but don't count on just one or two details to carry the weight of complex ideas. In an essay you will probably combine examples or illustrations with other methods of support.

Assignment 1 | **Using Examples and Illustrations**

Select two of the following general ideas and write them on your paper. For each, list at least three examples or illustrations that support the idea. Use a reference book if necessary.

1. Some TV commercials insult the intelligence of their viewers.
2. The language of teen-agers differs from that of adults.
3. With my closest friends, I express more with gestures than with words.
4. Power corrupts.
5. Our culture quickly turns luxuries into necessities.
6. I listen to music that reflects my changing moods.

Comparison and Contrast

? Critical Thinking:

Comparing

Sometimes an effective way to develop your subject is to hold it up to something else and show how the two elements are alike or different.

A **comparison** shows how two seemingly different items are really alike. You might compare last summer to an ice cube, yourself to a character in a story, or childhood to spring. Words such as *both, same, similar, too, also, alike, and, each, equally, just as, still,* and *common* establish comparisons.

? Critical Thinking:

Contrasting

What if two items that seem alike at first glance are really more interesting because of their differences? A **contrast** shows how two such items are dissimilar. You can contrast the personalities of your parents, conversing on a telephone with talking in person, or communism with socialism. Words such as *but, different, however, in contrast, on the other hand, yet, whereas,* and *while* signal contrast. Notice how these transitions are used in the following paragraph that describes a connection between present and past.

Every time I see a professional hockey game on television, I think of the hockey games we played on our frozen pond at home. The professionals, padded head to toe with the latest gear, glide neatly around the rink, guided by rules, penalties, and referees. On the other hand, I remember the days we raced over the rough ice of the pond, dressed in only our sweaters, mittens, and corduroy pants, slapping wildly at the puck with splintered and taped sticks. Our rule book was a short one: Don't get seriously hurt. In professional games, when a player gets hurt, a team of medics rushes to care for him. Our medical arrangements were different. One day, one of my brothers slid out of control and fell, hurting my other brother's leg with the blade of his skate. The two boys helped each other up and limped off the ice. In a professional game, there is a clear division between spectators and players, but in our games neighborhood dogs and smaller children skidded back and forth across the ice, chasing after the puck. When I watch the games on TV and reminisce, I am certain of one thing: the professionals don't have nearly as much fun.

Some pieces of writing combine comparison and contrast to develop their subjects. As you read this paragraph, notice that the subjects seem very different on the surface, yet their similarities and connection resulted in a great human achievement.

No two men could have looked more different or come from more different parts of the world, yet they united in a single, heroic effort. Edmund Hillary was over six feet tall, a light-skinned beekeeper from New Zealand. Tenzing Norgay was under five feet tall, a swarthy mountain guide from Nepal. Hillary came from a rolling country that had cars, planes, theaters, and universities. Tenzing (his family name) came from a world with no roads and no schools, but with the tallest mountains in the world. Both men shared a love of the mountains and great skill in climbing them. Both had climbed on Everest before the climb that made history. In May 1953, Hillary and Tenzing became the first people to stand at the summit of Mount Everest. Both published autobiographies in 1955 that recreated the adventure: Hillary's *High Adventure* and Tenzing's *Tiger of the Snows*. After serving as director of field training at the Himalayan Mountaineering Institute, Tenzing died in 1986; Hillary continued to write books while serving as New Zealand's ambassador to India.

Paragraphs that use comparison and contrast depend upon carefully chosen details that are presented in balance. In the preceding paragraph, numerous details about the lives of these two men have been omitted. For example, Hillary was a navigator during World War II, but this detail is not relevant to the paragraph. Each detail about Hillary is balanced by a corresponding detail about Tenzing, creating a clear balance between the two subjects. Here, the details are organized in alternating fashion: one about Hillary followed by one about Tenzing, then another about Hillary, and so on (ABABAB). A paragraph can also present all information about one of the subjects and then present all information about the other subject (AAABBB). Choose the organizational method that suits your subject, and balance your presentation.

Choose three of the following pairs. For each pair, list on your paper at least three points that would support a comparison of the items. Use a reference book if necessary.

1. Eyes and windows
2. A paper bag and a skull
3. A cradle and an ocean

4. A ship and a book
5. Fire and ice
6. Gravity and prejudice

Assignment 3 Using Contrast

Choose three of the following pairs. For each pair, list on your paper at least three points that would support a contrast of the items.

1. Your right hand and your left hand
2. A teacup and a mug
3. A rowboat and a canoe

4. Two pencils
5. A bass and a trout
6. Loneliness and solitude

Using Analogy

An **analogy** is a particular kind of extended comparison. In an analogy you explain or illuminate an unfamiliar process or idea in terms of something familiar to your audience. Imagine analogies such as these.

UNFAMILIAR	FAMILIAR
How the eye works	How a camera works
Writing an essay	Gardening
Military strategy	Playing checkers
Arteriosclerosis	Clogged pipes

An analogy does not prove anything; it merely explains. Like comparison and contrast, it depends on a point-by-point balance and carefully chosen details. If you use an analogy, be certain that your audience is familiar with the element that you are using to explain another less familiar element. In the following paragraph, the writer explains a kind of jazz in terms of cooking without a recipe.

How can musicians play with no music to guide them? Improvisational jazz is like cooking without a recipe. In either case, the artists work with whatever ingredients are available and simply begin to play. Just as foods combine to make a meal delicious, instruments blend as jazz music is created. Too much percussion? Add more brass. Add it slowly, then bring it to a boil. As a chef cooks, a plan for a main dish emerges. As musicians play, a dominant melody emerges. The other sounds or tastes all cluster around. Gourmet chefs and the masters of improvisation may never play the same piece twice because the pieces grow out of the moods and the environment at the moment of creation. It takes accomplished artists to improvise either jazz pieces or new dishes. They must trust their instincts and follow the flow.

Choose two of the following pairs of subjects. For each, write on your paper at least four points of comparison that could support an analogy. In each pair, assume that the unfamiliar item is the second one.

SAMPLE   A spider web and a corporation

ANSWER   Network branches out in all directions; disturbance anywhere can be felt everywhere; central seat of power can see all points; difficult to build but can be torn down quickly

1. Working a crossword puzzle and translating a foreign language
2. Saving money from a paycheck and preserving food from a garden
3. Getting new clothes and learning new vocabulary words
4. Prospecting for gold and getting ideas for writing
5. How a bakery operates and how a computer works

Using Cause and Effect

By nature, human beings like to know why things happen and what the consequences of certain events might be. Showing **cause and effect** in your paragraph can provide the answers. To be effective, this kind of elaboration depends on clear reasoning. You must look at all possible causes and not jump to hasty conclusions.

Cause-and-effect support can move in either direction. You can begin with causes and lead to an effect, or you can begin with an effect and show its causes. To make these relationships clear, use words such as *cause, reason, effect, result, because, so that, since, consequently,* and *therefore.*

Causes and effects often create chains of events. For example, each effect in the list below in turn becomes a cause.

? Critical Thinking:
Determining cause / effect relationships

Reference Point:
pages 438–439

Sub-zero temperatures → Frozen water in cellar pipes → Broken pipes → Flooded basement → Rusted tools → A new drill for a birthday gift

In this paragraph, the actions of human beings are connected to a life-threatening effect.

There is a hole in the sky, and we have created it. Earth's atmosphere contains a layer of ozone that shields us from harmful ultraviolet radiation from the sun. In 1985 scientists discovered a gaping hole in the ozone layer above Antarctica. Since then the hole has been growing wider; by 1988 it had become as large as the continental United States. Scientists know that the hole is caused by chemical chlorofluorocarbons

(CFCs), which are manufactured by humans. CFCs are released into the atmosphere during the manufacture and destruction of styrofoam fast-food containers. In addition, every time we turn on an air conditioner or use an aerosol spray can, we contribute to the breakdown of atmospheric ozone. We are responsible for opening the hole in the protective layer of our atmosphere; we must be responsible for closing it.

Assignment 5 Determining Causes and Effects

? **Critical Thinking:**

Determining cause / effect relationships What are possible reasons and outcomes?

On your paper, copy three of the following items, leaving six lines between them. List three possible causes for each and three possible effects for each.

1. Electrical failure in your house
2. Closing a neighborhood market
3. High school graduation
4. Lower taxes
5. A broken ankle
6. A drought

Classification and Definition

? **Critical Thinking:**

Classifying

When you **classify,** you divide a broad subject into smaller parts, groups, or categories according to characteristics shared by members of that smaller group. For example, if you are writing about sports medicine, you might classify according to sport: baseball, basketball, football, hockey. You might also classify according to medical functions: prevention of injuries, emergency care, therapy and rehabilitation. Your choice of classifications depends on the purpose that you have identified.

Reference Point: *pages 436–437*

? **Critical Thinking:**

Defining

Whereas classification breaks a subject into parts or subsets, **definition** places a subject in a class and shows how that subject differs from other members of its class. Frequently you will define terms that are unfamiliar to your audience. Other circumstances may demand more complex definitions that extend throughout a paragraph or an essay. Longer definitions may use one or more of these techniques.

▶ **Strategies**

1. *Give the historical background* of the word, showing where or when it originated and how it developed its present meaning.
2. *Explain the use of the word* by certain groups in society and the values and attitudes attached to it.

   What is *macho?*
3. *Tell what the word does not mean.*

   A true friend does not lie.
4. *Use a narrative to illustrate the meaning of the word.*

   How I first learned the meaning of *SOS*

5. *Explain a process that the word involves.*

   What is photosynthesis?

6. *Use an analogy* to define a word *(page 32)*.

This paragraph presents an extended definition of a fish called a "coelacanth," a living connection to a prehistoric past.

(sē′ lə-kănth′)

> More than 400 million years ago, before humans or even dinosaurs inhabited Earth, a fish called a "coelacanth" swam along the floor of what is now the Indian Ocean. Although scientists have known of its existence since the late 1930s, not until 1987 were they able to study live coelacanths in their habitat. Few organisms have endured for such a long time without evolving, or changing, and certain specific characteristics identify the fish as one that has existed for hundreds of millions of years. At the tip of its snout, a jelly-filled organ detects prey. A hinge in the head allows the fish to open its mouth very wide in order to collect food. Further along the body, a fat-filled sac helps to keep the fish afloat. The fin at the tip of the tail, which waves back and forth as the fish swims, helps it to navigate through deep, dark waters. Finally, the coelacanth, unlike most other fish, bears live young rather than eggs. For this reason, scientists suspect that it may be the ancestor of later reptiles and amphibians. It is truly a living link to an ancient past.

Assignment 6 | Classifying

On your paper, name a class that each of the following groups of items belongs to, based on a common characteristic. Then add at least two new members to the class.

SAMPLE rotisserie, campfire, hot plate, hibachi
ANSWER *Class:* Cooking devices
           Additions: oven, griddle, toaster

1. cravat, boa, noose, collar
2. thread, rope, twine, shoelace
3. plumage, jewelry, façade, garnish
4. salute, handshake, wave, applause
5. zipper, staple, glue, ligament

? Critical Thinking:
Classifying
What do these items have in common? What other items go with them?

Assignment 7 | Defining

From the following list, choose four words that are unfamiliar to you. For each, (1) state the class that the item or idea belongs to and (2) give the characteristics that distinguish the word from other members of that class. Use a dictionary for reference.

1. Laconic
2. Schooner
3. Castanets
4. Burnoose
5. Sampan
6. Whydah
7. Hemlock
8. Judo
9. Lambaste

? Critical Thinking:
Defining
What class does this item belong to? How does it differ from other members of its class?

For writing
a **paragraph**
or an **essay**

For the idea that you focused in the Continuing Assignment on page 29, choose the kind of support that best fits your topic, your purpose, your audience, and the length of the piece that you will draft. Look at the kinds of details that you have accumulated, and determine whether they are best suited for examples, illustration, comparison, contrast, cause and effect, classification, definition, or a combination.

Prewriting

Ways to Organize Support

Sometimes order will grow naturally from your limited topic; your details will almost arrange themselves. At other times, various choices may seem possible, and each will create a unique effect. For example, you may arrange an essay about your childhood memory of a snowstorm *chronologically* from the first snowflake to the roar of the snowplow. You may arrange the details *spatially* from near to far as you saw them from your bedroom window. You might arrange the advantages of such a storm in *order of importance* to a child, from good to better to best.

Critical Thinking:
Organizing

Choose a method of organization before you begin to draft. Your writing will be **coherent** if it moves in a clear, logical flow with connections among your supporting details.

Chronological Order

If your details tell a story, explain a process, or occur over time, **chronological order** will be a logical choice. For example, an essay on the history of helicopters may begin with Leonardo da Vinci's sketch in 1483 and move to helicopters of the present. A historical summary may span centuries; a personal experience may cover only a few brief moments.

Signal chronological movement with carefully chosen **transitions,** words or phrases that help readers to move with full understanding from one detail to the next. Transitions include *after, as soon as, before, during, finally, later, meanwhile, next, now, soon,* and *when.*

Critical Thinking:
Organizing
What order of
details is
logical?

Write a paragraph using the following supporting details. Use at least three transitional words or phrases to emphasize chronological order and to link the events.

Topic sentence: For most of her adult life, Frances Perkins tried to improve working conditions in the United States.

Supporting details:

— In 1933 became secretary of labor under President
  Roosevelt; first woman cabinet member; helped draft
  labor legislation, build Department of Labor; held
  post until 1945
— In 1910 took volunteer job as secretary of Consum-
  ers' League, New York City; worked to eliminate bad
  working conditions in bakeries
— Became professor at Cornell University's School of
  Industrial and Labor Relations in 1957 at age 77
— Appointed member of Civil Service Commission by
  President Truman in 1945, held position until 1953
— As member of NY Industrial Commission in 1918, set-
  tled strikes, helped pass a law reducing the work week from 54
  to 48 hours
— In 1912 became director of investigation for NY's Factory and
  Investigating Commission, helped identify employers who jeopar-
  dized health of workers

Spatial Order

When you arrange details about places, objects, or persons according to their locations in space, you are using **spatial order.** This organization paints a picture for your reader, directing his or her mind's eye in
a logical, smooth path.

Different spatial arrangements create different effects. For example, describing a space shuttle from its tail to its nose will highlight its
enormous height. Showing a rope bridge from side to side will emphasize the expanse that it covers.

Using transitional words and phrases such as *above, across,
among, behind, below, in front of, in the middle of, over, toward,* and
within can ensure coherence and will signal the relationships among
your details.

Assignment 2 Using Spatial Order

Write a paragraph arranging in spatial order the topic sentence and the
supporting details here and on the next page. Use at least three transitional words or phrases.

> *Topic sentence:* Descending into the subway is like descending into
> a typical fantasy of the underworld.

Supporting details:

— Trains below sound like subterranean earthquake.
— Transit employee takes tokens like a mythological gatekeeper.
— Entrance like the mouth of a cave; people pour in
— Smells of coffee and exhaust replace sulfur and brimstone.

**? Critical
Thinking:**
Organizing
What order of
ideas is
logical?

— Stairs, like the River Styx, descend into darkness.
— Trains: like modern-day ferries of the Underworld
— Air hot and stifling
— Sign above entrance: "Entrance Only"
— Another level below first one

Order of Importance

If some of your details have more value or significance to your focusing idea than others, arrange them by their **order of importance.** For example, a piece of writing may criticize college testing programs, beginning with the idea of stress to an individual and moving to broader concerns, such as the possibly unfair representation of a student's potential.

Particularly useful for arranging a series of reasons, causes, effects, accomplishments, or criticisms, order of importance depends upon transitions such as *above all, better, finally, furthermore, of major concern, equally important,* and *moreover.*

Critical Thinking:

Organizing
What details are most important?

Assignment 3 Using Order of Importance

On your paper, write a paragraph using the following supporting details arranged in their order of importance. You may combine details in one or two of the sentences. Use at least three transitional words or phrases to emphasize degree of importance.

Topic sentence: Essay exams can be intimidating, but you can ensure your best performance by practicing a few techniques.

Supporting details:
— Allow time for reading answers, revising.
— Attention to exact wording of questions
— Budget time carefully.
— Don't pad weak answers.
— Cross out if necessary; better right than neat
— Write topic sentence for each answer.
— First, answer questions you know.
— Make rough outline before starting.
— Survey entire exam before beginning.

Continuing Assignment Select a Pattern of Organization

For writing a **paragraph** or an **essay**

Look over your prewriting notes from the preceding Continuing Assignments, and review your purpose and the kind of support that you plan to use. To arrange supporting details, select the order that best suits your material: chronological order, spatial order, order of importance, or another logical order. Then arrange your notes according to the pattern that you choose. Save your notes.

Drafting

The word *draft* is related to the word *draw*, as in drawing water from a well. This is just what you'll do when you draft: dip into the rich well of your prewriting notes and draw out a series of sentences or paragraphs.

When drafting, you are creating a preliminary organization for your writing, not a final product. Don't be concerned with grammar, punctuation, or spelling; simply be concerned with getting your ideas down in a tentative shape that you can change and polish later. Don't get bogged down trying to revise your words or sentences.

Drafting

Drafting a Paragraph

Whether you write a single paragraph or a multiple-paragraph essay, paragraphs are the most important unit of organization. Each must have its own clear scope and purpose.

A well-constructed paragraph has three components. A **topic sentence** states the limited topic of the paragraph and indicates the **focusing idea,** the main point that you want to make about your topic. The topic sentence gives your readers an overview of what they're about to read. **Supporting sentences** explain or develop what you've stated in the topic sentence. Your **concluding sentence** brings the paragraph to a close, coming back full circle to the idea introduced in the topic sentence. When each sentence in your paragraph clearly contributes to the unit of thought by saying something about the topic, then the paragraph has **unity.** A unified paragraph will capture your readers' interest and attention, develop a topic fully, and build toward a conclusion.

Notice how the topic sentence, the supporting sentences, and the concluding sentence work together in the following paragraph about the value of baseball cards.

If you saw several kids riding their bikes up your street, baseball cards clipped to the spokes with clothespins, you might wince if you knew how much those cards were worth. Believe it or not, baseball cards are hot items. Dealers devote entire shops to baseball cards, and nearly every major city has a baseball card show at least once a month. People flock to these shows to trade cards, to find out how much their collections are worth, and to search for the one missing card from their collections. The most valuable cards are the oldest ones — as long as they are in good condition. For example, the 1910 Honus Wagner card is worth at least $10,000. Other valuable cards include entire team sets and cards of famous players. Investors have paid $1200 for a 1933 set and expect the price to double. A 1952 Mickey Mantle in good condition is worth thousands of dollars. A 1954 Hank Aaron is worth as much as some cars or houses. Consequently, if you're an active baseball card collector, don't stop. If you used to collect them, raid your attic; those old cards might be worth a lot more than the price of a pack of gum.

Topic sentence with focusing idea

Supporting sentences, including examples

Concluding sentence with focusing idea

The Topic Sentence

A topic sentence tells your readers what to expect in the paragraph and how the details are related. In it, state your limited topic and clarify your focusing idea. Notice how these topic sentences from earlier sample paragraphs state a limited topic (in boldface type) and direct the readers' attention to the focusing idea (in italic type).

Customs often have *roots that extend for centuries.*

Every time I see a **professional hockey** game on television, I *think of the hockey games we played on our frozen pond at home.*

Improvisational jazz is *like cooking without a recipe.*

Drafting a Topic Sentence

A topic sentence must fit its paragraph snugly, being neither too broad nor too narrow. Often, this means adjusting the topic sentence after the paragraph is drafted. Consider the following limited topic, list of details, and possible topic sentences. Which one is the best fit?

Limited topic: Life cycle of tarantulas

Supporting details:

— Live in deep cylindrical burrows
— Emerge at dusk, retire at dawn
— After mating, male dies within a few weeks
— Live no more than 20 years
— Fertilized female lays 200–400 eggs at a time
— Female weaves cocoon to enclose eggs

— As eggs hatch, young walk away and find places to dig burrows
— Live in solitude

Possible topic sentences:

A. Female tarantulas live longer than males.
B. Tarantulas can sting, but they cannot kill a human.
C. The life cycle of a tarantula is interesting.
D. Tarantulas are extremely antisocial creatures.

Sentence A is too narrow for at least two reasons: (1) its subject is even more narrow than the limited topic, and (2) only one of the details supports its idea. Sentence B reflects the limited topic, but it is irrelevant to any of the details. Sentence C is closer since all of the details deal with the life cycle of the tarantula, but the sentence is weak. *Interesting* is a vague, limp focusing idea; it provides no clear direction. Sentence D contains the limited topic and draws a conclusion from the supporting details. The focusing idea, *antisocial*, entices an audience to continue to read to find out "How are they antisocial?" It also gives the details a common direction. Sentence D is the best fit.

Topic sentences most commonly appear at the beginnings of their paragraphs. In some cases, though, a short opening can grab your audience's attention and then lead to the topic sentence, as in this beginning of a paragraph connecting faces with personalities.

Faces are all the same, right? Each face has two eyes, a nose, a mouth, a chin, cheeks, and a brow. Despite this consistency, like signatures, every face is different. *In fact, you can tell a great deal about people by studying their faces.*

Assignment 1 Drafting Topic Sentences

The following paragraphs have no stated topic sentences. For each paragraph, write two topic sentences. On your paper, write one that could appear as the first sentence in the paragraph. Then write one that could appear somewhere later in the paragraph.

1. My idea of paradise is a dance floor with bright flashing lights, loud music, and people dancing forever without getting tired. It's a bookstore filled with all of the books ever written and all eternity to read. It's a lifelong camping trip with perfect weather and an endless supply of large, hungry fish. Paradise is eating pizza every day. It's sailing in turquoise water with all your friends on board.

2. My grandmother drove a sports car until she was eighty-five; she even wore black leather gloves behind the wheel. She loved rock-and-roll music, and played it louder and LOUDER the more hard of hearing she became. She wore brightly colored tights and miniskirts while her friends wore cotton dusters and stretch pants. When she was well past eighty, she marched in a women's rights demonstration and nearly got arrested for disorderly conduct.

The Implied Topic Sentence

A topic sentence may be **implied,** or suggested, rather than explicitly stated in your paragraph if your topic and focusing idea are clear from the content of your writing. Consider the following example.

> On December 23, 1986, the world's largest paper airplane, *Voyager*, landed at Edwards Air Force Base. On board were pilots Dick Rutan and Jeana Yeager, who had flown the fragile craft around the world, a distance of 25,012 miles, without stopping or refueling. Their journey had lasted nine days, three minutes, and forty-four seconds. A difficult plane to fly even in the smoothest weather, *Voyager* met and survived some brutal weather on its journey, including typhoons, and aerial lightning storms.

Does this paragraph have a clear limited topic and focusing idea? Look carefully at the sentences. *The flight of the Voyager* is, in some form, the subject of each sentence; the limited topic is clarified through this repetition. The focusing idea emerges from the details given: the flight was a historic first, but it was difficult and dangerous.

Narrative writing often includes paragraphs with implied topic sentences that continue a lengthy description or story line established in preceding paragraphs. They have implied topic sentences like "This is what happened next" or "The place looked like this."

Assignment 2 **Understanding Implied Topic Sentences**

In each of the following paragraphs, the topic sentence is implied. On your paper, write a sentence that states the limited topic and the focusing idea as you understand them from the details given.

1.

> *F*or a number of months I imitated the gorillas' chestbeats by slapping my hands against my thighs in studious mimicry of their rhythm. The sound was instantly successful in gaining the gorillas' attention, especially when they were at distances over one hundred feet. I thought I was very clever but did not realize that I was conveying the wrong information. Chestbeating is the gorillas' signal for excitement or alarm, certainly the wrong message for me to have sent as an appeasement signal. I stopped mimicking chestbeating and only use it now when trying to hold newly encountered groups, whose curiosity upon hearing chestbeats from a human being nearly always overcomes their instinct to flee.
>
> Dian Fossey *(1932–1985)*
> from *Gorillas in the Mist*

2.

> *T*he room into which she led Molly was crammed with overstuffed furniture. The chairs wore doilies crocheted in green and lavender and gold on their arms. And photographs were everywhere, stuck in cheap frames and propped on the table or taped to the walls: snapshots of Grandma and Grandpa in Florida, of Betty and Molly blowing out the candles on their birthday cakes, of Betty diving, of Molly dressed as Scrooge for the school play two years before. Piles of magazines and newspapers rose in neat columns against one wall, and every table, every bookcase, was crammed with knickknacks, colored glass bottles, and salt and pepper shakers.
>
> Nancy Willard *(1936–   )*
> from *Firebrat*

Developing the Paragraph

As you turn your list of supporting details into supporting sentences, maintain your limited topic and focusing idea. When you combine and shape details into sentences, you are **synthesizing.** As you synthesize, use transitions *(pages 36–38)* to connect your ideas and to signal the method of organization that you have chosen. Each sentence should flow smoothly and naturally into the next.

If you discover gaps in your thinking as you draft the body of your paragraph, write yourself a note in brackets or on a tag. Later, return to prewriting techniques *(pages 8–15)* to explore your topic further.

Encourage yourself to revise later by giving yourself room now. Double- or even triple-space your drafts so that you'll have room to add words, sentences, or notes to yourself in between the lines.

? **Critical Thinking:**

Synthesizing

Assignment 3 **Drafting a Paragraph**

Step 1: Read the following set of details. On your paper, write a topic sentence that includes the limited topic and a focusing idea. *Step 2:* Eliminate any details that do not apply to your topic sentence. *Step 3:* Decide on a way of organizing the remaining details, and use them to draft a paragraph. (Details continue on the next page.)

Limited topic: Beliefs about forecasting a hard winter in the Northeast

Supporting details:

— Squirrels gather nuts early, in large quantities.

? **Critical Thinking:**

Synthesizing
Which details go together to support the topic sentence?

— Beaver lodges have more logs on north than south.
— Snow kills many common viruses.
— Horses, sheep, cows, and dogs grow thicker coats.
— Wild berries thicker and larger
— Winters milder — possibly caused by greenhouse effect
— Frost before October 1
— Crows gather.
— Hoot owls call late in fall.
— Hard winter likely

The Concluding Sentence

You know the importance of the last scene of a film, the last chapter of a novel, or the final song of a concert. The concluding sentence of your paragraph has a similar goal: to leave your readers with a sense of completion, or **closure,** and a clear echo of the focusing idea. Save a particularly fine phrase or an especially rich detail for the end of your paragraph. Always leave your audience with a fresh, creative final impression; never resort to mere repetition.

The following paragraph explains an unusual connection between shopping bags and art. Specific examples support the focusing idea, but the paragraph lacks the closure of a concluding sentence.

Some shopping bags are no longer plain, anonymous, brown sacks; they are works of art. They can portray everything from reproductions of fine art to commercial art advertising the store that distributes them. For example, the Museum of Fine Arts in Boston distributes shopping bags printed with reproductions of art work displayed in museum exhibits. The Cooper-Hewitt Museum in New York has even presented an exhibit of the artistic shopping bags themselves. Some bags are designed so that they advertise stores or manufacturers blatantly; others don't include the name of the store at all. Offering these designer bags costs money, but marketing experts claim that they are actually "money in the bank." On their way home, shoppers are walking billboards. Consumers also tend to keep the special bags rather than throw them away; this means increased exposure for the museums and the stores.

Concluding sentences can take several forms. Which of the following possibilities do you consider most appropriate and effective for the preceding paragraph?

1. *The concluding sentence can restate the focusing idea in an interesting way.*

   Shopping bags are no longer just a simple way to carry purchases; they are a new form of advertising — and art.

2. *The concluding sentence can ask a question.*

   If shopping bags are now a legitimate canvas for art, what's next?

3. *The concluding sentence can state a personal impression or a feeling.*

   I'd rather carry my purchases home wrapped in a glossy Monet painting than in a flimsy brown bag.

4. *The concluding sentence can state a logical conclusion.*

   The new bags prove that beautiful art can be exhibited on any surface, anywhere.

5. *The concluding sentence can be a call for action.*

   We should save these new displays of art; someday they may be valuable collectors' items.

Assignment 4 **Drafting Concluding Sentences**

On your paper, draft five possible concluding sentences for the paragraph that follows. Write one sentence of each of the following types:

   a. one that restates the focusing idea in a new way
   b. one that asks a question
   c. one that states a personal impression or a feeling
   d. one that states a logical conclusion
   e. one that uses a quotation

   Something ancient is enjoying a renaissance, something that could make history more accurate and well rounded. That something is *oral history*, and it depends on the tape recorder rather than the written page. Traditionally, history has only been recorded by educated "people of letters." The perspective of the less educated working class has been ignored. The movement started in 1948 when historian Allan Nevins established the first oral history program. This program helped record the words of Mennonite conscientious objectors during World War I. It also supported Studs Terkel's research for books like *Hard Times* and *Working*, both based on interviews of working class citizens. Oral histories often focus on themes, such as music or crafts in a community or region. In 1967 the National Oral History Association was founded; it now has thousands of members.

Continuing Assignment **Draft a Paragraph**

In the previous Continuing Assignments, you have selected and explored a subject, focused your topic, and decided on kinds of support and a method of organizing your support. Review your prewriting material. Then draft a paragraph. Include a topic sentence that incorporates your limited topic and your focusing idea. Draft a concluding sentence to bring your paragraph full circle.

For writing
a **paragraph**

Drafting an Essay

Obviously, an essay differs from a paragraph in its length and the complexity of its ideas. Because you have any number of paragraphs in an essay in which to treat your topic, you may select a broader subject and a wider focus. Build an essay paragraph by paragraph. In addition to having its own unity and coherence, each paragraph must flow naturally from a preceding paragraph and lead gracefully into the next.

The components of an essay are comparable to those of a paragraph. The thesis statement, like the topic sentence, identifies the limited topic and the focusing idea. It is contained in an opening paragraph that grabs your readers' attention and establishes your tone. Body paragraphs, like supporting sentences, clearly support the focusing idea and follow a logical order, using transitions as connectors. Finally, an essay needs a strong concluding paragraph that, like a concluding sentence, provides closure and echoes your main idea.

The Thesis Statement

The **thesis statement** controls and directs an essay the way that a topic sentence rules a paragraph. Like a topic sentence, it must fit snugly, being neither too broad nor too narrow to cover the supporting paragraphs filled with supporting details. In the following thesis statements, the limited topics are in boldface type and the focusing ideas are in italic type.

You, too, can predict the weather by *making* **a simple barometer** *out of common household supplies.*

Over time, **the pet owners in our neighborhood** *have begun to resemble their pets.*

In a courtroom, witnesses swear to tell "the whole truth," but **some conversations** can remain secret, *expressly protected by law.*

In these cases, the focusing ideas can be more fully developed in a series of paragraphs than in a series of sentences. Notice that each thesis statement not only contains a topic and a focus but also predicts the kinds of paragraphs that will follow: the steps involved in making a simple barometer, examples of people who resemble their pets, and the kinds of relationships that the law declares confidential. As you draft your own thesis statements, use the following strategies.

▶ **Strategies**

1. *Decide what your prewriting details have in common, and write a statement that summarizes their significance.* A good thesis statement is *derived from* your material, not *imposed on* it.

2. *Include the impression that you want these details to make on your audience.* A good thesis statement is more than a statement of fact, a title, or an announcement of your subject.

3. *Make sure that your thesis statement is specific and is suitably limited.* It should accurately portray what your essay will cover: no more, no less.

4. *Make your thesis statement foreshadow the organization of your essay.* Word it so that the number and the subjects of your paragraphs follow naturally from it.

Assignment 1 Drafting a Thesis Statement

On your paper, write two possible thesis statements for each of the following sets of limited topics and details.

1. *Topic:* Hannibal, Missouri, today

   Supporting details:
   — Nestled in notch of steep bluffs of Mississippi River
   — Highway 61 parallel to river
   — Fast-food chains, gas stations, motels
   — Mark Twain's house now a museum
   — Mark Twain's Cave — gift shop, snack bar, playground
   — Waterslides on Mark Twain Lake
   — Becky Thatcher Restaurant and Mark Twain Dinette

2. *Topic:* Children and television

   Supporting details:
   — Average 13-year-old watches 30 hours per week.
   — '82 NIMII Report links TV violence and aggression.
   — Over 98% of population has TV sets.
   — Studies show TV second only to parents' influence on children.
   — Replaces reading, outdoor play, solitude
   — Australian study: viewing induces slow, trancelike brain waves
   — Instills attitude of "spectatorship," not active involvement
   — TV as babysitter
   — VCRs alternative

Outlining

Before building something, architects draw plans or blueprints that they will refer to throughout the building process. These plans are visual representations of what they intend to build; they show the relationship of rooms to one another and the relationship of parts to the whole. Similarly, you can find an outline helpful to the process of building an essay.

There are many kinds of outlines; four will be treated in the following pages. Choose one that is appropriate to your topic and to your individual preferences. Before you begin, write *a thesis statement*, not just a limited topic. Every point in your outline should have clear and direct relevance to your thesis statement.

Mapping

? **Critical Thinking:**

Organizing

Of all the outlining forms, **mapping** is the most creative and visual kind of outline; it invites experimentation. Use it when you need to continue to organize and insert details as you plan; also use it if you like to see the progression of your ideas grow from the center outward.

Maps can take the form of clustering *(page 14)* — with circles and arrows; they may use lines and geometric figures; or they may resemble trees with branches and twigs. For any form, visually attach every detail, fact, quote, or example to your thesis statement. You can use single words, phrases, sentences, or a combination of these. The following map outlines an autobiographical essay for a college application.

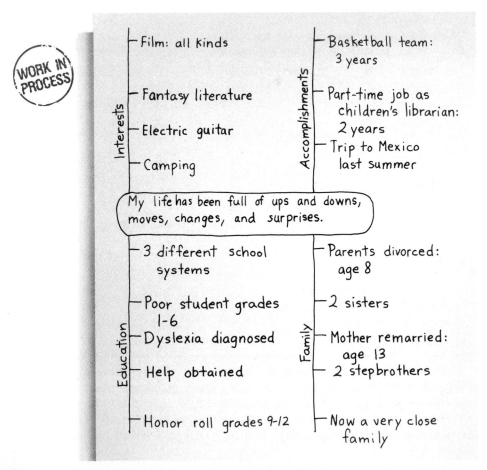

On your paper, arrange the following details into a map.

> *Thesis statement:* Because so many arteries in the human body perform such critical functions, disease of the arteries is always serious.

Supporting details:

— Kinds of arteries
— Pulmonary artery: blood from heart to lungs
— Smaller arteries named for body parts they serve
— Diseases of the arteries
— Arteriosclerosis or hardening of the arteries common in old age
— Largest arteries connected to heart
— Aorta: blood from heart to body parts
— Over-accumulation of cholesterol: cause of arteriosclerosis
— Intercostal arteries: rib area
— Embolism: obstruction of an artery by a blood clot
— Facial artery: head and jaw
— Hepatic artery: liver
— Lumbar arteries: back region

? Critical Thinking:

Organizing
What is the most logical arrangement of details?

The Rough Outline

If the organization of your essay is simple, making a rough outline is probably the best way to plan. It involves two organizing steps: (1) eliminating weak and irrelevant details and (2) arranging the remaining details into a logical sequence.

? Critical Thinking:

Organizing

Using your thesis statement as your guide, begin by crossing out any details in your prewriting notes that don't belong. Then number the remaining notes in a sequence that makes sense to you. Think about the relationships among ideas and how one will flow into the next. If necessary recopy the list, leaving space to add notes and details that you want to remember.

The following rough outline explains the process of planting a vegetable garden. The outline continues on the next page.

Thesis statement: Planting a vegetable garden can be easy if you follow a few tips about preparation, planning, and organizing.
Possible details:
⑨ Follow directions on seed packets carefully.
⑤ Plan perrenial bed: dimensions and details.
~~Enjoy home-grown salad!~~
④ Draw rows and spaces between rows to scale.

② *Vigorously hoe and then rake soil.*
⑥ *Plan annuals in separate space.*
⑦ *Use string and poles to mark off rows before planting.*
~~*Thin seedlings to recommended distances*~~
③ *Draw plan of garden on paper.*
⑧ *Use 3×5 cards to label each row.*
~~*Can grow a small garden in a windowbox.*~~
① *Have soil tested; recommended fertilizer*

Assignment 3 Making a Rough Outline

? Critical Thinking:

Organizing
What is the
most logical
arrangement of
details?

On your paper, copy the following thesis statement and the list of details. Then cross out any details that do not relate to the thesis statement. Finally, number the remaining details in the order that makes sense for their presentation.

Thesis statement: Looking out the window of a city skyscraper, I feel as though I can see the whole world.

Supporting details:
— Roofs with exhausts, skylights, occasional gardens
— Pedestrians like insects
— Sun pours through crack in dark clouds.
— 19 floors below mine
— Rose of sunset meeting blue-gray of hills
— Edges of city — chips of color (mosaics?)
— Tiny cars on highways and streets
— Can't see harbor, wrong side of building
— Beyond dark clouds is clear blue sky, puffs of white.
— Jets poke through clouds.
— Blue hills beyond city like huge giants lying down to rest
— Dark clouds above horizon seal in city.

The Topic Outline

? Critical Thinking:

Organizing

A **topic outline** uses headings, subheadings, Roman and Arabic numerals, and letters to organize the relationships and the progression of your ideas. Use these guidelines to develop a topic outline.

▶ **Strategies**

1. *Write your thesis statement at the top of your paper.*
2. *Write the main ideas from your notes* as the **main headings** of your outline. Think of these headings as whole paragraphs or as blocks of two or three paragraphs. Number them with Roman numerals.

3. *List the introductory and the concluding paragraphs of your essay as main headings.* Identify the introduction with the Roman numeral I and the conclusion with the last Roman numeral.

4. *Fill in the supporting details for each Roman-numeral heading.* Identify these **subheadings** with capital letters. Indent them beneath the Roman-numeral headings. Think of subheadings as representing sentences in a paragraph.

5. *Add supporting details for each subheading if you wish your outline to be specific.* Identify these details with Arabic numerals and, if you have even more specific details, use lower-case letters.

6. *Review your outline.* Make sure that each subheading supports its main heading and that each main heading supports the thesis statement. Make sure that each section has at least two headings; that is, each *I* needs a *II*, each *A* needs a *B*, and so forth.

Notice how these strategies are used in the following topic outline about the connection between the mind and the body.

```
Thesis statement:  Researchers have proven that emotions
affect the body's immune system.

  I.  Introduction
 II.  Loneliness--negative effects on health
      A.  Family ties
      B.  Social Activities
      C.  Retirement communities
      D.  Pets
III.  Feeling control over one's life
      A.  Intensive care patients--depression
      B.  More control--longer life, fewer illnesses
 IV.  Stress
      A.  Holmes and Rahe stress-rating scale
      B.  Ailments with direct connections
      C.  Study of air traffic controllers
      D.  Cause--chemicals shut down immune system
  V.  Positive emotions--good health
      A.  Relaxation therapy
      B.  Art and Music
      C.  Exercise and dance
      D.  Programs that foster relationships
 VI.  Norman Cousins
      A.  Life-threatening illness
          1.  Anecdote
          2.  Vitamin C and laughter
      B.  Recovery
          1.  Resumed busy life
          2.  Wrote book
VII.  Conclusion--future?
```

On your paper, copy the following partially completed topic outline. Insert the missing main headings, subheadings, and details from the list that precedes the outline.

Thesis statement: The Bushmen of the Kalahari Desert provide archeologists with insight into early cultures and their major goals: survival and pleasure.

Headings, subheadings, and details:
— Rainfall in short season in summer — 13″ at most
— Excellent musicians
— Combination of sounds, clicks, and syllables
— Sweet outer husks boiled for gruel
— Food
— Antelope — a prestigious kill
— Hundreds of signs understood by all members of group
— Musical bow like two flutes played together
— Dances: some all night
— Pools below surface in clefts in rocks

   I. Introduction

  II. Finding water
     A. Most of the year, little or no rain
     B.   ?
     C. Wring pulp of plants that store water in roots
     D.   ?

 III.   ?
     A. Plants as most of diet
     B. Mungongo nuts — staple — gathered by women
        1.   ?
        2. Grow along sand dunes
     C. Men as hunters
        1. Common prey — hares, guinea fowl
        2.   ?

 IV. Communication
     A. Chatterlike language
     B.   ?
     C. Use sign language when hunting
        1. Use hands, arms to depict animals
        2.   ?

  V. Recreation and relaxation
     A.   ?
        1. Singing and clapping
        2. Thumb pianos
        3.   ?

B. Dancing when food is abundant
1. Magical and medical functions too
2. Accompanied by jokes, storytelling
3. __?__

VI. Conclusion

The Sentence Outline

You can think of the sentence outline as an expansion of the topic outline. It uses complete sentences instead of words and phrases. Some writers find this cumbersome; others find it useful since it combines outlining and much of drafting into one step.

In the following example, expressing the ideas in phrases and words might have been difficult. Casting complex details into sentences allows you to see how they will relate and connect.

Thesis statement: The history of printing techniques illustrates publishers' two main concerns: ease and speed.

I. Introduction
II. Johann Gutenberg of Germany invented movable type in 1440.
   A. His press used "punches," bars of steel with letters engraved on their ends.
   B. A skilled hand caster could set 4000 characters a day.
   C. Gutenberg's technique didn't change much for the next four and a half centuries.
III. In 1884, Mergenthaler developed a Linotype machine that could set an entire line of type in a single operation.
   A. Mechanized typesetting can set fifteen to sixteen newspaper lines per minute.
   B. This advance resulted in a tremendous expansion in all printing fields.
IV. In 1950 the first successful phototypesetter applied photographic principles to the printing process.
   A. Phototypesetters use printing plates instead of metal type.
   B. They increased productivity to about thirty newspaper lines per minute.
V. Today, computerized typesetters have increased output ten times over.
   A. Computer programs store various type styles, illustrations, and formats.
   B. Characters and images are flashed on a cathode ray tube as editors "set the type."
VI. Conclusion

On your paper, use the following headings, subheadings, and details to write a sentence outline that has a logical order. Use at least two subheadings for each main heading and two details, if any, for each subheading.

Thesis statement: Winslow Homer's entire life was directed toward being a New England landscape painter.

Headings:

Later years as painter   Introduction
Younger years as illustrator   Conclusion
Childhood and early years

Subheadings:

At age 21 sold first illustration to *Harper's Weekly*
Painted during summer wanderings, from Maine to North Carolina
Born February 24, 1836, in Massachusetts
Sent by *Harper's* to Civil War front to do illustrations
Civil War illustrations outstanding in realism
Painted unsentimentalized country life scenes
Watercolors began at age 37, became modern master
Almost entirely self-taught
Apprenticed at age 19 to Boston lithographer
Wood engravings used to reproduce many illustrations

Details:

Uncouth rural figures in tattered clothes
Illustrations of soldiers' everyday camp life
Avoided romanticized view of war
Painted haymakers, farmers' wives, children in fields

Parts of an Essay

Like paragraphs, essays have a three-part organization: the introductory paragraph, the supporting body paragraphs, and the concluding paragraph. Smooth transitions through the three parts are crucial to the success of a longer, more complex piece of writing. Draft your paragraphs, and then pay particular attention to the connections from one to another.

The Introductory Paragraph

Have you ever picked up an essay or a story and put it down after reading only the first few sentences? Introductions can make or break an essay. They should attract attention and arouse curiosity. Grab your readers with a surprising statistic, a humorous anecdote, or a lively quotation. Make sure, also, that your opening is consistent in tone with the rest of your essay.

Once you have their attention, hand your readers your thesis statement. It will point their reading in your intended direction.

These introductory paragraphs use a variety of techniques to catch and hold their readers' interest. The first uses humor and hyperbole *(page 93)* to introduce a moving personal essay expressing a change of heart about summer.

*I*t has taken me a good number of years to come to any measure of respect for summer. I was, being May-born, literally an "infant of the spring" and, during the later childhood years, tended, for some reason or other, to rather worship the cold aloofness of winter. The adolescence, admittedly lingering still, brought the traditional passionate commitment to melancholy autumn — and all that. For the longest kind of time I simply thought that *summer* was a mistake.

Lorraine Hansberry *(1930–1965)*
from *To Be Young, Gifted, and Black*

Sometimes a single word can have so much connotative weight that it conveys an entire focusing idea. This introductory paragraph to an essay about Little League baseball begins with a simple historical fact, but consider what this writer does with the judgmental word *monster*.

*I*n 1939, Little League baseball was organized by Bert and George Bebble and Carl Stotz of Williamsport, Pa. What they had in mind in organizing this kid's baseball program, I'll never know. But I'm sure they never visualized the monster it would grow into.

Robin Roberts *(1926–   )*
from "Strike Out Little League"

This writer begins with a call to action followed by a new definition of an old, familiar word.

*O*ne of the major pleasures in life is appetite, and one of our major duties should be to preserve it. Appetite is the keenness of living; it is one of the senses that tells you that you are still curious to exist, that you still have an edge on your longings and want to bite into the world and taste its multitudinous flavours and juices.

Laurie Lee *(1914–   )*
from "Appetite"

This writer begins with a personal anecdote. Notice how the paragraph narrows to the focusing idea, its final phrase.

> I slid off the ski lift, skidded across the crusty snow and collapsed. Tangled in a jumble of skis, poles, and pole straps, I struggled to a sitting position. I tried kneeling and fell down again. I quickly realized that it was impossible for me to get up. People behind glided off the chair lift and swept by me with ease. Others stopped to watch, amused. They'd all been there before; lying in a heap in the snow was the first step in learning to ski.

Assignment 6 The Introductory Paragraph

Each of these introductory paragraphs needs a thesis statement in one of the locations indicated by a blank. From the three choices after each paragraph, select the most appropriate thesis statement, and write the letter on your paper. Then write the number of the position that you think is most appropriate.

1. <u>(1)</u> Infernos swept across 3.7 million acres in the western United States. <u>(2)</u> Nearly one million acres were destroyed in Yellowstone National Park alone, and firefighting efforts involved 30,000 people and cost $600 million. <u>(3)</u> Not since the early 1700s had such a vast area of the country been destroyed by fire. <u>(4)</u>
    a. The smoke from these fires drifted across the nation from coast to coast.
    b. The forest fires of 1988 caused unprecedented destruction and expense.
    c. Forest fires can cause great damage.

2. <u>(1)</u> Lydia is ninety-five years old. <u>(2)</u> She lives alone. <u>(3)</u> She orders her groceries and medicine over the telephone. <u>(4)</u> She and two friends call each other every day just to check up and chat. <u>(5)</u> In case of an emergency, Lydia has a telephone beside her bed, and the touch of one programmed button will alert the local hospital. <u>(6)</u> Her extended family of over fifty relatives call her often so she knows she's never forgotten. <u>(7)</u>
    a. At this old age, Lydia is still independent and active.
    b. Lydia uses the telephone in many ways.
    c. For Lydia and others like her, the telephone is a life line to the outside world.

Body Paragraphs

Once you've drafted your opening paragraph, draw on your notes and outline to draft the supporting body paragraphs. Continue the tone that you've established in your opening, and always keep your audience clearly in mind. Serve your purpose and your focusing idea as you **synthesize** your ideas into sentences and your sentences into paragraphs.

Critical Thinking:
Synthesizing

As you draft the body of your essay paragraph by paragraph, make sure that each has a clearly stated or implied topic sentence *(pages 40–42)*, ample supporting sentences, and a concluding sentence. In an essay, the concluding sentence of each body paragraph has an additional duty: it should lead the reader naturally to the next paragraph. Use transitions *(pages 36–38)* to connect your paragraphs.

An essay will usually use a combination of patterns of organization to support its thesis statement. For example, if you were writing an essay on the women's movement in the United States, you could arrange the paragraphs chronologically on a time line as they are on page 21. Each paragraph, then, could discuss the significance of an event with its details arranged from least important to most important.

Let your outline be a guide, not a dictator. If new ideas occur to you, explore them by returning to prewriting techniques *(pages 8–15)*. If sections of your outline seem weak, make additions and adjustments.

As you draft an essay, always keep your purpose, audience, voice, and focusing idea uppermost in your mind. Every sentence that you draft should clearly support these choices.

Assignment 7 **Drafting the Body Paragraphs**

On your paper, write three body paragraphs to follow this opening paragraph. Use the points from the outline given, adding any necessary details from your own imagination. Match the tone and the style of the opening paragraph, and use transitional words and phrases to ease the flow of ideas in the paragraphs.

> **Critical Thinking:**
> **Synthesizing** How can I combine ideas into a logical whole?

> It was love at first sight. She is gorgeous: perfect body, perfect personality. I spent my entire savings account on her, but she is worth every cent. The thought of her makes my head swim and my knees buckle. The sight of her, her smells, her sounds all drive me wild. I confess: I am hopelessly and obsessively in love with my new car.

I. Interior
   A. Black leather upholstery
   B. Bucket seats
   C. Tinted windows
   D. Stereo system
   E. Air conditioning
   F. Four-on-the-floor
   G. Cruise control

II. Exterior
   A. Red paint with black pin stripes
   B. Retractable headlights
   C. Electric sunroof
   D. Steel-belted radial tires with custom wheel covers

III. V-8 engine
    A. Fuel injection
    B. Dual exhaust
    C. Idles soundlessly

IV. Conclusion

The Concluding Paragraph

Like a concluding sentence of a paragraph, a concluding paragraph of an essay should convey a sense of closure *(page 44)* and contain a clear echo of the thesis statement.

Your concluding paragraph need not be dramatic or loud; neither should it be a repetition of your opening paragraph. Be creative. Pick up a thread from your opening paragraph and return your reader to your focusing idea; make your last effort strong and clear.

The techniques for drafting a concluding sentence of a paragraph *(pages 44–45)* also apply to drafting a concluding paragraph. Additionally, when you write an essay, you can save a series of details to wrap up the essay and lead to an echo of your thesis statement.

The following paragraph concludes the essay whose opening paragraph appears on page 56. The pronoun *That* in the first sentence has the entire essay as its antecedent; it gathers into one word all the paragraphs that precede it. Notice, too, how the phrase *lying in a heap in the snow* recalls the action in the first paragraph, and *was there once too* echoes the clause *They'd all been there before* in the opening. This echo brings the essay full circle.

> That was five years ago. After a few ski lessons, I went back to the mountain again and again to practice. I learned how to snowplow, then how to turn and stop. I progressed from the novice slopes to the intermediate slopes. Now I do smooth, easy parallel turns down the most difficult slopes. I know that beginners, nervous and shivering, look down from the chairlift with envy as I glide down the mountain. Whenever I see one of them lying in a heap in the snow, I stop to see if I can help. After all, I was there once too.

Assignment 8 The Concluding Paragraph

For each of the following paragraphs, on your paper write one of these phrases to show which method or methods the paragraph uses for its conclusion.

Restates focusing idea in a new way   *Asks a question*
Gives a personal impression   *Calls for action*
Draws a logical conclusion   *Adds additional details*

1.   As I stood at the window of the skyscraper, I leaned against the cool glass. I felt as though I could step right out into the sky. If the world seemed so peaceful and silent from twenty stories above, I wondered, how must it look from space?

2. The life is disappearing from the centers of small towns as shopping malls emerge along strips of highway outside the towns. No one sits on the park benches at lunch time. No one slides into the booth at the downtown diner for a toasted cheese sandwich and a chat with the cook. No one stops to buy fresh flowers at the flower stand. If we don't stop the proliferation of malls, we will lose the heart of our small towns.

3. Some people believe that building a new school in our town is necessary. Others believe that the current population boom will decline in a few years and the proposed new school will eventually stand empty. The fact is, no matter what the townspeople decide, it is too late for those of us who are in school now.

Analyzing a Complete Essay

Before you draft your own essay, study the following annotated essay. It was developed from the topic outline on page 51 that explores the connections between body and mind.

Is Laughter the Best Medicine?

Questions narrow readers' focus.

Was your last cold preceded by feelings of loneliness, depression, or anxiety? Have you ever suffered a serious illness on the heels of a major family crisis? These common situations are not mere coincidence. Researchers have been studying the link between mind and body for the past ten years. Through experimentation, they have demonstrated that emotions affect the immune system, the organs, glands, and cells that the body uses to fight infection.

Thesis statement

Because of this mind-body connection, negative emotions can promote illness, and positive emotions can foster good health.

Topic sentence introduces order of importance.

Scientists now believe that loneliness, or social isolation, is one of the greatest risks to a person's health. One

Example #1

study has shown that people with close ties to their families have fewer cases of heart disease than people whose families are scattered. Doctors may prescribe involvement in a social

Example #2

club or organization, volunteer work, or even shopping or a bridge game as steps to better health. Retirement communities

Example #3

offer elderly people the opportunity to socialize. Even own-

Example #4

ing a pet can provide isolated persons with companionship and affection, and hence, better health.

Transition to
next paragraph
—Another contributor to poor health is feeling a lack of control over one's life. Patients in intensive care units suddenly have little control over their diets, their routines, and even their ability to sleep and move around. They often fall into deep depressions and develop resulting side illnesses. On the other hand, even institutionalized persons who have some say in their daily diets and activities have fewer illnesses and live longer.

Transition to
next paragraph
—Poor health can also be the direct result of high stress. Two psychiatrists, Thomas Holmes and Richard Rahe, have compiled a stress-rating scale that ranks common experiences on a numerical scale of Life Change Units. The death of a spouse ranks highest (100), and forty-three factors follow in descending order, including marriage (50), change in job (36), change in schools (20), and even minor law violations (11).

Specific
example
Ailments such as headaches, backaches, ulcers, and high blood pressure have undisputed connections with accumulated stress. One study involving one of the most stressful professions, air traffic controllers, showed that these individuals exhibit four times more cases of high blood pressure and twice as many instances of diabetes and ulcers as their pilot counterparts.

Cause and
effect
Why? Chronic stress causes the adrenal gland to release into the bloodstream chemical messengers that shut down the immune system. In addition to poor eating and sleeping habits that usually accompany periods of high stress, this shutdown can lead quickly to illness. Illness, in turn, causes more stress, and the cycle continues.

Transition
between
paragraphs
—If all of this sounds hopeless, don't despair. There is a positive flip side to these recent discoveries. Since negative emotions contribute to illness, researchers look for ways to create positive emotions that will lead to good health.

Supporting
examples
Some physicians use relaxation therapy to help patients overcome insomnia and migraine headaches. Art and music therapies

give patients creative outlets for stress. Physical exercise
and dance can contribute to a positive outlook and in turn
contribute to a healthier body. Certain programs even pair
children with elderly people, creating revitalizing relationships for both that can create well-being.

Of all the specific testimonies to the connection between
good health and positive attitude, that of Norman Cousins is
the most dramatic. Cousins is often described as the man who
laughed his way to health. In the mid-'60s, the author/editor
was diagnosed as having a life-threatening disease that left
him almost completely paralyzed. He was given only a few
months to live. Instead of following the traditional medical
treatments, he developed his own, based on a firm belief in
the mind-body link. Combined with high doses of Vitamin C,
Cousins exposed himself to high doses of humor: old "Candid
Camera" tapes, Marx Brothers movies, and books by Robert
Benchley and James Thurber. "I made the joyous discovery that
ten minutes of genuine belly laughter had an anesthetic effect
and would give me two hours of pain-free sleep," writes
Cousins in *Anatomy of an Illness*. His condition steadily improved; Cousins slowly regained control of his limbs and resumed his busy life.

As Cousins notes in his book, "the will to live is not a
theoretical abstraction, but a physiologic reality with therapeutic characteristics." What does all this mean for the future of medicine? Some scientists believe that someday we
will actually be able to train the immune system to prevent
illness and even to repair damaged tissue. "Emotions affect
wound healing," reports scientist Theodore Melnechuck, "We are
beginning to see a parallel story in repair of tissue." Maybe
laughter, combined with factors such as security, autonomy,
and companionship, really is the best prescription.

Supporting examples

Movement to a specific example

Anecdote: arranged in chronological order

Quotation adds variety and authority.

Transition between paragraphs

Question echoes opening paragraph.

Echo of title

For writing
an **essay**

In the Continuing Assignments on pages 22, 29, 36, and 38, you have selected and explored a subject, focused your topic, and decided on kinds of support and a method of organizing your support. *Step 1:* Review your prewriting material, and write a thesis statement that includes both your limited topic and your focusing idea. *Step 2:* Make a map, a rough outline, a sentence outline, or a topic outline to organize your ideas. *Step 3:* Draft your essay. Be sure that your introductory paragraph grabs your readers' attention and clearly states your limited topic and your focusing idea. Your body paragraphs should develop your thesis statement, and your concluding paragraph should achieve closure while maintaining your readers' interest. Save your notes and your draft.

Revising

The words *visible*, *vision*, and *visit* derive from the Latin verb *videre*, meaning "to see." Now that you've drafted your paragraph or essay, it's time to re-see, or revise, your writing by looking at it in a new way.

At this stage, look at your writing not as creator, but as critic. Try to imagine that it's not your own. Work to develop a questioning attitude, always asking, "How can I make this writing clearer, stronger, and more precise?"

Revising is the time for change. Some changes may be dramatic and broad. You may delete entire passages or add new ones, or you may move sentences or paragraphs to different locations. Other changes will be subtle and specific: a livelier verb, an adjustment for variety, a splash of style. The techniques in this section will help you to re-see and re-shape your writing until every paragraph, every sentence, and every word is just right.

A major influence on revising is time. When you're under pressure, working against a tight deadline, it's difficult to be objective and careful about perfecting your writing. Always invest enough time to read, evaluate, and change your writing — on your own and with a reader.

Revising on Your Own

First, revise your own writing. The more you practice, the better you'll get at seeing your writing with an objective eye. These strategies will help.

▶ **Strategies**

1. *Let your draft settle.* Because shifting from the role of writer to that of reader in one sitting is difficult, let your draft cool, at least overnight.

2. *Read your writing aloud* to develop a sensitivity to its sound. Good writing has a rhythm that is pleasing to the ear. Like music, it rises and falls, speeds and slows. Additionally, you'll hear weaknesses that your eyes miss. Reading aloud also slows your pace so that you don't race past a problem.

Critical Thinking:

Analyzing

3. *Develop efficient ways to make changes.* As you read, analyze each part of your paragraph or essay. Make notes in the margin of your paper or on tags so that you won't forget first impressions before you rewrite. If you left ample margins and double-spaced your draft, you'll have room for changes. Also, use a different writing tool or a different color for revising so that your changes show up easily. Don't erase, black out, or throw away anything in case you change your mind.

Use proofreading symbols *(page 99)* to show yourself where to insert or delete material or how you want to change what exists. Use arrows and circles to show where to move passages.

Reference Point:
pages 514–515

If possible, learn to use a word processor. It eliminates tiresome recopying and makes correcting and improving your writing quick and easy.

4. *Deal with broad concerns first; then move to narrower ones.* The techniques in this section are arranged from general to specific. Conduct your revising in the same order.

5. *Use a checklist to make the steps of revising more manageable.* A general revising checklist appears at the end of this section on page 97 and at the very end of the book. Once you have practiced revising, you can tailor this checklist to your own tendencies and weaknesses.

Using Peer Review

Writing can be a lonely task; it's difficult to know whether your thoughts are clearly expressed or if your writing is interesting to read. Peer review involves testing your draft on a trusted reader. A fresh mind and eye can spot strengths and weaknesses that you never suspected were there.

The connection that you make with someone who can read your drafts critically and constructively is mutually beneficial. Because it's so difficult to be objective about your own work, peer review can make the revising process more efficient and productive. If you trade drafts with another writer, both of you can get suggestions. Also, by reading another writer's draft, you develop critical skills that you can use when you are revising on your own.

Guidelines for the Writer Use the strategies on the next page when you ask a classmate to review your paragraph or essay.

► Strategies

1. *Give your reader specific written questions.* It's often difficult to remember oral instructions. Keep in mind that your reader can't look at everything. General questions like "Is this good?" won't provide useful responses. Instead, ask specific questions: Does this metaphor work? Have I offered enough support for this opinion? Is this word too strong?

2. *Ask your reader about any comments that you don't understand.* Otherwise, you may dismiss comments without considering their worth. If your reader responds orally, take accurate notes to guide your revision later.

3. *Don't take comments about your writing personally;* responses and criticism are meant to make your writing better, not to make you feel worse. If you disagree with a response, discuss the point with your reader. It's up to you to evaluate your readers' reactions just as they have evaluated your draft.

? Critical Thinking:
Evaluating

Guidelines for the Reviewer Your goal as the reviewer is to improve the piece of writing by evaluating what you read. Always remember that you are reviewing the writing, *not* the writer. Keep a healthy balance between praise and criticism, and try to make suggestions for possible changes. Use the following strategies when you review someone else's work.

? Critical Thinking:
Evaluating

► Strategies

1. *Read the draft at least twice.* First, concentrate on the whole piece of writing and offer a general comment about how it affects you. As you read it a second time, answer the specific questions that the writer has asked.

2. *Make your comments constructive.* Always begin by praising something that the writer has done well. Phrasing your comments about weaknesses as questions prompts the writer to rethink. Notice how the tone *(pages 87–89)* of your questions can inspire creativity rather than bruise a writer's ego. Ask "Can you think of a better word?" rather than writing "wrong word." Ask "How is this detail relevant to your topic sentence?" instead of responding "This doesn't fit."

3. *Make your comments specific.* Vague comments such as "I like this" or "Add more here" don't give the writer much guidance or direction. Explain why you like something or what kind of information the writer should add. Ask yourself, "If this draft were mine, what changes would I make?" Offer your ideas to the writer as suggestions.

Revising for Focus: Unity, Clarity, and Coherence

Begin your revising by addressing the most general concerns. Think of the paragraph or essay as one whole unit and ask the following questions: Does this writing have a clearly expressed topic and focus? Does every sentence contribute to the main idea? Do the sentences flow in a logical order?

Unity

Your first concern should be weeding irrelevant details from your writing and making sure that it holds together around a clear focusing idea. A piece of writing has **unity** when all the supporting sentences are related to the topic sentence or to the thesis statement. Use these strategies to revise for unity within paragraphs.

▶ **Strategies**

1. *Remove any sentence that does not support its topic sentence or thesis statement.*

2. *Rewrite any sentence that is not clearly related to the topic sentence or thesis statement.* If you're unable to shape the sentence so that its relevance is clear, delete it.

3. *If your supporting details seem weak or sparse, return to prewriting techniques to add information.* Use brainstorming, clustering, cubing, or changing viewpoints *(pages 13–20)* to generate new details. Try to have at least three details to support a point.

4. *Make sure that your conclusion echoes your topic and your focusing idea.*

Here is the first draft of a paragraph that explores fabric, a connection between humans and the natural world. To the left are the writer's notes on needed revisions for unity.

Revise to clarify topic sentence ———

Unrelated sentence — delete

Unrelated sentence ———

Modern science has learned to produce fibers by chemical and technical means. Many people prefer natural fibers from plants and animals for their durability and textures. I know my mother does. They may also want to support a simpler, less technology-dependent lifestyle. Cotton accounts for more than 95 percent of the natural fibers used in the United States. China produces more cotton than any other nation. Cotton fibers produce soft, absorbent fabrics that are widely used for clothing, sheets, and towels. The strength and beauty of linen, made from flax fibers, make it popular for fine tablecloths and handker-

<table>
<tr><td>Is this related? Revise?</td><td>chiefs. My grandfather's handkerchiefs were all made of fine Irish linen. Fibers of the jute plant are woven into burlap, used for sacks, rugs, and carpets. Animals also supply natural fibers. Sheep supply most of our wool, but some</td></tr>
<tr><td>Unrelated sentence</td><td>comes from certain kinds of camels and goats. Goats produce milk too. Wool provides warm, comfortable fabrics</td></tr>
<tr><td>Is asbestos a fiber? Do I want to include it?</td><td>for clothes and sweaters. Asbestos is used for brake linings and fire-retardant hoses; it comes from several varieties of rocks. Silk comes from cocoons spun by silkworms.</td></tr>
<tr><td>Add concluding sentence</td><td>Because its long filaments have great luster and softness and can be dyed brilliant colors, silk is popular for scarves and neckties.</td></tr>
</table>

Assignment 1 **Revising for Unity**

On your paper, revise the following paragraph for unity. Use the strategies on page 66 to guide your decisions, and be prepared to explain your choices.

> The purpose of commercial television is not really to entertain or to inform. Its purpose is to attract huge mass audiences, hold them to the screen for long hours, and then sell those captives to the highest bidder. The advertiser uses TV programs as billboards — something to attract the crowd of potential buyers. Billboards are usually owned by marketing companies and rented to advertisers. In this sense, the shows are just extensions of commercials; instead of being thirty seconds long, commercials are stretched into ten- or fifteen-minute segments. Commercials range from five seconds to thirty seconds. Of course, the audience seldom suspects this. People actually believe that they can avoid the commercialism of television by leaving the room when the commercials appear. My brother simply turns down the sound during commercials. The advertiser may not be at all concerned with the quality of the show. He or she simply wants a program that will attract the most — and repel the fewest — members of the audience. That's why we are bombarded year after year with incredibly bland programming.

Revising for Coherence and Clarity

Once you have weeded unnecessary and irrelevant ideas from your writing, check for logical order and connective threads. Read your draft to make sure that the sentences move clearly from one to the next and that there are connections between your sentences.

If your writing has clarity, your reader will proceed through it smoothly, without hesitation or confusion. The sentences will flow logically, and your topic and focusing idea will be apparent. Use the following strategies to analyze for clarity.

Critical Thinking: Analyzing

▶ **Strategies**

1. *Check to see that you have strategically positioned your topic sentence or your thesis statement.* Make sure that this sentence is rich, clear, and evident. In a paragraph, first sentences and last sentences are positions of emphasis.

2. *Check the organization of each paragraph to see if it follows chronological order, spatial order, order of importance, or another logical order.* An essay will usually combine patterns of organization; a paragraph will usually follow one pattern.

3. *Make sure that you have discussed a series of items in the same order in which you introduced them.* For example, if you promise in your thesis statement to discuss the origins of zippers, grippers, and buttons, do not begin with buttons.

4. *Check to make sure that you have defined unfamiliar or unusual terms the first time that you use them.* Be aware of your readers' level of knowledge at all times. Always consider what *they* may not know.

5. *Check to make sure that each sentence is connected to the sentences around it.* Use transitional words and phrases to show movement in time, direction, or importance, and to show how one sentence relates to the next *(pages 36–38)*.

The final strategy in the preceding list will also provide **coherence,** connections between ideas. The repetition of key words can also weave connective threads through your sentences and paragraphs. Consider the following paragraph.

> I stared into the dirty cell. I had never seen a jail before. It looked so small, too small for a person to live in for more than an hour or so. Why, it was so small that the walls would push a person's thoughts right in. The mattress on its painted metal cot was thin and stained; its sink was more brown than white; its bars were crisscrossed, not just up and down like in the movies. As I stood there, I promised myself that I would never be so bad or so unlucky as to go to jail.

Notice how repetition of the words *jail, person,* and *small* pull the sentences together, echoing and reinforcing these key images and the focusing idea. Such careful, deliberate repetition contributes to coherence. Similarly, words that refer to the same thing or idea provide links between sentences. For example, notice how *cell* and *jail* connect the first two sentences.

Reference Point:
pages 647–652

Pronouns also provide coherence. Notice how the clause *It looked so small* and the details *its cot, its sink,* and *its bars* are connected to the topic sentence by the pronoun-antecedent relationship.

In a coherent paragraph, these techniques create a network of connections between sentences. The following paragraph is tightly woven, its threads many and varied.

Television and radio are the only media under direct government control; they are regulated by the Federal Communications Commission because broadcasting uses public airwaves. The basis of the nation's broadcasting system was set with the passage of the Radio Act of 1927. This act declared that the airwaves belong to the people and that service should be equally distributed across the country. Additionally, freedom of expression in broadcasting is covered by the First Amendment. The government's regulatory power over broadcasting is not absolute but can be appealed. Its control is based on its power to grant and renew licenses.

Assignment 2 Analyzing for Clarity and Coherence

On your paper, copy the following paragraph and analyze it for coherence. Circle and connect transitions, pronouns, words that refer to the same thing or idea, and repetitions of key words.

> And after all the weather was ideal. They could not have had a more perfect day for a garden party if they had ordered it. Windless, warm, the sky without a cloud. Only the blue was veiled with a haze of light gold, as it is sometimes in early summer. The gardener had been up since dawn, mowing the lawns and sweeping them, until the grass and the dark flat rosettes where the daisy plants had been seemed to shine. As for the roses, you could not help feeling they understood that roses are the only flowers that impress people at garden parties; the only flowers that everybody is certain of knowing. Hundreds, yes, literally hundreds, had come out in a single night; the green bushes bowed down as though they had been visited by archangels.
>
> Katherine Mansfield *(1888–1923)*
> from ''The Garden Party''

(ärk'ān'jəlz)

Assignment 3 Revising for Clarity and Coherence

The following paragraph about family connections lacks clarity and coherence. Read it and decide what type of organization would best serve its topic and focusing idea: chronological order, spatial order, order of importance, or another logical order. On your paper, rewrite the paragraph, rearranging the sentences in a logical order. Include transitions, pronouns, words that refer to the same thing or idea, and repetitions of key words to provide coherence.

In the center of the big, black leather book are two pages that trace our family tree. The left page is my mother's branch and the right page is my father's. My mother's page is filled with small scrawlings, for she had seven brothers and sisters, each of whom had three or four children. Names of my maternal aunts and uncles are squished in the margins and in the center crease. They seem to spill over the edges of The Great Book, like a crowd of immigrants. My father's family has fields of white between their names. His only brother has just two children. Their parents descended from proper New England families who each had only one offspring. My mother's parents each sprang from large Wisconsin families. My father's relatives' names are broadly scrolled and connected with thick calligraphic strokes, names like Crawford, Robb, and Burke. My mother's family has names like Schneider, Vollenegger, and Rosenstein. I always find comfort in looking at these two soft pages. Somehow I reaffirm my parents' marriage every time I shut the book.

Assignment 4 Revising for Unity and Coherence

The following paragraph lacks both unity and coherence. *Step 1:* Read the paragraph and determine whether its topic sentence contains the limited topic and focusing idea. Also decide what order of organization is most appropriate. *Step 2:* On your paper, make a rough outline of a revised paragraph that arranges the sentences in a logical order and includes only those points that support the topic and the focusing idea. *Step 3:* Rewrite the paragraph, including at least three transitional words and phrases to clarify the order and to show connections between the ideas.

Most historians agree that the French played the earliest form of tennis during the 1100s or 1200s. They called it *jeu de paume,* meaning "game of the palm." The players batted the ball back and forth over a net with the palm of their hands. Today, people play handball this way. In 1881 the United States Lawn Tennis Association sponsored the first championship in Newport, Rhode Island. Newport is famous for its spectacular ocean views and its elegant mansions. Major Walter Clopton Wingfield of England is considered the father of modern tennis. Until the 1950s, France, Great Britain, and the United States produced almost all of the game's major players. From 1950 to 1967, Australian teams won the Davis Cup fifteen times. In 1874 Wingfield patented tennis equipment and rules for playing on grass courts. Tennis soon replaced croquet as

England's most popular outdoor sport. The most popular outdoor sport in the United States today is baseball. In 1874, Mary Ewing Outerbridge introduced tennis into the United States. She purchased equipment from British army officers in Bermuda and set up the first United States tennis court in New York City. Bermuda is an archipelago of about 300 islands.

Continuing Assignment **Revise for Focus**

Use the strategies on page 66 and 68 to revise your paragraph or essay for focus, unity, and coherence. Aim for a topic sentence or a thesis statement that is precise and that includes the main impression that you want your readers to get. Check your details to make sure that they support your main idea and that they are arranged in a logical order. Check for transitions, pronouns, words that refer to the same thing or idea, and repetition of key words that interconnect your sentences. Revise your conclusion so that it brings your reader back to your focusing idea. Write specific questions for peer review that address general issues of focus, unity, and coherence.

For revising
a **paragraph**
or an **essay**

Revising

Revising Sentences

When you are satisfied with the general organization of your paragraph or essay, look again at each separate sentence. Adjust each sentence until it achieves the exact effect that you want.

A complete thought can be expressed in many different ways. By combining, splitting, trimming, expanding, and rearranging words, phrases, and clauses, you can fine tune your sentences. For example, although the following sentences convey the same idea, they convey a variety of meanings and effects.

> Mort's Market is the place where folks congregate. Here, they talk about the weather. They discuss local politics. They chat about their latest family news.

> Neighbors love to chat about the weather, confide their family's latest news, or gossip about local politics; Mort's Market provides them with warmth and opportunity.

> If we want to chat about politics, families, or weather, we head to Mort's Market.

> Why go to Mort's Market? You can gab about politics, weather, or even your family's latest antics.

Experiment with the structure of your sentences as you revise. Let clarity, variety, and sound be your guides.

Combining Sentences to Show Connections

Combining two or three sentences into one longer one can clearly show connections among your ideas, eliminate unnecessary repetition, and help you to vary the lengths of your sentences for the sake of emphasis and pace. Consider these short sentences. Because they are related, they can be effectively combined.

This was my first job interview.
I was very nervous.
I carried my good-luck penny in my pocket.

The way that you combine sentences depends upon the details that you want to emphasize and the effect that you want to create. Note the differences in the following combinations.

I was nervous, for this was my first job interview, and I carried my good-luck penny in my pocket.

Since this was my first job interview and I was very nervous, I carried my good-luck penny in my pocket.

I carried my good-luck penny in my pocket because this was my first interview; I was very nervous.

Critical Thinking:
Determining relationships

Notice how the emphasis shifts among these sentences. In the first, all three details hang in perfectly coordinated balance; all three are valued equally. In the second sentence, the writer has determined that "I carried my good-luck penny" is the most important detail and has placed it in the independent clause. In the final sentence, "this was my first interview" is subordinate to "I carried my good-luck penny." Connecting "I was nervous" with a semicolon coordinates it with the action of carrying the coin. As you revise your sentences, decide which details are most important. Then use a variety of the combining methods described in the following pages to reflect the judgments that you make.

Combining Ideas of Equal Importance

Reference Point:
pages 587–588

If your shirt, pants, socks, and shoes go together, if none of them sticks out wildly from the others, your clothes are coordinated. Similarly, in writing, **coordination** is the process of combining related elements of equal importance or value. When you coordinate elements, one does not stand out as most important. Coordination of words, phrases, or clauses creates a sense of equal weight and balance. Use the following strategies to form coordinated structures in your writing.

▶ ### Strategies

1. *Experiment with several of the following strategies.* Test the combinations by reading the newly combined sentences aloud with the preceding and following sentences. Use a variety of strategies rather than depending on just one or two.

2. *Use a semicolon alone to coordinate complete sentences that you want to combine.*

Reference Point: *pages 721–722*

I don't like picnics; potato salad bores me.
Cut dahlias when they are fully open; cut gladioli when the first floweret is open; cut roses before the buds are open.

3. *Use a coordinating conjunction that conveys the appropriate kind of balance.* The coordinating conjunctions are *and, but, or, nor, for,* and *yet.* Each sets up a different relationship between coordinated elements, as shown on page 72. If you are coordinating two independent clauses, use a comma before the coordinating conjunction.

Reference Points: *pages 559 and 718*

Sumo wrestlers are obese by our standards, **but** they are athletic heroes in Japan.

If you are coordinating words or phrases, no comma is necessary.

Sumo wrestlers are obese by our standards **but** are athletic heroes in Japan.
He was obese **but** incredibly strong.

4. *Use a semicolon and a conjunctive adverb to coordinate independent clauses.* Adverbs that join ideas include *consequently, furthermore, however, nevertheless, otherwise, therefore,* and *thus.* Put a comma after the conjunctive adverb.

Reference Point: *pages 562–563*

On bad days the Long Island Expressway is like an enormous parking lot; **consequently,** we call it the "Long Island Distressway."

The various coordinating words and the relationships that they indicate are shown below.

ADDITION   *and, furthermore, in addition*

Lee enjoys spending money, **and** he enjoys saving it. He loves shopping sprees; **in addition,** he loves a fat bank account.

CONTRAST   *but, yet, however, instead, nevertheless*

He tries hard to be frugal, **but** he simply can't help himself when he gets near a record store.

ALTERNATIVE   *or, nor, otherwise*

"I can buy two albums **or** one compact disk!"

RESULT   *therefore, thus, consequently, accordingly*

The record store is next to his bank; **therefore,** paydays are difficult.

CAUSE   *for*

There is little hope for virtue, **for** he has to pass Rick's Records before he gets to the First National Bank.

Critical Thinking:

Determining Relationships
How can I show the appropriate relationship between ideas?

On your paper, coordinate the following pairs of sentences if their ideas are related. Use a variety of the strategies on pages 72–73. If the ideas are unrelated, write *Unrelated* on your paper.

1. My favorite foods are pizza, garlic bread, and onion soup. My least favorite foods are liver, broccoli, and anchovies.
2. Excavators unearthed papyrus documents from ancient Egypt. They are as legible today as they were when they were written.
3. Julian fell asleep before he could study. He failed his final exam.
4. The tow rope from the speed boat snapped. My first water-skiing adventure didn't last long.
5. The office was decorated with Asian art. His handshake felt like a wet fish.
6. I could go to a two-year college. I could enter a four-year college. I could get a job.
7. The Brooklyn Bridge cost nearly $18 million to build. Today, it would cost $700 million.
8. About 10,000 to 30,000 years ago, Cro-Magnon ancestors began to paint and sculpt. They left cave paintings in Western Europe.

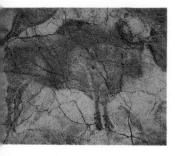

Combining Ideas of Unequal Importance

Reference Point:
pages 588–594

Emphasizing certain ideas requires de-emphasizing others. **Subordination** involves combining elements that you do not consider equal in value. It shows how the main idea in a sentence is supported, developed, caused, or undercut by other *subordinate*, or dependent, ideas.

Critical Thinking:

Determining relationships

After you determine the relationship between your ideas, use these strategies to combine sentences using subordination. In each example, the subordinate idea is in boldface type.

▶ **Strategies**

1. *Experiment with several of the following strategies.* Test the combinations by reading the newly combined sentences aloud. Make sure that they fit smoothly with preceding and following sentences and that they express the meaning that you intend.

Reference Point:
pages 588–589

2. *Put a related idea in an adjective clause.* Adjective clauses, which modify nouns or pronouns, often begin with relative pronouns *(that, which, who, whom, whose).*

   TWO SENTENCES
   Hands-on museums connect visitors directly with the world of knowledge. They are popular alternatives to "don't touch" museums.

   REVISED SENTENCE WITH ADJECTIVE CLAUSE
   Hands-on museums **that connect visitors directly with the world of knowledge** are popular alternatives to "don't touch" museums.

3. *Turn one idea into a participial phrase.* By doing so, you can express your thoughts more directly.

Reference Point:
pages 581–582

TWO SENTENCES

These museums operate according to the principle of learning through doing. They encourage participation and play.

REVISED SENTENCE WITH PRESENT PARTICIPIAL PHRASE

Operating according to the principle of learning through doing, these museums encourage participation and play.

TWO SENTENCES

In one museum a wave machine shows how turbulence can create huge recurring waves. It is activated by a visitor turning a wheel.

REVISED SENTENCE WITH PAST PARTICIPIAL PHRASE

In one museum a wave machine, **activated by a visitor turning a wheel,** shows how turbulence can create huge recurring waves.

4. *Include a detail of one sentence as an appositive phrase in another.* Place an appositive phrase just before or after the word that it identifies.

Reference Point:
pages 579–580

TWO SENTENCES

Air pressure is a relatively abstract concept. It becomes concrete when a person is hit with a low-pressure blast.

REVISED SENTENCE WITH APPOSITIVE

Air pressure, **a relatively abstract concept,** becomes concrete when a person is hit with a low-pressure blast.

5. *Use a subordinating conjunction that conveys the appropriate kind of relationship between your ideas.* Just as coordinating conjunctions *(pages 72–73)* show a separate but equal relationship between ideas, subordinating conjunctions combine ideas that are integrated and dependent. Different subordinating conjunctions express different relationships.

Reference Point:
pages 561–562

TIME *after, as, as long as, before, since, until, whenever, while*

When a visitor can play with a computer, the technology is much less intimidating.

MANNER *as, as if, as though*

One hands-on museum lets blindfolded children touch rough bark, brush foliage, and a fur-lined hole, **as if the children were dependent only on their sense of touch.**

CONDITION *although, as long as, even though, if, provided that, though, unless, while*

Although they can't swim in the shark tank, visitors to many aquariums can touch live crabs, starfish, urchins, and shrimp.

CAUSE   *because*

> **Because the concept of an assembly line is difficult for some children to understand,** one midwestern museum lets a dozen children manufacture a top by performing one step each.

PURPOSE   *in order that, so that*

RESULT   Another museum has built a jungle gym inside a huge plastic model of a protein molecule **so that visitors can appreciate the strength of its structure.**

Assignment 2   Combining Ideas of Unequal Importance

Critical Thinking:

Determining Relationships
What idea is most important?

Step 1: On your paper, rewrite each of the following sets of sentences as one sentence, using subordination to combine their ideas. You may combine subordination and coordination. *Step 2:* Indicate the strategy or strategies that you use by writing one or more of the following next to the sentence: *Adjective clause, Participial phrase, Appositive phrase,* or *Subordinating conjunction.*

1. Just about every world cuisine has a dish made with meat, fruit, cheese, or vegetables. These are wrapped in dough. The names reflect their ethnic flavor.
2. Pita from the Middle East is a round, flat bread with a pocket. The pocket can be filled with fried chickpeas and spices. This is known as "falafel." Greeks stuff the pita with souvlaki. Souvlaki is usually lamb.
3. French cooks put fillings into folded pancakes. Doing so produces a crepe. Crepes can contain fruit, vegetables, meats, or cheeses. Eastern Europeans call such pancakes "blintzes."
4. Mexico has given its neighbors the taco and the enchilada. Both are made from tortillas stuffed with beef or chicken. They are covered with tomatoes, onions, cheese, and lettuce.
5. Americans stuff meats into dough. They call them hamburgers.

Assignment 3   Revising: Coordination and Subordination

On your paper, revise the following paragaph. Use coordination and subordination to combine related sentences so that the paragraph is clear and the sentences are smooth.

> People speak different languages. They conduct business, scientific, and diplomatic meetings. They must talk with one another. L. L. Zamenhof wanted to fill the need for a universal language. He was a Polish physician and linguist. He developed Esperanto in 1887. Its basic vocabulary consists of root words common to the Indo-European languages. About half the people in the world speak languages in this family. They can easily recognize many Esperanto words. Zamenhof gave all the nouns and verbs consis-

tent forms. Thousands of works have been translated into Esperanto. More than one hundred magazines and newspapers are published in Esperanto. Schools do not require students to learn Esperanto. It may not succeed as the universal language.

Revising Sentences for Parallel Structure

Often, when combining sentences, you'll create a series of coordinated items. In addition to choosing an appropriate coordinating strategy, you also need to write the coordinated elements in the same grammatical forms. In other words, the parts need to be parallel in structure. Noun phrases must be balanced with other noun phrases, participles with other participles, gerunds with other gerunds, and so on. For example, in this sentence three sources of pleasure are coordinated.

Reference Point:
pages 578–586

> NOT PARALLEL **An overstuffed chair, a murder mystery,** and **listening to symphonies** are all that Helen needs to be content.

The first two elements are parallel, for both are simple noun phrases. The phrase *listening to symphonies* is not parallel, for it is a gerund with a prepositional phrase, rather than a noun and its modifiers. Removing the gerund and leaving only the noun, *symphonies,* will begin to solve the problem, but there is still an imbalance in the rhythm of the sentence. Adding the adjective *Beethoven's* before *symphonies* helps. Finally, seeing that the first two elements are singular nouns and making the necessary adjustment to the third element creates the following sentence, which is parallel in structure and in sound.

> PARALLEL **An overstuffed chair, a murder mystery,** and **a Beethoven symphony** are all that Helen needs to be content.

In the following sentences, notice how imbalanced structures and rhythms have been revised to be parallel.

> NOT PARALLEL Word processors make revision **quick, simple,** and **without pain.**

> PARALLEL Word processors make revision **quick, simple,** and **painless.** [parallel adjectives]

> NOT PARALLEL Tony has tried **to roller-skate, bicycling,** and **swimming,** but he still prefers **to jog.**

> PARALLEL Tony has tried **roller-skating, bicycling,** and **swimming,** but he still prefers **jogging.** [parallel gerund phrases]

When you use correlative conjunctions like *either . . . or* and *not only . . . but also,* you must not only use them with parallel elements but also place the two parts of the conjunctions carefully. Try to put them immediately before the sentence parts that are parallel in form.

Reference Point:
pages 560–561

European trains run not only frequently but also run on time.

She wants to play either the drums or play the electric guitar.

Similarly, if you use a preposition, an article, a pronoun, or the infinitive *to* more than once in a parallel series, you must include it in all items in the series. Otherwise, only use it with the first item.

I am most connected with my family, with my friends, and my dog.

We searched in the garage, in the pantry, and *in* the basement.

Assignment 4 Revising for Parallel Structure

On your paper, revise the following sentences so that phrases and clauses are parallel in structure and in sound.

SAMPLE   Sean was afraid that his father didn't know the way and he was going to be too proud to ask.

ANSWER   Sean was afraid that his father didn't know the way and that he was too proud to ask.

1. To learn French, you can either take courses or you can visit a French-speaking country.
2. The ballpark was filled with avid statisticians, people who just liked the fresh air, and infatuated fans.
3. To type accurately, taking shorthand, and knowing bookkeeping were the requirements for the job.
4. George was pleased with both the atmosphere at the Thai restaurant and how the food tasted.
5. The photographer caught long jumpers in midair, sprinters in full stride, and took shots of pole vaulters suspended in space.
6. My family has lived in Maine, in Ohio, in Texas, Nevada, and Alaska.
7. Admission depends on your high school transcript, your entrance-exam scores, your teachers' recommendations, and activities that you have participated in.
8. Verbose writers use many words to say very little; good writers use words economically and sparingly to convey a lot of information.

Revising Sentences for Coherence and Clarity

Like any other writing technique, sentence combining can be overdone. As a reader you quickly recognize a **rambling sentence** as one that is too long and complex. Although they may be grammatically correct, sentences that ramble on and on lose their readers' interest as their meaning becomes muddled. Notice how the overload of clauses and phrases creates a verbal traffic jam in the following sentence.

RAMBLING

Los Angeles, once called "twenty suburbs in search of a city," never felt the need to develop the usual system of public transportation because its roughly three million inhabitants own roughly three and a half million automobiles, and between a quarter and a third of the city's land is monopolized by the automobile and its needs, that is, by its freeways, highways, garages, gas stations, and parking lots.

COHERENT

Los Angeles, once called "twenty suburbs in search of a city," never felt the need to develop the usual system of public transportation because its roughly three million inhabitants own roughly three and a half million automobiles. Between a quarter and a third of the city's land is monopolized by its freeways, highways, garages, gas stations, and parking lots.

Blurred sentences occur when the relationship in a combined sentence is not clear. If you rely on *and* or *so* to join ideas without carefully considering the relationship between them, the meaning of your sentences can become muddled. To correct blurred sentences, use precise combining techniques that make relationships clear.

? **Critical Thinking:**

Determining relationships

BLURRED   Threads connect pieces of fabric, and ligaments connect muscles and bones.

CLEAR   Just as threads connect pieces of fabric, ligaments connect muscles and bones.

BLURRED AND RAMBLING

He heard the scream and ran into the museum, so the only clue that anything was wrong was the broken statue of Nefertiti.

CLEAR AND COHERENT

When he heard the scream, he ran in to the museum. The only clue that anything was wrong was the broken statue of Nefertiti.

Assignment 5 Revising for Coherence and Clarity

On your paper, revise the following paragraph to eliminate rambling sentences and blurred sentences. Divide sentences as necessary, and use phrases and subordinating conjunctions to make your sentences more precise. Read your completed revision aloud to check for clarity and smoothness.

? **Critical Thinking:**

Determining Relationships Which sentences need to show a clearer relationship among ideas?

My seventh grade French teacher arranged pen pals for our class in France, and mine was named Collette Bergeron. During the next three years, we exchanged polite, one-page letters about once a month containing lists of favorites, brief autobiographies, and superficial summaries of our days, and soon after our sixteenth birthdays, our letters began to change, and we began to confide secrets and dreams and hopes and fears to each other, things we would never say to our parents or the friends that we saw every day. These weekly letters were sometimes six pages long, and we were separated by an ocean and had never met, but we were best friends with much in common, for we both worried about school-work and nuclear war, loved romantic movies with strong, indepen-dent women, and wrote poems that we shared with no one but each other. We graduated, and we unknowingly sent each other the same book as a gift: *Everybody's Autobiography* by Gertrude Stein, our mutual heroine. We're both working now, and we still correspond, but less frequently, and after six years, we've both begun to save money for a transatlantic trip so that we might finally meet *vis à vis.*

Revising Sentences for Conciseness

Farmers prune trees in the spring; they cut off unnecessary growth to improve productivity. Similarly, if you prune unnecessary and weak words, your writing will thrive. When you've eliminated wordiness, your writing will be **concise.**

Reducing Phrases and Clauses

Concise writing is effective writing. To start, you can often reduce clauses and phrases without significantly changing their meaning. As you revise your own writing or review another writer's sentences, put brackets around words that could be eliminated. Then, later, you can decide what should be revised.

CLAUSE TO APPOSITIVE PHRASE

Henriette Wyeth, [who is] the sister of the painter Andrew Wyeth, is also an accomplished artist.

CLAUSE TO WORD

[It is] obvious [that] his taste in movies was very different from mine.

CLAUSE TO PREPOSITIONAL PHRASE

After a few agonizing seconds [had gone by], I reached for the rope.

CLAUSE TO INFINITIVE PHRASE

Because he had a tight schedule [that he had] to follow, Mr. Liu always carried a bag lunch.

CLAUSE TO PARTICIPIAL PHRASE

[Since] caterpillars eat heartily, they leave only skeletons of the leaves.

CLAUSE TO GERUND PHRASE

Before (the veterinarian) examin~~ed~~ *ing* the German shepherd, ~~she~~ patted the dog.

PHRASE TO WORD

Claudia dropped the (wheel) [to the] motorcycle /on her foot.

Assignment 6 | **Reducing Phrases and Clauses**

On your paper, revise the following sentences, reducing phrases and clauses as necessary.

SAMPLE   Before Mr. Andrews, who was Alice's father, left for work, he always jogged three miles.

ANSWER   Before leaving for work, Mr. Andrews, Alice's father, jogged three miles.

1. When I have a test that I have to take, my palms sweat and my mouth goes dry.
2. The beggar who is blind held out a cup that was dented and dirty.
3. Mark Twain, who is the author of *Huckleberry Finn*, relived his childhood by writing about it.
4. Viewers who are connected to the world through the miracle of television can considerably widen their circle of experience.
5. After he read the horror story by Edgar Allan Poe, Marvin had a great plan for his revenge.
6. We read *Walden*, a book that was written by Henry David Thoreau, which we liked.

Revising for Word Economy

Concise writing does not necessarily use the fewest possible words; then the best writing would always be the shortest writing. Concise writing uses only necessary words. Here are strategies for word economy. In short, cut waste.

▶ **Strategies**

1. *Do not mistake flowery expressions and pretentious words for good writing.* Beware of language that is overloaded with vague, uncommon, or technical words. At its best, this language is confusing; at its worst, it is downright comical, as in this example.

> Without a doubt, the course of action undertaken by a young adult who has recently or will soon matriculate from high school to seek either employment or to extend the range of his or her education can be one of the most challenging and complex decisions of the young adult's life.

Keep your writing direct and simple. Beware of expressions such as the following; replace them with their more succinct counterparts, listed on the right.

institution of higher learning	university
a person in the arts	artist
the members of our family	our family
functioning in the capacity of	working as
is desirous of	wants

2. *Be suspicious of certain fixed expressions that provide nothing but padding.* Replace phrases like these with more concise expressions or eliminate them altogether.

this kind of situation	at the present time
I want to make the point that	it is true that
one aspect of this	due to the fact that
in and of itself	to make a long story short
of all of the possibilities	one thing I'd like to say

Reference Point: page 546

3. *Use the active voice* rather than the wordier passive voice to make your writing more direct and forceful.

   PASSIVE London Bridge was built by the children's lifted arms.

   ACTIVE The children's lifted arms built London Bridge.

4. *Eliminate weak repetition.* Not all repetition is weak; strong repetition is at the heart of coherent writing *(pages 67–69)*. Useless repetition, however, emphasizes details that are not important and can bog down your readers.

   WORDY Writers in the writers' group brought their writing every week for the other writers to read.

   CONCISE Every week, writers brought their work to the group for other writers to read.

5. *Eliminate redundancy,* the needless repetition of ideas. If words are alike in meaning, use one, not both. Do not use a word that is part of the meaning of another word; *retreated back, my aunt is a woman who,* and *ten in number* repeat ideas. In the following redundant expressions, the italicized words should be eliminated.

return *back*	each *separate* thing
mix *together*	heavy *in weight*
connective link	8:00 P.M. *at night*
wearing a hat *on her head*	scrutinized *carefully*

Assignment 7 Revising for Conciseness

On your paper, revise the following paragraph to make it concise and direct. Refer to the preceding strategies.

Caricature is a way of connecting the art of portraiture with the art of satire. In modern times today, with the easy and widespread availability of printed materials, we have gotten used to seeing caricature in all popular forms of mass media, magazines, and newspapers. Many well-known famous personalities, such as presidents, entertainers, and athletes, are more readily identified with caricatures than with serious sketches or photographs. Caricaturists seek and search for an idiosyncracy of their subject; then they exploit it and use it to their advantage. They can transform an eyebrow, a lower lip, an ear lobe, or a lock of hair into a statement of personality. The person in the arts must take care not to overdo the exaggeration too much, for while an effective caricature must be outrageous, funny, and comical, it must also be instantly recognizable in a moment. Because of the fact that a bold line here and a sharp angle there can create a strong satirical statement, the formula for fine caricature seems to be a mysterious mixture of combining abbreviation and exaggeration.

NO MOLLY-CODDLING HERE (*This is the prevailing Wall Street notion of President Roosevelt's attitude toward corporate interests.*)
  From the Globe
  (*New York*)

Revising for Emphasis

In speech, gestures and intonations create emphasis. If an idea is important, you can pound your fist, slowly enunciate, or raise the pitch or level of your voice. In writing, position, structure, and repetition are the writer's tools for emphasis. Before you choose from among these strategies, think carefully about the ideas that you want to stress and the effect that you want to create.

▶ Strategies

1. *Place the most important ideas at the beginning and at the end of your sentences.* These positions emphasize whatever details occupy them. Weak words and ideas in these positions weaken sentences. The end of a sentence is often the most emphatic position.

  WEAK   He discovered that he had one too many pearls when he counted them. [weak idea at end]

  EMPHATIC   When he counted the pearls, he discovered that he had one too many. [important idea at end]

  WEAK   After a trying day, Lynne was relieved to be home from school. [weak idea at end]

  EMPHATIC   After a trying day at school, Lynne was relieved to be home. [strong idea at end]

2. *Use periodic sentences.* Because the end position in a sentence is often the most emphatic, sentences can build, with subordinate elements first and the main idea near the period. **Periodic sentences** dramatically build to such a climax. Use them sparingly.

PERIODIC SENTENCES

With the score tied, the bases loaded, and two out, Wade stepped up to the bat, took two called strikes, watched three balls sail by, and then smashed the home run.

After we'd waited all day long, flipping through magazines, sipping iced tea, weeding the garden, even dusting the furniture, we finally heard it — the creak of the mailbox.

3. *Repeat key words and phrases or key ideas.* Pointless repetition is wordy, but deliberate repetition of key words and phrases can be powerful and emphatic.

John was an average student, an average basketball player, and an average pianist, but he was an extraordinary inventor.

Grandma danced with Grandpa; my mother danced with my father; Aunt Marion danced with my cousin, Sam; and the cat danced for its dinner.

4. *Use a short sentence for emphasis.* You can capture your readers' attention with a short sentence that follows a group of longer sentences.

We polished the long table until it shone like a mirror, and the floors were so clean and waxed that they still looked wet. No newspapers, pencils, or wrappers lay about; we dusted the lamps and cleaned the fish tank. The house was ready.

Assignment 8 Revising for Emphasis

On your paper, revise each group of sentences to emphasize the words or the phrases that you consider most important. You may separate sentences or combine them.

1. Less interest has been shown in the candidate's political history than in his personal relationships in recent months.
2. Because the garage repaired Ms. Casazza's car, she can drive us to the softball game this afternoon.
3. His parents did not allow Stan to drive, so he bicycled the entire twelve miles by himself.
4. No one can enter the darkroom until the photographers turn off the light above the door to say that they're done.
5. Of course, all day the sun shone because Vanessa wore a stiff raincoat, floppy rubber boots, and a silly plastic hat.
6. When I forgot my keys, I was not angry at my brother. I was not angry at the cab driver. I was angry at myself. I was not angry with the television host who had distracted me.
7. Before we finally found the keys, we looked everywhere: in the glove compartment, in the cupboards, in the drawers, in the breadbox, and in the laundry basket.
8. If you want to see some powerful waves, go to the end of the peninsula and face outward.

Revising Sentences for Variety

You wouldn't want to sit down to a meal in which each dish was the same color, texture, and taste, all served in the same kind of bowl. Such repetition is boring in a meal or in a piece of writing. Variety is spice. It can give dull, choppy sentences rhythm and life. As you revise, vary the beginnings, the structures, and the lengths of your sentences.

Revising Sentence Beginnings

The monotonous repetition of grammatically perfect simple sentences will lull your readers to sleep. Vary the normal subject-verb-complement order of your sentences by trying some of the following sentence beginnings.

ADJECTIVE PHRASE	*Connecting 159 member nations*, the United Nations works for the betterment of the world community.
ADVERB PHRASE	*Shortly after World War II*, the nations that opposed Germany, Italy, and Japan decided that such a full-scale war must never happen again.
PREPOSITIONAL PHRASE	*In June 1945*, fifty nations signed the UN charter in hopes that the organization would keep peace.
PARTICIPIAL PHRASE	*Headquartered in New York City*, the United Nations seeks the causes of war and tries to find ways to eliminate them.
ADVERB CLAUSE	*If fighting between two or more countries breaks out anywhere*, the United Nations may be asked to stop it.
APPOSITIVE PHRASE	*The world's peacekeeper*, the United Nations tries, above all, to deal with problems and disputes before they turn into active aggression.
INFINITIVE PHRASE	*To honor the UN peacekeeping forces*, the Nobel Committee awarded them the 1988 peace prize.

Inverting normal sentence order is another way to vary sentence beginnings. Note the variety achieved by inverting the following sentence.

Reference Point: *pages 636–637*

NORMAL ORDER	Peace and human dignity are on the United Nations' agenda.
INVERTED ORDER	On the United Nations' agenda are peace and human dignity.

Be careful, though; changing the order of your sentence parts does *not* work for sentences whose modifiers will be misplaced as a result. Consider the following problem.

Reference Point: *pages 667–668*

Revising Sentences   85

| NORMAL ORDER | Visitors can see the flags of all member nations flying in front of the headquarters. |
| INVERTED ORDER | Flying in front of the headquarters, visitors can see the flags of all member nations. [Suddenly, the visitors, not the flags, are doing the flying; this is not the intention!] |

Variety in Sentence Length and Structure

Probably the simplest way to achieve sentence variety is to vary the length of your sentences. In general, long sentences slow down reading and suit the more formal styles of analysis or explanation. Short sentences are quick to read. They emphasize.

Reference Point:
pages 595–596

Varying sentence beginnings will result in varied sentence structure. Using coordination and subordination, you can create a mixture of simple, compound, and complex sentence structures. Note how the sentences in the following paragraph change the pace of your reading. The paragraph begins with analytical, informative sentences, then moves to shorter sentences that express a series of simple yet meaningful actions.

Complex	Because I had been the older kid next door for seven of his eight years, Kevin had always been somewhat suspicious of me. His handicap isolated him somewhat, I suspected, for he had never had a best friend the way I had at his age. He wheeled across his front lawn, and he carefully parked next to me in the darkness. Quietly, he reached for my hand.
Compound-Complex	
Compound	
Simple	

Assignment 9 Revising for Sentence Variety

On your paper, revise the following short essay. Provide sentence variety by combining sentences and varying their beginnings, structures, and lengths. Check for meaning and pace by reading your revised essay aloud.

Scrap collection for reuse or resale is not new. Today it is an environmental necessity. People born sixty or seventy years ago remember a time when little was thrown away. Ashes became soap. Old clothes became patchwork quilts. Organic garbage became compost. The compost fertilized the garden for next season's food. Organized recycling reached a peak during World War II. No patriotic citizen would throw away newspapers or pieces of metal. We have become adept at many things since that time. We have become adept at waste making most of all. The last few years have brought a heightened awareness. There are serious problems being generated along with the prodigious amounts of trash. Problems arise from locating waste disposal sites. Problems also arise from financing its transportation. Recycling is one way to start reducing these problems. It reduces the amount of trash.

Revise Your Sentences

Once you have revised your piece of writing for content, focus, unity, clarity, and coherence (in the Continuing Assignment on page 71), look next at your sentences. Read your writing aloud so that you can hear how the ideas sound. When necessary, make the relationships between ideas clearer by combining sentences. Combine ideas of equal importance by using coordination; check for parallel structure. Combine ideas of unequal value by using subordination. Eliminate rambling and blurred sentences. Eliminate wordiness, redundancy, and weak repetition. Finally, revise for variety in sentence beginnings, structure, and length. Ask a classmate to evaluate your revised sentences, using the strategies for peer review on pages 64–65.

For writing
a **paragraph**
or an **essay**

Revising

Revising for Style and Tone

Your signature is unlike anyone else's. Similarly, your writing style is exclusively yours. **Style** is that quality that makes your writing unique. It must be consistent throughout a piece of writing and be appropriate to your purpose, audience, and voice. Your style is reflected in the words that you choose, the sentences that you construct, the details that you include, the punctuation and phrases that you favor, and the kinds of paragraphs that you like to write.

Using an Effective Level of Formality

Your style is partially reflected in the level of formality that you choose. Evaluate your writing to make sure that the level of formality you have chosen is consistent and appropriate. Whether you've dressed your ideas formally, informally, or casually will strongly affect the tone *(page 27)* of your writing and the effect it has on your readers.

Formal language, appropriate for a research paper, a ceremonial speech, or a letter of application, serves a serious purpose. It avoids slang, contractions, and conversational expressions; its sentences are usually longer, more complex, and highly structured. Be cautious with formal language, however, for it can become wordy and unclear *(pages 81–82)*. In the hands of a seasoned writer, however, formal language can border on poetry, as the following example illustrates.

Critical Thinking:
Evaluating

*I*t was the best of times, it was the worst of times, it was the age of wisdom, it was the age of foolishness, it was the epoch of belief, it was the epoch of incredulity, it was the season of

Light, it was the season of Darkness, it was the spring of hope, it was the winter of despair, we had everything before us, we had nothing before us, we were all going direct to Heaven, we were all going direct the other way — in short, the period was so far like the present period, that some of its noisiest authorities insisted on its being received, for good or for evil, in the superlative degree of comparison only.

Charles Dickens *(1812–1870)*
from *A Tale of Two Cities*

Informal language presents ideas in a simpler, conversational way. Used to express personal experiences and the feelings of the writer, it uses contractions, first-person and second-person pronouns, some slang, and even colloquialisms. Its sentence structure is varied and lively but complete and grammatically correct.

When I left Lake Wobegon, I packed a box of books, two boxes of clothes, and two grocery sacks of miscellaneous, climbed in my 1956 Ford, and then, when my old black dog Buster came limping out from under the porch, I opened the door and boosted him into the back seat. He had arthritic hips and was almost blind, and as Dad said, it would be better to leave him die at home, but he loved to go for rides and I couldn't see making the long trip to Minneapolis alone. I had no prospects there except a spare bed in the basement of my dad's old Army buddy Bob's house. Buster was company, at least.

Garrison Keillor *(1942–   )*
from *Lake Wobegon Days*

Casual language is even more informal. In its attempt to capture a live speaker's voice, it might contain sentence fragments, run-on sentences, regional expressions, and contractions. Sometimes, standard spelling is changed to capture the sounds of speech. Often used in dialogue, poetry, short stories, and plays, casual language often rambles like conversation, as in the following example.

You were asking about highlights in my life. Significant moments. I don't know if there are highlights. Divisions, yes, highlights, no. These divisions of mine are not chronological.

> Life goes back and forth, life selects. For instance, my Aunt
> Arlette — a woman whom I knew for a short time but long
> enough — if you listen to her, you realize that jewelry separates
> her life. Forget greed, this is not about greed. Take her conver-
> sations, the way they begin — When I bought the bracelet or Be-
> fore my necklace clasp broke in the lobby of that theatre or When
> the rings were stolen.
>
> Bette Pesetsky (1932–   )
> from *Midnight Sweets*

Assignment 1 Formal, Informal, and Casual Language

On your paper, write whether each of the following paragraphs uses
formal, informal, or casual language. Be prepared to discuss the advantages of each level of formality.

? Critical Thinking:

Evaluating
What is the ef-
fect of each
level of
language?

1.   The corner market and variety store is fading into the photo
        album of history, part of a bygone era before the advent of shop-
        ping malls. Gone are the days when parents send their children
        running to the corner for a quart of milk or a dozen eggs. Gone are
        the days when men gather there to discuss local politics or nearby
        fishing. Gone are the days when ladies gather in the afternoons to
        discuss wedding showers and Founders Day picnics. These cen-
        ters of small-town social life have been replaced by trendy bou-
        tiques or shopping malls, and with them has passed a spirit of
        community, sharing, and openness that this generation will be the
        last to recall.

2.   Mort's Market has stuck in my memory all these years. I
        dream about its big freezer beside the wooden check-out counter.
        On sticky July afternoons, I'd slide back the freezer's silver top and
        the cold vapor would billow out into my hot face. Inside was fro-
        zen relief in infinite variety: tall and thin, short and fat, creamy,
        icy, red, and blue. I'd reach down, pull up a treat, inspect it, then
        replace it, repeating this action several times in order to prolong
        the cold blast. In those days, these decisions were the only diffi-
        cult ones.

Revising for Effective Word Choice

As you read your writing aloud, question each word that you have
written. Is it necessary? Is it strong? Is it clear? Is it precise? Are
you satisfied with it? Make an effort to use words that your audience is
familiar with, but also search for words that will surprise and delight
your readers.

Using Strong Words

Be specific when you write. Strong, specific details will pull your readers into your writing and point them toward the broader ideas that you want to support. The following sentences contain limp words that convey little information and almost no emotional temperature.

The children stood in a circle.
Basketball is an exciting sport.
Pollution on beaches is disgusting.

Sentences like these *tell* rather than *show*. They tell abstract truths, but they fail to make a particular reality come alive for readers. What are the children doing in a circle? Don't tell your readers that basketball is exciting; show them a game. Don't say that pollution is disgusting — show a particular beach scattered with litter. Always make a sensory connection with your readers by offering a series of colorful, specific details.

▶ **Strategies**

1. *Choose strong nouns and verbs.* Strengthen sentences by replacing weak adjective-noun combinations with precise nouns. Change weak adverb-verb combinations to vivid verbs.

   ORIGINAL A black bird smoothly flew over the small house and the young cat looked hungrily after it.

   REVISED As a raven glided over the cottage, the kitten licked its tiny pink chops.

Reference Point:
pages 540–548

2. *Replace forms of the verbs* go, get, *and* be *with precise verbs that show action.* Lively verbs have punch, movement, and emotional color. They allow readers to see, touch, smell, taste, and hear what you describe.

   ORIGINAL The platoon went into the jungle.

   REVISED The platoon stormed the jungle.

   ORIGINAL Jan is a strong singer.

   REVISED When Jan hits a high C, crystal glasses shatter and neighborhood dogs howl.

3. *Choose verbs in the active voice to show who does what.*

   ORIGINAL Webs are spun from the outside in.

   REVISED Spiders spin webs from the outside in.

Reference Point:
pages 623–625

4. *Select verbs in the simple present tense or in the simple past tense.* Because they are more direct, they convey more energy than verbs accompanied by auxiliary verbs, as this example shows.

ORIGINAL	Before he was nineteen, Jack London had canned fish, had manufactured rope, and had sold ice.
REVISED	Before he was nineteen, Jack London canned fish, manufactured rope, and sold ice.

5. *Use specific nouns, verbs, adjectives, and adverbs to make your ideas come alive.* The sentences from page 90 are revised here to *show* concrete images.

ORIGINAL	The children stood in a circle.
REVISED	A dozen preschoolers fidgeted in a bean-shaped ring, waiting to play dodge ball.

ORIGINAL	Basketball is an exciting sport.
REVISED	Guards steal the ball and score faster than the crowd can react; forwards block sure bets and pass downcourt to turn the tide; centers can foul or be fouled; in a close game, one second, one elbow, one lay-up can win or lose the game.

ORIGINAL	Pollution on beaches is disgusting.
REVISED	On Rockport Beach, tin foil, styrofoam, cigarette butts, and cellophane blended in a sand-based stew.

Assignment 2 **Choosing Strong Words**

On your paper, rewrite each of the following sentences so that they show instead of tell. Choose precise, concrete nouns and strong verbs. If you use adjectives or adverbs, be sure that they really add meaning to your sentence.

SAMPLE The autumn sky was beautiful.
ANSWER The turquoise sky was interrupted only by tufts of milkweed, popcorn clouds, and memories of passing jets.

1. The garage is cluttered.
2. The library book looked as though it had been read often.
3. The circus delighted the children.
4. The woods were lovely.
5. The woods were scary.
6. A spider web hung in the doorway.
7. Her bathrobe was ugly.
8. I went upstairs and went to bed.

Using Precise Words

Words represent ideas in at least two ways. First, words have a meaning that you can look up in a dictionary. This **denotation** is essentially the same for every user of the language. Second, the **connotation** of a word is its associations — the feelings, attitudes, and opinions that

Reference Point:
page 481

it suggests. Most nouns, verbs, adjectives, and adverbs carry connotations that differ somewhat from person to person because each reader has unique experiences with certain words.

Writers choose words for their denotations, their connotations, and their sounds. The combination of these components results in meaning. For example, the following sentences have similar denotations but very different sounds and connotations.

> The couple was married in June.
> The bride and groom took nuptial vows at the summer solstice.
> The pair got hitched when the daisies bloomed.
> The betrothed were wed in the sixth month.
> The lovebirds tied the knot when the weather was hot.

Each sentence expresses the same idea — or does it? Much of the meaning is carried by the connotations and sounds of the sentences, far beyond the denotations of the words. Strong words carry weighty connotations; use them wisely and they will serve you well.

Assignment 3 **Using Precise Words**

Step 1: On your paper, explain what denotation the words in each group have in common. If necessary, use a dictionary for reference. Then explain how the connotations differ. *Step 2:* Choose two of the groups and write a sentence for each word, illustrating its connotations.

1. language, speech, lingo, native tongue, jive
2. support, flatter, boost, whitewash, encourage
3. gallop, dash, scamper, whiz, hasten
4. strong, mighty, invincible, courageous, hardy
5. peace, quiet, harmony, truce, concord
6. blend, mixture, alloy, fusion, conglomerate

Using Figurative Language

The following sentences use language in a **literal** way. In these sentences, language means just what it says.

> I prefer staying up late to getting up early.
> Man Ray's well-known photograph of Ernest Hemingway shows a banjo behind his head.
> Yeast needs water and carbohydrates to grow.

In contrast, this sentence uses language in a different way.

> Our friendship is an oasis.

This sentence goes beyond what is literally true and suggests a rich comparison between a friendship and a green and fertile spot. To understand this **figurative language,** readers must use their imaginations. It may take an entire paragraph of literal explanation to express what these five simple words suggest. Clearly, the friendship is a blessing; it is nourishing and rehabilitating. It is also lush and productive. It can be returned to again and again; it will not run dry. Compared with this friendship, other relationships may be arid and barren. Probably when these friends are not together, they want to be.

The rich meaning of figurative language demands careful and active readers. For this reason it can be the most creative — and challenging — kind of language to read and to write. Experiment with various forms of figurative language as you revise your writing.

Simile and Metaphor   The most common forms of figurative language are simile and metaphor. Consider the following sentences.

> Relief poured in like butterscotch.
> Her criticisms were as gentle as bee stings.
> My thoughts, like gerbils, keep me awake.

These sentences are **similes**, figures of speech that use *like* or *as* to compare two essentially unlike elements. Again, readers must explore the language to unearth its meaning. For example, the third sentence does not show how thoughts can be like gerbils; you must use your own imagination to compare the two. Obviously, this writer's mind is active at night. Maybe it moves in endless circles like gerbils on an exercise wheel. Maybe it chews at the events of the day, trying desperately to make a soft nest for sleep.

Critical Thinking:
Comparing

The sentence "Our friendship is an oasis," a **metaphor,** compares directly without using *like* or *as.* Simple combinations of words may be metaphorical, such as *popcorn clouds, peppermint words,* or *a plastic personality.* The dense language of metaphors conveys much meaning in a small space.

When you use similes and metaphors, avoid using phrases that have a familiar ring, such as *raining cats and dogs, chip off the old block,* or *solid as a rock.* These are worn out, overused expressions called **clichés.** Figurative language is effective only when it is fresh and original.

Personification   When you give human characteristics to inanimate objects or to animals, you are using **personification.** Personification makes clouds mime, toasters belch, and oak trees moan as they dance in the wind.

Hyperbole   Exaggeration comes naturally to most of us, as in proclamations like, "If I don't eat soon, I'll die." In writing, **hyperbole** goes beyond literal language to emphasize and entertain. Try a splash of hyperbole to make a strong point in a light spirit, as in these examples.

(hī-pûr′bə-lē)

> My closet has been declared a disaster area.
> In all of her eighty-seven years, she has never cracked a smile.

(sûr′ bər-əs)

Allusion Another example of compact figurative language, **allusion** uses specific references to literature, history, or popular culture in a kind of metaphorical comparison. Never explain an allusion; choose references that you are sure your readers will be familiar with, as in the following examples.

> They were the Beatles of Dennison High School.
> Rita has a Wall Street mentality.
> When it comes to holidays, William is a Scrooge.
> Brian followed his Jack Sprat diet for only a week.

Allusions are an "inside joke" that can range from the very familiar to the highly literary. Do you recognize the references in these allusions?

> He guarded the door like Cerberus.
> How do I hate geometry? Let me count the ways.
> Give me science fiction, or give me death.
> Kurt has the humility of Muhammad Ali.

Assignment 4 Using Figurative Language

? Critical Thinking:

Comparing
What vivid comparison can I make?

On your paper, use fresh and lively figurative language to express the ideas in the following simple sentences. Rewrite at least four of the sentences, using at least one simile, one metaphor, one example of personification, and one example of hyperbole.

1. The cat entered the room.
2. Henry is grumpy every morning.
3. A single light bulb hung in the attic.
4. A string connected me with my kite.
5. The sky was gray and stormy.
6. The motorcycle was very loud.
7. From the moon, Earth looked small.
8. The blade of grass was tall and straight.

Assignment 5 Using Allusion

On your paper, create allusions by copying the following sentences, filling in the blanks. Use the bracketed comments as guides.

1. He had _?_ eyes. [a person with gorgeous eyes]
2. She could play the _?_ [a musical instrument] well, but she was no _?_. [accomplished musician on that instrument]
3. Evenings with the newlyweds were like evenings with _?_. [a couple famous for their fights]
4. She was a twentieth-century _?_. [pre-twentieth-century woman who overcame great odds]

5. Faster than __?__, she told the secret to everyone she knew. [a fast runner]
6. He had a peanut-butter salary but __?__ tastes. [a brand name that suggests great wealth]
7. In his dreams Carl was __?__ [a famous, sophisticated movie star], but in reality he was __?__. [an awkward, comic character]
8. When I won the award, I felt like __?__. [a great achiever]

Reconsidering Factors That Influence Your Writing

During prewriting and drafting, you made decisions about purpose, audience, and voice. Use the following questions to return to these major decisions and analyze their effectiveness. Make sure that your choices translate clearly into your piece of writing.

Critical Thinking:

Analyzing

Reconsidering Prewriting Decisions

- Who is your **audience?** What response to your topic are you seeking from your readers?
- What is the **purpose** of your writing? Have you served this purpose throughout your paragraph or your essay?
- How would you describe your **position as a writer?** Do you play the role of storyteller, expert, explorer, reporter, or some other role? How does this role relate to your topic, your purpose, and your audience?
- Is your **voice** personal or impersonal? How is your voice appropriate to your topic, your purpose, and your audience?
- Is your **tone** positive, negative, or neutral (objective)? Is the tone consistent throughout?
- What **pronouns and verb tense** have you chosen? Are they suitable for your topic and your audience? Are they consistent with your purpose?
- Are your **level of formality** and your **word choices** suitable for your topic, your purpose, your audience, and your tone?

Assignment 6 | Factors That Influence Writing

Working alone or with a partner, use the questions in the preceding chart to analyze the following opening paragraph written for a high school audience. On your paper, answer the questions.

Critical Thinking:

Analyzing
How do purpose, audience, and voice work together?

Fare Share Food Cooperative offers you good health, lower prices, and political comfort. Remember that good looks grow from the inside out. Snacks such as granola, sunflower seeds, raisins, peanuts, and dates make people feel and look better than ever. Fare Share's fruits, vegetables, and grains are organically grown; that means no chemical fertilizers or preservatives. Choosing organically grown produce will lengthen your life, for many pesticides have been proven to cause serious illnesses. Fare Share buys food in bulk and sectionalizes it into smaller portions on the premises. All the work is done by members of the co-op who volunteer their time in exchange for even lower prices. Because co-op foods do not come in ostentatious packages or offer plastic toys or seductive contests, their prices are lower. The costs of labor and packaging are not passed on to the customer. Fare Share gave you the chance to say NO to high-tech farming and YES to the small, local farmer, for local products fill the shelves. It allowed you to say NO to chemical pesticides and YES to safe and natural produce. It allows you to say NO to conglomerate corporations who raise prices and cloud issues of product safety, health, and nutrition and YES to the spirit of volunteerism and self-sufficiency. Try Fare Share; it offers you more than food.

Composing a Title

Good titles have two jobs: to interest and to inform. They arouse your readers' curiosity and hint at your focusing idea. For example, "Is Laughter the Best Medicine?" *(pages 59–61)* pulls readers in by directly asking them a question. Additionally, both laughter and medicine become major ideas in the essay.

Good titles grow from various seeds. Some reflect main characters, such as *Medea, Don Quixote,* or "Rapaccini's Daughter." Others reflect settings, such as *Island of the Blue Dolphins* or "Dover Beach." You can call attention to a central image, as in *The Glass Menagerie* or "The White Heron." You can also foreshadow an important action, as in "The Jilting of Granny Weatherall," "The Lottery," or "Shooting an Elephant." A title can be mysterious — *Rumble Fish, The Lord of the Flies* — but at some point the writer must reveal its meaning.

A good title fits the scope of the piece of writing. *War and Peace* is a sprawling Russian novel of thousands of pages, whereas "The Eye of a Deer" is a short personal essay. Compose an effective title by making it reflect your topic and your tone — with a splash of word play to delight your audience.

Assignment 7 Composing Titles

Reread the untitled paragraphs on the pages indicated below. For each one, compose a title that reflects its topic and its tone. Make each title interesting as well as informative.

1. The paragraph on Hillary and Tenzing *(page 31)*
2. The paragraph on improvisational jazz *(page 32)*
3. The paragraph on the hole in the ozone layer *(page 33)*
4. The paragraph on collecting baseball cards *(page 40)*
5. The paragraph on shopping bags *(page 44)*
6. The paragraph on oral history *(page 45)*

Continuing Assignment **Revise for Style and Tone**

Reread your revised draft from the Continuing Assignment on page 87, this time examining its style and tone. Check to see that the level of formality is appropriate. Use specific nouns and verbs to make your writing lively. Also, be sure that the connotations and sounds of words are suitable. To make your writing more vivid, try using figurative language. Look again at the questions on page 95 and reconsider the factors that influence your writing, making any necessary changes. Then compose a title that indicates your topic and attracts your readers' attention. Finally, ask a classmate to evaluate the style and tone of your draft, using the guidelines for peer review on pages 64–65. Be sure that your final draft is neat enough for you to proofread.

For writing
a **paragraph**
or an **essay**

Revising Checklist

Focus *(pages 66–69)*	• Does the topic sentence or the thesis statement clearly indicate the topic and its focusing idea?
	• Does each sentence develop and support the topic sentence or the thesis statement? What, if anything, might be cut?
	• Is the writing clearly organized? What, if anything, might be moved?
	• Is there enough support for the topic sentence or the thesis statement? What, if anything, might be added?
	• Are there clear connections between sentences and paragraphs?
	• Does each paragraph build toward a closing sentence?
	• Does the conclusion create a sense of closure? Does it echo the topic and its focusing idea?
Sentence Structure *(pages 71–86)*	• Are sentences combined effectively?
	• Are combined sentence parts parallel in structure?
	• Are all sentences as concise as possible?
	• Are all sentences clear and coherent?
	• Do the most important ideas receive emphasis?
	• Are the sentences varied in their beginnings, structure, and lengths?
Style and Tone *(pages 87–96)*	• Is the choice of words accurate, effective, and appropriate?
	• Is figurative language used effectively?
	• Is the level of formality appropriate?
	• Is the tone consistent?

The goal of proofreading is to have no errors in your final copy. Errors in writing are as annoying as static in an electrical connection. If your readers have to reread a sentence or to look twice at a word to decipher it, their line of thought will be broken, and you'll appear to be a careless writer. Before you publish, scrutinize every detail of your writing. Its effectiveness depends on each sentence, each word, and each punctuation mark working together in perfect harmony.

Good proofreading takes time. Don't leave it until just before a deadline; invest enough time to proofread carefully. Like revising, proofreading demands objectivity. You're more likely to spot errors if you can put your writing aside and come back to it with a fresh eye.

These strategies will help you to develop good proofreading habits.

▶ Strategies

1. *Proofread your paper at least three times.* First, read *each sentence*, checking structure, agreement, and usage. Second, proofread for *mechanics:* capitalization and punctuation. Finally, look at *each word* for errors in spelling.

2. *Proofread forward and backward.* First, proofread your writing from the beginning to the end to catch the most obvious errors. Then proofread from the end to the beginning, using an index card to cover all but the sentences or the words that you are proofreading. The second pass will force you to look at each sentence or word independently, eliminating the context of the others around it.

3. *Read your writing aloud;* read it slowly. If a sentence sounds clumsy, even if it is correct, refine it to satisfy your ear. Perfect the sound of your writing as well as the sense.

4. *Have someone else proofread your writing.* Trade your final copy with another writer after proofreading it yourself. A new pair of eyes and ears will pick up errors that you have missed.

5. *Develop and use a proofreading checklist.* A general checklist appears on page 105. Supplement this checklist with additional, personalized reminders.

6. *Use symbols to identify and correct errors.* As you proofread, mark your writing with the following proofreading symbols.

Proofreading Symbols

∧ insert something   ⌒ close up letters

⌗ add a space   c̲ capitalize

¶ begin a new paragraph   M̲ make this letter lower case

∿ reverse letters or words   .... let it stand as it was

✗ delete   (under something crossed out)

Note how these symbols are used in the following paragraph.

Not so long ago the peace corps looked like a dream whose whose time had passed, its idealism merely a shadow against the harsh reality ofthe late Twentieth century. After Surviving a childhood bliss in the '60s and a pain ful adolescence in the '70s, it has grown more professional and more practical as it approaches its third decade. Although Hubert humphrey proposed the Peace Corps in the late 1950s, it was not until John F. Kennedy's presidency that the idea became a reality.

Proofreading

Proofreading Your Writing

Proofreading is a skill that requires concentration and acute attention to fine detail. Read with a skeptical attitude, and be suspicious of every sentence. Hardly any piece of revised writing is mechanically perfect. Errors are bound to be there; find them and correct them.

Proofreading for Correct Sentence Structure

As you read your sentences aloud, look carefully at how you have connected their parts. Look for omitted words. Read slowly, or your mind will automatically correct the mistakes or fill in the gaps. Specifically, look for the following common sentence errors.

Reference Point:
pages 598–600

- *Sentence Fragments.* Make sure that each group of words that you've written as a sentence is a complete sentence. Fragments will make your readers stop, reread, and guess at your intentions.

> When I donate blood twice a year, making es me woozy but proud.

Reference Point:
pages 600–602

- *Run-On Sentences.* Run-ons lose your readers' attention and create confusion. For example, somewhere in the middle of this sentence, readers would get muddled without the correction.

> Uncle Sam gave his niece a walkie-talkie for her birthday; from her room she could talk to her friend Arnie next door.

Reference Point:
pages 559–562

- *Faulty Conjunctions.* Check all conjunctions, making sure that you've used coordinating conjunctions to connect equal ideas and subordinating conjunctions to connect a dependent idea to another dependent idea.

- *Nonparallel Structure.* Faulty parallelism *(pages 77–78)* creates a feeling of imbalance and disharmony. Make sure that the structures of items in a series are grammatically balanced.

> We fly from Boston to Atlanta, from Atlanta to Dallas, from Dallas to Houston, and from Houston to Galveston; we'll be there in no time!

Assignment 1 Proofreading for Sentence Structure

The following paragraph contains errors in sentence structure. On your paper, rewrite the paragraph, correcting all sentence fragments, run-on sentences, inappropriate conjunctions, and nonparallel structure.

Imagine a race in which the competitors raced toward each other instead of beside each other. In 1862 two railroad companies, the Union Pacific and the Central Pacific, were hired to build a transcontinental railroad starting from both ends of the country — East and West. The Union Pacific pushing westward from Omaha, Nebraska, the Central Pacific building eastward from the California city of Sacramento. They raced to connect, thousands of Chinese and Irish workers were hired to lay track across broad prairies, swift rivers, and across mountain peaks. At the height of the race nearly 20,000 workers toiling and sweated, suffered scorching heat and blinding snowstorms, mile by mile the two railroads grew closer. On May 10, 1869, two locomotives — Number 119 and Jupiter — touched noses at Promontory Point near Ogden, Utah. The Union Pacific won the race with 1089 miles of track, and it crossed level country for most of the way. The Central Pacific had to cross the Rockies and laid only 689 miles of track. There was great rejoicing all over the country as Governor Stanford

of California drove the famous golden spike into the final tie. This
connection, a victory for the whole country.

Proofreading for Correct Usage

After concentrating on whole sentences, proofread inside your
phrases and clauses to evaluate the connections among your words. As
you proofread for correct usage, concentrate on the following areas.

Correcting Verb Usage

Since each sentence contains at least one verb, evaluating verbs
will focus your attention on sentence parts and consistency. For each
sentence, locate and question each verb form.

- *Consistent Tense.*   Unless you have a specific reason to shift tenses,
  use one tense throughout your piece of writing. Notice how shifts in
  tense blurred the feeling conveyed in the original sentence.

  > As a child, I loved connect-the-dots books; they seem_ed_ so orderly and
  > predictable.

- *Subject-Verb Agreement.*   For each clause, make sure that the subject agrees in number with the verb, especially when they are sepa
  rated from each other. If one is singular, both must be singular.
  Your readers' attention would be interrupted by the original verb in
  the following sentence.

  > Only a thin string, which dips in the air and bends in strong winds,
  > connect_s_ me to the enormous kite.

Correcting Pronoun Usage

Used correctly, pronouns create coherence and eliminate wordiness. Used incorrectly, they only confuse. As you proofread, scrutinize
all pronouns.

- *Clear Antecedents.*   Each pronoun's antecedent should be as close
  to it as possible. Work for clarity as well as for correctness.

  > Sylvia's hat matched her shirt, but not her jacket; her jacket matched
  > her tights, but not her vest; her scarf matched her belt, but clashed
  > with her hat; it _her outfit_ looked like a kaleidoscope.

- *Pronoun-Antecedent Agreement.*   Make each pronoun agree with its
  antecedent in number and in gender. Slips in agreement will distract
  your readers and expose your carelessness.

  > Each leaf clung to _its_ ~~their~~ branch, fearing the fall.

Reference Point:
pages 653–660

- *Pronoun Case.* Because pronouns have different forms to show their grammatical use in a sentence, you also need to proofread for correct form or case. Be especially careful with compound objects and with *who* and *whom.*

She offered fruit to~he~ and~I,~ but we refused.

(him / me above)

The teacher who~I~ remember most is retiring.

(m above)

Correcting Usage of Modifiers

As you proofread, check the form and placement of each modifier.

Reference Point:
pages 667–669

- *Placement of Modifiers.* To be clear, modifiers must closely precede or follow the words that they modify. Pay close attention to prepositional phrases and participial phrases.

Doug caught the football with a cracked collarbone.

Reference Point:
pages 664–667

- *Modifiers in Comparisons.* Check modifiers used to compare two or more elements. Catch errors such as *most perfect* or *more warmer.* Remedy comparisons that are illogical because of missing or faulty elements.

Jeff's snowmobile wasn't as fast as Carl~'s~.

Correcting Word Usage

Reference Point:
pages 492–495

As you proofread, check all homophones and words with similar sounds for errors in usage. Be careful: incorrect usage may escape you unless you are reading words in their full context. For example, there are no misspelled words in the phrase *piece and quite*, but it does not accurately refer to a calm state of mind.

Assignment 2 Proofreading for Correct Usage

The following paragraph contains errors in the use of verbs, pronouns, and modifiers. On your paper, rewrite the paragraph to correct errors in tense, agreement, clarity, placement, and word usage.

Looking out to sea, the tides are far more than the rise and fall of the ocean waters. They regulate the days of people who inhabit the seacoasts of the world. They are more important than a clock to the child whom plays along the shore when the tide is in and dig clams on the bear flats when they are out. The tides were the morning and evening whistle of the workday to fishing cruise who need high water to leave or enter a harbor. They are assurances that nature's pace is more regular and predictable than people. The tides reminds us that we are connected to the rest of the universe, that there are cosmic pulls and tugs that effect our tiny planet.

They are mirrors of human emotions that wax and wane. Because it both falls away and rises again — like voices, like luck, like entire earthy kingdoms — tides are a constant reminder to us that life moves in recurring cycles that seam to have no end.

Proofreading for Correct Mechanics

After you've proofread your sentences for clarity, correctness, and sound, carefully proofread them for mechanics: capitalization, punctuation, underlining, and numbers.

- *Capitalization.* Check the beginning of each sentence, each proper noun, and each proper adjective for capital letters. Words like *china* and *rose* change meaning dramatically with capitalization. Also, carefully check capitalization in titles.

Reference Point: *pages 710–715*

- *Punctuation.* Like traffic signs, punctuation shows the junctions, turns, and merges in your writing. Inaccurate signals in a congested city could be deadly; so could writing with haphazard punctuation. Check each comma, semicolon, and colon for accuracy.

Reference Point: *pages 715–737*

Give quotations special attention. A reader should never have to guess where a quotation begins and ends.

"After college," Carol mourned, "I never lived at home again."

Similarly, possessives and contractions require special attention. For example, without apostrophes "the travel agents ad" or "Wed already locked the doors" will make readers pause and guess.

- *Underlining.* Foreign words and the titles of books, films, plays, magazines, and newspapers require underlining or italics. Omitting this distinction can be misleading.

Reference Point: *pages 737–738*

The most exciting part of my visit to New York was seeing Cats.

- *Numbers.* If you use numbers in your writing, handle them accurately. Decide carefully whether to use words or numbers, and be consistent throughout a piece of writing.

Reference Point: *pages 739–741*

Assignment 3 Proofreading for Mechanics

The following paragraph contains errors in mechanics. On your paper, rewrite the paragraph, making the necessary corrections in capitalization, punctuation, underlinings, and numbers.

There have been many famous student-teacher connections: Socrates and Plato, Anne Sullivan and helen keller, Yoda and Luke Skywalker but mine with Mr Willard tops them all. As a freshman I entered his class hating grammar hating writing, and hating litera-

ture. On that first day, Mr. Willard simply read us Poes poem *An-nabel Lee.* In a short 45 minutes, he nudged ideas from us that we never dreamed we were capable of thinking. His writing assignments were always the same: "Write an essay to prove an idea. His quiet, dry wit, and his easy manner made us all comfortable in his classroom. Wed never get out the door without at least 1 uproarious communal laugh and 1 moment of quiet awe at the splendor of the written word He pushed us to think more deeply, more completely. In class, when we'd answer, he'd often reply, "Comma"? to tell us that we should continue our thought rather than end it. Today, when I read a Poem or I finish the last line of a Novel, I recall mr. Willard. I picture him leaning his slight frame against the chalkboard, rubbing his chin as he listened to a humble adolescent discuss a timeless work of art, taking it as seriously as he would a soliloquy by Shakespeare himself

Proofreading for Correct Spelling

When you are satisfied that your sentences are correct, proofread the words in your piece of writing to nab spelling errors. Increase your efficiency by reading backward from the last word to the first. When you see a word that you use infrequently or that looks questionable, consult a dictionary. There are no excuses for any spelling errors in your final copy.

Assignment 4   Proofreading for Correct Spelling

On your paper, list the words that are misspelled in the following paragraph, correcting their spellings. If necessary, use a dictionary for reference.

Conections between two different plants or animals whose survival is interdependant are forms of *symbiosis.* Like the relationship between two human beings, symbiosis can take sevral forms. In *paracitism,* one organism obtains food or shelter at the expence of the other, somtimes even destroying the host. For example, hookworms that live in the digestive sistems of mamals can cause disease and even death. In *commensalism,* one organism gets the leftovers from the host's food and is sheltered by the host. Little, if any, harm is done. For example, small fish attatch themselves to the bodies of sea turtles. They get free transportation and protection, and they gobbel tidbits that the turtles drop. In *mutualism,* both partys benifit. For example, when an alga and a fungus grow together to form a licken, the fungus gets food from the alga, who, in turn, gets pretection from the fungus. Probably every organism experiences symbiosis in some form.

Proofreading

Making a Proofreading Checklist

The suggestions on the preceding pages can be combined into a Proofreading Checklist. Once you're comfortable with the proofreading process, a checklist can serve as a quick reminder of what to look for in a thorough proofreading.

Proofreading Checklist

- Have I eliminated **fragments** and **run-ons?**
- Have I checked **conjunctions** for effectiveness and clarity?
- Have I used **parallel structure** for items in a series?
- Have I used correct and consistent **verb tense?**
- Have I made all **subjects and verbs agree?**
- Have I used pronouns with **clear antecedents?** Do they agree?
- Have I eliminated misplaced **modifiers** and used correct forms?
- Have I used correct **capitalization?**
- Have I used correct **punctuation?**
- Have I handled **quotation marks** correctly?
- Have I checked all **word usage?**
- Have I used **apostrophes** correctly?
- Have I used **underlining** correctly?
- Have I correctly used **numerals** or spelled out **numbers?**
- Have I **spelled** all words correctly?

You can apply these general questions to any piece of writing. In addition, like most other writers, you probably repeat certain errors. Therefore, supplement this checklist to address your own weaknesses. Review several past writing assignments, noting repeated errors in grammar, usage, and mechanics. Then, in your writer's notebook, keep a personal checklist. Your additions might include notes such as these:

Don't use "It is a fact that...."
Check spellings of effect and affect.
Avoid words like good, bad, nice, and fine.
Don't underline titles of poems.

Assignment · Making Your Own Proofreading Checklist

Review several of your past writing assignments, looking for errors in grammar, usage, and mechanics that you have missed more than once. In your writer's notebook, develop at least four personalized reminders, addressing the repeated errors that you have noted.

Continuing Assignment | Proofread Your Writing

For writing a **paragraph** or an **essay**

Step 1: Use the preceding checklist and your own additions to proofread your revised draft from the Continuing Assignment on page 97. Use the proofreading marks on page 99 to identify and correct all errors that you locate. Make all the necessary corrections, and make a clean copy. *Step 2:* Proofread your clean copy at least once more to catch any copying errors. *Step 3:* Trade your final copy with another writer and do a final proofreading. Make all the necessary corrections. Save your final copy.

Publishing

Publishing brings to reality the connection between you and your readers. After you've planned, organized, drafted, revised, and proofread your writing, it's time to share it with an audience, to publish it for others to read. For most writers, the act of writing is incomplete until the words are read by others. By publishing your writing, your ideas can live — and grow — in your readers' minds.

Look around at the abundance of written material in the world today. Computers have helped to make this the most prolific generation of writers in history. Suddenly, countless private individuals have the power and the technology to generate professional-looking newspapers, magazines, letters, newsletters, greeting cards, books, memoranda, ads, and fliers. You, too, will want to share your best writing, so join in.

Reference Point:
pages 510–517

Publishing

Preparing Your Manuscript for Readers

Can you accurately judge a book by its cover? — a product by its label? — a food by its packaging? Probably not, but we all are very much influenced by such initial visual impressions. Whether you like it or not, first impressions affect your credibility as a writer and may even determine whether your readers will bother to read your work.

Take care, then, to present a manuscript that is clean, neat, and visually appealing. Polish your manuscript's appearance by following these guidelines.

▶ **Strategies**

1. *Write, type, or print out your work on standard paper — 8½″ by 11″.* Use one side of the paper only. If you use a typewriter or a word processor, double-space your final copy for easier reading. Always proofread this final copy with care.

2. *Use blue or black ink* that is clear and dark.
3. *Leave even margins* of one inch on the left side, the right side, the top, and the bottom of all pages.
4. *Center your title on the top line.* Double-space from the title to the first line of your writing. Do not put quotation marks around your title, and do not underline it or type it in all capital letters.
5. *Indent the first line of every paragraph five spaces.*
6. *Write your name and the date in the upper left corner of the first page.* If the piece of writing is for a class, include the name of your teacher and the course in this heading. On every page except the first page, put your last name and the page number (in Arabic numerals) in the upper right corner.
7. *Attach multiple pages at the upper left corner* with a staple or a paper clip.
8. *Above all, follow any special guidelines or instructions given by a teacher, an editor, or a committee* even if they differ from the strategies offered here. Details matter a great deal. For example, some editors refuse to read manuscripts that don't conform to their specified guidelines.

Continuing Assignment **Prepare Your Manuscript**

For a
paragraph
or an **essay**

Using your revised and proofread piece of writing from the Continuing Assignment on page 106, prepare your manuscript for publication. Follow the preceding strategies, and pay close attention to detail.

Publishing

Publishing Opportunities for Student Writers

For a writer, there is nothing more rewarding than publishing a piece of successful writing. If you feel proud of a piece of writing, take steps to get it published. Find out what opportunities are available to you, and submit your best work for consideration.

Publishing for an Audience of One Some writers write primarily for themselves in order to explore their thinking or to probe their experiences. Occasionally these self-addressed writings, such as *The Diary of Anne Frank* and *A Writer's Diary, Extracts from the Diary of Virginia Woolf,* are later published for a wider audience. In a sense you've been publishing for another reader since first grade; whenever you've handed a final copy to a teacher or showed your writing to a classmate, you have published. When you send a letter, you also publish for an audience of one. College essays and job application letters are among the most important pieces of writing you'll ever publish. For many writers, letter writing is a way to explore and try out ideas. You may want to look at collections such as *The Letters of Walt Whitman to His Mother* or *The Letters of Katherine Mansfield* to observe how writers develop their ideas and styles in their letters.

Publishing for a Limited, Familiar Audience   When you've completed a piece of writing that you are particularly proud of, consider having it read by a small but familiar audience, as well as keeping a copy in your portfolio. For example, class anthologies are excellent means of preserving personal bests and reflecting the interests of classmates. Your school may fund a student newspaper, a literary magazine, or a yearbook. Such publications may accept **free-lance writing,** done by writers who are not on their staff. Submit an article to a newsletter covering your favorite hobby or interest, or even start one of your own. Word-processing technology puts the power to publish at anyone's fingertips.

Reference Point: *pages 516–517*

Publishing for a Large, Unknown Audience   As your confidence grows, so will your desire to share your best work with an even broader audience. Editors of local newspapers often welcome students' perspectives; some even run special columns for student news and features. Send a piece of writing to a favorite magazine; first, though, inquire about guidelines for free-lance writers and then follow them meticulously. Watch for posters or announcements about writing contests for high school students. Many such contests reward outstanding poetry, drama, short stories, essays, or even novels, and they may offer scholarships, cash, or publication as awards. Publications such as *Writers' Market* list opportunities and specific details that can guide you to match your best work with an appropriate publication.

Continuing Assignment   **Publish Your Writing**

Choose one or more of the preceding opportunities, and publish the manuscript that you prepared for the Continuing Assignment on page 108.

For a **paragraph** or an **essay**

Publishing

Responding: The Writer as Reader

When one writer publishes and someone reads the published writing, the reader is often inspired to write a response. In this way, the reading-writing cycle continues. As you read any published piece of writing, you react to the ideas and the images expressed. They blend with ideas and images of your own. Even reading your own writing — especially if time has passed since you published it — can spark reactions and generate new ideas. Such reactions will lead you right back to prewriting, and the writing process truly comes full circle.

Varieties of Response

Good writing may evoke your laughter, anger, sympathy, suspicion, determination, or amusement. If you invest your attention and your imagination in what you read, allowing yourself to get involved with the words and the ideas, your first and immediate response to powerful writing is likely to be an emotional one. Later, in retrospect, you may ask yourself why you reacted that way. What personal experience or attitude contributed to your emotion?

Your response to writing will not only be emotional, however; you will also react critically and objectively. As you read—or afterwards—you may evaluate, synthesize, interpret, compare, contrast, or determine relationships. As a critical reader, you can also observe and analyze the writing techniques that convey the ideas. What metaphors does the writer use? How effective is the opening sentence? Would another method of organization have been more effective? Sensitivity to writing techniques will broaden your own horizons as a writer. Let your own writing be inspired by what you read — by both its content and its form.

No two readers will ever have identical responses to a piece of writing. Your response — conditioned by your unique personality and experience — is as individual as your signature. Additionally, there is never a right or wrong way to respond. The important question is not "What does this piece of writing mean?" but "What does this piece of writing mean to you?"

Forms of Response

How do you express your responses to a piece of writing? Forms of response vary. Sometimes, responses are expressed orally. For example, you may discuss a piece of writing in a classroom or with friends at lunch. You may recommend a novel or an article to another reader. In the working world, you may be asked for your reaction to a memorandum, a business plan, or a press release. Discussing a piece of writing will help you to see that various people have various responses and that no one response is right or wrong.

As a student you will often be asked to express your responses in writing. Writing forces you to defend your responses, to show why you responded in a certain way. Similarly, you may write a letter to a writer to argue a point or to congratulate a position or a style. Reading might inspire a memory, a poem, or a story. Use your writer's notebook to record your strongest responses to what you read while your reactions are fresh in your mind. You can return to your notebook later and build on these immediate reactions.

Responses are not limited to speaking and writing. For example, many films are interpretations of literature: *The Grapes of Wrath, Ordinary People, One Flew Over the Cuckoo's Nest,* to name just a few. Responses can be expressed through the visual arts. Painter Paul Klee's *Sinbad the Sailor* interprets the legend of *The Arabian Nights;* in *Don Quixote Attacking the Windmills,* French artist Honoré Daumier portrays Cervantes's hero. Your response might be expressed in music, such as Dire Straits' "Romeo and Juliet," folk singer Steve Goodman's "Call Me Ishmael" based on *Moby-Dick,* or Felix Mendelssohn's familiar opera *A Midsummer Night's Dream.* In all of these situations, readers have allowed their responses to pieces of writing to initiate new creative processes.

Reading as a Writer

Human beings are creatures who learn by example. When you experience something that you like or admire, you may try to emulate it. When you experience something that you loathe or reject, you remember never to repeat it. Reading is an imaginative experience that follows these patterns. Your reading experiences can serve as examples to you as a writer.

How can you make this process work for you? Take notice of writers' techniques. How do they accomplish their craft? For example, after discovering the writer's topic, you will probably recognize the writer's *purpose.* You might notice how a writer uses *voice* to appeal to a particular *audience.* Thinking about the writer's *tone* and *style* might lead you to discover new ways to use language. You might even wonder why the writer chose this particular form of *publication.*

As you think about your reading, you make meaning. By reading thoughtfully and creatively, you actually become a part of the author's writing process, because meaning is a blend of the writer's words and the reader's imagination. In this sense, the meaning of a piece of writing changes with every reader. Meaning is not fixed and indisputable; it is individual and variable. The meaning in a piece of writing is not a lock that requires a special key; rather it is a coat that fits various readers in various ways.

As you read, keep the writer in mind. Imagine the process of writing behind the words on the page. When you *read as a writer,* you continue the reading-writing cycle by paying close attention to the writer's craft and learning from it. When you *write as a reader,* too, you keep your audience in mind, imagining their experience as readers.

Reading as a writer means asking certain questions as you reflect on a piece of writing. Since your first response is likely to be emotional, consider the following response questions first.

- What is my first impression of the piece of writing? Do I like it? — dislike it? — feel neutral toward it?

- What mood does the writing put me in? Bored? Confused? Delighted? Angry? Sad? Dismayed?

- Does the writing remind me of any personal experience or memory — or of the experience of someone I know? In what ways are the situations similar? In what ways are they different? How do I feel about the experience or the memory?

- Does the writing remind me of something else that I have read? How are my reactions to the two pieces similar? How are they different?

- What is the central meaning of the piece of writing? Do I agree or disagree with the point that the writer seems to be making? Why?

- Does the writing cause me to see things from a new perspective? Does it cause me to re-examine an opinion or a belief that I have previously held?

- Would I recommend this piece of writing to someone else? Why or why not?

Once you have responded to the writing in terms of your feelings and your experience, ask yourself critical, analytic questions about what the writer has done to inspire your responses. Answers to these questions may help you to discover techniques for your own writing.

Reading Critically

- Does the writing leave me with a dominant impression? Does it leave me feeling that my attention was scattered and diffused? Can I describe that singular focus so that someone else can experience it?

- Does the writing satisfy all my expectations? Does it contain "loose ends" that never get tied up? Does it raise issues and expectations and resolve them satisfactorily, or does it leave me "hanging" by failing to resolve all the questions?

- Does the writing place unfair demands on me by assuming that I already have certain information or facts? Does it attempt to provide me with sufficient information to form opinions and to make judgments? Does it assume that I have certain technical expertise or know special terms?

- Does the writing require me to take notes or to mark key points for further study?

- Does the writing capture my attention from the outset and sustain it to the end, or does the pace change, flowing quickly in some places, plodding in others? Which elements help to focus my attention? — the writer's word choice? — the vividness of details? — the method of organization? — the inherent interest of the topic?

- Does the writing offer me any clues about the writer's attitude toward the topic? Does the writer take the point of view of an expert, a novice, or an observer? Is the writer sympathetic toward the topic or neutral and disinterested? Are there any clues as to why the writer has taken this stance?
- Can I convey the overall mood of the writing to someone else, using my own words?
- What traits of this writing do I consider noteworthy and memorable?
- Are there elements of this writing that are similar to how I write? — its choice of words? — its imagery? — its method of organization? — its format and style? Does it contain traits and techniques that I want to imitate or any that I want to avoid?

Considering and discussing these questions can help your writing in two ways. First, you will find ideas in your reading that you will want to explore in your own writing. In addition, by discovering and analyzing another writer's techniques, you'll discover new ways to develop your own craft.

In the units that follow, use your responses to other writers' published work as part of your own prewriting. Use both kinds of experience — *reading as a writer* and *writing as a reader* — to inspire you as a writer, extending the limits of your own techniques, imagination, and understanding.

Continuing Assignment **Read as a Writer**

Exchange with a classmate the pieces of writing that you have published in the Continuing Assignment on page 109. Read each other's writing carefully and respectfully — analyzing it as writers. As you read, ask yourself the questions for Responding to Writing on page 112 and those for Reading Critically on pages 112–113. Write down your responses, along with other questions and answers that occur to you as you read. Then write one or more paragraphs to the writer, expressing your response. If possible, get together with your classmate to talk over each other's responses. Keep this reader's response to your writing in your portfolio or your writer's notebook. From time to time, record in your notebook other questions and comments that will help you to view your writing as both a writer and a reader. Continue to respond as a writer when you read, and record your responses as prewriting for other pieces of writing.

For a **paragraph** or an **essay**

Applying *the* Writing Process

CONTENTS

UNIT **1**

Writing with a Descriptive Focus

Before TV, radio, films, and photography, people relied almost exclusively on descriptive writing to form images of people, places, and things outside their own experience. In fact, over the centuries, description may have done more to shrink the world than any of our modern technologies. In this unit you'll test your powers to observe and to translate what you see, feel, hear, taste, and smell into writing that's as clear—or clearer—than the original. You'll study techniques for seeing even workaday objects with new eyes, and you'll gain strategies for communicating the freshness of your vision to your readers.

In reading or writing descriptive passages, you become an armchair traveler leaving your own time and place far behind. This unit gives you a taste of *travel* to other places as you read models of effective description and do some descriptive writing of your own. One of these places is Egdon Heath, Thomas Hardy's imaginative composite of several heaths of Dorset County in the English countryside. As you read the passage shown here, focus on the techniques that Hardy uses to breathe life into the "haggard" landscape. Focus, too, on how the description makes you feel.

Montréal, QUE.
–Central Sta./Ga
Cantic, QUÉ.

(NYS & W)
Rouses Point, NY

Plattsburgh, NY
Port Kent, NY (Bur
Westport, NY (Lake
Saranac Lake

1 17A
0 49A
448
3 55P
3 50P
3 10P
2 25P
1 00P

A Saturday afternoon in November was approaching the time of twilight, and the vast tract of unenclosed wild known as Egdon Heath embrowned itself moment by moment. Overhead the hollow stretch of whitish cloud shutting out the sky was as a tent which had the whole heath for its floor.

The heaven being spread with this pallid screen and the earth with the darkest vegetation, their meeting-line at the horizon was clearly marked. In such contrast the heath wore the appearance of an installment of night which had taken up its place before its astronomical hour was come: darkness had to a great extent arrived hereon, while day stood distinct in the sky. Looking upwards, a furze-cutter would have been inclined to continue work; looking down, he would have decided to finish his faggot and go home. The distant rims of the world and of the firmament seemed to be a division in time no less than a division in matter. The face of the heath by its mere complexion added half an hour to evening; it could in like manner retard the dawn, sadden noon, anticipate the frowning of storms scarcely generated, and intensify the opacity of a moonless midnight to a cause of shaking and dread.

In fact, precisely at this transitional point of its nightly roll into darkness the great and particular glory of the Egdon

Great image! Cloud = tent.

Egdon _tells_ a tale — it's like a person.

Tone is like the Heath— majestic but mysterious.

waste began, and nobody could be said to understand the heath who had not been there at such a time. It could best be felt when it could not clearly be seen, its complete effect and explanation lying in this and the succeeding hours before the next dawn: then, and only then, did it tell its true tale. The spot was, indeed, a near relation of night, and when night showed itself an apparent tendency to gravitate together could be perceived in its shades and the scene. The sombre stretch of rounds and hollows seemed to rise and meet the evening gloom in pure sympathy, the heath exhaling darkness as rapidly as the heavens precipitated it. And so the obscurity in the air and the obscurity in the land closed together in a black fraternization towards which each advanced half-way.

The place became full of a watchful intentness now; for when other things sank brooding to sleep the heath appeared slowly to awake and listen. Every night its Titanic form seemed to await something; but it had waited thus, unmoved, during so many centuries, through the crises of so many things, that it could only be imagined to await one last crisis —the final overthrow.

It was a spot which returned upon the memory of those who loved it with an aspect of peculiar and kindly congruity. Smiling champaigns of flowers and fruit hardly do this, for they are permanently harmonious only with an existence of better reputation as to its issues than the present. Twilight combined with the scenery of Egdon Heath to evolve a thing majestic without severity, impressive without showiness, emphatic in its admonitions, grand in its simplicity. The qualifications which frequently invest the façade of a prison with far more dignity than is found in the façade of a palace double its size lent to this heath a sublimity in which spots renowned for beauty of the accepted kind are utterly wanting. Fair prospects wed happily with fair times; but alas, if times be not fair! Men have oftener suffered from the mockery of a place too smiling for their reason than from the oppression of surroundings oversadly tinged. Haggard Egdon appealed to a subtler and scarcer instinct, to a more recently learnt emotion, than that which responds to the sort of beauty called charming and fair.

Indeed, it is a question if the exclusive reign of this orthodox beauty is not approaching its last quarter. . . .

The most thorough-going ascetic could feel that he had a natural right to wander on Egdon: he was keeping within the line of legitimate indulgence when he laid himself open to influences such as these. Colours and beauties so far subdued were, at least, the birthright of all. Only in summer days of highest feather did its mood touch the level of gaiety. Intensity was more usually reached by way of the solemn than by way of the brilliant, and such a sort of intensity was often arrived at during winter darkness, tempests, and mists. Then Egdon was aroused to reciprocity; for the storm was its lover, and the wind its friend. Then it became the home of strange phantoms; and it was found to be the hitherto unrecognized original of those wild regions of obscurity which are vaguely felt to be compassing us about in midnight dreams of flight and disaster, and are never thought of after the dream till revived by scenes like this.

It was at present a place perfectly accordant with man's nature—neither ghastly, hateful, nor ugly: neither commonplace, unmeaning, nor tame; but, like man, slighted and enduring; and withal singularly colossal and mysterious in its swarthy monotony. As with some persons who have long lived apart, solitude seemed to look out of its countenance. It had a lonely face, suggesting tragical possibilities.

Thomas Hardy *(1840–1928)*
from *The Return of the Native*

Like looking in a mirror?

Like a person again.

Responding to Literature

You know from reading imaginative literature that animals, objects, and even natural phenomena are sometimes given human attributes, or are personified. Thomas Hardy uses personification to give Egdon Heath its ominous character. Read the selection again and find several examples of this technique. Then choose one or two that you find particularly eloquent, and respond to each by brainstorming or clustering. Focus your response on the descriptive possibilities for your own writing. For instance, the heath has a *face* and a *complexion* that reflect its mood. How would you use similar terms to describe a scene from your experience? How does the face of your favorite mountain, say, change with the time of day, with the season, or with *your* mood? Keep your prewriting notes in your writer's notebook.

Discovering and Exploring Ideas

Think about a passage in a novel, a biography, a story, an essay, or a magazine article that you especially liked. Chances are the passage you liked was a passage of descriptive writing. You use description when you write a story, when you do a character study, when you write about a trip or an event, when you describe a scene or locale, and in many other writing situations. Whether your purpose is to stimulate your readers' imaginations with a piece of fiction or to re-create a scene or an event with a factual description, you need to develop your descriptive powers.

Discovering Ideas

One ability to develop is your power of observation. Examine your daily experiences to find ideas for descriptive writing. Keep your writer's notebook or journal with you and record vivid impressions that you encounter: sights, sounds, tastes, smells, textures, and other sensations. You can get ideas for writing by observing people in various places. Watch their movements and gestures; listen to their words and their voices. Record your observations in your writer's notebook. Also record details of interesting places and objects; don't rely on your memory to re-create important details.

Record in your writer's notebook ideas that you get while reading books, magazines, and newspapers, while listening to the radio, or while watching TV. Include pictures, poems, and clusters of associations *(pages 14–15)* that interest you.

Make an interest inventory. List people whom you admire, places that appeal to you, and things that you like to do in your leisure time. All are potential subjects for descriptive writing.

Use freewriting *(pages 11–12)* to generate ideas for descriptive writing. The advantage of freewriting is that it can be done anywhere, at almost any time. Do some freewriting at the end of a study period or while you're waiting in a doctor's office. Freewrite the last thing at night before going to sleep, or take your notebook or journal with you on a walk and freewrite some of your observations. Begin with a word or an idea: *hero, birch,* or *dawn.* Write whatever comes to mind — words, phrases, sentences. Later, mine your writing to find idea gems for descriptive writing.

Assignment 1   Recording Observations

During the next week, record in your writer's notebook details that you observe about people, places, and objects. As you gather impressions, use all your senses, and include at least one conversation. Record one set of details each day.

Assignment 2 Practicing Freewriting

Look over the observations that you have recorded in your writer's notebook. Choose a single observation or an idea that is common to several of your observations and do a page or two of freewriting about it.

Exploring Ideas

Observation and freewriting usually generate many ideas. How can you determine which ideas are worth developing? Try asking yourself the following questions. Consider a *no* answer to be a danger signal.

- *Will the subject be interesting to explore and write about?* If you aren't enthusiastic about your subject, your writing may lack energy and detail.
- *Do you think of the subject in terms of images?* If not, it will probably be difficult to describe.
- *Is the length of the subject appropriate for the assignment?* If not, your treatment of the subject may suffer by being padded or cut to fit the required length.
- *Is the subject potentially rich in sensory detail?* Remember that providing your readers with a variety of sensory detail is fundamental to good descriptive writing. If you don't provide enough sensory detail, you risk writing a composition that is bland or one-dimensional.

Using Prewriting Techniques

Once you have chosen a subject, you can use a prewriting technique such as brainstorming, clustering, asking questions, or changing viewpoints to explore your ideas and to gather descriptive details. Since you'll be writing a description, you'll want to include many sensory words in your prewriting.

Brainstorming *(pages 16–17)* produces a list of all the details that come to mind about the person, place, object, or event that you have chosen. You write words and phrases that tell how the subject looks, sounds, tastes, smells, and feels. Write each detail as you think of it, without stopping to evaluate your writing.

Clustering *(pages 16–17)* creates a sort of map of the details that come to mind about your subject. In your cluster, circle each word and use arrows to show the relationships or the associations among the words in the cluster.

Critical Thinking:
Determining relationships

Another prewriting technique is finding the answers to the questions that begin with *who, what, where, when, how,* and *why (page 18)*. You'll ask questions like these, for example: *What* is the Palace of Westminster? *Where* is it located? Asking and answering questions will supply you with concrete details for your description.

Critical Thinking:
Analyzing

Critical Thinking:

Determining relationships; Analyzing
What details are related to my subject? What questions lead to details?

Choose three of the following subjects, and write them on your paper. Using a different prewriting technique for each subject, generate concrete details, especially details that appeal to the senses.

1. A police officer
2. A photograph
3. A statue
4. A shopping mall
5. A room in an inn
6. A tour guide

Changing Viewpoints to Gather Sensory Details

Another prewriting technique for exploring ideas for descriptions is changing viewpoints. Observing a subject from different viewpoints may call your attention to details that you have overlooked.

For example, in describing an airplane, you could choose to see it from the inside or the outside; from the front, the rear, or the side; from the ground or the air. You could describe the plane as it taxis, takes off, flies, or lands. Each time you change viewpoint, you will find the details somewhat changed. Choose a viewpoint that will add interest to your description. Look at these four viewpoints of an island.

From a plane: a small patch of trees and rocks with a narrow sandy beach
From a distant boat: clumps of trees and rocky ledges, dense vegetation, rimmed by white sand
Closer (thirty yards): tall palms rising out of dense undergrowth, pinkish sand, rocky ledges studded with tough little trees, red blossoms, tall grass
Inside (on the island): enormous trunks of the palms, bright colored birds, strange calls of birds and animals, waving grasses, heavy sweet smell of brilliant red flowers, rocky slopes, pink sand with scattered shells

Assignment 4 Changing Viewpoints

Choose one of the following subjects to explore for a descriptive passage, and write it on your paper. View the subject from at least three positions and list details from each viewpoint.

1. A cruise ship
2. A statue
3. An outdoor market
4. A painter
5. A marathon
6. A formal fountain garden

Continuing Assignment Find a Subject for Description

For writing a **paragraph** or an **essay**

In this unit you will develop a paragraph or an essay with a descriptive focus. Begin by reviewing the contents of your writer's notebook.

Then brainstorm to find suitable subjects to write about. After you have chosen a subject, use freewriting, clustering, answering questions, and changing viewpoints to develop sensory details about your subject. Save your notes.

Focusing Ideas

Now that you have chosen your subject and begun to find some details, you need to explore your subject thoroughly to bring it into sharp focus. Then, at the drafting stage, you will know which details to keep and which to discard.

Establishing Purpose, Audience, and Point of View

Think about your purpose and your audience as you plan your descriptive writing. You may need to include a descriptive passage in a persuasive essay or in a personal narrative. Consider how you use description in a report or in instructions, where concrete physical details describe objects or processes. On the other hand, if your purpose is to tell a story, you may use vivid sensory details to describe characters and settings. Note how the writer of the following selection brings actions to life for the reader.

> *I*t was a day to be nearly free; a day to stay in London and dream of the country. In Saint James's Park the premature summer was entering its third week. Along the lake girls lay like cut flowers in the unnatural heat of a Sunday afternoon in May. An attendant had lit an improbable bonfire, and the smell of burnt grass drifted with the echoes of the traffic. Only the pelicans, hobbling fussily around on their island pavilion, seemed disposed to move; only Alan Turner, his big shoes crunching on the gravel, had anywhere to go; for once not even the girls could distract him.
>
> John le Carré *(1931–   )*
> from *A Small Town in Germany*

Your audience also determines the kind of description you write. If it is likely that your readers will be unfamiliar with your subject, you will want to use details that give essential facts simply and that relate your subject to more familiar experiences. On the other hand, if your readers are likely to know something about your subject, you can use unusual details or express the familiar in a fresh, creative way.

The **tone** of your description is the voice or the attitude that you employ. Tone depends on both your purpose and your audience. For example, you may use limited vocabulary and simple concepts to explain something to young children, informal language to amuse your friends, and formal language and technical terms to report abstract ideas or complicated processes to a general audience.

You may also need to consider the point of view of your composition. In addition to position (describing something from above or below, for example), you can select a **point of view,** which is the person of the narrator. As you describe someone or something, are you putting yourself into the picture or referring to yourself *(page 26)?* If so, your description will come from the first-person viewpoint. If you are creating your description without referring to yourself, then you are using the third-person viewpoint. For some descriptive passages, you might need the **omniscient,** or all-seeing, point of view.

(ŏm-nĭsh′ənt)

FIRST PERSON   I stood at the edge of the silent, frozen lake, thinking how different the scene had been in July, with brightly clad sunbathers stretched out on the beach, swimmers churning the water, and everything hot and bright.

THIRD PERSON   Now, in winter, the lake was frozen, windswept, and deserted, cottages were boarded up, and all was silent.

OMNISCIENT   In summer the lake was lively, a favorite spot for swimmers and sunbathers, but its winter aspect was quieter. Frozen from December until March, it was invaded on Saturdays by groups of skaters from nearby neighborhoods, all young, strong, and very noisy.

Assignment 1   Purpose, Audience, and Point of View

Two purposes are listed for each of the following subjects. First, write each subject on your paper, leaving space between. Then explain how your two descriptions of that subject would differ, based on each purpose and audience. Explain the tone and the point of view that you would use for each description.

1. An interesting tour guide
   a. To describe that person in a travel brochure written for prospective customers of a travel agency
   b. To describe in a letter to a friend your experience with that person on a recent trip
2. A colonial herb garden
   a. To suggest to your town council that they establish a similar garden on the property of the antique house that they recently restored and opened to the public
   b. To describe the plants and their placement to a botany class

3. A castle high above a small village

    a. To describe your impressions of the castle and its surroundings to readers of the travel section of a newspaper

    b. To use the castle and the setting in a picture book for preschool children

Limiting Your Description

Before writing any description, you will need to limit your subject to a topic that you can comfortably handle in the space allowed. For example, the subject "European travel" is much too large to cover in a paragraph or an essay — and probably even in a book. The subject "The French Riviera" can be handled in a book and, perhaps sketchily, in a lengthy essay. On the other hand, "The architecture of hotels on the French Riviera" lends itself well to an essay, and "The Architecture of the Carlton in Cannes" could be described in one paragraph.

The following steps will help you to limit your subject and to choose a title for your writing.

▶ **Strategies**

1. *Determine how long the finished piece of writing should be.* Is a paragraph required? Two or three paragraphs? A short story? A long essay? Your answer to this question will indicate how many words or pages you will need to write.

2. *Decide what portion of the writing will be description.* If your purpose is primarily to describe, all your writing will be directed toward that goal. On the other hand, if your purpose is to tell a short story, you will devote lines and whole paragraphs wherever you need them to describe characters, settings, and actions.

3. *Choose a working title that reflects the content that you will cover.* Your title needs to reflect the whole piece of writing. It should be appropriate, but it should provoke your readers' interest. Your title should not be lengthy unless you mean it to be humorous.

Assignment 2   Limiting Topics for Description

Choose three of the following subjects. For each subject, write on your paper the title for two limited topics: one that you could cover well in a paragraph and another that you could cover in an essay of five or six pages.

SAMPLE   Train travel
ANSWER   *Paragraph:* The Advantages of Traveling to Work by Train
         Essay: Eating and Sleeping on Long-Distance Train Trips

1. Wide-body planes	**3.** Automobile travel	**5.** Guided tours
2. Big airports	**4.** Bus terminals	**6.** Restored trains

Supporting by Details and Examples

Your descriptive paragraph or essay will center on a general statement characterizing the topic. That statement cannot stand alone without "proof." Consider these general statements, which need details or examples to prove or support them. "A desert can be as varied and interesting as any forest." "The beauty of the Alps should not be underestimated." The first general statement invites examples, developed by comparison and contrast, that tell how a desert and a forest are alike and different. The second general statement calls for examples of the beauty of the Alps. Depending on the length and purpose of the descriptive composition, you may have to provide many brief details or several longer examples.

Using Examples

An example *(pages 29–30)* is a case or a sample that illustrates a general statement. In the following selection, note how the author uses examples to demonstrate and amplify the statement about Mexican fiestas and the surprises they offer.

> • • • *T*he art of the fiesta has been debased almost everywhere else, but not in Mexico. There are few places in the world where it is possible to take part in a spectacle like our great religious fiestas with their violent primary colors, their bizarre costumes and dances, their fireworks and ceremonies, and their inexhaustible welter of surprises: the fruit, candy, toys, and other objects sold on these days in the plazas and open-air markets.
>
> Octavio Paz *(1914–   )*
> from *The Labyrinth of Solitude*

Assignment 3 **Using Examples**

On your paper, write four topics from the following list or four of your own choosing, and state whether you would develop each topic as an essay or as a single paragraph. Then list at least three examples that you might use to support each topic.

SAMPLE   A strange vacation
ANSWER   an essay
               Locked out at midnight
               Unexpected guests, two-legged and otherwise
               The cottage with talking doors

1. My favorite place
2. A guided tour
3. Survival training
4. A jungle adventure
5. Foods of another country
6. Traveling with a pet
7. A river trip
8. A day in a strange city

Using Comparison and Contrast

You can use comparison and contrast *(pages 30–32)* to organize the details of your description. Use comparison to show how two things are alike, contrast to show how they are different. Use comparison and contrast only when there is an important link between the two people or objects. Suppose that you compare a winding road to a snake. Like a snake, a dirt road can twist and turn. Both are long and thin; both may be difficult to follow and might even present danger. Unlike the snake, however, the road is unvarying, never changing its course.

Since a bus and a bicycle are both vehicles, they invite comparison. Can you compare daily living with riding a bicycle? Both require effort, both will get you there — if you know where you want to go — and both can be dangerous if you are reckless. Creativity can make interesting connections between seemingly dissimilar things, amusing and instructing the reader in the process.

What comparison does the writer make in the following selection?

> *J*ust then a distant whistle sounded, and there was a shuffling of feet on the platform. A number of lanky boys of all ages appeared as suddenly and slimily as eels wakened by the crack of thunder; some came from the waiting-room, where they had been warming themselves by the red stove, or half asleep on the slat benches; others uncoiled themselves from baggage trucks or slid out of express wagons.
>
> Willa Cather *(1876–1947)*
> from "The Sculptor's Funeral"

Similes and metaphors are brief comparisons. A **simile** uses the word *like* or *as* when comparing two people or objects: a cough that rattled *like* dried beans in a paper cup; a promise as reliable *as* New England weather. A **metaphor** also compares two things, but unlike a simile, a metaphor does not use the word *like* or *as:* birthday candle stars blown out by a breath of cloud.

Critical Thinking:
Comparing / contrasting
How are the two alike? How do they differ?

Assignment 4 Using Comparison and Contrast

Choose a subject from the following list or one from your imagination. On your paper, write the subject that you have chosen and another person, place, object, or action that you will use for a comparison and contrast paragraph. List similarities and differences, and then write a paragraph comparing and contrasting these two objects, places, actions, or persons.

1. An astronaut
2. A postcard
3. An airport
4. A backpacker
5. A campground
6. A hotel lobby

Choosing the Best Descriptive Details

Once you have chosen your subject and limited the scope of your description, you will be ready to select the best descriptive details. Begin by looking over the details that you generated while discovering and exploring ideas through brainstorming, clustering, asking questions, and changing viewpoints. You will want to keep some of those details and discard others. Keep only those details that conform to your purpose, audience, and point of view. If you need additional details, use brainstorming or other prewriting techniques to generate them.

The details that you choose should be rich in sensory words. They should stimulate your readers' imaginations through appeals to their senses. You may want to describe music filling a concert hall, the spicy aroma of cookies baking, or the sight of a butterfly newly unfolding itself on a leaf. You need to think about all of the senses, and you may even want to include some sensory details that are unpleasant, even painful. Your imagination and your memories will help you to provide your readers with vivid experiences.

Notice the variety of details in the following passage.

> *T*he next evening when Joe Willow passed the gate, I got up and ran to hang on it as I watched him pass on up the road. The sun, being low and to his back, sent a long finger of shadow ahead of him. I could hear the crunch and whisper of his footsteps between the squeaks of the bucket he carried until they began to fade with the coming of the breeze through the tall grass alongside the road. The bucket creaked faintly and the breeze dropped for a moment.
>
> Durango Mendoza (1945–   )
> from "The Passing"

Precision in your choice of details will make your description vivid, helping your readers to see and feel the images and the sensations that you want to evoke. Instead of using general attributes such as "tall" or "heavy," include unusual details in your description or make comparisons with similes or with metaphors. A few well-chosen details will suggest the personality of the subject. It is always better to show than to tell.

Notice the precise descriptive details in the next passage.

. . . *B*ut Abba stubbornly rose at dawn and continued at the shoemaker's bench. Although yellow hair does not readily change color, Abba's beard had turned completely white, and the white, staining, had turned yellow again. His brows had sprouted like brushes and hid his eyes, and his high forehead was like a piece of yellow parchment. But he had not lost his touch. He could still turn out a stout shoe with a broad heel, even if it did take a little longer. He bored holes with the awl, stitched with the needle, hammered his pegs, and in a hoarse voice sang the old shoemaker's song.

Isaac Bashevis Singer (1904   )
from "The Little Shoemakers"

Assignment 5 Choosing Descriptive Details

Choose three of the following subjects or three of your own choosing. On your paper, list at least ten descriptive details about each subject, using as many senses as you can. Include at least one comparison, if possible, as a simile or a metaphor.

SAMPLE A bakery

ANSWER A rich cloud of aromas: yeast bread, cinnamon, apple and vanilla; gleaming glass cases with rows of lustrous golden rolls and croissants; the proprietress in starchy white, her cheeks like apples; the tinny sound of a radio from the kitchen.

1. An amusement park
2. A tour bus
3. A museum
4. A souvenir stand
5. A diver
6. An orange
7. A flower
8. A bonfire
9. A hiker

Using Descriptive Language

Once you have noted the details that make your subject unique, you will need to find the best words to describe that uniqueness to your readers.

Using Effective Nouns and Verbs

Specific nouns and strong verbs help your readers to form a mental picture of the person, place, or object that you're describing. Since specific nouns create precise images, words such as *snowshoe hare, knotty pine,* and *monarch* rather than *animal, woods,* and *butterfly* will make your descriptions more effective.

Verbs describe motion; strong verbs describe motion exactly. Remember as you focus your description on actions to indicate whether a

Reference Point: *pages 540–543 and pages 546–548*

person *edged* or *burst* into a room. Flowers that *rocket skyward from a tangled bed* are not the same flowers as those that *creep unobstructed across the warm soil.* If you wrote "The man walked across the street," your readers would not get a clear picture of the way the man crossed the street. Did he *shuffle, scurry, limp, stroll, stagger,* or *weave?* Readers will know only if you show them.

Note what a difference a strong verb makes in each of the following pairs of sentences.

VAGUE   The angry man entered the room.

CLEAR   The angry man burst into the room.

VAGUE   In her excitement, she took the gift.

CLEAR   In her excitement, she snatched the gift.

Reference Point:
pages 546–547

Use verbs in the active voice rather than in the passive voice.

PASSIVE   The Battle of the Bands contest was won by our school.

ACTIVE   Our school won the Battle of the Bands contest.

In addition, choose action verbs rather than forms of the verb *be* such as *am, are, was,* and *were:* "His plan excited us" rather than "His plan was exciting."

Assignment 6   Using Specific Nouns and Strong Verbs

On your paper, rewrite each of the following sentences twice. Use specific nouns and strong verbs to create two different situations.

SAMPLE   The animal came out of its house.
ANSWER   The squirrel leaped out of its nest.
The python slithered out of its tank.

1. A person fastened the sign.
2. Flowers were gathered by her.
3. Animals are chased by others.
4. The people greeted the ship.
5. Someone read a map.
6. He is fond of shopping.

Using Effective Modifiers

Words that add to or limit the meaning of other words are **modifiers.** As you know, adjectives modify nouns and pronouns; adverbs modify verbs, adjectives, and other adverbs; prepositional and participial phrases modify various parts of speech.

Reference Point:
*pages 549–556
and pages
578–582*

Similes and metaphors also modify words by comparing them to other things.

SIMILES   as impenetrable as Alaskan soil in January

danced like a wounded bear

METAPHORS   a thin wafer of a moon

the flat landscape of her life

Original similes and metaphors add zest to your writing, but familiar ones have become clichés. Try always for freshness.

Well-chosen modifiers add strong details to the words they modify. Note how effectively the writer of the following selection used modifying words and phrases.

> Nine hours later we lay anchored in Mudros harbour, waiting to tranship. Never before had I seen so many vessels of all kinds, great and small, old and new, British and French and Levantine. Hospital ships gleamed white and enormous above the small black cargo-boats that ran inconspicuously through the Mediterranean to take refuge in the estuaries of large rivers; gaunt Dreadnaughts lay close beside little sailing vessels, with ancient rigging so fantastic that they seemed, in the brilliant incredible light which flooded the harbour, to be no longer the property of the Levantines from the tumble-down village on the sinister shore, but the old beautiful ships of the Greeks awaiting the Persian fleet.
>
> Vera Brittain *(1893–1970)*
> from *Testament of Youth*

Be careful not to overdo your use of modifiers. You will be guilty of overwriting if you attach a string of modifiers to every noun and verb. Overusing modifiers will weaken the effect of your nouns and verbs.

OVERWRITTEN   The young, speckled fawn fearfully listened to loud thrashing in the surrounding brush and unsteadily struggled to its tiny feet.

BETTER   The speckled fawn, alarmed at the thrashing in the brush, wobbled to its feet.

Assignment 7   Using Modifiers Effectively

On your paper, choose three of the following topics or three of your own and create a list of details with modifiers for each. Use phrases as well as single words.

SAMPLE   A storm
ANSWER   Gusty winds, jagged streaks of lightning, a ripping of thunder, rain in sheets, and then a sudden storm of marble-sized hailstones clattering on the roof and gutters

1. A mountain
2. A bicyclist
3. A church
4. A sailor
5. A workshop
6. A letter
7. A restaurant
8. A flag
9. A sky

For writing
a **paragraph**
or an **essay**

Using your prewriting notes from the Continuing Assignment on page 122, make notes to focus your ideas. First, keeping your purpose and audience in mind, select an appropriate point of view and tone. Next, limit your topic for either a one-paragraph description or a longer descriptive essay and choose an appropriate working title. Then decide what kind or kinds of supporting details you will use, such as examples or comparisons. Finally, jot down precise nouns, strong verbs, similes and metaphors, and modifying words and phrases that will help you to write an effective description. Save all your notes for later use.

Prewriting

Organizing Ideas

Now that you have a subject and some good details, you need to find a pattern to organize your material effectively in order to make your descriptive paragraph or essay striking and vivid to your readers. There are a number of organizational patterns that will help you to do that.

Patterns of Organization

? Critical Thinking:

Organizing

You need to organize your general statements and details in a pattern that creates the effect that you want and is easy for your readers to follow. Three good patterns for descriptive writing are spatial order, order of importance, and chronological order.

Using Spatial Order

You can use spatial order *(page 37)* to arrange details as they exist in space. Spatial order is especially useful for describing rooms and scenes. When using that organization, present each detail as it would be seen by a person who observes something from top to bottom, from side to side, or from near to far.

To help readers follow your spatial route, use transitional words and phrases such as *above, below, next to, behind, in front of,* and so on. Notice how spatial order and directional transitions clarify the following passage.

> *T*he small toy train climbs up on its narrow gauge from the Umzimkulu valley into the hills. It climbs up to Carisbrooke, and when it stops there, you may get out for a moment and look down on the great valley from which you have come. . . .

If there is mist here, you will see nothing of the great valley. The mist will swirl about and below you, and the train and the people make a small world of their own. Some people do not like it, and find it cold and gloomy. But others like it, and find in it mystery and fascination, and prelude to adventure, and an intimation of the unknown. The train passes through a world of fancy, and you can look through the misty panes at green shadowy banks of grass and bracken. Here in their season grow the blue agapanthus, the wild watsonia, and the red-hot poker, and now and then it happens that one may glimpse an arum in a dell. And always behind them the dim wall of the wattles, like ghosts in the mist.

(ăg′ə-păn′thəs)

(ăr′əm)

Alan Paton *(1903–1988)*
from *Cry, the Beloved Country*

Assignment 1 Using Spatial Order

? Critical Thinking:
Organizing
How can I put details into spatial order?

Think of a store or a section of a store that you can describe. Locate yourself somewhere in or near the store: for example, in or approaching a doorway, in the middle of the floor, or on a stairway or escalator. Brainstorm and list on your paper the details that you could observe from that vantage point, using as many of your senses as possible. Then arrange your details in the spatial order that you would follow in a description.

Using Order of Importance

Another useful pattern for descriptions is order of importance *(page 38)*, which presents details in ascending or descending order. You may begin with the least important detail and end with the most important detail, or you may present the most important detail first and work your way down to the least important. You can also indicate order of importance through the use of transitional words or phrases such as *better yet* or *more important*.

The writer of the following paragraph uses order of importance to describe a room.

*M*issy had her own room, timber-panelled and as brown as the rest of the house. The floor was covered in a mottled brown linoleum, the bed in a brown candlewick spread, the window in a brown Holland blind; there was an ugly old bureau and an even older, uglier wardrobe. No mirror, no chair, no rug. But the walls did bear three pictures. One was a faded and foxed

(də-gâr'ə-tĩp)

daguerreotype of an incredibly shrivelled, ancient first Sir William, taken about the time of the American Civil War; one was an embroidered sampler (Missy's earliest effort, and very well done) which announced that THE DEVIL MAKES WORK FOR IDLE HANDS;

(păs pär-tōō'dĭd)

and the last was a passe-partouted Queen Alexandra, stiff and unsmiling, but still to Missy's uncritical eyes a very beautiful woman.

Colleen McCullough (1938–   )
from *The Ladies of Missalonghi*

Notice how the writer focuses the description on less important details such as the walls and the floor first, leading up to the most important feature, the three pictures. The repetition of the color brown tends to reduce the importance of individual features of the room by blending them. Even the pictures are described in order of importance, the last being a picture of a woman whom the character Missy regards with admiration and perhaps envy.

Assignment 2 Using Order of Importance

Choose a place that is familiar to you and your classmates. Then brainstorm vivid details to describe it. Write the details on your paper and number them in order from least to most important. Draft a paragraph that describes but does not give the name of the place. Exchange papers with a classmate and see if you can identify the places.

Using Chronological Order

A third organizational pattern is chronological order. When you use chronological order, arrange details in the order in which they are observed. Although time passes while these details are being observed, the details themselves, not the passage of time, are the focus of your description. Transitional words such as *first, then, next,* and *finally* help your readers to follow the order.

Notice how the element of time is used in the following passage.

A Saturday afternoon in November was approaching the time of twilight, and the vast tract of unenclosed wild known as Egdon Heath embrowned itself moment by moment. Overhead the hollow stretch of whitish cloud shutting out the sky was as a tent which had the whole heath for its floor.

The heaven being spread with this pallid screen and the earth with the darkest vegetation, their meeting-line at the horizon was clearly marked. In such contrast the heath wore the appearance of an instalment of night which had taken up its place before its astronomical hour was come: darkness had to a great extent arrived hereon, while day stood distinct in the sky.

Thomas Hardy *(1840–1928)*
from *The Return of the Native*

Assignment 3 | **Using Chronological Order**

Think of a subject that you might observe and describe using chronological order. After limiting your subject to a topic, list details on your paper in any order. Then number the details in the order in which they would be observed. Write your description in chronological order, using transitional words and phrases such as *first, next, finally, after that,* and *in the meantime* to guide your readers.

Using Mixed Order

Not all descriptions can be classified neatly into one of the orders described here. It is often necessary to combine spatial and chronological order, chronological order and order of importance, and so forth. It is even possible to find all three orders in one paragraph. It is more likely that you will use all three types of order during a longer piece of writing such as an essay. Notice how the writer uses chronological order combined with spatial order and order of importance in the following passage.

*T*here stood the house, waiting. Why should a house wait? Most pretty scenes have something passive about them, but this looked like a trap baited with beauty, set ready to spring. It stood back from the road. Lou put her hand on the gate and, with a touch of bravado, the two filed up the paved path to the door. Each side of the path, hundreds of standard roses bloomed, overcharged with colour, as though this were their one hour. Crimson, coral, blue-pink, lemon and cold white, they disturbed with fragrance the dead air. In this spell-bound afternoon, with no shadows, the roses glared at the strangers, frighteningly bright. The face of the house was plastered with tea-roses: waxy cream when they opened but with vermilion buds.

Elizabeth Bowen *(1899–1973)*
from ''Look at All Those Roses''

Using Mixed Order

Choose one of the following topics or one of your own choosing. On your paper, list details that you will use in your description. Then arrange details using mixed order: spatial order and order of importance, for example. Write your descriptive paragraph using the mixed order you have chosen.

1. A public garden
2. A sculpture
3. An unusual building
4. A procession or parade
5. A store
6. A ship

Outlining and Mapping

Having decided on a pattern of organization, you are ready to arrange your notes so that you can follow your pattern easily during drafting. You may decide to use a topic outline *(pages 50–51)* or a map *(page 48)* to organize your notes. You might even draw a rough sketch of the person, place, or object that you are describing — especially if you are using spatial order — to remind you of the order in which you will present details.

Rough outlining *(page 49)* is a good way to organize your notes, especially when you are using spatial order or order of importance. To make a rough outline, begin by rereading your prewriting notes. Next, cross out any details that don't fit your organizational scheme and add others if they are needed. Finally, number the details according to the sequence that you have chosen.

Making a Rough Outline

Copy the following prewriting notes on your paper. Then make them into a rough outline that follows either spatial order or order of importance. Cross out notes that do not belong; number the rest according to the order that you have selected. Save your paper.

Topic: California's Big Sur: something for everyone
Details:
— 90-mile stretch of rugged seacoast
— huge redwoods, hundreds of years old
— swimming, beachcombing, fishing, birding, horseback riding
— named by Spanish priests sometime around 1770
— a day's drive or a month's vacation
— highway fog-shrouded in mornings, clear in afternoons
— three natural hot springs to soak in
— twisting, cliff-hugging Highway 1 along entire stretch
— taking photographs of Santa Lucia Mountains rising above the Pacific
— Big Sur: area from about 10 miles south of Carmel to about 5 miles south of Lucia

Organize Your Description

Using your prewriting notes from the Continuing Assignments on pages 122 and 132, proceed according to the following steps to organize details for your descriptive paragraph or essay. *Step 1:* Select the sensory details that best describe your subject. If necessary, use prewriting techniques to generate additional or more specific details. *Step 2:* Decide whether to use spatial order, order of importance, chronological order, or a combination of orders. *Step 3:* Organize your details into a rough outline, a topic outline, or a map, using the order that you have chosen. Make a sketch if that will help. Save all your work for later use.

For writing a **paragraph** or an **essay**

Drafting

Drafting a Descriptive Paragraph

All kinds of paragraphs, including descriptive paragraphs, can either stand alone or be part of a longer piece of writing. A paragraph needs a topic sentence, usually at least three supporting sentences, and a concluding sentence or a transition sentence to the next paragraph.

When drafting a descriptive paragraph, write as quickly as possible, letting your ideas flow freely. You will revise your writing later.

Notice the structure and the effect of the following paragraph. How does the first sentence, the topic sentence, set the stage for the supporting sentences that follow?

*T*here are times of great beauty on a coffee-farm. When the plantation flowered in the beginning of the rains, it was a radiant sight, like a cloud of chalk, in the mist and the drizzling rain, over six hundred acres of land. The coffee-blossom has a delicate slightly bitter scent, like the blackthorn blossom. When the field reddened with the ripe berries, all the women and the children, whom they call the Totos, were called out to pick the coffee off the trees, together with the men; then the waggons and carts brought it down to the factory near the river. Our machinery was never quite what it should have been, but we had planned and built the factory ourselves and thought highly of it. Once the whole factory burned down and had to be built up again. The big coffee-dryer turned and turned, rumbling the coffee in its iron belly with a sound like pebbles that are washed about on the sea-shore. Sometimes the coffee would be dry, and ready to take out of the dryer, in the middle of the night. That was a picturesque moment, with many hurricane lamps in the huge dark room of the factory, that was hung everywhere with cobwebs and coffee-husks, and with eager glowing dark faces, in the light of the lamps, round the dryer; the factory, you felt, hung in the great African night like a bright jewel in an Ethiope's ear.

Isak Dinesen *(1885–1962)*
from *Out of Africa*

In this passage, the writer has used a wealth of sensory detail to create some striking scenes that are bound up with memories of a place and a time. Notice the images of color, scent, sound, and contrasting dark and light to create a vivid impression of the coffee farm.

The Topic Sentence

Your topic sentence *(pages 40–43)* identifies your topic, sets the tone of your description, and suggests what you plan to say about it. For example, the topic sentence of the passage from *Out of Africa* tells readers to look for examples of beauty in the sentences that follow. The opening line of *The Return of the Native (pages 134–135)* also reveals the subject clearly: Egdon Heath as the setting of the novel, and in a sense, Egdon Heath as a character in the novel.

By looking at some of the other topic sentences in this unit, you'll see the vital role they play in descriptive paragraphs and essays. You can use the following guidelines to help you to craft effective topic sentences.

▶ **Strategies**

1. *Write a topic sentence that conveys a general impression of your topic.* Usually your topic sentence tells your readers what you are going to tell them. Your other sentences will "prove" your topic sentence.

   The moon illuminated the courtyard.
   Mr. Muttock was not an ideal neighbor.
   As she entered, she realized with a shock that her room had changed.

2. *Convey your personal feelings about your topic if it is appropriate to do so.*

   Yesterday Walter Howe's long-awaited trip turned into a tragic tale.
   I know of no hobby more satisfying than travel.
   To me, the beauty of Paris on an April morning is unsurpassed.

3. *Place the topic sentence effectively.* Most topic sentences are placed at the beginning of paragraphs, but occasionally you may have reason to place a topic sentence later in the paragraph, even at the end.

4. *Try out several topic sentences.* Experiment by writing a number of topic sentences. Select the one that you feel best suits the focus of your paragraph.

Assignment 1 **Drafting Topic Sentences**

On your paper, draft an effective topic sentence for each of the following limited topics.

SAMPLE A lake under a full moon
ANSWER The reflection of the full moon lay like a river of molten silver on the surface of the lake.

1. A firefighter at work
2. A crowded beach
3. Motorists at a rest area
4. A tourist in a large city
5. Baseball players during a game
6. A grassy pasture

Supporting Sentences

As you know, supporting sentences support or prove the statement made in your topic sentence. Supporting sentences contain details that you identified during prewriting: comparisons, examples, and so forth. These detail sentences provide the color and texture of your description. If your description is to be delightful, or funny, or grim, it will probably be your detail sentences that make it so.

The following strategies will help you to write effective supporting sentences.

▶ **Strategies**

1. *Write supporting sentences that contain sensory details to describe an object's color, shape, size, and weight.* Draw on your sense of touch to describe its texture. If appropriate, also describe its sound, taste, and smell.

2. *Write supporting sentences that describe a place by using details that help the reader "see" its location and understand its significance.*

3. *Write supporting sentences that describe a person by using details that reveal personality as well as physical characteristics.*

4. *Organize your supporting sentences in the order that best suits your topic and purpose.* Present your details in spatial order, order of importance, chronological order, or mixed order — whichever arrangement that you think makes your description most effective.

5. *Add transitional words and phrases* such as *to his left, more important,* and *finally* to help readers to follow your order of presentation.

Drafting Supporting Sentences

Choose one of the topics listed in Assignment 1 on page 139. On your paper, write an effective topic sentence for that topic. (You may use one of the sentences that you wrote during Assignment 1, or create another.) Use prewriting techniques to generate details to "prove" your topic sentence. Write supporting sentences containing those details and arrange them in the order in which you plan to present them.

The Concluding Sentence

If you begin your descriptive paragraph with a topic sentence, you will usually need to end it with a concluding sentence *(pages 44–45).* A concluding sentence can restate your topic sentence, summarize your thoughts about the topic, or add a new insight on the subject. In the last sentence of the Thomas Hardy passage that begins this unit, the narrator reflects on Egdon Heath: "It had a lonely face, suggesting tragical possibilities." You can also conclude with a final example or an important detail. Good examples of such important concluding details are seen in the passage by Elizabeth Bowen on page 135 and in the one by Isak Dinesen on pages 137–138.

Assignment 3 **Drafting Concluding Sentences**

Review the topic sentence and the supporting sentences that you wrote for Assignment 2 above. Review how you numbered supporting sentences to recall the organization that you chose for your descriptive paragraph. Now write three or four concluding sentences to close the paragraph. Choose and mark the best sentence.

Continuing Assignment **Draft Your Descriptive Paragraph**

For writing
a **paragraph**

Review your notes from the Continuing Assignments on pages 122, 132, and 137. You have outlined or mapped your details or perhaps made a sketch. If you have limited your details to those that will suit a paragraph, you will now write the first draft. Begin with a topic sentence, follow with supporting sentences, and end with an effective concluding sentence. Simply develop your ideas into sentences according to your plan. You will revise and proofread later. Save your papers.

Drafting

Drafting a Descriptive Essay

When you draft your descriptive essay, concentrate on following your outline and capturing your thoughts on paper quickly. Let your words flow; you will revise the style and the content later.

A descriptive essay usually consists of three or more paragraphs that describe a person, place, or object in detail. A paragraph contains a topic sentence, supporting sentences, and a concluding sentence. An essay is constructed similarly: it contains an introductory paragraph, body paragraphs, and a concluding paragraph.

Read the essay that follows.

*V*ermont is a rural landscape of changing colors that gloriously signal the time of year. As the winter snow melts, springtime brings the excitement of white water and a countryside splashed with apple blossoms and wild flowers.

With summer the myriads of greens deepen and the velvetlike hillsides are strewn with red clover, buttercups, and daisies. The sunset silhouettes a mowing machine or a hay baler left in a field for another day.

From mid-September to mid-October the fiery yellows and reds of deciduous trees move up the mountain slopes, and the air is pungent with dry leaves and ripened crops.

When the leaves have fallen, snow blankets the rolling hills and mountains and the New England villages snuggled in their valleys. The world becomes blue and white with accents of dark evergreen and barn red.

The impact of seasonal change is heightened by the mountainous terrain. "The surface of Vermont is generally uneven," wrote a historian back in 1842. It is that "uneven-ness," so laconically stated, that provides such beauty from the road.

from "A State for All Seasons"
in *America from the Road (1982)*

(mĭr′ē-ədz)
(dĭ-sĭj′ōo-əs)

The Introductory Paragraph

Your introductory paragraph should capture your reader's attention and focus it on your subject. Although most of your details come in later paragraphs, there should be some striking statement or some provocative element in the introductory paragraph that tugs at your readers, making them want to know what follows. Just as a topic sentence limits the topic of a descriptive paragraph, the introductory paragraph *(pages 54–55)* limits the subject and sets the tone of the descriptive essay. It contains a **thesis statement,** which often is the first sentence of the paragraph, but which can also come last. You might want to begin your introductory paragraph with a quotation, a line from a poem or a story, for example, or a vivid detail.

As the topic sentence tells what is coming during the paragraph, the thesis statement tells — or at least hints at — what is coming during the entire essay. The thesis statement introduces the topic of the essay and focuses on the writer's approach. In the essay about the landscape of Vermont *(page 141)*, the thesis statement is simple and clear: the writer tells readers that it is a landscape of changing colors. Some thesis statements may not entirely give the subject away, however. You may prefer to write a thesis statement that hints at a quality to be revealed or one that creates a little mystery at first.

A good introductory paragraph will build on the thesis statement. It may, however, build up *to* the thesis statement, in an essay that begins with a striking detail, a quotation, or some other attention getter. Often the introductory paragraph sets up areas or subtopics that you will expand upon during the rest of the essay. Whatever else your introductory paragraph does, it must capture your readers' interest and create a "need to know," making them read on.

The Body Paragraphs

Now that you have an introduction that commands your readers' attention, you must deliver what the introduction promises: a vivid description of your subject. Have your lists of details and your outline in front of you as you draft your body paragraphs *(pages 56–57)*. Your writing should flow with no interruption.

Each of your body paragraphs treats a part of your subject, so let each one have its own flavor and its own coherence. Make sure also that the body of the essay is a unified treatment of your subject. For example, each paragraph in the essay about Vermont treats a separate season, but all deal with the landscape. As you know, you can make your description clearer by using transitional words and phrases *(pages 36–38)* to connect paragraphs, just as you do to link sentences within a paragraph.

The tone of your body paragraphs should indicate your attitude toward your subject. It is likely you have chosen to describe the subject because you find it fascinating, or humorous, or strikingly beautiful. Your enthusiasm for your subject should fill your writing and give it spark and energy.

The Concluding Paragraph

Your concluding paragraph *(page 58)* should summarize the outstanding characteristics of the topic that you are describing. It may also give some added insight to give meaning to the subject. In the concluding paragraph of the essay about Vermont, the writer sums up its beauty and color. Quoting a historian, the writer then concludes that the variety of terrain in that state contributes to the beauty that travelers experience. As you conclude, remind your readers of the topic's importance or express your personal feelings about it. Just as it is a good technique to find an attention getter for your opener, it is wise to find something — or to save something — for your conclusion. Here again, a quotation from another writer can end your essay on just the right note. Find a line from a poem, a story, a song, or a play — it might be just what your essay needs. Remember that your conclusion makes a final impression on your readers. What do you want that impression to be?

Assignment 1 Drafting an Introductory Paragraph

Step 1: For a descriptive essay of five paragraphs, choose a topic from items 1–5 on the following list or choose one of the literary selections in items 6–8 for your inspiration. To find your topic from a descriptive passage of literature, reread the piece at least twice, and think about a place or a person that the passage brings to mind. *Step 2:* Brainstorm a list of details that you would use in your descriptive essay. *Step 3:* Decide on the order that you would use, putting your headings and details into outline form. *Step 4:* Draft an introductory paragraph for your essay.

Topics:

1. A hike in the woods or the mountains in a colorful season
2. An air terminal just before a busy holiday
3. A whale-watching trip
4. A violent storm viewed from a safe place
5. A holiday or a festival celebration in another country

Literature passages:

6. from *The Return of the Native* on pages 134–135
7. from "Look at All Those Roses" on page 135
8. from *Out of Africa* on pages 137–138

Assignment 2 Drafting a Concluding Paragraph

Using your outline and your introductory paragraph from Assignment 1, write a concluding paragraph. Sum up your topic, restate your topic's importance, and add some personal insight to the description to make it meaningful to your readers.

Continuing Assignment Draft Your Descriptive Essay

Use your outline and your notes from the Continuing Assignments on pages 122, 132, and 137 to write a first draft of your descriptive essay. Be sure that your essay has an introductory paragraph with a thesis statement, body paragraphs, and a concluding paragraph. Save your notes and your draft.

For writing
an **essay**

Revising for Content

**? Critical
  Thinking:**

Evaluating

After you have written the first draft of your descriptive paragraph or essay, set it aside for at least an hour before revising it. Refer to the guidelines for revision on pages 63–64. As you revise, you should look first at the content of your paragraph or essay. Once you are satisfied with the content, you should give it a second revision for style and tone.

The following strategies will help you to revise the content of your descriptive writing.

▶ **Strategies**

1. *Read your description several times.* Focus on a different concern each time: introductory, body, and concluding paragraphs; order of presentation; number and kind of details, and so on.
2. *Determine whether your reader will be able to see what you have described.* Make sure that you have *shown* rather than *told about* the person, place, or object being described.
3. *Check for unity and coherence.* All descriptive details should relate to the subject, all sentences should be fully developed, and all paragraphs should be presented in the best order. Transitions between sentences and paragraphs should be smooth.
4. *Check for clarity.* Will readers be able to follow your focus, your details, and your order?
5. *Add details if necessary.* Do additional brainstorming or clustering to generate more specific details.

Assignment Revising for Content

**? Critical
  Thinking:**

Evaluating
How can I improve the content of the draft?

On your paper, revise the following paragraph for unity, coherence, and clarity. Eliminate unnecessary information. Change or rearrange sentences to follow spatial order. Add transitional words or phrases to smooth out the flow of sentences and to help readers follow your order of presentation.

Along the far side of Aaron's hotel room sprawled a huge bed, its covers neatly tucked beneath the mattress as though awaiting inspection. I wondered how the mirror had been cracked. The bed was reflected in a cracked, narrow mirror above a dusty dresser whose half-open drawers threatened to spill socks and underwear onto the polished floor. The room was a study in contrasts. From the door where I stood I could see to my left a painting of flowers, hung against an expanse of grimy wallpaper. The walls would have looked better painted. Opposite the dresser was a scarred oak desk with knobs missing from two drawers, topped with a single pile of neatly arranged papers. Oak dressers are hard and durable.

For writing
a **paragraph**
or an **essay**

Continuing Assignment **Revising for Content**

Review the draft of the paragraph *(page 140)* or the essay *(page 143)* that you wrote for previous Continuing Assignments. Using the strategies on page 144, revise the content of your paragraph or essay. Save your drafts and your notes.

Revising

Revising for Style and Tone

After revising your descriptive paragraph or essay for content, you should turn your attention to revising its style and tone. You may need to choose more specific words, make your point of view more consistent, or choose a title that better reflects the focus of your description. You may need to eliminate clichés or trite figures of speech. You may also need to revise to enhance the atmosphere or the mood. The following strategies can help you to revise your writing for style and tone.

Strategies

1. *Reread your description several times.* Concentrate each time on a different element: words, point of view, mood, and so on.

2. *Check your sentences.* Be sure that they offer variety in structure and length. Combine some sentences *(pages 71–76)* if necessary.

3. *Check your transitions.* Do sentences and paragraphs flow easily from one to another? Use transitional words and phrases to make your description clear and your organization easy to follow.

4. *Check your point of view.* Be sure that it is consistent throughout the description. Do not refer to yourself unless you are using the first-person point of view.

5. *Check your nouns and verbs.* Are the nouns precise, the verbs strong?

6. *Study your similes, metaphors, and other comparisons to make sure that they are original.* If you suspect that one of your comparisons may be a cliché, consult a dictionary or a handbook for a list of overused expressions.

7. *Check your modifiers.* Have you used only enough adjectives and adverbs to strengthen your description? Revise overwritten passages by eliminating unnecessary modifiers.

8. *Choose an effective final title.* Perhaps your working title is no longer appropriate or is not effective. Make your title provocative but relevant.

Assignment Revising for Style and Tone

On your paper, rewrite the following description to vary sentence structure and to replace inappropriate or ineffective language. Use a dictionary and a thesaurus to help you to improve word choices. Combine some sentences to provide variety. Replace clichés with fresh, original comparisons. If necessary, provide transitions between sentences. Finally, write an interesting title for the description.

I was hungry as a bear. The stew the trapper was cooking smelled neat. He was cooking it on top of the wood stove. The wood stove was old and rusty. I had to wait a half hour. Then the trapper decided the stew was done. He ladled out a dish for me. Then ladled out one for himself. The stew was a deep brown, thick, aromatic liquid in which there were clustered reddish-yellow, tender, fresh-picked carrots, generous chunks of well-cooked but still stiff white potatoes, and bite-sized pieces of venison that would melt in your mouth. I forgot my manners. I forgot to thank the trapper. I dived into the stew. I ate like a horse until I was full.

Continuing Assignment Revise for Style and Tone

For writing a **paragraph** or an **essay**

Reread your revised draft from the Continuing Assignment on page 145. Using the guidelines on page 145, revise your paragraph or essay for style and tone. Do not be concerned at this stage with spelling or mechanics; you will correct those errors when you proofread. Save your latest revision for later use.

Proofreading

Proofreading Your Description

Reference Point:
pages 598–602

After you have revised your descriptive writing for content and for style and tone, you are ready to proofread it. During proofreading, check for all mechanical errors: grammar, usage, punctuation, spelling, and capitalization. Also check to be sure that you have not used any sentence fragments or run-on sentences. After you have made all the necessary corrections, proofread your description to be sure that you have not overlooked anything. Then make a final copy and proofread it again.

As you proofread your descriptive writing, give special attention to the following points.

Subject-Verb Agreement Be sure that your subjects and verbs agree in number.

Reference Point: *pages 636–647*

> Our first view of the snow-covered Alps, dazzling in the
> was
> sun, ~~were~~ one of the most spectacular sights on our trip.

Commas Use commas to show a pause after introductory prepositional, participial, and adverbial phrases of four or more words.

Reference Point: *page 718 and pages 578–586*

> After a wonderful breakfast at our hotel^we bundled up and
> set out for the slopes.

Assignment Proofreading a Descriptive Paragraph

The following paragraph contains a number of errors. On your paper, rewrite the paragraph, correcting all errors that you find in it. After you have made your final copy, proofread it again to make sure that no errors remain.

A hugh tree had toppled onto a parked car Its heavy trunk had struck the hood first. With what must have been great force. Putting a long crease down the center of the hood flattening the metal and forcing the edges of the hood to curl toward the tree trunk. One branch had smashed a large hole in the window. on the dirver's side. And the glass had flown into the car and bits of glass had penetrated the front seat and a shower of glass had flown into the car. And a fire engine was at the scene and two fire fighters from across the street was checking to be sure that no one was in the car. As luck would have it the driver had been in a neerby store when the tree fell.

Continuing Assignment Proofread Your Description

Proofread the descriptive paragraph or essay that you revised for the Continuing Assignments on pages 145 and 146. After you have made your final copy, proofread it again or have a classmate proofread it for you to make sure that no errors remain.

For writing
a **paragraph**
or an **essay**

Publishing Your Descriptive Writing

Now that you have written, revised, and proofread your descriptive paragraph or essay, you are ready to share it with others. Here are some of the many ways you can publish your work.

- Illustrate the subject of your description or ask an artistic friend to illustrate it for you.
- Exchange papers with classmates and respond.
- Find research topics by reading your classmates' descriptions of objects or places.
- Submit your writing to your school's newspaper or literary magazine.
- Use a classmate's description as inspiration for a drawing, a painting, a story, a song, or a poem.

Continuing Assignment **Publish Your Descriptive Writing**

For writing
a **paragraph**
or an **essay**

Using one or more of the ways suggested here, publish your descriptive paragraph or essay. Also make a copy to keep in your portfolio.

Student to Student

Reading and Responding to Writing

Description often focuses on nature. Margarett Hopewell, a student at Borrego Springs High School in Borrego Springs, California, wrote this descriptive essay about sunrise. Consider the questions in the margin as you read her essay. Then follow the directions for *Responding to Writing* and *Reading Critically*.

Sunrise in Borrego

In the mornings of spring in Borrego, the sunrise is magnificent. The sky is lit up with brilliant colors of lavenders and yellows. The sun sitting on the horizon looks like a giant ball of flames with a lot of life and energy. The sight is so lovely I used to get up very early just to see the sun come up.

I used to believe that one day the sun would come to life and talk to me, but the morning peace was never disturbed by anything. All around I could hear the sounds of nature starting over in a new light and baby birds crying to be fed. All around, the mountains enclose all the new life and protect it from the dangers of the city. Now I know that the sun is a giant ball of gas and will only talk with the moon and stars.

Every time I see the sun rise, it is very different. The sun is some days cast out by clouds, making it seem dark and dull. On clear days the sun seems to change colors from orange to red and then yellow to white and back again. The sun gives me a feeling of happiness and cleanliness. It introduces a new day with new life awakening.

The sunrise is very memorable to me because it seems like a dove flying high in the sky. It burns bright with energy. Throughout the day it travels and sleeps through the night; then when it's morning it wakes the whole world and every form of life.

What image does this simile create?

What sense does Margarett appeal to here?

How does Margarett feel about her subject?

Responding to Writing   In your writer's notebook, describe how you feel about Margarett's images and tone. What is their impact?

Reading Critically   In a discussion or in a written analysis, respond to these questions: What similes and metaphors does Margarett use? How does she use personification? How is a mood evoked?

The Literature Connection

The English word *describe* comes from the Latin word *scribere* meaning "to write" or "to delineate." When you use description, then, you are molding your impressions and giving them a kind of reality through writing. In fact, if you don't capture them in writing, most of your impressions are lost, except to memory. You've already described your sensory impressions in vivid language, but what about your feelings, thoughts, intuitions, and premonitions? Of course, you can describe these mental occurrences in abstract terms; however, you can convey them much more effectively in sensory terms or images, as the passage by Joseph Conrad on this page illustrates.

Guided Reading   On the surface, Joseph Conrad wrote stories about travel and adventure, and very rousing ones at that. Below the surface, however, his stories probe various emotional states and make them "visible" for readers. In this selection from *Heart of Darkness*, the narrator, Marlow, describes his childhood fascination with Africa and his response to the troubling stillness he found when he finally traveled to the "dark continent." In your first reading, look for images that describe mental impressions and create a distinctive mood. Then reread the passage and answer the questions at the right.

"*N*ow when I was a little chap I had a passion for maps. I would look for hours at South America, or Africa, or Australia, and lose myself in all the glories of exploration. At that time there were many blank spaces on the earth, and when I saw one that looked particularly inviting on a map (but they all look that) I would put my finger on it and say, 'When I grow up I will go there.' The North Pole was one of these places, I remember. Well, I haven't been there yet, and shall not try now. The glamour's off. Other places were scattered about the Equator, and in every sort of latitude all over the two hemispheres. I have been in some of them, and . . . well, we won't talk about that. But there was one yet — the biggest, the most blank, so to speak — that I had a hankering after.

What is the point of view?

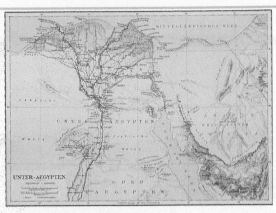

UNTER-AEGYPTEN.

"True, by this time it was not a blank space any more. It had got filled since my boyhood with rivers and lakes and names. It had ceased to be a blank space of delightful mystery — a white patch for a boy to dream gloriously over. It had become a place of darkness. But there was in it one river especially, a mighty big river, that you could see on the map, resembling an immense snake uncoiled, with its head in the sea, its body at rest curving afar over a vast country, and its tail lost in the depths of the land. And as I looked at the map of it in a shop-window, it fascinated me as a snake would a bird — a silly little bird. Then I remembered there was a big concern, a Company for trade on that river. Dash it all! I thought to myself, they can't trade without using some kind of craft on that lot of fresh water — steamboats! Why shouldn't I try to get charge of one? I went on along Fleet Street, but could not shake off the idea. The snake had charmed me. . . .

What is the analogy here? What does it suggest?

"Going up that river was like travelling back to the earliest beginnings of the world, when vegetation rioted on the earth and the big trees were kings. An empty stream, a great silence, an impenetrable forest. The air was warm, thick, heavy, sluggish. There was no joy in the brilliance of sunshine. The long stretches of the waterway ran on, deserted, into the gloom of over-shadowed distances. On silvery sand-banks hippos and alligators sunned themselves side by side. The broadening waters flowed through a mob of wooded islands; you lost your way on that river as you would in a desert, and butted all day long against shoals, trying to find the channel, till you thought yourself bewitched and cut off for ever from everything you had known once — somewhere — far away — in another existence perhaps. There were moments when one's past came back to one, as it will sometimes when you have not a moment to spare to yourself; but it came in the shape of an unrestful and noisy dream, remembered with wonder amongst the overwhelming realities of this strange world of plants, and water, and silence. And this stillness of life did

What key words set the tone?

not in the least resemble a peace. It was the stillness of an implacable force brooding over an inscrutable intention. It looked at you with a vengeful aspect. I got used to it afterwards; I did not see it any more; I had no time. I had to keep guessing at the channel; I had to discern, mostly by inspiration, the signs of hidden banks; I watched for sunken stones; I was learning to clap my teeth smartly before my heart flew out, when I shaved by a fluke some infernal sly old snag that would have ripped the life out of the tin-pot steamboat and drowned all the pilgrims; I had to keep a lookout for the signs of dead wood we could cut up in the night for next day's steaming. When you have to attend to things of that sort, to the mere incidents of the surface, the reality — the reality, I tell you — fades. The inner truth is hidden — luckily, luckily. But I felt it all the same; I felt often its mysterious stillness watching me at my monkey tricks, just as it watches you fellows performing on your respective tight-ropes for — what is it? half-a-crown a tumble — "

> What does the stillness "say" to Marlow?

> Why "luckily"? Paraphrase the last three sentences.

Joseph Conrad (1857–1924)
from *Heart of Darkness*

Enrichment Connections

Choose one or more of these activities to do on your own or as a group.

Giving Directions

To explain effectively how to do something requires that you use description within your explanation. Write a brief set of directions (no more than two pages) for some activity such as riding a bicycle, making a meal from scratch, reading, or some imagined undertaking. Assume that your audience knows nothing about the process and doesn't have time to read a book about it. Be sure that your explanation includes lots of descriptive detail. The more your readers *see* of the process, the better they will understand how to do it. As a class, you might read your sets of directions aloud — and even try to put some of them to the test.

Using Personification

Read over your notes for *Responding to Literature* on page 119 and do some more prewriting if necessary. Then write a one- to three-paragraph description of the scene that you've chosen. Be sure that you describe at least one aspect in human terms: "the tops of the trees chattered riotously or bowed courteously," for example. You might even write from the point of view of some feature of the scene (a mountain, a river, a cloud), describing the world as *it* sees things.

A Travel Brochure

Imagine that you've just received your first big assignment as a travel writer. You're to *sell* your community to the world. Brainstorm to generate ideas and images. Then write a one- to two-page descriptive brochure that focuses on two or three unforgettable features. Consider what concerns tourists — sightseeing, shopping, dining, accommodations, transportation, and unusual customs.

A Variation on a Theme

Develop the descriptive paragraph or essay that you wrote for this unit into a story, a poem, or a short play. First, do some prewriting to get new images bubbling on the surface of your imagination. Then write at least two drafts, being selective about what details from the original paragraph or essay you include. Your present creative effort may take you in a direction that requires fresh details. When you are finished (including proofreading), compare the two works. Decide which one you prefer and jot down in your writer's notebook your reasons for preferring it.

Speaking and Listening

An Interview Interview a classmate about a particularly humorous childhood memory. Prepare a list of questions that will elicit rich descriptive detail and his or her feelings about the event. Take careful notes as you listen. Then, using your notes and your own imagination, write a brief story that narrates the comical event. You may choose to write from the first- or third-person point of view; let the nature of the material determine which is better. Ask this same classmate to proofread your essay, and, with his or her permission, read it to the class.

Writing Comparison and Contrast

In *Heart of Darkness*, Marlow fulfills a childhood dream and travels to Africa, but the Africa he discovers is more nightmarish than dreamlike. Often, however, one's expectations are satisfied — or even exceeded. Reflect back on a place that you wanted to visit and finally did, and do some prewriting to evoke vivid images. Then write a two- to three-page story or essay that compares and contrasts what you expected and what you actually experienced. Was the reality better or worse, and why? How did you form your expectations? Include answers to these questions in your essay or story. If you prefer, write about a person whom you wanted to meet and later did. In either case, bolster your work with well-drawn descriptive passages.

How do you feel about travel? If you have taken a long journey, how did you like it? If you haven't, does the thought of one fill you with excitement—or with dread? What would it be like actually to move to another country?

For Ernesto Galarza (ār nĕs´ tō gä lär´ zä) the first journey was one from which he never returned. When he was six years old, Galarza left his home in western Mexico with his mother, Doña Henriqueta (dō´nyä ān rē kā´ tä), to begin a new life in the United States. In the following selection, you will join these travelers and get a glimpse of the culture of the United States in 1910 through their eyes. As you read, notice how important a role language plays in their travels. Then do one or several of the activities that follow the selection. Working on them may help you to increase your understanding of other places and other lives.

CELEBRATING DIVERSITY

In the sunny morning of the next day we walked back to the station. Our train was still there, the flats and boxcars and coaches deserted, Mexican and American soldiers walking back and forth. "Look, the American flag," my mother said. It was flying over a building near us. Down the street, beyond the depot, there was a Mexican flag on a staff. "We are in the United States. Mexico is over there."

It took further explaining to clear up certain points to my satisfaction. The North was the same place as the United States, and we had finally arrived. The Americans never drew an eagle on their flag. The red and the white were the same as on ours but why they liked blue better than green was just one of those peculiar things about Americans. Where did Mexico begin? Just beyond the railway station. How far did it go? "A long way," said Doña Henriqueta,[1] "far down the track, farther than Jalcocotán."[2] It was the closest thing we did to saying good-bye to our country.

1. *Doña Henriqueta* (dōn' yä ān rē kā'tä)
2. *Jalcocotán* (häl kō kō tän´)   a mountain village in western Mexico

That evening at the *mesón*,[3] José and my mother and I reread Gustavo's letter, the last we had received in Mazatlán.[4] José was to work his way on the railroad to a place called Sacramento.[5] My mother and I were to go to another city called Tucson[6] and wait there until another pass and money could be obtained.

José then explained a remarkable thing about our money. Mexican centavos and tostones and pesos[7] were good for nothing in the United States. He had already exchanged some of our Mexican currency for dollars. "Listen carefully," he told us. "You have to give two pesos for one dollar. For one tostón you get one quarter. For ten centavos you get one nickel." On the table he laid out the coins, in rows two for one.

He turned to me.

"Now, Ernesto, you are the man of the family. You will take care of your mother until we are together in Sacramento. How do you say *por favor?*"[8]

"Plees."

"Right, how do you say *cuánto es?*"[9]

"Hau-mochee."

"How do you say *qué hora es, por favor?*"[10]

"Hua-tinees, plees."

"Correct."

"Now say the numbers."

"Huan, too, tree."

"Correct. If you don't know the numbers, hold up your fingers and count in Spanish."

In Nogales[11] we sold the extra blankets. José bought us two cardboard suitcases and one for himself, and an alarm clock like the one we used to try to win in the lottery tent in Mazatlán. With our new luggage and the tin trunk, we set off for Tucson, saying good-bye to José. In one of the suitcases there was a brown folder tied with a blue tape. In it were the pass, the letters from Gustavo with certain names and addresses, and the instructions for our arrival in Sacramento. The suitcase with its precious papers was never out of our sight, and the American paper money that José had exchanged. Gustavo's forwarding address was puzzling. The best we could make out it

3. *mesón* (mā sōn') Spanish for "inn"
4. *Mazatlán* (mä zät län') a city on the west coast of central Mexico
5. *Sacramento* (sä krä měn' tō) city in central California, the capital of the state
6. *Tucson* (tōō' sŏn) a city in southeastern Arizona
7. *centavo* (sěn tä' vō), tostón (tōs tōn'), peso (pä' sō) Mexican money. The peso is the monetary unit and contains one hundred centavos. A tostón is a fifty centavo piece.
8. *por favor* (pōr fä vōr') Spanish for "please"
9. *cuánto es* (kwän' tō ěs) Spanish for "how much"
10. *qué hora es, por favor* (kā ō' rä ěs, pōr fä vōr') Spanish for "what time is it, please"
11. *Nogales* (nō gä' läs) a Mexican city on the border with Arizona

was a General Delibri. It sounded as if generals were in charge of the mail in the United States, nothing like our *lista del correo*[12] in Acaponeta. . . .

Our temporary home was halfway down the alley between two streets. Our landlady was plump, quiet, slow-moving, and wore her greying hair in two thick braids. The husband, a fat man with sad eyes who talked even less than his wife, did odd jobs around town. . . .

Privately we called the old couple *los abuelitos*,[13] and our visit with them gave me some idea of what it was like to have a grandfather and grandmother in the house. They were not our kinfolk but the *respeto*[14] I felt for them, after Doña Henriqueta's lectures, was genuinely Mexican.

Except for the quiet company of the *abuelitos*, we were locked in the alley, my mother with no work and I with no friends. The Mexican boys who lived in the other row houses had no place to play where we could become acquainted. The one time I ventured out of the alley and down the street I was chased back by three American boys who yelled something I could not understand but which didn't sound friendly. . . .

Regularly we went to the hotel to ask for mail from Gustavo. Almost always there was a letter with money, but it was many weeks before we received the most important one of all, the one that had the pass and the instructions for the trip. We were to take the train to Sacramento, go to the Hotel Español and stay there until Gustavo and José came for us.

The *abuelitos* walked us to the railroad station, helping us with our tin trunk and suitcases. As if we had lived together all our lives everybody embraced everybody and the old couple waited to wave good-bye as our train pulled out of the station.

As soon as we were in the coach I knew we were riding first-class. The seat was a green felt cushion, plump and comfortable. The packages and suitcases were placed on the racks and under the seats, not in the aisles, so I could walk up and down when I felt stiff or when I wanted a drink of ice water which came out of a silver faucet. . . .

12. *lista del correo* (lēs′tä dĕl kōr rä′ō) Spanish for "general delivery"; general delivery is a postal service that delivers mail to a post office where the addressee calls for it.
13. *los abuelitos* (lōs ä bwä lē′tōs) Spanish for "grandparents"
14. *respeto* (räs pā′tō) Spanish for "respect"

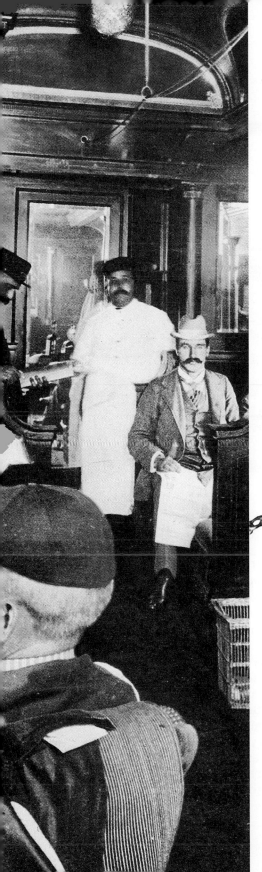

When the conductor came by to check tickets, he punched two colored tabs and slipped them through a metal frame on the seat in front of us. I discovered to my delight that the brass letters on his cap were exactly like those of the conductor in Mazatlán. I spelled them out silently as I watched him—c-o-n, con, d-u-c, duc, t-o-r, tor, conductor. In a whispered conversation with my mother over the subject, we agreed that a gringo conductor would not be wearing Mexican letters on his cap, and that *conductor* in Spanish was the same as conductor in English. This started a guessing game that kept us amused the rest of the trip. Some words worked out neatly in both languages, like *conductor*, others failed to match by a syllable or a letter, in which case we thought English spelling idiotic.

I had never moved as fast as on this train which sped along faster even than the *diligencia*.[15] The telephone poles whizzed by, making me dizzy if I watched them, and around the curves the coach leaned a little. . . .

I asked the conductor several times while we were on the long journey, "hua-tinees, plees." One conductor pulled the watch out of his vest pocket, flipped open the gold lid and read the time to us, which meant nothing at all since we didn't know the numbers in English. Another, after looking us over and guessing our difficulty, snapped his watch open and held the face up for us to read.

Ernesto Galarzo *(1905–   )*
from *Barrio Boy*

15. *diligencia* (dē lē hĕn' syä)   Spanish for "stagecoach"

A Multicultural Experience **A4**

Taking Another Look

Ernesto's great adventure has its practical side; he and his family must adjust to many bewildering new customs and situations. What are some of the adjustments they have to make? What things puzzle them about their adopted home? How do the people they meet respond to them? Characterize Ernesto's family. What holds the family together? What values are reflected in the actions of José and Gustavo, Ernesto's two uncles? What makes you think that this family will succeed in building a new life?

Changing Places

While the journey was full of wonders for Ernesto, it might have been different if he'd been older and more aware of what such a trip meant. If you were moving to a foreign country where you didn't speak the language, how would you feel? What hopes and fears would you have? How would you handle your homesickness? If you were responsible for a younger sibling, what would you say and do to make leaving home easier for him or her?

WRITING

Culture Shock   You don't have to travel thousands of miles from home to experience culture shock. Sometimes just entering someone else's home can leave you feeling disoriented—pleasantly or otherwise. Write a brief essay or a story in which you describe a memorable encounter that you have had with another culture. Because your focus is descriptive, think about the experience in sensory terms. What did you see, hear, taste, feel, and smell? Don't let your readers get away without sharing in the intensity of your response.

LANGUAGE

Echoes seohcE Did you know that the English word *echo* is *eco* in Spanish or that the English word *poem* is *poema*? Words like these that share a common root are called *cognates*. Find examples of cognates in the selection from *Barrio Boy*, and begin a list of them in your writer's notebook. Then check textbooks and dictionaries for five or ten additional words. Look for cognates in a number of different languages, noting how the meaning of each word varies from language to language. Your list can help you to build a vocabulary in other languages and to appreciate the history and richness of your own.

DID YOU KNOW? Ernesto Galarza's family left Mexico to escape the Mexican Revolution of 1910. This revolution successfully removed the dictator Porfirio Díaz (pŏr fēē' ryō dēē' äz) from office; however, another dictator, Victoriano Huerta (vēēc tō ryä' nō wär' tä), soon replaced him. Revolutionary fervor increased again, and Huerta's government fell in 1914 through the military efforts of such Mexican leaders as Pancho Villa (pän' chō vēē' yä) and Zapata (sä pä' tä) and through the political aid of President Woodrow Wilson of the United States.

Skill WORKSHOP

General Delibri Gustavo, one of Ernesto's uncles who has gone ahead to Sacramento, seems to know a little more about the North than Ernesto's mother does; he gives her a letter with names and addresses and instructions for their trip to Sacramento. What else might he have told her? Imagine that friends from another culture are coming to visit you. What will they need to know to get from the airport or the train station to your house? Are there any customs or practices that they should be aware of in order to make the trip on their own? Write the instructions in a letter, using modified block style.

UNIT 2

Writing with a Narrative Focus

We all tell stories for a variety of reasons about things that happen to us or to other people. These stories narrate an event or a series of events that is somehow significant or important. Narratives can be brief or long, serious or funny, all depending on the purpose of the story. The best narratives, however, grab readers' interest and inspire them to respond in a certain way. To elicit this response as a writer, you must bring to life vivid action and compelling characters with dramatic dialogue and colorful, descriptive language.

Although these details are essential to both fiction and nonfiction narratives, this unit concentrates on narratives about real people and real events: stories about *change*. You can narrate changes in the course of history, changes throughout a person's life, and changes in a particular individual. The narrative shown here is from the memoirs of composer Hector Berlioz. The single incident, which involves the narrator and another composer of the same period, is significant to Berlioz as an ironic preview to his future relationship with this man. As you read the passages, see whether you can guess at certain aspects of both personalities by the way the two men behave during the encounter.

Now that I had made some progress in the study of harmony, Lesueur wished me to have a recognised position as one of his pupils in the Conservatoire. He spoke to Cherubini, who was then director, and I was admitted. Fortunately no one suggested that I should be introduced to the terrible author of *Médée,* for the previous year I had put him into one of his white-heat furies by opposing him in a matter which I shall now narrate, and which he probably had not forgotten.

No sooner was Cherubini appointed director, after the death of Perne, than he at once set to work to signalise his accession to power by the introduction of all sorts of restrictions in the internal economy of the school, which had not, up to that time, been organized on exactly puritan principles. In order to prevent the intermingling of the two sexes, except in the presence of the professors, he issued an order that the men were to enter by the door in the Faubourg Poissonière, and the women by that in the Rue Bergère; the two being at opposite ends of the building.

Wholly ignorant of this moral decree, I betook myself one morning to the library, entering as usual by the Rue Bergère, the female door, and was making my way to the library when I found myself suddenly confronted by a servant, who stopped me in the middle of the courtyard, and ordered me to go back and return to the very same spot by the other entrance. I thought this so absurd that I sent the liveried Argus about his business, and went on my way. The rascal, hoping to find favour in the eyes of his new master by emulating his severity, ran off to report the circumstance. I had forgotten all about it, and had been absorbed in *Alceste* for a quarter of an hour, when Cherubini entered the reading-room, his face more cadaverous, his hair more bristling, his eyes more wicked, and his steps more abrupt than ever. He and my accuser made their way round the table, examining several unconscious students, until the servant stopped in front of me and cried, "Here he is!" Cherubini was in such a passion that he could not utter a word. "Ah! ah, ah, ah!" he cried at last, his Italian accent comically intensified in his

Intro-duction makes me curious.

Implies some-thing about Cherubini's character.

Argus? His driver?

So dramatic!

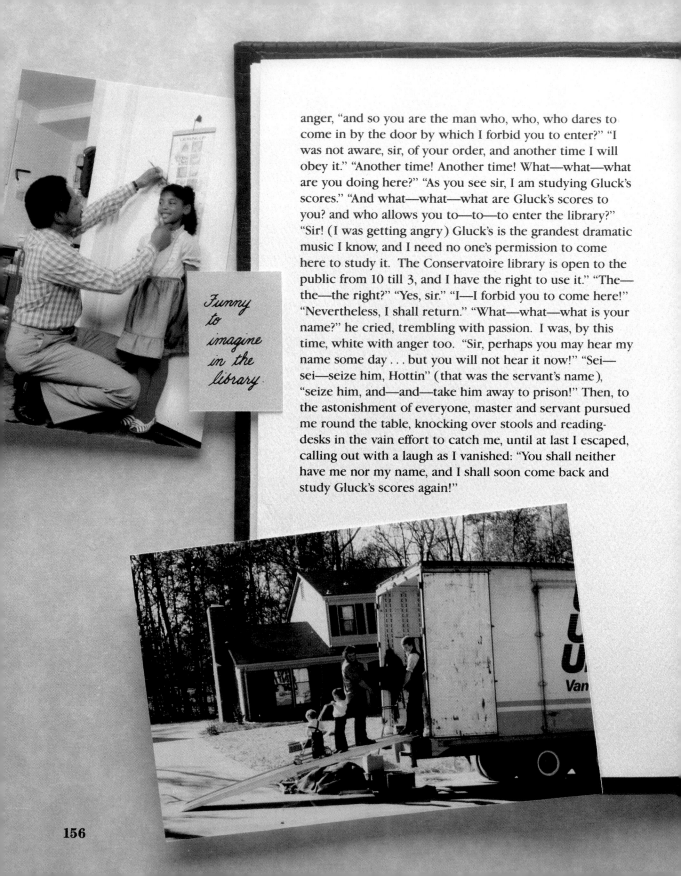

anger, "and so you are the man who, who, who dares to come in by the door by which I forbid you to enter?" "I was not aware, sir, of your order, and another time I will obey it." "Another time! Another time! What—what—what are you doing here?" "As you see sir, I am studying Gluck's scores." "And what—what—what are Gluck's scores to you? and who allows you to—to—to enter the library?" "Sir! (I was getting angry) Gluck's is the grandest dramatic music I know, and I need no one's permission to come here to study it. The Conservatoire library is open to the public from 10 till 3, and I have the right to use it." "The—the—the right?" "Yes, sir." "I—I forbid you to come here!" "Nevertheless, I shall return." "What—what—what is your name?" he cried, trembling with passion. I was, by this time, white with anger too. "Sir, perhaps you may hear my name some day . . . but you will not hear it now!" "Sei—sei—seize him, Hottin" (that was the servant's name), "seize him, and—and—take him away to prison!" Then, to the astonishment of everyone, master and servant pursued me round the table, knocking over stools and reading-desks in the vain effort to catch me, until at last I escaped, calling out with a laugh as I vanished: "You shall neither have me nor my name, and I shall soon come back and study Gluck's scores again!"

Funny to imagine in the library.

This was my first interview with Cherubini. I do not know whether he remembered it when, later on, I was presented to him officially. But it is curious that, twelve years afterwards, I should have been appointed, against his wish, to the charge of the library out of which he tried to turn me. As regards Hottin, he is now porter to the orchestra, devoted to me, and a most zealous partisan of my music; he used even to declare, before Cherubini died, that I was the only man who could take his place at the Conservatoire. M. Auber apparently thought otherwise.

I shall tell many more stories about Cherubini, from which it will be seen that though he gave me some bitter pills to swallow, he had to accept some unpalatable draughts in return from me.

Hector Berlioz *(1803–1869)*
from *Memoirs*

That's a twist!

Responding to Literature

First encounters are often embarrassing, funny, frustrating, or tense. Berlioz's first encounter with Cherubini is humorous, as it is described here, but it is also ironic because of the narrator's future appointment as head of the "forbidden" library. At the end of the passage, the author implies that he and Cherubini were at odds throughout their careers.

Your life may change in curious and surprising ways, and chance encounters may gradually take on significance over the course of time. Brainstorm about some first impressions that you have experienced. Perhaps some of your encounters led to a major change, or they may have turned out ironically, the way Berlioz's encounter with Cherubini did. Include in your brainstorming the people, the situations, and the results. When you have finished, circle the three incidents that are the most entertaining. Save the list in your writer's notebook.

JOB INTERVIEW

9:00 a.m. Monday Oct. 7
at ICG Corporation
see Daniel Del Valle

Selecting and Focusing Topics for Narratives

Every **narrative** tells a story, either about imaginary events or about true events in your life or in the life of someone else. Nonfictional narratives include histories, biographies, and autobiographies. Fictional narratives include drama, short stories, and novels. Both nonfictional and fictional narratives can be any length, from a single paragraph to a multi-volume series.

This unit concentrates on nonfictional narratives, stories about real people and actual events. When you write historical narrative, you can write about famous personages and places or the people and places that you know best, such as your family and your neighborhood. In this section, you will learn how to select and focus a narrative topic; how to develop setting, characters, and action; and how to organize your narrative.

Selecting Your Narrative Topic

Whether you are writing fiction or nonfiction, you need to select a topic that focuses on a significant event, one with historical importance or one with instructional value. At the same time, the topic should interest you and your audience. Suitable topics are those that include lively action or colorful characters. Several prewriting techniques will help you to explore possible topics for narratives: generating an interest inventory, developing a chronology, brainstorming, clustering, and asking questions. Not every prewriting technique will suit your needs; as you apply the techniques, you will discover which ones work best for you.

Generating an Interest Inventory

An abundant supply of suitable writing ideas can be culled from your personal interests, activities, and experiences. An **interest inventory** *(page 12)* is a record of real or imaginary people, places, activities, and events that you keep as a source of interesting topics, many of which will have a narrative focus.

Dedicate a section in your writer's notebook for your inventory and allow room to keep adding new interests. A complete and up-to-date inventory will furnish you with numerous narrative topics.

Developing a Time Line

A second way to find appropriate topics for narratives is to develop a **time line** *(page 21)*, a chronological list that highlights important events in someone's life. A time line helps you to concentrate on those events that interest you the most. You can construct your time line vertically or horizontally and divide the line into days, months, years, or ages. The following is a time line of the life of Louis Braille, the teacher who invented a reading system for the blind.

1809	Born near Paris
1812	Blinded from accident while playing in father's workshop
1819	Earned musical scholarship; attended school for the blind in Paris
1821	Met Army Capt. Chas. Barbier, who taught him night writing (code punched in thick paper)
1824	Invented alphabet based on night writing
1826	Became teacher at school he had attended
1829	Published Braille system
1852	Died of TB, alone and penniless

When you have completed your time line, highlight the events that you consider to be the most important or interesting.

Assignment 1 Developing a Time Line

Select an event from your interest inventory and sketch a vertical or horizontal time line. Include as many dates as you can recall or do any research that is necessary. Review the time line and mark those incidents that you might like to explore for a narrative.

Critical Thinking: Sequencing What events happened? In what order?

Brainstorming and Clustering to Identify Narrative Ideas

The prewriting techniques of brainstorming *(page 13)* and clustering *(page 14)* are effective ways to probe your memory for narrative topics. Begin by selecting a broad subject, such as "turning points" or "European history." Then quickly write your thoughts down regardless of any apparent irrelevance; you will soon discover that even the smallest incident may prove to be something worth writing about. Review your notes and mark the most interesting facts. Include them in a time line, or copy them in your writer's notebook.

Assignment 2 Brainstorming and Clustering

Step 1: Choose an interesting person from the past or the present who has made a contribution to the world or has produced an important change. You may select this person from your interest inventory, from a time line, or from one of the following categories. *Step 2:* On your paper, brainstorm to collect all the details that you can about this person. *Step 3:* On a second piece of paper, begin a cluster with the words "How *(name)* Changed the World." Cluster ideas about specific things that this individual accomplished or contributed to society. Save your notes in your writer's notebook.

1. A famous athlete
2. A famous entertainer
3. A famous artist
4. A famous politician
5. A famous scientist
6. A famous author

Asking Questions to Find Narrative Topics

Ask questions that begin with *who, what, where, when, why,* and *how* — in the manner of journalists — to collect ideas for narrative topics. Keep in mind that your purpose is to generate ideas; therefore ask questions that will produce informative answers. Use the following questions as a guide for gathering interesting topics.

- *Questions About People:* Who has impressed me with his or her professional or personal achievements? What impressed me the most or the least? Why am I impressed? What mark did this person leave on the world?
- *Questions About Events:* What past or current event has aroused my rage, excited my curiosity, or increased my understanding of something? What are the facts — the *who, what, when, where,* and *how* — of the event? Why do I feel as I do about the event? What are the opinions of others concerning the event? What are the consequences of the event? — for myself? for others?
- *Questions About Historical Periods:* What period of history fascinates me? Why am I interested in this period? What preceding events influenced this period? How have the events from this period influenced events that followed?

Assignment 3 Asking Questions

Select an event that caused a pivotal change in the life of someone whom you know or admire. Ask and answer questions to collect as much information as you can about the event. Mark those answers that you consider to be interesting topics for narratives. Save them in your writer's notebook.

Focusing Your Narrative Topic

Once you have selected a narrative topic, you can turn your attention to selecting those details that express your reason for writing the story and that motivate your audience to read what you have written.

Suppose that you have developed a time line on the life of the British bacteriologist Sir Alexander Fleming. You have highlighted his discovery of penicillin as the incident that most interests you. The details that you select to include will depend on your purpose for writing the story, the characteristics of your audience, and your point of view.

Determining Your Purpose

Evaluating what you want your readers to do, to feel, or to think after reading your story is crucial to determining your purpose. Narrative writing is basically storytelling, but you can also present a new idea, convince your readers of something, make comparisons or connections, or show changes. In a narrative about Fleming, for example, you might explain how his discovery of penicillin in 1928 changed the medical world. You could also describe medical science in his day.

Similarly, when you are writing an expository, descriptive, or persuasive paragraph or essay, you may need to use narrative writing to present an example or to help you to make a point. An expository essay on early twentieth-century medical advances, for example, could include a narrative about Fleming's accidental discovery of penicillin. Keep all your purposes in mind as you choose relevant details to include in your narrative.

In the following autobiographical narrative, the writer has added descriptive and expository details to show changes in the behavior of the chimpanzees that she was studying in the African jungle and to explain why she preferred to name, rather than number, the animals.

*A*s the weeks went by the chimpanzees became less and less afraid. Quite often when I was on one of my food-collecting expeditions I came across chimpanzees unexpectedly, and after a time I found that some of them would tolerate my presence provided they were in fairly thick forest and I sat still and did not try to move closer than sixty to eighty yards. And so, during my second month of watching from the Peak, when I saw a group settle down to feed I sometimes moved closer and was thus able to make more detailed observations.

It was at this time that I began to recognize a number of different individuals. As soon as I was sure of knowing a chimpanzee if I saw it again, I named it. Some scientists feel that animals should be labeled by numbers — that to name them is anthropomorphic — but I have always been interested in the *differences* between individuals, and a name is not only more individual than a number but also far easier to remember.

Jane Goodall (1934–   )
from *In the Shadow of Man*

(ăn′thrə-
pə môr′fĭk)

Determining Your Audience

The focus of your narrative will vary depending upon your audience. For example, if you were writing a narrative about the Battle of Dunkirk, you might tailor your focus to fit the needs of an audience of English war veterans, an audience of students, and an audience of historians. To identify your audience, create a reader profile, including the likely ages of your readers, their knowledge of the subject, and what their expectations might be as they read your narrative.

Determining Your Point of View

After you determine your purpose and audience, you can concentrate on your role, or your narrator's role, in the narrative. What relationship do you want to establish with your readers? When you wish your readers to see the story from the viewpoint of a participant, use the **first-person point of view,** which is standard in autobiographies and in many fictional narratives. When you write in the first person, using pronouns like *I* and *we*, you establish a close relationship with your readers and create an informal tone.

When you wish your readers to see the story from a more objective standpoint, use the **third-person point of view,** with pronouns like *he, she,* and *they*. Histories and biographies are written in the third person. Writing in the third person, you create a more formal tone. A fuller explanation of point of view may be found on pages 26–27.

The following passages of historical narrative show how purpose and point of view can vary in consideration of the audience. The first narrative, in the third person, is intended to instruct high school history students about consequences of the Battle of Dunkirk.

> The fall of Belgium allowed the German army to move around the end of the Maginot Line. Tanks and motorized infantry burst through the French defenses near Sedan and raced toward the English Channel. This German advance drove a wedge between the French army defending Paris and the Allied (British, Belgian, and French) forces on the coast. Some 330,000 Allied troops retreated to Dunkirk on the English Channel. To rescue the trapped soldiers, every available vessel set sail from England — fishing boats, tugboats, and private yachts, as well as merchant ships and navy destroyers. In about a week, ending on June 4, 1940, most of the soldiers were taken to England, though great amounts of valuable and badly needed equipment were left behind on the beaches. The "miracle of Dunkirk" inspired and united the British people in their resistance to Hitler.

By contrast, consider the following narrative, by C. P. Snow, written some years after the Battle of Dunkirk. In 1940 Snow had listened to Winston Churchill's speech following the battle. Snow's narrative is intended for an audience of his fellow Britons for the purpose of describing what he and his colleagues thought of the event when it occurred and what he thinks years later. As a result, Snow places into perspective the significance of the event. He uses the first-person point of view to create a closeness between himself and his audience.

> *O*ddly enough, most of us were very happy in those days. There was a kind of collective euphoria over the whole country. I don't know what we were thinking about. We were very busy. We had a purpose. We were living in constant excitement, usually of an unpromising kind. . . .
>
> Looking back, perhaps one reads into our mood of those months elements which were not there. Did we really have a sense of last things, as I have now? The last fight of Britain as a solitary great power (I think we knew that whatever happened, we should not after this ever be, in the full sense, a great power again).
>
> C. P. Snow *(1905–1980)*
> from "Churchill"

Plan your narrative by focusing on a purpose, an audience, and a point of view that work in harmony. At the same time, maintain a consistent point of view throughout to help your readers to follow your narrative.

Assignment 4 Purpose, Audience, and Point of View

Step 1: From your interest inventory or from your knowledge of history, select an important historical event. *Step 2:* On your paper, brainstorm, cluster, or ask and answer questions about the event. *Step 3:* Draft two paragraphs, each one narrating the incident from a different point of view and for a different audience. *Step 4:* Below each narrative paragraph, provide a brief audience profile and explain your purpose and your choice of a point of view.

Limiting Your Topic

The length of your narrative will determine how many details you can include. A brief, one-paragraph story necessitates your limiting the topic to a few details. Longer narratives allow you to expand the topic. Regardless of the length of the narrative, you must carefully select an appropriate number of details that will tell about the event in a given amount of space.

An effective way to select an appropriate number of details is to ask yourself questions such as these: How much information do I have about the event? What is the length of the narrative if a length is predetermined? What interests me the most about the subject? What will interest my audience the most? These questions will help you to write focused and unified narratives.

Creating a temporary working title is another way to help you to concentrate on the main point of the narrative and to determine which details to include. You can revise the title if your focus changes or when you complete the narrative.

Assignment 5 | **Limiting Your Topic**

Number your paper from 1 to 5, leaving three blank lines between each number. After each number write one of the topics provided or select topics from your writer's notebook. Then, beneath each topic, limit the topic by listing two possible main points — one for a one-paragraph narrative and one for a three-page narrative essay. Use reference materials if necessary.

1. The 1969 test flight of the British-French supersonic *Concorde*
2. The knighting of Francis Drake by Queen Elizabeth I on board his ship the *Golden Hind*
3. The wedding of Lady Diana Spencer and Prince Charles
4. William of Normandy (France) becomes ruler of England (1067)
5. The publication of the first book by Gutenberg (1450)

Continuing Assignment | **Select and Focus Your Topic**

For writing a **paragraph** or an **essay**

In this series of Continuing Assignments, you will develop and publish a narrative paragraph or essay. *Step 1:* Review your interest inventory and other prewriting notes in your writer's notebook and choose an event to narrate. You may want to deal with a significant historical event in the life of a figure from English history or from English literature, or an event in the life of someone whom you know well — even yourself. *Step 2:* On your paper, use prewriting techniques such as brainstorming, clustering, and asking questions to gather the details relating to the event. *Step 3:* Focus your topic by writing your purpose, your audience, and your point of view. *Step 4:* Limit your topic in two different ways: for a one-paragraph narrative and for a two- to three-page narrative essay. Save your notes.

Prewriting

Planning Your Narrative

Developing Narrative Details

Perceptive and dramatic descriptions of the settings, the characters, and the actions in your narrative can make your writing fun and interesting to read. Use the questioning techniques given on page 18 to help you to develop clear and accurate narrative details.

Developing the Setting

Narrative events usually take place in a **setting** — a certain time and a certain place. Paint a vivid picture for your readers by precisely describing the physical and emotional surroundings of a scene in your narrative. Imagine the setting in your mind and write every detail that you see — furnishings, landscape, architecture, weather — anything that is essential to the action of the narrative. Ask yourself such questions as "When did the event occur?" "How long did the action last?" "Which physical features contribute to the action?" "Is the mood subdued, intense, alarming, or peaceful?" Answer your questions, review them, and select those that create the desired impression.

The following passage illustrates how the details of a setting contribute to the mood of a scene. This passage is taken from a longer narrative about the events leading to the abdication of King Edward VIII.

*T*he gloom of the events of December, 1936, was intensified by the pathetic fallacy, dear to authors of detective stories, of the dank London winter and its enshrouding fogs. . . . It is the London whose winter evenings Hollywood loved to re-create with offstage machines pumping clouds of fog onto the silhouettes of Basil Rathbone and Nigel Bruce as they strode off for the eight twenty-nine from Paddington in pursuit of some horrific mischief in the West Country — a London that on the fairest days glimmered with a rusty light and by night simmered in a stew of gray mist through which such a landmark as the Tower or the Houses of Parliament loomed up like the prow of an oncoming liner.

Tuesday, the first of December, 1936, ended in such an evening, though one strangely aglow on the southeastern horizon with the still-burning inferno of the old Crystal Palace, the glass-and-iron masterpiece of Victorian festival architecture in whose charred remains clergymen, reporters, and other amateur sociologists were soon to recognize an omen of the collapse of the Victorian ideals of duty and domestic tranquility.

Alistair Cooke *(1908–   )*
from *Six Men*

Assignment 1 Details of Setting
_____

Choose one of the following settings or choose one from a topic in your writer's notebook. On your paper, write seven to ten narrative details that describe the physical and emotional setting. Use reference materials for information if necessary. Review your list and highlight those details that you consider to be the most descriptive and interesting.

1. The deck of the *Pinta* when sailors first sighted land (1492)
2. The scaffolding used by Michelangelo to paint the ceiling of the Sistine Chapel
3. The underground shelters used during the blitz in England
4. A dining car on the *Orient Express*
5. The lab in which the compact disc player was perfected

Developing Characters

Performing the actions of your narrative are characters with individual physical features, personality traits, and motivations. These traits often help to explain the characters' words and behavior. To help your readers to understand your characters, you need to include physical and emotional profiles for the major performers in your narrative.

Description Narrative writing lends itself perfectly to colorful character descriptions. Whether you directly describe your characters — "She looked like a beggar but spoke like a lawyer" — or let them speak for themselves through dialogue — "I abandoned my reserve and laughed till it hurt" — vivid descriptions provide your readers with insight into those characteristics that make a character special or unusual. Complete instructions on writing descriptively can be found on pages 120–149.

Freewriting *(page 11)* is a productive way to generate descriptive details. When you freewrite, create a mental image of a character's looks and behavior and then write freely about him or her. Review your notes, marking the details that match your image. The following is a description of Queen Victoria (1819–1901) as a teen-ager.

Yesterday, going thro' one of the Parks, I saw the poor little Queen. She was in an open carriage, preceded by three or four swift red-coated troopers; all off for Windsor just as I happened to pass. Another carriage or carriages followed with maids of honour, etc: the whole drove very fast. It seemed to me the poor little Queen was a bit modest, nice sonsy [cheerful] little lassie; blue eyes, light hair, fine white skin; of extremely small stature: she looked timid, anxious, almost frightened. . . .

Thomas Carlyle *(1795–1881)*
from *Portraits of His Contemporaries*

Motivation The catalyst behind your characters' words and actions is motivation. Without motivation your characters may appear to be performing actions capriciously or arbitrarily. There are as many sources of motivation as there are human emotions. Love, fear, hate, compassion, anger, and joy name just a few of the motivations that push people into action. Read the following autobiographical passage to see how the writer expresses the driving force behind his effort to succeed.

I felt at that moment that it was my chance to do one thing supremely well. I drove on, impelled by a combination of fear and pride. The air I breathed filled me with the spirit of the track where I had run my first race. The noise in my ears was that of the faithful Oxford crowd. Their hope and encouragement gave me greater strength. I had now turned the last bend and there were only fifty yards more.

Roger Bannister *(1929–   )*
from *The Four-Minute Mile*

Personality In addition to detailing the physical characteristics and the personal motivations of your characters, you can add a third dimension to their identity by describing their personalities. Personalities, which can range from the sublime to the ridiculous, are the behavioral traits of a person. Your character could be a daring hero or heroine, an animated eccentric, or an unassuming soul. By providing succinct details of your characters' personalities, you make them come to life for your readers. Often, in fact, insights into personality are more important than physical description in a narrative about a person's bringing about some change. Read how this writer reveals her personality in the following autobiographical passage.

*S*omebody with a flair for small cynicism once said, "We live and do not learn." But I have learned some things.
I have learned that if you must leave a place that you have lived in and loved and where all your yesterdays are buried deep — leave it any way except a slow way, leave it the fastest way you can. Never turn back and never believe that an hour you remember is a better hour because it is dead. Passed years seem safe ones, vanquished ones, while the future lives in a cloud, formidable from a distance. The cloud clears as you enter it. I have learned this, but like everyone, I learned it late.

Beryl Markham *(1902–1986)*
from *West with the Night*

On your paper, make three columns: One headed *Physical characteristics*, one headed *Motivation*, and one headed *Personality traits*. Then in each column list expressive details that describe someone whom you know or admire. Include anything that will give an accurate and a complete picture of that person. When you have finished, tell in a few sentences which details would be appropriate to the actions in a narrative, and explain why.

Developing the Action

Make your narrative exciting and enjoyable for your readers by including lively, entertaining action — the sequential account of an event or a series of events. Vital to narrative action is **conflict** — a physical or emotional struggle between the central character and another person or a situation. Within a conflict there will be **rising action,** a series of actions that build in intensity or suspense to the **climax,** or high point of the conflict. After the climax comes **falling action,** those incidents during which a resolution is (or is not) achieved and a conclusion is reached. Gather ideas and details for narrative action by clustering *(page 14)*, brainstorming *(page 13)*, asking questions *(page 18)*, or any other prewriting technique that works best for you. Once you have gathered the details, review them for appropriateness and completeness. Read the following passage about Beryl Markham's first terrifying flight and notice how the conflict and the action are developed.

*T*he little plane was doing a respectable eighty miles an hour — hardly record speed even then, but still fast enough to make me appreciate the sad and final consequences of not getting over that close horizon. As I blundered on, the trees of the Ngong Hills began to separate one from another, to stand out individually — even magnificently; the ravines got deeper.

More stick, more throttle.

I was calm. Most beginners, I thought, might have got a bit rattled — but not I. Certainly not Tom. He sat in front of me motionless as a drowsing man.

You can open a throttle just so far and increase the angle of a joy-stick to just such a degree — and if your plane does not respond to this, you had better think of something else. The Moth was not gaining altitude; she was losing that, and her speed. She was heading straight for the implacable hills like a moth hypnotized by light. There was a weight on her wings that I could feel, bearing her down. She could not lift the weight. Tom must have felt it, but he never moved.

When you can see the branches of trees from a cockpit, and the shape of rocks no bigger than your own hands, and places where grass thins against sand and becomes yellow, and watch the blow of wind on leaves, you are too close. You are so close that thought is a slow process, useless to you now — even if you can think.

The sound of our propeller got trapped between a wall of rock and the plane before Tom straightened in his seat and took the controls.

He banked sharply, dusting the trees and rock with blue exhaust. He put the nose of the Gipsy down and swung her deep into the valley while her shadow rode close on the hill. He lost altitude until the valley was flat. He climbed in spirals until we were high above the Ngong Hills, and then he went over them and home.

It was all so simple.

Beryl Markham *(1902–1986)*
from *West with the Night*

Assignment 3 Developing Action

From the following types of events, choose one specific event that interests you. On your paper, list the details of the action. Then identify the action by bracketing each part of the action and labeling it *Rising action, Climax,* or *Falling action.*

1. A well-known event in British history
2. A well-known event in international politics
3. A well-known event in contemporary music
4. A well-known event in literature

Organizing Narrative Details

Chronological order, the organization of events according to when they occurred, is particularly useful in narrative writing. Look back to the narrative about Hector Berlioz on pages 155–157 to see a narrative written in chronological order.

Before you begin to draft a brief narrative, group your prewriting notes chronologically in an informal or rough outline, or a map of the incident. An **informal outline** or a **rough outline** *(pages 49–50)* is a numbered list of events in chronological order. For **mapping** *(page 48),* you draw a plan or a diagram of the main elements of the narrative. In longer, more complicated narratives, you may want to use a topic outline *(page 50).* Begin your outline with character descriptions and a setting since these details are presented first in a narrative.

? **Critical Thinking:**

Organizing

The following topic outline shows how one writer organized her notes chronologically.

FLEMING DISCOVERS PENICILLIN

1. <u>Characters</u>--Sir Alexander Fleming

2. <u>Setting</u>--1928, medical research lab in London

3. <u>Events</u>

   a. Fleming at work on discovery of treatment of infectious diseases

   b. On lab bench, had culture broth of staphylococcus (infectious microbe)

   c. During the day, Fleming opened window for fresh air

   d. A particle of mold--<u>Penicillium notatum</u>--floated in through open window and landed on culture dish containing staphylococcus

   e. Fleming noticed culture began to dissolve

   f. Examined culture under microscope and saw mold killing the culture; named his discovery <u>Penicillin</u>

(stăf'ə-lō-kŏk'əs)

Later on, when you draft the action in your narrative, you will need to use transitional words and phrases, such as *began*, *before*, *during*, *first*, and *in the meantime*, to reinforce the sense of a flow of time. Using transitions will make your narrative more coherent and therefore easier for your readers to follow.

Assignment 4 | Chronological Order

? Critical Thinking:

Organizing What sequence is logical?

If you have not already done so, make a topic outline showing the chronological order of events that take place in the topic that you chose for Assignment 3 on page 169.

Continuing Assignment | **Plan Your Narrative**

For writing a **paragraph** or an **essay**

Using your prewriting notes from the Continuing Assignment on page 164, elaborate on your descriptions of the characters, the setting, and the action. Then organize your narrative into chronological order, using a map or a formal or informal outline of the events. Save all your notes.

A Brief Narrative

While most narratives run from several pages to thousands of pages, as few as one or two well-constructed paragraphs can make a fine narrative.

I remember an old prospector came to our farm one evening when I was a child. He had spent all his life wandering around Africa. He said he had just gone home to England for a holiday of six months; but left at the end of a week. Too many people, he said; a tame little country, catching trains and keeping to time-tables. He had learned his lesson; he would never leave the highveld again. "People," he said, shouting at himself — for he was certainly arguing against his own conscience — "people are mad, wanting to change Africa. Why don't they leave it alone? A man can breathe here, he can be himself. And," he went on, getting angrier and angrier, "when we've filled Africa up, what then? The world is only tolerable because of the empty places in it — millions of people all crowded together, fighting and struggling, but behind them, somewhere, enormous, empty places. I tell you what I think," he said, "when the world's filled up, we'll have to get hold of a star. Any star. Venus, or Mars. Get hold of it and leave it empty. Man needs an empty space somewhere for his spirit to rest in."

That's what he said. I remember every word, for he made a great impression on me.

Doris Lessing *(1919–   )*
from *Going Home*

When you first draft a brief narrative, just get your ideas onto paper. Refining them will come later. Try the following strategies when drafting your narrative.

▶ Strategies

1. *Start with a topic sentence.* Set forth the topic and your specific, focused idea on that topic at the beginning of your paragraph.
2. *Choose your point of view and use it consistently.*
3. *Tell* who, what, where, when, why, *and* how *at the start.*
4. *Use chronological order.* Present action and details chronologically.

5. *Use transitional words and phrases such as* first of all *or* as a consequence.

6. *Summarize your reactions to the event in a concluding sentence.* If you provide a personal viewpoint or a final comment in your concluding sentence, you will help your reader to understand your narrative more clearly.

Assignment 1 Introductory and Concluding Sentences

On your paper, draft three alternative introductory sentences and three possible concluding sentences for the following paragraph. Then place a check next to the most effective introductory sentence and another next to the most effective concluding sentence.

> When, around 1850, Florence announced to her parents that she wanted to serve as a nurse, they protested. No respectable lady would consider such a thing. Nightingale was determined, however. She learned from the religious orders in Europe how to care for the sick. She was sent to the Crimea to tend the wounded there despite loud protests that the front lines were no place for a woman. The conditions that she found there were horrifying, but to Florence Nightingale these were compelling reasons for committing herself totally to healing the sick.

Assignment 2 Drafting a Narrative Paragraph

Use the following notes to draft a brief narrative about the situation described in them. Write a topic sentence and several supporting sentences that give the facts in chronological order.

Notes:
— After 1818, Ludwig van Beethoven had people write in notebooks instead of speaking to him.
— Born 1770, Bonn, Germany; died 1827, Vienna, Austria
— Had about 400 notebooks when he died.
— Well-meaning friend destroyed some 250 of them because of criticisms of the imperial family
— First recital at age 8
— 1797, first signs of deafness; by age 48, completely deaf
— From 1818 on he carried notebooks everywhere.
— People would write in the notebooks; Beethoven would look over their shoulders as they did.
— Many sentences in the notebooks are incomplete. (B. probably stopped writers once he knew what they meant.)
— Had composed piano and chamber works — and one symphony — before becoming deaf

Draft a Brief Narrative

Use your prewriting from the Continuing Assignments on pages 164 and 170 to draft your narrative paragraph. Present the setting and characters clearly in the first sentence or two, and write supporting sentences by following your map or outline. Sentences should follow chronological order. Finally, conclude your draft with a sentence or two that give a particular perspective on the topic. Save your notes and your draft.

For writing
a **paragraph**

Drafting

An Extended Narrative

The Elements of a Narrative Essay

To present an interesting yet minor incident, such as Beethoven's use of notebooks, described in Assignment 2 on page 172, you can limit yourself to one or two paragraphs. If, however, you need to tell a more elaborate story, the extended narrative affords you the opportunity to develop your writing more fully and to use dialogue.

In an extended narrative, each paragraph has a single action or several related actions. Using appropriate transitions between the paragraphs, your aim will be to create a coherent, logical narrative that allows your readers to learn and to draw conclusions from the events that you narrate.

Once you have focused your idea, limited your topic, and organized the details for your narrative, you can begin your first draft. Write down everything that seems appropriate in light of your topic and your outline. Now is not the time to worry about style or mechanics; after writing your draft, you will be able to revise it as much as necessary.

Using Dialogue

Dialogue is usually inappropriate in very brief narratives. Longer narratives, however, often include **dialogue,** the direct presentation of the speech of your characters, or **indirect discourse,** the speech of the characters presented in the narrator's words. Use dialogue when you wish to reveal the behavior of your characters; use indirect discourse when you wish instead to focus on the narrator's perception of that behavior.

INDIRECT DISCOURSE Mai's eyes widened as she set foot in her new homeland; she asked her mother if they had indeed finally arrived in America.

DIALOGUE Mai stared out at the hall at Ellis Island and then gazed up at her mother. She asked in a voice both fearful and excited, "Are we there yet? Is this really America?"

The Purposes of Dialogue   Dialogue affords you opportunities to reveal the style and the manner of your characters' speech.   You can use slang, contractions, fragments, and other peculiarities of speech to give your readers a clearer picture of the characters portrayed in your narrative.   Furthermore, in historical narrative, dialogue usually provides greater vividness than a paraphrase does.

In the following dialogue, a young soldier attempts to comfort his pregnant wife the night before his black army outfit ships out for action in the Korean War.

*S*he was in his arms, and her shoulders shook.   "It isn't fair!   Why can't they take the ones that aren't married?"

He hugged her tight, feeling a great fullness in his throat.   "Come on now, stop crying, hon.   Cut it out, will you?   I'll be back home before little Joey sees daylight."

"You may never come back.   They're killing a lot of our boys over there.   Oh, Joe, Joe, why did they have to go and start another war?"

In a gruff voice, he said, "Don't you go worrying about Big Joey.   He'll take care of himself.   You just take care of little Joey and Cleo.   That's what you do."

"Don't take any chances, Joe.   Don't be a hero!"

He forced himself to laugh and hugged her tighter.   "Don't you worry about the mule going blind."

She made herself stop crying and wiped her face.   "But I don't understand, Joe.   I don't understand what colored soldiers have to fight for — especially against other colored people."

"Honey," said Joe gently, "we got to fight like anybody else. We can't just sit on the sidelines."

But she just looked at him and shook her head.

"Look," he said, "when I get back, I'm going to finish college.   I'm going to be a lawyer.   That's what I'm fighting for."

John Oliver Killens (1916–   )
from "God Bless America"

The Format of Dialogue   Make sure that when you include dialogue in your narrative, you transcribe it properly so that your readers can follow the changes from one speaker to another as the dialogue progresses.   Be sure to use quotation marks and other punctuation correctly and to begin a new paragraph each time the speaker changes.

Reference Point:
page 725

Select precise and interesting expressions when you are describing how the speakers make their comments.   Verbs such as *say* and *ask* are appropriate for making neutral statements, but they do not convey much information with regard to how the characters spoke or to how they behaved while speaking. Compare the following two passages to see the difference that using precise expressions can make.

DULL   "Wilma," Joe said, "if you're going to kick up a fuss whenever you've got to churn the butter or get the tarps drawn, you're sure to find this frontier living pretty mean."

Wilma said, "I, I don't mean nothing by it, Joe, it's just that it's so, well, different here from Baltimore. I know this is our future, but just be patient with me."

VIVID   "Wilma," Joe snapped, irritable after the long journey, "if you're going to kick up a fuss whenever you've got to churn the butter or get the tarps drawn, you're sure to find this frontier living pretty mean."

Wilma was taken aback and stammered, "I, I don't mean nothing by it, Joe, it's just that it's so, well, different here from Baltimore. I know this is our future, but just be patient with me, Joe."

Assignment 1 **Drafting Dialogue**

Imagine that you could arrange a meeting between the two people named in any of the four following items. Draft an imaginary dialogue about their similar areas of expertise and the differences between them that result from their having lived in different eras. Use reference materials if necessary.

1. Shakespeare and Mark Twain
2. Disraeli and Margaret Thatcher
3. Washington and King Arthur
4. Robin Hood and Jesse James

Using Description

Careful description is indispensable to well-crafted narrative, for it aids the progression of narrative details, maintains your readers' interest, gives insight to characters' motivation, and contributes to the mood of the story. Notice the mood conveyed in this passage.

*T*his is what he finally found, down a solitary side street lit faintly by a single street lamp at the middle of the block; the house, set back on a short hill that surely, in the spring and summer, would be a thick lawn, perhaps bordered with flowers. Snow clung to the empty, blackened branches of a hedge concealing a grotesque iron fence. The house too was grotesque, painted gray, its gables hung with daggerlike icicles.

William Melvin Kelley (1937–   )
from "A Good Long Sidewalk"

Drafting Paragraphs: Characters

Draft an introductory paragraph for a narrative about an event in the life of a well-known historical figure. Within the paragraph, provide descriptive details that have a bearing on how the person acts in the event. Do research if you require additional information about your subject.

Drafting Paragraphs: Setting

Draft a narrative paragraph that describes the setting of an important historical event. If you wish, use the event that you introduced in Assignment 2. You may need to do research to gather information about the event you choose.

Drafting Your Narrative Essay

A narrative essay contains a number of well-written, logically related paragraphs. You present your topic and your focusing idea in the introductory paragraph and then develop that topic in precise and interesting ways in the supporting paragraphs that follow. In your concluding paragraph, you bring your narrative to a close and may express a particular attitude that you have toward the topic.

The Introductory Paragraph   Establish the topic, purpose, point of view, and tone of your narrative in the introductory paragraph and thus capture the interest of your readers. Include the principal characters and a brief description of the setting if it is significant to the event. The **thesis statement** should state clearly the topic of your essay and the aspect of that topic upon which you intend to focus. You may wish to set forth in this paragraph any conflict to be developed or to identify what it is that makes the narrative worth telling.

In the following introductory paragraph to a study of ancient history, note how the author invites his readers to play an active part in this project.

Thesis
statement —
> The reader is asked, for the moment, to accept this as a reasonable statement of fact, that in a part of the world that had for centuries been civilized, and quite highly civilized, there gradually emerged a people, not very numerous, not very powerful, not very well organized, who had a totally new conception of what human life was for, and showed for the first time what the human mind was for. This statement will be amplified and, I hope, justified in what follows. We can begin the amplification now by observing that the Greeks themselves felt, in quite a simple and natural

way, that they were different from any other people that they knew. At least, the Greeks of the classical period habitually divided the human family into Hellenes and barbarians. The pre-classical Greek, Homer for instance, does not speak of "barbarians" in this way; not because he was more polite than his descendants, but because this difference had not then fully declared itself.

H. D. F. Kitto *(1897–1982)*
from *The Greeks*

The Body Paragraphs The body paragraphs present chronologically the component actions of the event. Usually each paragraph contains one narrative action. Several related actions, however, may be developed together within a single paragraph. To emphasize the chronology and to clarify the sequence of actions for your readers, use transitional words and phrases such as *first, then, in the beginning, years later,* and *prior to (page 36).*

In most narratives, the body paragraphs end with the climax, after which follow the resolution of the conflict and the conclusion of the narrative.

The Conclusion The climax is the last major action in a narrative. In the conclusion you need to resolve any action that the climax has not resolved. Furthermore, try to include in the conclusion your thoughts and assessments — or those of your narrator — with regard to the narrative episode. Look at this concluding paragraph to a chapter of Berlioz's memoirs. Upon completing his symphonic work *Romeo and Juliet*, Berlioz realized that, because of the realities of the musical world there, any orchestra that played it in London would practically have to memorize it.

*I*t will never, therefore, be played in London, where the necessary rehearsals are not to be had. In that country, musicians have no time to make music.

Hector Berlioz *(1803–1869)*
from *Memoirs of Hector Berlioz*

When you have completed your draft, take another look at your working title if you have one. Is it still appropriate? If not, you may wish to replace it with another title, which better fits the content of your draft.

Assignment 4 Drafting Paragraphs

By talking to long-time residents of your neighborhood, gather details about any changes that they have observed in the community over the years. Select the choicest details, organize them chronologically, and then draft a three-page narrative, including an introductory paragraph, several supporting paragraphs, and a conclusion.

Continuing Assignment **Draft an Extended Narrative**

For writing an **essay**

Refer to your prewriting notes in the Continuing Assignments on pages 164 and 170. Review your notes and your outline and then draft your extended narrative. Write as clearly and as logically as you can from the introduction through the body of the essay to its conclusion, but do not stop now to revise or refine your draft. Include dialogue if you wish. Save your notes and your draft.

Revising Your Narrative

? **Critical Thinking:**

Analyzing

After you have written your first draft, your next step will be to revise your narrative. Revising entails assessing your work and reorganizing and rewriting it so that the results express your thoughts in a clear and effective manner. To revise completely, you will have to read your draft through many times, each time evaluating a particular aspect of your writing and making improvements where needed.

Several aspects of narrative writing require especially close attention during revision. In addition to reviewing the Revising Checklist on page 785, think of questions such as the following to ask yourself when you revise. Then read through your draft with one question in mind, and revise for that one element. Repeat the process; you might lose the focus of your work if you try to revise everything at the same time. After revising, seek out readers who can offer constructive criticism. Their responses may lead you to see your work in a new way and, quite possibly, to discover further improvements that you can make.

- Do you present your topic, characters, and setting in the introduction?
- Is there a conflict? Do you resolve it at the conclusion of your narrative?
- Is there a climax or a turning point?
- Have you arranged the actions in chronological order?
- Are related actions grouped into paragraphs?
- Is your point of view consistent?
- If you have used dialogue, does it reveal the personalities of the characters and move the action along?

Revising the Content of Your Narrative

Begin with revising the content of your narrative. Add details or explanations if necessary, and remove anything superfluous. Use these strategies when you are revising your narrative.

▶ **Strategies**

1. *Consider purpose, audience, and point of view.* Is your narrative likely to interest your readers? Have you made clear its significance? Are your facts accurate, and do they suit your purpose? Is your language appropriate for your intended audience? Do you avoid shifting your point of view?

2. *Check unity and focus.* Does the narrative make clear your focusing idea about the event? Are all the details that you have included necessary and sufficient? After deleting any superfluous details and adding any needed information, does the narrative remain unified? If there is dialogue in your narrative, does it move the action along? Have you accurately transcribed any dialogue that you do use?

3. *Revise for coherence and transitions.* Do you present your ideas logically? Do you explain everything that might not be immediately clear to your intended readers? In narrative essays, do you present your thesis, develop your topic, and include at the conclusion of your essay a particular perspective on your essay? Have you checked for lapses of logic, clarity, and consistency? Have you used transitional words and phrases to help your narrative to flow smoothly?

Assignment 1 **Revising for Content**

On your paper, revise the content of the following paragraph to make it appropriate for the audience and the purpose specified. Correct any lack of unity, incoherence, or inconsistency in point of view.

Critical Thinking:
Analyzing
Does everything here belong? Does it make sense?

Topic: Madame de Sévigné

Audience: Students in a Western Civilization class

Purpose: To provide a brief biography of an important woman in seventeenth-century France

Point of View: Third person

Palaces and paintings and politics are what most people think of when they think of the age of Louis XIV. But what about the human element? That is what interests me, and among the most "human" of the humans of that age was Marie de Rabutin-Chantal, the marquise de Sévigné. She was born in 1626 in Paris to a family

Françoise Marguerite
de Sévigné Comtesse de
Grignan.

of the provincial nobility. At eighteen she married the marquis de
Sévigné, and all I know about him was that he was a scoundrel. He
was killed in a duel in 1651. They had two children, a girl and a
boy, and after the death of the marquis, they were the very center
of her existence. Court life meant little to her. It probably meant a
lot to a lot of people back then, though. When Françoise, the
daughter, married, she moved to Provence in southern France, far
from Paris. Madame de Sévigné was a well-educated woman,
which was unusual then. Because she missed her daughter so intensely, she began a twenty-five-year correspondence with her, and
those letters today contain the most magnificent and detailed history we have of the court of Louis XIV as viewed by an insider.
Madame de Sévigné had no literary aspirations. The letters are
marked not only by a remarkable intelligence and wit, but also by
an intimate conversational style and by the warmth of maternal
affection.

Revising the Style and Tone

You should review the style and tone of your work as well as its
content. Use these strategies to look over your narrative for stylistic
qualities.

▶ **Strategies**

1. *Check for sentence variety and tone.* Are your sentences sufficiently varied to maintain your readers' interest in your story?
   Have you written only simple sentences? Are any of your sentences too complex, confusing your readers? Does the tone that
   you have chosen — whether serious or humorous, critical or lauda-
   tory — suit your purpose?

2. *Examine word choice and clarity.* Are your words precise? Do
   they say what you mean, and, furthermore, will they make clear
   your meaning to your readers? Do you use words that are understandable and appropriate for your purpose and your audience?
   Will the language that you use help to keep your readers interested
   in your writing? If you have included dialogue, is it accurate and
   intelligible?

| Assignment 2 | Revising for Style and Tone |

On your paper, revise the following narrative for sentence variety, tone,
word choice, and clarity.

Agatha Mary Clarissa Miller was born in 1890 to an English
mother and a Yankee. Mrs. Miller, her mom, thought a girl's mind

should be challenged with more than the usual stuff, so she tutored her at home, giving her, among other things, Charles Dickens's novels to read.

Well, Agatha tried her hand at writing. Stories and poems, nuanced with Gothic undercurrents, flowed from her pen. Coarse though these preliminary attempts may have been, good stuff soon followed. Agatha married Colonel Christie, and in 1916 when he was off fighting World War I, Agatha's sister challenged her to write a detective story. The resulting book, *The Mysterious Affair at Styles*, received excellent reviews and sold two thousand copies. Nevertheless, Christie earned no royalties from it.

But that challenge changed her life, and she wrote more than one hundred mysteries. Two of her detectives are particularly memorable. She created Hercule Poirot in her first book. Later, she came up with Miss Jane Marple, feeling that an elderly woman detective would give the genre a little pizzazz, and boy, did she.

Christie's talents were not limited to novels alone. At one point in the early 1950s, three of her plays were running simultaneously in major theaters in London.

Try one of her books! They're great!

Continuing Assignment Revise Your Narrative

Use either the narrative paragraph that you drafted in the Continuing Assignment on page 173 or the narrative essay that you drafted in the Continuing Assignment on page 178. Evaluate the appropriateness of your writing for your intended purpose and audience. Make any needed changes so that a clear, well-focused narrative with a consistent point of view results. Read your narrative again to revise its style and tone. Consider the structure of your sentences and the clarity of the result. Read your revised narrative through again to make sure that the result is successful. If further changes are needed, either note them in pencil or make a new draft. Save your revised draft.

*For writing a **paragraph** or an **essay***

Proofreading

Proofreading Your Work

Having completed your revisions, you need to proofread your narrative by reading through it at least three times: once to check grammar, once for spelling and usage, and once for mechanics. Writers are unlikely to catch all these different kinds of errors by proofreading just once. Remember to proofread your final copy when you have completed it. Refer to the guidelines for proofreading on page 105 for a list of the kinds of questions to ask yourself when proofreading.

The Grammar Connection

Reference Point:
pages 661–662

As you proofread your narrative writing, give special attention to the following.

Pronoun Reference Make sure that your pronouns are unambiguous.

> He read her "Mariana," but she didn't like it. *that poem*

Here, readers cannot be sure whether the word *it* refers to the poem or being read to. You must avoid such ambiguity in your writing.

Assignment Proofreading a Paragraph

On your paper, rewrite the following paragraph, correcting all errors in grammar, usage, spelling, capitalization, and punctuation.

Every age seems to have one person that best represents that age. Samuel Johnson epitomizes the spirit of 18th century England. He was born in seventeen nine in Lichfield, a small Village, where his father was a booksseller. The younger Johnson learned his lessons well, and was sent to Oxford university. He didn't get his degree (though the school gave him a honorary degree of doctor of laws in 1775). When he was 24 he married a 46 year old widow woman with two teen-age children! It proved to be a blisful marrige though it ended when Mrs. J died seventeen years later. They had moved to London where he wrote prolifically and participated in the literary life of the capitol. The 1700s were the age of the dictionary and the encyclopedia, and Johnson's *Dictionary* is one of the monuments of that age. Johnsons masterpiece tries to incorporate all that was worth knowing during his age. As Shakespere had before, Johnson profoundly effected the language, and shaped the literary taste of the English people for generations to come.

Continuing Assignment Proofread Your Narrative

For writing
a **paragraph**
or an **essay**

Look at your revised draft from the Continuing Assignment on page 181, and proofread it for punctuation, capitalization, spelling, usage, and grammar errors. Once it is free of errors, make a clean, final copy and proofread it once more.

Publishing Your Narrative

You have a number of options to consider when publishing the final version of your narrative. First of all, think of the most effective way of communicating your work to your intended audience. If, for example, your narrative recounts a particularly dramatic historical episode, a well-delivered oral presentation might prove memorable. A narrative of a notable Civil War battle, on the other hand, would probably be improved with the addition of maps that show through pictures the advances and the retreats of the opposing sides. Consider additional ways of keeping your readers interested when you are ready to publish your work.

Your classmates, friends, and relatives can often give suggestions of ways to publish your work so that you communicate your ideas in the most effective way possible.

Continuing Assignment **Publish Your Narrative**

Publish a neat copy of your narrative for its intended audience. Seek publishing suggestions from anyone that you feel might offer good advice. Try getting your readers' responses as well. Keep this and other samples of your writing in your writer's portfolio.

For writing
a **paragraph**
or an **essay**

Student to Student

Reading and Responding to Writing

English is spoken throughout the world but in many different dialects. Carolyn Clark, a British student at Cambridge Rindge and Latin High School in Cambridge, Massachusetts, learned something about differences in English dialects when she tried out for football at her new American high school. Read Carolyn's narrative and think about the questions in the margins as you read. Then answer the questions that follow the essay.

American Football

As a nine-year-old growing up in Liverpool, England, I had the reputation of being the finest football player in the girls grammar school league. I played goalie and defense better than anyone. Out of the twelve games I played as goalie, a total of only fifteen points were scored by the opposing team. As you can see, I was pretty happy growing up in Liverpool.

When my dad, who was a pilot for British Airways, took a new job with TWA in Boston, we had to move to the United States, and I would have to go to school there.

On the first day of school in Cambridge, Massachusetts, I wasn't very happy with the way things were. I was surrounded by strangers, I couldn't find my classes, people made fun of the way I talked, and worst of all, I walked into the boys changing room! I'd have preferred getting nine demerits in Liverpool than to go to school in Cambridge.

Things actually started lightening up when the teacher announced that football tryouts would be held next period in the field. I can't even explain how I felt right then. Now would be my chance to have some fun. I felt so confident in the changing room. I quickly changed into my gym shorts and a T-shirt. I couldn't believe this was happening to me!

The sun blinded my eyes as I ran out onto the field. All I could see were shadows. I felt something hit me in the head

What clue do you get here about language differences?

How does Carolyn organize her narrative? What transitions does she use?

184

and then bounce onto the ground. It was a strange egg-shaped ball. I picked it up to examine it, and the next thing I knew I was on the ground with about thirty people on top of me all grabbing for the ball! I heard a whistle blow, and everyone got up. Everybody was dressed in big bulky costumes and helmets. The man with the whistle said in so many words that he had never had a girl try out for the team and he was proud to have me and he wished me luck with the tryouts. Then he said I'd better get some equipment before I got hurt. I told him I didn't have any. He told me that was okay because this was only the tryouts. During tryouts I realized that Liverpool football was almost like Cambridge football in that you have to get goals. I was starting to get the hang of Cambridge football.

I got home all sweaty and dirty. I told my father everything that happened, starting with the egg-shaped ball. He was smiling a knowing smile all the time that I was telling him what happened. I asked him what was so funny. He told me that what was called football in Liverpool was called soccer in Cambridge and that what I tried out for was an all-American sport.

I went upstairs to shower and change. I thought about what Dad had said. Soccer, I said to myself over and over. It sounds like someone that makes socks. I decided that I liked American football better than English football.

When I got out of the shower, Dad told me that I had got a phone call from the coach saying that I made the team. I was so happy. By the next week I was known all over school as the "First, yet Finest, Female Quarterback ever"!

What is the rising action? Where is the climax?

How does the conclusion provide a personal slant?

Responding to Writing Have you or has anyone you know ever had a similar experience? How do you think that the narrator's success in American football might have helped her to gain acceptance at her new school in a new country? What advantages and disadvantages might Carolyn have had during her first season playing American football?

Reading Critically How does Carolyn set the scene for her narrative in the introductory paragraph? Where does she introduce conflict? Where does she resolve it? What tone does she use? Does she vary the tone? How does she vary the structure of her sentences?

The Literature Connection

When you tell a story to friends about an experience that you've had, how do you recreate the event so that they respond to it in the same way that you did? How do you make them feel as if they were there? Obviously there are many ways to tell a captivating story, but you need to establish your own personal style by finding and using techniques that work best for you. Pay attention to what makes an audience hungry for more when you or someone else is telling a story. When you read, note any methods that the author uses to keep you interested and involved.

Guided Reading   In the passage that follows, Eva Hoffman tells about a single moment that marked a vital change in her life. In the first paragraph, she not only draws her readers in, but she also subtly informs them of the *who, what, when, where, why,* and *how* of her narrative. After you read the passage once, read it again and answer the questions at the right.

*I*t is April 1959, I'm standing at the railing of the *Batory*'s upper deck, and I feel that my life is ending. I'm looking out at the crowd that has gathered on the shore to see the ship's departure from Gdynia — a crowd that, all of a sudden, is irrevocably on the other side — and I want to break out, run back, run toward the familiar excitement, the waving hands, the exclamations. We can't be leaving all this behind — but we are. I am thirteen years old, and we are emigrating. It's a notion of such crushing, definitive finality that to me it might as well mean the end of the world.

How does this paragraph tell *who, what, when, where, why,* and *how?*

My sister, four years younger than I, is clutching my hand wordlessly; she hardly understands where we are, or what is happening to us. My parents are highly agitated; they had just been put through a body search by the customs police, probably as the farewell gesture of anti-Jewish harassment. Still, the officials weren't clever enough, or suspicious enough, to check my sister and me — lucky for us, since we are both carrying some silverware we were not allowed to take out of Poland in large pockets sewn onto our skirts especially for this purpose, and hidden under capacious sweaters.

When the brass band on the shore strikes up the jaunty mazurka rhythms of the Polish anthem, I am pierced by a youthful sorrow so powerful that I suddenly stop crying and try to hold still against the pain. I desperately want time to stop, to hold the ship still with the force of my will. I am suffering my first, severe attack of nostalgia, or *tęsknota* — a word that adds to nostalgia the tonalities of sadness and longing. It is a feeling whose shades and degrees I'm destined to know intimately, but at this hovering moment, it comes upon me like a visitation from a whole new geography of emotions, an annunciation of how much an absence can hurt. Or a premonition of absence, because at this divide, I'm filled to the brim with what I'm about to lose — images of Cracow, which I loved as one loves a person, of the sun-baked villages where we had taken summer vacations, of the hours I spent poring over passages of music with my piano teacher, of conversations and escapades with friends. Looking ahead, I come across an enormous, cold blankness — a darkening, an erasure, of the imagination, as if a camera eye has snapped shut, or as if a heavy curtain has been pulled over the future. Of the place where we're going — Canada — I know nothing. There are vague outlines of half a continent, a sense of vast spaces and little habitation. When my parents were hiding in a branch-covered forest bunker during the war, my father had a book with him called *Canada Fragrant with Resin* which, in his horrible confinement, spoke to him of majestic wilderness, of animals roaming without being pursued, of freedom. That is partly why we are going there, rather than to Israel, where most of our Jewish friends have gone. But to me, the word "Canada" has ominous echoes of the "Sahara." No, my mind rejects the idea of being taken there, I don't want to be pried out of my childhood, my pleasures, my safety, my hopes for becoming a pianist. The *Batory*

How do the narrator's visions of Poland and Canada differ from those of her parents? Why do they differ so?

187

pulls away, the foghorn emits its lowing, shofar sound, but my being is engaged in a stubborn refusal to move. My parents put their hands on my shoulders consolingly; for a moment, they allow themselves to acknowledge that there's pain in this departure, much as they wanted it.

Many years later, at a stylish party in New York, I met a woman who told me that she had had an enchanted childhood. Her father was a highly positioned diplomat in an Asian country, and she had lived surrounded by sumptuous elegance, the courtesy of servants, and the delicate advances of older men. No wonder, she said, that when this part of her life came to an end, at age thirteen, she felt she had been exiled from paradise, and had been searching for it ever since.

No wonder. But the wonder is what you can make a paradise out of. I told her that I grew up in a lumpen apartment in Cracow, squeezed into three rudimentary rooms with four other people, surrounded by squabbles, dark political rumblings, memories of wartime suffering, and daily struggle for existence. And yet, when it came time to leave, I, too, felt I was being pushed out of the happy, safe enclosures of Eden.

Eva Hoffman (1946–   )
from *Lost In Translation*

What is paradise to the woman at the party? To the narrator? Are their ideas of paradise different? If so, in what way?

Enrichment Connections

Choose one or more of these activities to do on your own or as a group.

Narrative Writing

In her narrative, Eva Hoffman describes a monumental change in her life that symbolizes a step from childhood to adulthood. Describe in three or four paragraphs a moment in your own life when you felt that you had made this step. If you wish, you may write about a moment that another person has told you about.

Speaking and Listening

Storytelling Techniques   Choose a first-impression encounter from the brainstorming that you did for *Responding to Literature* on page 157. Write a three- or four-paragraph entry in your writer's notebook about what happened and why the incident became significant. Freewrite before you draft in order to develop interesting ways to bring your main character to life. Read your entry aloud to some classmates. Watch their reactions to find clues for effective storytelling techniques.

A Letter

Choose a place you remember that has either changed or that you imagine has changed. Write a letter to a real or imaginary friend who has moved away, and describe how this place has changed. The place can be a building, a field, or any other spot that was important to you when you were younger. The place can change physically, or it can *seem* different to you. Organize the details by mapping or outlining before you begin to write. Revise carefully to make sure that your description of change is clear and vivid. Send the letter to your friend or exchange it with a classmate when you have revised and proofread it.

Creative Writing

Writing a Poem   Write a poem about change. You may choose from the interest inventory that you developed at the beginning of the unit or from prewriting in your writer's notebook. Cluster around the topic to generate some material for your poem. When you have revised and proofread your poem, publish it by using one of the suggested methods in the unit.

Writing a Fantasy   A variety of stories tell about people who have undergone some kind of change. One of the most famous stories is "The Metamorphosis" by Franz Kafka. In this story the main character wakes up one morning to discover that he has turned into a giant bug. Write a brief narrative about a metamorphosis of your own in which you change into something or someone else. Brainstorm on what you think it would be like to discover this change. Think about the feelings and sensations and also about the way other people would react to you.

An Autobiography

What do you foresee for the next ten years? Suppose that your high-school reunion chairperson has contacted you to announce the approach of your tenth reunion. In the reunion information packet is a request for a brief autobiography that will bring your classmates up to date on what you have been doing over the ten years since you were graduated. Write a description of what you think (or hope) that the next ten years will hold for you. Make logical and coherent transitions among the significant events. When you have finished, gather future autobiographies from your classmates and publish a collection.

CELEBRATING
DIVERSITY

What aspects of your way of life do you take for granted? How well could you adapt to a world without electricity or to a world where all communication is done by computer? What changes do you anticipate in your lifetime? Do you think they will change your life for the better or for the worse?

In the following two selections from a novel about the Chippewa people, the elderly narrator Nanapush tells his granddaughter about the changes he has seen. As you read, notice which changes represent the end or the "last" of something, which are natural occurrences, and which are created by human beings. Then work on one or more of the activities that follow the selection. Working on them may give you new insight into a way of life that is now gone.

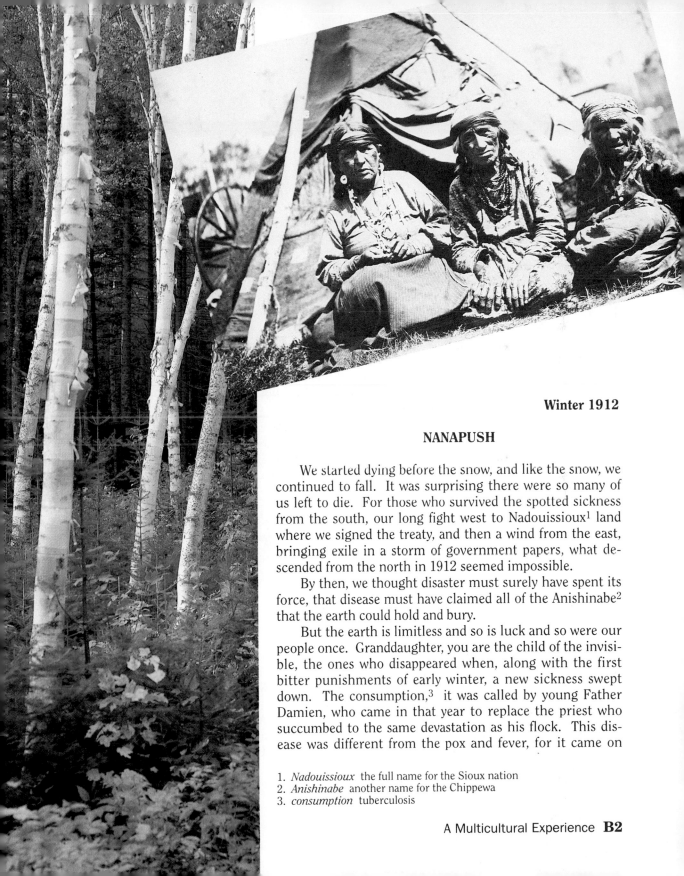

Winter 1912

NANAPUSH

We started dying before the snow, and like the snow, we continued to fall. It was surprising there were so many of us left to die. For those who survived the spotted sickness from the south, our long fight west to Nadouissioux[1] land where we signed the treaty, and then a wind from the east, bringing exile in a storm of government papers, what descended from the north in 1912 seemed impossible.

By then, we thought disaster must surely have spent its force, that disease must have claimed all of the Anishinabe[2] that the earth could hold and bury.

But the earth is limitless and so is luck and so were our people once. Granddaughter, you are the child of the invisible, the ones who disappeared when, along with the first bitter punishments of early winter, a new sickness swept down. The consumption,[3] it was called by young Father Damien, who came in that year to replace the priest who succumbed to the same devastation as his flock. This disease was different from the pox and fever, for it came on

1. *Nadouissioux* the full name for the Sioux nation
2. *Anishinabe* another name for the Chippewa
3. *consumption* tuberculosis

slow. The outcome, however, was just as certain. Whole families of your relatives lay ill and helpless in its breath. On the reservation, where we were forced close together, the clans dwindled. Our tribe unraveled like a coarse rope, frayed at either end as the old and new among us were taken. My own family was wiped out one by one, leaving only Nanapush. And after, although I lived no more than fifty winters, I was considered an old man. I'd seen enough to be one. In the years I'd passed, I saw more change than in a hundred upon a hundred before.

My girl, I saw the passing of times you will never know.

I guided the last buffalo hunt. I saw the last bear shot. I trapped the last beaver with a pelt of more than two years' growth. I spoke aloud the words of the government treaty, and refused to sign the settlement papers that would take away our woods and lake. I axed the last birch that was older than I, and I saved the last Pillager[4]. . . .

Fall 1913—Spring 1914

NANAPUSH

Before the boundaries were set, before the sickness scattered the clans like gambling sticks, an old man never had to live alone and cook for himself, never had to braid his own hair, or listen to his silence. An old man had some relatives, got a chance to pass his name on, especially if the name was an important one like Nanapush.

My girl, listen well. Nanapush is a name that loses power every time that it is written and stored in a government file. That is why I only gave it out once in all those years.

No Name, I told Father Damien when he came to take the church census. *No Name*, I told the Agent when he made up the tribal roll.

"I have the use of a white man's name," I told the Captain who delivered the ration payout for our first treaty, "but I won't sign your paper with that name either."

4. *Pillager* Fleur's family name

The Captain and then the lumber president, the Agent and at last many of our own, spoke long and hard about a cash agreement. But nothing changed my mind. I've seen too much go by unturned grass below my feet, and overhead, the great white cranes flung south forever. I know this. Land is the only thing that lasts life to life. Money burns like tinder, flows off like water. And as for government promises, the wind is steadier. I am a holdout, like the Pillagers, although I told the Captain and the Agent what I thought of their papers in good English. I could have written my name, and much more too, in script. I had a Jesuit[5] education in the halls of Saint John before I ran back to the woods and forgot all my prayers.

My father said, "Nanapush. That's what you'll be called. Because it's got to do with trickery and living in the bush. Because it's got to do with something a girl can't resist. The first Nanapush stole fire. You will steal hearts."

Not Fleur though, getting back to her. Your mother both clung to and resisted me, like any daughter. Like you're doing now.

"Stay here with me," I said to Fleur when she came to visit.

She refused.

5. *Jesuit* a Roman Catholic order of priests

"The land will go," I told her. "The land will be sold and measured."

But she tossed back her hair and walked off, down the path, with nothing to eat till thaw but a bag of my onions and a sack of oats.

Who knows what happened? She returned to Matchimanito and stayed there alone in the cabin that even fire did not want. A young girl had never done such a thing before. I heard that in those months she was asked for fee money on all four allotments, even the island where Moses hid. The Agent went out there, then got lost, spent a whole night following the moving lights and lamps of people who would not answer him, but talked and laughed among themselves. They only let him go at dawn because he was so stupid. Yet he asked Fleur again for money, and the next thing we heard he was living in the woods and eating roots, gambling with ghosts.

Every year there are more who come looking for profit, who draw lines across the land with their strings and yellow flags. They disappear sometimes, and now there are so many betting with sticks and dice out near Matchimanito at night that you wonder how Fleur sleeps, or if she sleeps at all. Why should she? She does without

so many things. The company of the living. Ammunition for her gun.

Some have ideas. You know how old chickens scratch and gabble. That's how the tales started, all the gossip, the wondering, all the things people said without knowing and then believed, since they heard it with their own ears, from their own lips, each word.

I was never one to take notice of the talk of those who fattened in the shade of the new Agent's storehouse. But I watched the wagons take the rutted turnoff to Matchimanito. Few of them returned, it is true, but those that did were enough, loaded high with hard green wood. From where we now sit, granddaughter, I heard the groan and crack, felt the ground tremble as each tree slammed earth. I weakened into an old man as one oak went down, another and another was lost, as a gap formed here, a clearing there, and plain daylight entered.

Louise Erdrich *(1954–)*
from *Tracks*

Taking Another Look

What disasters occurred before consumption struck Nanapush's people in 1912? In what sense is the granddaughter "the child of the invisible"? What do you think the metaphor of the frayed rope means? Nanapush lists a number of "last" events; what type of world or way of life do the first three add up to? What threatened and eventually destroyed that way of life? In the second selection, why does Nanapush refuse to give his name? How does he contrast the value of land and money? What does he think of the treaties the government made with the Indians? What are the Captain, the lumber president, and the Agent trying to get Nanapush to do? How has he lived up to his name?

Changing Places

Imagine that you are Nanapush's granddaughter, listening to his story of your people. What would you think of Nanapush? How would you feel about your heritage? Would you be curious to find out more details about your people? Now consider your own life. What stories have older friends or relatives told you about your background? How do you usually react to them? What things in your family background would you like to know more about? Keep these questions in mind as you choose one or more of the following activities.

WRITING

Considering Heritage

Everyone has a heritage. Nanapush describes many things to his granddaughter that are part of her heritage. How would you describe *your* heritage? Do you know enough about your family background to make an attempt? List any information that comes readily to mind, and write down questions that you would like to have answered. Then interview relatives and old family friends, and take notes on what you learn from them. Write a narrative of your family's history, describing your heritage and the significant changes that your family has undergone. Share your narrative with classmates by reading it aloud or by posting it on the bulletin board.

SPEAKING and LISTENING

Making a Speech   Prepare a speech about some aspect of American Indian life in your own state. (If no American Indians live in your area now, you can select another part of the country to write about.) Choose a specific nation and research facts about their history, their lifestyle, and their current communities and organizations. Record the information you discover on notecards and practice delivering your speech. Perhaps you can actually deliver it to a history class or a local historical organization.

LANGUAGE

Force-ful Metaphors   Look at the first paragraph of the selection, and notice how Nanapush uses weather metaphors involving snow and a windstorm. In the second selection, he uses fire, water, and wind metaphorically to make a point about economics. Brainstorm or cluster to think of events, situations, or emotions that you could describe using metaphorical comparisons to the basic forces of nature and weather. Then select one topic, and write a short narrative, an essay, or a poem based on one or several nature-related metaphors.

UNIT 3

Writing with an Expository Focus

An expository writing assignment can be a chance for you to write about something that you already know. Such an assignment is also an opportunity for you to learn more about the subject that you're writing about. After all, the process of expository writing is a way of *thinking* on paper.

What's more, when it's appropriate to your purpose and your audience, the very *process* of coming to a conclusion can become part of your final essay. In this kind of writing, the persona, or voice, of the essay reaches a new understanding at the end of the piece, just as the reader does. In addition, the persona can contribute warmth, humor, outrage, or simply a quirky new way of looking at the world. In the selection shown here, note how the persona's attempt to mark and measure leads her to an unexpected conclusion. As you examine this expository piece and the other measurement techniques on these pages, think about how you might approach writing about *measurement* and think about what kind of persona you could use to enliven your expository writing.

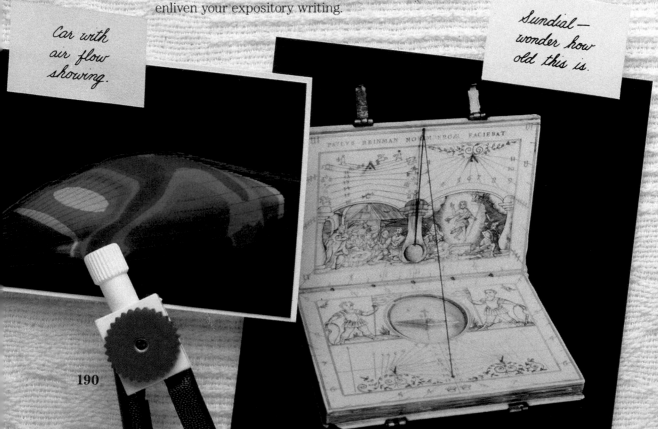

Car with air flow showing.

Sundial— wonder how old this is.

Yesterday I set out to catch the new season, and instead I found an old snakeskin. I was in the sunny February woods by the quarry; the snakeskin was lying in a heap of leaves right next to an aquarium someone had thrown away. I don't know why that someone hauled the aquarium deep into the woods to get rid of it; it had only one broken glass side. The snake found it handy, I imagine; snakes like to rub against something rigid to help them out of their skins, and the broken aquarium looked like the nearest likely object. Together the snakeskin and the aquarium made an interesting scene on the forest floor. It looked like an exhibit at a trial—circumstantial evidence—of a wild scene, as though a snake had burst through the broken side of the aquarium, burst through his ugly old skin, and disappeared, perhaps straight up in the air, in a rush of freedom and beauty.

The snakeskin had unkeeled scales, so it belonged to a nonpoisonous snake. It was roughly five feet long by the yardstick, but I'm not sure because it was very wrinkled and dry, and every time I tried to stretch it flat, it broke. I ended up with seven or eight pieces of it all over the kitchen table in a fine film of forest dust.

The point I want to make about the snakeskin is that, when I found it, it was whole and tied in a knot. Now there have been stories told, even by reputable scientists, of snakes that have deliberately tied themselves

She'll compare season and snake-skin?

Hard to measure.

Tries to measure seasons exactly.

Great image!

in a knot to prevent larger snakes from trying to swallow them—but I couldn't imagine any way that throwing itself into a half hitch would help a snake trying to escape its skin. Still, ever cautious, I figured that one of the neighborhood boys could possibly have tied it in a knot in the fall, for some whimsical boyish reason, and left it there, where it dried and gathered dust. So I carried the skin along thoughtlessly as I walked, snagging it sure enough on a low branch and ripping it in two for the first of many times. I saw that thick ice still lay on the quarry pond and that the skunk cabbage was already out in the clearings, and then I came home and looked at the skin and its knot.

The knot had no beginning. Idly I turned it around in my hand, searching for a place to untie; I came to with a start when I realized I must have turned the thing around fully ten times. Intently, then, I traced the knot's lump around with a finger: it was continuous. I couldn't untie it any more than I could untie a doughnut; it was a loop without beginning or end. These snakes *are* magic, I thought for a second, and then of course I reasoned what must have happened. The skin had been pulled inside-out like a peeled sock for several inches; then an inch or so of the inside-out part—a piece whose length was coincidentally equal to the diameter of the skin—had somehow been turned right-side out again, making a thick lump whose edges were lost in wrinkles, looking exactly like a knot.

So. I have been thinking about the change of seasons. I don't want to miss spring this year. I want to distinguish the last winter frost from the out-of-season one, the frost of spring. I want to be there on the spot the moment the grass turns green. I always miss this radical revolution; I see it the next day from a window, the yard so suddenly green and lush I could envy Nebuchadnezzar down on all fours eating grass. This year I want to stick a net into time and say "now," as men plant flags on the ice and snow and say, "here." But it occurred to me that I could no more catch spring by the tip of the tail than I could untie the apparent knot in the snakeskin; there are no edges to grasp. Both are continuous loops. . . .

Time is the continuous loop, the snakeskin with scales endlessly overlapping without beginning or end, or time is an ascending spiral if you will, like a child's toy Slinky. Of course we have no idea which arc on the loop is our time, let alone where the loop itself is, so to speak, or down whose lofty flight of stairs the Slinky so uncannily walks.

Comparison comes together.

Annie Dillard *(1945   )*
from *Pilgrim at Tinker Creek*

Responding to Literature

Did the persona of the preceding selection eventually do what she set out to do? What did she do—or discover—instead? Notice how Dillard's initial comparison finally leads her to a metaphorical definition of time.

Some changes are so gradual that they cannot be measured, just as Dillard couldn't "stick a net into time and say 'now.'" Human beings, however, continue to try to mark their beginnings and their endings. Think of some other gradual changes, such as from day to night or from childhood to adulthood. Choose one, and freewrite about it. Include at least one metaphor to sum up your feelings about trying to measure that change. Save your prewriting in your writer's notebook.

193

Getting and Exploring Ideas for Expository Writing

The Nature of Exposition

Exposition is one of the oldest and most important kinds of writing. From Thucydides' chronicles of the Peloponnesian Wars in the fifth century B.C. to Einstein's essays on relativity in the twentieth century, exposition has recorded the history of great minds at work. Less exalted but no less important is the role of exposition in everyday life. From a letter of application to a how-to book on gardening, exposition helps you to go about the business of life.

In this unit, you will learn to become a better user of exposition. You will use expository writing to explain what something is, to explain causes and effects, and to explain an idea or an opinion. In addition, you will examine the role of exposition in writing within the various subjects in your school.

All your life you've been explaining. The following questions about the metric system, for example, lead to answers that are expository.

What is the metric system?
How can we make a shift to the metric system easier?
Why was the metric system designed?

To answer each of these questions, you would write an expository paragraph or essay.

The following paragraph is an example of exposition. It explains how the distribution of wealth in the United States is changing.

According to the United States Bureau of the Census, the size of the middle class in the United States is shrinking while that of the upper and lower ends is expanding. From 1973 to 1982, the percentage of families earning under $20,000 a year grew from 28.4 percent to 34 percent. Between the years 1970 and 1987, the percentage of families earning more than $50,000 a year grew from 15.4 percent to 22.9 percent. Middle-income families now constitute fewer than half of the families in the United States. This shift in income is likely to have profound social effects in years to come.

When you tackle expository writing situations, various approaches to your topic will help you to find the best way to accomplish your task. Use *process analysis* when the topic or the problem has a sequence of events that needs to be explained. When physical details are essential to your explanation, use *description*. To cite specific cases that help to explain the topic, try *illustration and example*. *Comparison and contrast* can help you to explain topics by pointing out their similarities and differences. When your readers need to know what a term or an idea means, use *definition*. If the sources or the results of a topic are essential to your explanation, use *cause and effect*. *Classification* can assist you in dividing a topic into categories. When an anecdote or a story would help your explanation, use *narration*. Use these approaches to clarify your thinking on expository topics. As you explore your subject, you may find that a combination of approaches works best.

Assignment 1 Approaches to Expository Answers

Reread the paragraph on the distribution of wealth on page 194. On your paper, list the approaches that the writer uses: *Process analysis, Narration, Description, Illustration and example, Classification, Comparison and contrast, Definition,* or *Cause and effect*. Explain your answers.

Getting Started with Expository Writing

When you write exposition, you're often assigned a specific topic. Perhaps your boss needs a report on the latest salary figures, or your math teacher wants an explanation of your problem-solving techniques. Prewriting techniques such as brainstorming and clustering *(page 16)* can help you to explore ideas on these assigned topics.

When you aren't assigned a topic, prewriting can also help you to discover one. Brainstorming *(pages 13–14)*, freewriting *(pages 11–12)*, clustering *(pages 14–15)*, keeping an interest inventory *(pages 12–13)*, and other prewriting techniques can give you ideas for expository writing, and your writer's notebook *(pages 8–9)* can be the perfect place to save your prewriting notes.

Writer's Notebook

Your best source for expository topics is the world around you. Become a careful observer, with your eyes open to the wonders and the delights of the world. How does your neighborhood change in the summer? Do different foods affect the way you feel, perform, and interact with friends and family? What is your best time of day? Why? Then record those details in your writer's notebook.

Use your writer's notebook to explore your world. Include your thoughts and your comments on the day. Don't worry about how you sound — use your own words to explore ideas for future expository writing. In the following excerpt from a writer's notebook, for example, a student writes random thoughts and then looks back at them, considering whether they suggest good topics for expository writing.

January 1: New year — what's new about it except the last digit of the date? By the time it comes, I don't feel new at all — just exhausted from the hectic pace of the holidays, with family celebrations, parties, and my part-time job. Maybe that's why we <u>need</u> the new year — if we're "old" and worn out, we need rejuvenation and renewal. Of course, nature would renew itself whether or not we marked the cycle. Interesting — in the depths of winter, we celebrate the newness that's still months away.

Why is January the first month? Why not March, with spring and the vernal equinox? In fact, why not March 21? I guess I like having the year begin in the winter though. Part of newness, after all, is promise — promise of spring, change, growth, and new opportunities. I wonder if people in other climates find life awfully dull — and depressing — without seasonal cycles.

January 4: What about a topic? I don't want to write about "what the new year means to me" — at least not in the way that silly title implies. And yet I really got into thinking about newness. Maybe I could write something about the psychology of renewal — why I need the new year to come along after the holidays and why it's important to me to have the new year begin just when everything in nature seems most dead. Or I could write about why January is the first month — that's less personal but still interesting. Maybe I could write something humorous entitled "Make March 21 the New New Year's Day!"

Although your writer's notebook is composed of notes to yourself, it also asks you to look at the world with a writer's eyes. Its purpose is to help you to focus on ways that you can turn your experiences or your thoughts into writing. Use your writer's notebook to experiment with various ideas before you write for an audience.

Beginning with a Title   Writers who already know what they plan to write often create a working title to focus their minds on the topic and the possible approach. If you choose this option, try to make your title reflect your plan and capture your readers' interest.

Assignment 2 Writer's Notebook

Do some freewriting in your writer's notebook. Then examine your freewriting for questions that require expository answers. On your paper, write five questions that your thoughts and your observations suggest. Save your questions to give you ideas for further writing.

Continuing Assignment **Find Ideas for Expository Writing**

For writing a **paragraph** or an **essay**

In the series of Continuing Assignments in this unit, you'll be defining, explaining causes and effects, presenting an idea or an opinion, and practicing the kind of writing that you do for school subjects. As an alert and interested observer, record your reflections in your writer's notebook. Write down bits of conversation, surprising billboards that you see, or questions that occur to you as you read your physics textbook, for example. Include anything that might generate some interesting ideas for expository writing. Then reread your entries, considering them from a writer's point of view. On your paper, list ten expository topics that you see in the material in your writer's notebook. Save your list to help you with ideas for later Continuing Assignments.

Prewriting

Focusing Ideas for Expository Writing

Once you have an expository topic — one that you've been assigned or one that you've chosen — focusing your ideas will overlap with deciding what kind of exposition to write. Like your topic, the type of exposition may often be out of your hands. A fellow employee may ask you for a written definition of the RAM (random-access memory) in your computer, or your math teacher may want you to explain the metric system. Decide simultaneously or in any other workable order what kind of exposition to write and how to focus your ideas.

Decisions That Affect Your Writing

Who's going to read your explanation? What do you expect your readers to do after they've read it? What is your role as the writer? Answer these questions carefully before you write, but don't worry about the order in which you answer them.

Identifying Your Audience

Who will read your expository essay? What do they already know about your topic and how will they use the explanation that you provide? A well-informed audience will expect original support and complex thinking but won't need very much background material, definition, and general explanation. A less informed audience, on the other hand, will need a considerable amount of background material, definitions of key terms, and thorough explanation.

Consider also whether your readers have a natural interest in your topic. If they don't, you'll have to generate ideas that will build their interest. Show them, for example, how they'll be affected by the topic or how important it is.

Identifying Your Purpose

Once your readers have read your explanation, what do you want them to do? When you define something to satisfy your readers' curiosity or to convey general knowledge, for example, you don't need to write a complex definition. On the other hand, if your audience needs the information in your definition to act successfully, you'll write a more detailed explanation.

When you explain causes and effects, you'll want to provide your readers with enough information to understand why something happens, to comprehend the results of an action, to cause some result to occur, or to avoid certain results of an action. In explaining an idea or an opinion, you'll try to give your readers sufficient material to make intelligent decisions about your topic. Perhaps, too, you believe that sharing your ideas and your opinions will help others.

When you write for various school subjects, you'll usually write for three basic reasons. You'll write to learn and understand the subject, with yourself as the audience; you'll write to be evaluated by your teacher, who is your only audience; or you'll write for interested, curious readers who are very similar to those who read your other kinds of expository writing.

Identifying Yourself as the Writer

Your readers will want to know something about you as the writer. Can you be counted on, do you have the knowledge to present a strong explanation, and have you thought seriously about your subject? Your job is to inspire confidence in your readers.

If your audience knows you well and if your purpose is within the context of your normal, friendly relationship, choose an informal tone — relaxed and colloquial. On the other hand, use a more business-like, formal tone for a less familiar audience.

To establish or maintain a personal relationship with your readers, choose a personal tone, addressing your readers as *you* and even using the first-person pronoun *I* for very personal writing. Use an impersonal tone, though, when you want to establish distance between you and your readers, to emphasize the seriousness of your purpose, or to emphasize your authority on the subject.

For each of the following expository topics, write on your paper a possible purpose, a potential audience, and your role as a writer for a paragraph or an essay.

SAMPLE How to measure success

ANSWER *Purpose:* to define success; *Audience:* high school students who believe that expensive clothes and cars are everything; *Role as writer:* personal and informal

1. Computer memory
2. Measuring intelligence
3. The effects of stress
4. The real value of money
5. Civic responsibility
6. Measuring friendship
7. The meaning of time
8. Choosing a college
9. The use of sundials
10. Designing an exercise program

Limiting Your Topic

To write a paragraph or an essay, you'll need a topic that's limited enough for the length that you choose. Often your audience and your purpose work to limit your topic naturally, with little effort on your part. There will still be occasions, however, when you'll need to limit a topic before you begin to write. In those cases try using these questions: *Who? What? Where? When? Why? How?*

For example, suppose that you decide to write about time. Since the subject obviously needs to be limited, you might start by asking yourself some questions.

Who?	Who invented the way that we measure time?
What?	What does Einstein's theory of relativity have to do with time?
Where?	Where is the world's most accurate time kept?
When?	When have the ways that we measure time changed?
Why?	Why is time so important? Why do we have leap year?
How?	How have various societies measured time? How does time affect our lives?

Answering these questions can begin the limiting process and give you many different ideas for expository writing.

On your paper, limit the following topics for a paragraph or an essay. Use the preceding questions to guide you.

1. Light
2. Success
3. Earthquakes
4. Temperature
5. Intelligence
6. Morality
7. The metric system
8. Freedom
9. Financial security

Selecting a Kind of Exposition

While you're limiting your topic and focusing your ideas, think carefully about what kind of exposition you'll write. Sometimes you don't have a choice: your teacher assigns an essay defining probability, or you need to explain to a friend what a Geiger counter is. At other times you don't decide what kind of exposition to write until much later. Whenever you make your decision, however, it will dramatically affect the writing that you do. In this following section, you'll examine and practice four different types of expository writing.

Explaining What Something Is

One purpose of expository writing is to explain what something is. This kind of writing is often called **definition.** You probably encounter brief definitions of words or terms all the time. For your six-year-old brother, for example, you might define a *thermometer* as "something that shows whether you're sick." This explanation is probably complete enough to satisfy your brother, but usually you'll need an expanded definition. To define *mercury thermometer* for a relatively sophisticated audience, one writer wrote the following paragraph.

*T*he commonest type of thermometer is the mercury thermometer. It consists of a capillary tube (a tube with a very small bore) which is sealed at its upper end and is enlarged into a spherical or cylindrical bulb at its lower end. This bulb is filled with mercury. When this is heated, it expands and rises in the tube. Because of the very small bore of the latter, even a small increase in the volume of the mercury will cause it to rise quite appreciably. The thermometer is calibrated between two fixed reference points: the freezing point and the boiling point of water at normal atmospheric pressure. . . .

from *The Way Things Work: An Illustrated Encyclopedia of Technology*

Explaining Causes and Effects

Sometimes expository essays explain either causes — why something happens — or effects — what happens as a result *(page 33)*. When you ask, for example, how radiation is produced, you are searching for causes. When you ask what happens when radiation levels are too high, you are concerned about effects.

Be sure to make distinctions between a cause and an effect. Clarify the relationship between the two. Make it as clear as you can that a cause doesn't just precede an effect; it produces the effect.

In *The Measure of the Universe*, for example, science writer Isaac Asimov defines temperature as "the measure of the average energy of motion possessed by each particle of a mass." Then he explains one effect of decreasing temperatures on cold-blooded land animals.

Cold-blooded animals (that is, all animals but birds and mammals) usually have their body temperature equal to the environmental temperature about them. This means that, as the temperature drops at night or in the winter, the energy content of the body sinks and the cold-blooded land animal grows sluggish. (Water animals that are cold-blooded, such as fish, are adapted to a surrounding temperature that is *always* cold and are lively enough.)

Isaac Asimov (1920–   )
from *The Measure of the Universe*

Explaining an Idea or an Opinion

You've had a great deal of practice explaining your ideas and your opinions. After all, ever since you began conversing intelligently with family and friends, you've done this kind of explaining. All the practice that you've had keeps it from being too difficult.

Although explaining an idea or an opinion may seem close to persuasion *(page 230)*, your purpose here is to explain. Don't worry about whether your readers agree with you, but do everything that you can to be sure that they understand you. The following paragraph, for example, explains the writer's opinion of a human need.

The need to verify one's competence is strong, deep, and universal. Young children demand to be quizzed: "Ask me about such-and-such!" Older children and adults play quiz games and solve puzzles. Half the attractions in amusement parks are tests of skill; the other half are tests of aplomb. This need is not only an appetite for admiration but a hunger for reassurance, a drive that springs from events in the earliest months of an infant's consciousness, when he learns of the existence of a world outside himself and struggles confusedly to know and control it. "Do I really know what I know?" and "Does the world know me?" are two questions the infant asks himself before he has words to ask them with. *Not* to be examined in a subject leaves the competent student frustrated.

Donald Barr (1921–   )
from *Who Pushed Humpty Dumpty?*

Step 1: On your paper, write the kind of exposition that you would choose for each listed topic: *To explain what something is, To explain an idea or an opinion,* or *To explain causes and effects.* *Step 2:* Write your anticipated audience and your role as writer for each topic.

SAMPLE Getting measured for a tuxedo

ANSWER *Expository purpose:* to explain effects; *Audience:* friends going to the prom; *Role as writer:* informal and personal

1. Meter in poetry
2. IQ tests
3. The gross national product
4. A Geiger counter
5. Carbon dating

6. Calories
7. Baseball statistics
8. Deficit spending
9. Clocks
10. The stock market

Writing for Various Disciplines

Writing can play an important role in all school subjects. Many teachers give essay exams, assign book reviews, require lab reports, assign research papers and essays, include short-answer questions on their tests, and include logs or notebooks as a part of their daily requirements. Writing, these teachers realize, is not only a way to measure knowledge but also a powerful way to learn and to gain understanding. Writing something down makes it even more completely yours than thinking or talking about it does.

When you write for school subjects, you often begin prewriting long before you settle on a topic. Use your prewriting to explore material that might later be turned into an expository essay. Here are some of the forms that your prewriting might take.

- *Class notes.* Take notes in class to record the points that your teacher and your classmates make and to clarify your own responses to the material. Use any form that works for you: incomplete sentences, phrases, maps, or diagrams.
- *Summaries.* An excellent way to become familiar with the subject matter of a course is to summarize the reading material and the class discussions. A summary is a condensed version, written in your own words, of the material. When you write a summary, refer to your class notes to jog your memory.
- *Reading logs.* Discussing a subject with someone else is a good way to get and develop ideas for writing about it. A reading log allows you to have a sort of discussion with yourself. To make such a log, divide your paper in half lengthwise. In the left-hand column, write facts, statistics, comments made by your teacher and your classmates, questions that you have, ideas from your textbook, and ideas that you have. Use the right-hand column to write the things that you discover as you write and do research. Write the answers that

you find to your questions, qualifications of your earlier opinions, conclusions that you draw, and examples from your own life. Try to write information on the same points opposite one another. Whenever you use an outside source, be sure to document *(pages 405–408)* it carefully.

Class notes, summaries, and reading logs can be valuable forms of prewriting for lab reports, research papers, and essay exams. Other prewriting techniques, such as charting *(page 17)*, brainstorming *(page 13)*, or making a time line *(page 21)*, can also help you to generate ideas for expository writing for school subjects.

Assignment 4 Expository Topics for Various Disciplines

Step 1: On your paper, brainstorm a list of topics for paragraphs or essays that you could write for various school subjects. *Step 2:* Choose three topics from your list and limit them carefully for a paragraph or an essay. *Step 3:* On your paper, identify the audience, the purpose, and your role as the writer for each topic.

Continuing Assignment Focus Your Ideas

Step 1: Choose one topic for each of the following types of exposition: explaining what something is, explaining causes and effects, and explaining an idea or an opinion. Select the topics from those that you generated for the Continuing Assignment on page 197, from other topics in your writer's notebook, or from topics suggested to you by teachers in various classes. *Step 2:* Using a separate sheet of paper for each topic, write your purpose, your audience, and your role as writer. *Step 3:* Limit each topic based on your purpose and your audience and write the limited topic on your paper. Save your papers.

For writing a **paragraph** or an **essay**

Prewriting

Planning Your Expository Writing

Outstanding expository writing requires thorough, detailed information and effective, logical organization. Consider your topic carefully, generate interesting ideas about it, compile convincing supporting details, and organize your ideas appropriately.

Choosing a Prewriting Technique

Your earlier prewriting may have already generated enough support to develop your ideas in a paragraph or an essay. When you choose a type of exposition, however, your perspective on your topic changes.

Additional prewriting at this stage may very well yield new ideas and a different slant on your information. You've probably found that some types of prewriting work better for you than others and that some work better on certain topics than on others. Choose a prewriting technique, then, that suits your style and your topic.

To explain what something is, for example, try asking questions *(page 18)* or charting *(page 17)*. Use clustering *(page 14)* or freewriting *(page 11)* in your writer's notebook to get ideas for explaining causes and effects. Brainstorming *(page 16)* and changing viewpoints *(page 20)* can help you to explore ideas to explain an idea or an opinion.

Writing for various disciplines requires a prewriting technique appropriate to the subject. Charting *(page 17)*, for example, might be effective for explaining a concept in economics, while a time line *(page 21)* could help you to generate ideas for a history topic.

Assignment 1 Prewriting for Exposition

Choose three of the topics in Assignment 3 on page 202. On your paper, explore each topic by using a different prewriting technique for each one. Choose from a variety of prewriting techniques: brainstorming, freewriting, clustering, asking questions, cubing, changing viewpoints, charting, or making a time line.

Ways to Order Your Ideas

Critical Thinking:
Organizing

Readers like to be directed through a piece of writing in an orderly fashion. Order helps them to follow your ideas and to understand them. The nature of your topic frequently controls the order of your support, but you can choose to direct your readers through your writing by using chronological order, spatial order, order of importance, and order of generalization, among others.

Chronological Order   Use chronological order *(page 36)* whenever your purpose demands that your readers move on a step-by-step or event-by-event basis through your essay or your report. Put first things first, arranging your supporting sentences in the order that the events or the steps have to happen to produce the anticipated result. Highlight chronological order by using transitional words such as *first, as, then,* and *before.*

Spatial Order   Use spatial order *(page 37)* whenever it's important that your readers get a picture in their minds. Organize by location: from left to right, from top to bottom, and so forth. Emphasize spatial order with transitional phrases such as *on your left* and *straight ahead.*

Order of Importance For support that clearly has various levels of importance, use order of importance *(page 38).* Begin with your most important support to capture your readers' attention immediately; then move toward the least important. Alternatively, move from the least important support toward the most important to build your readers' interest in your ideas. Indicate order of importance by using adjectives in the comparative or superlative degree, such as *better, best, worse,* or *worst,* or use transitional words and phrases such as *furthermore, moreover,* and *finally.*

Order of Generalization When your supporting details are at different levels of abstraction or when none of the previous orders of arrangement would effectively serve your purpose, try using order of generalization. Begin your supporting sentences with your most specific support and move toward your most general, or begin with your most general support and move toward your most specific. Transitional phrases such as *in general* and *specifically* will guide your readers as they follow your ideas.

In the following paragraph, for example, the supporting sentences are arranged from general to specific — from a characteristic that is shared with other things found in nature to a characteristic that is specific to plants.

> Long ago, seeds were often used as measures of weight. Like stones, another unit of weight, they occurred naturally and plentifully. Unlike stones, however, seeds of the same plant tended to be of a standard size no matter where or under what conditions the plant that produced them grew. This specific feature of plants ensured that two people in different regions could weigh out something and end up with approximately the same amount. Thus the *grain,* which is the weight of a grain of wheat, was used in the measurement of small amounts of medicine, and the *carat,* the weight of the seed of the carob tree, was used in the measurement of precious gems.

You might find paragraphs organized by order of generalization difficult to recognize; they can be confused with paragraphs developed by order of importance. The important thing, however, is that you as a writer are able to organize a paragraph using order of generalization. Whether or not your readers notice its particular method of organization, they will recognize that the paragraph is logical and effective.

Assignment 2 **Ordering Ideas**

Step 1: Choose one expository topic from your writer's notebook, from Assignment 3 on page 202, or from another source. On your paper, do some prewriting on the topic and write your purpose, your audience, and your role as writer. *Step 2:* Arrange the ideas in your prewriting notes in an order that works effectively with your topic. Use chrono-

? **Critical Thinking:**
Organizing
What is the best order for your ideas?

logical order, spatial order, order of importance, or order of generalization. *Step 3:* Discuss the arrangement of your ideas with a classmate to be sure that it clearly supports your intended purpose.

Structuring Your Expository Paragraph or Essay

Critical Thinking:

Classification

At this stage you have a topic and you've used prewriting techniques to generate support for your ideas. It's time now to write a topic sentence *(page 40)* for your paragraph or a thesis statement *(page 46)* for your essay, and to develop a plan to direct your writing. Classify your ideas, arranging them into groups or categories, and then choose an appropriate order for the categories.

One method of developing a preliminary plan is making an outline *(pages 47–54)*. When you've examined and ordered the categories of your ideas, label each category. Ask yourself whether your ideas and your details support your topic sentence or your thesis statement, and eliminate unnecessary or irrelevant details. Determine whether your main and supporting ideas are arranged in a logical and workable order. As you draft, use your outline to check for unity and coherence.

Assignment 3 Planning Expository Writing

Critical Thinking:

Classification
What categories do you see in these ideas?

Examine the following thesis statement and notes generated during brainstorming for an essay on ways of measuring time. On your paper, list the information in a logical order and label categories appropriately. Then turn the information into a rough outline for an essay.

Thesis statement: Throughout history societies have developed a variety of ways to measure the passing of the days, months, and years.

Notes:
— Ancient calendars
— The Babylonian calendar was based on the moon and occasionally corrected itself by inserting an extra month.
— Month measured by appearance of moon
— Measures time within year
— 1582: Gregorian calendar
— Religious calendars: Hebrew, Islamic, Christian
— The week is a manmade unit of time.
— The Egyptian calendar was based on the sun and was six hours shorter than Earth's revolution.
— 46 B.C.: Julian calendar designed to correct confusion of ancient calendars. It disregarded periods of the moon; its year lasted 11 minutes and 14 seconds longer than solar year.
— Day and year each measured in relation to sun

Step 1: Reread your notes for the Continuing Assignment on page 203.
Step 2: Using separate paper for each topic, choose a prewriting technique and use it to explore each topic, writing your ideas on your paper. Choose from brainstorming, clustering, freewriting, asking questions, cubing, changing viewpoints, charting, or making a time line. *Step 3:* Look closely at your prewriting notes and arrange your ideas in an order that works with your topic. Select chronological order, spatial order, order of importance, or order of generalization. *Step 4:* Then categorize your ideas and label the categories, generating a plan for a paragraph or an essay on each topic. Save your papers.

For writing
a **paragraph**
or an **essay**

Drafting

Drafting Your Expository Writing

The first draft of a paragraph or an essay is an opportunity to test your ideas, your support, and your organization. It's not the time to try to get everything perfect. Keep your writing plan beside you to guide your writing, but if you get a new idea, feel free to modify the plan as you go. Make notes to yourself in the margins or on tags. If you don't like something, don't worry about fixing it unless you have an immediate idea. You'll have time to fine tune and to correct during revising and proofreading.

Drafting an Expository Paragraph

Occasionally an expository paragraph is a complete piece of writing, a short essay in itself. It's more usual, however, for an expository paragraph to form part of the support for a longer essay. In either case an expository paragraph will have a topic sentence, supporting sentences, and a concluding sentence.

The Topic Sentence

Your topic sentence *(page 40)*, often the first sentence of your paragraph, prepares your readers to think about the information and the ideas that follow it. As a guide for your readers, it shows them what to expect and how to read what follows. It needs to announce the topic and make your purpose clear to your readers.

A topic sentence should be neither too general — "Time is important" — nor too specific — "There are twenty-four hours in a day." For a paragraph explaining what something is, for example, the topic sentence usually forecasts the topic being explained.

For the retired person, the word *time* takes on new meaning.

The topic sentence for a cause-and-effect paragraph, on the other hand, often introduces the general causes or effects of an action.

The time limitations imposed by part-time employment result in less study time and lower grades for many students.

For a paragraph explaining an idea or an opinion, the topic sentence usually states the opinion or the idea that the writer is developing.

For a high school student with a demanding academic schedule, the limits of a twenty-four-hour day make holding a part-time job a juggling act.

Assignment 1 Writing a Topic Sentence

On your paper, draft potential topic sentences for each of the following topics. Use each type of exposition — explaining what something is, explaining cause and effect, and explaining an idea or an opinion — at least once. Some topics may need to be limited.

1. Urban transportation
2. Modern heroes
3. Sailing with a compass
4. Deficit spending
5. Automobile safety devices
6. Assessing political leadership
7. Dating archeological finds
8. The energy-efficient house
9. How pilots plot their courses
10. Today's football statistics

Supporting Sentences

? Critical Thinking:
Distinguishing among methods

The sentences that accomplish the purpose of your paragraph and that develop your topic are called supporting sentences *(page 43)*. You can use a variety of methods of development for these supporting sentences. You'll quickly see, for example, that when you're writing to explain something that involves steps, you'll have to develop the steps in their proper and most effective order by using *process analysis*. To show your readers what terrible things can happen if they don't understand the causes of something, use *narration* to tell what happened to you when you didn't. If you realize that there are two similar parts in something that you are defining, carefully tell what each part looks like using *description*. When you are explaining the differences between two computer networks to a group of your friends, use *comparison and contrast* to show how the two are similar and different.

To explain ideas, concepts, or words that might be unfamiliar to your readers, use *definition*. Use *cause and effect* to show that an action has a direct consequence, or that there is a reason why something happened. When you need to establish why something or someone does or does not belong to a particular category or group, use *classification*. *Illustrations and examples* can provide concrete details to prove a point that you're making.

Often several different methods of development would work in a given paragraph. Select your method, then, by considering your purpose, your audience, and your own experience reading effective expository writing. If your topic sentence introduces an explanation of the fascination of the heavens, for example, the supporting sentences could use *illustrations and examples* of civilizations that were interested in the heavens.

TOPIC SENTENCE
The heavens have long fascinated us.

SUPPORTING SENTENCES
Even before the invention of the telescope, stars were the object of our study. The Druids, the ancient Egyptians, and the Mayans all studied the stars.

A supporting sentence such as "An observatory is a building where astronomers study the heavens," on the other hand, would confuse your readers because it announces another topic. Use your supporting sentences to focus your readers' attention on your topic. Don't distract them with irrelevant details that draw them away from the topic and undermine your explanation.

Assignment 2 Examining Methods of Development

On your paper, identify the methods of development that you see in the following passages. Choose from process analysis, narration, description, comparison and contrast, illustrations and examples, definition, cause and effect, and classification.

1. To measure the amount of money that workers in the United States make, economists use the concept of "real" wages. As opposed to money wages, real wages are the sum of money one earns measured in terms of the amount and value of goods and services that can be purchased with the wages. Another way to define real wages would be to say that they are those wages one earns "adjusted for inflation." For example, a worker earning $22,000 yearly receives a 5 percent raise. At the same time, costs for goods and services rise by 9 percent. The worker may feel as though he or she has an extra $1100 to spend. The real wages, however, have gone down by 4 percent, or $880.

2. Many of us are slightly mystified by the word *machine*. It suggests gears, engines, and blueprints. The simplest machines, however, freed humanity from the burden of backbreaking work and allowed us to develop the sophisticated technology that we now have. These simple machines — the inclined plane, the lever, the pulley, the screw, the wedge, and the wheel and axle — multiply the energy of our bodies, giving us the ability to work beyond our physical capacity. In hundreds of small ways, these simple machines affect our lives.

Critical Thinking:
Distinguishing among methods
What methods of development are used in each passage?

The Concluding Sentence

Your concluding sentence *(page 44)* is the last chance that you have to communicate with your readers. It becomes, then, one of your most important sentences. Use this opportunity to leave your readers with the primary impression of your paragraph. Send a clear message of closure, and stress the sense that you've finished your task and reached your goal.

The concluding sentence of the following paragraph, for example, refers to the point made in the topic sentence and provides closure by assuming that the writer has proven the point.

> The abundance of solid-state electronic equipment and appliances in the average household has made a voltage surge suppressor a necessity. Solid-state technology can be damaged by upward fluctuations in the electrical current caused by static electricity, lightning, or equipment switching. Even turning the air conditioner off and on can shorten the life of solid-state equipment. The surge suppressor helps to keep the electrical output to and from such equipment at a safe level. For the home computer user, the surge suppressor not only protects equipment, but also can prevent a nightmare — the loss of large chunks of memory. *A surge suppressor, then, is a necessity rather than a luxury in modern households.*

Assignment 3   Writing Concluding Sentences

On your paper, write three potentially effective concluding sentences for the following incomplete paragraph.

> How can you measure the value of a national park? You can write that Yosemite has over 700,000 acres, hundreds of miles of hiking trails, and enough campgrounds for a small city. You could cite the numbers of animal and bird species that live within the park. You could list the varieties of trees and flowering plants or count the groves of sequoias. None of these calculations, however, measure the value of El Capitan, a jagged crag of rock that dominates the valley and that awes both climber and casual tourist alike. None of them measure the beauty of the Merced River when the late autumn sun turns it into a road of sparkling diamonds. None measure the silence of a fresh winter snow that intensifies our experience of the new landscape.

Drafting an Expository Essay

The process of drafting an expository essay is very much like drafting an expository paragraph. In an essay, however, you'll be more likely to use more than one method of development — narration, process analysis, description, comparison and contrast, classification, definition, cause and effect, or illustrations and examples — and to develop more supporting details for a more complex topic.

The Introductory Paragraph

Your introductory paragraph creates your readers' initial interest in your essay and introduces them to your view of the topic. It prepares your readers to read your essay, develops their expectations about what is to come, and begins to establish your relationship with them. A poorly written introductory paragraph can undermine an otherwise brilliantly written essay.

Your introductory paragraph includes your **thesis statement,** a sentence that states the main idea of your essay *(page 46)*. Be sure to evaluate your preliminary thesis statement; change it if it is no longer effective and appropriate.

Try one or more of the following approaches for writing an effective introductory paragraph.

▶ Strategies

1. *Clearly state your topic and your focusing idea about the topic in your thesis statement.*
2. *Show why your topic and your main idea are important* to create interest in your readers.
3. *Demonstrate ways in which the topic affects your readers.*
4. *Use a quotation that summarizes and captures the spirit of your thesis statement.*
5. *Begin with a challenging thought or a question.*

If your readers begin your essay interested in what they'll encounter as they read, you'll have a better chance of accomplishing your purpose. The following paragraph, for example, introduces an essay on the development of the calendar.

> One of humanity's great achievements, the development of the calendar, remains one of its most elusive and troublesome. Somehow, we just can't seem to get it right. After more than sixty centuries — yes, sixty — we still don't have a calendar that accurately measures the passing of the days, the months, and the years. We measure the year in terms of how long it takes Earth to revolve around the sun. As any encyclopedia will tell you, this journey lasts 365 days, 5 hours, 48 minutes, and 45.7 seconds — or one solar year. Accounting for this extra five-plus hours has caused eternal difficulty.

Assignment 4 Analyzing an Introductory Paragraph

On your paper, answer the following questions to analyze the preceding introductory paragraph.

1. What techniques does the writer use to capture the reader's immediate attention?

2. What is the author's tone: formal or informal? personal or impersonal?
3. What are the methods of development and organization suggested by the introduction?
4. What is the thesis statement that will control the essay?

Body Paragraphs

The body paragraphs of your expository essay are the meat of your essay. They develop the important details of your explanation and provide further explanation of your main idea.

Making Transitions Between Paragraphs Sometimes the ideas in two paragraphs so logically follow each other that you don't need any special transitions. At other times your readers will need help to move from paragraph to paragraph, and you'll have to provide transitional words or phrases *(pages 36–38)* to direct their thinking.

Take particular note of the transitions in the following paragraphs about the calendar.

Our current calendar, the Gregorian calendar, was developed in the sixteenth century. In order to account for the odd hours, minutes, and seconds, February gains a day every fourth year — except, of course, in those century years that cannot be divided by 400, such as 1800 and 1900. Confusing? Yes, and it's made even more confusing by the fact that not all countries adopted this calendar at the same time. Consequently, historians looking at dates in historical documents must know what calendar was in effect in a particular country at a particular time. For example, we all know that George Washington was born on February 22. Or was he? Which calendar was in effect, the Gregorian calendar or the Julian calendar?

A previous calendar, the Julian calendar, was created by Julius Caesar in the first century B.C. It attempted to account for the solar year's extra time by dividing the year into twelve months alternating in length between thirty and thirty-one days — except for poor February, which received only twenty-nine days. This calendar ran into immediate difficulty when Augustus replaced Julius Caesar as emperor of Rome. Augustus added an extra day to the month of August so that it would be as long as July. The Julian calendar was actually worse than the one we have now; by the time that the Gregorian calendar was developed, the Julian calendar was ten days off "real" solar time.

If we look at the calendars that predated the Julian calendar, though, we see that its confusion was significantly better than what had come before. One of the old Roman calendars, for example, had ten months based on the appearances of the moon. Then two more months were added, but the time measurement was so inexact that an additional month had to be added every other year. This same description applies to one of the ancient Greek calendars, except that the Greeks omitted the extra month every eight or nine years. During the eras of these calendars, only mathematicians and astronomers remembered birthdays.

Analyzing Body Paragraphs

On your paper, answer the following questions about the body paragraphs on page 212.

1. What are the main divisions of the essay?
2. Which methods of organization — chronological order, spatial order, order of importance, or order of generalization — does the writer of the essay use?
3. Which methods of development — narration, description, process analysis, comparison and contrast, illustrations and examples, definition, cause and effect, or classification — does the writer use?
4. What transitional words or phrases does the writer use between paragraphs?

The Concluding Paragraph

Your concluding paragraph is your last opportunity to make contact with your reader. Don't waste it. Make the paragraph as interesting and important as the rest of your essay. Generally, don't introduce new supporting evidence or new ideas that go beyond the scope of your purpose. On the other hand, don't simply write the introduction again using different words. Give your readers a clear sense of closure by referring to the ideas in your introductory paragraph, by answering a question that you asked in your introduction, or by summarizing your own reaction to your topic.

If you read your essay as if you were your intended reader, your response to the ideas in the essay can often be turned into a successful concluding paragraph. The following paragraph, for example, concludes the essay on calendars.

> Now that scientists and mathematicians have developed such precise instruments of measurement, we might expect that they could develop a new calendar that wouldn't need the adjustments that we now make. It can be confusing, for example, when we have to move the celebration of national holidays from their "real" calendar dates to more convenient days like Mondays. Indeed, from time to time proposals for a new calendar have emerged. Human nature, however, clings to the familiar. In all probability, people will still be having leap-year parties when our children are grandparents.

Assignment 6 Examining a Concluding Paragraph

On your paper, answer the following questions about the concluding paragraph shown above.

1. What concrete details were used to maintain the reader's interest?
2. What is the author's attitude toward the confusion in calendars?
3. What has the author done in addition to simply restating points?
4. Does this paragraph provide an effective conclusion for the essay?

For writing
a **paragraph**
or an **essay**

For the Continuing Assignment on page 207, you wrote a writing plan for a paragraph or an essay explaining what something is, explaining causes and effects, and explaining an idea or an opinion. Choose the topic that you would like to work with further. Draft an expository essay or a paragraph on your topic and save your draft.

Revising

Revising for Content, Tone, and Style

When you've completed a draft, you're ready to revise. Drafting gave you the chance to get your ideas down on paper. Now revising will allow you to decide whether you've made the best choices and to make necessary changes.

Revising can be demanding. You've completed a draft and feel relieved that your effort is over. Thinking about going back to the first draft is almost painful. A good writer knows, however, that revision makes the difference between mediocre writing and successful writing.

When you revise, look carefully at the content, the organization, the tone, and the style of your writing. Examine each element separately, but don't worry about errors in grammar and mechanics until later when you proofread. Review the guidelines for revising and the suggestions for peer reviewing on pages 64–65 and consult the Revising Checklist on page 97.

Revising for Content

Critical Thinking:

Evaluating

Start the revising process by evaluating your paragraph or your essay. Check the accuracy of your information and the clarity and the organization of your ideas. Be sure that you've considered your purpose and your audience.

Purpose and Audience   Find a reader who can act as your intended audience. Ask this reader to check that you have focused your essay accurately for your purpose and your audience by responding to the following questions.

- What is the main idea?
- What does the writer want you to do with this idea?
- Are there any places where you were confused?
- Who would enjoy reading this paragraph or essay?
- What title would you give it?

If the answers to these questions don't correspond to your intentions, examine where the differences lie. Check the clarity of your introduction, your topic sentence or thesis statement, your supporting evidence, the level of your vocabulary, and your conclusion.

Unity and Coherence   Good writing is unified, with all main and supporting ideas relevant to your main point; it's also coherent, with logical organization and clear transitions. To check each sentence and paragraph for unity and coherence, ask yourself the following questions.

- Does each sentence or paragraph appeal to your readers and help you to accomplish your purpose?
- Is your organization logical and clear?
- Is all your supporting information relevant to your topic sentence or your thesis statement?
- Have you used clear and appropriate transitions?
- Have you defined any unusual or unfamiliar terms?

Assignment 1   Considering Purpose and Audience

The following paragraph discusses good health for a general audience. On your paper, answer the questions on page 214 about this paragraph.

? **Critical Thinking:**
Evaluating
Is the appeal to a general audience?

> How do we measure good health? Most people measure their health in two ways: their physical appearance and their ability to do exercise. When they were teen-agers, most out-of-shape adults failed to take care of their bodies. They ate too much, they had unhealthy diets, they smoked, and they failed to exercise. They may not look fat, but they can't do simple exercises without difficulty and they aren't very limber. Commitment to a healthy diet and regular exercise early in life can improve health for everyone.

Assignment 2   Revising the Content

On your paper, revise the following paragraph for content. Make sure that it has a clear purpose for an identifiable audience and that all the information is relevant and appropriately organized. Use effective transitional words and phrases. (*Hint:* A more specific topic sentence would help.)

> There are differences in the heights of tides. The positions of the sun and the moon and the shapes of the coastlines cause the variations. When the sun and the moon line up, their gravitational forces pull together, causing the tides to rise. When they do not

line up and, therefore, pull in different directions, the tides are lower. All bodies small and large are subject to the sun and the moon. The sizes and the shapes of coastlines have almost as great an effect on the heights of tides. For example, because the Bay of Fundy in eastern Canada is shaped like a funnel, the height of the tides there has risen as much as fifty feet in height. Even though the tides are irregular, scientists who analyze the data about the sun, the moon, and the coastlines can predict the height of each tide. Sometimes an extremely destructive wave, called a tidal wave, can be generated by an undersea earthquake.

Revising for Tone and Style

In an effective paragraph or essay, the words and the sentences work with the organization and the paragraphing to produce an effect on your audience. It's important, therefore, to pay attention to the quality of your sentences and to the words that you use.

Critical Thinking:
Determining relationships

Combining Sentences To communicate your intended meaning directly and precisely to your audience, be sure that all sentences in each paragraph work together smoothly. Use sentence combining *(pages 72–76)* to indicate the relationship among your ideas and to eliminate short, choppy sentences. Careful use of sentence combining can produce more stylistically interesting writing.

Word Choice Examine each word carefully. Does it convey your meaning accurately in the appropriate tone for your purpose and your audience? Slang in a formal essay, for example, or overly formal language in an informal paragraph would be distracting. Have you used a variety of words? Using a good dictionary or a thesaurus can help you to reduce repetition in your word choices.

Creating a Title If you've written a preliminary title, examine it carefully now and make any necessary changes. If you don't yet have a title, create one after you revise your draft. Sometimes a few key words from your introduction or your conclusion make a good title. Try to make your title compelling enough to excite your readers' interest.

Critical Thinking:
Determining relationships
How are the ideas related?

Assignment 3 Combining Sentences

Read the following pairs of sentences carefully. On your paper, combine the sentences to make them more effective.

1. Many early measurements were based on practical activities. Other early measurements were based on tools close at hand.

2. The *furlong* was the approximate distance that a horse could pull a plow without stopping. The *acre* was the amount of land that a pair of yoked oxen could plow in a day.

3. The *stadion* was the distance a person could run without getting out of breath. The *stadion* actually measured about 200 meters.

4. The *yard* is a unit of length. The *yard* was originally the length of a stick about three feet long.

5. The *palm* was the width of a human hand. The *palm,* now called the *hand,* is still used to measure the height of horses.

6. The *foot* is another unit of length. A *foot* was originally based on the length of a person's foot.

Assignment 4 Checking for Appropriate Word Choice

Read the following paragraph carefully and revise it. Is the tone of each word appropriate? Can you eliminate repetition by replacing repeated words with synonyms or by eliminating them? Write the revised paragraph on your paper.

> Most teen-agers consider themselves to be generally healthy and fit, but many of them cannot climb stairs without puffing or even touch their toes without straining. Specific physical fitness, the ability of different systems of the body to meet the specific demands placed on them, is different from general good health. This specific kind of fitness can be determined by three measures. One is agility, the ability to move quickly and easily. One specific measure is endurance — whether the body can sustain an activity over a period of time. Endurance depends largely on how efficiently the heart and the lungs can operate. Another measure is flexibility, the specific ability of the muscles and the connective tissue to stretch and elongate. Most people are not physically fit specifically because they don't get enough exercise. An additional measure is strength, the ability of the muscles to lift heavy objects — or to hoist the body. Therefore, if one wants to be healthy, one must eat right, get enough sleep, and exercise regularly.

Continuing Assignment Revise Your Expository Writing

Reread the draft of the expository paragraph or essay that you wrote for the Continuing Assignment on page 214. Revise your draft carefully. Be sure that you have fulfilled your purpose for your intended audience. Check the unity and the coherence of your writing. Look carefully at your sentences and your word choice. Save your revised draft for future reference.

For writing
a **paragraph**
or an **essay**

Proofreading Your Expository Writing

Careful proofreading considers the needs of your readers. No one enjoys reading a paragraph or an essay filled with distracting errors in grammar, usage, spelling, capitalization, or punctuation. When you proofread thoroughly, you convey your ideas more efficiently and more clearly. Consult the proofreading guidelines on pages 98–99 and the Proofreading Checklist on page 105. When you've made the necessary corrections on your paper, make a clean copy and proofread it again to check for new errors that may have crept in.

The Grammar Connection

As you proofread your expository writing, pay particular attention to these points.

Semicolons Be sure to use a semicolon to connect independent clauses joined by a conjunctive adverb or by an explanatory expression.

Reference Point:
pages 721–722

> The university's seismograph measured fourteen tremors in three hours ;consequently, the story dominated the evening news.

Sentence Fragments Incorporate any sentence fragment into a related sentence, or rewrite it to make it a complete sentence.

Reference Point:
pages 598–599

> We
> ∧Took the rock samples to the lab. ∧The teacher weighed and measured them.

Assignment Proofreading Practice

On your paper, rewrite the following paragraph, correcting errors in spelling, grammar, usage, and mechanics.

No matter which of the radon test kits you use to assure the safety of your House. There is right and wrong ways to conduct the test. First, you should know that radon rates varies therefore testing should be done over a period of time. if your house tests even mildly positive, you should repeat the test a second or even a 3rd time to see if it might be more positive at a later date. In addition, you should test one's basement in a variety of different places. raddon ratings, for example, can be much higher near a crack in the concret floor. radon rates can also vary at different heighths depending on where unseen foundation cracks may be located in short, if you want to assure that your structure is free from radon contamination, make sure that you test a vareity of locations at a variety of heights over a period of time.

Continuing Assignment **Proofread Your Expository Writing**

On your paper, proofread the draft of the expository paragraph or the essay that you've been working on in the preceding Continuing Assignments. Make a clean copy and proofread it again. Save your completed writing.

For writing
a **paragraph**
or an **essay**

Publishing

Publishing Your Expository Writing

Now that you have a finished paragraph or an essay, it deserves to be read. Publish *(pages 108–109)* your writing to share it with an audience. Try one of the following methods.

- Read your essay aloud to your family. Encourage them to share their reactions or to ask questions.
- Be on the lookout for contests that award scholarships and other prizes for good student writing. Submit your work for consideration.
- Start a writing group with your friends. Read and respond to one another's writing.
- Send your essay to a business, a government agency, or a civic organization that has a related interest or concern.
- Ask your teacher for a list of publications that accept student writing and submit your best writing for consideration.
- Submit your writing to the student newspaper or the literary magazine in your school.
- If you wrote for a subject other than English, ask a teacher of that subject to read and respond to your writing.
- Submit your essay as a sample of your writing with a job application or with an application for college admission.

Continuing Assignment **Publish Your Expository Writing**

Publish your paragraph or your essay, using the method of your choice. Write a note to your teacher describing your method of publication, how you felt about publishing your work, and how your audience responded. Keep this note and your writing in your portfolio.

For writing
a **paragraph**
or an **essay**

Student to Student

Reading and Responding to Writing

Why hasn't the United States gone metric? In the following essay, Deborah Black, a student at Colorado City High School in Colorado City, Arizona, explains the benefits of the metric system. As you read her essay, think of answers to the questions in the margin. Then perform the activities in *Responding to Writing* and *Reading Critically*.

Think Metric!

How many of you actually like to do fractions? If you're like most people, you don't. Well, how would you like to do your math or science entirely by calculator with no fractions involved? It is simple. To eliminate fractions and all those difficult conversions, all you have to do is think metric! Just convert to the simplest measurement system in the world.

If the metric system is so very simple, why hasn't the United States converted to it? One main reason is <u>tradition</u>. The people of the United States are a very traditional people. To take the English system of measurements away from them is like taking a security blanket away from a child. People are afraid that if we convert to the metric system, our whole way of life will change. Yes, our way of life will change--for the better. Because they have no real knowledge concerning the metric system, people continue to believe that it is a strange and mysterious creation. However, many will find that it is a modernized system established by international agreement to provide a logical, uniform system of measurement.

Other people are concerned with the expenses and difficulties of switching to the metric system. As for expenses, some costs will be involved as road signs, tool sizes, and clothing sizes are altered. However, as American industry takes its first steps into the metric age, companies from IBM to General Mills are finding to their complete surprise that the shift does not bring the expense that has been feared. As for the

What strategies does Deborah use to make you want to read the remainder of her essay?

Why is it important to state reasons for opposition?

actual conversions, the metric system is greatly simplified because of the convenient decimal system it consists of.

The basic units of the metric system are meter for length, gram for weight, and liter for volume. By adding prefixes milli-, meaning one thousandth; centi-, meaning one hundredth; deci-, meaning one tenth; deka-, meaning ten; hecto-, meaning one hundred; and kilo-, meaning one thousand, you can easily convert from one unit to the other. Try converting fifty-five inches to yards. You would first have to know that there are thirty-six inches in one yard. You would then have to divide fifty-five by thirty-six. It is rather complicated, isn't it? Now try converting fifty-five centimeters to one meter. It's easy; all you have to do is move the decimal point two places to the left to get 0.55 meters.

Why is this particular sequence of detail logical?

As you can see, the metric system has many advantages. First, it can be very efficiently used in education. Conversion from unit to unit is greatly simplified, and fractions are completely eliminated! It is estimated in the course of getting through elementary and high school, a student can save between six months and a year in learning math and science because of the simplicity of the metric system. Also, the metric system is very similar to our monetary system. Both are simple and can be used hand in hand. Another advantage is that the metric system is understood worldwide. Every nation in the world has adopted or is now committed to the metric system except three: Burma, Brunei, and the United States. Approximately 90 percent of the world's population now uses the metric system.

Why will this be a persuasive detail for most of Deborah's readers?

By using the metric system, you can help pull that old, useless security blanket, the English system of measurements, out from under the U.S., helping it to become more efficient. Then think metric!

Responding to Writing How does Deborah's essay encourage you to "think metric"? What difficulties do you expect to encounter?

Reading Critically In writing or in a group discussion, answer these questions: How has Deborah organized her essay? Why is it effective? What assumptions has she made? What techniques has she used?

As you know, expository writing sometimes makes a brief appearance in writing with a different purpose and focus. The novel *Moby-Dick*, which is often regarded as the story of a certain whaling voyage, actually contains much more than that story — including a number of expository chapters on the natural history of the whale.

Throughout the novel, Ishmael, the narrator, struggles to understand the whale. For example, he tries to make literal and symbolic sense of his voyage on the *Pequod* and of Ahab's battle with the great white whale Moby-Dick. This is not the only way that Ishmael approaches the problem of understanding the whale, however. Every so often he takes time out from the story and explores the whale in art, literature, religion, and science. In the chapter shown here, he tries to take the measure of the whale, both literally and figuratively.

Guided Reading   As you read this selection and answer the questions, think about the narrator's attitude toward his subject and toward you, the reader. Note his vocabulary, his expository methods, and his "asides" where he strays from measuring to expand upon his larger purpose.

Chapter CIII
Measurement of the Whale's Skeleton

In the first place, I wish to lay before you a particular, plain statement, touching the living bulk of this leviathan, whose skeleton we are briefly to exhibit. Such a statement may prove useful here.

> What is the narrator's tone?

According to a careful calculation I have made, and which I partly base upon Captain Scoresby's estimate, of seventy tons for the largest sized Greenland whale of sixty feet in length; according to my careful calculation, I say, a Sperm Whale of the largest magnitude, between eighty-five and ninety feet in length, and something less than forty feet in its fullest circumference, such a whale will weigh at least ninety tons; so that, reckoning thirteen men to a ton, he would considerably outweigh the combined population of a whole village of one thousand one hundred inhabitants. . . .

In length, the Sperm Whale's skeleton at Tranque measured seventy-two feet; so that when fully invested and extended in life, he must have been ninety feet long; for in the whale, the skeleton loses about one-fifth in length compared with the living body. Of this seventy-two feet, his skull and jaw comprised some twenty feet, leaving some fifty feet of plain back-bone. Attached to this back-bone, for something less than a third of its length, was the mighty circular basket of ribs which once enclosed his vitals.

To me this vast ivory-ribbed chest, with the long, unrelieved spine, extending far away from it in a straight line, not a little resembled the hull of a great ship new-laid upon the stocks, when only some twenty of her naked bow-ribs are inserted, and the keel is otherwise, for the time, but a long, disconnected timber.

What expository method is this?

The ribs were ten on a side. The first, to begin from the neck, was nearly six feet long; the second, third, and fourth were each successively longer, till you came to the climax of the fifth, or one of the middle ribs, which measured eight feet and some inches. From that part, the remaining ribs diminished, till the tenth and last only spanned five feet and some inches. In general thickness, they all bore a seemly correspondence to their length. The middle ribs were the most arched. In some of the Arsacides they are used for beams whereon to lay footpath bridges over small streams.

What is the purpose of this information?

In considering these ribs, I could not but be struck anew with the circumstance, so variously repeated in this book, that the skeleton of the whale is by no means the mould of his invested form. The largest of the Tranque ribs, one of the middle ones, occupied that part of the fish which, in life, is greatest in depth. Now, the greatest depth of the invested body of this particular whale must have been at least sixteen feet; whereas, the corresponding rib measured but little more than eight feet. So that this rib only conveyed half of the true notion of the living magnitude of that part. Besides, for some way, where I now saw but a naked spine, all that had been once wrapped round

Why are his measurements of the skeleton inadequate for Ishmael's purpose?

with tons of added bulk in flesh, muscle, blood, and bowels. Still more, for the ample fins, I here saw but a few disordered joints; and in place of the weighty and majestic, but boneless flukes, an utter blank!

How vain and foolish, then, thought I, for timid untravelled man to try to comprehend aright this wondrous whale, by merely poring over his dead attenuated skeleton, stretched in this peaceful wood. No. Only in the heart of quickest perils; only when within the eddyings of his angry flukes; only on the profound unbounded sea, can the fully invested whale be truly and livingly found out.

> How can the whale be "truly found out"?

But the spine. For that, the best way we can consider it is, with a crane, to pile its bones high up on end. No speedy enterprise. But now it's done, it looks much like Pompey's Pillar.

There are forty and odd vertebrae in all, which in the skeleton are not locked together. They mostly lie like the great knobbed blocks on a Gothic spire, forming solid courses of heavy masonry. The largest, a middle one, is in width something less than three feet, and in depth more than four. The smallest, where the spine tapers away into the tail, is only two inches in width, and looks something like a white billiard-ball. I was told that there were still smaller ones, but they had been lost by some little cannibal urchins, the priest's children, who had stolen them to play marbles with. Thus we see how that the spine of even the hugest of living things tapers off at last into simple child's play.

> What does the last sentence tell about the whole attempt to measure the whale?

Herman Melville *(1819–1891)*
from *Moby-Dick*

Enrichment Connections

Choose one or more of these activities to do on your own or as a group.

Experimenting with Time

You have probably heard the expression, "Time flies when you're having fun," and you know how time can drag when you're bored or anxious. React to this sense of

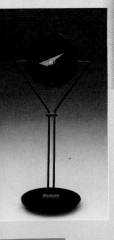

the relativity of time by writing either a poem, a short story, or a short play. Have your persona or your characters measure time both subjectively (how it feels) and objectively (by the clock or the calendar). Post your experiment with time on the bulletin board.

A Narrative

Ishmael's attempt to measure the whale (*pages 222–224*) fails for a different reason than does Dillard's attempt to measure the seasons (*pages 191–193*). Ishmael succeeds in getting the physical dimensions of the whale's bones, but he still cannot define or explain the "fully invested whale." Dillard fails to mark the beginning of spring but arrives at a new understanding of time. Write a brief narrative either about a "failure" that you have experienced that led to a more important success or about a task that you thought you had completed successfully only to find that you had "failed."

A Free-Verse Poem

Reread *Responding to Literature* on page 193 and the prewriting that you did for it. In your writer's notebook, list any new ideas that you have gained while studying this unit. Then write a free-verse poem based on your freewriting. Your poem should be a definition of the change that you measured in your prewriting. Use a simile or a metaphor to sum up or define that change.

Across the Curriculum

Science Do library research about a scientific achievement in measurement, such as the discovery of the speed of light or sound, the development of carbon dating, or the invention of the thermometer. As in Assignment 2 on page 197, ask questions to limit your topic. Finally, write a brief expository essay on what you learn.

Social Studies Fashion has long been studied by sociologists and others interested in cultural development. Some researchers have found sociological significance in the length of women's skirts and other fashion trends. Some even suggest that the stock market follows the change of women's hemlines up and down. Do research in serious books of fashion history and sociology. Investigate the hemline—stock market connection or another fashion trend involving measurement, such as the width of ties, the height of heels, or the length of hair considered suitable for men and women. Report orally to the class on what you learn, or write a brief essay to share with your classmates.

CELEBRATING DIVERSITY

What goals are you working toward right now? How are you preparing to reach those goals? Are you just dreaming about them or are you doing some serious planning? What preliminary steps have you taken that could lead to your goals?

In the following excerpt, a successful athlete reminisces about learning the proper techniques of her sport. While still in high school, Wilma Rudolph was spotted by Ed Temple, the coach of women's track at Tennessee State, and asked to attend his summer training session at the college. As you read this excerpt from *Wilma,* see if any of the techniques Rudolph learned that summer can be applied to activities and goals other than running track. Then do one or more of the activities that follow the selection. Working on them may help you see the relationship between training and performance in a new light.

So all the track girls settled in over the weekend, and on the first Monday morning, we went down to see the equipment manager, Pappy Marshall, and he issued us everything we would need. We each got a couple of T-shirts, a couple pair of shorts, a couple of sweatsuits, and heavy Converse basketball sneakers to run in. This was on purpose, and it would be a couple of weeks before we were issued our first pair of track shoes.

The next morning, we were roused out of bed a little before six, to do our first running. It was cross-country, and we would run a good six miles. We would run from about six in the morning to eight in the morning, then come

back in for breakfast. We would rest after breakfast until about ten thirty and then go out and run another six miles and come in for lunch. After lunch, we would rest up until about three in the afternoon, and then we would do the six miles again.

So, the routine settled in on us quickly: we were running about twenty miles a day, five days a week. It was all cross-country running, over hills and farmlands mostly, and there were these big oil tanks way out in the distance and we would run out to them, and this became known as "going to the tanks." On weekends, we went to the movies, and to church, and we rested.

After the first two weeks, the cross-country phase was over. Coach Temple explained to us that all of the cross-country running was for the purpose of building up our endurance. Then we started in on running different distances, and we started learning the various techniques of proper running. I can remember learning some of the basics of running right there, how to smooth out, how to stop fighting yourself, keeping the fists loose. That is a very small thing, but a very important thing. The less tense your muscles are, the better you can run; if you are running with clenched fists, it's an indication that the rest of your body is tight, too. Run with open hands and, chances are, the rest of you is just as loose. Some girls were running while leaning backwards, and this was no good. You've got to lean into your race, not away from it. We walked through everything dozens of times before we ran through it.

Always, Coach Temple kept things on a team basis; we were a team, not just a bunch of individuals. He kept the motivation high because under the team concept all of us became very competitive. In fact, the competition among us that summer was about as intense as any competition I can ever remember. Still, we all stayed friends.

Myself, all of the cross-country running did me a lot of good. It built up my stamina, and it got me to breathing free and easy, naturally. So when I finally started running the 100, or the 200, I didn't have to worry about my breathing patterns, they just came naturally. I learned certain tricks of breathing—taking long, deep breaths, take air in and let it out; doing this a couple of times relaxes everything. We also learned certain exercises that loosen up the body, make the arms and legs feel as light as feathers.

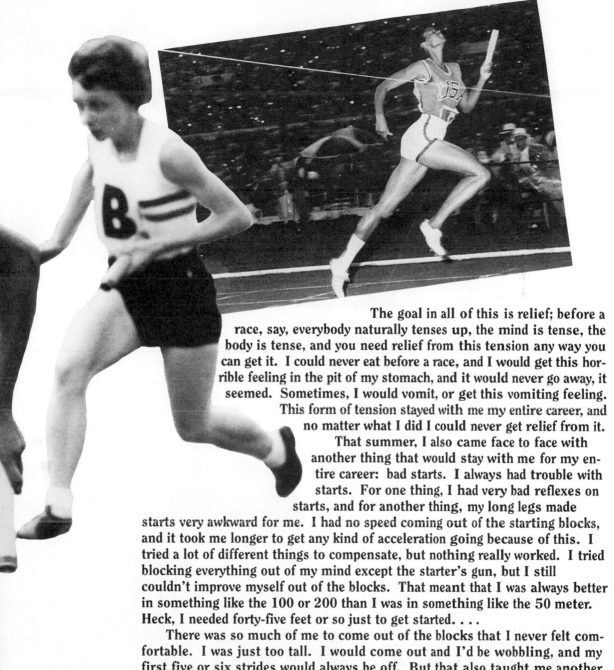

The goal in all of this is relief; before a race, say, everybody naturally tenses up, the mind is tense, the body is tense, and you need relief from this tension any way you can get it. I could never eat before a race, and I would get this horrible feeling in the pit of my stomach, and it would never go away, it seemed. Sometimes, I would vomit, or get this vomiting feeling. This form of tension stayed with me my entire career, and no matter what I did I could never get relief from it.

That summer, I also came face to face with another thing that would stay with me for my entire career: bad starts. I always had trouble with starts. For one thing, I had very bad reflexes on starts, and for another thing, my long legs made starts very awkward for me. I had no speed coming out of the starting blocks, and it took me longer to get any kind of acceleration going because of this. I tried a lot of different things to compensate, but nothing really worked. I tried blocking everything out of my mind except the starter's gun, but I still couldn't improve myself out of the blocks. That meant that I was always better in something like the 100 or 200 than I was in something like the 50 meter. Heck, I needed forty-five feet or so just to get started. . . .

There was so much of me to come out of the blocks that I never felt comfortable. I was just too tall. I would come out and I'd be wobbling, and my first five or six strides would always be off. But that also taught me another lesson about running: every runner is different, and every runner has different problems. What was a problem for me, starting blocks, was no problem for a lot of other girls; but, on the other hand, what bothered them, not being able to deliver a good finishing kick, never bothered me.

Wilma Rudolph *(1940–)*
from *Wilma*

In the preceding excerpt, Rudolph gives a fact-filled account of her summer experience. What do you find out about her personality through this account? How do you think she felt during that summer of hard work? What was the relationship among the girls? Which techniques of proper running did Rudolph learn first? In this summer of training, she obviously honed her running skills a great deal. What other, more personal things do you think Rudolph might have learned along with this physical expertise?

Changing Places

If you were already a good high-school runner in the 100- and 200-meter races, as Rudolph was, how would you react to being asked to run cross-country for two weeks and to walking through the most basic techniques? How do you generally react to "coaching"? Are you most likely to accept constructive criticism and suggestions from teachers, parents, or friends? Is there any activity in which you think you could benefit from review or rethinking of the basics? Consider these questions and do one or more of the following activities.

WRITING

Made to Measure

"Measure"— or meter— is very important to poetry. Some specific poetic forms, such as sonnets, limericks, and haiku, have strict rules for the number of syllables per line. There are even rules telling which syllables should be accented. Choose one of these verse forms, and write a poem in which you observe its rules of measurement exactly.

WRITING

Live and Learn Rudolph's summer internship taught her many things. Think of a similar training experience of your own (or another activity in which you participated) that left you equipped with a specific, practical skill. Make a list of your experiences and select one topic on which to write a paragraph explaining what you learned. As you write your paragraph, be sure to include the intangible things that you learned from your experience (patience, for example). Exchange papers with a classmate.

LANGUAGE

Be a Sport! Most sports have special jargon or expressions of their own, yet these expressions are often borrowed and used metaphorically for other activities. In a group discuss the meaning of the following sports-related expressions and the circumstances in which you've seen them used: *Don't jump the gun. He has two strikes against him. The ball is in their court.* To gather more sports-related expressions, first generate a list with your group. Then look through newspapers and listen to the evening news for other examples. Finally, make a master list of the expressions found by your group, including (1) the expression's original meaning in the context of its sport, (2) its metaphorical meaning, and (3) a sample of how the expression is used outside its own sport.

SPEAKING and LISTENING

Spotlight on Stage Fright
Rudolph's description of her pre-race jitters is similar to other forms of stage fright. Do you ever experience "butterflies"? What do you do to relieve that feeling? Are you successful? After jotting down your answers to these questions, use similar questions to interview at least three people about their particular forms of stage fright and how they deal with them. Try to find people who participate in different kinds of performances such as drama, music, athletics, or teaching. When you have taken notes on all the interviewees (including yourself), use that material to prepare a "How to Deal with Stage Fright" speech. Then present your speech to your class. (To inject humor into your speech, consider acting out the forms of stage fright for your audience's benefit.)

DID YOU KNOW? Wilma Rudolph could not begin kindergarten on time because of the results of polio and other childhood illnesses. Although she wore a brace on her right leg between the ages of six and twelve, she was playing basketball by seventh grade. By ninth grade, Rudolph was almost six feet tall and a local track star. At sixteen, while still in high school, she won a bronze medal in the 1956 Olympics. In the Rome Olympics of 1960, Rudolph became the first woman from the United States to win three gold medals.

UNIT 4

Writing with a Persuasive Focus

If persuasion were not an effective tool, people might still be living in caves and settling their differences of opinion with clubs. As you know from your own experience, though, people are much more likely to respond favorably to reason than to threats or subterfuge. In this unit you will develop your ability to write essays that effectively persuade others to accept an idea, take a particular action, or look at a situation in a new way. You will learn how clear, forceful language and logical argumentation can bring about more positive and lasting change than coercion or deception ever could.

Learning the dynamics of persuasion is particularly important in a democracy where individuals preserve freedom by exchanging ideas in a free market. Understanding the dynamics of *business and the economy* is also important; in the following pages, you will read about various trends and features of the economic marketplace. The selection shown here is part of an argument favoring "competitive capitalism" and the idea that economic freedom is essential to political freedom. Notice how the authors use analogy to make clear and interesting the complex operation of "voluntary exchange" within economies. Notice, too, their appeal to the authority of Adam Smith (1723–1790), the father of modern political economics. As you read, note any other strategies that the Friedmans employ to persuade you to consider their ideas seriously.

The Ne

47,790   Copyright © 1989 The New York Times

Consumer Index Increases 0.6%; Inflation Feared

Biggest Rise in 2 Years Led by Food and Fuel

By ROBERT D. HERSHEY Jr.
Special to The New York Times

WASHINGTON, Feb. 22 — In what many analysts considered strong evidence that inflation has accelerated, the Labor Department reported today that the Consumer Price Index jumped

Voluntary exchange —meaning? →

"Talking pencil" is effective. Pulls me in.

A delightful story called "I, Pencil: My Family Tree as Told to Leonard E. Read" dramatizes vividly how voluntary exchange enables millions of people to cooperate with one another. Mr. Read, in the voice of the "Lead Pencil — the ordinary wooden pencil familiar to all boys and girls and adults who can read and write," starts his story with the fantastic statement that *not a single person . . . knows how to make me.* Then he proceeds to tell about all the things that go into the making of a pencil. First, the wood comes from a tree, "a cedar of straight grain that grows in Northern California and Oregon." To cut down the tree and cart the logs to the railroad siding requires "saws and trucks and rope and . . . countless other gear." Many persons and numberless skills are involved in their fabrication: in "the mining of ore, the making of steel and its refinement into saws, axes, motors; the growing of hemp and bringing it through all the stages to heavy and strong rope; the logging camps with their beds and mess halls, . . . untold thousands of persons had a hand in every cup of coffee the loggers drink!"

And so Mr. Read goes on to the bringing of the logs to the mill, the millwork involved in converting the logs to slats, and the transportation of the slats from California to Wilkes-Barre, where the particular pencil that tells the story was manufactured. And so far we have only the outside wood of the pencil. The "lead" center is not really lead at all. It starts as graphite mined in Ceylon. After many complicated processes it ends up as the lead in the center of the pencil.

The bit of metal — the ferrule — near the top of the pencil is brass. "Think of all the persons," he says, "who mine zinc and copper and those who have the skills to make sheet brass from these products of nature."

What we call the eraser is known in the trade as "the plug." It is thought to be rubber. But Mr. Read tells us the rubber is only for binding purposes. The erasing is actually done by "Factice," a rubberlike product made by reacting rape seed oil from the Dutch East Indies (now Indonesia) with sulfur chloride.

After all of this, says the pencil, "Does anyone wish to challenge my earlier assertion that no single person on the face of this earth knows how to make me?"

None of the thousands of persons involved in producing the pencil performed his task because he wanted a pencil. Some among them never saw a pencil and would not know what it is for. Each saw his work as a way to get the goods and services he wanted — goods and services we produced in order to get the pencil we wanted. Every time we go to the store and buy a pencil, we are exchanging a little bit of our services for the infinitesimal amount of services that each of the thousands contributed toward producing the pencil.

It is even more astounding that the pencil was ever produced. No one sitting in a central office gave orders to these thousands of people. No military police enforced the orders that were not given. These people live in many lands, speak different languages, practice different religions, may even hate one another — yet none of these differences prevented them from cooperating to produce a pencil. How did it happen? Adam Smith gave us the answer two hundred years ago.

*   *   *

The key insight of Adam Smith's *Wealth of Nations* is misleadingly simple: if an exchange between two parties is voluntary, it will not take place unless both believe they will benefit from it. Most economic fallacies derive from the neglect of this simple insight, from the tendency to assume that there is a fixed pie, that one party can gain only at the expense of another.

This key insight is obvious for a simple exchange between two individuals. It is far more difficult to understand how it can enable people living all over the world to cooperate to promote their separate interests.

The price system is the mechanism that performs this task without central direction, without requiring people to speak to one another or to like one another. When you buy your pencil or your daily bread, you don't know whether the pencil was made or the wheat was grown by a white man or a black man, by a Chinese or an Indian. As a result, the price system enables people to cooperate peacefully in one phase of their life while each one goes about his own business in respect of everything else.

Adam Smith's flash of genius was his recognition that the prices that emerged from voluntary transactions between buyers and sellers — for short, in a free market — could coordinate the activity of millions of people, each seeking his own interest, in such a way as to make everyone better off. It was a startling idea then, and it remains one today, that economic order can emerge as the unintended consequence of the actions of many people, each seeking his own interest.

Milton Friedman and Rose Friedman
from *Free to Choose: A Personal Statement*   (1980)

Responding to Literature

In many books, articles, and lectures, the Friedmans have argued for a "truly" free market system, and their ideas have persuaded such world leaders as Great Britain's Prime Minister Margaret Thatcher and former United States President Ronald Reagan to establish policies that limit government intervention in the marketplace. Brainstorm on business and economics, focusing on the free market. Ask yourself such questions as: What is it? Who profits from it? What would be the consequence of complete freedom from government control? Then, based on your brainstorming, list all the pros *and* cons to a free market economy that you can come up with, including your response to this selection and to other arguments that you've read or heard. Save your paper in your writer's notebook.

Understanding Your Purpose, Audience, and Position

Your purpose in persuasive writing is to convince your readers that they should accept an idea, take action, or do both. You do this primarily by presenting a reasonable argument that supports the position that you are concerned with. Before focusing on your argument and on how to persuade, clarify your audience and your position.

Your understanding of your audience will affect both your content and your approach. Therefore, it is important that you fully appreciate your audience's point of view before you begin to write. The fact that your audience even needs persuading means that they do not think about the topic exactly as you do. Knowing how their thinking differs from your own will tell you what to emphasize in your position and how to focus your argument.

As you consider different audiences, think about how helpful each one might be in supporting your position and how difficult they might be to persuade. Some audiences present greater challenges than others.

Your position on a persuasive topic is usually based on an **opinion** — a view or a belief that is open to disagreement. Most opinions either explain, evaluate, predict, or advise. The following opinion makes a prediction.

> Hypermarkets — gigantic stores that sell groceries, clothing, and housewares — will replace supermarkets and department stores by the 1990s.

Proving opinions may be difficult because they are often based on personal feelings and judgments, and people are likely to differ in these. Most people, however, don't demand proof of an opinion to accept it; they are satisfied if they are shown through reason and evidence that it is probably true.

? Critical Thinking:
Evaluating opinions

In persuasive writing, the opinion that you are defending should be based on a logical idea, not on a personal preference, a feeling, or a hunch. It should also be specific and clear.

PERSONAL PREFERENCE
Office work is more relaxing than factory work.

FEELING OR HUNCH
I'll bet that robots will eventually do all factory work.

TOO VAGUE
Large corporations should pay more taxes.

When you write down your opinion or your position, you establish a **preliminary position statement.** This statement can be revised later if your view of your topic or your position itself changes.

You can be persuasive in as little as a single paragraph if you have a fairly limited topic. In this unit, however, your focus will be on writing a persuasive essay. Even in an essay, you need to limit your topic if you are to discuss it thoroughly, especially if the length of your essay is restricted. When stating your position, therefore, be aware of the area that you can reasonably expect to cover in the space that you have.

Assignment 1 Identifying Audiences

On your own or with classmates, identify two possible audiences for each of the following opinions: one audience that would agree with the opinion and one audience that would strongly oppose the opinion.

SAMPLE   International companies should have computers that can translate technical material from one language to another.

ANSWER   *Likely to agree:* Business executives
Likely to oppose: Professional translators

1. The average cost of homes and condominiums is too high; housing costs must be reduced.
2. To help reduce the national budget deficit, the tax on gasoline should be increased.
3. Malls are frequently crowded and noisy; it is more convenient and comfortable to shop through mail-order catalogues.
4. Raising the minimum wage will attract more workers to service industries such as restaurants and supermarkets.

Assignment 2 Recognizing Suitable Opinions

For each of the following opinions, write *Suitable* if the opinion is appropriate as the basis of a persuasive composition. Write *Unsuitable* if it is not appropriate, and explain your answer.

SAMPLE   Someone should change the mandatory age for retirement.
ANSWER   Unsuitable — This opinion is too vague.

1. Automobiles produced in Japan are better than those made in the United States.
2. Vocational training provides students with an excellent opportunity to learn job skills.
3. I think that mobile cellular telephones will be installed in all cars in the future.
4. Students receive important knowledge at business schools.
5. To encourage health and fitness, employers should provide exercise facilities for their employees.
6. With increasing malpractice insurance rates, many medical students will probably avoid specialization in high-risk fields of medicine.

? Critical Thinking:

Evaluating opinions
Can the opinion be supported with reasons?

Assignment 3 Limiting Your Topic

On your paper, write a more limited topic for each opinion. (The topics are in italic type.)

SAMPLE *Credit cards* should be used sparingly to avoid serious debt and overspending.

ANSWER Major credit cards from banks

1. *Military spending* should be limited.
2. *Equipment* has revolutionized business communication.
3. *Advertisements* should include truthful, accurate information.
4. *Public transportation* is one way to solve commuting problems in large cities.
5. *Organizations* should assist hungry and needy people worldwide.

Continuing Assignment Select a Position and an Audience

For writing an **essay**

Step 1: Look into your writer's notebook for ideas that could serve as the topic of your persuasive essay. Also review your responses to the passage on pages 227–229. On your paper, list five changes that you would like to see occur. Select one of the changes as the topic of your persuasive essay, and write it on your paper under the heading *Purpose.* *Step 2:* Under the heading *Audience,* list three possible audiences for the purpose that you have selected. Consider whether each audience might support your position or be difficult to persuade. Select one of the groups as your audience and circle your choice. *Step 3:* Try to predict the most important objection that your audience would raise about your position. Under the heading *Preliminary Position Statement,* write a sentence stating the main opinion that you want your audience to accept. Limit your topic so that you can treat it effectively. Save your paper.

Prewriting

Preparing Your Argument

Once you have determined your audience and your position, you need to prepare a convincing **argument** — a line of reasoning that supports your position through the logical presentation and development of ideas.

Discovering Ideas

Explore ideas about your topic before you begin to draft your essay. First, list information that you already know about it and make notes on ideas that you want to include in your argument. Use prewriting techniques to discover additional information that will support your argument *(pages 8–22).* You can then do research to expand on these basic ideas and to learn about aspects of your topic that may not have occurred to you. Reading articles and books, consulting reference materials *(pages 385–387),* conducting experiments, or interviewing knowledgeable people will give you evidence for your position and a deeper understanding of your topic.

Reference Point: *pages 442–445*

Assignment 1 Planning Research

Select two of the following opinions and copy them on your paper, leaving plenty of space between them. Under each opinion, list three questions whose answers would require research. After each question, briefly indicate the kind of research needed.

SAMPLE Certificates of deposit, or CDs, provide bank customers with a risk-free way to invest their money.

ANSWER
   a. What interest rates do bank customers receive from CDs? — Refer to a newspaper's financial section; check interest rates at a bank.
   b. What are the restrictions applied to a bank CD? — Interview the manager or customer service representative of a local bank.
   c. What are the possible risks of investing in a CD? — Consult a magazine article on financial planning.

1. Following airline deregulation, passengers benefited from competitive fares among airlines.
2. Serious investors should always consult a reputable financial planner before buying stocks and bonds.
3. The trend toward entrepreneurship will continue to grow in the 1990s.
4. As increasing numbers of women join the work force, the need for adequate day-care facilities has become critical.

Looking at Opposing Views

An important part of preparing your argument is becoming aware of viewpoints opposed to your own. Whether you foresee them when you establish your position or uncover them in the course of your research, make notes on what they are and consider the best way to respond to them in your argument. When you discuss them in your essay, you can then present your opposing evidence, called a **rebuttal.**

By discussing opponents' views knowledgeably and by defending your own position in light of them, you demonstrate to your audience that you are confident of your own position and can deal with opponents openly. Including a rebuttal also gives you the opportunity to respond to questions that your audience may have about your argument.

? Critical Thinking:
Predicting outcomes

Understanding opposing views may even change your approach to your topic. If this happens, rewrite your position statement to be more effective or defensible, or write a new position statement.

? **Critical Thinking:**

Predicting outcomes What is the audience's viewpoint?

Step 1: On your paper, list an audience that probably would disagree with each opinion that follows. Leave plenty of space between your answers. *Step 2:* For each audience, state the opposing view or the question that you think that the audience would raise. *Step 3:* Write a likely response to each opposing view.

SAMPLE The rates charged by alternative operator service (AOS) companies are too high; customers should use regular telephone companies.

ANSWER *Audience:* Owners of AOS companies
Opposing view: AOS companies are new and must charge higher rates to cover operating expenses and start-up costs.
Answer to opposing view: AOS companies cannot gain public confidence and grow unless their rates compete with those offered by established telephone companies.

1. Retail stores are better than factory outlets because they are more conveniently located, provide delivery service, and have extensive sales help.
2. Renting an apartment is a better investment than buying a home; renters are not responsible for maintenance, repair, or taxes.
3. Economical shoppers should join food cooperatives, in which members stock shelves, run cash registers, and bag their own groceries in return for member discounts.
4. Most third-world countries are not industrialized; to create a mutually beneficial relationship with them, the United States should offer them technology and equipment in exchange for raw materials.

Providing Reliable Evidence

In your argument you must include evidence that convincingly supports your position. Facts, common beliefs, and expert opinions are three kinds of evidence that readers will find reliable.

Facts — since they can be objectively verified through observation, measurement, experimentation, or research — can serve as reliable evidence in any argument. They provide support for major ideas or opinions and serve as specific examples or explanations for general statements.

Opinions can also be useful evidence, provided that they have a high degree of reliability. Among such opinions are common beliefs and experts' opinions.

Common beliefs are values or ideas shared by most people. For instance, most people believe that children should be educated and that honesty is a desirable quality. The Declaration of Independence contains statements of many common beliefs — that all people are entitled to certain rights, such as "Life, Liberty, and the pursuit of Happiness," for example. Common-sense notions — such as the idea that you shouldn't drive when you are tired — also rely on common, accepted beliefs. These common beliefs are not verifiable in the way that facts are, but they have the status of wisdom and thus are rarely challenged.

Experts' opinions are also regarded as trustworthy by most people. An **expert** is an accepted source of special knowledge or advice, someone considered to be an **authority** in a field of knowledge. You can find the opinions of experts by consulting the experts directly or by referring to their scholarly and scientific works, other highly respected documents or books, and reputable organizations. Because experts base their opinions on knowledge acquired through education, research, first-hand experience, or a combination of these, their opinions are generally thought to contain a higher degree of truth than most. When researching your topic, look for experts' opinions that support your own opinions; plan to include them in your argument as evidence.

The following prewriting notes show how facts and opinions can be used together to provide solid evidence for an argument.

Position statement: By linking their products with worthwhile causes, businesses can increase the sales of their products and help charitable organizations raise money at the same time.

FACTS:
Cause-marketing (products linked with specific causes) raises about $100 million each year for charitable causes. Easter Seals, March of Dimes Birth Defects Foundation, and Cystic Fibrosis Foundation participate in cause-marketing.

OPINIONS:
Belief — Helping the less fortunate is everyone's responsibility.
Belief — Serving others is a source of satisfaction.
Expert — American Red Cross representatives state that cause-marketing will raise $10 million for national disaster relief by 1993.
Expert — Jay Clara, president of Saucy Salsa, Inc., says, "Sales for our new Saucy Salsa skyrocketed after we teamed up with Food for Thought, the local food bank."

Each of the following statements expresses a belief. On your own or with classmates, decide whether you think that a majority of people would accept each statement as true without serious question. Identify each belief as *Widely accepted* or *Not widely accepted*.

SAMPLE   All employed people in the United States should receive free health insurance.

ANSWER   Not widely accepted

1. Buying gold is the most profitable way to invest money.
2. People's reputations are determined largely by how well they keep their word.
3. Government employees should always keep in mind that they are public servants.
4. Holding a part-time job is an excellent way for a teen-ager to learn discipline.
5. Mortgage rates for first-time home buyers should be lowered.
6. Shoppers should compare the prices of similar consumable goods to find the best value for their money.
7. It's foolish to make high-risk investments if you can't afford to lose much money.
8. In general, government programs should avoid doing what people can do for themselves.

Step 1: On your paper, identify a person likely to be considered an expert on each opinion. Leave space between your answers. *Step 2:* Research the opinions and list three pieces of supporting evidence for each one. Include at least one expert opinion in your evidence.

1. Workers need unions to protect their interests with regard to pay, working conditions, and job benefits.
2. The rising cost of houses has led home owners to renovate their current homes instead of buying new residences.

Planning a Logical Argument

An effective argument consists of a convincing line of reasoning as well as sound evidence. As you prepare your argument, therefore, think through the line of reasoning that you will present. The relationships that you develop and the conclusions that you draw must follow logically from your supporting statements. In other words, your reasoning must be **valid.**

There are two fundamentally different types of reasoning: inductive reasoning and deductive reasoning. Since most arguments employ both kinds, it is important to understand the rules that govern each.

Inductive Reasoning

When you use **inductive reasoning,** you draw a general conclusion from a set of specific experiences or observations. Much of what people know comes from inductive reasoning. For example, as a child, you probably saw the surface of a pond, a lake, or a river become icy when the air temperature dropped. Based on this limited observation, you formed an idea about cold weather in general: Cold temperatures can cause water to freeze.

Many other experiences have taught you other things — that chili peppers taste hot and spicy, for instance, or that certain name-brand clothes are expensive. From each experience or set of experiences, you formed a generalization about a whole class of objects or events based on your specific experiences with members of that class.

In inductive reasoning, certain members of a class are assumed to represent the entire class. Such an assumption, of course, may or may not be justified. The absolute truth of a generalization can only be established by (1) observing every possible member of the class being discussed, which is often impossible; or (2) by using deductive reasoning, which demonstrates that the members must operate according to a rule. (Deductive reasoning is discussed on pages 239–241.) The validity of a generalization depends on the amount and the quality of the experience on which it is based.

The most logical application of inductive reasoning is usually found in science. When scientists observe a pattern in nature, for example, they form a tentative, or temporary, generalization known as a **hypothesis.** The scientists then devise experiments to determine whether the hypothesis holds true in all cases and under varying conditions. Depending on the results of their experiments, they either accept, reject, or modify the hypothesis. In some cases, modifying the hypothesis may simply involve making it more specific, as in this example.

PATTERN OBSERVED   Water turns into ice at a certain temperature.

HYPOTHESIS   Water freezes at 32 degrees Fahrenheit.

MODIFIED   Water freezes at 32 degrees Fahrenheit under standard
HYPOTHESIS   atmospheric pressure.

Keep these guidelines in mind as you plan the logic of your argument.

▶ **Strategies**

1. *Make sure that your generalization is based on a sufficiently large and representative sampling of cases.* Generalizing from a very small number of experiences is not a sound way to reason since the similarities may be only coincidental. If your own experience is too limited to provide adequate evidence, look for and cite as additional

? **Critical Thinking:**

Inductive reasoning / generalizing

Reference Point: *pages 436–438*

evidence studies that support your generalization. Your evidence, at the very least, must show that a clear pattern exists within the class of objects being discussed and that this pattern does not depend on changing circumstances such as place or time.

2. *Limit your generalization to reflect only what is justified by the evidence.* Be certain that your generalization is based on an accurate interpretation of your facts or your evidence. Avoid distorting or exaggerating the real meaning of your evidence. In your research, you may discover evidence that clashes with your own observations. If this happens, adjust your generalization to make sure that it reflects all of your information. Rather than claiming that something is always the case, for instance, suggest that it is usually or probably the case. Remember that one exception will disprove a generalization about an entire class.

Assignment 5 | Using Inductive Reasoning

? Critical Thinking:
Inductive reasoning / generalizing
Does the evidence support the generalization?

Read the statements of information and the generalizations that follow them. On your paper, write the letter of the generalization that is clearly justified by the information.

1. Colorblindness affects seven out of every hundred men and one out of every thousand women.
   a. Women have better eyesight than men.
   b. A person's sex has little to do with the quality of his or her eyesight.
   c. Men are more likely to be affected by colorblindness than women are.

2. In 1988 in the United States, 217 savings-and-loan institutions failed, the highest number since 1938.
   a. The large number of savings-and-loan institution failures in 1988 means that the country is heading into another depression.
   b. 1988 was a disastrous year for many savings-and-loan institutions.
   c. Today's savings-and-loan industry is in serious financial trouble.

3. Every year 20 percent of the families in the United States change their place of residence.
   a. These days it is unusual for a family in the United States to remain in the same residence for more than five years.
   b. A typical person in the United States lives a fast-paced life.
   c. Families in the United States tend to change their residences fairly frequently.

Assignment 6 | Identifying Generalizations

On your paper, copy the generalization stated in each argument. On your own or with classmates, decide whether you think that the generalization is justified by the given evidence. Write *Justified* or *Unjustified* on your paper. If you indicate *Unjustified*, write an alternative that would be justified by the evidence.

1. In laboratory experiments, scientists have observed that objects moving at 86 percent of the speed of light have doubled their weight. These findings support the theory that an object's mass increases with its velocity.
2. Today's filmmakers present a largely negative view of the business world. Last year a dozen major movies were released involving corporate executives or business persons. In all but one, the characters were portrayed as greedy and corrupt.
3. Between 1984 and 1988, the sale of minivans in the United States rose from approximately 200,000 to 700,000. In the same period, the sale of station wagons declined by nearly 40 percent. Clearly, most drivers in the United States today prefer minivans to station wagons.
4. Contrary to what most people think, earthquakes are not an uncommon phenomenon. Every year more than 50,000 earthquakes occur somewhere in the world.
5. Most people in the United States suffer from faulty eyesight. Approximately two out of every three adults wear eyeglasses at one time or another.

Assignment 7 Justifying Generalizations

On your paper, write *Yes* or *No* to indicate whether you think that evidence could be obtained to justify each generalization. Next to each *No*, briefly explain why it would be difficult or impossible to obtain the evidence. Work on your own or with classmates.

SAMPLE   The labor-union movement in the United States today is not as interesting as it was in the 1950s.

ANSWER   No — The word *interesting* cannot be measured in a clear-cut way. People differ about what is interesting.

1. In the last decade catalogue shopping has become quite popular among consumers.
2. People in the United States are not as concerned about social injustice today as they were in the 1960s and the 1970s.
3. The cost of basic foods is lower in the United States than in any other major industrial nation.
4. Professional football players are vastly overpaid.

Deductive Reasoning

Whether you are conscious of it or not, you use **deductive reasoning** all the time. This means that you put ideas together in such a way that a necessary conclusion follows. In a sense, deduction is done "in your

Critical Thinking:
Deductive reasoning

head" rather than through observation or research. You may think, for example, "Dolores isn't at school again today; she must still be sick," or "The post office will be closed on Monday — it must be a federal holiday." As a further example, if you know that drivers in your state must be sixteen years old to obtain a license, and you also know that your neighbor Eli has obtained a license, you can put these pieces of knowledge together and **deduce** — or reach the conclusion — that Eli is at least sixteen years old.

In your daily encounters, like most other people you probably present your deductions as educated guesses rather than as logical arguments with necessary conclusions. In formal persuasion, however, where your statements may be examined closely by your audience, it is important to be aware of your deductions and how you reach them.

(sĭl′ə-jĭz′əm)

The standard method for testing the logic of a deductive argument is to express the argument as a **syllogism,** a set of three logically related statements. The first two statements in a syllogism are **premises,** statements assumed to be true. The third statement is a conclusion that follows necessarily from the two premises. The following are syllogisms.

PREMISE   All dinosaurs existed during the Mesozoic Era.

PREMISE   Tyrannosaurus rex was a dinosaur.

CONCLUSION   Tyrannosaurus rex existed during the Mesozoic Era.

PREMISE   No financial investment is ever 100 percent safe.

PREMISE   Buying stocks is a financial investment.

CONCLUSION   Buying stocks is never 100 percent safe.

Critical to any syllogism is the way that words or ideas are joined to one another. The use of qualifying words — *all, always, any, every, each, many, some, a few, hardly any, no, none,* and *never* — is also vital. These qualifiers specify the exact relationships among the ideas of a syllogism and make the conclusion possible. In the syllogism about dinosaurs, for instance, if the qualifier *All* were replaced by the qualifier *Some,* no conclusion would follow from the premises.

PREMISE   Some dinosaurs existed during the Mesozoic Era.

PREMISE   Tyrannosaurus rex was a dinosaur.

CONCLUSION   No conclusion is possible. [If only *some* dinosaurs existed during the Mesozoic Era, tyrannosaurus rex may have existed during another era.]

While a syllogism can clarify how an argument works, it is an artificial structure and is not commonly used in everyday conversation or writing. People almost always express their deductions informally, without stating their premises clearly or completely, either because they are unaware of their premises or think that they are obvious. The value of a syllogism is that it permits you to see any hidden premises, or assumptions, in an argument. Consider the following example.

ARGUMENT AS STATED
Congressional filibusters should be prohibited since they slow down the pace of governmental business.

ARGUMENT EXPRESSED AS SYLLOGISM

HIDDEN PREMISE Any activity that slows down the pace of governmental business should be prohibited.

PREMISE Congressional filibusters slow down the pace of governmental business.

CONCLUSION Congressional filibusters should be prohibited.

Check the logic of your argument by identifying any hidden premises involved in your reasoning. If you have made an assumption that your readers are likely to question, you will need to support the assumption with additional evidence. If you find that the assumption is questionable or incorrect, you may need to rethink and possibly revise your argument.

Assignment 8 **Using Deductive Reasoning**

Read the following syllogisms. On your paper, write the missing premise or conclusion that would complete each syllogism logically.

? Critical Thinking:

Deductive reasoning
What is the missing idea?

SAMPLE *Premise:* Disability insurance should be a standard benefit for working people.
Premise: All employers should provide standard benefits to their employees.
Conclusion: __?__

ANSWER All employers should provide disability insurance to their employees.

1. *Premise:* No government should tax the sale of necessary items.
Premise: For many people today, gasoline for automobile travel to and from work is a necessity.
Conclusion: __?__

2. *Premise:* __?__
Premise: Refined sugar has no nutritional value.
Conclusion: People should not eat refined sugar.

3. *Premise:* Inflation is hardest on people living on fixed incomes.
Premise: __?__
Conclusion: Inflation is hardest on some older citizens.

4. *Premise:* __?__
Premise: The 55-mph speed law passed in 1976 helped save lives.
Conclusion: The 55-mph speed law should be maintained.

The following syllogisms are logically flawed. On your own or with classmates, briefly explain the logical error involved in each one.

1. *Premise:* Lack of exercise is a major cause of illness in people.
   Premise: My grandparents have been ill for the past month.
   Conclusion: My grandparents obviously have not been getting enough exericse.

2. *Premise:* Every citizen should keep informed about current events.
   Premise: Reading a daily newspaper is a way of keeping informed about daily events.
   Conclusion: Every citizen should read a daily newspaper.

3. *Premise:* Many politicians are more interested in exercising power than in serving constituents.
   Premise: Mayor York is a politician.
   Conclusion: Mayor York is more interested in exercising power than in serving constituents.

4. *Premise:* All charitable organizations in the United States are exempt from taxes.
   Premise: All nonprofit organizations in the United States are exempt from taxes.
   Conclusion: All nonprofit organizations in the United States are charitable organizations.

Each of the following deductive arguments contains a conclusion and a single premise. Working on your own or with classmates, write on your paper the conclusion of each argument, leaving space between your answers. Under each conclusion, write the argument's missing premise or hidden assumption. Then indicate your attitude toward the assumption by writing either *Agree* or *Disagree*.

1. TV commercials for alcoholic beverages may entice minors to drink illegally. Clearly, networks should prohibit all such commercials.
2. Since one of the purposes of high school is to prepare students for the duties of citizenship, every high school should require its students to take civics.
3. The United States should not impose any additional tariffs, or duties, on imports. Tariffs inevitably result in higher prices for consumers.
4. Business monopolies have no place in a free-market system. They restrict or eliminate competition.

Outlining and Organizing Your Evidence

A poorly organized argument may confuse, rather than persuade, your audience. Outlining your essay before you draft will help you to organize your evidence and your ideas into a logical and effective argument. You may need to write only a rough outline for a short, fairly simple argument. A longer, more complex argument may require a topic or a sentence outline. (See pages 47–53 for specific instruction on outlining.) Follow this procedure to arrange your ideas.

▶ **Procedure**

1. *Discuss ideas completely, one at a time.*
2. *Present first things first.* For instance, if you plan to propose a solution to a problem, define the problem before presenting the solution.
3. *Maintain a clear line of reasoning.*
4. *Develop a preliminary plan for dividing your composition into paragraphs.*
5. *Construct your actual outline.*

Your persuasive argument presents your readers with a **line of reasoning** — a series of related ideas and evidence. To be effective, your line of reasoning must be clear, easy to follow, and logical. The organization of your essay, therefore, is very important.

Consider how to arrange your ideas before you begin to draft. In order to organize your thoughts, select from your notes the information that best supports your position. Identify main ideas and combine closely related secondary ideas or facts into groups under them.

You can use any order to arrange ideas or reasons of equal importance. In grouping your ideas, however, you will find that certain arrangements work for certain kinds of ideas, depending on how they are related. Order of importance, chain of reasoning, and rebuttal using comparison and contrast are useful arrangements in persuasive writing.

? Critical Thinking:
Determining relationships

Order of Importance Independent reasons of varying importance can be arranged in the order of least-to-most important, as in this paragraph.

Position statement	Businesses should supplement their full-time work force by employing retired people on a part-time basis. As
1st reason	the average life span increases, there are greater numbers of older, retired people who wish to fill their time and supplement their incomes. They generally have flexible sched-
2nd reason	ules and can work part time or on weekends. Furthermore,
3rd reason	hiring retired people can be cost-effective — companies may avoid paying employment agency fees, retirement benefits, and training costs. Finally, older workers offer valua-
4th reason	ble years of experience to employers.

Chain of Reasoning   In a chain of reasoning, the ideas are interrelated; each statement is connected to the next one, with the position statement representing the final link in the chain. To build this kind of chain, you must be able to arrange your supporting sentences in their logical sequence.

The following chain of reasoning links causes with effects in a chronological order.

Position
statement
(final link)
1st link
2nd link

3rd link
4th link
5th link

> One of the most serious threats to sea life in our oceans is land pollution created by both agriculture and urban industry. Farmers use pesticides and chemical fertilizers, and factories produce toxic by-products. Rain and snow carry pollutants from industrial and agricultural areas, and runoff eventually contaminates local rivers and streams. In time, this polluted fresh water flows into salt water. Chemical pollutants settle on the sea bottom, and may eventually result in deadly, explosive growths of algae, known as *red tides*. These red tides poison and kill fish and shellfish.

This chain of reasoning demonstrates connections made by linking more abstract concepts.

Position
statement

Chain of
reasoning

Logical
conclusion

> People who abuse the rights of others forfeit their own rights. For instance, you can hardly complain about the loud music coming from your neighbor's house at 2:00 A.M. if you have been guilty of the same offense. By ignoring your neighbor's right to peace and quiet, you have given your neighbor license to ignore *your* right to peace and quiet. What is it that entitles you to a particular right in the first place? If it is the fact that you are a citizen, then you must acknowledge that all other citizens possess the right too. If it is the fact that you are a human being, then you must grant the right to every other human being. Thus, in claiming a right for yourself, you also grant it to your neighbor. What is more to the point, in denying a right to your neighbor, you also deny it to yourself.

Rebuttal   When you include a rebuttal *(page 233)* in your argument, you compare and contrast your opponents' evidence with your own. You can do this in one of two ways: (1) present all of your opponents' points first and then follow with your own or (2) alternate the individual points. The writer of the following persuasive essay uses the first type of rebuttal.

Introduction

Position
statement

> Counterfeiters duplicate and sell billions of dollars' worth of goods — everything from shampoo to helicopter parts — each year. To stop this practice, manufacturers should fight back with the newest technology.

Some manufacturers may believe that customs agents, private detectives, and trademark and copyright laws protect them adequately. Other business owners just refuse to believe that their products will be copied and are unwilling to spend money on new technology.

Although traditional methods slow counterfeiters, they do not stop them. Counterfeiters now use computers and other sophisticated techniques to make believable fakes that they can sell as genuine articles. Overworked customs agents search only about 5 percent of foreign goods for counterfeits. Also, while trademark laws are strict, in most cases manufacturers settle out of court to save time and money.

In the long run, the cost of newer methods for marking products — invisible inks, laser etchings, and hidden micro computer chips — is a small price to pay for protection of profits and reputations.

Assignment 11 Ordering Ideas

On your own or with your classmates, identify the best method for ordering each group of ideas. Write *Order of importance*, *Chain of reasoning*, or *Rebuttal*. Leave room between your answers. After each answer, list the supporting ideas in the order that you chose.

**? Critical
Thinking:**

**Determining
relationships**
How do the
ideas relate
to one
another?

1. *Position statement:* High-speed trains, which travel over 100 mph, should be used in the United States.

   — Railroad officials claim that costly track improvement is required for faster trains.
   — High-speed trains operate safely in Japan and Europe.
   — Consumer groups concerned about risk of more frequent, serious train accidents with faster speeds
   — More than a dozen trains in United States regularly travel over 80 mph
   — More passengers attracted by faster train service: would increase ticket sales, railroad revenues

2. *Position statement:* The development of Alaska's natural resources is important to the state's economic success, but it should not be achieved at the loss of two other valuable assets, a beautiful environment and an extensive wildlife population.

   — Has 104 billion acres of national parks and wildlife preserves
   — Tourism, second major industry, attracts thousands of people to Alaska.
   — Environmentalists concerned that development could damage land and wildlife
   — Great economic expansion because of many mineral resources
   — Coastal waters support salmon, cod, halibut, herring, and shellfish.

3. *Position statement:* The workfare program, which provides skills training, educational assistance, and work experience to the working poor, must include services as well if it is to succeed in helping disadvantaged citizens in any lasting way.

— Some politicians believe that workfare will end unemployment.
— Child-care services, a higher minimum wage, and more government benefits necessary for workfare participants to benefit in long run
— Workfare programs alone will not replace welfare.
— Most workfare participants have children and need child-care services, which are expensive and scarce.
— Workfare primarily trains people for low-paying jobs.
— Government benefits end when workfare "graduates" have jobs.

4. *Position statement:* A single world currency should be adopted.

— International currency would simplify buying and selling of goods; would encourage world trade
— Economists warn that one country, government, or agency would control world's money
— International Monetary Fund and the Bank for International Settlements have both handled world finances for over 40 years
— Dollar might be pooled with currency of less value — bankers in United States object, claiming that country would lose money

---

Continuing Assignment   **Prepare and Organize Your Argument**

For writing an **essay**

Step 1: Using your work from the Continuing Assignment on page 232, write the heading *Argument Notes* below your position statement. List three or more major reasons for believing that your position is correct. Leave space between the reasons. *Step 2:* List supporting details after each reason, including facts and opinions among them. Do additional research to discover other facts or supporting opinions. *Step 3:* Under the heading *Conclusions from Evidence,* list conclusions that you have reached from examining your evidence. *Step 4:* Using these prewriting notes, outline your persuasive essay on separate paper. Follow the procedure on page 243. Your outline should indicate the sequence of paragraphs in your essay. Save your notes and outline.

Drafting

Drafting Your Persuasive Essay

When you draft, you organize the ideas in your notes according to your outline and attempt to express those ideas in an effective way to your readers. In the process of drafting, if you find that you need examples or explanations that are not in your notes, you can always do more research and include them. You can also adjust your outline to make your line of reasoning clearer to your readers if necessary.

Drafting Your Introduction

In your introduction, you should present your topic, state your position on the topic, and clarify that position as needed. You want your position to be clear and specific in the beginning of your essay so that your readers will understand the purpose of your argument and its direction.

Use these strategies to help you to express your position effectively.

▶ **Strategies**

1. *Convey your position directly, preferably as a statement or a command.* While you may introduce your topic with an interesting question, your position statement itself should be direct and decisive.

   NOT EFFECTIVE Why should people be forced to retire because they have reached a certain age?

   EFFECTIVE People should not be forced to retire because they have reached a certain age.

2. *Select words that express your ideas precisely.* Avoid vague or unnecessarily general language.

   LESS PRECISE National organizations should ban harmful consumer goods.

   MORE PRECISE The Consumer Product Safety Commission should ban consumer goods that may cause death, injury, or illness.

3. *Clarify your position statement with additional sentences as needed.* Define key terms, provide vital background information, give examples, or limit your opinion if necessary.

   Position statement
   Clarifying remark
   Our local library should launch a fund-raising program to improve its facilities. For example, donations should be sought so that carrels for private study can be built.

4. *Present your topic in an interesting manner.* To interest your reader, precede your position statement with a question, a little-known piece of information, a striking image, or an unusual point of view.

   Unusual point of view
   Position statement
   In the United States these days, a typical citizen wakes up to a Taiwanese-made clock radio, dresses in a Korean-made suit and Italian-made shoes, warms breakfast in a Japanese-made microwave oven, and drives a German-made car to his or her job. While this portrait may be exaggerated, the point behind it is not. Foreign manufacturers are endangering the future of those in the United States and unless companies here become more competitive, the trend will continue.

Drafting Position Statements

The following position statements are either vaguely worded or indirect. On your paper, rewrite each sentence to make it an effective position statement. Work on your own or with classmates.

SAMPLE   Why should airlines continue their frequent-flyer programs to attract passengers?

ANSWER   Airlines should continue their frequent-flyer programs to attract passengers.

1. What can be done to improve emergency procedures for workers stationed on offshore oil rigs?
2. Banks should encourage entrepreneurs.
3. Congress should help farmers during a weather crisis.
4. What kinds of trade agreements should the United States have with Canada?
5. Fine-art collectibles make good investments.

Assignment 2 **Drafting an Introduction**

Step 1: Copy the following position statement on your paper and write one or two clarifying remarks for it by following the directions in parentheses. Use a dictionary or an encyclopedia to obtain information if necessary. *Step 2:* Using your position statement and clarifying remarks, draft an introductory paragraph of four to seven sentences for a persuasive essay. Use the strategies on page 247.

> *Position statement:* Since toll-free numbers are one of the most effective and least expensive ways to boost consumer satisfaction, businesses should include them in their customer-service programs. (Describe two positive effects of consumer satisfaction. Define *customer-service programs* and *toll-free numbers.*)

Drafting Your Argument

The largest part of your persuasive essay is your argument, in which you present the ideas and reasoning that support your position. In order to maintain a clear line of reasoning *(pages 236–241)*, follow your outline carefully as you write your argument, especially if your argument is a long one. Read the following introduction and argument from an essay, and notice how the parts of the outline (on the left) shape its organization. You will read its conclusion later.

Introduction

Imagine buying antifreeze, bread, fashionable clothing, and a dishwasher all in one store. Giant stores called *hypermarkets* bring together under one roof these products and many others traditionally sold separately in supermarkets, retail stores, and appliance stores. While these stores offer consumers

Position
statement

I. Threat to
   competitive
   market
   A. Capacity of
      hypermarkets
      to absorb
      consumer pool
   B. Loss of
      shopping
      diversity

   C. Value of
      entrepreneurs
      and specialty
      stores

   D. Loss of
      retailers and
      entrepreneurs

II. Threat to
    community and
    environment
    A. Size
    B. Number of
       shoppers
    C. Parking and
       traffic
       problems
    D. Malls as
       example
    E. Appearance
       of community

III. Evidence
     supporting
     opponents'
     views
     A. Lower costs

     B. Convenience

     C. Time saved

     D. Quick and
        efficient
        service

huge discounts and the ultimate in "one-stop shopping," they are a threat not only to the survival of the entrepreneur and the independent retailer, but also to the quality of life in the United States.

Despite some arguable advantages, the phenomenon of hypermarkets raises some serious issues. Because of their size, their mass-market appeal, their unbeatable prices, and their capacity for absorbing a large share of the consumer pool, hypermarkets threaten the continuation of healthy competition in the marketplace, as well as the shopping diversity that consumers have come to expect. A competitive, entrepreneurial business spirit has always been encouraged and protected in the United States, and the result has been the growth of original and creative enterprises of varying scale — including everything from specialty bookstores to fashionable clothing boutiques to gourmet shops. Ultimately, hypermarkets endanger the future of these entrepreneurial enterprises, as well as small-store chains and independent retailers.

Hypermarkets also present problems for communities and the environment. These stores take up a great deal of land, covering as much as 200,000 square feet, or about five football fields. They attract as many as 50,000 shoppers per week and therefore require large parking areas. Placing a hypermarket in the midst of a community is likely to create traffic problems, general congestion, and noise. Existing malls clearly exhibit this problem already. Hypermarkets will also have an obvious impact on the appearance of a community; a building the size of five football fields is hard to make attractive and hard to maintain.

Developers of hypermarkets and many consumers, as well, will claim that these stores present distinct advantages for shoppers. The most important advantage put forth by hypermarket proponents is the huge savings available to consumers at these stores, which can offer discounts up to 40 percent below regular retail stores. Convenience, or "one-stop shopping," is another proclaimed advantage for consumers, who can find almost everything they need — groceries, clothing, appliances, household items — in one location. In relation to convenience, there is the claim that consumers will save a great deal of time by shopping at hypermarkets. Finally, quick and efficient service is also offered as an attraction. Generally equipped with more than fifty cashiers and staffs of at least six hundred people,

hypermarkets are capable of serving enormous numbers of customers.

Hypermarkets have an obvious appeal for consumers who consider cost the only priority in shopping. Many consumers, however, will agree that cost is not the only or the most important consideration in shopping, and that many of the "advantages" of hypermarkets can be disputed. One-stop shopping can increase the stresses of shopping because it increases expectations. People attempting to meet all of their shopping needs in one trip to one store need to be well organized. Also, once they are there, they need a great deal of stamina and patience to accomplish all of the shopping that they have planned.

Are hypermarkets, in fact, convenient? The answer depends on how people define convenience, and even on the kinds of things that they value in life. For some consumers, hypermarkets are too large for convenience or comfort, leaving shoppers tired, lost, or simply overwhelmed. In one sense, hypermarkets are actually inconvenient because of their size, since they are not easy to get into and out of on the spur of the moment. This is the value of the "convenience" store. Finally, the convenience and diversity that hypermarkets seem to offer exist already in large supermarkets and discount department store chains, as well as in shopping centers and malls, where shops are clustered in one convenient location.

Hypermarkets have attempted to alleviate some of the problems associated with their size. Strategically placed benches appear in many stores for the use of weary shoppers. To lessen confusion, some stores organize products into color-coordinated zones — green for groceries, for example — that make finding particular areas easier. Hypermarkets may also feature telephone hot lines that give assistance and information to customers.

Benches are a convenience, but sitting down for a few minutes' rest in the midst of a long shopping chore is not likely to be refreshing and only prolongs the time spent in the store. Furthermore, the fact that services such as color coding and telephone hot lines are needed at all demonstrates the strain and confusion involved in this kind of shopping.

IV. Rebuttal countering opponents' evidence

   A. Stresses of one-stop shopping

   B. Not really convenient

   C. Size causes problems

   D. Convenient alternatives exist

V. Other evidence supporting opponents' views

VI. Rebuttal

As you draft your argument, keep the following strategies in mind.

▶ Strategies

1. *Concentrate on one major point of your argument at a time.* Do not take up the next major point until you have discussed the pre-

ceding one completely. Support each point with at least three details. Use your outline as a guide for ordering your major points.

2. *Present supporting details in such a way that readers can grasp information clearly.* Use transitional expressions *(pages 36–38)* to specify connections between ideas.

3. *Provide frequent examples.* Examples illustrate the meaning of general statements and show that the opinions are based partly on specific cases or facts.

4. *Include language that emphasizes the reliability of your ideas.* Naturally, you should use expressions that stress the certainty of your ideas only if they are justified.

Assignment 3 Drafting an Argument

Use the following topic outline to draft two body paragraphs of an argument to follow the introduction that you drafted in Assignment 2 on page 248. Use the strategies for drafting an argument on this page and on page 250. Do research on the topic if you need further information.

Position statement: Since toll-free numbers are one of the most effective and least expensive ways to boost consumer satisfaction, businesses should include them in their customer-service programs.

I. Best way to satisfy consumers — provide quality products and excellent customer services
  A. 54 percent of customers try products and services again if complaints are resolved; 19 percent give brands or companies second chance if complaints not resolved
  B. Example — British Airways: lost money in 1982; extensive customer-service program (video complaint booths, full refunds, personal letters of apology) helped turn company around; result — airlines' 1988 net income topped other international carriers
  C. Effective customer-service programs boost brand loyalty
  D. Money invested in customer-service programs increases profits
II. Value of toll-free numbers
  A. Toll-free numbers
    1. Most widely used customer service
    2. Cost less to operate than other customer services
    3. Telephone representatives trained to handle complaints or inquiries; receive 4–5 weeks' training
    4. Give consumers free personal response and offer company chance to explain position or product
  B. Half of companies earning more than $10 million each year have toll-free numbers.
  C. Dissatisfied consumers who use toll-free numbers — 30 percent more likely to try product again than consumers who receive letter replies to complaints

Drafting Your Conclusion

It is important to leave readers with your most important thoughts on your topic as you conclude your essay. When you write your conclusion, therefore, you should restate your position, briefly summarize the major points of your argument, and link them to your position statement. Following is a possible concluding paragraph for the essay on pages 248–250.

Conclusion

Summary of
main points

Tie-in to
position statement

> The real value of hypermarkets depends on the values of the consumer. If cost is the first, and possibly only, priority, then hypermarkets have a proven value. However, if consumers are concerned with other aspects of shopping, such as personal service, a pleasant environment, and the ability to give full and thoughtful attention to one or two shopping tasks at a time, they may question the benefits of the hypermarket. Consumers should also be concerned about more long-term considerations such as variety in shopping alternatives, the survival of local neighborhood stores, and the unique benefits and pleasures to be reaped from businesses run by creative entrepreneurs. In conclusion, hypermarkets are a creation for a hyperactive society, as the term *hypermarket* itself reveals. Their economic benefits are gained at the expense of diversity and individuality and, ultimately, at the expense of a healthier, slower-paced lifestyle.

If it is appropriate, you can also recommend some action that is based on your position and that is justified by the reasons that you have given.

> Concerned citizens should strive to be aware of plans for the development of hypermarkets in or near their communities. By banding together, they can make their opposition to such developments clear to their local zoning boards.

Assignment 4   Drafting a Concluding Paragraph

Write a summary concluding paragraph of three to five sentences for the argument that you drafted in Assignment 3 on page 251. In your summary briefly refer to the major points of the argument, linking them to the position statement.

Continuing Assignment   Write Your First Draft

For writing
an **essay**

Use your notes and the outline that you constructed for the Continuing Assignment on page 246 to write your first draft. As you compose your introduction and position statement, your argument, and your conclusion, use the strategies suggested on pages 250–251. Save your notes and outline, as well as your draft.

Revising

Evaluating Your Content

**? Critical
Thinking:**

Evaluating

In the process of revising your essay, you have the chance to improve its language, content, and organization. You can, in fact, make any changes that you think necessary or desirable. The key to effective revision is to examine your draft from the point of view of your audience. A good way to do this is to read it aloud or to have someone else listen to it or read it aloud.

Concentrate first on content when you revise — that is, on your ideas and your evidence and how you present them. First, ask yourself these general questions about your introduction.

Checking Your Introduction

- Is the topic introduced near the start of the essay?
- Is an attempt made to arouse the reader's interest in the topic?
- Does the introduction include a clear and specific position statement that is adequately clarified?
- Does the introduction prepare readers for the argument that follows?

You should examine areas specific to persuasion in your review of your argument. Give attention to the quality of your evidence in particular. If you are to succeed in persuading, your readers must consider your evidence reliable. Contradictory statements and inaccurate information could undermine their confidence in you and make them question the care with which you've thought out your argument. Use these questions to check the soundness of your argument.

Checking Arguments for Accuracy and Consistency

- Have you maintained a single position throughout the argument?
- Have you defined terms clearly and used those definitions consistently?
- Do your examples agree with your definitions?
- If you have offered separate reasons for your position, are they consistent with one another (or does accepting one reason rule out accepting another)?
- Have you clearly distinguished between facts and opinions in your argument?
- Have you verified your facts, checking the accuracy of statistics and other information?
- Have you correctly quoted sources?
- Have you accurately presented opposing views and claims?

Checking for Genuine Evidence

In addition to making sure that you include consistent and accurate information in your argument, you need to examine the quality of your argument itself. First, verify that you have actually offered genuine evidence.

Some arguments appear to provide evidence when they actually do not. To serve as genuine evidence, supporting statements must differ in content from your position statement; in other words, they must offer new information. Failure to provide genuine evidence is known as **begging the question.** Begging, in this sense, means sidestepping or avoiding an issue by either repeating your position, distracting the reader with irrelevant material, or casually assuming the truth of what you are saying. There are several ways to "beg" a question.

1. *Repetition.* Merely repeating your position in different words does not establish the truth of your position. The supporting statements in the following paragraph, for example, simply repeat the position taken in the first sentence rather than offering evidence that supports that position.

> To compete with North American and Asian markets, members of the European Economic Community (EEC) should unify their trade practices. Currently, the twelve EEC nations have different trade practices. The twelve countries in the EEC operate separately. If EEC countries continue to trade individually, foreign markets will prevail.

Contrast the preceding repetitive argument with the following revised version, in which meaningful evidence is given.

> To compete with North American and Asian markets, members of the European Economic Community (EEC) should unify their trade practices. EEC nations now duplicate efforts in product research, development, manufacturing, advertising, and shipping. Each EEC nation operates independently, with different safety and technical regulations, customs procedures, price standards, brand names, and product labels. Trade consolidation among the twelve EEC nations would save time and money. By working together and forming a single, unified European marketplace, EEC countries would multiply their individual strength in the world marketplace and reap many benefits.

2. *Argument from character.* When you argue from character, you attempt to prove or disprove a position by describing the merits or the faults of the person holding the position. The only sound way to determine the truth of a position, however, is to examine the position itself.

> According to John Candotti, owner of Frolic Fashions, domestic plants will soon manufacture almost 50 percent of all apparel sold in the United States. Yet Mr. Candotti can hardly predict clothing-production trends. He wears unattractive and unfashionable clothing himself.

Revise your argument if you find that you have relied on character rather than evidence in making a point.

3. *Distraction or "red herring."* When you argue by distraction, you divert your readers' attention from one point by introducing another issue that has little or nothing to do with the first one. You present the two issues as though they are connected but, in fact, do not show a connection.

> Corporations should offer flextime — the option to begin and end work at varying times. The United States Labor Department predicts a shortage of workers under the age of thirty-five by the year 2000. It is essential for companies to attract new employees by providing generous health and retirement benefits.

The writer doesn't give a reason for favoring flextime and establishes no connection between that issue and those mentioned later. The latter issues cannot serve as evidence for the first.

4. *Arguing with words, or name calling.* When you argue with words, you support a position simply by describing the subject in favorable or unfavorable terms, but without justifying the description. Using highly positive or negative terms — or **loaded words** — is simply a form of begging the question.

> Irresponsible banks should not finance hostile takeovers planned by corporate raiders. This senseless practice allows greedy buy-out experts to borrow money and then to seize defenseless companies. Such unconscionable loans threaten our economy and free enterprise. Ethical bankers wouldn't encourage this kind of irresponsible activity.

(ŭn-kŏn′shə-nə-bəl)

This writer uses loaded words — *irresponsible, senseless,* and *unconscionable,* for instance — to describe banks' practice of lending money for corporate takeovers. While there may be valid criticisms of takeovers, readers are given no real basis — or evidence — on which to judge the accuracy of the writer's viewpoint.

Assignment 1 Identifying Genuine Evidence

On your own or with your classmates, evaluate each argument by writing either *Offers genuine evidence* or *Begs the question.* Then identify each argument that begs the question as *Repetition, Argument from character, Distraction,* or *Arguing with words.*

? **Critical Thinking:**

Evaluating
How reliable is
the evidence?

1. The national budget deficit, which is projected to reach $128 billion in a few years, should be reduced. Certainly, the federal government must stop spending more money than it earns. Congress needs to find a way to balance the budget so that the United States will have a surplus of money rather than a debt.

2. The government should ban the use of plastic-foam packaging by fast-food restaurants. Most fast-food businesses throw away or burn food containers, thus contributing to landfill shortages and to air pollution. These businesses must begin to practice recycling.

3. Executives often schedule breakfast meetings at restaurants and then demand pencils, pads, and mobile telephones. No business really takes place at these meetings. This is just another example of the way that executives throw their weight around.

4. United States consumers should limit spending and start saving more. When consumers don't save money, the national savings reserves decrease. Consequently, less money is available for new businesses and projects. The United States is thus forced to borrow money from foreign sources. Between 1984 and 1987, the foreign debt in the United States rose from zero to $400 billion.

5. Professional musicians should violently protest the pirating of popular tunes for radio and TV ads. This sleazy gimmick may catch public attention, but it is unfair for product manufacturers to cash in on classic songs. Talented artists must force money-hungry ad agencies to stop this musical highway robbery.

Assignment 2 **Revising Arguments**

Select one argument from Assignment 1 on page 255 and write the number on your paper. Then indicate the kind of revision that is needed to make it a sound argument. (The revision may include changing the position statement.)

Providing Sound Reasoning

Critical Thinking:

Analyzing for fallacies

To ensure that you reach sound conclusions in your persuasive argument, you must start with true or correct ideas in the first place. However, even if your supporting statements are true, an error in logic can easily lead to a false conclusion. Therefore, you must check your reasoning, as well as your information, when you review your argument. In particular, look for **fallacies** — methods of reasoning that violate the rules of logic. Explanations of some common fallacies follow.

1. *Hasty generalization.* A generalization based on too few experiences or facts is called a hasty generalization.

   All third-world countries have a serious debt crisis. Mexico and Brazil, among the world's top debtor nations, each owe billions of dollars to banks in the West.

   This generalization is hasty, since Mexico and Brazil obviously are not *all* third-world countries. If you find an unsound generalization in your argument, include more information to support it or revise your generalization.

2. *False causality.* False causality is the error of concluding that because one event occurs after another event, the earlier event must be the cause of the later one.

> Following passage of the Tax Reform Act of 1986, the unemployment rate steadily dropped from 7 percent in 1986 to 5.8 percent in 1988. Undoubtedly, this new, simplified code encouraged people to work.

No evidence is included to show the connection between the first event and the second. Other factors may have caused unemployment to drop. If you find this fallacy, revise to show precisely how the first event caused the second. If you are unable to do so, present the first event as a possible cause of the second.

3. *Unnecessary either / or.* Either / or reasoning works if there are only two possible answers to a question — if one of them is proven false, the other one must be true. The fallacy of unnecessary either / or occurs when a person applies either / or reasoning to a problem that has more than two solutions.

> Canada has recently increased exports of natural gas to the United States. Either Canadians suddenly have a natural gas surplus, or demand in the United States has recently risen sharply. The Department of Energy reports no unusual increase in consumption of natural gas. Obviously, Canada has unearthed new fuel sources.

The writer ignores the possibility of other causes for the increased export of natural gas to the United States. Since the two alternatives identified are not the *only* possible answers, eliminating one alternative does not establish that the other one is correct.

4. *Circular reasoning.* Circular reasoning consists of using two ideas to prove each other. If you argue that Idea A is true because Idea B is true, you cannot then turn around and say that Idea B is true because Idea A is true.

Idea A	TV advertising must be extremely effective; otherwise, com-
Idea B	panies would not spend more than twenty billion dollars
Idea B	each year on commercials. Companies obviously budget
	billions of dollars for TV ads each year because these com-
Idea A	mercials are so effective.

Neither Idea A nor Idea B can be proved if the truth of each depends on the other. To break this circle of reasoning, the writer must introduce a third idea (Idea C) to support Idea B. Idea C may be that, on average, companies spend twice as much money on TV ads as they do on magazine and radio ads. If you spot circular reasoning in your writing, determine what critical piece of evidence you have left out and add it to the argument.

5. *Hypothesis contrary to fact.* A **hypothesis** is a conditional statement. When you hypothesize, you temporarily assume the truth of an idea and then make a prediction or draw a conclusion based on that idea. Most hypothetical statements begin with expressions such as *If, Assuming that,* or *Supposing that.*

   A hypothesis contrary to fact contradicts or disagrees with a verifiable truth. The statement "If Orville and Wilbur Wright had not been keenly interested in flying machines . . ." is a hypothesis contrary to fact since it is verifiable that the Wright brothers did have such an interest. People often like to hypothesize about certain changes in history and then guess what the world would be like based on those changes. To draw a conclusion from a hypothesis known to be false, however, is a fallacy.

   If Orville and Wilbur Wright had not been keenly interested in flying machines, people today would not be traveling in airplanes.

   The preceding argument is illogical because it excludes the very real possibility that airplane travel might have developed even without the Wright brothers. Given this possibility, the conclusion of the argument ("people today would not be traveling in airplanes") is open to question.

   If your argument contains a hypothesis contrary to fact, make sure that any conclusion that you draw is presented only as a possible or a probable consequence ("*perhaps* people today would not be traveling in airplanes"), not as a certainty.

6. *False analogy.* Arguing by analogy is attempting to make a point about something by comparing it to a similar item. You make a false analogy if you compare two items in a way in which they are not truly similar. The writer of the following passage makes a false comparison.

Reference Point:
pages 239–240

   The Consumer Product Safety Commission has banned future sales of three-wheel all-terrain vehicles (ATVs) because they are unsafe. Since three-wheel ATVs are a cross between a motorcycle and a dune buggy, sales of the latter two should also be banned.

   The analogy is false because, although three-wheel ATVs are a cross between a motorcycle and a dune buggy, the three vehicles are distinctly different in their designs, their safety problems, and the level of regulation under which they can be operated. The dissimilar points of comparison make the argument faulty.

Assignment 3 Identifying Problems in Reasoning

On your paper, identify the error in reasoning involved in each statement by writing one of the following: *Hasty generalization, False causality, Unnecessary either / or, Circular reasoning, Hypothesis contrary to fact,* or *False analogy.*

1. If the homeless population had not increased, funds for shelters and "soup kitchens" would be used to expand other programs.

2. West Virginia and Maryland both earmark taxes for specific uses by their state governments. Beverage taxes in West Virginia help support its state medical schools. Therefore, Maryland should also institute a beverage tax.

3. Following the deregulation of the airlines, airports began using more sophisticated security systems. Deregulation, which resulted in lower fares and a greater number of passengers, undoubtedly provided the funds to develop new surveillance technology.

4. Book-size, portable videocassette players will soon be the new craze in electronic entertainment. Kreeger's Video King has more mini-videocassettes in stock than pocket-size TVs and personal stereos combined.

5. The number of workers between the ages of sixteen and twenty-four who are entering the job market has recently dropped. Either young people do not need money as much as they used to, or companies are not hiring inexperienced help. Since the United States Department of Labor reports that companies have raised hourly pay in order to attract young employees, it must be true that young people do not need money as much anymore.

6. Hotel guests must really like exercise facilities in hotels; otherwise, hotels would not provide complimentary sports equipment and clothing. Naturally, hotels provide free sports equipment and gear because guests use the workout rooms and equipment so much.

Assignment 4 Revising to Eliminate Fallacies

Select one argument from Assignment 3 on pages 258–259 and write the number on your paper. Then indicate the kind of revision that is needed to make it a sound argument. (The revision may include changing the position statement.)

Continuing Assignment Revise Your Writing for Content

Evaluate your first draft from the Continuing Assignment on page 252. Make notes on it to indicate needed content changes. Use first the chart on page 253 to check your introduction. Use second the chart on page 253 to check the consistency and accuracy of your content. Then focus on the quality of your argument. Does it offer genuine evidence? Is your reasoning sound and free of fallacies? If possible, have one or more other people read your composition and evaluate its content. Once you have completed your review, write a second draft of your paragraph or essay. Save your papers.

For writing an **essay**

Revising for Tone and Style

Critical Thinking:

Evaluating

In addition to examining the content of your essay, evaluate its tone and style to see if they are appropriate and effective. **Tone** is the attitude and feeling that your writing conveys to your audience. In persuasive writing, you want to establish a tone of thoughtfulness, fairness, and sincerity. Ask yourself these questions:

Reviewing the Tone of Your Essay

- *Is your point of view consistent?* Don't confuse your audience by changing from one point of view to another.
- *Is your argument fair?* Your argument may appear one-sided or biased unless you show your audience that you are aware of views opposed to your own. Be sure to represent others' views fairly and to address your rebuttal *(pages 244–245)* to real points in the opposing argument.
- *Do you express feelings appropriately?* While emotions often have an appropriate place in persuasive writing, do not use them as a substitute for reason. Avoid exaggerating your feelings, playing unfairly on readers' desires or fears, or making offensive or inflammatory remarks.
- *Are your opinions well considered and moderate?* If so, your audience will be more likely to accept them.

Style — the way that you use words and construct sentences to express your ideas — also plays an important part in persuasion. As you review the tone in your essay, pay attention to style as well.

In checking your style, be especially careful to select words that convey your thoughts exactly. Using precise language is important in persuasive writing since argument often involves making fine distinctions among ideas. You should also be sensitive to **connotation** — that is, the special meanings of words and the emotional responses that they evoke in readers.

Reference Point:
page 481

As you review the style of your essay, keep the preceding points in mind and answer these questions.

Reviewing the Style of Your Essay

- Do you use coordinating and subordinating conjunctions to provide proper emphasis and to show the relationships among ideas?
- Do you use transitional words *(pages 36–38)* to connect sentences and paragraphs, allowing ideas to flow logically and smoothly?
- Do your word choices reflect your meaning precisely?
- Do your sentences vary in length?

Assignment Revising for Tone and Style

Step 1: On your paper, write the headings *Tone* and *Style*, and number 1 through 4 under each heading. *Step 2:* Review the following persuasive paragraph and answer the four questions in each chart on page 260 by writing *Yes* or *No* after each number under the appropriate heading. (The questions apply to paragraphs as well as to essays.) For each *No*, briefly describe the revision that is needed. *Step 3:* On a separate piece of paper, revise the paragraph, making all the changes that you indicated.

? **Critical Thinking:**
Evaluating
Are transitions in the paragraph smooth?

Every business in the United States, from the largest corporation to the smallest neighborhood store, should provide flextime and job-sharing opportunities for its employees. Each business should provide maternity and paternity leave. It's the least that we can expect in this day and age when, as you know, most families need two incomes just to survive. Both of the parents are usually working forty-hour weeks. Each business should also be responsible for providing on-site day-care facilities. If businesses provided flextime and job-sharing options, as well as maternity and paternity leave, employees would save money on commuting and day-care expenses. They would save time. They would be happier and more productive on the job. Some people say that small businesses cannot afford to offer all these options, but I don't agree. I think that it is irresponsible for businesses to fail to respond to the needs of their employees. By responding to the needs of their employees, businesses ensure their own health and prosperity.

Continuing Assignment Revise for Tone and Style

Review your second draft from the Continuing Assignment on page 259, noting possible improvements in tone and style. Answer the questions in both charts on page 260. Then write a third draft. Compose a title for your essay if you have not already done so. Save all your papers.

For writing an **essay**

Proofreading

Proofreading Your Essay

When you have finished revising your draft and have made a clean copy of it, proofread it carefully to catch oversights or any new errors that you may have accidentally introduced. Check your essay for correct spelling, grammar, usage, punctuation, and capitalization. Also make sure that your writing is free of sentence fragments and run-on sentences.

As you proofread your persuasive essay, give special attention to these points.

Reference Point:
page 538 and
pages 600–602

Indefinite Pronouns Be sure that indefinite pronouns are used correctly as antecedents in your writing and that their use is consistent with the point of view that you have chosen.

```
One may be able to invest money in an individual
                                   he or she has
retirement account even if you have a pension plan at
work.
```

In the preceding example, a third-person pronoun, not *you,* must be used to refer to the indefinite pronoun *one.* Also, *you* and *one* reflect different points of view and cannot be used interchangeably.

Run-on Sentences Eliminate any run-on sentences in your writing by breaking them into two separate sentences or by rewriting the run-on sentence.

```
Laptop computers weigh less than twenty pounds,
executives can easily transport them.
```

Assignment **Proofreading a Paragraph**

Proofread the following paragraph. Rewrite it on your paper, correcting any errors that you find, including incorrect pronoun usage, run-on sentences, and errors in spelling and punctuation.

Is the office obsolete. Portable electronics — laptop computers, mobile phones, telephone-answering systems, and facsimile machines — have radically alterred the traditional workplace. One can send their documents in minutes and give and receive messages with portable electronics, offices can be located any where in the World, whether employee's work in Hawaii, Hartford, or helsinki. Portable electronics enable him to receive and convey important information. Moreover, portable electronics eliminate time and distance limitations you may work on business trips, on commuter trains and busses or in home offices. Electrical and steam power gave rise to the factory during the Industrial revolution, portable electronics will probably give rise to the mobile, transportable office.

Continuing Assignment **Proofread Your Persuasive Essay**

For writing
an **essay**

Proofread your third draft from the Continuing Assignment on page 261. Then make a clean copy of your essay, correcting faulty mechanics, spelling, grammar, and usage. Proofread this final copy and save your paper.

Publishing

Publishing Persuasive Writing

When you have completed your essay, you may wish to share your view with an audience other than your teacher and your classmates, especially since your goal has been to persuade. Here are some suggestions for publishing your composition.

- Send your essay to a magazine that deals with subjects related to your topic and whose readers may or may not share your view.
- Submit your essay to the editor of your local newspaper for publication in the letters-to-the-editor section.
- Submit your essay to your school newspaper or magazine for publication.
- If the topic of your essay is appropriate, send a copy of it to your local chamber of commerce or a local civic or citizens' group.

Continuing Assignment **Publish Your Persuasive Essay**

For writing
an **essay**

Choose an audience that you think will be interested in the composition that you completed in the preceding Continuing Assignment. Give or send a copy of your composition to the readers that you have chosen, explaining briefly why you wish them to read it and requesting a response, if appropriate. Save your essay and any helpful response in your writer's portfolio.

Student to Student

Reading and Responding to Writing

Is there anything about the modern world that you'd like to change? In the following persuasive essay, Paul Sasaura, a student at Hayward High School in Hayward, California, expresses his views about a change that he'd like to see. As you read Paul's essay, consider possible answers to the questions in the margin. Then do the activities in *Responding to Writing* and *Reading Critically*.

The Snooze Syndrome

Picture this: It's a cold and dreary Monday morning. You are still recuperating from the previous night's madcap party, but you know you must get up and out of bed, for life does go on. True, life can go on without you, but this is no excuse; school still beckons you. After every endeavor to open your eyes proves futile, something terrifying happens. In a last ditch attempt to get up, you fool yourself into believing that you will get up as soon as your alarm clock starts buzzing one more time. Consequently, almost by instinct, your hand reaches for the dreadful, evil snooze button. Being late to school because of thirty consecutive snooze button delays is my greatest fear.

The habit of abusing the snooze button, commonly called the snooze syndrome, can be rather detrimental to one's life. I don't know who invented the snooze button, but it obviously was not someone with brains. Just imagine what the inventor said when he proposed this ill-conceived idea. "Mr. Alarm Clock Maker, I've got this great idea. Let's make a button that people can push in order to wake up later than the time they originally wanted to wake up at." Sheer brilliance. How little this person knew of human nature is vastly apparent. After hitting the snooze button thirty times, one is not only late for school, but is late for dinner as well. It is my

What techniques does Paul use to introduce and make his topic interesting? Who is Paul's audience?

How would you characterize the tone and the style of Paul's essay?

strong opinion that the snooze button be destroyed before more fall to the perils of the notorious snooze syndrome.

As a victim of the snooze syndrome, I must now set my alarm clock hours before I intend to get up. Such are the consequences of the snooze button. Someday, it may get to the point where I have to set my alarm a day earlier and snooze for twenty-four hours in ten-minute intervals. How appalling! Someone has to put an end to snooze button production immediately. The active lives of millions of people are at stake.

What kind of relationship does Paul establish with his audience?

Responding to Writing   Do you like the tone and the style of Paul's essay? Do you take his position seriously? Why? Have you ever felt the kind of frustration that he describes about something else? Write your own persuasive essay about a device or a recent invention that you would like to see abolished. Think about using techniques that will make your essay amusing and convincing at the same time.

Reading Critically   In a discussion or in a written analysis, respond to these questions: How does Paul's essay differ from what you expect in a persuasive essay? What line of reasoning does he present in his argument? Is it logical? Is it meant to be logical? Explain. What kind of evidence could be included in a different treatment of this topic?

The Literature Connection

By now you know that much of what passes for persuasion — including advertising, political debates and commentaries, and editorials — is full of logical holes. You have analyzed arguments, including your own, for such weaknesses as red herrings, loaded words, and hasty generalizations. You have also studied how deductive and inductive reasoning can help you to build *valid* arguments, and you have seen how tone and style can turn bland arguments into colorful ones. Your new level of awareness will help you to produce authentic persuasive writing and to resist misleading arguments wherever you meet them.

Guided Reading Talk of the economy is becoming as common as talk of the weather. Even strangers will debate about what should be done to reduce the deficit or unemployment. In the selection shown here, Art Buchwald, a syndicated columnist, records a humorous exchange with a taxi driver named Rico on whether members of Congress should get a pay raise. Read the column and answer the questions at the right, focusing on Rico's argument. What reasons does he give for being against an across-the-board raise? Under what conditions would he give a raise and why? Does he have a "hidden agenda"? Are there any logical fallacies lurking in the dialogue?

Good Work, Good Pay

*T*here has to be a solution to the congressional pay gridlock. Congressmen and senators need more money and the taxpayer is adamant about not giving it to them.

Is there any truth to this claim?

There are some people who are against the raise because they think it's too much. Then there are others who are against it because this is the first time in their lives that they have been in a position to turn down *anyone* for a pay increase. Consequently, they want to make the most of the opportunity.

My taxi driver is one of them. "I say no raise," he declared, as we started out for the office. "They get too much money anyway, and they don't do a thing for it."

What logical fallacy do you detect here?

"That's a harsh judgment, Rico. Many legislators work day and night, and then have to travel long distances on weekends in order to give the American people the best laws that money can buy. Would you prefer that they be paid the same wages as the workers at McDonald's?"

"They tried to sneak the raise in behind our backs because they were too chicken to vote on it up and down. If Congress had come to me and said, 'Rico, we need this to educate our children and feed our families,' I might have given them the increase."

"That's very good of you, Rico. How many raises have you handed out in your life?"

"That doesn't matter. I'm a good judge of character, and I know when someone should have a pay increase and when he shouldn't. I read the papers like everybody else. Besides, I never thought an across-the-board raise was a good idea. I'd like to see the lawmakers paid on a piecework basis. Members of Congress would be rewarded according to their level of production. If a legislator shows up every day on the Hill, he is given a standard fee. If he introduces a bill in Congress, he gets an extra amount for it, and if the bill is passed, he receives a bonus."

"Would you give them anything for attending a PAC breakfast to raise money for their election campaigns?"

"No, they would be on their own for all fundraisers. At the same time I might offer them a fee for going to a prayer breakfast."

"How much should they get for waging a filibuster?"

"In that situation we would be very generous because it puts a lot of wear and tear on the body. I'd also pay piecemeal for those who give speeches on the floor of the Senate, but I would like to see a system

Does Rico's plan make good economic sense?

whereby the person making the shortest speech gets the most money."

"Would I be correct if I presumed that each time a representative voted, he'd get a stipend?"

"Yes. I'd have the sergeant at arms sit at a table and pay everyone in cash as they came down the aisle."

"Rico, I think you're on to something. No one has ever thought of compensating lawmakers for what they actually did — not even Trotsky."

"It's the only way Congress is going to get a raise from me."

"You're a good man and a fair man, but suppose they don't accept your plan?"

"They have no choice. I don't think anyone has been fairer than I have to the people on Capitol Hill. But I can't justify throwing money away on large pay raises when there are so many potholes in this country still waiting to be filled."

Why does Buchwald give Rico the last word?

Art Buchwald *(1925–   )*

Enrichment Connections

Choose one or more of these activities to do on your own or as a group.

Creative Writing

A Short Story   Imagine a country without money, banks, Wall Street, the IRS, credit cards, bills — in short, a utopia. Write a short story about this economic experiment including a description of how people get what they need and how they are paid for their labor (if they work). Through your tone and style and your use of metaphor, irony, or satire, try subtly to persuade your readers that life under your imagined conditions would or wouldn't be an improvement over actual conditions.

Speaking and Listening

An Economic Summit   What will the business and economic world look like in the twenty-first century? You are going to role-play a group of leaders (local, national, or international) to find out. To prepare, your class will need to decide on two or three major issues (such as women in the work place or the "graying" of the work force), designate the summit participants and establish their positions, and conduct the necessary research. In addition to using the library, consider interviewing local businesspeople and government officials. Try to make the summit as authentic as possible, including having some students role-play the news media.

A Mock Trial   Some of the most profound social issues are settled through persuasion in courtrooms. As a class, conduct a mock trial around some issue of common concern. You will need two teams — the prosecution and the defense — a judge, and a jury. Focus your efforts on each team's closing statement, which should be able to stand alone as a persuasive essay. The jury should deliberate not only about *what* each team says but also about *how* it says it.

Detecting Logical Fallacies

Advertising attempts to persuade people that one product or service is superior to others. Are the "arguments" sound, however? Review pages 256–258 and then analyze several advertisements or commercials to discover what strategies advertisers use to *appear* logical and how these strategies fail or succeed. Present your findings, summarized in graphic handouts if possible, to your English class and, if appropriate, to your civics or history class.

Discussing Business

Read over the pros and cons to the free market system that you listed for *Responding to Literature* on page 229 and do some research on the subject. You might start by reading the entry for "Capitalism" in a good encyclopedia. Then write a short dialogue between two or more people who are discussing the pros and cons of this system. Be sure to give both sides credible arguments. Your tone can be serious and academic or light and satirical. Art Buchwald's column is an example of how to lighten a debate on a weighty issue. Like him, you might give your debaters an interesting setting or context.

CELEBRATING DIVERSITY

What's your business forecast for the future? Will the workplace look the same as it does now? Will the work force look the same? What part will *you* play in the economy at the turn of the century?

Here's one educated guess about the work force of the future in the United States. The authors of the selection that follows argue that it will be anything but "business as usual" when we reach the year 2000. As you read, try to determine what the authors mean by "managing diversity" and how they suggest that businesses go about it. Then work on at least one of the activities that follow the selection. Working on these activities may help you to value the differences among people even more and to understand the world of work that you will be entering.

WORKFORCE 2000

IS TODAY

Managing Diversity. Valuing Differences. Valuing Diversity. Whatever the name of the initiative may be, corporate America is slowly waking up to the fact that the changing employee demographics outlined in the landmark Hudson Institute report "Workforce 2000: Work and Workers For the 21st Century," is already a reality. The ground-breaking 1987 report forecasted widespread shortages of skilled labor and pointed out that between 1985 and the year 2000, 85% of the entrants into the work force will be women, minorities and immigrants. The report also said that older workers and disabled employees will require more of their employer's attention.

Despite the fact that this report was issued three years ago, a recent survey of 645 organizations conducted by the management consulting firm Towers Perrin and the Hudson Institute, a policy research firm, revealed that although nearly three out of four companies noted some level of management concern over the added complexities of managing a culturally diverse work force, only 42% have minority recruiting programs in place. Even more disheartening is the fact that the survey, titled "Workforce 2000 Competing in a Seller's Market: Is Corporate America Prepared?" reports that although 57% of the respondents claim that diversity issues affect management decisions and corporate strategy, only 29% actually train managers to value diversity.

The report signals that the American business community is making feeble attempts to synthesize an increasingly diverse work force. It's obvious that if top management does not firmly believe that: 1. diversity is a business issue that affects the company's ability to effectively compete, and 2. comprehensive training programs are necessary to make this happen, then the diversity issue will disappear like many of the cultural awareness programs of two decades ago. . . .

AFFIRMING DIVERSITY

Sheryl Hilliard Tucker & Kevin D. Thompson
from
"Will Diversity = Opportunity and Advancement for Blacks?"
in
Black Enterprise, November 1990

It's no longer good enough, say leading authorities on diversity such as R. Roosevelt Thomas, director of the Atlanta-based American Institute For Managing Diversity Inc. at Morehouse College, for companies to wear their affirmative action and equal employment opportunity statistics as badges of commitment to minorities and women. For the past 30 years, companies have tried to enforce affirmative action and EEO[1] policies designed to institutionalize the recruitment, retention and promotion of minorities and women. For some, affirmative action initiatives were developed as a matter of common decency; others proclaimed that EEO made good business sense; but for many, compliance requirements for lucrative government contracts was the overriding impetus.

Regardless of what initiated a company's EEO efforts, even affirmative action's staunchest critics can't deny its success in bringing substantial numbers of black professionals into corporate America since 1970. However, statistics aren't so encouraging when looking at the movement of blacks up the corporate ladder. African-Americans comprise 10.1% of the nation's 112.4 million employed civilians; 6.2% of its nearly 28 million managers and professionals and 8.5% of its 3.3 million technical and related support staff.

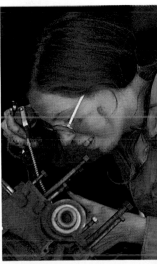

In his breakthrough article "From Affirmative Action to Affirming Diversity," which appeared in the March-April 1990 issue of the *Harvard Business Review,* Roosevelt Thomas took a less confrontational approach: "Affirmative action gets the new fuel into the tank, the new people through the front door. Something else will have to get them into the driver's seat. That something else consists of enabling people, in this case minorities and women, to perform to their potential. This is what we now call diversity. Not appreciating or leveraging diversity, not even necessarily understanding it. Just managing diversity in such a way as to get from a heterogeneous work force, the same productivity, commitment, quality, and profit that we got from the old homogeneous work force." The new litmus test of the progressive organizations of the '90s is reflected by not only how well companies recruit and attract minorities and women, but whether or not the company's corporate culture truly respects and promotes people who differ from the majority of managers and executives throughout corporate America.

Taking Another Look

According to the Hudson Institute report, how is the work force changing? How have United States corporations responded to these changes thus far? Why did companies develop affirmative action initiatives in the past? Why will such initiatives be advantageous in the future? What success have African Americans had in "climbing the corporate ladder"? What does R. Roosevelt Thomas mean by "managing diversity"? Do companies need to understand or appreciate diversity in order to manage it? What might companies gain by a campaign to manage cultural diversity?

1. EEO equal employment opportunity

Changing Places

If you were a typical manager—a white male—how would you deal with the changing face of the work force? How would you help men and women with widely different backgrounds, values, and interests to work together? How could you make cultural diversity work *for* your company? What advantages could having a diverse work force give you in the global marketplace? How might developing the potential of people different from you affect you personally? What might be your fears? Your hopes? What might happen if you decided to resist the challenge or to take a laissez faire attitude?

WRITING

Beyond the Melting Pot The selection suggests that by the year 2000 the work force will be far more heterogeneous than ever before. If this is so, then the society that produces the work force will also be more diverse. What has happened to the idea of "the melting pot"? Should the United States encourage cultural homogeneity? Is the United States on its way to becoming a "nation of little nations"? Think about these questions, and then write a persuasive essay, a story, or a poem that takes a position on the question of the nation's growing diversity. Focus on whether you favor strengthening or weakening the effects of cultural diversity, not on whether the nation is, in fact, becoming more diverse. If you write a story or a poem, you might want to imagine that you are a recent immigrant who plans to live and work in the United States from now on and then write from that perspective.

CRITICAL THINKING

Numbers Don't Lie Study the chart of information that has been taken from another part of the article in *Black Enterprise*. Then analyze and interpret the data in order to answer the questions that follow. In what area have all companies with diversity programs (A and B) made the most progress? In what area is the difference between the efforts of "A" companies and "B" companies the greatest? The smallest? What do you think accounts for the great disparity in the percentages in column 1 and column 5? Overall, what type of company has responded better to the issue of diversity in the workplace?

Company Response to Cultural Diversity in the Workplace					
	1	2	3	4	5
	Recruit Minorities Explicitly	Train Managers to Value Diversity	Train Minorities for Supervisory Positions	Provide Minority Support Groups	Provide Immigration Assistance
A. Companies with Diversity Programs	42%	29%	ca. 12%	ca. 12%	ca. 11%
B. Companies with Management Involvement in Diversity Programs	60%	ca. 37%	ca. 14%	ca. 16%	ca. 9%

LANGUAGE

The Care and Feeding of People   The English word *culture* has a variety of meanings. Its most basic meaning, though, may be the one people are least familiar with. Look up *culture* and read all of the definitions. Pay particular attention to its root meaning. How does learning or being reminded of the origin of the word change your perception of the culture (or cultures) you live in? Does the root suggest that a culture is a fixed, inherited thing or that it is organic and changing? What are the implications for managing diversity? Jot down the definition for future reference, and keep your answers to the above questions.

WRITING

Manager for a Day   Imagine that you are the editor-in-chief of your school newspaper. Your staff of student reporters includes boys and girls of various cultural and ethnic backgrounds, not all of whom speak and write English as well as others. The faculty advisor to the newspaper wants your input on how to make the experience of working on the paper a positive one for all while maintaining high journalistic standards. What can you do to insure staff equality in terms of story assignments, story placement and space, and workload? How can you promote the development of your reporters who have more trouble with English? What can you do with the paper that will allow not only your staff but the entire school to benefit from the staff's cultural diversity? Write a memo to the advisor detailing your thoughts on these questions.

DID YOU KNOW?   In the past decade, African-American-owned businesses in the United States grew in number and made record profits, and this trend is expected to continue into the twenty-first century. The top one hundred businesses had revenues of nearly $7 billion in 1989. This figure represents a 10.2 percent increase over the previous year and compares very favorably with the 7.6 percent growth rate of Fortune 500 companies for the same period.

UNIT 5

Writing Stories, Plays, and Poems

Have you ever watched a child playing alone and talking and gesturing animatedly? Such a child seems to be completely absorbed in an imaginary world. Perhaps you can remember going to far-off places with exotic make-believe friends to face some exciting adventure during the fantasies of your own childhood. Your imagination is a valuable resource. Even as you get older, you use your imagination to envision people, places, and encounters. Your imagination uses your creative energy and lets you contemplate, even stretch, all the possibilities that life offers.

Your imagination will be vital when you are writing stories, plays, and poems. Your power to create believable characters, scenery, and action will depend upon your ability to let your mind run wildly over the endless images in your head and pluck out the most effective ones to express your ideas.

You can find material for writing within you or all around you. Stories about relatives (their belongings, habits, traditions, decisions) pass through generations and come to represent the spirit of a family. It is often interesting to think about your *roots*—the people and the events that make up your past—and to consider what parts of them have become a part of you. As you read the story shown here, note what the main character realizes about himself and about his future when he takes a long, close look at his father.

Shaving

*E*arlier, when Barry had left the house to go to the game, an overnight frost had still been thick on the roads, but the brisk April sun had soon dispersed it, and now he could feel the spring warmth on his back through the thick tweed of his coat. His left arm was beginning to stiffen up where he'd jarred it in a tackle, but it was nothing serious. He flexed his shoulders against the tightness of his jacket and was surprised again by the unexpected weight of his muscles, the thickening strength of his body. A few years back, he thought, he had been a small, unimportant boy, one of a swarming gang laughing and jostling to school, hardly aware that he possessed an identity. But time had transformed him. He walked solidly now, and often alone. He was tall, strongly made, his hands and feet were adult and heavy, the rooms in which all his life he'd moved had grown too small for him. Sometimes a devouring restlessness drove him from the house to walk long distances in the dark. He hardly understood how it had happened. Amused and quiet, he walked the High Street among the morning shoppers.

He saw Jackie Bevan across the road and remembered how, when they were both six years old, Jackie had swallowed a pin. The flustered teachers had clucked about Jackie as he stood there, bawling, cheeks awash with tears, his nose wet. But now Jackie was tall and suave, his thick, pale hair sleekly tailored, his gray suit enviable. He was talking to a girl as golden as a daffodil.

"Hey, hey!" called Jackie. "How's the athlete, how's Barry boy?"

He waved a graceful hand at Barry.

"Come and talk to Sue," he said.

Barry shifted his bag to his left hand and walked over, forming in his mind the answers he'd make to Jackie's questions.

"Did we win?" Jackie asked. "Was the old Barry

As if he can feel himself growing.

He sees change in others too.

271

Wow!
Bleak!

Stanford magic in glittering evidence yet once more this morning? Were the invaders sent hunched and silent back to their hovels in the hills? What was the score? Give us an epic account, Barry, without modesty or delay. This is Sue, by the way."

"I've seen you about," the girl said.

"You could hardly miss him," said Jackie. "Four men, roped together, spent a week climbing him—they thought he was Everest. He ought to carry a warning beacon, he's a danger to aircraft."

"Silly," said the girl, smiling at Jackie. "He's not much taller than you are."

She had a nice voice too.

"We won," Barry said. "Seventeen points to three, and it was a good game. The ground was hard, though."

He could think of nothing else to say.

"Let's all go for a frivolous cup of coffee," Jackie said. "Let's celebrate your safe return from the rough fields of victory. We could pour libations all over the floor for you."

"I don't think so," Barry said. "Thanks. I'll go straight home."

"Okay," said Jackie, rocking on his heels so that the sun could shine on his smile. "How's your father?"

"No better," Barry said. "He's not going to get better."

"Yes, well," said Jackie, serious and uncomfortable, "tell him my mother and father ask about him."

"I will," Barry promised. "He'll be pleased."

Barry dropped the bag in the front hall and moved into the room which had been the dining room until his father's illness. His father lay in the white bed, his long body gaunt, his still head scarcely denting the pillow. He seemed asleep, thin blue lids covering his eyes, but when Barry turned away he spoke.

"Hullo, son," he said. "Did you win?"

His voice was a dry, light rustling, hardly louder than the breath which carried it. Its sound moved Barry to a compassion that almost unmanned him, but he stepped close to the bed and looked down at the dying man.

"Yes," he said. "We won fairly easily. It was a good game."

His father lay with his eyes closed, inert, his breath irregular and shallow.

"Did you score?" he asked.

"Twice," Barry said. "I had a try in each half."

He thought of the easy certainty with which he'd caught the ball before his second try; casually, almost arrogantly he had taken it on the tips of his fingers, on his full burst for the line, breaking the fullback's tackle. Nobody could have stopped him. But watching his father's weakness he felt humble and ashamed, as if the morning game, its urgency and effort, was not worth talking about. His father's face, fine-skinned and pallid, carried a dark stubble of beard, almost a week's growth, and his obstinate, strong hair stuck out over his brow.

"Good," said his father, after a long pause. "I'm glad it was a good game."

Barry's mother bustled about the kitchen, a tempest of orderly energy.

"Your father's not well," she said. "He's down today, feels depressed. He's a particular man, your father. He feels dirty with all that beard on him."

She slammed shut the stove door.

"Mr. Cleaver was supposed to come up and shave him," she said, "and that was three days ago. Little things have always worried your father, every detail must be perfect for him."

Barry filled a glass with milk from the refrigerator. He was very thirsty.

"I'll shave him," he said.

His mother stopped, her head on one side.

"Do you think you can?" she asked. "He'd like it if you can."

"I can do it," Barry said.

He washed his hands as carefully as a surgeon. His father's razor was in a blue leather case, hinged at the broad edge and with one hinge broken. Barry unfastened the clasp and took out the razor. It had not been properly cleaned after its last use and lather had stiffened into hard yellow rectangles between the teeth

Compares himself to his father.

of the guard. There were watershaped rust stains, brown as chocolate, on the surface of the blade. Barry removed it, throwing it in the wastebin. He washed the razor until it glistened, and dried it on a soft towel, polishing the thin handle, rubbing its metal head to a glittering shine. He took a new blade from its waxed envelope, the paper clinging to the thin metal. The blade was smooth and flexible to the touch, the little angles of its cutting clearly defined. Barry slotted it into the grip of the razor, making it snug and tight in the head.

The shaving soap, hard, white, richly aromatic, was kept in a wooden bowl. Its scent was immediately evocative and Barry could almost see his father in the days of his health, standing before his mirror, thick white lather on his face and neck. As a little boy Barry had loved the generous perfume of the soap, had waited for his father to lift the razor to his face, for one careful stroke to take away the white suds in a clean revelation of the skin. Then his father would renew the lather with a few sweeps of his brush, one with an ivory handle and the bristles worn, which he still used.

His father's shaving mug was a thick cup, plain and serviceable. A gold line ran outside the rim of the cup, another inside, just below the lip. Its handle was large and sturdy, and the face of the mug carried a portrait of the young Queen Elizabeth II, circled by a wreath of leaves, oak perhaps, or laurel. A lion and unicorn balanced precariously on a scroll above her crowned head, and the Union Jack, the Royal Standard, and other flags were furled each side of the portrait. And beneath it all, in small black letters, ran the legend: "Coronation June 2nd 1953." The cup was much older than Barry. A pattern of faint translucent cracks, fine as a web, had worked itself haphazardly, invisibly almost, through the white glaze. Inside, on the bottom, a few dark bristles were lying, loose and dry. Barry shook them out, then held the cup in his hand, feeling its solidness. Then he washed it ferociously, until it was clinically clean.

Methodically he set everything on a tray, razor, soap, brush, towels. Testing the hot water with a finger, he filled the mug and put that, too, on the tray. His care was absorbed, ritualistic. Satisfied that his preparations were complete, he went downstairs, carrying the tray with one hand.

His father was waiting for him. Barry set the tray on a bedside table and bent over his father, sliding an arm under the man's thin shoulders, lifting him without effort so that he sat against the high pillows.

"You're strong. . . ." his father said. He was as breathless as if he'd been running.

"So are you," said Barry.

"I was," his father said. "I used to be strong once."

He sat exhausted against the pillows.

"We'll wait a bit," Barry said.

"You could have used your electric razor," his father said. "I expected that."

"You wouldn't like it," Barry said. "You'll get a closer shave this way."

He placed the large towel about his father's shoulders.

"Now," he said, smiling down.

The water was hot in the thick cup. Barry wet the brush and worked up the lather. Gently he built up a covering of soft foam on the man's chin, on his cheeks and his stark cheekbones.

"You're using a lot of soap," his father said.

"Not too much," Barry said. "You've got a lot of beard."

His father lay there quietly, his wasted arms at his sides.

"It's comforting," he said. "You'd be surprised how comforting it is."

Barry took up the razor, weighing it in his hand, rehearsing the angle at which he'd use it. He felt confident.

"If you have prayers to say . . ." he said.

"I've said a lot of prayers," his father answered.

Barry leaned over and placed the razor delicately against his father's face, setting the head accurately on the clean line near the ear where the long hair ended. He held the razor in the tips of his fingers and drew the

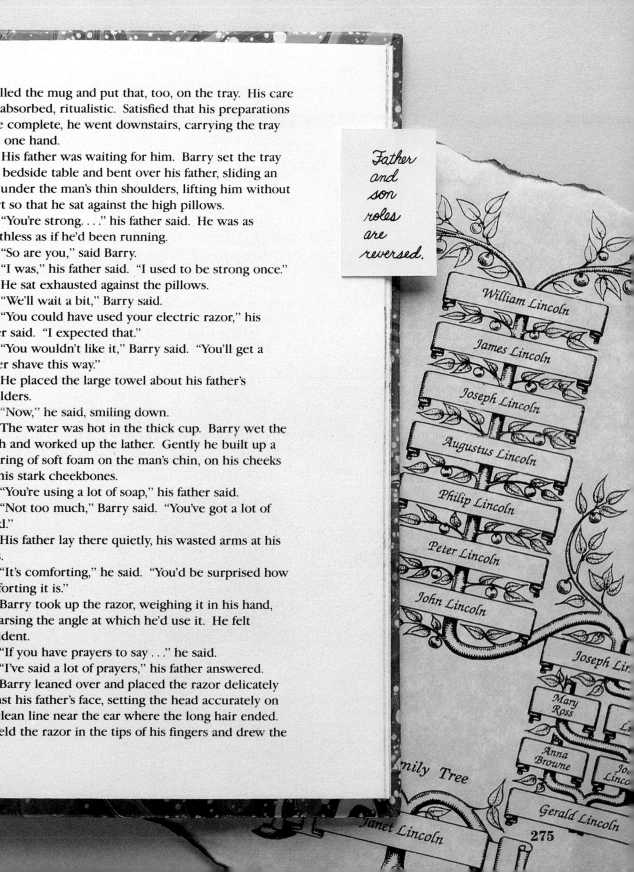

Father and son roles are reversed.

William Lincoln

James Lincoln

Joseph Lincoln

Augustus Lincoln

Philip Lincoln

Peter Lincoln

John Lincoln

Joseph Lir.

Mary Ross

Anna Browne

Jo Lince

..mily Tree

Gerald Lincoln

Janet Lincoln

275

He is so close, so careful.

Why "bigger"?

blade sweetly through the lather. The new edge moved light as a touch over the hardness of the upper jaw and down to the angle of the chin, sliding away the bristles so easily that Barry could not feel their release. He sighed as he shook the razor in the hot water, washing away the soap.

"How's it going?" his father asked.

"No problem," Barry said. "You needn't worry."

It was as if he had never known what his father really looked like. He was discovering under his hands the clear bones of the face and head, they became sharp and recognizable under his fingers. When he moved his father's face a gentle inch to one side, he touched with his fingers the frail temples, the blue veins of his father's life. With infinite and meticulous care he took away the hair from his father's face.

"Now for your neck," he said. "We might as well do the job properly."

"You've got good hands," his father said. "You can trust those hands, they won't let you down."

Barry cradled his father's head in the crook of his left arm, so that the man could tilt back his head, exposing the throat. He brushed fresh lather under the chin and into the hollows alongside the stretched tendons. His father's throat was fleshless and vulnerable, his head was a hard weight on the boy's arm. Barry was filled with unreasoning protective love. He lifted the razor and began to shave.

"You don't have to worry," he said. "Not at all. Not about anything."

He held his father in the bend of his strong arm and they looked at each other. Their heads were very close.

"How old are you?" his father said.

"Seventeen," Barry said. "Near enough seventeen."

"You're young," his father said, "to have this happen."

"Not too young," Barry said. "I'm bigger than most men."

"I think you are," his father said.

He leaned his head tiredly against the boy's

shoulder. He was without strength, his face was cold and smooth. He had let go all his authority, handed it over. He lay back on his pillow, knowing his weakness and his mortality, and looked at his son with wonder, with a curious humble pride.

"I won't worry then," he said. "About anything."

"There's no need," Barry said. "Why should you worry?"

He wiped his father's face clean of all soap with a damp towel. The smell of illness was everywhere, overpowering even the perfumed lather. Barry settled his father down and took away the shaving tools, putting them by with the same ceremonial precision with which he'd prepared them: the cleaned and glittering razor in its broken case; the soap, its bowl wiped and dried, on the shelf between the brush and the coronation mug; all free of taint. He washed his hands and scrubbed his nails. His hands were firm and broad, pink after their scrubbing. The fingers were short and strong, the little fingers slightly crooked, and soft dark hair grew on the backs of his hands and his fingers just above the knuckles. Not long ago they had been small bare hands, not very long ago.

Barry opened wide the bathroom window. Already, although it was not yet two o'clock, the sun was retreating and people were moving briskly, wrapped in their heavy coats against the cold that was to come. But now the window was full in the beam of the dying sunlight, and Barry stood there, illuminated in its golden warmth for a whole minute, knowing it would soon be gone.

Leslie Norris (1921–   )

Like his father.

Responding to Literature

In "Shaving" Barry experiences a personal, memorable moment in time. During the shaving, what happens between Barry and his father? Freewrite in your writer's notebook on the exchange that takes place during the shaving. Go back and reread the story and note any clues in the dialogue. Although Barry and his father seem to say very little to each other, their words are loaded with double meanings. As you freewrite, record quotations from the story that influenced your understanding. Save these quotations in your writer's notebook.

Writing a Short Story

Somerset Maugham notes of his own story writing, "I have taken living people and put them into the situation, tragic or comic, that their characters suggested. I might say that they invented their own stories." This sounds simple enough, but no doubt you will find that writing a short story demands all of your imaginative powers.

Your short story can create an experience so vivid that your readers will laugh, shudder, or even cry. This story will be your own unique creation, shaped partly by your background and experiences, but for the most part an invention of your imagination. Although they are as varied as other art forms, all short stories share certain elements.

Characters are people whose lives and conflicts form the action. The **plot** is the series of actions in your story and the sequence or order of these actions. The time and place of a story comprise its **setting,** an element that often includes atmosphere. The point of view that you choose for the narrator determines how you present the story.

Like all short stories, "Shaving" *(pages 271–277)* has **conflict.** Conflict is the characters' struggle to confront a problem, find a solution, and come to terms with the resulting changes in their lives. In "Shaving," Barry courageously faces his father's terminal illness and the changes in his own and his mother's lives. As you know, the significance or meaning of the story is its **theme.** In most stories the theme and the outcome of the conflict are closely related.

Prewriting

Getting an Idea for a Story

By drawing on your experience and using your imagination, you can find an idea for your story. The seed of the story may lie in something that has actually happened to you. By asking "what if," you can create several outcomes for an event and decide which one would make the most effective short story.

Ingredients of a Story

Where do stories begin? Some stories begin in the author's mind as a setting with a certain atmosphere. Many stories, notably mystery stories, begin with a plot. Perhaps your story will begin with a character who has a problem to solve. You may have a theme that you want to treat in your story. Any one of these elements or ingredients may lead you to the others. As you begin to relate characters to settings and conflicts, you will begin to imagine the plot of a story.

? Critical Thinking:
Determining relationships

Setting The setting for your story may be important for atmosphere, or it may be necessary for other reasons, such as appropriateness for characters or historical accuracy. What is most important about the setting in "Shaving" is not that it takes place in England, but that it takes place in a home. The conversion of the family dining room into a sickroom is an important detail of setting. As you plan, ask yourself whether your story idea demands a particular setting.

Characters Your treatment of characters includes personality traits, habits, and experiences. Be concerned about a character's appearance only when it figures in the story. "Shaving" is told from Barry's perspective, and there is no reason for Barry to be thinking about his looks, but his awareness of his increased size is a part of his character. Barry's observations about his father's appearance, on the other hand, tell us how ill his father is and express Barry's deep love for his father as he tenderly shaves him. As you plan your characters, ask yourself which of their character traits will be most important in your story.

Conflict Readers enjoy stories with intense conflicts. You can create a strong story by making your characters' conflict clear to the reader. Life is full of conflict; one reason to read stories, beyond the pleasure they give, is to gain understanding of what life is about. In your story, characters will have to confront issues and make decisions involving their deepest feelings as they struggle to overcome obstacles and seek happiness.

Conflict forms the plot and moves your story forward. Think about how your characters struggle within themselves, against other characters, or against forces beyond their control. One type of conflict may set off another, or a character may be subject to more than one conflict at a time. A character's internal conflict, such as fear, jealousy, or disappointment, may be heightened by an accident or by pressure from school or a job, for example. The most important kinds of conflicts are human conflicts, that is, conflicts that involve human feelings. A character's being swept off a mountain slope by an avalanche may be a spectacular event, but not in itself a very meaningful one.

? Critical Thinking:
Determining relationships
What conflicts go with these characters and settings?

Assignment 1 Characters, Setting, and Conflict

Step 1: On your paper, make a list of characters and then a separate list of settings. Choose one character and one setting from your lists, and relate a conflict to this character in this setting. *Step 2:*

Write a sentence or two describing the person, the setting, and the conflict. *Step 3:* Repeat this process with two or three more characters and settings. Share your paper with one or more classmates and talk over story ideas.

SAMPLE   *Character:* high school girl, athlete
                     Setting: Midwest, suburban

ANSWER   Julie is a better-than-average student, especially in mathematics, but her real love is soccer. Julie's mother, a former concert pianist, has insisted that Julie continue her piano lessons, and Julie has dutifully obeyed. The conflict that Julie is experiencing has begun to surface.

Getting Started

As you prepare to write a story, you need to develop powers of observation, to pay close attention to details around you. Not every detail that you observe will be valuable, but it is important to develop a sharp eye. Keep a writer's notebook to record impressions and events, interesting things that you see everywhere: at an outdoor event, on a walk, in store windows, or in your reading.

Besides having sharp eyes, try to develop a good ear for dialogue. An overheard conversation can help you to create strong characterization through dialogue. Keep your writer's notebook with you to record what you hear.

You can use the techniques of freewriting, brainstorming, clustering, and charting *(pages 11–17)* to discover characters, conflicts, and plot. Suppose that you have an idea for a character based on a person you know or based on characteristics of several people you have known. You could brainstorm character traits and then look for a set of characteristics that might be found together in the character you have in mind. You might then list these character traits as you see the character emerging.

CHARACTER TRAITS	*Never loses temper*
	Patient
	Efficient: gets work done on time
	A perfectionist
	Meets obstacles head-on
	Must be in control

Taking a character trait that might cause some conflict, you could cluster on that trait.

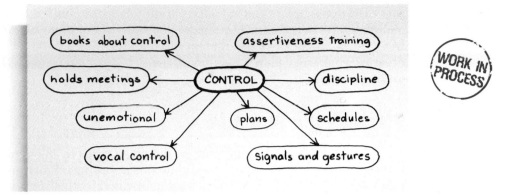

Another strategy would be to brainstorm or cluster about ordinary, everyday events that might take on unusual significance — as shaving does in the Norris short story.

Assignment 2 Using Prewriting Techniques

Following is a list of common personality traits. *Step 1:* On your paper, cluster around one trait that you think has possibilities for a story. *Step 2:* Give this trait to a character, and list two or three other traits that you might find in the same person. *Step 3:* Brainstorm three or four situations that this character might find difficult.

apologetic   loves to gossip, spreads rumors
manipulative   withdrawn, shy
competitive; usually wins   easygoing; almost lazy
intellectual   witty; talkative

Continuing Assignment Find an Idea for a Story

In this series of Continuing Assignments, you will write a short story. In your writer's notebook, use brainstorming, clustering, and charting to explore potential characters, conflicts, and settings for your story. Answer in writing the questions on setting and characters on page 284. Keep experimenting until you find the characters, the conflict, and the setting for your story. Write them down and save your notes.

Prewriting

Developing Your Story Plan

Some writers finish a draft of a story in one sitting after doing some prewriting. Others write a story in stages: first the beginning, then the middle, then the end. Whether you write your story in one sitting or in stages, you need to make careful plans for conflict, characters, and structure, and you need to make decisions about point of view and tone. As you plan the development of your story, it's a good idea to organize your story plan with a chart *(page 17)*, a map *(page 48)*, or an outline *(page 47)*.

Planning the Structure

? Critical Thinking:

Determining
cause / effect
relationships

The events in your story must be linked so that one happening causes another. Story events should be linear, propelled forward by other events. Characters in stories are motivated by their drives, by their emotions, and by events in their lives. A story is more believable and more exciting if cause and effect greatly influence the development of plot, characters, and conflict. Planning your structure carefully will help you to make your story believable, to eliminate gaps, and to build suspense.

Developing the Plot

Working out a story plan can help you to decide on the order of events in your story. In "Shaving," Barry's meeting with his friends helps the author to bring out the fact that Barry's father is dying. Barry's decision to shave his father is brought about by several incidents, the most obvious being the fact that the man who is supposed to shave him has not come for three days. Barry's approach to the act of shaving his father lends weight and significance to this seemingly ordinary act. Each event leads into the next by a linkage carefully constructed by the author.

The high point of the action is the **turning point** or **climax.** In "Shaving," the turning point comes while Barry shaves his father, and his father recognizes Barry's ability to carry on after he is gone. After the climax, the story must end with a **resolution,** which is the solution to the problem or the end of the conflict. In "Shaving," the resolution is peace of mind for Barry's father and Barry's new self-assurance that he is strong enough to handle what is to come. In your own story, the beginning must lead to a complication, and the ending must solve that complication. The story will flow logically because one event leads to — or causes — the next.

? Critical Thinking:

Sequencing

Most likely, you will arrange the events of your plot in **chronological order,** the order in which they occurred. Even if you sequence events this way, however, you won't include every event in your character's day. The structure of a whole day includes many routines that are neither interesting nor relevant to your story. For example, you would not include what your character is wearing unless it has some significance to the story. Building a good plot requires careful selection of events.

You might consider using an order of events that is not entirely chronological but makes use of **flashbacks** or memory sequences. A memory can be very effective in revealing a past event that influenced the main character. Suppose, for example, that your main character excuses himself from going with a group of friends to a restaurant. One friend suggests that it's time he got over the past. A flashback here might reveal your main character's reason for not going to this restaurant (or perhaps for not going to any restaurants) by showing what happened in his past.

Critical Thinking:
Cause and effect; Sequencing
What is the sequence of these events? How does one cause another?

Assignment 1 Ordering the Plot

Choose one of the following situations or one of your own. On your paper, list at least five incidents for the plot, using chronological order. Then make a second sequence in which you use a flashback. Consider cause and effect as you sequence the actions.

1. In Shana's gym class, a student new to the school loses consciousness during an activity.
2. Four young people go sailing on a very windy day with rough seas.
3. Without asking his parents, Emilio has volunteered his recreation room as a practice room for his newly formed band.
4. Alexandra's exhibit for the science fair isn't finished, and she plans to stay up all night Sunday to get it in Monday.
5. Carla's brother asks if he can borrow two hundred dollars from her. He says that he needs the money desperately, but he will not tell her what it is for and he begs her not to tell their parents about it.

Planning Details: Character, Conflict, Setting

As you develop your story plan, consider your characters from several angles. To develop your major characters fully, think about different sides of their personalities. Imagine details of their lives outside the events that you use in your story. For example, consider how your main character would respond to a great success of some kind. Imagine your main character or characters in an uncomfortable or embarrassing situation. Think about the way that your main character would face a difficulty or suffer a great loss. To get to know your characters better, try writing a letter from one character to another, or do some freewriting or write journal entries from the viewpoint of one or more of your characters.

Before drafting, you must also imagine details of setting. If setting is important in your story, choose details that will make it vivid. Listing details or clustering will help you to plan your setting. If you like to draw, do a sketch or two of your setting.

Ask yourself the questions on the next page as you plan your characters and setting.

- What do I know about my characters' pasts?
- What details do I know about them beyond those that I will use in my story?
- Which of my characters are minor and need less development?
- What traits in my characters could create conflict?
- How can I tell when I have made a character do something out of character?

- How important is a particular locale to my story? Could this story take place almost anywhere?
- When does the story take place? Is the specific year or season important to the story?
- What details will make the setting vivid and create the atmosphere I want?
- Does my story require more than one setting?
- Will I have to research my setting?

Assignment 2 Planning the Conflict

On your paper, state the conflict that the character faces in each item. Then write two or three possible actions for a plot. An item may have more than one possibility for the conflict.

SAMPLE Raul and his best friend Taro both work after school in a nursing home. One day when they are playing games with a wheelchair instead of working, Raul is fired.

ANSWER Taro feels that he is just as guilty as Raul, but he doesn't want to get fired too. Raul tells him not to feel bad and just to keep on working there. Taro decides to go to the manager of the nursing home to talk things over. The manager listens and then tells Taro that to be fair, he has to fire him also.

1. Alita and her sister have been sneaking food out of the house to help a runaway whom they know slightly from school.
2. Enrico and his sister get onto the wrong train and are separated from their parents while they are vacationing in France.
3. Maria's parents don't want to allow her to go on an outing in a mountain cabin because the only chaperone is a student teacher.
4. Meiko helped Lucian with his essays at the beginning of the school year, and now Lucian seems dependent on her.

Assignment 3 Planning Details of Setting

Choose a time and a place from the following lists and write them on your paper. Then brainstorm details for the setting that you have chosen. Do this with three other combinations of time and place.

TIME	PLACE
late fall, the present	Rocky Mountains, a resort
storm, spring, 1890s	city high school, locker room
holiday, the present	New England, large town
February, 1930s	mountain cabin
August, the present	New York City, an apartment

Planning Other Story Elements

Once you have made decisions about characters, conflict, and setting, you should give careful thought to point of view and tone.

Point of View of Narrator   When you choose your **point of view,** you decide on a narrator, a decision that determines what parts of the action the reader will witness. You will want to decide between first-person and third-person point of view — the two most common viewpoints for short stories. **First-person point of view** uses *I* for the narrator, giving a degree of immediacy and intimacy with the reader. In many cases, this narrator is the main character, but in others the first-person narrator is someone close to the main character, a reliable observer.

Third-person point of view refers to the main character by name and by *he* or *she*. The third-person narrator is an invisible observer, usually viewing events through the main character's eyes and expressing his or her thoughts and feelings. In "Shaving," for example, the narrator has Barry's consciousness. In some stories there is a greater distance between the narrator and the main character. The result of this distancing is a more detached point of view and possibly a lower degree of emotional involvement between reader and main character. You need to think carefully about how the point of view you choose will affect your story. Look at the following passages to consider each point of view.

> *T*hey came in the night while we slept. We knew they were coming, but not when, and we expected to see them when they did. We never thought that they would come at night. When we got up, well, when John, my brother, got up (he was always getting up early), when he got up, he looked out of the window and ran and jumped back in bed and shook me and called my name.
>
> Junius Edwards (1929–   )
> from "Mother Dear and Daddy"

Notice that in this passage the narrator is a first-person narrator and seems to be fully involved in the story. This is the opening passage to a short story, and we sense immediately that the events happen to this character, rather than to someone else. Notice the differences in the next passage, also an opening.

*M*ashenka Pavletsky, a young girl who had only just finished her studies at a boarding school, returning from a walk to the house of the Kushkins, with whom she was living as a governess, found the household in a terrible turmoil. Mihailo, the porter who opened the door to her, was excited and red as a crab.

Anton Chekhov *(1860–1904)*
from "An Upheaval"

In this story opening, you see that the third-person narrator establishes a certain distance from the main character, Mashenka, by noting details ("just finished her studies at a boarding school") that would not naturally be occurring in the character's mind at the time. Note, however, the observation that the butler was "red as a crab," which is comical in tone and might be the way Mashenka would think of him at this moment. You can maintain a greater or lesser distance from your main character by the observations that you allow your narrator to make.

As you plan, ask yourself these questions about point of view.

- Which character should tell this story?
- Is there any part of the story that this character cannot witness?
- Does this story happen *primarily* to this character?
- If the story mostly happens to another character, would that character be the better narrator?

Tone Your narrator's attitude gives your story its tone. Along with point of view, the tone of your story can strongly affect the reaction that you get from your readers. Perhaps you want to entertain your readers by making them laugh. Possibly you want to involve your readers through their sympathy for your characters. Reread the passages on this page and on page 285 and consider the differences in tone. For example, the narrator in the passage on page 285 recounts a moment from childhood. The reader senses the boys' excitement, wondering who "they" are and whether the boys are happy or scared. In contrast, the opening of "An Upheaval" is brisk and energetic. The house is described as being in a "terrible turmoil," and the reader senses that the outcome will be comical or ironic, rather than painful or sad.

Assignment 4 **Identifying Point of View and Tone**

On your paper, identify the point of view for each passage by writing *First person* or *Third person.* Then comment on the tone and state whether the narrator seems to be close to the main character or at a greater distance.

1.   *L*ord Strawberry, a nobleman, collected birds. He had the finest aviary in Europe, so large that eagles did not find it uncomfortable, so well laid out that both humming-birds and snow-buntings had a climate that suited them perfectly. But for many years the finest set of apartments remained empty, with just a label saying: "PHOENIX. *Habitat: Arabia.*"

Sylvia Townsend Warner *(1893–1978)*
from "The Phoenix"

2.   *T*his is not an easy story; not a road for tender or for casual feet. Better the meadows. Let me warn you, it is as hard as that old man's soul and as sunless as his eyes. It has its inception in catastrophe, and its end in an act of almost incredible violence; between them it tells barely how a man, being blind, can become also deaf and dumb.

Wilbur Daniel Steele *(1886–1970)*
from "Footfalls"

3.   *A*s Gregor Samsa awoke one morning from a troubled dream, he found himself changed in his bed to some monstrous kind of insect.

He lay on his back, which was as hard as armor plate, and, raising his head a little, he could see the arch of his great, brown belly, divided by bowed corrugations. The bedcover was slipping helplessly off the summit of the curve, and Gregor's legs, pitiably thin compared with their former size, fluttered helplessly before his eyes.

Franz Kafka *(1883–1924)*
from "The Metamorphosis"

Continuing Assignment **Develop Your Story Plan**

In the Continuing Assignment on page 281, you decided on the characters, the conflict, and the setting for your story. Now decide on the plot, the point of view, and the tone. Make an outline, a chart, or a map to complete the plans for your short story. Keep all your notes.

Drafting the Beginning of Your Story

Now that you have done your planning, you can begin the drafting process. You can do your drafting quickly, without making final word choices or polishing sentences. Although some writers draft an entire story in one sitting, try drafting your story in sections: the beginning, the middle, and the end.

As you draft the beginning of your story, you need to give your readers enough information to get them involved in the story. Reread the first three paragraphs of "Shaving" on page 271. As you read, look for important information or **exposition.** Also note the beginnings of the conflict and try to sense the mood or atmosphere.

Choose from these strategies one that is appropriate to your story.

▶ **Strategies**

1. *Create atmosphere by describing the setting in detail.*
2. *Open by involving the main character in an action that establishes the conflict.*
3. *Open with a dialogue that gradually reveals the narrator, the situation, and the conflict.*

The beginning of your story is crucial. You need to capture your readers' attention, drawing them into your characters' world.

Establishing Setting: Time, Place, and Atmosphere

Notice how quickly time and place are established in "Shaving." The writer includes such details as "brisk April sun" and "spring warmth" to show the season. The fact that the shaving mug (dated 1953) is much older than Barry gives a clue to an approximate year. We also recognize that the setting is England, since the mug commemorates the coronation of Queen Elizabeth II. Whatever details of setting you include in your story should occur naturally through the narrator's observations. Just as the main character would not normally be thinking of his hair color or height, he would not under ordinary circumstances be thinking of the exact dimensions of his desk or kitchen table or the name of his town. Barry's thoughts are on his father, not on the sickroom itself. The fact that the room had been a dining room is just a passing thought for Barry, but it is important for the reader.

Assignment 1 Establishing Atmosphere and Setting

Choose a setting from the list on the next page or one from Assignment 3 on pages 284–285, and write two different story openings. First, write an opening that creates a cheerful atmosphere, and then write one that creates a gloomy or frightening atmosphere.

the living room of an apartment
a. Afternoon sun streamed in the tall windows on either side of the bookcase, making the whole room bright. A vase of daffodils brightened the coffee table.

b. The ragged curtains at the window might have moved had there been any kind of breeze. A dull yellow light fell upon the faded carpet and filled the cheerless room.

a car lot	a library	a parking garage
a lake or pond	a doctor's office	a garden or orchard

Developing Characters

You will catch and hold your reader's interest if you develop your characters and conflict early in the story. By combining dialogue, description, and interior monologue, you can get your readers involved with your character in a single page.

Leslie Norris, the author of "Shaving," creates Barry's character quickly. In the brief conversation between Barry and his friends, Barry has little to say. The difference between Barry and his friend Jackie highlights Barry's conflict. Jackie is interested in the opposite sex and in fashion; he's able to joke and have a good time. For the time being, Barry's world is focused on his father. Notice how his mother's feelings are revealed: "She *slammed* shut the stove door." She continues with everyday chores in her home, but her movements express her anger and frustration.

You can reveal characters by dialogue and by **interior monologue** — the observations, reactions, and physical sensations of the main character. Early in "Shaving," the interior monologue reveals that as he flexes his shoulders, Barry is "surprised again by the unexpected weight of his muscles, the thickening strength of his body."

Physical description of your characters is not as important as personality traits. Introduce such details only if they reveal character. The physical description of Barry's father reveals that he is near death: gaunt body, dry voice, irregular and shallow breathing, frail temples. In contrast, Barry's mother *bustles* with "orderly energy."

Establishing the Conflict

Your conflict should be clearly established and easy for your readers to grasp. In "Shaving," Barry confronts the reality of death and acts with dignity and grace, easing his father's mind about the future of the family. His father's illness has made Barry find strength inside himself to assume a leadership role in the family and to assure his father that "there's no need" to worry. In your story, the main character may have to take steps — that is, take action — to solve the problem. In "Shaving," the action — Barry's shaving his father — provides the opportunity for closeness and for reassuring communication between father and son.

The following dialogue has no details or markers. To reveal character and conflict, copy the dialogue onto your paper, adding details of description and interior monologue. Choose a point of view and a tone, and make the conflict more or less intense through the details in the main character's thoughts and feelings.

"Well, I'm here."

"Just take a seat, Lloyd. I'll be with you in a minute."

"O.K. May I open a window?"

"Fine. Now, do you know why I asked you to stay after?"

"Yeah, I guess so. You thought I was out of line when I said you weren't being fair with Carlos."

"Well? Do you agree that you shouldn't have interfered in my discipline of another student?"

"Maybe I didn't handle it right, Mrs. Sampson, but I have to say it again, you aren't giving Carlos a chance. He's having a hard time."

"Does that mean he has to be fresh?"

"You think he's being fresh, but he's not. Let Carlos stay after with me tomorrow, please. I think I can help him explain what he meant."

"All right. I'd be glad to find out I was wrong, this time."

Continuing Assignment **Draft the Beginning of Your Story**

Using your notes from the Continuing Assignments on pages 281 and 287, draft the beginning of your short story. Establish the setting, the characters, and the conflict. Remember that this is a first draft. You will have plenty of opportunity to revise it later. Save your draft and your notes.

Drafting

The Middle: Building to the Climax

Having established your setting, characters, and plot in your opening, you are ready to draft the middle of your story. Now, as your conflict builds to the climax, you will see how your story plan works and how your characters react as you put them into action.

Revealing Characters and Relationships

You need to make clear how your characters act, react, and think. In "Shaving," Jackie is witty and talkative; in contrast, Barry is quiet and unassuming, and doesn't brag about his victory. He also refuses

Jackie's invitation to go for coffee, preferring to be by himself, or perhaps feeling an obligation to be at home with his father. Barry's actions in preparing the shaving equipment show how methodical he is and how he considers this event a ritual — of almost religious importance. Barry's thoughts early in the story about his greater size and weight tie in with a later remark he makes to his father: "I'm bigger than most men," which then takes on a deeper meaning. As you draft your story, look for opportunities to reveal depths of character and to reinforce your theme with the right details and the right words.

Creating Significant Events

In your story, one event must lead into another to move the plot along to the climax. You do not need many events, but each event must have some significance. Other events may occur in the lives of your characters, but the ones you include should be those that reveal character, bring out conflict, and move the plot forward. Characters make decisions about their actions, and those decisions advance the plot. These events and decisions are linked by the operation of cause and effect. What would have happened if Barry had opted to have coffee with his friends? What would have happened if he had not volunteered to shave his father? Decisions like these are important because they generate responses and emotions in your readers.

Critical Thinking:
Cause and effect

Assignment Creating Significant Events

Following is the first event in a plot. On your paper, write three or four paragraphs that advance the action and build conflict.

> Kiri asks her parents for permission to hold a garage sale with two of her neighborhood friends.

Continuing Assignment **Draft the Middle of Your Story**

Continue the draft that you began for the Continuing Assignment on page 290. Pay attention to how your characters act and react. Create events that advance the action to the turning point — a flash of recognition or insight. Continue to use interior monologue, dialogue, and description. Save your drafts.

Critical Thinking:
Cause and effect
How does one event cause another?

Drafting

Bringing the Story to a Close

As you draft the ending of your story, consider how your main character has been changed by this experience. Barry has accepted the mantle of adulthood by the end of "Shaving." Norris chooses to close

"Shaving" by having Barry reflect on the "dying sunlight . . . illuminated in its golden warmth, . . . knowing it would soon be gone." This comparison between the dying sun and the dying father is a metaphor implying a number of ideas to the reader: Barry values his father (he compares him to the sun); he will value the last days of his father's life; he will miss his father's "warmth." Having Barry say to another character, "I'm going to miss my father — he's very important to me" would be less effective.

The ending of your story may be a new beginning; it may resolve the conflict; or it may bring a recognition of some kind, a happy surprise, or an ironic twist of fate. Studying endings of short stories can help you to understand how endings work and to appreciate the skill of fiction writers.

Making the Theme Clear

As your story comes to a close, your theme should be clear to your readers. Although the theme, or meaning, should emerge from the whole story, you should emphasize it by details in the ending: a line of dialogue, a detail of the setting, or a thought in the mind of the main character. In "Shaving," Barry reflects on his hands, strong and capable now, but not long ago small boy's hands. He has been forced to grow up as he faces his father's imminent death. The theme is also underscored by Barry's comforting his father, telling him he has nothing to worry about, and in a sense, trading roles with him. The boy becomes a man, and in his helplessness, the father is dependent, like a child. Your theme should be clear through the details that you choose for your ending.

These strategies will help you to write the ending to your story.

▶ **Strategies**

1. *Make sure that the ending completes the action.* Even if it is not a "happy ending" for the main character, it must give a sense of completeness.

2. *Write the ending in terms of the characters whom you have created.* Do not have a character do something out of character for him or her.

3. *Look back at your chart, outline, or story map.* If the ending is not the one that you originally planned, is it a more satisfying ending?

4. *Show change in the main character as the result of the action of the story.* This change might be a new outlook, new maturity, or some personal satisfaction.

Assignment Reviewing the Ending of a Story

Reread the last five paragraphs of "Shaving" on page 277. On your paper, list at least three ways in which this ending is effective.

Decide how to end the story that you have developed in the preceding Continuing Assignments. Then draft the ending. Save all your drafts.

Revising

Revising Your Story

Think about the original directions for writing your short story. You were to (1) create characters and conflict through dialogue and interior monologue; (2) contribute to mood or atmosphere with setting; (3) maintain a consistent point of view; (4) create significant incidents to advance the conflict; and (5) bring the story to a close, achieving a change in the main character and resolving the conflict. To begin revising your story, first evaluate it in terms of these requirements. Later, you can further revise to improve tone and style.

? **Critical Thinking:**
Evaluating

Revising to Make Your Story Work Better

Stories are meant to be read by an audience. As you revise, try to put yourself into a reader's shoes. Ask yourself how a reader would answer these questions about your story.

- Is the setting clear and appropriate for the story?
- Are the characters developed? Are their actions motivated?
- Is it clear how characters feel about each other?
- Is the conflict interesting?
- Will the reader care about these characters and their story?
- Are time segments in the story clear?
- Is the ending satisfactory and prepared for by the beginning?

The answers to these questions will help you to revise. Later, have a classmate, a friend, or a family member read your story and respond to it. Consider having this reader answer the same questions.

Refining Characters and Conflict

You know your characters. With the right details, you will make your readers believe that these products of your imagination, your characters, are real. Although the scene between Barry and his mother is brief, readers get to know her immediately from details of her movements and from what she says. Remember that what your main character observes about another character can tell your readers a great deal about both the observed and the observer. Revising your story will help you to provide those details and observations.

The first draft of a passage from a story follows on the next page.

> David closed the door and stood in the hallway. He could hear the television. He knew his parents were still up. He wanted to go up to his room without talking to them. His mother came to the door of the family room. "Well," she said, "aren't you coming in?"

The revision provides better details of character and conflict:

> David closed the door as quickly and quietly as he could. Too much cold air could warn them he was home just as easily as the noise of a slammed door. The television was blaring in the family room. Good, he thought, maybe they won't hear me. He knew his mother would want to hear how things went tonight. He could imagine her very direct questions. "Well," she would say, "have you made up your mind?" He hadn't.
>
> He took a few steps toward the stairs. Maybe he could get up to his room. But it was too late. His mother was suddenly there, at the door of the family room.
>
> "Well," she said, "aren't you going to come in and talk to us? We want to hear what you've decided."

Notice what the writer has done to intensify the main character and the conflict. The detail suggesting that the cold air will give him away shows David's taking every precaution to avoid a confrontation with his parents. The detail of his mother's suddenly appearing suggests her direct approach to the confrontation. Sometimes refining your characters may mean doing a new cluster or list, or observing people further.

Assignment 1 Building Character and Conflict

? Critical Thinking:

Evaluating
What details
will develop
the character?

On your paper, revise the following passage, providing details in the description and interior monologue to develop the character and build the conflict. Add dialogue and action if you wish.

> The only good reason to get up in the morning is so that you can go back to bed later, thought Dayton. What was it Ovid said? "Sleep is death warmed up." Something like that. Ovid stunk. He could write a poem about the beauty of sleep, if only he could stay awake long enough to do so. His mother thought he was sleep-walking through life. What did she know, anyway?

Revising for Consistent Point of View

As you revise, make sure that you stay in the consciousness of one character for interior monologue. Remember to provide a way for this character to find out about events that he or she could not witness. In novels you will sometimes find the **omniscient point of view,** which uses an all-seeing narrator who can enter different characters' viewpoints at different points in the novel. Since there are no chapter breaks in a short story, however, a single point of view is more credible and easier to handle. Your revision should correct any weaknesses or inconsistencies in the point of view. Refer to the passages on pages 285–287 if needed.

Revising for Tone and Style

The tone of your story should be consistent with its plot, its characters, and its narrator. Of course, there can be serious undertones to a funny story, but even then the tone should not shift abruptly. Examine your sentence length, word choice, and images to see if they maintain the tone consistently.

During revision, you can make changes that improve the style of your story. Like other writers, you are developing a personal style of writing. Whatever your personal writing style, there are strategies that you can use to improve your story's tone and style.

▶ **Strategies**

1. *Use active verbs.* Replace lifeless "be" verbs such as *is, are, was, were, be, being, been,* and *am* to give your sentences more punch.
2. *Use specific nouns.* You may be able to avoid extra modifiers.
3. *Vary the length and style of your sentences.* You may find that you can change the mood and rhythm of your story by altering and combining sentences *(pages 72–76).*
4. *Eliminate trite expressions and clichés.* If you are not sure if an expression is a cliché, consult a style guide, or have a classmate or your teacher read the passage and respond.

Assignment 2 Revising for Tone and Style

The following passage contains weaknesses in style and inconsistencies in tone. On your paper, rewrite the passage, eliminating the inconsistencies and improving the style.

Lara really loved to go to the cottage alone on the weekends. It was really a complete change of scenery. It was a wonderful restorative after the pressure of work and the conflicts at home. Her mother thought it was pretty keen, too, and wondered why they hadn't thought of it before. Sunday afternoons seemed to last forever, Lara thought delightedly. Really, it was swell being here at

Blue Lake with just the songs of birds and the gentle lapping of the waves breaking the silence.

Continuing Assignment **Revise Your Story**

To revise the story that you have drafted in previous Continuing Assignments, answer the questions on page 293, follow the strategies on page 295, and make needed changes. After you have revised your story once, have at least one person read it and respond to it. Such responses should help you to revise the story further. You should revise to improve interior monologue, to refine character, to maintain a consistent point of view, and to improve style and tone. Save your papers.

Proofreading

Proofreading Your Story

After revising your story, you are ready to proofread it for errors in grammar, punctuation, capitalization, and spelling. Proofreading is important. Make sure that you take the time to eliminate every error. Then write your final copy and proofread it again.

The Grammar Connection

When you write dialogue, there are a few rules to remember:

Paragraphing Begin a new paragraph and use a separate set of quotation marks each time the speaker changes. When one speaker continues for more than a paragraph, reopen the quotation marks at the beginning of each paragraph. Do not close the quotation marks until the speaker finishes or until words such as *she continued* break the speech.

Reference Point:
pages 725–727

Punctuation Place a period inside closing quotation marks. Question marks and exclamation points go inside quotation marks *if* they apply to the spoken words. Use a comma or commas to separate an explanatory phrase, such as *Rita asked* or *he said*, from the quotation itself. Place the commas outside the opening quotation marks but inside the closing quotation marks.

> "Are you going away next week for winter vacation"?/ Chung asked. ¶ "We were supposed to go skiing,"∧Miwa said,"∧but my father might have to work."

Proofreading a Passage

The following passage contains errors in punctuating and paragraphing dialogue, as well as other errors in capitalization and punctuation. Rewrite the dialogue correctly on your paper.

> "Hey, need a ride?" Derek asked. "Sure, that'd be great." Robin replied. "Neat car. Your mom's"? "Yeah, she loves sport cars. we like them, too." "I especially like the sun roof." "She calls it a moon roof. Says looking at the stars is a lot better than blinking at the Sun.

Continuing Assignment **Proofread Your Story**

Carefully proofread your own story now, paying close attention to punctuation and paragraphing in dialogue. You may have a partner read it also to check for correct spelling, capitalization, punctuation, and grammar. After the final version is written or typed, check it one more time to make sure that no errors remain.

Publishing

Publishing Your Story

A story is meant to be read. Once you have a final copy of your short story to share, you can publish it in many ways, as well as keeping a copy in your portfolio. Here are a few suggestions for publishing.

- Hold classroom response groups to discuss your classmates' stories.
- Exchange stories with students in other classes.
- If some stories were written for a younger audience, share them with students in the elementary school.
- As a class, collect your stories, bind them in an anthology, and catalogue the book for your school library.
- Hold a readers' theater performance of some of the stories for an audience of students, teachers, and parents.
- Submit the best stories to a literary magazine. If there is no literary magazine in your school or town, you may want to use your stories to start one.
- If your school newspaper or a local newspaper publishes creative writing, submit some stories for publication.

Continuing Assignment **Publish Your Story**

Choose one or more of the suggestions given here to share stories with an audience of your friends, other classes, teachers, and parents.

Writing a Short Play

When you write a play, you create characters, plot, and setting just as you do writing a story, but you work within the elements of a performance. Although you can use many of the same prewriting activities that you use for stories to get ideas for a play, you will find that drafting a play differs greatly from drafting a story. The greatest difference is that there is no narrator, making the dialogue and action even more important than they are in a story. The audience's knowledge of time and place is limited to what they see on the stage, what is revealed in the dialogue, and perhaps what is given in program notes.

Ideas for scripts come from many of the same sources as ideas for stories: everyday conflicts — serious or comical, newspaper stories, observations of people and situations, and other personal experiences. Sometimes a central setting can be the focus of an idea for a play, as in *The Dining Room*, a play by A. R. Gurney, Jr. Following is a description of the set and a portion of the play.

[The play takes place in a dining room — or rather, many dining rooms. The same dining room furniture serves for all: a lovely, burnished, shining dining room table; two chairs, with arms, at either end; two more, armless, along each side; several additional matching chairs, placed so as to define the walls of the room. Upstage somewhere, a sideboard, with a mirror over it.]

FATHER: I'll tell you one thing. If there's a war, no one gets cream. If there's a war, we'll all have to settle for top of the bottle.

GIRL: Mother said she was thinking about having us eat dinner in here with you every night.

FATHER: Yes. Your mother and I are both thinking about that. And we're both looking forward to it. As soon as you children learn to sit up straight . . . *(They quickly do.)* . . . then I see no reason why we shouldn't all have a pleasant meal together every evening.

BOY: Could we try it tonight, Dad? Could you give us a test?

FATHER: No, Charlie. Not tonight. Because tonight we're giving a small dinner party. But I hope very much you and Liz will come down and shake hands.

GIRL: I get so shy, Dad.

FATHER: Well you'll just have to learn, sweetie pie. Half of life is learning to meet people.

BOY: What's the other half, Dad? [Pause. The Father fixes him with a steely gaze.]

FATHER: Was that a crack?

BOY: No, Dad . . .

FATHER: That was a crack, wasn't it?

BOY: No, Dad. Really . . .

FATHER: That sounded very much like a smart-guy wisecrack to me. And people who make cracks like that don't normally eat in dining rooms.

BOY: I didn't mean it as a crack, Dad.

FATHER: Then we'll ignore it. We'll go on with our breakfast. [Annie comes in.]

ANNIE: [To Girl] Your car's here, Lizzie. For school. [Annie goes out.]

GIRL: [Jumping up.] O.K.

FATHER: [To Girl] Thank you, Annie.

GIRL: Thank you, Annie . . . (Kisses Father) Goodbye, Daddy.

FATHER: Goodbye, darling. Don't be late. Say good morning to the driver. Sit quietly in the car. Work hard. Run. Run. Goodbye. [Girl goes off. Father returns to his paper. Pause. Boy sits watching his father.]

BOY: Dad, can I read the funnies?

FATHER: Certainly. Certainly you may. (He carefully extracts the second section and hands it to his son. Both read, the Son trying to imitate the Father in how he does it. Finally:) This won't mean much to you, but the government is systematically ruining this country.

A. R. Gurney, Jr. (1930–   )
from The Dining Room

Dramatists reveal character primarily through dialogue and action. First, the audience learns about characters from **dialogue,** what they say and what others say about them. Sometimes one character has to give background on another character. This necessary background information is called **exposition.** A second way the audience gains information is through stage business and props. **Stage business** is an action or set of movements often involving **props,** objects or furniture used onstage. Notice the stage business with the newspaper, for example.

As you draft a play, you write several kinds of **stage directions.** Besides giving actors directions for tone of voice and movement, stage directions also give the time of day or year, describe the set and even hint at the atmosphere. The **set** is the stage itself after the setting has been translated into what is put up, constructed, or carried on. You will probably need to draw a basic floor plan to help you decide on characters' movements.

Just as observations in your writer's notebook helped you to create characters for your short story, notes on the way people speak and move can help you to create characters for your play. Make note of mannerisms, gestures, and nervous habits that might provide good stage business.

The following strategies will help you to set up your script.

▶ **Strategies**

1. *Put stage directions in italics to set them off from the speeches.* Underline such material in your manuscript.

2. *Set stage directions off from the text of the speeches by brackets or parentheses.* Use brackets when the stage directions are separate from dialogue. Use parentheses when the stage directions are inserted into the middle of a speech.

3. *Put characters' names in all capital letters. Follow names with colons preceding a speech.*

4. *Indent all but the first line of each speech to make your script easier to follow.*

5. *Use the terms* **stage right** *and* **stage left** *to refer to the actors' right and left, not the audience's.*

Assignment | **Write a Dramatic Scene or a Short Play**

Using some of the same ideas about conflict, characters, and setting that you learned in writing a short story, write a short play. After you have drafted your play, hold a classroom run-through to show you what needs revision. Once you have revised and proofread your script, publish it by giving a performance for an audience of students, teachers, and parents. Remember also to keep a copy of your script in your portfolio.

Like a painting, a poem is an interpretation of experience. A poem is intense in its use of language and immediate in its emotional and sensory appeal. When you write a poem, you create a single impression or a series of impressions, carefully selecting words and details, and narrowing the focus of your subject. Your poem can give a unique view of human experience and can, through its images and details, delight your readers as well.

Prewriting

Getting and Developing an Idea for a Poem

You don't have to go far for subjects for your poems. Sometimes a simple scene at home can be the inspiration for a poem. For example, the following poem speaks of a family setting.

Boy with His Hair Cut Short

Sunday shuts down on this twentieth-century evening.
The El passes. Twilight and bulb define
the brown room, the overstuffed plum sofa,
the boy, and the girl's thin hands above his head.
A neighbor radio sings stocks, news, serenade.

He sits at the table, head down, the young clear neck exposed,
watching the drugstore sign from the tail of his eye;
tattoo, neon, until the eye blears, while his
solicitous tall sister, simple in blue, bending
behind him, cuts his hair with her cheap shears.

The arrow's electric red always reaches its mark,
successful neon! He coughs, impressed by that precision.
His child's forehead, forever protected by his cap,
is bleached against the lamplight as he turns head
and steadies to let the snippets drop.

Erasing the failure of weeks with level fingers,
she sleeks the fine hair, combing: "You'll look fine tomorrow!
You'll surely find something, they can't keep turning you down;
the finest gentleman's not so trim as you!" Smiling, he raises
the adolescent forehead wrinkling ironic now.

He sees his decent suit laid out, new-pressed,
his carfare on the shelf. He lets his head fall, meeting
her earnest hopeless look, seeing the sharp blades splitting,
the darkened room, the impersonal sign, her motion,
the blue vein, bright on her temple, pitifully beating.

Muriel Rukeyser *(1913–1980)*

Poetry has a way of looking inside the experience, looking beyond the surface, exploring deeper levels of emotion. A poem can begin with an image and expand to include an experience, or it can begin with an idea and find the images to express it. A poem can begin with an emotion or a mood, or it can begin with a setting that leads to that emotion or mood. A poem can look outward at a landscape, or inward at the speaker's mind or heart. When you write a poem, you can assume a character, or persona, making the speaker someone you imagine, not necessarily yourself. There are many decisions for you to make before you draft your poem, and others that you'll make as you draft. Probably the first decision you will make is your choice of subject.

Thinking of Subjects and Images

Sometimes you may find that your subject comes to you as an image or a cluster of images. An **image** is an appeal to the senses in concrete language. Although you may first think of visual images, you should also consider the experience of other senses: hearing, taste, smell, and touch. Sensations such as heat and cold, lightness and heaviness, and motion can also enhance the imagery in your poem.

Perhaps your subject will be an activity: parachuting; skating; skipping rocks; refinishing furniture; watching an animal, a bird, or even an insect; painting; writing; planting seeds; or repairing an engine. Maybe you prefer writing about a place: a room, the beach, a meadow, a park bench. Perhaps a person will be your subject: a parent, grandparent, or ancestor; a brother or sister; a teacher; a friend; a famous person.

Assignment 1 Thinking of Images

On page 303 are four types of subjects for poems. *Step 1:* On your paper, write an example for each type of subject. *Step 2:* Following the subject that you have chosen, make a list of images that come to mind. Try to think of images that appeal to at least two different senses.

SAMPLE Significant places
ANSWER Grandmother's storeroom: a dress form draped with an old sheet, an old black sewing machine, cold dry air, hat boxes with cords and tassels, a faint spicy smell mixed with musty odors, dust coating everything, a cracked mirror on a stand, some postcards from Florida, a little locked box.

1. Significant places
2. Significant people
3. Significant moments
4. Significant activities

Developing Your Idea

Once you have decided on a subject, you'll probably need to use some prewriting strategies to develop your ideas for the poem. For instance, you may want to do some freewriting *(page 11)* to explore a significant memory in your writer's notebook, as the writer of this passage has done.

> An exhibit I saw at a Natural History Festival made me think of something that happened when I was about 10. My father, sister, and I — along with our old dog Jip — were out back of the house in the woods looking for mushrooms. My Dad told me to go over and look for mushrooms in a certain spot. I started over to the maple he had pointed to and then stopped. There was a snake coiled in front of me. Jip ran over, grabbed the snake, and shook it in her mouth. I was petrified. I've always been afraid of snakes, and I think this incident was particularly bad because my Dad had made a joke out of it — had pushed me toward something I feared. It made me trust him a little less.

An entry in your notebook can provide a subject, can inspire a poem through recorded details and images, or can itself become the poem through revision for line breaks and language.

Other prewriting notes may look more like grocery lists — notes and ideas scratched on paper. Brainstorming *(page 13)* follows this pattern. For example, you may begin thinking about your subject by freewriting in your notebook and then brainstorming to generate a list of specific details. These details form a sort of data bank from which you can withdraw words and phrases to use in your poem.

If you have decided to write a poem about an ancestor, you can develop your subject by interviewing members of your family. In an interview, you are looking for details about a specific ancestor as well as incidents that can provide material for a poem. Read the following portion of an interview.

J: Could you tell me some more about that Civil War incident? You know, I've heard you talking to Uncle George about it at family reunions.

F: Do you mean about Buddy?

J: Yeah, that's the one.

F: Well, you know this was a border state during the war, so there were sympathizers for each side in the area, and sometimes things got a little rough. There was a group from town rode out to take Flavius--he was nicknamed Buddy--and his brother into jail. The men that rode out didn't have any charges, but that didn't stop them. Buddy and his brother were at the smokehouse helping their mother with the butchering. She told them to go on in so there wouldn't be trouble. They did. A couple of days later, they were carrying wood into the jail, and one of the men on guard said, "You all can leave." As the brothers turned away, they were both shot. Someone went out to the farm and told the womenfolk to come collect the bodies. Their mother brought in the wagon, but when she got them loaded, she saw Buddy wasn't dead yet. She drove her team down to the railroad station and took him by train to the city where a doctor patched him up pretty good. He lived 'til '88. And he never went back into town.

This family story could be the basis for an effective poem. Consider point of view when you write an ancestor poem. You could use the first-person point of view, taking on the persona of your ancestor. You could also write the poem from your perspective as a grandchild or great-grandchild. Another possibility is to use a third-person narrator as an observer.

Suppose you decided to explore "the relatives" as a topic for a poem. Clustering *(page 14)* might produce a subject such as "big weddings" that could be explored in a further cluster. Maybe the second cluster gets you wondering why anyone wants a public wedding. When you start thinking about the *why* behind events, then you're not just generating words for a poem but thinking, too, about theme.

Practice using freewriting, listing, brainstorming, or clustering by exploring one or more of the following topics or one from your imagination.

a family pet	backyard of your house
a memory	a holiday important to your family
family tradition	a family vacation
siblings	the family tree

Considering Meaning and Theme

Even though the language of a poem gives pleasure in itself, you want to leave your reader with a sense of having gained some insight or having grasped the meaning and significance of your poem. Part of planning your poem, then, is giving thought to meaning and theme. Consider the theme of the following poem.

That Dark Other Mountain

My father could go down a mountain faster than I
Though I was first one up.
Legs braced or with quick steps he slid the gravel slopes
Where I picked cautious footholds.

Black, Iron, Eagle, Doubiehead, Chocorua,
Wildcat and Carter Dome —
He beat me down them all. And that last other mountain,
And that dark other mountain.

Robert Francis *(1901–1987)*

This poem has as its subject the relationship between a father and son and their shared experience of climbing mountains. The title of the poem indicates its emphasis: not the real mountains — Black, Wildcat, Carter Dome — but the *dark* mountain of death. This poem is about the significant relationship the speaker had with his father. It is also about the recognition most people have of their own mortality after they experience the death of a parent. As you draft your poem, you may find that it expresses more than one meaning.

Read the poem on the next page carefully. On your paper, write first the literal meaning of the poem. Then write what you see as the symbolic meaning and the theme of the poem.

River Skater

*B*ound to a boy's swift feet, hard blades of steel
   Ring out a brutal rhythm from black ice.
A gawky skater with a godlike heel,
   He cuts a clear and convolute device,
A foliated script, nor looks around
   To see what letters twine where he has come,
But, all delighted with the savage sound,
   His body beats from such a solid drum,
He springs into a faster pace, and then,
   Far down the pastures, paper-white and pure,
You see his figure, slanted like a pen,
   Writing his own and winter's signature.

Winifred Welles (1893–1939)

Considering Point of View

As you know, when you choose a speaker or **persona** for your poem you are free to adopt another voice, unlimited by your age, sex, or education. Read again "Boy with His Hair Cut Short" *(page 301)* and "That Dark Other Mountain" *(page 305)*. In the former poem, you might assume that the "I" is a son, but there are no clues as to whether the speaker is male or female. In the latter poem, the speaker is an unseen observer, like a third-person narrator of a story. Just as you consider point of view in writing a story, you need to choose the speaker or persona for your poem.

Assignment 4 Persona in a Poem

Reread "River Skater," above, and write on your paper a description of the speaker. Note whether the speaker uses the first-person or is an anonymous onlooker. Also include your opinion on the speaker's attitude toward the subject.

Choosing an Appropriate Tone

Tone is the attitude that you reveal toward the subject of your poem. The tone of your poem might be ironic, joyful, angry, romantic, peaceful, or somber. In "That Dark Other Mountain," the speaker has a sense of wonder and pride at his father's ability to climb — and go down — mountains. The second stanza begins with a strong, sure voice listing the names of conquered mountains and then takes on a note of awe toward "that dark other mountain." The speaker in "River Skater" expresses a sense of wonder and admiration at the skater's artistry.

Strong word choices bring out sharp images: *hard blades, brutal rhythm, foliated*, and *paper-white.* You will find that the tone of your poem comes mostly from the language that you use: images, figurative language, and word choices. You will need to focus on these elements of poetic language as you draft your poem.

Assignment 5 Identifying Tone

Read "Symptoms of Love," below, and "The Market Man," below and on the next page. Decide on the tone of each. Record your decisions on your paper and explain them with a sentence or two.

1.
Symptoms of Love

*L*ove is a universal migraine,
A bright stain on the vision
Blotting out reason.

Symptoms of true love
Are leanness, jealousy,
Laggard dawns;

Are omens and nightmares —
Listening for a knock,
Waiting for a sign:

For a touch of her fingers
In a darkened room,
For a searching look.

Take courage, lover!
Could you endure such grief
At any hand but hers?

Robert Graves *(1895–1985)*

2.
The Market Man

*T*he walnut brains think moist
in their light tan skulls;
the apples croon redly
of their tooth white pulp;
and the squash curves voluptuously
in its yellow skin.

It is cold and the market man
burns an orange crate;
it is dark and bare bulbs hang down
like fiery glass pears.
The market man has big blunt thumbs,
he feels chapped melons;
the market man has a strong mouth,
dry as potato dust;
the market man has black grape eyes,
no seeds show in them.
The market man has lonely shanks,
he splats lemons against a wall;
the market man is angry at the cold,
he strips the heads of lettuce down
and throws the green leaves on the cobble street;
the market man smells the salty river,
he bites an onion open with his teeth
and floods the black night with tears and burning.

John Ratti (1933–   )

Thinking of Form

The **form** of your poem is the shape or arrangement of words on the page. As you draft, you will make decisions about line breaks and stanzas. Your readers will notice the form of your poem immediately, but they will feel the influence of the form on the meaning only as they read and reread the poem. The lengths of your lines and certain combinations of words can actually carry tension, which creates a powerful effect. A line that is too short can fail to build the desired tension, whereas a line that is too long can collapse under its own weight. Think about how your poem should look on the page, and whether you might break the poem into stanzas.

Assignment 6 Analyzing the Form of a Poem

Choose one of the poems in this unit and analyze its form. On your paper, write the title of the poem. Then write a short paragraph about how the poem looks on the page and how the arrangement contributes to its meaning.

Continuing Assignment Develop an Idea for a Poem

Using one or more of the prewriting techniques suggested in this section, find a subject for your poem. Decide on the meaning, or theme, the point of view, the tone, and the form of your poem, and write these decisions down. Save your notes.

Drafting Your Poem

Having decided on a subject, and having considered tone and form, you are ready to draft your poem. Draft your poem quickly several times, letting the momentum carry you through to the end. Although images and details will probably come to you during drafting, you needn't make final word choices until you revise.

Here are some guidelines to help you as you draft your poem.

▶ **Strategies**

1. *Draft your poem quickly several times.*
2. *Experiment with form.* Move lines and whole sections around. Experiment with the lengths of the lines.
3. *To get images flowing when you get stuck, do a new cluster or brainstorm list for that part.*
4. *Don't stop to make final decisions on word choices.*
5. *If you are writing about a scene, try to be there or have a photograph in front of you.* In the same way, if you are writing about an object or a painting, try to have it with you as you write.
6. *If you are writing about a family member or an ancestor, work from facts in your notes.* Photographs of ancestors can be helpful.

Creating Images and Sound

The images and the sound in your poem can create powerful effects and can delight your readers. The language of poetry is often rich and intense, and one of its most delightful qualities is found in figures of speech and in sound effects.

As you draft, try creating images through similes and metaphors. **Metaphors** directly compare two seemingly unlike things by saying that one *is* the other. **Similes** are also comparisons but use *like* or *as* to connect the objects. For example, read the following poem, in which simile and metaphor create sharp images and an amusing ironic tone.

Word

*T*he word bites like a fish.
Shall I throw it back free
Arrowing to that sea
Where thoughts lash tail and fin?
Or shall I pull it in
To rhyme upon a dish?

Stephen Spender *(1909–   )*

Notice the strong simile created in the first line: "The word bites like a fish." Note also the metaphor "arrowing to that sea" as well as the metaphor of the sea itself "Where thoughts lash tail and fin."

Another figure of speech used frequently to create images in poetry is **personification,** which gives human qualities to inanimate objects or animals. The following example is the first stanza of "Hunger in New York City," by a contemporary Native-American poet.

> *H*unger crawls into you
> from somewhere out of your muscles
> or the concrete or the land
> or the wind pushing you.
>
> Simon Ortiz *(1941–   )*

You can also add to the pleasure that your poem gives to your readers by using various sound effects, or sound devices. **Rhythm** is the beat formed by stressed and unstressed syllables in words. It may form a regular pattern in a poem — such as iambic pentameter, the rhythm Shakespeare chose for his plays. Even everyday speech has rhythm, as does prose, but rhythm is usually more pronounced in poetry. Although rhythm is often combined with rhyme, it can also be part of a poem without rhyme. A **rhyme scheme** is a pattern of rhyming words that fits into, and emphasizes, a set rhythm. Another kind of rhyme is **internal rhyme,** the effect created by two words rhyming within a line. If you choose to use a set pattern of rhythm and rhyme, be careful not to sacrifice your meaning in order to keep the rhyme.

Three other sound devices that you might like to use are alliteration, assonance, and onomatopoeia. **Alliteration** is the repetition of initial sounds. Notice the repeated sound of hard *c* and *k* in the beginning line from Alfred, Lord Tennyson's "The Eagle": "He clasps the crag with crooked hands." The repetition of vowel sounds is called **assonance,** which is seen in the repeated *a* sound in *clasps, crag,* and *hands,* in the same line. When you use words that suggest their meaning through their sound, you are using **onomatopoeia,** which is a kind of sound imagery. Words like *buzz, moan, whirr,* and *rattle* are examples of onomatopoeia.

(ŏn'ə-măt'ə-pē'ə)

Assignment 1 Creating Figurative Language

Reread "Symptoms of Love" on page 307, "The Market Man" on pages 307–308, "Word" on page 309, and the excerpt from "Hunger in New York City" by Simon Ortiz, looking especially at figurative language. Then, using one of the poems as a model if you like, write a poem of your own using figurative language to create imagery.

Reread "River Skater" on page 306 and "The Market Man" on pages 307–308. Look for examples of rhythm, rhyme, alliteration, assonance, and onomatopoeia. On your paper, write the words, phrases, or lines in which each sound effect occurs. After each example, write a sentence or two explaining the effect that it gives in the poem.

Continuing Assignment Draft Your Poem

Study your prewriting notes, and think of additional ways to use language to enhance your poem. Create strong images through figurative language and precise word choices. Think about how you will use sound in your poem. Then draft your poem several times. Save all your notes and drafts of your poem.

Revising

Revising Your Poem

If you have drafted your poem several times, you have already done some shaping of the original. Now you are ready to read your poem carefully and begin revising it. First, consider the impact or immediate impression that your poem gives. Make sure that the format of your poem fits the subject. Second, consider the details of the poem, the parts that make up the whole: images, figurative language, word choices, and arrangement. Read your poem aloud, listening to how individual words sound together. Try doing your revision in stages: a first revision to enhance the meaning and the tone, a second to improve poetic devices and polish word choices. Give your poem a title that enhances the meaning. A title should be relevant, provocative, and brief. After these revisions, you may be ready to have someone respond to your poem before you make further changes. Reader response can help you to evaluate your work in a new way and give you some direction for revision.

? Critical Thinking:
Evaluating

Considering the Meaning and the Tone What do you want your readers to feel as they read your poem? Probably you want them to delight in your words, to find your images or word choices particularly striking. Beyond the pleasure in the words or sounds or images, however, you want your readers to find meaning in your poem, to come away from the experience of your poem with an insight into some aspect of human experience. Ask yourself the questions at the top of page 312 about the meaning and tone of your poem. If your answers show you areas to revise, you may wish to make those changes before showing your poem to anyone else.

- Allowing for some differences in interpretation, have I conveyed my meaning clearly?
- What is the tone that I wanted to convey in my poem? Is this the tone that my readers will sense?
- If I have not conveyed the meaning or tone I wanted, what do I need to change?

Considering the Poetic Devices   You may find that you must revise or omit an image, a simile, or a metaphor that you really like because it does not reinforce your meaning. Save pieces that you like in your writer's notebook for possible use in the future. You may decide to revise a simile so that it becomes a metaphor, which is a more direct comparison. A thesaurus will help if you want words that will achieve a particular effect, such as alliteration or assonance. Be sure to use a dictionary along with the thesaurus to check the precise meanings. Ask yourself these questions about poetic devices.

- Do similes, metaphors, or other figures of speech contribute to the over-all effect of the poem?
- Are sound devices used effectively in the poem?
- Would the poem be more effective with an additional metaphor or simile?
- Does any poetic device used in the poem sound strained or contrived?

Considering Individual Words   You will have already been thinking about changing individual words to achieve effects in figurative language and sound. Continue your revision by scrutinizing each word in your poem. Replace or cut words that do not contribute to the poem. Articles, prepositions, *and*'s, linking verbs, and some modifiers can often be deleted without changing the meaning of the poem.

Response Groups and Revision   Responses that you get from classmates or family members who read or listen to your poem can help you as you revise. Sharing a poem with a response group will also give you ideas for revision as others offer comments and suggestions.

Read the following first draft of a poem and the suggestions that readers made for revisions.

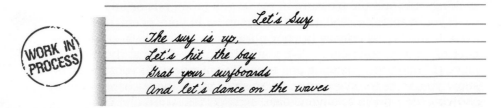

Let's Surf

The surf is up,
Let's hit the bay
Grab your surfboards
And let's dance on the waves

Ride your board
Set yourself free
Ride the tide in luxury.
Hit the pipe as fast as you can
Cause the waves will hit you and smash you man.
So be cool
Let's surf.

Some of the suggestions for revision follow. Notice that responses often begin with a positive comment.

> The "insider's" language — like pipe — sounds authentic; I also like the idea of "dancing" on a board. Could you emphasize that?

> There's a lot of action here — the poem moves quickly — and yet there's a sense that a surfer has to still be cool. Can you play that up? I mean, that this is dangerous but the surfer can't let on that it is.

> I'd like to see more description of the scene so I'd have a better sense of where this poem is set.

> This is kind of way-out, but could you put the poem in the form of waves?

Using these suggestions, the writer makes another draft of the poem, knowing that this one will need more revision too.

Let's Surf

Cries of "surf's up" echo across the white sands.

Fit, bronzed bodies grab their boards, custom-designed.

Hit the bay,

Blue-white waves leaping up to slap high 5's

Then it's get on the pipe as fast as they can,

Some ripped beneath the surf,

Coming up, fused to boards that float coffinlike.

Others dance on the waves, taking a ride, being cool.

A luxury. Their feet boogie on down the wall of water.

WORK IN PROCESS

Assignment Altering Word Choices and Word Order

The author of "Let's Surf" is still not satisfied with the second draft. How would you revise the poem? Rewrite the poem on your paper, making changes in form, figurative language, and word choices.

Critical Thinking:
Evaluating
How can the poem be improved?

Continuing Assignment | **Revise Your Poem**

If you have not already done so, show your poem to classmates or family members and make notes about their responses. Ask yourself the questions on page 312 about meaning and tone, poetic devices, and individual words. Using your answers to these questions and the checklist on page 97, revise your poem. Save your notes and your most recent drafts.

Proofreading Your Poem

Once you have revised your poem completely, you are ready to proofread it for spelling, punctuation, and grammatical correctness. Make sure that if you have violated any rules, you have done so intentionally. Analyze the capitalization and the punctuation in your poem to see whether they contribute to the total effect of your poem or detract from it.

The Grammar Connection

As you proofread your poem, give special attention to these points.

Commas Use commas to separate introductory words and phrases and to set off nonessential phrases and clauses from the rest of the sentence. Do not overuse commas.

Reference Point:
pages 716–721

```
On the history class bulletin board
I find a cartoon which the teacher
invites us to caption.  It shows
an elderly lady grimly watching
the evening news  On the table
next to her is a battered globe
in her hand a hammer.
```

Assignment | Proofreading a Poem

The poem on the next page has no punctuation. Following normal rules for punctuation, copy the poem onto your paper, adding the punctuation that you think makes the poem most effective. Also change capitalization as needed. Be prepared to explain why you made the changes that you did.

> Sunset tints the end of the day
> A restless breeze ruffles tall grass
> Blue sky blanches watching
> the hazy sun abandon it
>
> A black shadow detaches itself
> from dark trees edged in gold
> A leaf falling to earth
> No a bird making a last flight
>
> Jaded the brilliant sun
> vacates its airy spot
> A pale moon drained by envy
> rules the brief night

Continuing Assignment   **Proofread Your Poem**

Paying careful attention to capitalization, punctuation, spelling, and grammar, get your poem into final form for publishing. After you have made your final copy, proofread it again, or have a classmate proofread it for you. Then make your final copy, making sure that no errors remain.

Publishing

Publishing Your Poem

Like other forms of literature, poetry is meant to be shared with an audience. Now that you have finished your poem, share it with an audience by using one or more of the following publishing strategies.

▶ **Strategies**

1. *Set up a poetry reading just for your class, or with an audience of other classes, faculty, and parents.*
2. *Hold poetry response groups to get your poems before an audience and to exchange ideas.*
3. *Share your poems with readers by displaying poems on bulletin boards in classrooms as well as in the library and other common areas around your school.*
4. *Publish your poems in a classroom anthology illustrated by artists in your class or other classes.*

5. *If your school has a literary magazine, submit your poetry to it.* If there is no school magazine at present, this might be a good time to start one.

6. *Publish your poetry in your area newspaper.* Many newspapers have a page for local poets.

7. *Submit your work to national student magazines.* Many of these magazines also hold poetry contests.

8. *Send poems in to poetry magazines.* These magazines, also called "little magazines," often publish the work of young writers.

Continuing Assignment **Publish Your Poem**

Use one of the methods suggested here to share your poem with a variety of audiences. You and your classmates may also find other sources by brainstorming or by consulting your teachers and librarians. In addition, make another copy to put into your writer's portfolio.

Student to Student

Reading and Responding to Writing

Do you ever gaze at your inner landscape? Glenna Sue Murray, a student at Norwood High School in Norwood, Ohio, published this poem about introspection in her school's literary magazine, *Reflections of Young Writers*. As you read the poem, ask yourself the questions beside it. Then follow the directions for *Responding to Writing* and *Reading Critically*.

```
                A Desolate Island

        A desolate island--
        I sat all alone.
        Drawing pictures in the sand,
        I looked to the future;
        My ocean, there, stretched beyond sight.
        It was
        Time for concentration;
        Meditate and conclude
        For the past lay behind.
        The jungle stretched thick;
        Vines intertwined
        And clouds, silent, hovered above.
        They were reminders of history's hurt--
        Small pieces left;
        Part of imbedded storm
        But ahead lay my ocean,
        Awaiting only me.
        Enough, enough
        Let go of tight strings.
        Plunge into unknown
        To discover the best,
        The worst,
        Or whatever shall be.
```

What is the subject of the poem? What details reveal the subject?

Which details of the setting seem also to have a second function? What is the second function?

What is the tone of the poem? Is the speaker pessimistic or optimistic? Is the theme implied or stated directly?

Responding to Writing   Does Glenna's poem make you feel peaceful? — sad? — hopeful? What times in your own life does her poem bring to mind? What parts of the poem are especially significant to you?

Reading Critically   In a brief paragraph or in a class discussion, answer these questions: Does the tone of Glenna's poem change at any point? Where? What are the strongest images? Do these details seem to function as metaphors or, in a wider sense, as symbols?

The Literature Connection

You have exercised your imagination in this unit by creating believable places, people, and conflicts. You also experimented with many devices that complement your creativity, such as selective word choice, similes, metaphors, and tone. These devices help you to build whole, round, living, breathing characters who face situations in a world that your audience should almost be able to feel, smell, and touch.

Guided Reading   The passage that follows describes a grandmother at a distinct, significant moment. Notice the ways in which the author brings her to life. What aspects of her character are the most telling? Is her physical appearance vitally important? What can you find in the passage that will help you to draw a picture of her in your mind?

*O*ne year my grandmother had three quiet daughters and the next year the house was empty. Her girls were quiet, she must have thought, because the customs and habits of their lives had almost relieved them of the need for speech. Sylvie took her coffee with two lumps of sugar, Helen liked her toast dark, and Molly took hers without butter. These things were known. Molly changed the beds, Sylvie peeled the vegetables, Helen washed the dishes. These things were settled. Now and then Molly searched Sylvie's room for unreturned library books. Occasionally Helen made a batch of cookies. It was Sylvie who brought in bouquets of flowers. This perfect quiet had settled into their house after the death of their father. That event had troubled the very medium of their lives. Time and air and sunlight bore wave and wave of shock, until all the shock was spent, and time and space and light grew still again and nothing seemed to tremble, and nothing seemed to lean. The disaster had fallen out of sight, like the train itself, and if the calm that followed it was not greater than the calm that came before it, it had seemed so. And the dear ordinary had healed as seamlessly as an image on water.

> What habits and customs make her girls quiet?

One day my grandmother must have carried out a basket of sheets to hang in the spring sunlight, wearing her widow's black, performing the rituals of the ordinary as an act of faith. Say there were two or three inches of hard old snow on the ground, with earth here and there oozing through the broken places, and that there was warmth in the sunlight, when the wind did not blow it all away, and say she stooped breathlessly in her corset to lift up a sodden sheet by its hems, and say that when she had pinned three corners to the lines it began to billow and leap in her hands, to flutter and tremble, and to glare with the light, and that the throes of the thing were as gleeful and strong as if a spirit were dancing in its cerements. That wind! she would say, because it pushed the skirts of her coat against her legs and made strands of her hair fly. . . .

So the wind that billowed her sheets announced to her the resurrection of the ordinary. Soon the skunk cabbage would come up, and the cidery smell would rise in the orchard, and the girls would wash and starch and iron their cotton dresses. And every evening would bring its familiar strangeness, and crickets would sing the whole night long, under her windows and in every part of the black wilderness that stretched away from Fingerbone on every side. And she would feel that sharp loneliness she had felt every long evening since she was a child. It was the kind of loneliness that made clocks seem slow and loud and made voices sound like voices across water. Old women she had known, first her grandmother and then her mother, rocked on their porches in the evenings and sang sad songs, and did not wish to be spoken to.

And now, to comfort herself, my grandmother would not reflect on the unkindness of her children, or of children in general. She had noticed many times, always, that her girls' faces were soft and serious and inward and still when she looked at them, just as they had been when they were small children, just as they were now when they were sleeping. If a friend was in the room her daughters would watch his face or her

Describe the setting in your own words.

Define *cerements*.

What kind of loneliness is this? Why do old women know it?

face intently and tease or soothe or banter, and any one of them could gauge and respond to the finest changes of expression or tone, even Sylvie, if she chose to. But it did not occur to them to suit their words and manners to her looks, and she did not want them to. In fact, she was often prompted or restrained by the thought of saving this unconsciousness of theirs. She was then a magisterial woman, not only because of her height and her large, sharp face, not only because of her upbringing, but also because it suited her purpose, to be what she seemed to be so that her children would never be startled or surprised, and to take on all the postures and vestments of matron, to differentiate her life from theirs, so that her children would never feel intruded upon. Her love for them was utter and equal, her government of them generous and absolute. She was constant as daylight, and she would be unremarked as daylight, just to watch the calm inwardness of their faces. What was it like. One evening one summer she went out to the garden. The earth in the rows was light and soft as cinders, pale clay yellow, and the trees and plants were ripe, ordinary green and full of comfortable rustlings. And above the pale earth and bright trees the sky was the dark blue of ashes. As she knelt in the rows she heard the hollyhocks thump against the shed wall. She felt the hair lifted from her neck by a swift, watery wind, and she saw the trees fill with wind and heard their trunks creak like masts. She burrowed her hand under a potato plant and felt gingerly for the new potatoes in their dry net of roots, smooth as eggs. She put them in her apron and walked back to the house thinking, What have I seen, what have I seen. The earth and the sky and the garden, not as they always are. And she saw her daughters' faces not as they always were, or as other people's were, and she was quiet and aloof and watchful, not to startle the strangeness away. She had never taught them to be kind to her.

— What has she seen?

Marilynne Robinson (1944–   )
from *Housekeeping*

Enrichment Connections

Choose one or more of these activities to do on your own or as a group.

Speaking and Listening

A Play   Write a play based on a story. If you wrote a short story for this unit, turn it into a play. If you prefer, use the story "Shaving" on page 271. Include all of the necessary stage business and create any dialogue that is needed to explain the action. When you finish, choose a cast and perform the drama.

A Poetry Reading   Find any poem that you have written or one by your favorite poet. Prepare this poem for a poetry reading by rehearsing your delivery a number of times before presenting it. Check your pronunciation carefully and be certain that you make appropriate pauses.

A Narrative Paragraph

Passing down from one generation to the next is a familiar concept. Many cultures transfer belongings, customs, traditions, and even traits. Brainstorm on specific things that have been handed down to you. Choose one item from your brainstorming and write a paragraph about the moment when you received it, or if it is a trait, on the moment when you became aware of it. Narrate your feelings and whether or not the event held significance for you, now that you look back on it. After revising and proofreading your paragraph, gather ones that other classmates have written and make a narrative collection.

A Poem

Write a poem that the passage from *Housekeeping* inspires. Select one dimension to write about, for example, the scenery, or the grandmother, or an idea from her thoughts. Freewrite to come up with colorful ways to express yourself. When you have completed the writing process, publish your poem by using one of the suggestions on pages 315–316.

A Descriptive Paragraph

In the passage from *Housekeeping*, the setting, actions, and thoughts are so clearly explained that this woman is alive in the readers' minds. Notice that the grandmother's appearance is not the most important aspect of her characterization, but other details help to make her whole. Choose a relative of your own and describe that person in a paragraph. Brainstorm on actions, gestures, and expressions that make the person you are describing unique. After you revise and proofread your writing, send it to your relative or to someone who knows the person whom you are describing.

E1 Celebrating Diversity

How did you get to be the person you are? Where did your sense of humor or your taste in clothes come from? Why do certain people interest you while others leave you cold? What makes you *you*?

Events and impressions from childhood, of course, shape people, but so can things that happened even before a person was born. In the following selection, Zora Neale Hurston explores the sources of her more "spirited" characteristics. As you read, make a mental note of the people, places, things, and conditions that may have helped to make Hurston who she is. Then work on one or more of the activities that follow the selection. Working on these may help you to use the literature and your own experience to see the roots of personality and culture in new ways.

CELEBRATING DIVERSITY

J ohn Hurston [my father], in his late twenties, had left Macon County, Alabama, because the ordeal of share-cropping on a southern Alabama cotton plantation was crushing to his ambition. There was no rise to the thing. . . .

It was after his marriage that my father began to want things. Plantation life began to irk and bind him. His over-the-creek existence was finished. What else was there for a man like him? He left his wife and three children behind and went out to seek and see.

Months later he pitched into the hurly-burly of South Florida. So he heard about folks building a town all out of colored people. It seemed like a good place to go. Later on, he was to be elected Mayor of Eatonville for three terms, and to write the local laws. The village of Eatonville is still governed by the laws formulated by my father. The town clerk still consults a copy of the original printing which seems to be the only one in existence now. I have tried every way I know how to get this copy for my library, but so far it has not been possible. I had it once, but the town clerk came and took it back.

When my mother joined Papa a year after he had settled in Eatonville, she brought some quilts, her featherbed and bedstead. That was all they had in the

house that night. Two burlap bags were stuffed with Spanish moss for the two older children to sleep on. The youngest child was taken into the bed with them.

So these two began their new life. Both of them swore that things were going to get better, and it came to pass as they said. They bought land, built a roomy house, planted their acres and reaped. Children kept coming—more mouths to feed and more feet for shoes. But neither of them seemed to have minded that. In fact, my father not only boasted among other men about "his house full of young'uns" but he boasted that he had never allowed his wife to go out and hit a lick of work for anybody a day in her life. . . .

There were eight children in the family, and our house was noisy from the time school turned out until bedtime. After supper we gathered in Mama's room, and everybody had to get their lessons for the next day. Mama carried us all past long division in arithmetic, and parsing sentences in grammar, by diagrams on the blackboard. That was as far as she had gone. Then the younger ones were turned over to my oldest brother, Bob, and Mama sat and saw to it that we paid attention. You had to keep on going over things until you did know. How I hated the multiplication tables—especially the sevens! . . .

Mama exhorted her children at every opportunity to "jump at de sun." We might not land on the sun, but at least we would get off the ground. Papa did not feel so hopeful. Let well enough alone. It did not do for Negroes to have too much spirit. He was threatening to break mine or kill me in the attempt. My mother was always standing between us. She conceded that I was impudent and given to talking back, but she didn't want to "squinch my spirit" too much for fear that I would turn out to be a mealy-mouthed rag doll by the time I got grown. . . .

This is all hear-say. Maybe some of the details of my birth as told me might be a little inaccurate, but it is pretty well established that I really did get born. . . .

They tell me that an old sow-hog taught me how to walk. That is, she didn't instruct me in detail, but she convinced me that I really ought to try.

It was like this. My mother was going to have collard greens for dinner, so she took the dishpan and went down to the spring to wash the greens. She left me sitting on the floor, and gave me a hunk of cornbread to keep me quiet. Everything was going along all right, until the sow with her litter of pigs in convoy came abreast of the door. She must have smelled the cornbread I was messing with and scattering crumbs about the floor. So, she came right on in, and began to nuzzle around.

My mother heard my screams and came running. Her heart must have stood still when she saw the sow in there, because hogs have been known to eat human flesh.

But I was not taking this thing sitting down. I had been placed by a chair, and when my mother got inside the door, I had pulled myself up by that chair and was getting around it right smart.

As for the sow, poor misunderstood lady, she had no interest in me except my bread. I lost that in scrambling to my feet and she was eating it. She had much less intention of eating Mama's baby, than Mama had of eating hers.

With no more suggestions from the sow or anybody else, it seems that I just took to walking and kept the thing a-going. The strangest thing about it was that once I found the use of my feet, they took to wandering. I always wanted to go. I would wander off in the woods all alone, following some inside urge to go places. This alarmed my mother a great deal. She used to say that she believed a woman who was an enemy of hers had sprinkled "travel dust" around the doorstep the day I was born. That was the only explanation she could find. I don't know why it never occurred to her to connect my tendency with my father, who didn't have a thing on his mind but this town and the next one. That should have given her a sort of hint. Some children are just bound to take after their fathers in spite of women's prayers.

Zora Neale Hurston *(1903–1960)*
from *Dust Tracks on a Road*

Taking Another Look

Think about Zora Neale Hurston as an adult. What can you tell about her grown-up personality from her narrative voice and from the events that she chooses to narrate? Now think about Zora the child. Was her childhood happy? Characterize her parents and the life they lived before she was born. Is Hurston more like her father or her mother, or is she like each of them? Explain your response. Why does she tell the tale of the sow? Find passages that make you smile or laugh. What do these passages reveal about Hurston's perspective on life?

Changing Places

Imagine that you are creating a narrative about your childhood. How would you describe it? What do you see when you look at yourself as a child? What traces do you see of your mother or your father? Which aspects of their personalities do they claim to have passed on to you? What are their values, and how do they communicate them? Would they raise you differently if they could turn back the clock? If so, how? Consider these questions as you do one or more of the following activities.

Skill WORKSHOP

Letters and Forms In this selection, Hurston tells the story of her family, one generation back. You, too, can explore your family history, either by interviewing relatives or by researching your family's genealogy. Write a letter requesting information about genealogy research—how to begin, what sources are available, and what methods are used. You may be able to find local sources in your telephone directory under "Genealogy." You can also look into the resources at your local public library.

WRITING

"Jump at de Sun" Have you ever received mixed messages from your parents or from other people in positions of authority? Has one person said "Do this" while the other said "Do that"? Hurston's mother told her to "jump at de sun"; her father told her to slow down and keep her eyes on the ground. What was her response? What have your responses been in similar situations? Write a story, a poem, or a play in which you or another main character is torn in two directions but finds a self-affirming way out of his or her dilemma.

WRITING

Walking, Talking—and Writing What stories have your relatives or family friends told about your first step, your first word, or another early, memorable incident? Some people would rather forget these affectionate anecdotes, but you can turn them into an engaging piece of writing. If you haven't already been told stories about your early attempts to master the world, ask several people who knew you as an infant or a child for their recollections. Then write a short, *focused* story, poem, or play based on the tales you've been told.

LANGUAGE

Making a Purse from a Sow's Ear You might expect to see a statement such as "Hog teaches child to walk" in a tabloid at the supermarket, but perhaps not in a piece of literature. In a sense, though, Zora Neale Hurston *was* taught to walk by a hog. How does Hurston turn a hog into a successful teacher? The answer lies in the language of metaphor. Look up *metaphor* in the Glossary of English Terms at the back of this book and read about this special form of figurative language. Then look for at least four examples of metaphor in the Hurston selection or in other literary selections in the book. Use each metaphor you find as a model and create your own. Personalize your work by dipping deeply into your own experience.

UNIT 6

Writing About Literature

In this unit, you will experiment with literature about *time.* You will read about the passage of time and the sense of mortality that it brings. You will look at the subjectivity of time, the difficulty of waiting, and the uneven pattern of growing up. Reading this literature will allow you to look through the eyes and into the hearts of writers who have expressed their insights about time in carefully crafted literature. Writing about this literature will give you not only new perspectives on time but also on the use of language to discover and express meaning.

You will also learn to take time—to read carefully and slowly and to notice the craftsmanship of each literary work. You will see how the writer heightens the meaning and the emotional effect of the literary work through its style and structure. Taking the time to craft your own responses to literature carefully will make you a better reader as well as a better writer.

Spend some time now looking over these pages and reading the story shown here. Think about how time passes and how it affects different people at different stages of their lives. What fiction, poetry, and drama can you think of that provide a new or special insight into the actual and symbolic importance of time?

Books are what you did before TV.

Some homes still have a few lying around.

WE HAVE TO WRITE A BOOK REPORT!

Araby

North Richmond Street, being blind, was a quiet street except at the hour when the Christian Brothers' School set the boys free. An uninhabited house of two stories stood at the blind end, detached from its neighbors in a square ground. The other houses of the street, conscious of decent lives within them, gazed at one another with brown imperturbable faces.

The former tenant of our house, a priest, had died in the back drawing room. Air, musty from having been long enclosed, hung in all the rooms, and the waste room behind the kitchen was littered with old useless papers. Among these I found a few paper-covered books, the pages of which were curled and damp: *The Abbot*, by Walter Scott, *The Devout Communicant*, and *The Memoirs of Vidocq*. I liked the last best because its leaves were yellow. The wild garden behind the house contained a central apple tree and a few straggling bushes, under one of which I found the late tenant's rusty bicycle pump. He had been a very charitable priest; in his will he had left all his money to institutions and the furniture of his house to his sister.

When the short days of winter came dusk fell before we had well eaten our dinners. When we met in the street the houses had grown somber. The space of sky above us was the color of everchanging violet and toward it the lamps of the street lifted their feeble lanterns. The cold air stung us and we played till our bodies glowed. Our shouts echoed in the silent street. The career of our play brought us through the dark muddy lanes behind the houses where we ran the gantlet of the rough tribes from the cottages, to the back doors of the dark dripping gardens where odors arose from the ashpits, to the dark odorous stables where a coachman smoothed and combed the horse or shook music from the buckled harness. When we

He's older than I thought. In love —or a crush?

returned to the street, light from the kitchen windows had filled the areas. If my uncle was seen turning the corner we hid in the shadow until we had seen him safely housed. Or if Mangan's sister came out on the doorstep to call her brother in to his tea we watched her from our shadow peer up and down the street. We waited to see whether she would remain or go in and, if she remained, we left our shadow and walked up to Mangan's steps resignedly. She was waiting for us, her figure defined by the light from the half-opened door. Her brother always teased her before he obeyed and I stood by the railings looking at her. Her dress swung as she moved her body and the soft rope of her hair tossed from side to side.

Every morning I lay on the floor in the front parlor watching her door. The blind was pulled down to within an inch of the sash so that I could not be seen. When she came out on the doorstep my heart leaped. I ran to the hall, seized my books, and followed her. I kept her brown figure always in my eye and, when we came near the point at which our ways diverged, I quickened my pace and passed her. This happened morning after morning. I had never spoken to her, except for a few casual words, and yet her name was like a summons to all my foolish blood.

Her image accompanied me even in places the most hostile to romance. On Saturday evenings when my aunt went marketing I had to go to carry some of the parcels. We walked through the flaring streets, jostled by drunken men and bargaining women, amid the curses of laborers, the shrill litanies of shop boys who stood on guard by the barrels of pigs' cheeks, the nasal chanting of street singers, who sang a *come-all-you* about O'Donovan Rossa, or a ballad about the troubles in our native land. These noises converged in a single sensation of life for me: I imagined that I bore my chalice safely through a throng of foes. Her name sprang to my lips at moments in strange prayers and praises which I myself did not understand. My eyes were often full of tears (I could not tell why) and at times a flood from my heart seemed to pour itself out into my bosom. I thought little of the future. I did not know whether I would ever speak to her or not or, if I spoke to her, how I could tell her of my confused adoration. But my body was like a harp and her words and gestures were like fingers running upon the wires.

One evening I went into the back drawing room in which the priest had died. It was a dark rainy evening and there was no sound in the house. Through one of the broken panes I heard the rain impinge upon the earth, the fine incessant needles of water playing in the sodden beds. Some distant lamp or lighted window gleamed below me. I was thankful that I could see so little. All my senses seemed to desire to veil themselves and, feeling that I was about to slip from them, I pressed the palms of my hands together until they trembled, murmuring: O love! O love! many times.

At last she spoke to me. When she addressed the first words to me I was so confused that I did not know what to answer. She asked me was I going to *Araby*. I forget whether I answered yes or no. It would be a splendid bazaar, she said; she would love to go.

—And why can't you? I asked.

While she spoke she turned a silver bracelet round and round her wrist. She could not go, she said, because there would be a retreat that week in her convent. Her brother and two other boys were fighting for their caps and I was alone at the railings. She held one of the spikes, bowing her head toward me. The light from the lamp opposite our door caught the white curve of her neck, lit up her hair that rested there and, falling, lit up the hand upon the railing. It fell over one side of her dress and caught the white border of a petticoat, just visible as she stood at ease.

—It's well for you, she said.

—If I go, I said, I will bring you something.

What innumerable follies laid waste my waking and sleeping thoughts after that evening! I wished to

Unpleasant sounds except for her "music"

He's got it bad!!!

"He's one thousand years old today!"

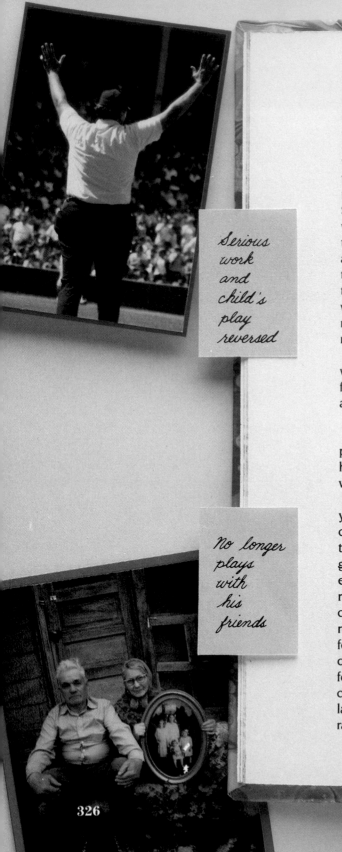

Serious
work
and
child's
play
reversed

No longer
plays
with
his
friends

326

annihilate the tedious intervening days. I chafed
against the work of school. At night in my bedroom
and by day in the classroom her image came between
me and the page I strove to read. The syllables of the
word *Araby* were called to me through the silence in
which my soul luxuriated and cast an Eastern enchant-
ment over me. I asked for leave to go to the bazaar on
Saturday night. My aunt was surprised and hoped it
was not some Freemason affair. I answered few questions in class. I watched my master's face pass from
amiability to sternness; he hoped I was not beginning
to idle. I could not call my wandering thoughts
together. I had hardly any patience with the serious
work of life which, now that it stood between me and
my desire, seemed to me child's play, ugly monotonous child's play.

On Saturday morning I reminded my uncle that I
wished to go to the bazaar in the evening. He was
fussing at the hall stand, looking for the hat brush, and
answered me curtly:

—Yes, boy, I know.

As he was in the hall I could not go into the front
parlor and lie at the window. I left the house in bad
humor and walked slowly toward the school. The air
was pitilessly raw and already my heart misgave me.

When I came home to dinner my uncle had not
yet been home. Still it was early. I sat staring at the
clock for some time and, when its ticking began to irritate me, I left the room. I mounted the staircase and
gained the upper part of the house. The high cold
empty gloomy rooms liberated me and I went from
room to room singing. From the front window I saw my
companions playing below in the street. Their cries
reached me weakened and indistinct and, leaning my
forehead against the cool glass, I looked over at the
dark house where she lived. I may have stood there
for an hour, seeing nothing but the brown-clad figure
cast by my imagination, touched discreetly by the
lamplight at the curved neck, at the hand upon the
railings and at the border below the dress.

When I came downstairs again I found Mrs. Mercer sitting at the fire. She was an old garrulous woman, a pawnbroker's widow, who collected used stamps for some pious purpose. I had to endure the gossip of the tea table. The meal was prolonged beyond an hour and still my uncle did not come. Mrs. Mercer stood up to go: she was sorry she couldn't wait any longer, but it was after eight o'clock and she did not like to be out late, as the night air was bad for her. When she had gone I began to walk up and down the room, clenching my fists. My aunt said:

—I'm afraid you may put off your bazaar for this night of Our Lord.

At nine o'clock I heard my uncle's latchkey in the hall door. I heard him talking to himself and heard the hall stand rocking when it had received the weight of his overcoat. I could interpret these signs. When he was midway through his dinner I asked him to give me the money to go to the bazaar. He had forgotten.

—The people are in bed and after their first sleep now, he said.

I did not smile. My aunt said to him energetically:

—Can't you give him the money and let him go? You've kept him late enough as it is.

My uncle said he was very sorry he had forgotten. He said he believed in the old saying: *All work and no play makes Jack a dull boy.* He asked me where I was going and, when I had told him a second time, he asked me did I know *The Arab's Farewell to his Steed.* When I left the kitchen he was about to recite the opening lines of the piece to my aunt.

I held a florin tightly in my hand as I strode down Buckingham Street toward the station. The sight of the streets thronged with buyers and glaring with gas recalled to me the purpose of my journey. I took my seat in a third-class carriage of a deserted train. After an intolerable delay the train moved out of the station slowly. It crept onward among ruinous houses and over the twinkling river. At Westland Row Station a crowd of people pressed to the carriage doors; but the

Agony of waiting

Why has he lost the sense of his mission?

TIME PIECES
Clock Repairing

328

porters moved them back, saying that it was a special train for the bazaar. I remained alone in the bare carriage. In a few minutes the train drew up beside the improvised wooden platform. I passed out on to the road and saw by the lighted dial of a clock that it was ten minutes to ten. In front of me was a large building which displayed the magical name.

I could not find any sixpenny entrance and, fearing that the bazaar would be closed, I passed in quickly through a turnstile, handing a shilling to a weary looking man. I found myself in a big hall girdled at half its height by a gallery. Nearly all the stalls were closed and the greater part of the hall was in darkness. I recognized a silence like that which pervades a church after a service. I walked into the center of the bazaar timidly. A few people were gathered about the stalls which were still open. Before a curtain, over which the words *Café Chantant* were written in colored lamps, two men were counting money on a salver. I listened to the fall of the coins.

Remembering with difficulty why I had come I went over to one of the stalls and examined porcelain vases and flowered tea sets. At the door of the stall a young lady was talking and laughing with two young gentlemen. I remarked their English accents and listened vaguely to their conversation.

—O, I never said such a thing!

—O, but you did!

—O, but I didn't!

—Didn't she say that?

—Yes. I heard her.

—O, there's a . . . fib!

Observing me, the young lady came over and asked me did I wish to buy anything. The tone of her voice was not encouraging; she seemed to have spoken to me out of a sense of duty. I looked humbly at the great jars that stood like eastern guards at either side of the dark entrance to the stall and murmured:

—No, thank you.

The young lady changed the position of one of the vases and went back to the two young men. They began to talk of the same subject. Once or twice the young lady glanced at me over her shoulder.

I lingered before her stall, though I knew my stay was useless, to make my interest in her wares seem the more real. Then I turned away slowly and walked down the middle of the bazaar. I allowed the two pennies to fall against the sixpence in my pocket. I heard a voice call from one end of the gallery that the light was out. The upper part of the hall was now completely dark.

Gazing up into the darkness I saw myself as a creature driven and derided by vanity; and my eyes burned with anguish and anger.

James Joyce (1882–1941)

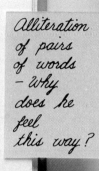

Alliteration of pairs of words — why does he feel this way?

Responding to Literature

After you have read "Araby" carefully, close your eyes and try to picture the scenes in the story. What colors do you see? Where is there darkness or shadow? Where is there light?

As you know, color and lighting play an important part in theater, movies, and television drama. They are also important in literature that is not performed. In the latter case, the author relies upon you, the reader, to take the direct statements about setting as well as more subtle clues and "set the scene" yourself. To some extent, you do this unconsciously as you read, and it "colors" your response to the literature. If you pay particular attention to them, these mood-setting devices can increase your understanding and appreciation of what you read.

Reread "Araby" now and take notes on color and lighting as you go along. Include information that you think would be needed by the lighting director or set designer for a theatrical production of the story. This careful reading should help you to "see" the story more clearly; it may also help to illuminate its meaning. You will return to "Araby" in this unit; meanwhile, save your notes in your writer's notebook.

Writing a Literary Essay

Reading and Responding to Literature

Writers are adventurers. They write for a myriad of reasons — among them to discover, to persuade, to entertain, to inform, and to play with words. Like most readers, you probably read with a similar sense of adventure, looking for the many rewards that reading offers. Reading literature, of course, offers unique and memorable rewards. Literature can show you the countless ways that other people have thought, felt, wondered, dreamed, suffered, and tried to make sense of the world. To read literature is to discover — to find out what writers see in the world and to make connections between that vision and your own life and experiences.

To read literature is also to be fascinated by the way that other people have used words. You know the thrill of watching a perfectly executed double play or seeing a photograph that dramatically captures a mood. You get a similar pleasure from reading good literature. A beautifully phrased description, an exciting dialogue, or a remarkably appropriate metaphor can give you a special kind of aesthetic pleasure. Your delight in the aesthetics of literature makes you part of a long, productive human history.

In the sections that follow, you'll be writing to share your sense of discovery and delight. Writing about literature clarifies your reactions and expands your insights into what you've read. Use this opportunity to experiment. Try different ways of reading and thinking about litera-ture and various ways of interpreting, analyzing, evaluating, and making meaning of what you read.

Remember that poems, short stories, novels, plays, and essays can have several meanings. Because the meaning that you make is so much a part of who you are and the experiences that you've had, other read-ers may find very different, even contradictory, meanings in the same work of literature. Take your reading slowly, then; keep in mind that you're dealing less with right or wrong answers than with a variety of possibilities.

Techniques for Responding

Before you begin to make sense of a work of literature, you often need to read it several times. That's easy enough if you're reading a poem or even a short story, but it's more difficult if you're reading a novel or a play. To help you make sense of what you're reading, practice ways of slowing down your first reading. Allow yourself time to think actively and to construct meaning as you read.

Start by being aware of your expectations. Doing freewriting *(page 11)* to record those expectations at various points in your reading — after reading the title, a stanza in a poem, or a paragraph or a page in a story — can help you to become conscious of the meaning you're making. If you're reading something in an unfamiliar form or something about which you feel unsure, try asking and answering questions *(page 18)* as you read. The following questions will help you to begin to respond to what you're reading. You'll develop your own list of questions as you read and respond.

General Response Questions

- How do you feel about the work?
- In what ways can you relate the work to your own experience, to the experience of a friend, or to something else that you've read or seen?
- What do you like most about the work? What do you like least?
- What parts of the work puzzle you? What questions do you have that you'd like answered?
- What words or descriptions seem most striking to you?

Reading a work aloud or hearing it read aloud can also help you to structure your response, as can discussing it with classmates or friends. Notice where and how their responses differ from your own. Conflicting responses not only enrich your view of a work; they also emphasize that good literature unfolds and offers various meanings to various readers over time. If you read a poem today, for example, and then read it ten years from now, or read it every day for the next year, each subsequent reading would probably lead you to make variations on the meanings that you've made already.

In addition to freewriting and asking questions, other prewriting techniques can be helpful in constructing meaning as you read literature. These techniques are also the first steps in writing a more formal essay about a literary work. After all, any writing that you do begins with your discovering the meaning that you make as you read. Brainstorming *(page 13)* and clustering *(page 14)*, for example, can help you to record or to discover what you come to know about anything that you read. Use these and other prewriting techniques to lay the groundwork for an essay on a work in any **genre** or type of literature. (zhän′rə)

Once you've completed some initial prewriting, try responding in a **double-entry log.** To make such a log, draw a line vertically down the center of your paper. Label the left column *Facts* and the right column *Explorations*. As you read, stop occasionally to record a fact from the work in the left column — a quotation, a description, a comment about the story's content, or a summary — and the page number on which you found that fact. In the right column, explore the fact that you've recorded. Respond to it, question it, and try to make sense of it. A double-entry response to James Joyce's "Araby" *(pages 323–329)*, for example, might begin in the following way.

? **Critical Thinking:**
Analyzing

FACTS	EXPLORATIONS
North Richmond Street is "blind"; empty house "at the blind end"	Is it important that the story takes place on a dead-end street? Is Joyce hinting that "Araby" might be about other kinds of dead ends as well?
The neighborhood: "dark muddy lanes," "dark dripping gardens where odors arose from the ash pits," "dark odorous stables"	Sounds like a dirty, smelly place to live and play. Does this go with the "dead end" idea?

Use a variety of methods to slow down your first reading of a work of literature and to record your thoughts about what you're reading. No matter how sophisticated your understanding of the work later becomes, always begin by thinking and writing about your own reactions.

Assignment 1 First Impressions

On your paper, freewrite on the title "When You Are Old." (Do not read the poem first.) For five minutes, write as quickly as you can any associations that you have with the words of the title. Write what the words suggest to you, what the title suggests about the speaker of the poem, and what connections you see between the title and other things that you've read, seen, or thought. Share your freewriting with a group of your classmates and make a list of what the class already knows or suspects about the poem.

Read the poem "When You Are Old" carefully, one stanza at a time. After each stanza, freewrite a response to the questions in the margin, saving in writing the thinking that you engage in as you read.

? **Critical Thinking:**

Analyzing
What do you think the poem means?

When You Are Old

When you are old and grey and full of sleep,
And nodding by the fire, take down this book,
And slowly read, and dream of the soft look
Your eyes had once, and of their shadows deep;

How many loved your moments of glad grace,
And loved your beauty with love false or true,
But one man loved the pilgrim soul in you,
And loved the sorrows of your changing face;

And bending down beside the glowing bars,
Murmur, a little sadly, how Love fled
And paced upon the mountains overhead
And hid his face amid a crowd of stars.

William Butler Yeats *(1865–1939)*

What is happening here? Who is being addressed?

How are "many" different from "one man"? What is a pilgrim?

Describe the speaker of the poem. What feelings does the poem give you?

Assignment 3 **Clustering**

Read "When You Are Old" again. Cluster to identify and form your thoughts about the poem. Try one of the following ideas as a starting point: Remembering, Getting old, Pilgrim soul, The speaker.

Assignment 4 **Making a Double-Entry Log**

On your paper, make a double-entry log for the first fifteen paragraphs of "Araby" *(pages 323–329)*. If you wish, use the log on page 332 to help you get started.

? **Critical Thinking:**

Analyzing
What meanings can you see in the story?

Understanding Your Perspective

Has your best friend ever startled you by loving a poem that made you uncomfortable and sad? Is your favorite character in a play one that several of your classmates dislike intensely? How you respond to a work of literature and what meaning you make of it are very much a part of who you are: where you live, what kinds of experiences you've had, whether you're male or female, how much reading you've done — even the mood that you're in or something that happened to you yesterday. Your understanding of literature changes as you change. A novel that you read this week will mean something different to you if you read it again in ten years.

As you learn to know yourself, you'll deepen and enhance your responses to literature. Your dreams, your beliefs, your disappointments, and your successes will all affect how you feel about a work. If you're conscious of your preferences and your prejudices, you'll understand your reactions more fully and learn to appreciate the often very different responses of others.

Assignment 5   Your Perspective as a Reader

On your paper, list six characteristics that you have that you think will affect the way that you read and respond to literature. After each characteristic, explain how that characteristic might affect your reading.

Literary Elements

As you were writing about "When You Are Old" *(page 333)*, you probably mentioned the speaker or the situation of the poem, its theme, its structure, or its tone. These elements and others work together to help you make meaning. Being aware of literary elements helps you to improve and refine your ability to make meaning.

Helping to Make Meaning

Consciously or unconsciously, all writers use literary elements. The names of these elements constitute a vocabulary for talking about literature and for making meaning of it. As you read, discuss, and write, use the following terms and others that you've learned.

Literary Elements

- **Characterization** is the representation of people in a literary work. Characters are revealed by their appearance, their actions, their speech, their thoughts, what the author and other characters say about them, and what they say about other characters.
- The **situation** is the event or the action taking place or the condition of the speaker.
- The **plot** is the sequence of events: what happens, how it happens, and why it happens. The plot may include a **flashback,** presenting events that happen at some time before the story begins, and **foreshadowing,** hints of what will happen later.
- The **setting** is the time and the place in which a literary work occurs.
- In poetry the **speaker** is the voice created by the poet to speak the poem. This **persona,** or mask, helps readers to separate the speaker from the writer; the two are not always identical. In fiction, the speaker is the **narrator.**

- The **point of view** is the perspective from which a narrator tells the story. The narrator may be a character in the story, a spectator, or a persona for the author. The narrator usually speaks in the first or the third person and may be omniscient — all knowing — or limited in knowledge.
- The **form** or the **structure** is the organization or the arrangement of the work. Fiction is often organized by plot, drama is usually organized into acts containing several scenes, and most poetry is structured by stanzas.
- The **theme** is a central idea in a literary work. A work may have more than one theme; different readers may focus on different themes.
- The **tone** is the author's attitude toward the subject or the audience, an attitude revealed by a character, by direct comment, or by choice of words, rhymes, and literary devices.
- **Dialogue** is conversation. Most genres employ dialogue, but drama depends on it to reveal plot and character.
- An **image** is a word or a group of words that descriptively re-creates a sensory experience — an experience that we know through our sense of touch, taste, sound, smell, or sight.
- A **symbol** is something that stands for something else.
- **Figurative language** is used to make comparisons between dissimilar objects and to add description and intensity to your comparisons. **Figures of speech** are an important kind of figurative language.
- A **simile** compares two unlike things using the word *like* or *as*.
- A **metaphor** compares two seemingly unlike things by saying that one *is* the other.
- **Alliteration** is the repetition of an initial consonant sound in two or more words of a line or a phrase.
- **Personification** gives human qualities to non-human objects or to ideas.
- **Onomatopoeia** designates the use of words that sound like what they mean: *hiss, buzz, creak, sizzle, thud*.
- **Style** is a combination of the author's choice of words, or **diction,** the length and the complexity of the author's sentences, and the tone that the author creates.
- **Irony** is a figure of speech in which one thing is said but something else is meant. In most cases of irony, the intended meaning is the opposite of what is literally said. **Dramatic irony** occurs when the audience or the readers know something that the characters do not.
- **Stage directions** tell actors how to move around the stage, what facial expressions to make, and what tone to use. They also describe how the stage should look — where props are placed, what lighting is needed, and when music or special effects are used.

Assignment 6   Identifying Literary Elements

Step 1: Read the following poem carefully. *Step 2:* On your paper, list at least five examples of literary elements that you find in the poem. Identify the line or lines in the poem where these examples occur. *Step 3:* Then explain briefly how the literary elements affect the meaning that you make of this poem.

(chĭd'n)

Neutral Tones

We stood by a pond that winter day,
And the sun was white, as though chidden of God,
And a few leaves lay on the starving sod;
   — They had fallen from an ash, and were gray.   4

Your eyes on me were as eyes that rove
Over tedious riddles of years ago;
And some words played between us to and fro
   On which lost the more by our love.   8

The smile on your mouth was the deadest thing
Alive enough to have strength to die;
And a grin of bitterness swept thereby
   Like an ominous bird a-wing. . . .   12

Since then, keen lessons that love deceives,
And wrings with wrong, have shaped to me
Your face, and the God-curst sun, and a tree,
   And a pond edged with grayish leaves.   16

Thomas Hardy (1840–1928)

Taking Notes

As you read a work that you'll eventually discuss in a literary essay, take notes that can be used as evidence for the claims that you'll make. Record information from the work and provide an account of the connections that you make as you read. For example, note the page or the line numbers of images, ideas, or themes that seem to recur, or jot down scenes or passages in which a particular character appears. Record various literary elements that you notice and explain their impact on the work.

Keep a running account of what you're thinking about the work that you're reading. Write comments such as "This first line suggests that . . ." or "This character is just about to. . . ." Then begin to build categories. Examine your notes and decide whether your comments and your references to the work fall into recognizable groups. After you've taken notes on James Joyce's "Araby" *(pages 323–329)*, for example, you might group together all your references to passages in which the girl appears. Another category for that same story might be the references to light and dark. If you're working with a poem, you could isolate and list images that seem to connect in some way or note lines that seem especially important to the meaning that you're constructing. Informational notes of this kind will help you to support the assertions that you make in your literary essay.

Reference Point:
pages 436–437

? Critical Thinking:
Interpreting,
Classifying

Notes on a Poem

Step 1: Read the following poem, taking notes as you read. *Step 2:* Group your notes into categories, listing on your paper the line numbers from the poem that illustrate each category. Watch for recurring images, ideas, or themes.

> *L*oveliest of trees, the cherry now
> Is hung with bloom along the bough,
> And stands about the woodland ride
> Wearing white for Eastertide.   4
>
> Now, of my threescore years and ten,
> Twenty will not come again,
> And take from seventy springs a score,
> It only leaves me fifty more.   8
>
> And since to look at things in bloom
> Fifty springs are little room,
> About the woodlands I will go
> To see the cherry hung with snow.   12
>
>   A. E. Housman (*1859–1936*)

Continuing Assignment **Select a Work of Literature**

For the Continuing Assignments in the first part of this unit, you'll prepare for and write a literary essay on a novel, a play, an essay, a poem, or a short story. *Step 1:* From the library, your literature book, or another source, choose a work that interests, puzzles, or moves you. *Step 2:* As you read, take notes on your paper and begin to categorize the notes. *Step 3:* Write a double-entry log on the work. *Step 4:* Use a prewriting technique such as clustering or asking questions to generate ideas about the work. *Step 5:* List your characteristics as a reader that might affect the meaning that you are making. *Step 6:* List literary elements that you notice in the work. Explain how they influence the way that you are interpreting the work. Save your papers.

Prewriting

Exploring and Focusing Ideas

Literary essays discuss an aspect of a work of literature by making a claim or an assertion about the work and then proving the claim with support from the work itself — the **primary source** — and from **secondary sources** — essays, articles, or books about the work. The prewriting techniques that you use to respond to a work — freewriting, brainstorming, answering questions, clustering, discussing, and keeping a reading log — are all ways to begin your explorations of ideas for a literary essay.

Limiting your topic and developing support for your ideas are both necessary steps in exploring and focusing your ideas. As long as you complete each step, don't be concerned about the order in which you do them. The best order will depend on your topic, your resources, and your personal style.

Limiting Your Topic

It's important to limit your topic to a manageable size and to find an approach that fulfills the promises that you make to your readers. You must decide how much you need to write. For example, if your essay will discuss how the conflict in Joyce's "Araby" *(pages 323–329)* represents a move from childhood to adulthood, three to five pages might cover the topic adequately. If your teacher has limited you to two pages, however, you probably wouldn't be able to do justice to your topic. In a two-page essay you could probably discuss Mangan's sister as seen through the eyes of the narrator or do a reasonable analysis of the structure of the story.

Constraints of length can actually help you as you limit your topic. Because your careful reading and your prewriting have made you very familiar with the work that you intend to discuss, you can expand or narrow the scope of your essay as the assigned length requires. Use the raw material in your prewriting notes, the intended length of your essay, and your purpose, your audience, and yourself as writer to help you limit the focus for your literary essay.

Purpose

A literary essay, like any essay, has a purpose. As you review your responses to a story, for example, you may discover that your most interesting observations relate to one of the characters. If you decide to focus your essay on that character, you must still determine a purpose. What point do you want to make about the character? Will you analyze the way the character's development illustrates or communicates a theme, or will you evaluate the character's development, showing how it strengthens the story? Your literary essay should focus on one main point, expressed as a thesis statement, that you want to share with your readers. Your purpose then becomes to explain, support, and clarify your main point as a way of enhancing your readers' experience of the work that you discuss. Among others, a literary essay may have one of the following purposes:

- *Interpretation.* To interpret a work is to explain what it means. Interpretive essays focus on a major or a minor theme, explaining how that theme develops and answering the question "What does the work mean?"

- *Analysis.* To analyze a work, a literary essay isolates and discusses the techniques that the author uses to create the work. Analytical essays deal with the ways in which structure, imagery, point of view, or other elements of a literary work contribute to its meaning. An analysis answers the question "What techniques does the author use to create and develop the meaning?"

Reference Point: *pages 442–444*

- *Evaluation.* A literary essay that evaluates explains what is significant about a work — something about meaning, subject matter, or the way that its author has used literary elements. An evaluation *judges,* claiming that the work does something well or not so well and answering the question "What is significant about the work?"

In many cases these purposes are difficult, even impossible, to separate. Can you interpret a work without analyzing it? Is it possible for an evaluation not to interpret? It's a question of degree. As you become more experienced as a writer of literary essays, you'll probably find that one purpose appeals to you more than the others. Whatever your approach, remember that you are sharing your views in order to expand and enrich your readers' experiences of the work.

Audience and Writer

Although the readers of your literary essay will usually have read the work that the essay discusses, they will not have read it as you did. Be careful to guide them by explaining your points and giving support to your ideas with quotations, paraphrases, and references to the work. Find the balance between telling your readers enough about the work and telling them too much.

Identify yourself as the writer by selecting an appropriate voice *(page 26)* and tone *(page 27).* Since literary essays tend to be interpretive, analytical, or evaluative, they usually use a formal tone. Although your personal reaction to the work is always an important first step in constructing a literary essay, an impersonal voice is often more appropriate for a formal essay. Use the present tense to discuss the work itself; works of literature are thought of as continuously existing.

Assignment 1 Limiting Topics

On your paper, limit each of the following topics so that it would be suitable for a two-page literary essay.

1. Growing Up in Joyce's "Araby" *(pages 323–329)*
2. Time in Housman's poem *(page 337)*
3. Love in Yeats's "When You Are Old" *(page 333)*
4. Memory in Thomas Hardy's "Neutral Tones" *(page 336)*

Read the following poem carefully. On your paper, write three possible purposes and three possible audiences for a two- or three-page essay about the poem.

Time

'Established' is a good word, much used in garden books,
'The plant, when established' . . .
Oh, become established quickly, quickly, garden!
For I am fugitive, I am very fugitive —

Those that come after me will gather these roses,
And watch, as I do now, the white wistaria
Burst, in the sunshine, from its pale green sheath.

Planned. Planted. Established. Then neglected,
Till at last the loiterer by the gate will wonder
At the old, old cottage, the old wooden cottage,
And say, 'One might build here, the view is glorious;
This must have been a pretty garden once.'

Mary Ursula Bethell *(1874–1945)*

Developing Support for Your Ideas

Ideas for your literary essay probably do not occur to you automatically. Instead, you find a topic by reading a work, thinking about it, and prewriting on it. Remember that you don't need to know exactly what you're going to say before you start writing. Writing and reading are both paths to discovery. As you write about a work, you'll have thoughts and ideas about it that hadn't occurred to you before. Let your interest and your curiosity guide you. Focus on those parts of the work that seem most meaningful, puzzling, or relevant to you. No matter what you write, you'll write most effectively if you are truly interested in your topic.

Reviewing Your Notes

When you read and use prewriting techniques to respond to a work of literature, you accumulate quite a bit of material. Once you feel that you have enough material to work with, sort through your prewriting notes to see what ideas seem to dominate. Be guided at this point by your interests, your ideas, and your support. Read through all your material, trying to connect pieces of it. Look for patterns in the ideas and the information that you've recorded.

Do your prewriting notes suggest that your essay will be predominantly interpretive, analytical, or evaluative? What literary elements in the work will support the purpose that you choose? If the information in the category that interests you looks scanty, do more prewriting and notetaking before you draft. You may even need to return to prewriting and notetaking as you draft.

Generating a Thesis Statement

At this point you have read, used prewriting to take notes, limited your topic, and reviewed your support. Now begin to form a thesis statement *(page 46)* for your literary essay. The **thesis statement** is a one-sentence statement of the main point of your essay, a sentence in which you state the claim or make the assertion that you will prove. Because this is still an early stage in the writing process, you may find as you draft that you need to change your thesis statement or that you see your topic differently.

That's fine. Writing is discovering; as you write, you'll think of new ideas or make new connections. Following connections that seem better than your original ones will probably result in fresher, clearer ideas. Think of this first thesis statement as preliminary. Continue to assess and revise it until it accurately and effectively makes the assertion that you intend to establish and support in your paper. Here are some examples of topics and preliminary thesis statements for literary essays.

TOPIC
The theme of "The Eve of St. Agnes," by John Keats

PRELIMINARY THESIS STATEMENT
Keats highlights the uncertainty of first love by filling "The Eve of St. Agnes" with contrasts.

TOPIC
The use of poetic sound in "The Lake Isle of Innisfree," by William Butler Yeats

PRELIMINARY THESIS STATEMENT
In "The Lake Isle of Innisfree," Yeats's use of poetic sound helps to convey the sense of peace that the speaker hopes to find in this ideal place.

TOPIC
The theme of "The Rocking-Horse Winner," by D. H. Lawrence

PRELIMINARY THESIS STATEMENT
The main theme of "The Rocking-Horse Winner" is that when human beings indulge in greed, they often end up worse off than when they began.

Selecting a Working Title Titles often give important information about what's contained in an essay. They also give your readers early clues about the topic and the approach of your essay. Your title alone may motivate someone to read your essay.

A working title for a literary essay should include the name of the work that your essay discusses and some suggestion of the purpose or the approach of the essay. Even though you may revise it later, a working title reminds you as you draft of what you're trying to accomplish.

Assignment 3 Reviewing Prewriting Notes

Read the following poem and take notes on your paper. Examine your notes and decide whether they point to an interpretive, evaluative, or analytical essay. Write down your decision.

Not Waving but Drowning

Nobody heard him, the dead man,
But still he lay moaning:
I was much further out than you thought
And not waving but drowning.   4

Poor chap, he always loved larking
And now he's dead
It must have been too cold for him his heart gave way,
They said.   8

Oh, no no no, it was too cold always
(Still the dead one lay moaning)
I was much too far out all my life
And not waving but drowning.   12

Stevie Smith *(1902–1971)*

Assignment 4 Writing a Preliminary Thesis Statement

Reread "Not Waving but Drowning." On your paper, write three possible thesis statements for a three- to four-page literary essay on the poem. Discuss the statements with your classmates and choose the one that you think would produce the most interesting essay.

Continuing Assignment Focus Your Ideas

Step 1: Reread the prewriting notes that you did for the Continuing Assignment on page 337. *Step 2:* On your paper, write whether your notes point toward a literary essay that is interpretive, analytical, or evaluative. Limit your topic to one that can be handled effectively in three to four pages or in a length determined by your teacher.
Step 3: Write a preliminary thesis statement. *Step 4:* Be sure that you have enough support for your thesis statement. If you do not, do some additional prewriting. Save your papers.

Organizing Your Ideas

How to organize an essay before beginning to draft it is an individual decision. Some writers plunge in, relying on some inner instinct to guide their organization. Others make lists or notes; still others outline or map; some freewrite a short narrative on what they'll discuss at what point. All good writers, however, keep in mind the point that they want to prove and the prewriting that they've done. Try to find an organization that will make your ideas most accessible to your readers.

Readers bring their own skills and beliefs to anything that they read. To communicate clearly with your readers, adjust your supporting details in the way that will make the most sense while it accurately addresses the topic that you've chosen. Careful planning before you draft will result in a more effective essay.

Categorizing Your Notes   Examine your prewriting notes carefully. As a first step toward planning an outline, look for patterns in your notes. Group together ideas that have something in common and label the categories that you form. Use the categories that you created as you were taking notes, or name new categories to reflect the direction that you're taking in your essay. Keep identifying and labeling until most of the information has been categorized. Looking at the categories will help you to focus your ideas. Use the following suggestions to help you find patterns in your ideas.

Reference Point:
pages 436–437

▶ **Strategies**

1. *Reread your prewriting notes.* Think of a category into which some of the information would fit. Label your paper with the name of that category and copy the information that fits the category onto the paper; cut the information out of its original location and paste it under the category name; or use your computer's editing functions to move or copy the information.

2. *Name several additional categories* for other bits of information. Recopy the information that fits each category onto the paper labeled with the appropriate category name; cut and paste; or use your computer's editing functions.

Reference Point:
pages 513–515

3. *Freewrite a page* that focuses on the topics and the purposes that your categories suggest to you.

Methods of Development   Using a variety of methods to develop the argument of your literary essay can help you to establish your point. Certainly you'll use *illustrations and examples* from the work to support your ideas. To make a point about different kinds of imagery in a poem, you might also use *classification*. If you are discussing a character or examining the plot or the structure, you might use *cause and effect*. *Comparison and contrast* is a common method of development for literary essays, particularly essays that discuss works with similar characters, themes, or images.

Discussing a character might also involve *definition* of the character's function, *process analysis* of the character's development, or a *description* of the character. If a short plot summary is necessary, your literary essay will include *narration*. Any literary essay will probably include several methods of development. Select the methods that help you to say exactly what you intend to say.

Order of Ideas As you arrange the ideas or the subpoints of your essay, start with the most basic and then move to the more complicated. That is, look at your preliminary thesis statement and list what you must prove or explain to your readers. Start with the points that must be proved before the others can be proved. In a way, you are retracing your own pattern of thought.

? **Critical Thinking:**
Organizing

Another way of ordering your ideas is from weakest to strongest. Use this order of importance *(page 38)* to build toward your strongest idea and its support. Your readers will move with you through your explanations, but your strongest point will gain additional emphasis because it is placed near your conclusion.

If your essay uses comparison and contrast *(pages 30–31)* as a method of development, be sure that your discussion is balanced. Present all your points about one work or one interpretation of a work followed by the comparable or contrasting points of the other work or the alternate interpretation (AAABBB), or alternate your points of comparison and contrast (ABABAB). Whatever approach you choose, be sure to balance your discussion point by point.

You may also organize your literary essay by moving chronologically *(page 36)* through the work that you're discussing. Gather support for your thesis statement as you proceed through the work.

Outlining and Mapping To determine the best placement for your ideas, make an outline *(page 47)* or a map *(page 48)*. Because they are much easier to rearrange than the parts of an entire essay, outlines and maps stimulate experimentation. An outline or a map also helps if you get stuck while drafting. Since you've already planned an order for your ideas, you always know what to write next. Of course you may stray from an outline. As you draft, you may find that your original order just does not work. In that case, reorder your ideas and go on writing.

The Primary Source Always support your statements and your claims by providing details that prove their truth. In most cases these details will be references to your **primary source,** the literary work itself, but they can also be additional notes that you've made about the work, illustrations from your own experience or reading, and information from secondary sources.

Quote directly from your primary source when you want your readers to see exactly what the work says or to get the feel of the language used, or when the source expresses something so well that you really cannot put it into your own words. Enclose all direct quotations in quotation marks and include page or line references. Reference Point: *page 725*

Quote sparingly, and quote to support a point, not to make one. Enclose direct quotations of up to four lines of prose in quotation marks and incorporate them into the body of your essay. Begin quotations of more than four lines on a new line, indented ten spaces from the left margin. Indent each line of the quotation and use no quotation marks. As **documentation,** give a page or a line reference in parentheses at the end of the quotation. See page 405 for an example.

Quote poetry in a similar way. Incorporate a line or a part of a line into the body of your essay, enclosed by quotation marks. If you are quoting two or three lines, use slash marks (/) to indicate line divisions. Begin quotations of more than three lines on a new line, indenting each line ten spaces and using no quotation marks. Be careful to reproduce the passage exactly as it appears in the original; duplicate the spacing, the punctuation, and any other visual features of the poem. Document by giving a line reference in parentheses at the end of the quotation.

All **paraphrases,** or passages from the work that you express entirely in your own words, must be followed by a page or line reference. Signal the start of a long paraphrase by using a sentence such as this:

> The events at the bazaar illustrate the degree to which the young narrator's dreams and expectations have shaped his perceptions.

The next few sentences could then paraphrase the events at the bazaar. At the end of the last paraphrased sentence, signal the end of the paraphrase by citing in parentheses the page on which the original passage appears.

Secondary Sources Use **secondary sources** with caution. These writings by scholars who study and analyze literature can be valuable for providing additional support for your thesis statement and for giving you a different perspective on what you've read. Until you've read your primary source carefully and done extensive prewriting on it, though, don't read any secondary sources. Secondary sources should enhance, supplement, or challenge your own ideas, not substitute for them.

Secondary sources in scholarly journals or in books are usually available only in large public libraries or in university libraries, although you can often request them through a smaller library by means of an inter-library loan system. Collections of articles and excerpts from books, however, are frequently available in school libraries.

If you decide, with your teacher's guidance, to use secondary sources, be sure to document them carefully. Give writers credit for their ideas and words. Quote or paraphrase with care, as you do with your primary source, and always give accurate information in your citations and in your list of works cited *(pages 405–408)*.

Revising Your Thesis Statement As you're planning your literary essay, working to arrange your ideas, and selecting details that support those ideas, be aware of how much guidance and direction your preliminary thesis statement is providing. Your outline or your writing plan should list all the points that you must establish in order to prove your thesis statement. Be sure that your evidence supports those points. If you find that your essay is taking a different shape, revise your thesis statement to accommodate your new discoveries. First, though, make sure that the new shape is sensible, not the result of disorganized rambling.

Assignment Organizing and Outlining

? Critical Thinking:
Organizing
What is the best order for your ideas?

Step 1: Reread "Araby" *(pages 323–329)* and take notes on it. Then examine the following thesis statement for a literary essay on the story. *Step 2:* On your paper, list four or five details from the story that support the thesis statement. Construct an outline that orders those points in a way that seems most effective.

Thesis statement: The young narrator's confusion of fantasy and reality is used in "Araby" to develop the idea that a romantic will always be disenchanted in the end.

Continuing Assignment Organize Your Ideas

Step 1: Reread your notes for the Continuing Assignment on page 337 and the one on page 342. Examine your preliminary thesis statement and rewrite it if necessary. *Step 2:* Choose a method of development and an order for your ideas. *Step 3:* On your paper, construct an outline or a map for your literary essay. Save your paper.

Drafting

Drafting Your Literary Essay

You have details, you have a thesis statement, and you have a plan. Now it's time to draft. Drafting isn't your final step; it's your opportunity to see whether your plan and your thesis statement work well with your support. Keep your plan within reach, quote accurately, and document thoroughly. You'll have a chance to shape and adjust your ideas when you revise.

The Introductory Paragraph

Sometimes you won't write your introductory paragraph until after you've finished a draft of your paper; at other times you'll feel that you must get it right before you can go on. In either case, you should accomplish several things in your first paragraph.

In your introductory paragraph, include the title and the author of the work that you discuss. Express your thesis statement clearly so that your readers will know where you intend to go in your essay. You may begin your introductory paragraph with your thesis statement, although it's not necessary. Try beginning with a quotation, some dialogue, an interesting anecdote, some background information, or a startling or controversial statement. For example, critic Warren Beck began his essay on "Araby" with a quotation from another writer:

> "Araby," wrote Ezra Pound, "is much better than a 'story,' it is a vivid waiting."

In Beck's essay, the thesis statement is at the end of the introductory paragraph.

In your introduction, do your best to involve your readers in what you have to say. For a lengthy essay, you might write an introduction of more than one paragraph, but balance the length of your introduction with the length of your essay.

For a five-paragraph essay on "Araby," one writer drafted the following introduction. The thesis statement for the essay is in italic type.

> *The central character of James Joyce's "Araby" changes dramatically in the course of the story.* The boy's changes are illustrated by his actions and his thoughts at three points in the story: the beginning, before Mangan's sister speaks to him; the middle, after he has promised to bring her something from the bazaar; and the end, after he actually goes to the bazaar. Ultimately he comes to see himself more objectively.

The Body Paragraphs

Most of the paragraphs in your literary essay will be body paragraphs, those paragraphs in which you explain and support the points that prove your thesis statement. The number of body paragraphs that you write will vary. You'll usually devote at least one paragraph to each major point, but some points may require two or more paragraphs for adequate development and support.

Each body paragraph should contain one point or claim that is supported by explanatory or clarifying sentences or by supporting evidence. The evidence comes from the work itself, from your own experiences, and from secondary sources. Use quotations, paraphrases, and references to illustrate and prove your point.

As you draft body paragraphs, follow your outline. Stay on your topic, building evidence and support as you write. If you find as you write that some part of your outline does not make sense, resolve the problem by revising the outline. Rearrange the order of your points, insert new points or explanations, or delete irrelevant material. Use transitional words and phrases *(pages 36–38)* to guide your reader through your essay and to emphasize the relationship between what you have just said and what you will say next.

Literary essays tend to follow certain standard practices called **conventions.** Write your literary essay, for example, using a serious, rather formal tone. Keep your point of view in the third person and use the present tense when you discuss the work.

Examine the following body paragraphs from the essay about "Araby." Notice the logic of the developing argument, the transitions between paragraphs and sentences, and the effective integration of secondary sources into the essay. See pages 405–408 for information on how to document secondary sources.

(ĭ-pĭf′ə-nē)

> At the beginning of "Araby," the boy is part child and part adolescent. As a child he plays with other boys every night after dinner, racing around the neighborhood "till our bodies glowed" (323). As an adolescent he is hopelessly infatuated with his friend Mangan's sister, who comes to the doorstep every night to call her brother. The boy stares at her from the porch railings every evening, watches for her from his parlor every morning, and manages to pass her daily as they walk to their separate schools. When he is not watching or following Mangan's sister, he is daydreaming about her:
>
> > Her name sprang to my lips at moments in strange prayers and praises which I myself did not understand. My eyes were often full of tears (I could not tell why) and at times a flood from my heart seemed to pour itself out into my bosom. (324–325)
>
> Although this "emotionality goes beyond the normal level exhibited by the boy's peers" (Sosnoski et al. 242), the boy clearly enjoys being awash in a sea of "confused adoration," (325). He spends one evening murmuring "*O love! O love!*" many times so that he will not "slip from" his feelings (325).
>
> Midway through the story, Mangan's sister speaks to the boy about a traveling bazaar called Araby, and he is so overcome that he promises to bring her something from it. At this point he becomes even more self-absorbed, even feeling himself above some of the things that he had enjoyed earlier. Now he views his school work as "child's play, ugly monotonous child's play" (326), and on the evening of the bazaar he doesn't join his companions in the street, spending an hour gazing at the Mangan house instead.
>
> At the end of the story, the boy has a "Joycean epiphany" (Beck, 96), a revelation about himself. He has waited until nine o'clock for his uncle, been delayed by the train, and spent too much of his money just for admission to the bazaar. Once inside, he finds not only that most of the stalls have closed but that Araby is not the magical place that he'd imagined. Waiters in a café are counting money, and the girl running one of the few open stalls — a girl from England, not the exotic East — is flirting with two young men and obviously doesn't care whether the boy buys anything.

Overcome with "anguish and anger," the boy leaves the darkening hall, now considering himself "a creature driven and derided by vanity" (329). He has learned "from this epiphany that reality never comes up to life's promise" (Magalaner and Kain 79).

The Concluding Paragraph

A graceful conclusion *(page 58)* will leave your readers with a satisfying sense of closure and — what all writers of literary essays hope to produce — with a strong desire to read or reread the work that you've discussed. In your conclusion, look again at your thesis statement in the light of the points that you've presented and supported in your essay. Summarize the main points of your essay, return to a comment that you made in your introduction, or make some personal remarks about the work or about your discussion of it. Try to motivate your readers to experience the work themselves.

The concluding paragraph of the essay about "Araby," for example, refers to the changes in the boy that the writer mentions in the introductory paragraph and suggests what readers might feel about those changes.

> "Araby" has been called "an initiation story in which the protagonist moves from ignorance to knowledge, from innocence to the brink of maturity" (Collins 93). The changes in the boy support this interpretation: he has learned, painfully, to look at his feelings more objectively. Readers can react to the boy's self-discovery in different ways. We can feel sad at his disenchantment and his pain, or we can feel hopeful that this experience will help him in his next encounter with love. Perhaps we can even feel both.

Assignment Drafting a Comparison
_____

Step 1: Read and take notes on the following poem. *Step 2:* Reread Housman's poem on page 337 and take notes on the points of comparison between the two poems. *Step 3:* Plan and draft a literary essay of at least three paragraphs comparing Housman's poem with "From the North Terrace." *Step 4:* Exchange your essay with a classmate; discuss and take notes on the differences between your comparisons. (The poem continues on the next page.)

> ### From the North Terrace
> #### (Mid-afternoon, second Saturday in October)
>
> *L*ike a football team whose colors are gold and scarlet
> This wedge of trees in fall
> Troops out to the edge of the field, with one big fellow
> Looming above them all   4

Like a giant tackle whose name is Pug or Butch
And the smaller dark-green firs
Stand around the pack and get in the way
Like school-boy worshippers.   8

The resemblance will not hold another fortnight
When the leaves have left the bough;
It may not even look, tomorrow morning,
The way it seems to now.   12

Dismissed from the mind in winter, spring, and summer,
As sure as the year again
Reaches this point, it will bring this image with it,
Twenty more times, or ten,   16

Or maybe less, but if I am there to see it,
Each year, a bit more tall,
These trees will troop to the field, in gold and scarlet,
Like a football team in fall.   20

                                     Rolfe Humphries *(1894–1969)*

Continuing Assignment   **Draft Your Literary Essay**

Using your thesis statement, the plan for your essay that you generated
for the Continuing Assignment on page 346, and your prewriting notes,
draft your literary essay. Include a provocative introduction, solid and
detailed body paragraphs, and an effective conclusion. Save your notes
and your draft.

Revising

Revising Your Literary Essay

After you've completed a draft of your literary essay, you'll want to
evaluate carefully what you've written. Revising gives you the opportunity to be sure that you've said what you want to say as effectively as
possible.

Revise in steps. Examine content first: your purpose, your audience, your thesis statement, and your support. Be sure that your writing is effective, clear, and coherent. Then look at your tone and your
style. Revise a number of times, working to communicate your meaning clearly and to fulfill your intentions. Refer to the Revising Checklist
on page 97 and use the following strategies for revision.

▶ Strategies

To revise for content:

1. *Read your essay aloud.* Note any places where you stumble and rewrite them.
2. *Check your draft against your outline to be sure that your essay is complete.*
3. *Determine whether you have achieved your purpose.* Have you kept the promises that you made in your introduction? Have you interpreted, analyzed, or evaluated the work according to your thesis statement?
4. *Make sure that your essay is appropriate for your audience.*
5. *Decide whether your ideas are developed in a logical and appropriate order.*
6. *Check each sentence and paragraph to be sure that it supports your thesis.* Can you isolate the main point and the relevant support in each paragraph? Revise or eliminate unnecessary sentences.
7. *Check your essay for clarity and coherence.* Have you included sufficient detail? Are your transitions effective?

To revise for tone and style:

8. *Check your tone, your point of view, and your verb tenses.* In general, choose a formal tone, third-person point of view, and the present tense.
9. *Check your word choices and the phrasing of your sentences.* Have you chosen words that accurately express your meaning? Should you rewrite some sentences to improve them, to clarify their meaning, or to add variety?
10. *Be sure that your title is precise and appropriate.*

Assignment Revising a Rough Draft

On your paper, revise the following portion of a rough draft. Pay particular attention to the verb tenses, the point of view, and the tone.

> To be a tragic hero, a character must have a potential for greatness but be destroyed by a tragic flaw in his or her personality. I think Macbeth was certainly a tragic hero.
>
> In many ways, Macbeth was an admirable figure. The first act established that he is a great and respected general, who has earned the trust both of his men and of his king. He also had a powerful love for his wife, Lady Macbeth, as well as for his comrades. And I can't help but admire his sense of morality; he knew

that his actions were wrong, and he was plagued by guilt. At the end of Act I, his soliloquy revealed this self-awareness:

> . . . that we but teach
> Bloody instructions, which, being taught, return
> To plague th' inventor. This even-handed justice
> Commends th' ingredients of our poison'd chalice
> To our own lips. (I.vii.7–12)

But as I mentioned earlier, Macbeth's good qualities were outweighed by the powerful tragic flaw that destroyed him: ambition. The temptation of power was too great. He couldn't resist Lady Macbeth's own ambitious arguments. Macbeth committed a series of murders that would lead to the throne, for he believed "For mine own good / All causes shall give way" (III.iv.135–136).

Continuing Assignment Revise Your Literary Essay

Step 1: Reread the draft of the literary essay that you wrote for the Continuing Assignment on page 350. *Step 2:* Write the main point of each paragraph in the margin or on a tag next to that paragraph. Then list the paragraph's support for that point. *Step 3:* Underline any sentences that neither express the point nor provide support for it. Revise these sentences for coherence or eliminate them. *Step 4:* Check the order of your points and your support in each paragraph. If necessary steps or support are missing, add them. *Step 5:* Change any transitions that do not do what you intend and add transitions where necessary. Make a clean copy of your draft and save it.

Proofreading

Proofreading Your Literary Essay

To ensure that the final copy of your literary essay has no errors or omissions, proofread it carefully. Make sure that your final copy contains no errors in usage, mechanics, grammar, or spelling.

To proofread, read your essay slowly and carefully several times, looking for a different type of error each time. Start with the errors that are most common for you. Correcting the errors that you find while you are proofreading may be as simple as adding a forgotten letter or a set of quotation marks. If you find a large error, however, you might need to make a clean copy of that page so that your readers are not confused by your corrections. Refer to the Proofreading Checklist on page 105, and don't forget to make a final check of the clean, proofread copy.

As you proofread your literary essay, give special attention to this point.

Reference Point:
pages 667–669

Placement of Modifiers Be sure that you have eliminated any dangling modifiers. Provide a nearby word for the dangling word or phrase to modify, or rewrite the modifying phrase as a subordinate clause.

Dad saw

Arriving at the reunion, ∧his old classmates stood

before him.

While Dad and his friends were
∧Reminiscing about their teen-age years, three hours went by.

Assignment **Proofreading Practice**

Read the following paragraph from a literary essay on Thomas Hardy's poem "Neutral Tones" *(page 336)*. On your paper, rewrite the paragraph, correcting any errors in usage, mechanics, grammar, or spelling and paying particular attention to the placement of modifiers.

Hardy uses imagery in "Neutral Tones" to rienforce the scene of emotional desolation between the lovers. the season is winter; the sun, as though rebucked by God, is pale. An ash tree stands by a pond with naked branches; a few gray leaves lay on the "starving" ground (1–4). All of these images suggests emptiness and death and echo the poem's human drama: the speaker has been decieved in love, and the relationship is dead Hardy underscores the conection between the natural and human scenes by calling the deceiving lover's smile "the deadest thing / Alive enough to have strength to die" (9–10) and by comparing a grin to "an ominous bird a-wing . . ." (12). indeed, the two scenes become one striking image for the speaker, who recalls with every subsequent deception "Your face, and the God-curst sun, and a tree, / And a pond edged with grayish leaves" (15–16).

Continuing Assignment **Proofread Your Literary Essay**

Reread the literary essay that you revised for the Continuing Assignment on page 352. Proofread it carefully, checking for errors in grammar, usage, and mechanics. Make a clean copy and proofread it again, checking for new errors that you may have made.

Publishing Your Literary Essay

The ultimate step in your work with your literary essay is to share your ideas and your perspectives with your readers. If your essay is effective, their understanding and appreciation of what you've discussed will be enhanced. To publish your literary essay, try one or more of the following methods.

- Place your essay in a folder, design a cover, and make it available in your classroom or in the school library.
- Collect essays on similar topics from your classmates, fasten them in a folder, and provide a cover, a title page, and a table of contents. Make the collection available in your classroom or in the library.
- Literary critics often bring their papers to sessions at conferences and meetings all over the world, read them aloud, and answer questions from the audience. Publish your essay this way by reading it aloud to your classmates and encouraging their questions. Perhaps your class can hold a small-scale literary conference.
- Submit your essay to a writing contest or to a school publication such as the literary magazine.

Continuing Assignment **Publish Your Literary Essay**

Using one of the preceding methods or another that you think of, publish your literary essay. Also keep a copy of it in your writer's portfolio.

Writing a Critical Review

A critical review evaluates the ideas, the characteristics, and the techniques of a literary or artistic work, a performance, or a craft. Reviews of books, films, art, plays, television programs, and exhibits and performances of all kinds appear in newspapers and magazines, and you've probably heard or seen such reviews on radio and television. Your critical review should help your readers to decide whether to view or read the work that you discuss.

Prewriting

Getting and Exploring Ideas for a Critical Review

As a reviewer, concentrate on whether a work is worth your readers' time. In addition, provide readers who have seen or read the work with an opportunity to compare their own reactions to yours. Be aware of your audience and acquaint your readers with what is significant about the work, giving reasons why they should or should not spend time reading or viewing it. Your critical review may evaluate a work positively or negatively or may find a mixture of positive and negative features in the work.

Audience Professional reviewers often have early access to a work. They may receive advance copies of a novel, be invited to the preview of a film, or attend a private press showing of an exhibit. Although you probably will not have these opportunities, the readers of your critical review usually will not have read or seen the work before they read your review. They will, however, have an interest in the work and might consider reading or viewing it. As a reviewer, be careful to give your readers sufficient information to understand your judgment of the work but not enough to spoil their enjoyment of it. Don't give away the conclusion, for example, of a particularly suspenseful film.

Tone A serious, often rather formal, tone is usually appropriate to a critical review. If you are amused, delighted, or irritated, however, a serious tone may not be suitable. Let the nature of the work guide the tone that you convey. Remember, too, that your audience expects you to take your role as a reviewer seriously. Whether you find fault with a work or praise it highly, let your readers know with your tone that you are a thoughtful, reasonable reviewer.

Assignment 1 Examining a Critical Review

Locate a critical review and read it carefully. Sunday newspapers and general news or feature magazines usually print book, film, television, and concert reviews. On your paper, write the title and the subject of the review and answer the following questions about it.

1. Who is the audience for the critical review?
2. How much information about the plot or the theme does the review divulge?
3. According to the reviewer, what is the central idea or the theme of the work?
4. How does the reviewer evaluate the work? Does he or she recommend it?

Experiencing and Responding to the Work

As you read or view the work that you'll review, anticipate information that you may want to include in your review and make note of it. Use the following strategies for anticipating and noting relevant information. If you must rely on memory rather than on a fresh reading or viewing of the work, these strategies will help you to recall what you know about the work.

▶ Strategies

Before reading or viewing the work:

1. *Consider the title as a clue to its subject and meaning.* What do you expect of a book entitled *The Horse's Mouth*? Do you expect something different from a book entitled *A Portrait of the Artist as a Young Man*? Write your expectations and associations with the title.

2. *Review what you know about the author and — in the case of a film, a television program, or a play — the director and the principal members of the cast as well.* To some extent, you build your expectations upon what has happened in the past. Writing may help you to recall what you know and to shape your expectations.

3. *Consider the literary type or genre of the work,* such as novel, play, poetry, general nonfiction, romance, documentary, biography, or autobiography. Each genre has its **conventions:** accepted techniques, devices, characters, types of plots, or settings that appear in most examples of that genre. An adventure, for example, will move

quickly, be full of surprises, and generally focus on a conflict between something good and something wicked. Before you read or view the work, then, try to determine its type and the usual expectations that you have of that type.

As you read or view the work:

4. *Note any special or unusual features that the work contains,* such as uncommon imagery, startling metaphors, great special effects, outstanding acting, or unrestrained suspense.

5. *Record the meaning that you're making* so that you'll be able to determine what the central idea or the theme of the work is.

6. *Note whether the work is meeting the expectations of it that you had* when you considered the title, the author, or the conventions of its genre.

After you've read or viewed the work, continue recording your responses by prewriting. Analyze your own reactions to establish what effect the work had on you and how it created that effect.

A variety of prewriting techniques can help you to explore and develop your ideas for a critical review. To begin, for example, take notes or ask questions about the work. How do you feel about what you've seen or read? What do you like most about the work? What do you like least? Can you relate the work to your own experiences? Do you have any questions about the work? Do you think that others would share your response?

Before and after you read or view the work, use the strategies on pages 356–357. Freewriting *(page 11)*, brainstorming *(page 13)*, and clustering *(page 14)* may generate new ideas and provide creative connections to other works or to your own life. Brainstorm, for example, to list historical exaggerations that you noticed in a television miniseries, or cluster on the quality of the acting in a film. Your prewriting can give you an initial idea for your review and help you to select the details and the illustrations that you need to support your idea.

? Critical Thinking:
Analyzing

Assignment 2 Reacting to the Work

Select a short story or an episode of a television series to review, preferably one that a classmate has also chosen. Before and during your reading or viewing of the work, use the strategies on pages 356–357. On your paper, write notes on your reactions and your observations. Compare your reactions with your classmate's.

? Critical Thinking:
Analyzing
How does the work create its effect on its audience?

Focusing Your Ideas

Now that you have generated ideas by prewriting, examine your notes. Consider your ideas carefully, looking for ideas and thoughts that recur. Look for patterns that will help you to structure your critical review.

Would you recommend the work or works to others? Select from your prewriting notes information that will help you to explain why you can or cannot recommend the work. Use the information to assist you as you search for a focus for your review. If you are comparing two works, such as a book and its film adaptation or a play performed by two different groups of actors under different directors, use comparison and contrast *(page 30)* to consider each work separately (AAABBB). On the other hand, you could consider related elements of the two works, dividing your support according to those elements (ABABAB). If you are writing on one work, propose your evaluation of the work as a thesis statement and gather supporting details from the work.

Omitting Unnecessary Details   To ensure unity, omit details that do not belong. Remember that your purpose is to help your readers to decide whether they would like to read or view the work themselves. Select the information that will give them what they need to understand. Leave out even very interesting details that do not fit the scope of your review.

Taking Additional Notes   If you do not have enough detail to support your ideas, do some additional prewriting. If possible, go back to the work and take additional notes. If you cannot return to the work — a film that is no longer available, for instance — go back to your prewriting notes and your responses. Reread the material that you've gathered and let it help you to recall more information.

Assignment 3 Analyzing a Review

Find and read a book review in a newspaper or a magazine. On your paper, write the title and the author of the book review and the title and the author of the book being reviewed. Then analyze the review by answering the following questions.

1. What does the review include?
2. Does the reviewer recommend the work? Why or why not?
3. Does the review give you enough information to decide whether to read the book?
4. If you have read the book, do you agree with the reviewer's evaluation of it?

Planning Your Critical Review

Begin planning your critical review by organizing your information. Build a structure for your review that suits your material and your own style. One useful method is to include an introduction, a description of the work, the central idea, any special features, an evaluation, and a conclusion.

- *Introduction.* Early in a book review, name the author and the title of a book and identify it as fiction or nonfiction. For a review of a film or a television production, give the title and the names of the director and the principal actors. You might begin by narrating a scene or providing some background material to capture your readers' attention.

- *Description of the work.* Describe the work in a sentence or two. Mention the characters, the situation, and the setting of a novel, for example. Present only the facts that are essential to give your readers a general idea of the subject of a work. To describe a work of fiction, for example, you could write, "*Lord of the Flies,* a novel by William Golding, tells the story of a group of schoolboys stranded on a deserted island during a war."

- *Central idea.* Discuss the central idea of the work: for instance, an explanation of a natural phenomenon in a television series on science, a poet's perspectives on life and human dealings in a poetry collection, or a conflict with nature or other people in a novel.

- *Special features.* If an aspect of the work is unique or especially well done, describe it to your readers. An unusual style, a perfectly formed character, or uncommon camera angles might help your readers to decide whether to read or view a work.

- *Evaluation.* How well does the work accomplish what it sets out to do? Is the central idea or the theme presented in an interesting, knowledgeable way? As a result, is the work powerful or memorable? Include your reaction or a comment about how the work affected you, but refer also to specific passages or scenes as you give reasons that support your evaluation.

- *Conclusion.* At the end of your essay, emphasize your evaluation of the work. Discuss what is significant about it, describe the effect that it had on you, and suggest whether your audience should read or view the work.

Critical Thinking:

Interpreting

Critical Thinking:

Evaluating

Assignment 4 Notes for a Critical Review

Choose a short story, a film, or a television show. Read or watch the work, taking notes on your paper on its action, its central idea, and its special features. Afterwards, on separate paper, write more complete notes for each of the six categories of information that appear in a critical review: introduction, brief description, central idea, special features, evaluation, and conclusion.

Critical Thinking:

Interpreting, Evaluating
What does the work mean? Is it worth reading or viewing?

Organizing Your Ideas

To make sure that your critical review is coherent, plan the order of your main points. Remember that most of your readers will not have read or seen the work. Consider what they need to know when. For example, you could use chronological order *(page 36)* for a review of a film or a book review. Spatial order *(page 37)*, on the other hand, would be effective in a review of a painting or a sculpture. Order of importance *(page 38)* would be useful in a review of a documentary television series.

? Critical Thinking:

Sequencing

Then generate a writing plan for your critical review. Look carefully at the categories that occur naturally in your prewriting notes and arrange them in an order that makes sense. An outline *(page 47)* can provide a structured guide for drafting your critical review, but a formal outline isn't always essential. A clear writing plan is.

Assignment 5 Planning a Critical Review

? Critical Thinking:

Sequencing
What is the
best order for
your notes?

Read "Shaving" on pages 271–277, taking notes on your paper. Examine your notes and arrange them in a logical and appropriate order. Then generate a writing plan for a critical review of "Shaving."

Continuing Assignment Prepare for Your Critical Review

For the series of Continuing Assignments that begins here, you'll write a critical review that compares two books, a book and a film, or a book and a play. *Step 1:* Individually, in groups, or as a class, brainstorm a list of works that you'd be interested in comparing in a critical review. Select works that have some basis for comparison: two books on the same subject or by the same author, a book and its film adaptation, or a book and a play by the same author or on the same general subject. *Step 2:* After discussing the list and consulting your teacher or your librarian, choose the two works that you will compare. *Step 3:* Before and while you read or view the works, write responses on your paper to the strategies on pages 356–357. *Step 4:* Review what you've written and do some additional prewriting. For example, brainstorm a list of the elements that you can compare, or freewrite on aspects of the works that are similar. *Step 5:* Decide whether you will recommend one or both works to your readers. Review your prewriting notes and categorize your information according to the points that you want to make. *Step 6:* Write a plan for your critical review. Include the details that you'll need for an introduction, a description of the works, the central ideas, any special features, your evaluation, and a conclusion. Save your notes and your plan.

Drafting

Drafting Your Critical Review

Drafting is your chance to find out whether you can effectively support your evaluation of the work using the details that you've accumulated. As you draft, follow the format on pages 358–359 or choose a form that fulfills the special needs of your audience and your material. Keep your prewriting notes and your writing plan beside you as you draft, and use the following conventions of the critical review.

Conventions of a Critical Review

- *Point of view.* In general use the third-person point of view to highlight your objectivity as a reviewer. If you're discussing your personal reaction to the work, however, the first-person point of view is appropriate, even necessary.
- *Tone.* For your critical review, choose a serious, rather formal tone. Take your role as a reviewer seriously.
- *Tense.* Unless you're writing about an event that happened last week and is clearly over, such as a concert, use the present tense in your review. Stories, books, recordings, films, and television programs are seen as occurring in the present tense; use the present tense to discuss them.

Be aware of the goals of your critical review and of the route that you'll take to reach them. Use your writing plan as your guide, but be prepared to revise it if it isn't serving your purpose.

Use transitional words and phrases *(pages 36–38)* to get yourself and your readers from one point to the next. Effective transitions signal and emphasize relationships, remind you of logical connections in your writing, and clarify those connections for your readers.

Here is a critical review of a performance of *Hamlet*. Notice its transitions, its organization, and its use of the conventions of a critical review. This review happens to find fault with the production, but remember that a critical review does not have to be negative.

Alex Wainwright's production of *Hamlet* at the New Theater is a triumph of superb acting and direction over careless lighting and a flimsy, distracting set design. Wainwright has elicited excellent performances from his amateur theater group. Richard Yong's Hamlet appeals directly to the audience as a lost, grief-stricken son roused to action by the apparition of his dead father. Ophelia, played by Amelia Sweeney in a controversial interpretation of the role that includes a charged, moving mad scene, retains the sympathy of the audience even at her manipulative worst. The characters of Claudius (Geraldo Nunes) and Gertrude (Ellie Jones) also project an almost electric attraction that humanizes even Claudius's devious hunger for power and for Gertrude.

The exciting acting in this production is almost immediately undercut, however, by glaring inefficiencies in lighting and set design. The guard platform in the first scene, for example, rattles and shakes ominously as the two guards (Jake Kendrick and Jerry Fernandez) rush around in semidarkness. The appropriately dimmed spotlight never seems to be focused on the person speaking, and the overall effect of precarious scenery and poor lighting transforms the scene from one of dark foreboding and evil to one verging on the ludicrous and the ridiculous. Some in the audience were, rightly, moved to giggles and suppressed laughter.

Later, during Hamlet's famous "To be or not to be" soliloquy, the person in charge of the spotlight was much too slow in illuminating Hamlet, leaving the impatient actor to wait several minutes on the darkened stage and then, patience exhausted, to begin his speech in the dark. In the same scene, the arras behind which Claudius and Polonius (played as a wonderfully tiresome busybody by Norm Schumacher) were hiding was so unsteady on its frame that Nunes and Schumacher had to hold it up in full sight of the audience. Again, inappropriate but understandable laughter broke out.

A first-night performance, particularly by an amateur group such as this one, often runs into minor, unforeseeable problems, but the New Theater has such a strong history of interesting and well-rehearsed productions that we now hold Wainwright's group to a high standard. Although his direction has produced a wonderfully acted *Hamlet*, his low budget is no excuse for these production problems. By all means see *Hamlet*. Enjoy the fine acting and the fresh, even controversial interpretation of the characters, but if the lighting and set problems haven't been corrected, make your views known emphatically to the management. Support community theater, but demand quality productions.

Assignment Finding the Central Idea

Select a critical review from a newspaper or a magazine. On your paper, write the name of the work that is reviewed. Then explain the central idea of the review and tell whether the writer of the review evaluates the work positively or negatively.

Continuing Assignment Draft Your Critical Review

Examine your prewriting notes and the writing plan that you wrote for the Continuing Assignment on page 360. Then write a draft of your critical review. Be aware of your tone, your point of view, and your verb tenses. Save your notes and your draft.

Revising

Revising Your Critical Review

Revising gives you another chance to examine what you've written, checking carefully to be sure that your critical review accomplishes its purpose. Consult the Revising Checklist on page 97 and revise several times, evaluating the content, the style, and the tone of your draft. To get a reader's assessment of how effective your review is, ask someone to read and respond to your draft before you revise it. Then use the following strategies for your revision.

▶ Strategies

1. *Decide whether the review tells your readers what they want to know.* Add or rearrange ideas so that your readers will get the information that they need.
2. *Be sure that the review is coherent.* To be certain that your readers can follow your presentation, rearrange or add points if necessary.
3. *Make sure that every sentence is relevant to the review.* Cut digressions and clarify connections.
4. *Be sure that your transitions are clear.* Emphasize comparison, contrast, examples, additions, and notions of time or place.
5. *Check the appropriateness of the tone, the point of view, and the tense.* Does your word choice convey the proper tone? Have you used the third-person point of view and the present tense?
6. *Check the style for possible improvement.* Read your review aloud, marking places that just don't sound right. Then rewrite those sections.
7. *Give your review a precise, informative title.* If possible, include the name of the author, the director, or the title of the work.

Assignment **Revising a Rough Draft**

Read the following paragraph from a critical review of a television series. On your paper, revise the paragraph, using the preceding strategies. Then suggest a title that might be appropriate for the entire review.

> How many of us think about time except to wonder where it went and to wish that we had more of it? Hey, face it, you just don't often!!! A new public television series, which will have aired this Tuesday, looked at time from various perspectives. In segment one, for example, several leading physicists discuss Einstein and the theory of relativity as well as some of the instruments that have been developed to measure time precisely. Each segment will focus on what time means to a particular group: scientists, poets, philosophers, ordinary people, artists, and so on. In a later segment, anthropologists discuss cultural differences in the perception of time, and sociologists tell you about the way time drives people in the nineties.

Continuing Assignment **Revise Your Critical Review**

Step 1: Reread the critical review that you drafted for the Continuing Assignment on page 362. *Step 2:* Read the review again, one sentence at a time. If a sentence doesn't relate to the point that you're making in your review, rewrite it or omit it. *Step 3:* Now read your review aloud. Revise any sentences or paragraphs that don't read smoothly. *Step 4:* Make a clean copy of your revised draft and save it.

Proofreading

Proofreading Your Critical Review

After you have revised your critical review to your satisfaction, proofread it to make sure that you haven't made any errors in the final copy that others will read. Go through the review sentence by sentence, checking for one kind of error at a time. Check spelling, punctuation, grammar, and mechanics and make sure that you haven't omitted words. Make small corrections neatly on the copy, but correct major errors by preparing another clean copy.

The Grammar Connection

Reference Point:
pages 737–738

Underlining (Italics) Be sure that you have underlined (italicized) the titles of books, book-length poems, plays, magazines, movies, and so forth.

The Broadway revival of Thornton Wilder's play "Our Town"
was recently reviewed in <u>Newsweek</u>.

Assignment **Proofreading Practice**

Read the following paragraph from a critical review of a production of *Hamlet.* On your paper, rewrite the paragraph, correcting any errors in usage, mechanics, grammar, or spelling.

Set designers can, of course greatly enhance or deminish a production with their work. xavier White whose artistry enlivened last year's Macbeth and As you like It has clearly diminished the New Theater's "hamlet" his oversized sets with there giant-sized furnishings and garrish colors make the actors literaly look like children playing at being adults. Instead of conveying the sense that Hamlet is overwhelmed by events, as perhaps they were meant to do the sets create a comic, sometimes, surreal atmosphere, that both detracts from the action and the language of the play. Furthermore, the actors are physically hindered by the sheer size of the props that they have to manipulate.

Proofread Your Critical Review

Proofread the final draft of your critical review, checking for one kind of error at a time. Then ask a friend or a classmate to proofread it also. Make a clean copy and proofread it again. Save your paper.

Publishing

Publishing Your Critical Review

The main purpose of your critical review is to let your readers know whether a work is worth their time. Publishing your review is an important final step. To share your critical review with an audience, try one of the following methods.

- Exchange reviews with a classmate. Read each other's reviews; then read or view the work that your classmate reviewed. Comparing your impression of the work with what your classmate claims about it, write a reply, explaining ways that you agree or disagree with the review.
- Gather the reviews that the students in your class have written. Under the direction of a student editor, sort them according to the genre that they review. Then put together a collection of each genre to share with classmates.
- Your school literary magazine or a local newspaper may be very much interested in a review of a recent book or film. Submit your critical review for possible publication.
- Make an audio tape of your critical review and send it to a local radio station; or videotape yourself reading your review and send the tape to a local cable television station.

Publish Your Critical Review

Using one of the preceding methods or another that you think of, publish your critical review. Try to find out whether your readers agree with your evaluation of the work.

Student to Student

Reading and Responding to Writing

You might have a negative reaction if someone referred to you as a fool. Yet Kristen McMahon, a student at Masuk High School, Monroe, Connecticut, argues in her literary essay about Shakespeare's *King Lear* that every decent character in the play is a fool. As you read her essay, ask yourself the questions beside it. Then follow the directions for *Responding to Writing* and *Reading Critically*.

The Fools of King Lear

In the tragedy King Lear by William Shakespeare, the word fool relates to every decent character. The Court Fool, Kent, and Albany can be considered different types of fools for various reasons. Each of these characters possesses significant qualities which make the term fool applicable to him.

> **What is the thesis statement?**

The Court Fool can be referred to as a "wise, truthful fool" who cares about the plight of the King. This fool, a loyal follower of King Lear, exerts his unusual right to state and do many things that no other ordinary person dares to. He continually states the truth to ignorant Lear and the curious audience. The Fool also sheds new light on important areas of the play by restating previously given expressions. The Fool through sarcastic speeches gives the King valuable advice on how to deal with his mistakes.

> **What is the main purpose of this essay?**

Fool:	Canst tell how an oyster makes his shell?
Lear:	No.
Fool:	Nor I neither; but I can tell why a snail has a house.
Lear:	Why?
Fool:	Why, to put's head in; not to give it away to his daughters, and leave his horns without a case. (I.v.22-27)

> **Why is this quotation effective here?**

These lines show the Fool offering advice to Lear in relation to his two nasty daughters. The Fool points out that the King should not have given away all of his land and power, which provide him with protection, to his greedy offspring. Since the King has given Regan and Goneril all of his worldly possessions, they wish to dispose of their senile old father, who has nothing left to offer them. The Fool talks of an irrelevant subject (the snail) in order to present an analogy to the King's situation. The sagacious Fool tries to display Lear's situation for him to see more clearly through the idea that the snail no longer has any protection without his house.

> **What makes these details from the play more than simply plot summary?**

The profound Fool once again provides Lear with concrete, intelligent advice in the following speech:

Mark it, Nuncle.

> Have more than thou showest,
> Speak less than thou knowest,
> Lend less than thou owest,
> Ride more than thou goest,
> Learn more than thou trowest,
> Set less than thou throwest;
> Leave thy drink and thy whore,
> And keep in-a-door,
> And thou shalt have more
> than two tens to a score. (I.iv.111-121)

In this speech the court jester tells the King to act cautiously in all of his actions. The Fool, the all-knowing character, makes attempts to enlighten the King and the audience about the doom to come. He continually warns Lear about his two deceptive daughters and his ominous future. The Fool often states portentous warnings, which made the audience believe that he knows the exact outcome of the play.

Kent, the "loyal fool" of the tragedy, displays an intense loyalty to the King throughout this piece. Even after the King banishes him for speaking out on Cordelia's behalf, Kent still acts as Lear's protector (I.i.139-187). The nobleman disguises himself and becomes a mere servant to the King. In the following conversation, the Court Fool offers his coxcomb, the ridiculous hat worn by the fools, to Kent because he believes that others will consider the noble a fool for offering his service to a poor King.

> Fool: Sirrah, you were best take my coxcomb.
> Kent: Why, fool?
> Fool: Why? For taking one's part that's out
>   of favor. Nay, and thou canst not
>   smile as the wind sits, thou'lt catch
>   cold shortly. There take my coxcomb!
>   ...If thou follow him, thou must needs
>   wear my coxcomb. (I.iv.92-100)

This speech between the jester and Kent contains a double meaning in relation to the disguised servant. The Fool points out that a follower can receive no reward because the King has previously given away all of his valuables. The jester implies that, in the world's eyes, only a fool would help a King in this position. Yet the jester himself admires the foolishness practiced by Kent, who aids the King only in order to help the person he truly cares about.   (Essay continues.)

Does Kristen's discussion of the fool's character involve definition of his function, analysis of his development, or description of his character?

How does the initial sentence of this paragraph provide a transition?

How is this paragraph developed?

How would you expect the essay to continue? How might it conclude?

Responding to Writing   How does reading Kristen's essay make you want to read or reread the play? Are there modern fools? What writing idea concerning the word *fool* does the essay suggest to you?

Reading Critically   On your paper or in a discussion, answer questions such as these: Where does Kristen give you details about the plot? How is her tone consistent with the purpose of her essay? How is her argument as a whole developed? Why is it easy to follow?

Many people have a favorite author whose work is especially meaningful. Authors themselves are no exception; they often respond to another author's work. An **elegy,** a poem written in memory of a person who has died, is a way of not only responding to the loss represented by death but also praising the greatness and the immortality of the person's work. The following elegy is for the Irish poet and patriot William Butler Yeats. In it the poet W. H. Auden reflects on Yeats and his work and on the world situation, the function of the poet, and the nature of poetry.

Guided Reading   First, just look at the poem; notice how different each section is. Then read the poem several times, at least once aloud. Notice that each section has a different "sound," and even a different audience and point of view. One key to what links the sections is the date of Yeats's death. In 1939 Europe was already embroiled in World War II. Look for Auden's metaphorical references to the war in Section III (note the allusion to "the dogs of war" from Shakespeare's *Julius Caesar*). Then answer the questions that accompany the poem.

In Memory of W. B. Yeats
(d. January, 1939)

I

*H*e disappeared in the dead of winter:
The brooks were frozen, the airports almost deserted,
And snow disfigured the public statues;
The mercury sank in the mouth of the dying day.
5   What instruments we have agree
The day of his death was a dark cold day.

Far from his illness
The wolves ran on through the evergreen forests,
The peasant river was untempted by the
    fashionable quays;
10   By mourning tongues
The death of the poet was kept from his poems.

> Explain the metaphor in this line. How does it affect the mood?

But for him it was his last afternoon as himself,
An afternoon of nurses and rumors;
The provinces of his body revolted,
The squares of his mind were empty,
Silence invaded the suburbs,
The current of his feeling failed; he became his admirers.

Explain this extended metaphor.

Now he is scattered among a hundred cities
And wholly given over to unfamiliar affections,
To find his happiness in another kind of wood
And be punished under a foreign code of conscience.
The words of a dead man
Are modified in the guts of the living.

How does the word *guts* affect this stanza?

But in the importance and noise of to-morrow
When the brokers are roaring like beasts on the
    floor of the Bourse,
And the poor have the sufferings to which they are
    fairly accustomed,
And each in the cell of himself is almost convinced
    of his freedom,
A few thousand will think of this day
As one thinks of a day when one did something
    slightly unusual.
What instruments we have agree
The day of his death was a dark cold day.

                    II
You were silly like us; your gift survived it all:
The parish of rich women, physical decay,
Yourself. Mad Ireland hurt you into poetry.

To whom is the poet speaking here?

Now Ireland has her madness and her weather still,
For poetry makes nothing happen: it survives
In the valley of its making where executives
Would never want to tamper, flows on south
From ranches of isolation and the busy griefs,
Raw towns that we believe and die in; it survives,
A way of happening, a mouth.

In your own words, what does Auden say that poetry does? What is poetry?

369

III

Earth, receive an honored guest:
William Yeats is laid to rest.
Let the Irish vessel lie
Emptied of its poetry.

45

In the nightmare of the dark
All the dogs of Europe bark,
And the living nations wait,
Each sequestered in its hate;

50

Intellectual disgrace
Stares from every human face,
And the seas of pity lie
Locked and frozen in each eye.

In your own words, tell how the poet characterizes Europe at the beginning of World War II.

Follow, poet, follow right
55 To the bottom of the night,
With your unconstraining voice
Still persuade us to rejoice;

What does Auden say that a poet should do at times like these?

With the farming of a verse
Make a vineyard of the curse,
60 Sing of human unsuccess
In a rapture of distress;

In the deserts of the heart
Let the healing fountain start,
In the prison of his days
65 Teach the free man how to praise.

In the last two stanzas, what opposites are linked? Why?

W. H. Auden *(1907–1973)*

Enrichment Connections

Choose one or more of these activities to do on your own or as a group.

Writing About Writing

Reread "In Memory of W. B. Yeats" carefully. Take notes on the direct references to the art of poetry (what it is, what it does) and the function of the poet. You may want to include some of your answers to the questions about the poem. Then consider and freewrite about the overall meaning of the poem and how, by example, it shows what Auden thinks poetry is and what it should do. Use your prewriting to write a literary essay on the nature of poetry in Auden's "In Memory of W. B. Yeats."

Using Visual Elements

Select a painting, a photograph, a movie, or a television program in which the use of color and of light and shadow strikes you as particularly important. Take notes on how the artist, the photographer, or the director used these visual elements. Then write a brief narrative in which you use descriptions of color, light, and darkness to create the same effect. If you choose a movie or a TV show, use its story; if you choose a painting or a still photo, create your own narrative for it. Look back at "Araby" on pages 323–329 and the notes that you took for *Responding to Literature* to see how Joyce made these descriptive elements effective without being overwhelming. Post your narrative on the bulletin board. If possible, illustrate your narrative.

Taking a Survey

Perspectives on Time   You may have heard the expression, "Youth is wasted on the young." What do you think it means? Very likely, it has a different significance to people at different stages of their lives. Take a survey of at least one person in each of these age groups: fifth-sixth grade, your age, late twenties-early thirties, your parents' age, your grandparents' age. Ask each person to explain the expression and to give a short, illustrative anecdote. Take careful notes on your interviews. Then prepare an oral or written report to share with your classmates or participate in a panel discussion on "youth and the young."

Evaluating Titles

Good writers choose titles with care. After all, the title is the readers' first clue to the nature and meaning of a work as well as the way most people remember it. Of the literary works included in this textbook, select three whose titles you think are especially well chosen. Write a short essay explaining how each title affected your understanding and appreciation of the work. Be sure that you support your conclusions with specific references to the literary piece.

Manipulating Time

A Narrative   Two literary devices that manipulate time are flashback and foreshadowing. Do research to find some examples of each or gather examples from discussions with your classmates. Discuss the most effective ways to use these literary devices. Then write a brief narrative in which you use at least one flashback and one instance of foreshadowing. If you like, write a parody of a familiar children's story, such as "Goldilocks and the Three Bears" or "Little Red Riding Hood." Place your narrative in a folder that will be available to your classmates.

CELEBRATING DIVERSITY

How much time do you spend thinking about the past? How much time dreaming about the future? Do you ever live totally in the present? How would it feel to have time stand still—the moment stretching back endlessly into the past and going on forever?

As you know from your own experience, time can be at once rigid and flexible. Here are three poems about time—and about other things. As you read, think about how each persona reacts to the past, the present, and the future. Then do one or more of the activities following the poems. Working on these activities may help you to "stop the clock" and focus on the unique characteristics of your time and place.

WRITTEN IN THE SUNSET

Time is engraved on the pale green faces
Of the floating lotus leaves.
Our hearts are a sea, a lake,
Finally a little pond, where
Spider webs interlock over the round leaves,   5
And below them our longing
Is only a single drop of dew.

Sometimes, suddenly the old story overcomes us.
Time triumphs then.
And lets down its hair—   10
Shadowy black,
Trailing like a willow.

The old melancholy
Comes from the land of longing.
The colors of the sunset thicken.   15
The shadows grow fast on the water.
You can tear them,
But not tear them away.

Hsiung-hung *(1940–   )*

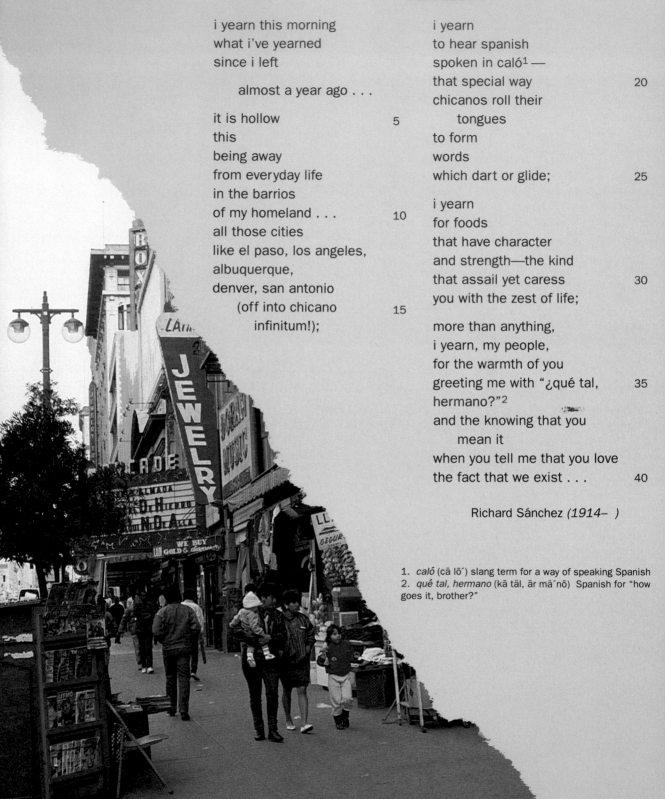

I YEARN

i yearn this morning
what i've yearned
since i left

   almost a year ago . . .

it is hollow   5
this
being away
from everyday life
in the barrios
of my homeland . . .   10
all those cities
like el paso, los angeles,
albuquerque,
denver, san antonio
   (off into chicano   15
     infinitum!);

i yearn
to hear spanish
spoken in caló[1] —
that special way   20
chicanos roll their
   tongues
to form
words
which dart or glide;   25

i yearn
for foods
that have character
and strength—the kind
that assail yet caress   30
you with the zest of life;

more than anything,
i yearn, my people,
for the warmth of you
greeting me with "¿qué tal,   35
hermano?"[2]
and the knowing that you
   mean it
when you tell me that you love
the fact that we exist . . .   40

      Richard Sánchez *(1914–)*

1. *caló* (cä lō´) slang term for a way of speaking Spanish
2. *qué tal, hermano* (kä täl, är mä´nō) Spanish for "how
goes it, brother?"

DAY-LONG DAY

Again the drag of pisca.[3] pisca
. . . pisca . . . Daydreams border
on sun-fed hallucinations, eyes
and hands automatically dis-
criminate whiteness of cotton
from field of vision. Pisca, pisca.

> "Un Hijo del Sol,"[4]
> Genaro Gonzales

Third-generation timetable.
Sweat day-long dripping into open space;
sun blocks out the sky, suffocates the only breeze.
From el amo desgraciado,[5] a sentence:

"I wanna a bale a day, and the boy here   5
don't hafta go to school."

In time-binding motion—
a family of sinews and backs,
row-trapped,
zigzagging through summer-long rows   10
of cotton: Lubbock by way of Wharton.
"Está como si escupieran fuego,"[6] a mother moans
in sweat-patched jeans,
stooping
with unbending dreams.   15
"Estudia para que no seas burro como nosotros,"[7]
our elders warn, their gloves and cuffs
leaf-stained by seasons.

Bronzed and blurry-eyed by
the blast of degrees,   20
we blend into earth's rotation.
And sweltering toward Saturday, the
day-long day is sunstruck by 6:00 P.M.
One last chug-a-lug from a water jug
old as grandad.   25
Day-long sweat dripping into open space:
Wharton by way of Lubbock.

> Tino Villanueva (1941–   )

3. *pisca* (pēs´ cä) picking cotton
4. *"Un Hijo del Sol"* (Ōon ēe´ hō dĕl Sōl) "A Son of the Sun"
5. *el amo desgraciado* (ĕl ä´mō dās grä syä´ dō) the despicable boss
6. *"Está como si escupieran fuego."* (Ĕs tä´ kō´mō sē ĕs kōō pyä´rän fwä´gō) "It's as if they're spewing fire."
7. *"Estudia para que no seas burro como nosotros."* (Ĕs tōō´dyä pä´rä kä nō sä´äs bōō´rrō kō´mō nō sō´trōs) "Study so you won't be a dumb beast like us."

In "Written in the Sunset," what over-all tone or feeling is established in the first stanza? How does Time triumph in the second stanza? What is the effect of the "old melancholy"? What cannot be torn away? Why? What does the speaker of "i yearn" miss most about the barrios? What do these three things add up to? How is "i yearn" similar to "Written in the Sunset"? How does the term "row-trapped" explain the situation of the people in "Day-Long Day"? According to line 1 and line 11, how do things change over time for these migrant workers? According to line 16, what is the way to break this cycle? Do you think the migrant workers of "Day-Long Day" could sympathize with the pain in the other two poems?

Changing Places

Imagine yourself as the persona in "Written in the Sunset." What do you think you might be longing for? If you were to go away from home for a year, as the persona of "i yearn" did, what do you think you would miss most? What sounds, what music, what accents speak to you most directly of home? How would the passage of time affect you? What customs and habits of family and friends would you miss most? Now put yourself into the shoes of the speaker in "Day-Long Day." How might you feel if you had to look forward to day after day of such heat and hard work? Jot down notes to answer these questions and reflect on them as you do one or more of the following activities.

LANGUAGE

Greetings! Notice the typical greeting quoted by Sanchez in lines 35-36 of "i yearn." Many groups and subgroups have distinctive ways of greeting one another. For example, Australians say "G'day" (Good day) while people in the United States say "Hello" or "Hi." Even within the United States, there are differences between regions, between age groups, and between close friends versus new acquaintances, to name only a few. Do two types of research to investigate the typical greetings in your area. First, spend a few days listening for greetings and noting the circumstances in which they're used. Second, take a survey asking people how they greet friends, coworkers, salespeople, their boss, their children, and so forth. Ask them how they would greet the President or their favorite movie star. Finally, working in a group, list and analyze your results. Write down your conclusions about which two or three greetings are most typical of your environment.

SPEAKING and LISTENING

Melodious Speech In "i yearn" Sanchez admires "that special way Chicanos role their tongues to form words which dart or glide." To get an appreciation for this musical language, listen to a recording of Chicano poetry. One is probably available at your library or in your school's Language Department. After listening, practice speaking the Spanish lines from "i yearn" and "Day-Long Day," using the pronunciation guides that accompany the poems. Finally, work with classmates to make a tape recording of "i yearn" and "Day-Long Day" using several voices.

WRITING

Capturing the Flavor Look again at Sanchez's description of the accents and the foods of his people, and notice the vivid words he uses. Choose an accent or foreign language that you're familiar with, or select a distinctive type of food that you either like very much or don't like at all. Then write as vivid a description as you can of the sounds or the tastes. Use either prose or poetry for your description.

WRITING

Running Hot and Cold "Written in the Sunset" and "Day-Long Day" present a contrast in color and temperature as well as in their view of time. Look carefully at the selections to see how the cool blue-green evening of one poem and the scorching, bleaching, blurry day of the other are created. Then choose an emotion or an activity that you could bring to life by linking it to a group of colors and temperatures. Brainstorm or cluster for vivid descriptive words and phrases that will help your reader see and feel your meanings. Finally, write the description either as prose or as a poem.

UNIT **7**

Writing a Research Paper

The desire to know more—to track an idea wherever
it may lead—is so strong in most people that it seems almost
instinctive. In this unit you will channel your drive for knowledge into
writing a research paper. By following the plan outlined here, you'll not only
reach your goal, a full-fledged research paper, but also enjoy yourself in the
process. While increasing your own knowledge, you'll be contributing to the
general store of knowledge about your subject. Your paper will provide a
resource for your readers, some of whom will want to explore the subject further.
As you experience the pleasure of "the hunt," then, be aware that you are also
opening the way for others.

While all fields of human endeavor require the probing mind, two fields are
particularly dependent on research: *science and technology.* In the following
pages, as you sharpen your research and writing skills, you'll read about past,
present, and future developments in the scientific and technological worlds. The
selection shown here takes an appreciative look at "the essential wildness of
science." Its author, Lewis Thomas, describes the seeming anarchy of scientific
pursuit and tries to interpret the method in this madness. As you read, be aware
of his tone and style. In your writer's notebook, jot down particular techniques,
such as the use of comparison, that you might want to use in your own writing.

*T*he essential wildness of science as a manifestation of human behavior is not generally perceived. As we extract new things of value from it, we also keep discovering parts of the activity that seem in need of better control, more efficiency, less unpredictability. We'd like to pay less for it and get our money's worth on some more orderly, businesslike schedule. The Washington planners are trying to be helpful in this, and there are new programs for the centralized organization of science all over the place, especially in the biomedical field.

It needs thinking about. There is an almost ungovernable, biologic mechanism at work in scientific behavior at its best, and this should not be overlooked. . . .

The most mysterious aspect of difficult science is the way it is done. Not the routine, not just the fitting together of things that no one had guessed at fitting, not the making of connections; these are merely the workaday details, the methods of operating. They are interesting, but not as fascinating as the central mystery, which is that we do it at all, and that we do it under such compulsion.

I don't know of any other human occupation, even including what I have seen of art, in which the people engaged in it are so caught up, so totally preoccupied, so driven beyond their strength and resources.

Scientists at work have the look of creatures following genetic instructions; they seem to be under the influence of a deeply placed human instinct. They are, despite their efforts at dignity, rather like young animals engaged in savage play. When they are near to an answer their hair stands on end, they sweat, they are awash in their own adrenalin. To grab the answer, and grab it first, is for them a more powerful drive than feeding or breeding or protecting themselves against the elements.

It sometimes looks like a lonely activity, but it is as much the opposite of lonely as human behavior can be. There is nothing so social, so communal, so inter-dependent. An active field of science is like an immense intellectual anthill; the individual almost vanishes into the mass of minds tumbling over each other, carrying information from place to place, passing it around at the speed of light. . . .

There is nothing to touch the spectacle. In the midst of what seems a collective derangement of minds in total disorder, with bits of information being scattered about, torn to shreds, disintegrated, deconstituted, engulfed, in a kind of activity that seems as random and agitated as that of bees in a disturbed part of the hive, there suddenly emerges, with the purity of a slow phrase of music, a single new piece of truth about nature.

In short, it works. It is the most powerful and productive of the things human beings have learned to do together in many centuries, more effective than farming, or hunting and fishing, or building cathedrals, or making money.

It is instinctive behavior, in my view, and I do not understand how it works. It cannot be prearranged in any precise way; the minds cannot be lined up in tidy rows and given directions from printed sheets. You cannot get it done by instructing each mind to make this or that piece, for central committees to fit with the pieces made by the other instructed minds. It does not work this way.

Effective analogies— very poetic style.

What it needs is for the air to be made right. If you want a bee to make honey, you do not issue protocols on solar navigation or carbohydrate chemistry, you put him together with other bees (and you'd better do this quickly, for solitary bees do not stay alive) and you do what you can to arrange the general environment around the hive. If the air is right, the science will come in its own season, like pure honey.

There is something like aggression in the activity, but it differs from other forms of aggressive behavior in having no sort of destruction as the objective. While it is going on, it looks and feels like aggression: get at it, uncover it, bring it out, grab it, it's mine! It is like a primitive running hunt, but there is nothing at the end of it to be injured. More probably, the end is a sigh. But then, if the air is right and the science is going well, the sigh is immediately interrupted, there is a yawping new question, and the wild, tumbling activity begins once more, out of control all over again.

Lewis Thomas (1913–   )
from *The Lives of a Cell*

More poetry

Possible research topics here.

Responding to Literature

Comparison, whether metaphor or simile, is an extremely useful tool in making a technical subject understandable, and it is one that you will often use in your writing. Besides helping to explain a process or a phenomenon, comparison can also help to enliven and enrich your writing style. Notice how comparison has brightened the passage by Lewis Thomas. Find as many metaphors and similes as you can in the selection, and analyze their effects. For instance, Thomas implies in the last paragraph that scientists are like yelping dogs ready to pounce. What associations does the simile "It is like a primitive running hunt" bring to mind? Using brainstorming or clustering, respond to each of the author's comparisons, and then try to create one of your own. Keep your responses in your writer's notebook.

Planning Your Research Paper

Creating a research paper will challenge your intellect, fuel your imagination, and strengthen your prowess as a writer as no other kind of writing assignment will. To create a research paper, you'll begin by thinking of a topic that you want to investigate. You'll focus on a point that you want to prove about your topic, and then you'll glean facts and information from library sources that support your point. Your investigation will culminate in a formal research paper.

Your research paper will begin with an introduction that states your point. In the body of your research paper, you'll present research findings that prove your point. You'll conclude your paper with a detailed list of your research sources. In this unit you will develop a research paper that is 2500 to 3000 words (twelve to fifteen typewritten pages) in length.

Selecting an Interesting Subject

Creating a research paper is an opportunity to gain in-depth knowledge and to satisfy your intellectual curiosity. Whether your subject is literary or comes from another academic area, select a subject that sparks your interest and that you'll enjoy sharing with your readers.

There are so many fascinating general subjects that you'd enjoy investigating, you'll want to cast a wide net in your search for ideas. Check your writer's notebook, textbooks, television and radio programs, magazines, newspapers, and encyclopedias for ideas. Sound out your friends, parents, and grandparents for ideas too.

Narrowing Your Focus

Suppose that you are interested in the general subject "Computer chips." That subject, however, encompasses topics that include history, the computer business, and uses in hundreds of kinds of computers and devices. A twelve-page research paper that includes all those topics would probably tell readers only surface information that they know already. You need to limit the focus of your paper to one topic within a general subject.

Although you can think of limited topics by brainstorming, it's often easier and more fun to do some preliminary reading to get an overview. You may find some unusual — and intriguing — limited topics.

Getting an Overview

Skim encyclopedias, books, and periodicals to get a quick overview of your subject and its limited topics. You will probably discover that your limited topic — and its subtopics — are broader than you thought.

Some limited topics may need to be limited even further. You should keep limiting a topic until you can thoroughly cover it in a twelve-page paper. As you narrow your focus, keep in mind your interests and those of your readers.

Here is how you might narrow your focus — and then further narrow it — on the subject "Computer chips."

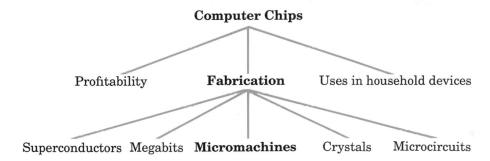

Evaluating Your Topic's Suitability

After finding a narrow topic, make sure that it is appropriate.

- *Is the breadth of your topic suited to the availability of research resources and the length of your paper?* Much information will be available for a broad topic, such as "Birds," but a twelve-page research paper cannot cover that topic in depth. A very narrow topic, however, such as "Computer analysis of the chirping patterns of sparrows" will have so little information that it cannot be researched in most school and community libraries. Try to strike a balance between available resources and the breadth of your topic.
- *Is the topic academic in nature?* An appropriate topic will be in an academic area that can be researched in a library. Don't waste your time or your readers' time on tabloid topics that are sensational, trivial, or silly, such as "Celebrity dating tips."
- *Is the topic objective?* Don't base your topic merely on personal knowledge, experience, or observation. A topic such as "Creating art on my computer" is fine for an essay, but not for a research paper.

You might evaluate the limited topic "Micromachines" as follows.

- Can the topic "Micromachines" be further limited? *Yes. It can be limited to the subtopics of sensor applications and micromotors.*
- Is enough information available on either subtopic for an in-depth research paper? *No. Micromachine technology is so new that most libraries have only limited information.*
- Is the topic academic in nature? *Yes. It is a respected area of study. Articles appear in reputable publications.*
- Is the topic objective? *Yes. It is not based on personal experience or observation.*

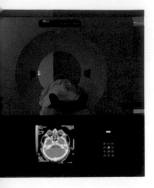

Assignment 1   Topics for a Research Paper

Six broad subjects follow. On your paper, list three topics for each that are sufficiently limited for a twelve-page research paper. You may consult outside sources for ideas.

SAMPLE   Space travel
ANSWER   Solar sails; Foods for space travel; Astronauts' training

1. Benefits of technology
2. Computers in the work place
3. Literary London
4. Medical technologies
5. Careers in writing
6. Environment and technology

Assignment 2   Evaluating Limited Topics

? Critical Thinking:

Evaluating
Which topics
are suitable?

On your paper, evaluate each of the following topics as *Satisfactory, Too broad, Too limited, Not academic,* or *Not objective.*

SAMPLE   *Topic:* Hydroponic farming
ANSWER   Satisfactory

1. How to design and build an orbiting space station
2. Measuring the heat output of medieval fireplaces in Scotland
3. Jane Austen's female view of society
4. Music synthesizers
5. This year's list of best-dressed persons
6. An obscure technique that uses electricity to stop rust on bridges
7. My uncle's computer animation techniques
8. The Franklin expedition to the Arctic
9. Robert and Elizabeth Barrett Browning: a literary marriage
10. Scientific prediction of earthquakes

Formulating the Point of Your Research

Before beginning your research, you should know what you want to accomplish. Formulate the point of your research in one sentence — for example, "The point of my research is to tell my readers about micromachine technology and its possible applications." If you know little about your topic, ask yourself what one question about your topic you would most like to answer. Finding the answer can guide your research — for example, "What are micromachines used for?"

If you cannot formulate the point of your research or state a specific question about your topic, read more about your topic until you can. If you try to do research without having a point, you'll waste time gathering information that you can't use. When you begin drafting your paper, you'll need a focusing idea so that your paper is not just an odd jumble of facts. If you don't know what you want to accomplish, neither will your readers.

Developing a Preliminary Thesis Statement

Once you have formulated the point of your research, write a preliminary thesis statement. A **thesis statement** is a single sentence that states the main idea that you intend to explain or prove in your paper. A thesis statement also reveals your focusing idea or position on your topic. For example, a writer may want to tell readers about the future of micromachines, but *what* about it? Is it important? unusual? good? bad? A thesis statement implies such a judgment.

Try some of these strategies to develop a focusing idea about your topic. Use the one that is most effective.

▶ Strategies

1. *Assert that there is a problem.*

   Laboratory test animals are often subjected to needless and cruel experimentation.

2. *Offer a solution to a problem.*

   Computers with speech recognition ability can eliminate the tiresome and time-consuming task of keyboarding.

3. *Make a statement of cause or effect.*

   Radon, a colorless, odorless gas that seeps through the foundations of many families' homes, is a major cause of lung cancer.

4. *Predict consequences.*

   Twentieth-century research will yield a twenty-first century automobile that is a marvel of microchip technology.

5. *Claim that there is information about which readers know little.*

   Computer software is now available that can teach users how to maximize their creative abilities.

The following example shows how you could develop a preliminary thesis statement from a limited topic.

LIMITED TOPIC	Micromachines
POINT OF RESEARCH	To tell readers about an important new field of technology and its potential
PRELIMINARY THESIS STATEMENT	Small machines, called "micromachines," could revolutionize technology in the twenty-first century as computers have in the twentieth century.

The focusing idea in this preliminary thesis statement is that micromachines will be important and will have a big impact on peoples' lives. Readers can anticipate that the paper will reveal how micromachines will affect life in the next century.

The focus of your preliminary thesis statement should guide your research. You may need to change your preliminary thesis statement after you learn more from your research, but for now it is a starting point for your investigation.

As you develop your preliminary thesis statement, evaluate it by asking yourself the following questions.

- Does my thesis statement make a point?
- Does my thesis statement establish my position on the topic?
- Can my position be supported or proved by research findings?
- Will my research paper convey new information to its readers?

The following poor thesis statement is a biographical statement. There is no point and no position to support.

POOR THESIS STATEMENT | Marie Sklodowska married Pierre Curie and then became known as Madame Curie.

REVISED THESIS STATEMENT | Although Madame Curie was honored for her discoveries, society in the 1700s and the 1800s scorned most women who took an interest in science.

The following poor thesis statement is a well-known fact. It does not establish a position nor does it imply that any new information will be presented.

POOR THESIS STATEMENT | The first powered flight was made at Kitty Hawk by the Wright brothers.

REVISED THESIS STATEMENT | It was only through an amazing series of circumstances and mistakes that the Wright brothers made the first powered flight.

The following poor thesis statement is a biased opinion that cannot be proved by research findings; *most fascinating* is a matter of opinion. State facts, not opinions, to convince your readers.

POOR THESIS STATEMENT | Raising chickens is the most fascinating activity anyone can ever hope to do.

REVISED THESIS STATEMENT | Poultry science has genetically engineered chickens that mature in half the usual time, lay twice as many eggs, and are more resistant to disease.

Assignment 3 Writing Thesis Statements

On your paper, write a possible thesis statement for each group of ideas that follows. To create a thesis statement, use one of the strategies on page 379.

SAMPLE *Limited topic:* Structural analysis by computers
Ideas: Engineers use computer analysis to predict dangerous stress points in high-rise buildings. Complex computer pro-

grams evaluate a building's construction materials and design as well as weather factors and terrain features. Analysis can be used in the design stage or for existing buildings.

ANSWER *Thesis statement:* Computers can now predict the safety — or the lack of safety — in high-rise buildings by analyzing their building materials, design, and physical environment.

1. *Topic:* Special effects in the movies
   Ideas: The field of "special effects" includes painted backgrounds, scale models, odd camera angles, and other effects that have been used for many years. Modern special effects include layering film images, computerized manipulation and fabrication of images, and Dolby sound. In the future, special-effects computer technology may allow filmmakers to create movies by using voices and images of actors from a data bank of stored images and voice prints.

2. *Topic:* Farming in the future
   Ideas: Future farm technologies may include driverless tractors guided by computers or satellites. Bioengineering will produce crops that are drought resistant, pest resistant, and high yielding. Some fruits and vegetables will be genetically altered to fit shipping containers.

Assignment 4 Evaluating Thesis Statements

On your paper, evaluate each of the following thesis statements as *Satisfactory* or *Unsatisfactory*. For statements that are unsatisfactory, tell how they could be improved.

SAMPLE Everyone has different fingerprints.

ANSWER Unsatisfactory — well-known fact without a point or a position. Create a revised thesis statement that makes a point, has a position, and gives readers new information.

? **Critical Thinking:**

Evaluating Does the thesis statement make a point that can be supported by facts?

1. The *Concorde* supersonic airliner travels in excess of fifteen hundred miles per hour.
2. A new computer technology will enable some people who are disabled by spinal injuries to walk again.
3. Vegetables grown with natural fertilizers taste better than those grown with chemical fertilizers.
4. Today we have more advanced technologies than ever before in history.
5. Most people do not think of insects as having complex societies, but some insects form highly structured societies that have queens, laborers, slaves, beggars, soldiers, police forces, jailers, and executioners.
6. Using genetic engineering, biologists have created square tomatoes, grains that grow in deserts, and other agricultural miracles.

You will now begin planning a research paper that you will continue to work on throughout this unit. *Step 1:* List three general subjects that interest you. *Step 2:* Select one general subject and do preliminary reading to get an overview of it and its topics. *Step 3:* Choose one limited topic and continue to narrow it until it is sufficiently limited to be the subject of your research paper. *Step 4:* Evaluate your topic's suitability. *Step 5:* Formulate the point of your research, a focusing idea. *Step 6:* Develop a preliminary thesis statement and evaluate it. Save all your work.

Prewriting

Researching Your Topic

Developing a Research Plan

Before you begin in-depth research, write your research plan on two 3″ x 5″ index cards. On one card, write your limited topic and your thesis statement. On the other card, write the points that you want to cover in your research. The following research plan is for the paper at the end of this unit.

Research Plan Cards

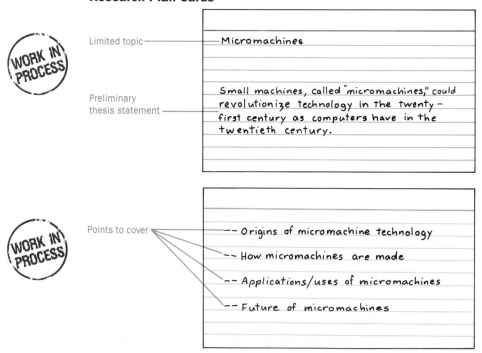

Limited topic — Micromachines

Preliminary thesis statement — Small machines, called "micromachines," could revolutionize technology in the twenty-first century as computers have in the twentieth century.

Points to cover
-- Origins of micromachine technology
-- How micromachines are made
-- Applications/uses of micromachines
-- Future of micromachines

Let your *Points to cover* be major chunks of information. In the preceding plan card, the points are arranged in chronological order: background, the present (how they're made and what they're used for), and the future.

Use logic to determine what points to cover. For example, if you explore a problem, you will want to describe it, get an overview of it, and examine possible solutions to it. Similarly, if you assert that there is a cause-and-effect relationship, you will want to cover the cause, the effect, the consequences, and alternative solutions.

Assignment 1 Organizing Information into Plan Cards

For each topic that follows, think of a thesis statement and points to cover. Then on your paper or on note cards, create two plan cards for each topic. On one card, write the limited topic and a thesis statement. On the other card, write a list of points to cover.

1. *Topic:* Lead poisoning
   Overview information: Lead poisoning is an illness caused by too much lead in the body. Lead poisoning comes from a variety of sources. Small children who eat chips of peeling lead-based paint are frequently the victims of lead poisoning. Such paint is commonly found in older homes. Children can be tested to detect lead poisoning. Lead poisoning over a long period of time can lead to permanent brain damage.

2. *Topic:* Computer viruses
   Overview information: Computer viruses infect computer programs. Viruses are often undetected for months or years. When they are triggered — by a word or a date — they sabotage or destroy computer programs. Losses from computer viruses cost millions of dollars. Some experts say that losses from viruses can be minimized.

Using a Library

You will do most of your research in libraries. Because libraries differ in the amount of material that they provide, it is important that you use the best libraries available to you. Use all the library resources that can help you to locate material related to your topic. Many large libraries also have a research librarian who can orient you to the research sources in the library.

Card Catalogs

A good place to begin your search for information is a library's card catalog. The **card catalog** is made up of cards, filed alphabetically, for every book in the library. Most books are listed in three ways: by author, by title, and by subject. Each catalog card contains the name(s) of the author(s), the complete title, the subject, the publisher, the publication date, the number of pages in the book, and the **call number** of the book — a number that enables you to find the book on the shelf. If the book contains illustrations, maps, bibliographies, or any other special features, these are indicated on the card.

Some libraries have filmed their catalog cards on microfilm. When the film is placed in a projector, you can read it. Other libraries use microcomputers to index their works. On-line computer databases contain the same information as card catalogs do. Ask your librarian for operating instructions.

The following are examples of catalog cards.

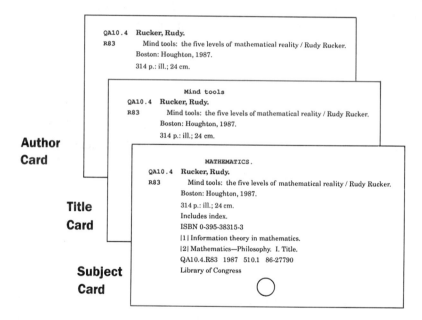

Author Card

Title Card

Subject Card

For general subjects, such as advertising, photography, and software, you will probably find subject cards when you look up the subject. When you look up other subjects, you may find a cross-reference card directing you to another subject heading in the catalog. For example, a card for "Aviation Engineering" may direct you to "Computers — Aviation Use." Books on the subject will be listed under that heading.

To find books in a library, you will need the call number that identifies each book. Nonfiction books are arranged on the shelves according to their call numbers. The call numbers follow one of two systems of classification, either the Dewey decimal system or the Library of Congress classification system.

The Dewey decimal system divides all branches of knowledge into ten parts according to hundreds, 000 through 900. These parts are then further divided into more specific areas of knowledge.

The Dewey Decimal System

000–099	General Works	500–599	Science
100–199	Philosophy	600–699	Technology
200–299	Religion	700–799	Fine Arts
300–399	Social Sciences	800–899	Literature
400–499	Language	900–999	History

The Library of Congress classification system divides all fields of knowledge into twenty lettered groups. These groups are then further divided into more specific subcategories.

Under the Library of Congress system, a book in the field of technology would be classified under the letter *T;* under the Dewey decimal system, the same book would be classified in the 600's section.

The Library of Congress Classification System

A	General Works	M	Music
B	Philosophy, Psychology	N	Fine Arts
C	History-Auxiliary Sciences	P	Language and Literature
D	History (except American)	Q	Science
E, F	American History	R	Medicine
G	Geography, Anthropology, and Recreation	S	Agriculture
		T	Technology
H	Social Sciences	U	Military Science
J	Political Science	V	Naval Science
K	Law	Z	Bibliography
L	Education		

General Reference Works

Some reference works give you information, and others tell you where to find information. Consult an encyclopedia for general information. Within a given article or in the index volume, you may find useful cross-references to related topics; some articles will also provide short bibliographies. Most libraries have general encyclopedias such as *The New Encyclopaedia Britannica, Collier's Encyclopedia,* and *The World Book Encyclopedia.*

Specialized encyclopedias such as the *Encyclopedia of World Art, Van Nostrand's Scientific Encyclopedia,* and *Grzimek's Animal Life Encyclopedia* may also be useful to you.

Other reference books that you should be aware of include *The Guide to Reference Books,* which lists both broad and very specific topics on every subject. *Books in Print* is a resource that indexes all books in print by author, title, and subject. When you need biographical information, consult biographical references such as *Who's Who in America, Who's Who in the World,* and *Current Biography.* If you need place names, consult atlases and gazetteers. Almanacs and yearbooks will give capsulized information for a given year.

Periodical Indexes

Periodical indexes list articles that have appeared in magazines, newspapers, and other publications. Magazines and newspapers provide current information on changing attitudes and new developments before this information is included in books. If your topic requires current information, use periodical indexes to begin your research. Most periodical indexes are published monthly or quarterly with cumulative annual volumes. At the front of each index is a list of abbreviations for the periodicals listed in the index. Authors and subjects are arranged in one alphabetical listing.

The *Readers' Guide to Periodical Literature* is an index to over 180 periodicals. Other indexes list articles in scholarly publications and specialized periodicals. These include the *General Science Index* and the *Social Sciences Index*. The two most popular newspaper indexes are *The New York Times Index* and the *Wall Street Journal Index*. Both of these newspapers cover a broad range of topics thoroughly.

Some libraries may have some periodical indexes on microfilm. Using a microfilm index is much faster than hand-searching a stack of bound indexes because one microfilm index contains the same information as several years' worth of bound indexes.

Entries in bound periodical indexes or on microfilm are similar in form to the following one from the *Readers' Guide:*

MICROMECHANICS
Micro machines. W. Hoffer. il *Popular Mechanics* 165: 79–81+ Jl '88

In the preceding example, the subject is **Micromechanics.** The title of the article is "Micro machines." The author is W. Hoffer. The article appears, with illustrations (il), in *Popular Mechanics* magazine in volume number 165. The article is on consecutive pages 79–81 and is continued on another page. The date of the issue is July 1988.

When using an index to periodical literature, look up your topic and related topics. Ask the librarian whether the library has back issues of the periodicals that you want. Some libraries allow back issues to circulate; other libraries do not.

Other Sources

The **vertical file** is a large file cabinet that contains material that is not kept on shelves. You will find pictures, pamphlets, newspaper clippings, and government pamphlets stored in folders arranged alphabetically by subject.

Many libraries have **nonprint resources** such as compact discs, videotapes, cassettes, and other materials. Ask your research librarian what materials your library carries.

For each topic that follows, write on your paper the letters of the three sources that would be most likely to guide you to useful information.

a. *The New York Times Index*
b. *Wall Street Journal Index*
c. *Social Science Index*
d. *Readers' Guide to Periodical Literature*
e. *General Science Index*
f. *Current Biography*
g. Card catalog

SAMPLE Recent disintegration of ozone layer
ANSWER a, d, e

1. Albert Einstein
2. Sports medicine
3. Nuclear waste disposal
4. Black holes
5. Music synthesizers
6. Industrial robots
7. Computerized code breaking
8. Flight simulators
9. Laser eye surgery
10. Authenticating art with computers

Making a List of Sources

The first step in your library research is to prepare a **working source list,** a list of books, magazines, and other research sources that you intend to use. You will prepare your source list by consulting the card catalog, indexes to periodical literature, and other reference works. You will probably want five to ten sources.

Using Source Cards

For convenience, use note cards (3″ x 5″ index cards) to record the information that identifies your sources. Your source cards will be used for two tasks: (1) to locate your sources on library shelves, and (2) to prepare a detailed list of sources later.

Use the formats that follow to record information on your source cards. You will need more information to prepare your detailed list of sources than you need to find the sources, so do not omit any categories of information. You may also need to get more information from a source later in your project. Make a separate card for each source.

Books and Pamphlets If the source is a book or a pamphlet, list information in the following order on your source cards.

1. *Author's name* (last name first). If there are two or three authors, write the authors' names in the order in which they are listed on the catalog card and on the title page of the book — which may or may not be in alphabetical order. Do not reverse the name of any authors except the first. If there are more than three authors, write the name of the first author and add *et al.,* which means "and others." If there is no author listed on the title page, begin with the

title of the work, unless the work is a government publication, in which case use this sequence of names in place of the author's name: the government, the agency, the subagency.

2. *Title of a work within a collection* (if using a collection of works or an anthology).

3. *Book title* (underlined — would appear in italic type in print). If a book has a subtitle — a title printed in smaller letters that appears under the main title — treat the subtitle as part of the title. Use a colon between the title and the subtitle. Underline the entire title.

4. *Edition* (only if the book is not a first edition or is a special edition).

5. *Name of editor, translator, or compiler* (if given).

6. *City where the publisher's headquarters is located.*

7. *Publisher's name* (shortened form — Columbia University Press becomes Columbia UP; Houghton Mifflin Company becomes Houghton; Funk and Wagnalls, Inc. becomes Funk). Usually, you will use only the first important word in a publisher's name. Federal government publications are usually printed by the Government Printing Office, abbreviated as GPO.

8. *Year of publication.*

9. *Page numbers — only for a work within a collection of works.* Write only the page numbers of the particular work that you are using.

A BOOK WITH ONE AUTHOR

Mortenson, Joseph. *Whale Songs and Wasp Maps: The Mystery of Animal Thinking.* New York: Dutton, 1987.

A BOOK WITH TWO OR THREE AUTHORS

Oberg, James E., and Alcestis R. Oberg. *Living on the Next Frontier.* New York: McGraw, 1986.

A BOOK WITH MORE THAN THREE AUTHORS

McLaughlin, Steven D., et al. *The Changing Lives of American Women.* Chapel Hill: U of North Carolina P, 1988.

A BOOK COMPILED BY AN EDITOR

Crump, Donald J., ed. *Builders of the Ancient World: Marvels of Engineering.* Washington: Natl. Geographic Soc., 1986.

A WORK IN AN ANTHOLOGY OR A COLLECTION OF WORKS

Walker, Alice. "Beyond What." *Images of Women in Literature.* Ed. Mary Anne Ferguson. 3rd ed. Boston: Houghton, 1973. 554.

A UNITED STATES GOVERNMENT PAMPHLET — NO AUTHOR GIVEN

United States. Dept. of Commerce. Patent Office. *Story of the United States Patent Office.* Washington: GPO, 1972.

**Source Card:
Book**

Author —————————— Mortenson, Joseph.

Title
(includes subtitle) ————— Whale Songs and Wasp Maps: The Mystery
                          of Animal Thinking.

City of publication ———— New York: Dutton,

Publisher (abbreviated) ——

Year of publication ————— 1987.

Magazines and Newspapers   To make a source card for an article from a magazine or a newspaper, list the information in the following order.

1. *Author's name* (last name first). If the author of the article is not given, begin the listing with the title of the article.

2. *Title of the article* (in quotation marks). Use upper-case and lower-case letters.

3. *Name of the magazine or the newspaper.* Drop articles such as *A* and *The*, and underline the name of the periodical.

4. *Date of publication.* Use the sequence of day-month-year; abbreviate the month except for May, June, and July.

5. *Edition* if given. Some newspapers have regional, national, international, or late editions. Abbreviate them as *eastern ed., natl. ed., internatl. ed.,* and *late ed.* If the edition is given, it will appear with the title and the date on the first page of the newspaper.

6. *Newspaper section number* in which the article appears. Use this number only if the newspaper begins each section with page 1 and does not include the section as part of the page number at the top of each page. Abbreviate the word *section* as *sec.* (sec. 2: 3). If a newspaper paginates each section separately and does include the section number or the letter as part of the page number at the top of each page, include the section letter as part of the page number (C4).

7. *First and last page numbers of the article,* for example, 44–46. If the pages are not consecutive (for example, the article begins on page 37 and skips to page 81), write the first page number and a plus sign (37+).

A MAGAZINE ARTICLE

Carpenter, Betsy. "Will Machines Ever Think?" *U.S. News and
    World Report* 17 Oct. 1988: 64–65.
Huyghe, Patrick. "Space Age Copters." *Discover* May 1988: 49+.
Sides, Franklin. "Varmints." *Mother Earth News* July–Aug. 1988:
    41–43.

A NEWSPAPER ARTICLE

Blakeslee, Sandra. "Researchers Detect Chemical Differences
in Muscle Fatigue." *New York Times* 27 Sept. 1988, natl. ed.: C3.
"'I Blew It,' Astronomer Says of Flawed Comet Study." *Boston
Globe* 3 Oct. 1988: 34.

Encyclopedias and Reference Books   To make a source card for
an article in an encyclopedia or a reference book, list the information as
follows.

1. *Author* (last name first). If the author is not named, begin the listing with the title of the article.
2. *Title of the article* (in quotation marks).
3. *Name of the encyclopedia or the reference book* (underlined).
4. *City where the publisher's headquarters is located — for reference
   books only.*
5. *Publisher's name — shortened form — for reference books only.*
6. *Year of publication of the edition* that you are using.

AN ENCYCLOPEDIA ARTICLE

Bergson, Tor. "Meteorology." *McGraw-Hill Encyclopedia of Science
and Technology.* 1987 ed.

A REFERENCE BOOK ARTICLE

Cassutt, Michael. "John Glenn." *Who's Who in Space: The First
Twenty-Five Years.* Boston: Hall, 1987.

Television and Radio Programs   If your source is a television or radio
program, list information in the following order on your source card.

1. *Title of episode* (in quotation marks).
2. *Optional information.* If you want to include the names of the
   writer, the narrator, the producer, the director, or the stars, include
   their names in the order just given, separated by periods, after the
   episode title.
3. *Title of program* (underlined).
4. *Network.*
5. *Local station and city.*
6. *Broadcast date.*

AN EPISODE IN A SERIES

"The Ancients." Narr. George Bainbridge. Written and prod.
Maria Estevez. *Search for the Stars.* PBS. WNET, New
York. 5 Jan. 1989.

A ONE-PART TELEVISION DOCUMENTARY OR SPECIAL PROGRAM

Slow Fires: On the Preservation of the Human Record. Narr.
Robert MacNeil. PBS. WGBH, Boston. 22 Dec. 1988.

Films   If your source is a film, list information in the following order on your source card.

1. *Title of film* (underlined).
2. *Optional information.*   If you want to include the names of the writers, the performers, or the producers, include this information in the order just given.
3. *Director* (abbreviated Dir.).
4. *Distributor* (abbreviate name of distributor when possible).
5. *Year of release.*
6. *Any additional information.*

> **A FILM**
>
> *The Caine Mutiny.*   Screenplay by Stanley Roberts.   Dir. Edward
>   Dmytryk.   Columbia Pictures.   1954.   Based on *The Caine
>   Mutiny* by Herman Wouk.

Interviews   If your source is an interview conducted by you, the researcher, list information in the following order on your source card.

1. *Name of interviewee.*
2. *Kind of interview* (personal, telephone, and so on).
3. *Date of the interview* (in day month year sequence).

> **AN INTERVIEW**
>
> Humphries, Lucinda.   Telephone interview.   12 Jan. 1989.

Assignment 3 Writing Source Cards

On your paper or on note cards, write source card listings based on the following information.   Book publishers' names are correctly abbreviated.   (The assignment continues on the next page.)

AUTHOR	TITLE	PUBLICATION FACTS
Book		
1. Thomas Pawlick	*A Killing Rain: The Global Threat of Acid Precipitation*	San Francisco, Sierra, 1984
Work in Anthology		
2. James Fleck, author. Brian P. Bloomfield, book editor	"Development and Establishment of Artificial Intelligence" in *The Question of Artificial Intelligence*	New York, Croom, 1987, pages 105-111
Pamphlet		
3. United States, Dept. of Interior, Fish and Wildlife Service	*Endangered Species*	Washington, GPO, 1979

Magazines

4. Lee Chan and   "How to Buy a   *Computer World* Feb-
   Jon Swensrud   Microcomputer"   ruary 1989, begins on
       page 89 and skips to
       page 106

5. Kenneth Bower   "The Wolf Man of   *Harrowsmith*, Sept-Oct
       Riding Mountain"   1987, pages 65-75 and
       then skips to page 86

Newspapers

6. none given   "Scientists Give   *New York Times*, natl.
       Wishbone New Twist"   ed., Oct. 4, 1988, page C7

7. Laura Landro   "Hopes Rise Again for   *Wall Street Journal*,
       Pay-Per-View TV"   eastern ed., Nov. 2,
       1988, page B1

Encyclopedia

8. Harold T. Meryman   "Freeze-drying"   *World Book Encyclopedia*,
       1988 ed.

Reference Book

9. Donald G. Groves   "Sea Ice"   *Ocean World Encyclo-*
   and Lee M. Hunt   *pedia*, New York,
       McGraw, 1980

Film

10. Fred Zinnemann,   *The Men*   produced by Stanley
    director   Kramer, starring Marlon
        Brando, United Artists,
        1950

Using Your Sources

After you prepare source cards, you will be ready to locate your
sources and to take notes from them.

Evaluating Your Sources

**Critical
Thinking:**
Evaluating

Take time to evaluate each source before you decide to take notes
from it. The notes that you take should support your preliminary thesis
statement. Follow these strategies to evaluate a source.

▶ **Strategies**

1. *Examine the table of contents and the index of a book to see
   whether the book contains information related directly to your
   topic.* Do not be misled by a related topic.
2. *Check the publication date of books and articles.* If your topic is in

a new or changing field, you should use the most current information available to ensure that your paper is accurate.

3. *Evaluate the author's expertise and the reputation of the publication.* Avoid sensational supermarket tabloids.

4. *Skim sources for information* that supports your main point.

Assignment 4 | Evaluating Sources

On your paper, tell whether each source (here and on page 394) would probably provide useful information in support of the given thesis statement. In a sentence or two, state a reason for each of your answers.

? Critical Thinking:

Evaluating Does the source support the thesis statement?

SAMPLE *Thesis statement:* Digitized computer simulations can improve an Olympic athlete's performance by analyzing a range of different body positions and game strategies and then projecting the best combination of factors.
   a. "Sports Schools Go High Tech" in *Fortune* magazine
   b. "Keeping Sports Scores with Computers" in *OMNI* magazine

ANSWER a. Probably useful. The article deals with high technology (which may include digitized computer simulations) and sports.
   b. Not useful. Keeping scores with computers has nothing to do with improving an athlete's performance.

1. *Thesis statement:* Winning at Grand Prix racing is not just an art but also an exacting science.
   a. "How to Officiate Auto Rallies" in *Car and Driver* magazine
   b. *The Art and Science of Grand Prix Racing*
   c. "All About the Grand Prix World Championship" in *Road and Track* magazine

2. *Thesis statement:* Experts predict that in twenty years, robots will be a part of most people's everyday lives.
   a. "Our Roboticised Future" chapter in *Robotics*
   b. "Exploring the Galaxy" chapter in *Future Space*
   c. "The Electrical and Mechanical Subsystems" chapter in *How to Design and Build Your Own Robot*
   d. Section on robots in the home in *Robots: Reel to Real*
   e. "Robots and the Future" chapter in *Robotics: Past, Present, and Future*

3. *Thesis statement:* Advances in bionic implants allow people to use artificial limbs as they did their natural limbs.
   a. "Parts Is Parts" chapter in a humor book *Laughing All the Way*
   b. "Restored Movement" chapter in *The Body Shop: Bionic Revolutions in Medicine*
   c. "Bionics" in *World Book Encyclopedia*

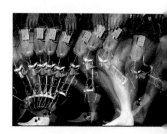

   d. "Bionic Human Is No Longer a Pipe Dream" in *U.S. News and World Report*

   e. Section on medical insurance in *The New Medicine*

   f. "Facts About Hearing Aids" chapter in *The Hearing Loss Handbook*

4. *Thesis statement:* Birds are more vital to the well-being of Earth's ecosystems than the small size of most birds would suggest.

   a. "Indirect Benefits: Life-Support Systems" section in "Why Should We Care?" chapter of *Extinction: The Causes and Consequences of the Disappearance of Species*

   b. "The Importance of 'Tweety Birds'" in *National Wildlife* magazine

   c. "Flocking Together: It May Help Ospreys to Fish More Efficiently" in *Scientific American* magazine

   d. "The Place of Birds in the Living World" chapter in *The Life of Birds*

   e. "Birds May Warn of Environmental Disaster" in *USA Today*

   f. "Why Living Things Are Where They Are" chapter in *Ecology*

Taking Notes on Note Cards

When you find a useful source, take notes on it. Write your notes on 3″ x 5″ or 4″ x 6″ index cards. Use the following guidelines to organize your note taking.

▶ **Strategies**

1. *Refer to your research plan cards as you take notes.* They will keep you on your topic.

2. *Read carefully through each source once for understanding.* Use only material that you understand. If you use information that you don't understand, you may unintentionally change the meaning of key ideas or facts.

3. *Read through each source once to record facts, ideas, statistics, and quotations* that support your thesis statement.

4. *Write the author's last name and an abbreviated title in the upper right corner of each card.*

5. *In the upper left corner of each card, write a subject heading to identify the main idea of the note.* You will later use these subject headings to develop a detailed outline. They will form some of the major headings and subheadings of your outline.

6. *Write only one idea on each card.* You will then be able to re-arrange your cards easily when you prepare your outline.

7. *Write on only the front of the card.* You might later overlook information written on the back of a card. If you need more room, use a second card.

8. *Write the number(s) of the page(s) from which you took the information.* List only the relevant page numbers. You will need the page numbers for references within your paper.

9. *On your source cards, record any other information needed to complete the formats on pages 387–391.*

Plagiarism   Using another writer's words or ideas without giving that writer credit is **plagiarism.** It is considered stealing and is against the law. Using as little as a clause from another writer's sentence is considered plagiarism. You cannot avoid plagiarism by rearranging words or substituting your own words in another writer's sentences. The only way to avoid plagiarism is to acknowledge your sources in the body of your paper and at its end.

Use one of the following methods of taking notes to avoid plagiarism. Choose the method best suited to your sources and your purpose.

Direct Quotation   If you use a **direct quotation,** copy the original author's words and punctuation exactly and enclose the passage in quotation marks. You should use a direct quotation when the author makes a point in an especially suitable, significant, or colorful way. If you leave out any words from within a quoted passage, insert ellipsis points (three spaced periods) in the appropriate spot to indicate that words have been omitted.

Reference Point: pages 733–734

If you quote only a word or a phrase rather than a complete sentence, you may omit ellipsis points if it will be obvious to your readers that you have omitted part of the sentence.

If you use a quotation within a quotation, be sure to use the correct format so that your readers won't be confused or misled. For example, if you are quoting a passage that contains a quotation, put single quotation marks around the quotation and double quotation marks around the passage.

Reference Point: pages 725–727

The note on the following card is from the article "Microbots" by T. A. Heppenheimer in *Discover* magazine. It shows a quotation within a quotation.

Note Card: Direct Quotation

Subject heading —— Mini robots   Heppenheimer, "Microbots"

Author ——
Abbreviated title —— Computer scientist Rodney Brooks:

Note —— "'These microbots won't make a big splash at first,' predicts Brooks. 'They'll probably start off doing very low-grade work, very mundane things, and doing it all in the background.'"

Page reference —— page 84

Paraphrase If you **paraphrase** sentences, you use your own words to restate an author's words. Crediting the source, you may paraphrase material that does not need to be stated in the exact words of the author. Keep the author's meaning without using the author's words.

The following sentences from a magazine article, "Thanks to 'Micromechanics,' Tires Can Check Their Own Air," edited by Emily T. Smith, are the basis of the paraphrase on the note card that follows them.

Squeaky wheels may get the grease, but tomorrow's noisy tires may want air instead. Neotech Industries Inc. is developing a little gadget that mounts on the wheel and vigilantly monitors the tire's air pressure. If the tire becomes dangerously under- or overinflated — conditions that could damage the tire or cause an accident — the tiny monitor would warn the driver with a beep and a flashing light.

The electronic pressure gauges are yet another application of micromechanics . . .

Note Card: Paraphrase

Sensor applications   Smith, "Thanks"
(Auto)

A microsensor was developed that mounts on a wheel and monitors a tire's air pressure. If the air pressure fluctuates dangerously, a warning signal is relayed to the driver.

page 105

Summary If you write a **summary,** you create in your own words a condensed version of a passage, giving just the main points and the essential details. You will still cite the source of the ideas. A page from "The Coming Age of Micromachines" by Jeanne McDermott in *Popular Science* is the basis for the two-sentence summary that follows.

Note Card: Summary

Development   McDermott, "Coming"

Micromachine technology began with silicon chips that were chemically etched to form grooves and channels. The success of chemical etching led to the next phase of development-- a pressure sensor on a chip.

page 91

Assignment 5 Taking Notes

On note cards or on your paper, take three notes on the following passage to support the given thesis statement. Make one note a direct quotation, one note a paraphrase, and one note a summary of the entire passage.

Thesis statement: Using special submersible chambers, researchers are now exploring Earth's last uncharted frontier, the depths of the oceans.

Half of Earth's surface is submerged under two miles or more of water. At its deepest, the ocean floor is almost seven miles below sea level.

The depths of the sea are dark, inhospitable, and mostly unexplored. Scuba divers can descend to only about 400 feet. No sunlight penetrates past a depth of 2500 feet. At this depth, pressure increases to 1000 pounds per square inch.

For years people assumed that no life could exist at such a depth. Exploration with submersible vehicles, however, has shown that even in the eternal darkness at 2500 feet, bizarre sea creatures thrive in abundance. In fact, submersibles have enabled scientists to discover sea life at 5000 feet, 13,000 feet, and most recently, at 35,800 feet. Most deep-sea creatures have adapted so well to the darkness and the pressure that they never rise to the surface and are being seen only for the first time with the aid of submersible vehicles.

In addition to discovering new species, scientists may also use submersible vehicles to record the dramas of the deep sea. At depths of 1500 feet and more, seventy-ton sperm whales seek their prey, giant squid. A giant squid, with its twenty-foot-long tentacles, thirty-foot-long body, and two-ton weight, is a worthy opponent, even for a whale. Sperm whales often bear three-inch-diameter battle scars from the squids' toothed suckers. In one case, however, a whale bore sucker marks that were eighteen inches in diameter. Scientists estimate that the giant squid that made those marks was two hundred feet long.

Continuing Assignment Research Your Topic

Step 1: Prepare research plan cards for the topic that you selected and limited in the Continuing Assignment on page 382. *Step 2:* Prepare source cards using the card catalog, periodical indexes, reference works, and the vertical file. Make a source card for each source that you will consult. *Step 3:* Using the sources listed on your source cards, take notes on note cards. Use the kind of note that is most appropriate for the information that you are recording. Save all your work for the next Continuing Assignment.

Organizing Your Information

Drafting a twelve-page research paper can be an intimidating task — unless your research notes are well organized. If you organize your note cards into an outline before you draft your paper, drafting your paper will be relatively easy.

Revising Your Preliminary Thesis Statement

From your research you will have gained significant knowledge, insight, and perspective on your topic. The next step is to compare your preliminary thesis statement with your notes. Revise your preliminary thesis statement so that it reflects what you have learned in the course of your research. Your revised thesis statement should accurately reflect the topic, the point or focusing idea, and the content of your paper. The amount of revision that you need depends on how much your research notes differ from your anticipated findings.

The following example shows the revision of a preliminary thesis statement for a paper on the topic "Micromachines." The revised thesis statement reflects the writer's increased knowledge.

PRELIMINARY THESIS STATEMENT

Small machines, called "micromachines," could revolutionize technology in the twenty-first century as computers have in the twentieth century.

REVISED THESIS STATEMENT

Tiny sensors and miniature motors, called "micromachines," are changing technology now and could revolutionize technology in the twenty-first century.

Making a Detailed Outline

Use the following procedure to organize your ideas into a detailed topic outline (pages 50–51) unless your teacher directs you to prepare a **sentence outline,** an outline written in complete sentences *(page 53).*

 Procedure

1. *To maintain your focus, write your thesis statement at the top of your paper before drafting your outline.*
2. *Sort your note cards into groups that have similar headings.*

3. *Use the subject headings for each group of similar note cards to select the main headings for your outline.* Arrange the headings in an order that best suits your topic, such as chronological order, order of importance, and so on. You may have to create new headings or reword note-card headings for your outline.

4. *Arrange subheadings and supporting details under the main headings that they support.* Use your note cards to form the headings. Be sure to eliminate those note cards that do not support your main headings.

5. *Draft your outline and number all headings.* Use a Roman numeral for each main heading. Use the Roman numeral *I* for the introduction to your paper and the final Roman numeral for the conclusion. Use a capital letter for each subheading, and use Arabic numerals for details and examples under the subheadings.

6. *Revise corresponding headings so that they are in the same grammatical form.* For example, if the heading for *A* is a phrase, the headings for *B*, *C*, and *D* should be phrases.

7. *When subdividing a main heading or a subheading, subdivide it into at least two sections.* Do not have an *A* without a *B*, for example, or a *1* without a *2*. You cannot logically subdivide a topic into only one part.

When you finish organizing your information, you should have a thesis statement and an outline similar to those that follow. The outline is for the research paper about micromachines, which appears on pages 424–427 and in the Appendix on page 751. (The outline continues on the next page.)

Thesis statement: Tiny sensors and miniature motors, called "micromachines," are changing technology now and could revolutionize technology in the twenty-first century.

    I.   Introduction
   II.   Background
  III.   Technology
         A. Building material
         B. Building processes
             1. Photolithography
             2. Sacrificial layers
         C. Classification of technology
   IV.   Microsensors
         A. Uses in medicine
             1. Blood pressure gauges
             2. Microelectrodes
         B. Uses in auto industry
             1. Tire pressure sensors
             2. Fuel injection devices
             3. Accelerometers
         C. Uses in robotics
         D. Miscellaneous uses
    V.   Micromachines
         A. Present research and development
             1. Bell Laboratories
             2. U. C. Berkeley

```
          B.  Method of propulsion
          C.  Uses in medicine
              1.  Surgery
              2.  "Smart" pills
          D.  Uses in industry
              1.  Micropumps
              2.  Alignment tools
              3.  "Gnat robots"
      VI.  The future
          A.  Anticipated problems
          B.  Anticipated impact on society
     VII.  Conclusion
```

You do not need to give equal development to each topic on your outline, but you may find that some topics need more support. If so, do additional research now. It will take less time to draft your paper if you have all the information that you need before you begin.

Number each of your note cards. As you use the information on each note card, write the number of the note card next to the sentence in which it appears in your first draft. This will save you time. When your draft is completed, you will not have to sort through your note cards to match your sources to the information in your paper.

Assignment **Sequencing Information into an Outline**

? Critical Thinking:

Organizing; Classifying What is the most logical sequence of ideas? Which material belongs together?

On your paper, copy the topic outline and fill in the blanks with the headings that follow it. Some headings are already in place. You will use all the headings.

Thesis statement: Oceans have been used as a dump to the extent that plastic garbage is now the most devastating manmade killer that marine creatures face.

    I.   _?_
   II. Annual production of plastic industry
      A. Industry production in dollars and product amount
         1.   _?_
         2.   _?_
      B. Annual industry production to increase in future
  III.   _?_
      A. Plastic garbage dumped by ocean-going vessels
         1. Dumped by ocean-going vessels from all nations
         2.   _?_
         3.   _?_
      B.   _?_
      C.   _?_
      D.   _?_
  IV. How plastic garbage harms marine creatures
      A.   _?_

       1.   ?

       2.   ?

   B. Plastic that kill creatures by entanglement or injury

       1.   ?

       2.   ?

       3.   ?

       4.   ?

V.   ?

   A.   ?

   B. Death estimates high

       1. Basing estimates on dead creatures that are found

       2. Estimate 40,000 seals die from being entangled in plastic

VI. What can be done

   A.   ?

   B.   ?

   C. Can eliminate port garbage disposal fees

VII.   ?

Headings:

Indigestible plastics that are swallowed

Plastic garbage spewed out by sewage treatment plants

Production of 1.2 trillion cubic inches of plastic goods

Clogs intestines and kills whales, turtles, porpoises

Vessels that dump garbage rather than pay port dump fees

After swallowing plastic, too buoyant to dive for food

Plastic garbage dumped by manufacturers

Plastic nets that entangle and drown creatures

Plastic beverage rings that strangle creature as it grows

Production of $13.8 billion in plastic goods

Estimates of how many creatures are killed

Can develop more biodegradable containers

Plastic garbage dumped by offshore drilling rig personnel

Can make international dumping penalties for ocean vessels

No accurate statistics on plastic-related deaths

Sources of plastic garbage

Plastic that cuts creature, causing it to bleed to death

Plastic debris that binds legs until atrophy sets in

Over 450,000 plastic containers dumped daily by ships

Introduction

Conclusion

Continuing Assignment **Organize Your Information**

Step 1: Read through the note cards that you prepared for the Continuing Assignment on page 397. If necessary, revise your thesis statement.

Step 2: Separate your note cards according to subject headings. Use your note cards to write a detailed topic outline for your paper.

Step 3: Examine your note cards and your outline. If any parts of the outline do not have sufficient support, find additional sources and take notes to complete your research. Save all your work for the next Continuing Assignment.

Drafting

Drafting Your Paper

Writing Your First Draft

Your goal in writing your first draft is simply to develop your ideas into sentences and paragraphs according to your outline. Expect the prose in your first draft to be rough; you'll revise and polish it in later drafts.

To make revisions easier, write your draft on only one side of your paper, and write on every other line. If you draft your paper on a word processor, double-space your hard copy. Number the pages of your draft as you write.

Be sure that you have completed your outline and have arranged your note cards before writing your first draft. If your information is well organized, writing your draft will be easier.

Try to write the first draft of each Roman-numeral section on your outline in one sitting. Your draft will be more coherent if you focus your attention on developing and supporting one main idea without interruption.

Drafting an Introduction to Your Paper

Begin your paper with an introductory paragraph of several sentences that lead to your thesis statement. In your introduction you should give enough background information so that your readers understand the importance of your topic and your approach to it. You should also create enough interest so that your readers want to read the rest of your paper. Even though the idea of what is interesting is subjective and varies from person to person, try using some of the following devices to improve your introductory paragraph's interest.

- Use action verbs, active voice, and lively language in your introduction as you do throughout your paper.
- Spark readers' imaginations with an interesting detail.
- Stir your readers' curiosity by revealing that the body of your paper contains very interesting or amazing information.
- Present a question or a puzzle that your readers can solve only by reading your paper.

The draft of an introduction follows.

> Computers were the technology of the 1970s and the 1980s.
> The same silicon-chip technology that made computers possible
> has made a new technology possible. ~~Computers are~~ This new
> technology, called "micromachine technology," consists of tiny
> sensors and miniature motors that are changing technology now
> and could revolutionize technology in the twenty-first
> century.

This introduction gives the topic, micromachines, and the position, that they are important. The thesis statement is the last sentence.

Assignment 1 Drafting an Introduction

On your paper, write an introduction to a paper about how advertising creates the illusion of need to spur demand for new products. Use the information in this outline and include a thesis statement.

I. Introduction
II. Personal care products that no one needs
   A. Cosmetics that do not do what they promise to do
      1. No instant romance from makeup
      2. Anti-aging creams that are proven to be ineffective
   B. Dental hygiene products that do not promote health
III. Household items with very limited uses
   A. Kitchen tools intended for obscure jobs
   B. Appliances that do unnecessary tasks
IV. Expensive entertainment items
   A. Toys for children that do not promote fun or creativity
   B. Electronics with features that have no real function
V. Conclusion

Drafting the Body of Your Paper

In the body of your research paper, you provide facts that support your thesis statement. Develop each heading on your outline into paragraphs by using the information on your note cards.

As you write, think about the meaning that you are creating. Don't blindly copy your note cards — make sure that what you write makes sense and is logically connected. Use transitional words and phrases *(pages 36–38)* to move smoothly from one idea to another.

Make sure that you have not overused direct quotations — your research paper is *your* writing, not an assembly of other writers' words.

Consider including in the body of your paper visual aids such as charts, graphs, and photographs to help your readers to understand the

information in your paper. For example, statistics are easier to comprehend when you show them in a table than when you try to express
them in words. Similarly, a process may be easier to visualize if you
present a diagram. Photographs or drawings may also enhance your
readers' understanding of physical settings or unfamiliar items.

Use the following guidelines when incorporating visual aids into
your paper.

▶ Strategies

1. *Make sure that a visual aid serves a real purpose.* Visual aids
   should not be mere decorations or padding.
2. *Place the visual aid near the text that it illustrates.* Refer to its
   position in your text — for example, "See the following chart."
3. *Make sure that your visual aids are clear and neatly labeled.* A
   confusing visual aid is worse than none at all.
4. *Give credit to the source of your visual aid.* If you copy a table or
   a diagram from a publication, acknowledge your source to avoid
   plagiarism.

Drafting a Conclusion to Your Paper

End your research paper with a concluding paragraph that restates
your main points. Your conclusion should convince your readers that
you have supported or proved your thesis statement.

Because the concluding paragraph is a summary, don't introduce
new information. Your readers should feel that your paper is completed. The draft of a conclusion follows.

> Micromachine technology is a technology of today and the
> future. At present, micromachine technology in the form of
> microsensors is used in a wide range of applications from
> medicine to the auto industry to the computer industry.
> Although micromachines with moving parts are still in ~~the
> developmental~~ the developmental stage, their potential uses
> seem unlimited. Although no one knows what the future of
> micromachine technology holds, it may well rival science-
> fiction fantasy.

Assignment 2 Writing a Conclusion

On your paper, write a conclusion for a research paper about how advertising creates the illusion of need to spur demand for new products.
Use the outline on page 403.

Documenting Your Sources

As you write your first draft, you must document the ideas that you incorporate from your notes. **Documenting** means acknowledging the sources of the information used in your research paper. You must acknowledge sources for several reasons.

- *Acknowledge sources to avoid plagiarism.* Give other writers credit for facts, statistics, opinions, and ideas that you take from their work.
- *Acknowledge sources for your readers' convenience.* Your readers may wish to read your sources of information.
- *Acknowledge sources as evidence.* Readers are more likely to believe a paper based on factual evidence.

Documentation takes two forms: citations within your paper and a list of sources, called a Works Cited page, at the end of your paper.

Citing Your Sources

A **citation** names the author and the page number(s) of your source in parentheses within the body of your paper. You should cite the sources that you quote, paraphrase, and summarize. The only information that you do not need to cite is that which is common knowledge and can be found in many sources. For example, it is common knowledge that Charles Goodyear invented the vulcanization process for rubber. If you are not sure whether you should cite a source, cite it. It is better to have too many citations than to risk plagiarism.

MLA Citation Format   There are several formats for citing sources. This textbook follows the guidelines set by the Modern Language Association (MLA). An alternative format uses footnotes or endnotes. Use the format that your teacher recommends.

Reference Point:
*Appendix:
Documentation
Styles*

▶ **Procedure**

1. *Within the body of your paper, cite the author's last name and the page number(s) on which the information is found* — for example, (Hoffer 79–80). If your source is an article in a collection, use the author of the article that you are citing. List only the relevant pages that you listed on your note cards. Use no punctuation between the author's name and the page number(s).

2. *If a work has two or three authors, list the last name of each author in the order listed on your source card, and then list the page numbers* — for example, (Angell, Terry, and Barth 44–46).

3. *If a work has more than three authors, list the first author's name followed by the notation* et al., *meaning "and others," and then list the page numbers* — for example, (Corbett et al. 21).

4. *If more than one source by an author is used, write the author's*

name, insert a comma, abbreviate the title of the source, and then write the page numbers. If the source is a periodical or an encyclopedia, use the title of the article — for example, (Davis, "Computing" 77).

5. *If there is no author listed or identified, abbreviate the title of the work and then write the page numbers* — for example, ("Seasons" 109).

6. *Omit the page number when citing an article that is only one page in length or when citing a source that arranges information alphabetically, such as an encyclopedia or a dictionary* — for example, (Schlender).

7. *If a newspaper has a section letter as part of the page number, include the letter in the page number* — for example, (Pollack C12).

8. *If the author's name is used within a sentence, list only the page numbers* — for example, (C12).

9. *When referencing an entire work, state the author's name in the sentence instead of creating a citation.* If you are summarizing an entire book or a lengthy article, a citation would not help readers to pinpoint the source of your information.

Placement of Citations The following guidelines will help you to determine where to place citations within paragraphs.

▶ **Strategies**

1. *Place a citation at the end of a sentence but before the final period.* Citations in that position are less likely to break the flow of your sentences.

"At Bell Labs researchers have designed a motor that will weigh just .013 ounce" (Heppenheimer 81).

2. *If you need to place a citation in the middle of a sentence to avoid confusion, place it at the end of a clause but before any punctuation.* For example, if you are using a fact from a source and drawing a conclusion from it, you will need to cite the source before stating your conclusion. Also use an internal citation if you use information from two sources in two parts of one sentence, as is the case in the following example.

Some gears and microparts are so small that they may be accidentally inhaled by a researcher (Pollack C1), or they may be blown off a laboratory table by a slight whiff of air (Marbach).

3. *For a quotation of five or more lines, indent the quotation as a block ten spaces from the left margin of the paper. Place the citation at the end of the quotation after the final period.*

Scientists believe more wonders are possible.

> Some turn their vision toward even smaller wonders,
> foreseeing computers a few hundred thousandths of an
> inch wide, with their atomic-scale components assembled
> using molecular wrenches; others look forward to
> cell-size, submarinelike robots that could be injected
> into the bloodstream to clean out cholesterol deposits
> or destroy viruses. (Heppenheimer 78)

Making a List of Works Cited

The list of **Works Cited** details all the sources that are acknowledged in the citations. It is the last page of your paper. Entries on the list of works cited follow the format that you used for source card listings on pages 387–391. You will prepare your list of works cited from the information on your source cards.

Use the following guidelines to prepare a list of works cited.

▶ **Procedure**

1. *Arrange the entries in alphabetical order by author's last name.* If an entry has two or three authors, invert the name of the first author, and list the names of the other author(s) as given on the title page. If an entry has more than three authors, write only the first author's name followed by the notation *et al.*

2. *An entry from an encyclopedia or a periodical with no author named is alphabetized by the first word of the article title,* not counting *A*, *An*, and *The*.

3. *If more than one source by an author is used, alphabetize those entries by their titles. For second and succeeding entries by the same author, put three dashes followed by a period where the author's name would appear.*

4. *Capitalize the first letter of each word in titles,* even if the author used all upper-case letters or all lower-case letters. The exceptions to this rule are articles, coordinating conjunctions, prepositions of fewer than five letters, and *to* when used as part of an infinitive — except if such words begin a title.

   Reference Point: *page 712*

5. *Underline book titles and enclose article titles in quotation marks.*

   Reference Point: *pages 737–738*

6. *Begin the first line of each entry at the left margin, and indent succeeding lines of each entry five spaces from the left margin.* Use the sample Works Cited on page 427 as a guide for spacing.

Note that the following entries are alphabetized and that all second and subsequent lines of entries are indented five spaces. Also note that page numbers are not given for books, although they are given for periodical articles.

Works Cited

Brown, Malcolm W. "Doctors Test New Plastics for Artificial Lenses and
    Corneas." *New York Times* 11 Oct. 1988, natl. ed.: C3.
"Cornea." *Encyclopaedia Britannica*. 1973 ed.
United States. Department of Health and Human Services. *Health: Car-
    ing for Your Eyes*. Washington: GPO, 1989.
Victor, Olivia E. *A New Way to Good Health*. Boston: Houghton, 1989.
---. *The Technology of Wellness*. New York: Macmillan, 1988.

Assignment 3 **Writing Citations**

On your paper, insert a citation in each of the following excerpts. Copy
just the word or words preceding the correct placement of the citation.

SAMPLE   People who have orbited Earth report having two main feel-
    ings: nostalgia for their home planet and a sense of
    brotherhood.
    *Source: The Overview Effect: Space Exploration and
    Human Evolution* by Frank White. Published by
    Houghton Mifflin Company in Boston,
    Massachusetts, in 1978. Information taken from
    pages 272–273.

ANSWER   brotherhood (White 272–273).

1. By measuring its growth layers, scientists have estimated that
a giant 580-pound clam was about one hundred years old.
Source: The Seven Mysteries of Life by Guy Murchie. Published
    in 1978 by Houghton Mifflin Company in Boston,
    Massachusetts. Information taken from page 111.

2. A human brain contains approximately 100 billion nerve cells. Authors Ornstein and Thompson state that in each of our brains "the
number of possible interconnections between these cells is greater
than the number of atoms in the universe."
Source: The Amazing Brain by Robert Ornstein and Richard F.
    Thompson. Published in 1986 by Houghton Mifflin
    Company in Boston, Massachusetts. Information taken
    from page 21.

3. Production-line efficiency has its drawbacks: Factory workers
who assemble just parts of a finished product may not feel as fulfilled by their work as craftspersons who create an entire product.
Source: "Technology" by Melvin Kranzberg in the *World Book*
    Encyclopedia, 1988 edition.

4. The over-application of the pesticide dieldrin on crops in Shelden,
Illinois, resulted in death for nearly all the birds and 90 percent of
the farm cats in the area.

Source: *Silent Spring* by Rachel Carson. Published in 1962 by
　　　　　Houghton Mifflin Company in Boston, Massachusetts.
　　　　　Information taken from pages 92–94.

5. A microchip that acts as a pet identification tag is injected under
   a pet's skin. When it is read with a special scanner at city animal
   shelters, lost pets can be reunited with their owners.

   Source: "High-Tech Tags for Pets" in *Newsweek* magazine, October
   　　　　　17, 1988, issue. A one-page article on page 61. No
   　　　　　author given.

6. Pigeons are diligent messengers. In one eight-hour workday, a
   messenger pigeon can fly three hundred miles without stopping to
   eat or drink.

   Source: "Pigeons and People" by Tony Soper on pages 162–164 in
   　　　　　Animal Stories: Tame and Wild, compiled by Gilbert
   　　　　　Phelps and John Phelps. Published by Sterling
   　　　　　Publishing Co., Inc., in New York, New York, in 1985.
   　　　　　Information taken from page 164.

7. "By 1982, 28 percent of the 80 million households in the United
   States subscribed to a cable television service"; even though, as
   many people know, cable television was originally intended only
   for those in areas too remote to receive broadcast signals.

   Source: *Teletext and Videotex in the United States* by John
   　　　　　Tydeman, Hubert Lipinski, Richard P. Adler, Michael
   　　　　　Nyhan, and Laurence Zwimpfer. Published in New York,
   　　　　　New York, by McGraw-Hill Publications Company in 1982.
   　　　　　Quotation taken from page 111.

8. Although the public tends to think of technology in terms of recent
   developments, such as machines or computers, not all scientists
   share that view.

   　　　　　Archeologists and linguists speak of the alphabet as a
   　　　　　technology because they see it as a tool that simplified
   　　　　　written language, making it more accessible to ordinary
   　　　　　people and more useful in commerce and the communi-
   　　　　　cation of ideas.

   Source: "Scholars Track the Alphabet with New Precision" by
   　　　　　John Noble Wilford in *New York Times* international
   　　　　　edition of November 8, 1988. The article begins on page
   　　　　　C1 and skips to page C8. Quotation is taken from
   　　　　　page C1.

Assignment 4 Prepare a List of Works Cited

On your paper, prepare a list of Works Cited using the information
contained in the numbered items on pages 408–409 in Assignment 3.

Abbreviate book publishers' names using the guidelines on page 388. Remember to put the entries in alphabetical order.

SAMPLE　A new, personal, hand-held computer analyzes diabetics' glucose levels so that they can adjust their daily insulin dosages to match their daily glucose levels.
Source: "This Computer is Made for Diabetics Only" by Charles W. Stevens in the eastern edition of the December 2, 1988, *Wall Street Journal* on page B1.

ANSWER　Stevens, Charles W. "This Computer Is Made for Diabetics Only." *Wall Street Journal* 2 Dec. 1988, eastern ed.: B1.

Continuing Assignment　**Acknowledge Your Sources**

Using your note cards and your outline, write your first draft. Using your source cards and your note cards, insert citations in your draft. Then prepare a rough draft of your Works Cited page. Save all your work.

Revising

Revising Your Paper for Content

Critical Thinking:
Evaluating

When you complete your first draft, put it aside for a few days so that you can distance yourself from your writing. You'll then be better able to evaluate objectively your draft.

Because of its length and complexity, your research paper deserves extra care and attention. You'll need to allow enough time for multiple revisions so that you can present your research findings in the most effective manner possible. You'll first revise your paper for content, then later for tone and style. For help in revising your paper, refer to the guidelines for revision on pages 63–86. In addition, use the following strategies.

▶ **Strategies**

1. *Update your outline if you departed from its organization when you created your first draft.* Referring to an outline is the quickest and easiest way to check the sequence of ideas in your draft.

2. *Make sure that your thesis statement accurately reflects the point and the content of your paper.* If you departed from the content of your outline, your thesis statement may need revision.

3. *Check assertions for adequate supporting details or facts.* An unsupported assertion may not be credible to your readers.

4. *Omit irrelevant information.* Ask yourself if each sentence directly supports the paragraph in which it appears.

5. *Read the draft for clarity.* Because of your research, you will

know more about your subject than your readers do. Make sure that you have no gaps in your explanations that will confuse your readers. Be sure to explain unfamiliar words and technical terms.

6. *Be sure that you have not quoted a source out of context.* Your excerpted quotations must accurately reflect their authors' views and the facts.

7. *Make meaningful comparisons to help your readers to understand technical or statistical information.* For example, in addition to stating that Jupiter has a gravitational force two and a half times stronger than Earth's, tell your readers that a horse on Jupiter would need legs as stout as those of an elephant to hold itself upright. You may even wish to omit a statistic and instead use a comparison: "A shrew is so tiny that it weighs less than a dime."

The following paragraph is marked for content revision. Notice that the events in the example will be resequenced to reflect the order in which they occur. The finished paper appears at the end of this unit.

> Micromachine sensors are used in a wide variety of
> *Name examples*
> products. Some (very important products) have been developed
> for use in the field of medicine. Other important products
> have also been developed for use the auto industry. For
> example, a microsensor for tires was developed that warns the
> ③ ← ——— *Put in chron. order*
> driver by relaying a warning signal. ╱ The microsensor mounts
> ① ← → ②
> on a wheel and knows when the tire is under- or over-inflated.
> Few service station attendants check tires' air pressure.

The following first draft of a paragraph uses statistics, but they won't be very meaningful to most readers.

> Bell Laboratories created a microturbine six hundred
> microns in diameter with blades that spin at the rate of four
> hundred r.p.s. Researchers at University of California at
> Berkeley developed an even smaller motor. The Berkeley motor
> is only one hundred microns in diameter and has extremely
> small gears.

In the revised draft, meaningful comparisons are added to enhance readers' understanding. If your source doesn't include such comparisons, you may need to do additional research to create them.

Bell Laboratories created a microturbine six hundred microns in diameter--about the width of six human hairs. The eight blades of the turbine spin at a rate of four hundred revolutions per second, which is faster than many jet engines. Researchers at the University of California at Berkeley developed an even smaller device--a motor that is the diameter of a single human hair. Their motor has gears that are so small that the "notched teeth are about the size of a red blood cell" (Anderson). Sixty thousand of these motors could fit in one square inch of space.

Assignment 1 Revising Body Paragraphs for Organization

Read the following paragraphs. Then on your paper, evaluate the sentences for proper sequence. Write the number of each sentence in the order in which it should be sequenced in revised paragraphs.

(1) Kenaf, a fast-growing woody plant that resembles bamboo, is a new source of paper pulp that could help to solve the world's timber shortage. (2) Newspaper made from the kenaf plant is strong, does not yellow with age, and holds ink so well that readers don't get smudged hands. (3) The paper that is made from the ground-up fibers of this ancient African plant is superior to that made from trees.

(4) In four months' time the kenaf plant grows from a seed to a height of eighteen feet; by contrast, a tree takes decades to mature. (5) The kenaf plant's main advantage over trees as a source of paper is its rapid growth. (6) In light of its potential for paper and other products, kenaf has researchers very excited.

(7) Besides being used to make paper, fibers of the kenaf plant have other applications. (8) In the future the kenaf plant may also be used for automobile parts, roofing materials, rope, and floor covering. (9) For the past six thousand years, the kenaf plant has been used in Africa for animal feed and for clothing. (10) In addition to rapid growth, kenaf plants also resist disease, grow in poor soils, and produce over three times as much paper pulp per acre as trees do.

? Critical Thinking:

Evaluating
Is each sentence clear, relevant, and well supported?

Assignment 2 Revising Body Paragraphs for Content

The following paragraphs are from the draft of a paper on Antarctic penguins. Number your paper from 1 to 8. Then evaluate each sentence by writing the letter of the suggested revision that you think would best improve the draft. If the sentence is effective as it stands, write the letter that indicates *Make no change.*

SAMPLE Unlike penguins, hummingbirds fly everywhere, even if their destination is only an inch away.
    a. Make no change.
    b. Delete as irrelevant. The topic is penguins, not hummingbirds.
    c. Add a comparison of how much larger a penguin is.

ANSWER b

(1) The physiology of Antarctic penguins puzzles scientists for several reasons. (2) For example, penguins cannot fly. (3) Penguins can, however, dive underwater to a depth of 350 feet and remain submerged for ten minutes. (4) Arctic waters are very cold. (5) Also, unlike most other creatures, penguins thrive in temperatures that range from −70 to 100 degrees Fahrenheit. (6) Moreover, penguins have high metabolisms; a colony of penguins can consume fish at a rate of nine thousand tons per day.

(7) Scientists now use a variety of technologies to probe the physiological secrets of penguins. (8) To track the travels and migrations of penguins, scientists glue transmitters to the birds' back feathers. (9) The transmitters do not harm the penguins, and at the end of a year's study, the transmitters drop off when the penguins molt. (10) The transmitters send signals to an orbiting satellite, which are then monitored by researchers.

1. Sentence 1
    a. Make no change.
    b. Revise the sentence as "Penguins puzzle scientists."
    c. As supporting detail, after *penguins* add , *which are located in the Southern Hemisphere,.*

2. Sentence 2
    a. Make no change.
    b. After *penguins* add *are technically birds, but they.*
    c. Delete the sentence as irrelevant.

3. Sentence 3
    a. Make no change.
    b. Delete *underwater* and *a depth of.*
    c. After *minutes* add *unaided* to clarify the meaning.

4. Sentence 4
    a. Make no change.
    b. As supporting detail, after *cold* add — *often below the freezing point.*
    c. Delete the sentence as irrelevant.

5. Sentence 5
    a. Make no change.

    b. To add supporting detail, revise *from −70 to 100 degrees Fahrenheit* as *from −70 degrees in the Antarctic to 100 degrees Fahrenheit in warmer environments.*

    c. To simplify, revise *temperatures that range from −70 to 100 degrees Fahrenheit* as *a wide range of temperatures.*

6. Sentence 6

    a. Make no change.

    b. To create a meaningful comparison, after *day* add , *which is the equivalent of a day's work for seventy modern trawlers.*

    c. To create a meaningful comparison, after *colony of* add *five million* and after *day* add , *which is the equivalent of a day's work for seventy modern trawlers.*

7. Sentence 7

    a. Make no change.

    b. As support after *penguins* add *including satellite transmitters, microchip implants, microphones, depth gauges, and speedometers.*

    c. Delete the sentence as irrelevant.

8. Sentences 8, 9, and 10

    a. Make no change.

    b. Resequence the sentences in this order: 8, 10, 9.

    c. Delete sentence 10 as irrelevant.

Continuing Assignment   **Revise Your Paper for Content**

Revise the first draft of your paper for content. Use the strategies given on page 410. Do not be concerned about matters of tone, style, and mechanics at this time. Save all your drafts.

Revising

Revising for Tone and Style

? **Critical Thinking:**

Evaluating

    Now that you have revised the content of your paper, you need to evaluate its tone and style. Refer to the guidelines for revision on pages 87–97. In addition, use the following guidelines.

▶ **Strategies**

1. *Make sure that your introductory paragraph creates interest.* Look again at the suggestions for creating interest on page 402.

2. *Read the draft for consistent tone.* Your paper should maintain a vigorous but formal tone throughout. Eliminate colloquial words, informal expressions, contractions, and words such as *I, me,* and *you.* If some direct quotations break the tone of your paper, consider paraphrasing them.

3. *Be sure that your tone is impartial.* Avoid extreme language; use facts, not emotions, to convince your readers. Your readers may resent attempts at manipulation and may become less receptive to your paper's position.

4. *Use gender-free words.* For example, use *businessperson* instead of *businessman;* use *flight attendant* instead of *stewardess.* Similarly, don't stereotype occupations: not all scientists are men, nor are all nurses women.

5. *Consider the impact that the connotation of words will have on your readers.* For example, *simple* means "uncomplicated," but it can also mean "trivial" or "stupid." Use words free of negative associations so that your paper will not seem biased, and to prevent your readers from misunderstanding your point of view.

Reference Point:
page 611

6. *Use transitional words and phrases* to guide your readers from main point to main point and from minor point to example *(pages 36–38)*. To connect sentences, use a pronoun that refers to a person or an idea just mentioned in the preceding sentence. To link paragraphs, repeat a key word or an idea from the previous paragraph.

7. *Replace vague words with specific terms or examples.* For example, instead of writing that paleozoic dragonflies were extremely large and flew at great speed, tell your readers how large and how fast: Paleozoic dragonflies had thirty-six-inch wingspans and flew an estimated forty-three miles per hour.

8. *Make sure that your conclusion leaves your readers with a sense of closure.* Your readers should not feel left dangling.

The following introduction from the draft of a research paper on the topic "Micromachines" is not as interesting as it could be.

> Computers were the technology of the 1970s and the 1980s. The same silicon-chip technology that made computers possible has made a new technology possible. This new technology, called "micromachine technology," consists of tiny sensors and miniature motors that are changing technology now and could revolutionize technology in the twenty-first century.

The preceding introductory paragraph has been revised to heighten readers' interest. Notice that in the revised version on the next page, the language is more vivid, a specific detail is included, and amazing applications within the body of the paper are previewed. The thesis statement is modified to suit the flow of the revised introduction.

> In the 1970s and 1980s, computers changed the way people lived, worked, and entertained themselves. A spin-off of computer chip technology called "micromachine technology" promises equally impressive changes for the twenty-first century. Tiny sensors and miniscule motors, some no wider than a human hair, are already displaying potential uses that rival science fiction.

The following paragraphs are marked for several kinds of changes. The revision will make the language more vivid and specific while eliminating wordiness and a stereotype. Added transitions improve the flow of the sentences.

> The National Science Foundation predicts ~~that~~ *the extensive use of* micromachines ~~will be used extensively~~ in medicine. Current plans call for ~~the~~ *tion of* mass producing micromachines for ~~next to nothing by manufacturers.~~ *less than a penny each.* A *disposable* machine that is ~~cheap and so tiny~~ *the size of a fly* ~~that it is nearly invisible could~~ *speck* *can* perform tasks that are not feasible with ~~the~~ larger, more costly mechanisms ~~that we now use.~~
>
> Microtools ~~could be~~ used with remote controls to *would* allow ~~a~~ *s* doctor to perform ~~various kinds of miraculous, life-saving~~ surgery from inside the body. ~~He could place~~ *For example,* micromachines *placed* inside fat-clogged arteries to *could* scrub away built-up fat. Fabricated as tiny cutting tools, (micromachines) ~~could be able~~ *will make* ~~to perform~~ *possible* delicate eye surgery. *In addition,* Micromachines with temperature sensors ~~could be shot~~ *injected* into tumors to *could* fight cancer by using *special freezing* ~~hypothermia~~ techniques.

Choosing a Title   You should now finalize the title of your paper if you have not done so already. Your title should provide a clue to the subject and the point of your paper — for example, "Micromachines: A Technology for the Twenty-First Century."

? Critical Thinking:

Evaluating
Are the style and the tone appropriate?

Assignment 1   **Revising for Tone and Style**

The paragraphs that follow are from a research paper about the cause of goosebumps. Number your paper from 1 to 8 *(see next page)*, and evaluate each sentence by writing the letter of the suggested revision that you think would best improve the draft. If the sentence is effective as it stands, write the letter that indicates *Make no change.*

(1) Scientists have long wondered why people have quivers and goosebumps, which are physical reactions to danger, when people hear sounds that don't signal danger. (2) Such physical reactions are automatically triggered by the fight-or-flight defense mechanism, which is a rush of adrenaline that spurs people to flee danger or defend themselves, but surprisingly the sound of something harmless, like the squeak of styrofoam, can trigger the same goosebumps. (3) There is a theory that may explain the connection between the fight-or-flight response and nonthreatening sounds.

(4) Because these physical responses to harmless sounds are instinctive, those who research theorized that the behavior is inherited from early ancestors. (5) Scientists first identified the sound wave pattern created by fingernails scratching a blackboard, the granddaddy of gross-outs. (6) The scientists then compared the sound wave pattern of fingernails scratching a blackboard to the sound wave patterns of threatening sounds from the wild that would have been known to early ancestors. (7) They discovered that a primate warning scream has a sound wave pattern a lot like that of fingernails scratching a blackboard. (8) In the distant past, warning cries by various species may have been so central to early ancestors' survival that an anxious, alert response to such cries became instinctive, and thus perhaps people's ability consciously to recognize such cries has dried up because it is no longer needed.

1. Sentence 1
   a. Make no change.
   b. Change *people* to *we.*
   c. Change *when people hear sounds* to *upon hearing,* and change *don't* to *do not.*
2. Sentence 2
   a. Make no change.
   b. To eliminate awkwardness, insert a period after *themselves,* delete *but,* and begin a new sentence with *Surprisingly,.*
   c. Replace *sound* with the more formal *auditory stimulus.*
3. Sentence 3
   a. Make no change.
   b. Replace *There is* with *Various scientists have come up with.*
   c. Replace *There is* with *Scientists developed.*
4. Sentence 4
   a. Make no change.
   b. Replace *those who research* with *researchers.*
   c. Replace *early ancestors* with the more colorful *our club-toting progenitors.*

5. Sentence 5
   a. Make no change.
   b. Delete *the granddaddy of gross-outs.*
   c. Before *Scientists* add *To test their theories,* and delete *the granddaddy of gross-outs.*
6. Sentence 6
   a. Make no change.
   b. Revise the sentence as "Then they compared that sound wave pattern to those of threatening sounds from the wild that early ancestors would have encountered."
   c. Revise as "Scientists compared it to threatening sound wave patterns from the wild."
7. Sentence 7
   a. Make no change.
   b. Replace *a lot like* with *very similar to.*
   c. Before *primate* add *bloodcurdling.*
8. Sentence 8
   a. Make no change.
   b. Insert a period after *instinctive,* delete *and thus,* and begin a new sentence with *Perhaps.*
   c. Insert a period after *instinctive,* delete *and thus,* begin a new sentence with *Perhaps,* and replace *dried up* with *diminished.*

Assignment 2 Revising Body Paragraphs for Transitions

Read the following paragraphs. Then on your paper rewrite them, creating transitions from sentence to sentence and from paragraph to paragraph.

By the year 2000, people may entertain themselves by recreating movies in the comfort of their own living rooms. A new digital computer technology may allow people to mix and match actors' images and voices from a data bank of stored images and voices to create movies on their home-computer screens. The movie *The African Queen* could be recast with different stars. A user would access that film with the actors' faces and voices erased. The user would fill in the blank faces and the sound track as desired. John Wayne could replace Humphrey Bogart as the leading character.

People could star in their own home-created movie. A computer-compatible image bank of a person would be created. The home users could add their images to a movie in the same way that actors' images and voices are added.

Assignment 3 Revising an Introduction

On your paper, revise the following introductory paragraph to create interest. Use the suggestions on page 402.

It has been revealed by research that there is no difference between the brain of an average person and that of a creative genius. Some researchers say that creativity is largely a function of individual motivation — some people have a big need to express their ideas and their feelings about what they think is significant around them in words, in painting, and other creative outlets. One of the centers of the brain that stimulates the need to create has recently been discovered by scientists.

Continuing Assignment **Revise for Tone and Style**

Reread your paper and revise it again — this time for tone and style. Do not be concerned yet with spelling or mechanics. Make sure that all citations are correct. Revise your Works Cited page, if necessary. Save all your work.

Proofreading

Proofreading Your Paper

The easiest and most effective way to proofread your paper is to proofread it several times, looking for just one kind of flaw each time. Each reading will go quickly. If you proofread your entire paper in a single reading, it will take you longer than several quick readings, and you are more likely to miss errors.

You will need to proofread your final paper before and after it is typed. Even if someone else types your paper for you, finding and correcting errors in your paper is still your responsibility.

Use the guidelines on pages 98–99 and 105 when proofreading your paper. Additional guidelines follow.

▶ **Strategies**

1. *Proofread your paper several times, looking for a different kind of error each time.* First, check for words or letters that are missing or added by mistake.
2. *Check your paper for errors in usage.* For example, check for agreement between subjects and verbs.

   Reference Point:
   pages 636–647

3. *Inspect your paper for errors in punctuation and capitalization.*
4. *Examine your paper for errors in spelling.*
5. *Proofread your paper once to make sure that all the citations are in place and that the information in them matches the information in your note cards.*
6. *Check your Works Cited page once for format, once for punctuation, and once for spelling.*

As you proofread, give special attention to these points.

Partial Quotations: Pronoun References Be sure that pronouns in quotations clearly refer to a particular person or object. One method of clarifying confusing pronoun references is to place the antecedent in brackets after the pronoun. Brackets (not parentheses) indicate that the material within them is your addition, not part of the source that you are quoting.

Reference Point: pages 661–662

> James Maxwell used Faraday's ideas to develop equations that
>
> formed the foundation of modern physics. It is probably
>
> "most fitting that in Albert Einstein's study, a picture of
> [Faraday]
> him was displayed" (Constable 56).

Measurements: Using Numbers In formal writing, spell out whole numbers up to one hundred and numbers rounded to even hundreds that can be written in one or two words. Do not mix numerals and words in the same category of measurement within a paragraph; write them all as numerals. Do not abbreviate units of measure such as *inches*, *feet*, or *seconds*.

Reference Point: pages 739–740

> 40,000
> There are approximately forty thousand living animals
> cubic foot
> in a cu. ft. of soil; about 25,000 of them are mites.

Assignment 1 Proofreading a Paper

Proofread the following paragraphs to find errors in spelling, usage, punctuation, and format. Number your paper from 1 to 10. If there is an error in a sentence, write just the words needed to correct the error. If there is no error, write *Correct.*

SAMPLE Consumers' may not want all the products that our advanced technologys can create.

ANSWER Consumers; technologies

    (1) In the 1970s, marketing experts predicted that the next consumer fad would be machines which use voice commands (Barron C1). (2) The experts was wrong. (3) Consumers were irritated by automobiles that gave them orders and insulted by apliances that stated the obvious such as "The drying cycle is completed" (Marsden 34).

    (4) Some consumer reactions exceded mere irritation. (5) One woman was so startled by her new cars unexpected voice com-

mand to "Fasten your seatbelt!" that he drove through the wall of her garage. (6) In another instance a man who was house-setting for a friend thought he had awakened to a robbery in progress when the friend's voice-alarm clock shouted at him, "Wake up! Wake up!" (Barron C12).

(7) Consumers' demonstrated their disdain by simply refusing to buy products with voice features. (8) As a result many manufacturers discontinued voice features in they're products. (9) Commando-voiced alarm clocks, talking Microwave ovens, and chatty clothes dryers have all met the fate of the buggy whip (C1–12 Barron).

(10) One auto executive, puzzle by customer resistence to an advanced technology, stated, "We thought a voice-warning system would be kind of fun, but the customers complained" (Hampton 70)

Assignment 2 Proofreading a List of Works Cited

Proofread the following Works Cited page. On your paper, rewrite all entries correctly.

Works Cited

Hampton, William J. "Smart Cars" *Business Week* 13 June 1988, 68+

Barron, James "Consumers Say No to Machines That Talk." *New York Times* Sept. 9, 1988, natl. ed.: C1+.

Guyon, Janet. "New Breed of Phone Service Riles Users. *Wall Street Journal* 9 Dec. 1988, eastern edition: B1.

Marsden, Allen. *The Machine Age.* 1989. New Haven: Yale UP.

Continuing Assignment Proofread Your Revisions

Proofread the revised draft of your paper and Works Cited page that you created in previous Continuing Assignments. Use the strategies on page 419 and refer to the formats on pages 405–408. Save your work.

Publishing

Publishing Your Paper

Congratulations! You have finally finished your research paper and are ready to share it with your readers. You may discover, as many writers have, that the best part of writing is having written.

Using Correct Manuscript Form

Your finished research paper should include the following parts in this order: (1) the title page, (2) the written or typed research paper, and (3) the Works Cited page. Your teacher may also want to see the supporting materials that you used to write your research paper: your source cards, your note cards, and your outline.

Reference Point:
pages 510–517

Write your research paper as legibly as you can. If at all possible, type your paper or use a word processor. You'll want your paper to make a good impression on your readers. Follow the guidelines on pages 107–108 to prepare your finished paper.

To prepare a title page, center the title about halfway down the page. Capitalize the first letter of the first word and all words except articles, conjunctions, and prepositions of fewer than five letters. Do not underline the title or put quotation marks around it. Double-space and center the word *by* under the title. Double-space again and center your name under *by*. In the lower right corner, put your teacher's name, the name of the course, and the date. For additional format information, refer to the guidelines for publishing on pages 107–108.

Place your name and the number of each page in the upper right corner of each page of your paper. If your pages become separated, they will not become mixed up with someone else's paper.

To make your paper more attractive and to protect it, you may also wish to place it in a folder or a slim binder.

Using Research Paper Headings   Your teacher may want you to use headings within your research paper. You may be able to use the same words for your headings that you used for your outline.

The most obvious benefit of using headings is to guide your readers through the content of a long research paper. The headings act as signposts that point out main ideas and subordinate ideas to your readers.

You may use two levels of headings. Headings of the same level in your paper should be parallel to each other in structure. For example, they should be all phrases or all single words. Headings are formatted as follows. For examples, see the sample research paper on pages 424–427 and in the Appendix, which begins on page 751.

Type first-level headings in all capital letters and center each one on a separate line. Use them for the main ideas listed on your outline as Roman numeral headings. You should have a corresponding first-level heading for each Roman numeral item except your introduction and conclusion; omit headings for these two because their subject matter will be obvious to your readers. Double-space twice before each first-level heading.

Type second-level headings in upper- and lower-case letters; underline them, and position at the left margin, each on its own line. Use them for the letter headings (*A*, *B*, and so on) of your outline. If you have only a few sentences for each second-level heading, you may wish to omit second-level headings and to use just the first-level heading. Do not add extra lines before or after these headings.

Ways to Publish Your Paper

Since you have spent so much time and effort creating your research paper, you should share it with as many readers as possible. Consider making your paper available to your classmates; if you think your topic is interesting, they probably will too.

Your teacher may suggest that you prepare an oral report based on your topic, or that you take part in a symposium with other students who wrote research papers on similar topics. If so, refer to pages 462–471 for listening and speaking strategies. If your teacher suggests that you exchange research papers with another class, use the opportunity to evaluate other students' papers. If they used strategies that you think are particularly effective, emulate those strategies.

You may also wish to submit your paper for publication in locally or nationally published periodicals. Books such as *Writer's Market* and *The Canadian Writer's Guide* list the names and the addresses of various periodicals and the kinds of freelance writing that they seek. You may be paid for the right to publish your paper.

You could also mail your research paper and a cover letter to your local newspaper. Depending on its topic, your paper could be published as a letter to the editor or even as a special feature.

Consider offering your paper to private businesses or government agencies that might be interested in using it as an information source. For example, suppose that you write a research paper about ways to save energy. Your local utility company may wish to use information from your paper as information for their customers.

Even if you don't submit your paper for publication now, save it. Later you can use your paper as a representative sample of your writing. If you apply to a college or a university, you may be asked for a sample of your writing. If you apply for a job that requires written communication, a prospective employer may want a sample of your writing.

Continuing Assignment | **Publish Your Paper**

Prepare your paper for readers, and then submit your paper for publication. You may use one of the preceding suggestions, or you may think of another approach. You will want to save your research paper — or a copy of it — in your portfolio as an important example of your writing.

Following is a portion of a sample research paper on micromachines and its complete Works Cited page. Use this portion as a guide when you format your paper for publication. Notice how the subheadings make the paper easier to follow. The complete research paper appears in the Appendix on pages 751–759.

Lavinia Washington

English 4

Mr. Martin

April 15, 19--

Micromachine Technology: The Small Revolution

In the 1970s and 1980s, computers changed the way people lived, worked, and entertained themselves. A spin-off of computer chip technology called "micromachine technology" promises equally impressive changes for the twenty-first century. Tiny sensors and miniscule motors, some no wider than a human hair, are already displaying potential uses that rival science fiction.

Background

Micromachine technology began in 1954 when researchers discovered that "it was possible to etch tiny valves, cantilevers, channels, and bridges into silicon" (Schlender). Because researchers had no use for their discovery, they did not pursue its development.

Micromachine technology got its next major boost in the 1970s. A scientist trying to develop an instrument for the National Aeronautics and Space Administration (NASA) needed to create a miniature valve--and could not. Although the deadline for NASA's project elapsed, the scientist continued to work on the problem. Finally, he succeeded. He created a valve that opened and shut in five thousandths of a second and let in ten billionths of a liter of gas (McDermott 90). Micromachine technology was born.

Technology

Today many laboratories make microparts, microsensors, and micromachines. All laboratories use very similar materials and processes.

Building Material

Like computer chips, micromachine devices are fabricated of silicon. The purity of silicon makes it an ideal building material for structures that cannot tolerate impurites, air bubbles, or other irregularities. Silicon is not only pure, but also it is stronger than stainless steel (Peterson and Barth 92).

Building Processes

A process known as photolithography is used to make microparts, such as valves. First, patterns for the parts are imprinted on silicon wafers. Then caustic chemicals etch away parts of the wafer to form three-dimensional shapes such as pits, pyramids, and walls. The cost to make each part is low because many parts are made at once in batches, just like computer chips (Angell, Terry, and Barth 44).

Since microparts are too small to assemble into a micromachine, another process is utilized to make devices that would normally require the assembly of several microparts. This process is called "sacrificial layering." Using this process, micromachines are built as completely assembled units. For example, to form a hub with a rotating arm, the whole assembly is constructed in layers of silicon separated by layers of silicon dioxide. When the assembly is completed, the sacrificed layers of silicon dioxide are etched away with acid, and the arm is free to move (Hoffer 80). Writer Andrew Pollack created an analogy of "a mechanic who builds a structure of alternating layers of metal and ice and then melts the ice, leaving only the metal" (C12).

Classification of Technology

Micromachine technology has two classifications: devices with moving parts and devices with nonmoving parts. Devices with nonmoving parts evolved first and are commonly used as sensors (Pollack C12).

Micromachines with moving parts are, for the most part, in the experimental stage. In fact, the definition of "micromachines" as tiny devices "distinguished as machines by their moving parts and their ability to do work" (Pollack C1) is relatively new. As recently as 1981, the term "micromachine" meant "microcomputer" in Tracy Kidder's Pulitzer Prize-winning book, <u>The Soul of a New Machine</u> (154-70). The ambiguity of the term decreased as the technology grew.

Microsensors

Microsensors perform a variety of tasks, including detecting heat, pressure, and sound (Schlender). They also measure vibration, liquid flow, chemical composition, infrared light, acceleration, and vacuum conditions (Peterson and Barth 93).

<u>Uses in Medicine</u>

In the field of medicine, microsensors are employed in a variety of products. For example, millions of microsensors are used each year in disposable blood pressure gauges (Schlender).

Microsensors in the form of microelectrodes greatly advanced the study of brain stimulation. With tips as small as one millionth of an inch in diameter, microelectrodes led the way to ground-breaking research by enabling scientists to study very small or very remote areas of the brain. For example, microscopic electrodes allow scientists to chart individual brain cell activity or to excite selected cells to prompt activity. In addition, tiny manipulators let scientists probe remote, previously inaccessible areas of the brain (Tether).

<u>Uses in Auto Industry</u>

The auto industry developed a host of sensor devices. One such device is a microsensor that mounts on a wheel and monitors a tire's air pressure. If the air pressure fluctuates dangerously, a warning signal is relayed to the driver (Smith). Auto makers also employ microsensors to

(The complete research paper appears on pages 751–759.)

Works Cited

Anderson, Ian. "Motors No Wider Than a Human Hair." New Scientist 1 Sept.
     1988: 44.

Angell, James B., Steven C. Terry, and Phillip Barth. "Silicon Micro-
     mechanical Devices." Scientific American Apr. 1988: 44-55.

Heppenheimer, T. A. "Microbots." Discover Mar. 1989: 78+.

Hoffer, William. "Micro Machines." Popular Mechanics July 1988: 79+

Kidder, Tracy. The Soul of a New Machine. New York: Avon, 1981.

Marbach, William D. "A Small World Grows Tinier." Newsweek 30 Nov. 1987:
     65.

McDermott, Jeanne. "The Coming Age of Micromachines." Popular Science
     June 1984: 87-91.

Peterson, Kurt E., and Phillip Barth. "Design Engineering." McGraw-Hill
     Yearbook of Science and Technology. New York: McGraw, 1988.

Pollack, Andrew. "New Generation of Tiny Motors Challenges Science to Find
     Uses." New York Times 26 July 1988, late ed.: C1+.

Schlender, Brenton R. "Microsensors Make Their Mark in a Wide Variety of
     Products." Wall Street Journal 21 Nov. 1986: 35.

Smith, Emily T., ed. "Thanks to 'Micromechanics,' Tires Can Check Their
     Own Air." Business Week 29 June 1987: 105.

Tether, J. Edward. "Brain: Brain Research." Encyclopedia Americana. 1987
     ed.

Waldman, Peter. "'Micromachines' Made from Silicon Crystals." Wall
     Street Journal 1 Apr. 1988: 13.

Student to Student

Reading and Responding to Writing

The question "How much land does a person need?" has served as the controlling idea for many stories and essays. A variation of that question that we as a species must now answer is "How much of Earth are we entitled to occupy?" An excerpted passage from a research paper about the destruction of tropical rain forests follows. The author, Andy King, is a student at Charlestown High School in Charlestown, Indiana. As you read Andy's paper, ask yourself the questions in the margin. Then follow the directions for *Responding to Writing* and *Reading Critically*.

The Plight of the Tropical Rain Forests

Tropical rain forests have circled Earth's equator for millions of years, creating a spectacular display of plant and animal life. These forests serve as a primary source for a wellspring of products that sustain our sojourn on Earth (Myers 6). Yet, their future existence appears quite bleak. Tropical rain forests are presently being destroyed at such an intense rate that they will be stripped bare within thirty years (Nalley 56). Unless man stops this thoughtless destruction now, mass extinctions of invaluable plants and animals will occur.

Scientists agree that deforestation of tropical rain forests is currently the number one environmental problem facing our planet today. Man is destroying them at a rate of fifty acres per minute without foreseeing the harmful consequences thereof (Nalley 56). This lack of foresight is partially due to ignorant people and to a lack of knowledgeable scientists capable of instructing them differently (Mitchell 229). Nonetheless, there are many other causes leading to the destruction of tropical rain forests.

The primary cause of disruption and deforestation of tropical rain forests is the small-scale farmer. Farming is the only means of making a living for many people living in typically poor, tropical countries. They seldom own land of their own, so they turn to the forests. Here, they fell virtually every tree within a small area and then burn the lot. After a few years of producing crops, the soil quickly loses its fertility and the farmers repeat the cycle in a new section of forest (Myers 143-8).

Like the small-scale farmer, the cattle rancher has also contributed to the problem. The cattle ranchers in Central

How does knowing the scope of the problem increase readers' interest?

What is Andy's thesis statement?

In what other ways can this statistic be stated?

Why is this background information needed?

America are destroying rain forests as a result of the currently high demand for inexpensive beef (Parker and Uhl 642). To meet this demand, cattle ranchers are clearing the rain forests to form pastures that are large enough to support their herds. Fifty-five square feet of grazing area is required to produce one four-ounce hamburger. This alarming figure is intensified since the United States buys ninety percent of Central America's beef, which is used primarily for the fast-food trade ("Hamburgers" 74). Thus, people in the United States are also responsible for the decline of tropical rain forests.

Another major cause of tropical deforestation is the over-exploitation of tropical hardwood timber by commercial loggers. The demand for hardwood timber has increased greatly over the past few decades. To keep up with the demand, commercial loggers are clearing large tracts of virgin forests without making an effort to replant the land with young trees (Myers 91).

The effects of small-scale farmers, cattle ranchers, and commercial loggers are having a tremendous impact on the plant and animal species that are native to the tropical rain forests. These plants and animals are rapidly becoming extinct as a direct result of tropical deforestation. Harvard Professor of Science Edward O. Wilson says that "The extinctions ongoing worldwide, promise to be at least as great as the mass extinction that occurred at the end of the age of dinosaurs" (Murphy 80), sixty-five million years ago. Environmentalist Norman Myers says that tropical deforestation may result in the eradication of one million species by the end of this century (53). This is quite frightening considering that naturalists have only formally named approximately 1.7 million species ("Biological" 126). However, scientists estimate that there are four million to thirty million undiscovered species living in tropical rain forests.   (Paper continues.)

Why is this information relevant? How are readers considered in the way in which statistics are stated?

Why is this person a credible source?

Responding to Writing   In groups or in a class discussion, state your opinion of the value of rain forests. Also consider what can be done about the problem. Do we have the right to take action to protect rain forests in another country? What would you do if another country's citizens decided that to control global air pollution, all people in this country should stop driving cars?

Reading Critically   On your paper, perform the activities and answer the questions that follow. Prepare an outline of this portion of Andy's research paper. How does Andy make transitions from paragraph to paragraph? Explain how Andy uses cause and effect and examples to support his thesis statement. What is Andy's attitude toward his topic? Give evidence from the paper. List three opinions that Andy states; then list the facts that support each opinion.

The Literature Connection

The completion of a research project is a major accomplishment. You started with an idea, a hunch, or even just a casual interest, and you turned it into a complete research paper. In the process, you've gained confidence in using the library and other resources, in synthesizing diverse bits of information, and in writing an extended investigation.

Guided Reading Bringing meaning to observations is as necessary to writers as it is to scientists and technicians. Whether you write a story, a poem, or an essay, you generally start by looking and listening. You then explore the connections between and among your observations, interpret their meaning, and finally select those that best fit your writing purpose. Scientists work in a similar manner: observing, finding connections, making meaning, and selecting. The following passage explains this process and argues that—down deep—research is really a search for similarities and order. Notice how the author supports his point with a colorful anecdote about Sir Isaac Newton's famous encounter with the apple. Why did Bronowski select this particular story? What likeness does he see between Hideki Yukawa and Sir Isaac Newton?

All science is the search for unity in hidden likenesses. The search may be on a grand scale, as in the modern theories which try to link the fields of gravitation and electromagnetism. But we do not need to be browbeaten by the scale of science. There are discoveries to be made by snatching a small likeness from the air too, if it is bold enough. In 1935 the Japanese physicist Hideki Yukawa wrote a paper which can still give heart to a young scientist. He took as his starting point the known fact that waves of light can sometimes behave as if they were separate pellets. From this he reasoned that the forces which hold the nucleus of an atom together might sometimes also be observed as if they were solid pellets. A schoolboy can see how thin Yukawa's analogy is, and his teacher would be severe with it. Yet Yukawa without a blush calculated the mass of the pellet he expected to see, and waited. He was right; his meson was found, and a range of other mesons, neither the existence nor the nature of which had been suspected before. The likeness had borne fruit.

What is a *meson*? What likeness did Yukawa see between light waves and the nuclei of atoms?

The scientist looks for order in the appearances of nature by exploring such likenesses. For order does not display itself of itself; if it can be said to be there at all, it is not there for the mere looking. There is no way of pointing a finger or camera at it; order must be discovered and, in a deep sense, it must be created. What we see, as we see it, is mere disorder.

Do you agree that order lies in the way you look at things, not in things themselves? Why or why not?

This point has been put trenchantly in a fable by Karl Popper. Suppose that someone wished to give his whole life to science. Suppose that he therefore sat down, pencil in hand, and for the next twenty, thirty, forty years recorded in notebook after notebook everything that he could observe. He may be supposed to leave out nothing: today's humidity, the racing results, the level of cosmic radiation and the stockmarket prices and the look of Mars, all would be there. He would have compiled the most careful record of nature that has ever been made; and, dying in the calm certainty of a life well spent, he would of course leave his notebooks to the Royal Society. Would the Royal Society thank him for the treasure of a lifetime of observation? It would not. The Royal Society would treat his notebooks exactly as the English bishops have treated Joanna Southcott's box.* It would refuse to open them at all, because it would know without looking that the notebooks contain only a jumble of disorderly and meaningless items.

How does this analogy apply to writers? Think about the observations that you have recorded in your writer's notebook.

Science finds order and meaning in our experience, and sets about this in quite a different way. It sets about it as Newton did in the story which he himself told in his old age, and of which the school-

---

*Joanna Southcott was a nineteenth-century English farm servant who claimed to be a prophetess. She left behind a box which was to be opened in a time of national emergency in the presence of all the English bishops. In 1927, a bishop agreed to officiate; when the box was opened, it was found to contain only some odds and ends.

books give only a caricature. In the year 1665, when Newton was twenty-two, the plague broke out in southern England, and the University of Cambridge was closed. Newton therefore spent the next eighteen months at home, removed from traditional learning, at a time when he was impatient for knowledge and, in his own phrase, "I was in the prime of my age for invention." In this eager, boyish mood, sitting one day in the garden of his widowed mother, he saw an apple fall. So far the books have the story right; we think we even know the kind of apple; tradition has it that it was a Flower of Kent. But now they miss the crux of the story. For what struck the young Newton at the sight was not the thought that the apple must be drawn to the earth by gravity; that conception was older than Newton. What struck him was the conjecture that the same force of gravity, which reaches to the top of the tree, might go on reaching out beyond the earth and its air, endlessly into space. Gravity might reach the moon: this was Newton's new thought; and it might be gravity which holds the moon in her orbit. There and then he calculated what force from the earth (falling off as the square of the distance) would hold the moon, and compared it with the known force of gravity at tree height. The forces agreed; Newton says laconically, "I found them answer pretty nearly." Yet they agreed only nearly: the likeness and the approximation go together, for no likeness is exact. In Newton's sentence modern science is full grown.

> Why is Newton's response to his observation (calculation) considered "modern"?

It grows from a comparison. It has seized a likeness between two unlike appearances; for the apple in the summer garden and the grave moon overhead are surely as unlike in their movements as two things can be. Newton traced in them two expressions of a single concept, gravitation: and the concept (and the unity) are in that sense his free creation. The progress of science is the discovery at each step of a new order which gives unity to what had long seemed unlike.

Jacob Bronowski (1908–1974)
from *Science and Human Values*

Enrichment Connections

Choose one or more of these activities to do on your own or as a group.

Covering the News

Based on the research that you did for this unit, write a one- to two-page cover story, news column, or press release on some exciting aspect of your general topic. Even if your topic is no longer newsworthy, imagine that the world is unaware of its existence or implications. Consider reading your "scoop" to your class, and have your research notes and your paper handy to handle questions from the audience.

Using Comparison

Read over your notes for *Responding to Literature* on page 375, and use them to generate ideas for a poem, a story, or a short play. For example, if you choose to write a story, you might *show* a group of scientists behaving like "bees in a disturbed part of the hive" through action and dialogue. Don't restrict yourself to Lewis Thomas's comparisons, but do use them if they serve your purpose.

Speaking and Listening

A Dramatic Soliloquy   Do enough research on Newton or on some other scientist who interests you to write a three- to five-page dramatic soliloquy that highlights your subject's contribution to science. You should focus on the events in his or her life of greatest historic and dramatic interest. Arrange to read your soliloquy or recite it from memory to your English and science classes, if appropriate. Be sure, however, to have several live rehearsals beforehand so that you can polish your writing and your presentation.

Across the Curriculum

Social Studies   As you know, research can involve experimentation and observation as well as library work. Set up a simple experiment that tests a hypothesis. Then write a short summary of your research that includes a statement of your hypothesis, a vivid description of your research method and what you observed, and a conclusion based on the evidence. You might, for example, test people's reaction to unusual foods or test the truth of some advertising claims.

What images come to mind when you hear words such as *eternity* and *universe*? How does your mind grapple with ideas that are so big that they can't easily be thought? How can science and technology give you a perspective on these "unthinkables" and help you bring them down to size?

In the following selection, you will hear from an eminent scientist, Stephen W. Hawking. He discusses the development and the trustworthiness of the scientific theories that help people talk about everything from atoms to white dwarfs (faint, dense stars). As you read, think about the ways in which your personal problem-solving approach is similar to or different from the scientist's. Then work on one or more of the activities that follow the selection. Putting the insights you have gained into action may give you a new perspective on the universe and your place in it.

A well-known scientist (some say it was Bertrand Russell) once gave a public lecture on astronomy. He described how the earth orbits around the sun and how the sun, in turn, orbits around the center of a vast collection of stars called our galaxy. At the end of the lecture, a little old lady at the back of the room got up and said: "What you have told us is rubbish. The world is really a flat plate supported on the back of a giant tortoise." The scientist gave a superior smile before replying, "What is the tortoise standing on?" "You're very clever, young man, very clever," said the old lady. "But it's turtles all the way down!"

Most people would find the picture of our universe as an infinite tower of tortoises rather ridiculous, but why do we think we know better? What do we know about the universe, and how do we know it? Where did the universe come from, and where is it going? Did the universe have a beginning, and if so, what happened *before* then? What is the nature of time? Will it ever come to an end? Recent breakthroughs in physics, made possible in part by fantastic new technologies, suggest answers to some of these longstanding questions. Someday these answers may seem as obvious to us as the earth orbiting the sun—or perhaps as ridiculous as a tower of tortoises. Only time (whatever that may be) will tell. . . .

In order to talk about the nature of the universe and to discuss questions such as whether it has a beginning or an end, you have to be clear about what a scientific theory is. I shall take the simple-minded view that a theory is just a model of the universe, or a restricted part of it, and a set of rules that relate quantities in the model to observations that we make. It exists only in our minds and does not have any other reality (whatever that might mean). A theory is a good theory if it satisfies two requirements: It must accurately describe a large class of observations on the basis of a model that contains only a few arbitrary elements, and it must make definite predictions about the results of future observations. For example, Aristotle's theory that everything was made out of four elements, earth, air, fire, and water, was simple enough to qualify, but it did not make any definite predictions. On the other hand, Newton's theory of gravity was based on an even simpler model, in which bodies attracted each other with a force that was proportional to a quantity called their mass and inversely proportional to the square of the distance between them. Yet it predicts the motions of the sun, the moon, and the planets to a high degree of accuracy.

Any physical theory is always provisional, in the sense that it is only a hypothesis: you can never prove it. No matter how many times the results of experiments agree with some theory, you can never be sure that the next time the result will not contradict the theory. On the other hand, you can disprove a theory by finding even a single observation that disagrees with the predictions of the theory. As philosopher of science Karl Popper has emphasized, a good theory is characterized by the fact that it makes a number of predictions that could in principle be disproved or falsified by observation. Each time new experiments are observed to agree with the predictions the theory survives, and our confidence in it is increased; but if ever a new observation is found to disagree, we have to abandon or modify the theory. At least that is what is supposed to happen, but you can always question the competence of the person who carried out the observation.

In practice, what often happens is that a new theory is devised that is really an extension of the previous theory. For example, very accurate observations of the planet Mercury revealed a small difference between its motion and the predictions of Newton's theory of gravity. Einstein's general theory of relativity predicted a slightly different motion from Newton's theory. The fact that Einstein's predictions matched what was seen, while Newton's did not, was one of the crucial confirmations of the new theory. However, we still use Newton's theory for all practical purposes because the difference between its predictions and those of general relativity is very small in the situations that we normally deal with. (Newton's theory also has the great advantage that it is much simpler to work with than Einstein's!)

The eventual goal of science is to provide a single theory that describes

the whole universe. However, the approach most scientists actually follow is to separate the problem into two parts. First, there are the laws that tell us how the universe changes with time. (If we know what the universe is like at any one time, these physical laws tell us how it will look at any later time.) Second, there is the question of the initial state of the universe. Some people feel that science should be concerned with only the first part; they regard the question of the initial situation as a matter for metaphysics or religion.

Stephen W. Hawking *(1942-   )*
from "Our Picture of the Universe" in *A Brief History of Time*

$$|0\rangle = \frac{1}{\pi^{1/4}} \int dq\, e^{-q^2/2} |q\rangle$$

$$|q\rangle = \frac{e^{-q^2/2}}{(\pi)^{1/4}}$$

Taking Another Look

Why does Hawking set the stage for his discussion with the anecdote about the "tower of tortoises"? What does his treatment of the story say about the permanence of *any* scientific theory? How does Hawking define a scientific theory? What makes a theory good? Why do scientists prefer to work with Newton's theory of gravity more than Einstein's theory of relativity, even though Einstein's is more accurate? What does Hawking mean when he says "single theory"? Would he say that one is possible? Would you?

Changing Places

How would some aspect of everyday life—the dating or eating behavior of a typical teen-ager, for instance—look to the trained eye of a scientist: random or predictable? Look through a scientist's lens at some custom or practice that particularly interests you. What do you see? Does looking through this lens make things clearer? Does it help you to see why people act the way they do? What are the advantages of looking at the world from a scientific perspective? What are the disadvantages? How would the world be different if everyone examined things from several angles—as scientists do—before making a judgment? Keep these questions in mind as you do one or more of the following activities.

 Stephen Hawking is a member of the Royal Society of London, the oldest scientific organization in the world. Sir Isaac Newton was one of its earliest members, joining its ranks in 1699. Professor Hawking has another connection with the "discoverer" of gravity: he is the Lucasian Professor of Mathematics at Cambridge University, a position once held by Newton.

WRITING

Mr. Einstein, meet Mr. Newton If Albert Einstein and Sir Isaac Newton were to meet at a casual gathering—a neighbor's barbecue, for instance—what might they say to each other? Would they "talk shop," or would they just try to get to know one another? Do some research on the lives and work of these two men, and then write a dialogue or a short story that records this historic event. Consider making yourself a participant in the meeting or an observer. As you prewrite, think about questions they might ask each other and about potential sources of rivalry, of friendship, or of both.

Technology
WORKSHOP

Using a Word Processor   Use a word processor—in combination with desktop publishing if it is available to you—to create a front page newspaper story covering a scientific discovery. (Use a real discovery, such as Newton's or Einstein's theory, or make one up.) Write a flashy headline. You can include quotations from an imagined interview with the famous scientist, facts that you find through research, or information from the preceding selection. Print the headline in a large type size and the story in columns, if possible. Experiment with various fonts and styles. If the technology is available to you, include a graphic to illustrate your article.

WRITING

A Cure for Prejudice?   What would happen to prejudice if people continually modified their theories about other people, as scientists continually alter theirs about the physical world? Concentrating on your own experience, think about how prejudice works, about how people's perspectives and attitudes become hardened. Think about how an open, "scientific" point of view might loosen things up. Then write an essay, a story, or a poem that offers your diagnosis and cure.

LANGUAGE

Did You Hear the One . . . ?   Have you noticed how many speeches begin with *anecdotes*, short accounts of some humorous incident? Anecdotes can do more than break the ice; they can also introduce a listener or a reader to some important aspect of your theme. Listen with an ear for engaging anecdotes to the stories that your friends and family members tell, and write the promising ones in your writer's notebook. Keep adding anecdotes from these and other sources and use them when they relate to your writing purpose and are appropriate for your audience.

Related Skills

C O N T E N T S

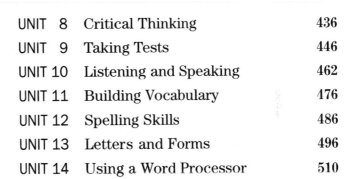

UNIT 8

Critical Thinking

The end of World War II marked the beginning of a revolution in communications technology. Television, satellite-communication networks, and computers transformed the way information is exchanged. Indeed, the second half of the twentieth century may be known in the future as the "age of information." Every week, the stream of facts, ideas, and opinions seems to grow larger. For some people this flow of information may be overpowering and perplexing.

Critical thinking is the tool that helps you to use this information to your advantage. In this unit, you will learn how to classify information, how to determine relationships between words and between ideas, and how to draw conclusions. Learning to classify will give you a foundation for identifying main ideas and for distinguishing between relevant and irrelevant details. As you study ways to determine relationships between words and between ideas, you will understand better how to recognize causes and effects and how to use analogies. Finally, studying strategies for analyzing and interpreting information will help you to draw reasonable conclusions. You will find that these skills are useful not only for doing your class work, but also for making decisions, solving problems, and understanding the complexities of the age of information.

How to Classify Information

Reference Point:
pages 34–35

Classifying, or sorting related items into groups, is the foundation for higher-level critical thinking. For instance, if you had a list of possible source books for a research paper on the colonization of North America, you could classify the books into related subject areas, such as Spanish settlements or the first English colonies. Classifying these books would prepare you to focus on topics of interest, to eliminate topics with little source material, and to brainstorm possible thesis statements.

The following classifications each have two parts: the **class name,** capitalized at the top of each column, and the **members,** listed in each column.

CENTRAL AMERICAN COUNTRIES	SHELLFISH	TROPICAL FLOWERS
Guatemala	shrimp	bougainvillea
Belize	lobster	African violet
Costa Rica	mussel	orchid

A **class** is a group of items sharing one or more features, such as place, physical characteristic, climate, size, color, texture, nationality, or time period. The **class name** describes the common features shared by members of the group. The members of the class *Tropical Flowers*, for example, have climate, location, and type of plant (flowering) in common. You can add new members if they share the group's common features. For example, you could add the pelican flower or the bird-of-paradise flower to the class but not the daisy or the tulip.

Effective classification, like good writing, depends on precision and accuracy. A classification is **precise** when the class name defines and also limits the features shared by class members. A class name should be as specific as possible, given the members of the group. *Central American Countries*, for example, is precise because it defines the general topic of countries and at the same time limits this subject to the category of countries in a specific region. If the class name were *Countries*, it would be so general that it would probably not be useful; the class would include every country in the world. However, if the class name were *Central American Countries Bordering Panama and Nicaragua*, it would be so specific that only Costa Rica would belong.

A classification is **accurate** when all the class members share certain common features. *Shellfish*, for example, is accurate because the members are aquatic animals that have shells or shell-like exoskeletons. Adding halibut or cod to the class would make the classification inaccurate because these fish do not have shells.

Classifying provides insight into paragraph organization. A paragraph, like a classification, has two parts: a main idea and details. The **main idea,** like a class name, defines and limits the topic and should be precise. The main idea is often stated in a **topic sentence,** which could be anywhere in the paragraph. **Irrelevant details** are comparable to inaccurate members in a classification. They distract, confuse, and mislead the reader by drawing attention away from the main idea.

Reference Points: *pages 40–41 and pages 66–67*

Assignment 1

Each of the following lists of class members has one member inaccurately assigned to it. On your paper, write the inaccurate member from each list. Then write a precise class name for the corrected list, and add two new members for each list.

SAMPLE crew, rigging, mast, deck, forecastle
ANSWER *Inaccurate member:* crew
Precise class name: Parts of Sailing Ships
New members: jib, keel

1. Shakespeare, Keats, Whitman, Shelley, Wordsworth
2. clogs, turban, hood, bonnet, helmet
3. violin, viola, guitar, oboe, harp
4. epic, sonnet, ode, haiku, novel
5. ruby, emerald, granite, opal, diamond

Assignment 2 Main Ideas and Irrelevant Details

On your paper, write the main idea and two irrelevant details from the following paragraph.

> In feudal times, noblewomen often had many duties outside the realm of household chores. To be sure, the lady of the castle supervised the household, oversaw the preparation of food, and kept a garden where she grew herbs to use in cooking and for medicine. However, she also taught young girls in her household how to sew, spin, and weave, and she tended the sick and wounded. A noblewoman's marriage was arranged by her father. When the lord was away from the castle, the lady took charge of his duties too. For example, she supervised the household officials, such as the record keeper and tax collector, and made financial decisions. For amusement, the noblewoman enjoyed chess and other board games. If the lord was taken prisoner in war, the lady raised the ransom to pay for his release. Sometimes she even put on armor and went to war. In short, everything from finances to health care and defense might fall on the shoulders of a noblewoman in feudal times.

Determining Relationships

Classifying can also help you to identify specific relationships between members in a classification or between ideas in a paragraph. Some examples of these relationships are fact / opinion, whole / part, relevant / irrelevant, and cause / effect. The following classifications illustrate cause / effect relationships.

Reference Point: pages 34–35

EFFECTS OF HUNGER	CAUSES OF MEMORY LOSS
dizziness	age
stomach pains	shock
fatigue	illness

A **cause-and-effect relationship** shows how one or more events bring about a situation. The **cause** is the reason for the situation, and the **effect** is the result — the situation itself. A classification may group single or multiple causes and effects. Read the following paragraph about the causes of the War of 1812.

In 1812, Americans went to war with Great Britain for several reasons. One factor was British impressment of American sailors. About 5000 American citizens had been forced to serve in the British navy. Naturally, Americans resented this. They said that Britain was acting like a bully and needed to be taught a lesson. Americans who lived on the frontier were also angry at Great Britain. The frontier settlers believed that the British in Canada were aiding Indian attacks on Americans; these Americans said that the Indians could be controlled only if the British were forced out of Canada. Other Americans were expansionists who wanted war with Britain so that their country could take over Canada and gain more land. In 1810, many "war hawks" were elected to Congress; they thought it would be easy for the United States to conquer Canada. For these reasons, the United States declared war against Britain on June 1, 1812.

In the preceding paragraph, the first sentence states that there were several causes of the War of 1812; it is the main idea of the paragraph. The rest of the sentences identify these causes. Together, all of the sentences of the paragraph describe a cause-and-effect relationship. Recognizing a cause-and-effect relationship in a paragraph can help you better to understand and recall main ideas and details.

Analogies

Recognizing relationships is crucial to the thinking process. By analyzing analogies, you can develop your ability to identify relationships. An **analogy** is a statement that defines the relationship between two pairs of words. The first pair of words and the second pair of words in an analogy both share the same or a similar relationship *(pages 451–453)*.

When you classify, you compare the members of a class to determine what common feature or features they share. Similarly, when you analyze an analogy, you compare the various parts to determine the relationships. Look at this example.

> *Loiter* is to *dawdle* as *accelerate* is to *hasten.*

Compare the first pair of words, *loiter* and *dawdle;* they are synonyms and words for "move slowly." Then compare the second pair, *accelerate* and *hasten;* they are also synonyms and words for "move more quickly." The analogy is correct because both pairs share the same relationship, synonyms referring to moving. If the second pair of words were *scream* and *howl,* however, the analogy would be incorrect; *scream* and *howl* are not words for movement, although they are synonyms. Analogies often appear in a shorthand style, like this:

> LOITER : DAWDLE : : accelerate : hasten

There are many kinds of analogies, just as there are many types of relationships in classification. Following are six of the many different kinds of analogy relationships.

TYPE OF ANALOGY	EXAMPLE
word : synonym	PATH : TRAIL :: freeway : expressway
whole : part	SLACKS : WAISTBAND :: shirt : collar
class : member	MAMMAL : WHALE :: tree : sequoia
worker : tool	GARDENER : HOE :: miner : pick
item : purpose	PEN : WRITING :: glue : binding
cause : effect	COWARDICE : SHAME :: bravery : pride

Analyzing analogies requires the same precision that you use in classifying. When you analyze the relationship between the first pair of words in an analogy, be as specific as possible. For example, look closely at the second type of analogy above, *whole : part*. *Slacks* is an item of clothing, and *waistband* is the top part of a pair of slacks, encircling the waist. Similarly, *shirt* is an item of clothing, and *collar* is the top part of a shirt, encircling the neck. Therefore, *collar* is a more precise choice than *sleeve*, *pocket*, or *cuff* would be.

The third type of analogy also illustrates the importance of precision. A *mammal* is a class of living things, and a *whale* is a member of that class, the largest member of all. Similarly, *tree* is a class of living things, and a *sequoia* is a member. A *sequoia*, like a *whale*, is the largest member of its class and, therefore, a precise choice.

Consistency is also necessary when you analyze analogies. If the first pair in an analogy is *verb : verb*, the second pair must also be *verb : verb*. The analogy *FOX : SLY :: lion : bravery* is incorrect. The first pair is *noun : adjective*, but the second pair is *noun : noun*.

Order must also be consistent in analogies. If the first pair in an analogy is *place : product*, then the second pair must also be *place : product*. For example, the analogy *GARDEN : VEGETABLES :: milk : dairy* is incorrect. The order of the first pair is *place : product*, but the order of the second pair is *product : place*.

Reference Point:
pages 32–33

To write a paragraph supported by an analogy, establish a comparison between two items that would not generally be thought of as similar. State the initial comparison at the beginning of the paragraph. Then extend the comparison to specific aspects of the items being compared. Notice how the writer of this paragraph develops the analogy between writing a poem and baking a blueberry pie.

> Words, like blueberries, can be baked into poems. Pick the plumpest, juiciest, ripest words from your field of thoughts and emotions. Weed out the green ones, the hard ones, and the bruised ones. Sugar them with your personality, and spice them with surprise. Pour them into dough, flat and white as parchment, and pinch the edges until you come full circle to the beginning. Cut holes to let the steam escape. Bake your poem in a hot oven until it is golden brown. Serve it to your family and friends; feed them with your words, warmed and transformed by your own hands.

Before starting to write a paragraph supported by analogy, list the similarities between the items to determine whether there are several points of comparison. Then develop the similarities in a block, or alternate between corresponding points for each item, as in a paragraph of comparison.

Reference Point: *pages 30–31*

Assignment 1 Cause and Effect

Step 1: On your paper, list four causes for the first item and four effects for the second item. *Step 2:* Select one of these classifications and write a paragraph explaining the causes or the effects. Use a reference book, if necessary.

1. Illness (causes) 2. Drought (effects)

Assignment 2 Analyzing Analogies

Study the first pair of words in the following analogies. On your paper, write the letter of the best word to complete the second pair. Check for precision and consistency. Then, identify the type of analogy.

SAMPLE CHAIR : THRONE :: hat : __?__
(a) derby   (b) plum   (c) staff   (d) head   (e) crown
ANSWER e; class: member

1. PICNIC : FEAST :: square dance : __?__
   (a) hop   (b) sociable   (c) ball   (d) jig   (e) waltz
2. TREE : BARK :: apple : __?__
   (a) seed   (b) skin   (c) core   (d) branch   (e) sauce
3. HOUSE : FLOOR :: ship : __?__
   (a) galley   (b) rigging   (c) deck   (d) mast   (e) ballast
4. SCULPTOR : CHISEL :: painter : __?__
   (a) brush   (b) canvas   (c) color   (d) spectrum   (e) subject
5. POD : WHALE :: pack : __?__
   (a) wolf   (b) clothes   (c) shark   (d) suitcase
   (e) passenger
6. SNOOP : NOSEY :: ignore : __?__
   (a) absent   (b) attentive   (c) curious   (d) kind
   (e) neglectful
7. SLIPPERS : MOCCASINS :: parka : __?__
   (a) shirt   (b) dress   (c) hood   (d) scarf   (e) jacket
8. DISOBEDIENCE : REVOLT :: defeat : __?__
   (a) fight   (b) enemy   (c) army   (d) rout   (e) victory
9. SYMPHONY : MOVEMENT :: novel : __?__
   (a) sitting   (b) paper   (c) chapter   (d) silence
   (e) writing
10. EDUCATION : OPPORTUNITY :: comedy : __?__
    (a) satire   (b) pleasure   (c) jokes   (d) tragedy
    (e) clown

Assignment 3 | Supporting a Paragraph with an Analogy

Step 1: On your paper, list four similarities for each of the following comparisons. *Step 2:* Select one of the two comparisons, and write a paragraph in which you develop the similarities by analogy.

1. Running a race is like taking a test.
2. Taking a walk through a park is like listening to a beautiful piece of music.

How to Draw Conclusions

Drawing conclusions is another important kind of critical thinking. When you draw a conclusion, you carefully examine evidence in order to figure out an explanation. A reasonable and consistent explanation of the evidence is a **valid conclusion.** An explanation that is inconsistent with the facts at hand is an **invalid conclusion.**

Reference Point:
pages 230–235

To draw a conclusion, evaluate the accuracy and reliability of your evidence. Knowing whether this information is fact or opinion can help you to make an evaluation. Opinions, because they cannot be proved, are generally less reliable sources of evidence than facts.

Analyzing and Interpreting

Analyzing and interpreting are the two basic steps required to draw a conclusion. **Analyzing** is a method of examining facts, details, or other evidence in order to get a better understanding of the whole. **Interpreting** is the process of clarifying the meaning or significance of the facts, details, or evidence. An effective way to analyze and interpret information is to ask questions. After you have analyzed and interpreted all the available facts and evidence, you are ready to draw a conclusion.

When you analyze, review information, determine whether the information is accurate, and look for additional sources of information. For example, if you were looking for an SAT review course, you would want to find the best one to suit your needs. To find it, you might examine the information by asking questions such as these: What is the price of the course? How long does it take each week? How long does the course last? What material is covered?

Reference Point:
pages 18–19

Interpreting the information that you gather would involve asking additional questions: Which course offers the best combination of length of time required and material covered? Which course suits my price range? Which is most highly recommended?

Analysis and interpretation are especially helpful in reading literature. Read this excerpt from the beginning of a short story.

*A*s she lay in her berth, staring at the shadows overhead, the rush of the wheels was in her brain, driving her deeper and deeper into circles of wakeful lucidity. The sleeping-car had sunk into its night-silence. Through the wet window-pane she watched the sudden lights, the long stretches of hurrying blackness. Now and then she turned her head and looked through the opening in the hangings at her husband's curtains across the aisle. . . .

She wondered restlessly if he wanted anything and if she could hear him if he called. His voice had grown very weak within the last months and it irritated him when she did not hear. This irritability, this increasing childish petulance seemed to give expression to their imperceptible estrangement. Like two faces looking at one another through a sheet of glass they were close together, almost touching, but they could not hear or feel each other: the conductivity between them was broken. She, at least, had this sense of separation, and she fancied sometimes that she saw it reflected in the look with which he supplemented his failing words. . . . The suddenness of the change had found her so unprepared. A year ago their pulses had beat to one robust measure; both had the same prodigal confidence in an exhaustless future. Now their energies no longer kept step: hers still bounded ahead of life, pre-empting unclaimed regions of hope and activity, while his lagged behind, vainly struggling to overtake her.

Edith Wharton *(1862–1937)*
from "A Journey"

(pĕch′ə-ləns)

To analyze the passage, ask such questions as these: Where does the story take place? What two characters are introduced in this excerpt? What time of day is it? What does the woman hear in the first paragraph? What does she see? What does she listen for in the second paragraph? How long has her husband been sick?

Then interpret by asking such questions as these: Why is the woman probably not sleeping? Why might she keep looking at her husband's curtains across the aisle? What effect does the illness seem to have had on her husband's temperament? How can you tell? How does she seem to feel about this change? How can you tell? What is the woman's health like? How can you tell? What was their relationship probably like before his illness struck? How can you tell?

Thoughtful analysis and interpretation, based on story facts and details, illuminate character, plot, and theme. The information you glean from this process is crucial to understanding the meaning of a story and to extracting the author's purpose.

Reference Point:
pages 338–339

On your paper, answer the questions that follow this excerpt from a short story. Save your papers.

I read about it in the paper, in the subway, on my way to work. I read it, and I couldn't believe it, and I read it again. Then perhaps I just stared at it, at the newsprint spelling out his name, spelling out the story. I stared at it in the swinging lights of the subway car, and in the faces and bodies of the people, and in my own face, trapped in the darkness which roared outside.

It was not to be believed and I kept telling myself that, as I walked from the subway station to the high school. And at the same time I couldn't doubt it. I was scared, scared for Sonny. He became real to me again. A great block of ice got settled in my belly and kept melting there slowly all day long, while I taught my classes algebra. It was a special kind of ice. It kept melting, sending trickles of ice water all up and down my veins, but it never got less. Sometimes it hardened and seemed to expand until I felt my guts were going to come spilling out or that I was going to choke or scream. This would always be at a moment when I was remembering some specific thing Sonny had once said or done.

James Baldwin *(1924–1987)*
from ''Sonny's Blues''

1. Where does the story open?
2. What is the narrator reading?
3. Whom did he read about?
4. How did he react to what he was reading?
5. Where did he go after he read the story?
6. What is he feeling in paragraph two?
7. What was his job?
8. What did his stomach feel like? Why?

Assignment 2 Interpreting

Reread your answers to the questions from Assignment 1. Then, on your paper, answer these questions.

1. Why do you think the narrator compared the feeling in his stomach to a block of ice?
2. How do his feelings fluctuate? How can you tell?
3. What kind of relationship did he probably have with Sonny? How can you tell?
4. Why do you think the story is called ''Sonny's Blues?''

Generalizing

One specific type of conclusion is a **generalization.** A generalization is an idea, a statement, or a rule that can be applied to more than one case or situation. A valid generalization has no exceptions. Here are some examples of generalizations:

> Squares always have four equal sides.
> All planets in the solar system revolve around the sun.
> All mammals have hair.

Whenever you see or write the words *always, all, every, never, none,* or *no,* your critical-thinking alert should go off. These words usually signal a generalization. Before making generalizations, be sure that you have considered enough cases so that you don't draw a **hasty generalization.** Use care and deliberation whenever you make a generalization because generalizations can lead to stereotypes. A **stereotype** is an unfair conclusion about all members of a specific group that is based on a limited number of cases. Stereotypes can be dangerous because they may lead to prejudice, intolerance, and injustice directed toward racial, ethnic, religious, or gender groups. Use qualifying words such as *some, many, most, often, few, seldom,* or *usually* if you have any doubts about whether a generalization is valid.

Reference Point: *pages 237–242*

Assignment 3 | Generalizations

On your paper, write *Valid* if the generalization is reasonable and *Invalid* if it is hasty, or unreasonable. Then briefly explain your reasoning. Identify any stereotypes that you find.

1. All children should have three glasses of milk a day.
2. March always has thirty-one days.
3. The circumference of a circle always equals the diameter multiplied by 3.1416.
4. Math tests are always difficult.
5. All nurses love working with people.
6. Parents are always taller than their children.
7. January is always colder than August.
8. Vegetarians never eat meat.
9. Lawyers are all rich.
10. No mammals live in water.

Taking Essay Tests

Essay tests ask you to write an essay, using a variety of thinking and writing skills. Several sample essay questions follow.

Discuss and illustrate the change in the standard of living of the average United States citizen between the years 1880 and 1920.

Explain the advantages and the disadvantages of using the Consumer Price Index to measure inflation.

Trace the development of synthetic vitamins.

Essay test questions often require you to display facts and concepts that you have learned in a course. You may be required to show general knowledge of a subject, to synthesize information and draw conclusions, or to defend a hypothesis. Read the directions for key words that will tell you what kind of answer is sought.

Key Words in Directions

Direction	Meaning
Compare	Point out similarities
Contrast	Point out differences
Criticize	Discuss the merits or value
Describe	Give details
Discuss	Consider various aspects of a subject
Explain	Give reasons
Illustrate	Provide examples
Name	List the names
Summarize	Give main points briefly
Trace	Present in logical or chronological order

Use the following strategies when answering essay questions.

▶ **Strategies**

1. *If you have a choice of questions to answer, read all of the questions before choosing one.*

2. *Allot the time that you will spend on each question according to the number of points that it is worth.*
3. *On scratch paper, jot down names, dates, facts, or formulas required in your answer, and arrange them in appropriate order.*
4. *Be specific in your answer, but do not pad it with unrelated details.*
5. *Proofread your answer for correct usage, spelling, and punctuation.*

Look at this example essay question.

Contrast aerobic and anaerobic exercise, and explain which is a better form of exercise. (ăn′ə-rō′bĭk)

This essay question asks you to do two things: point out differences and give reasons. If you only point out differences, you are answering only part of the question.

Because time is limited, you probably will not have the opportunity to revise your answer to an essay question. Preparing a rough outline of ideas, such as the one that follows, allows you to maximize your time and to create the most organized essay.

I. Anaerobic
   A — builds strength /spot-tones muscles
   B — requires little oxygen, but increases blood pressure
   C — not much caloric expenditure, but tires body fast
II. Aerobic
   A — tones muscles/improves circulation/lowers b.p.
   B — improves strength/functioning of heart and lungs
III. Aerobic better
   A — not as dangerous
   B — gives better all-over conditioning / benefits

Assignment Essay Questions

Write an essay answer to one of the following topics. Allow thirty minutes for planning, writing, and proofreading.

1. Describe one thing people can do to make their lives healthier.
2. Trace how the content of television programs changes from early evening to late evening.
3. Compare or contrast the qualities that make a person successful in professional sports with those that make a person successful in business.

Taking Standardized Tests

No matter what your future plans are, you will probably have to take a standardized test at some point in order to achieve your educational or career goals. Most colleges and many technical and vocational schools use scores on standardized tests as a basis for admission or placement. The United States military services also use test scores to determine placement for recruits.

One of the most frequently administered tests is the Scholastic Aptitude Test (SAT), given by the College Entrance Examination Board. The following pages are based on the verbal skills and written-English sections of the SAT, but this material will be helpful in preparing for other standardized tests as well.

Preparing for any standardized test takes time. Last-minute cramming is not helpful. The best way to prepare for a test is to use the strategies in this unit and to read widely. Through reading you can enlarge your vocabulary, broaden your appreciation of well-written prose, and develop your ability to comprehend what you read.

Note: Always find out if there is a penalty for wrong answers. If there is no penalty, guess at answers that you are unsure of after you eliminate choices that you know are wrong.

Vocabulary Questions

Most standardized tests have at least one section designed to measure the extent of your vocabulary. This section may include test items covering antonyms, analogies, and sentence completions. These test items measure the extent of your vocabulary and your ability to differentiate relationships between words.

Antonym Questions

Antonym test questions require you to select the word *most nearly opposite* in meaning to a given word. Most antonym items follow the format shown here.

PONDEROUS: (a) delicate (b) unthinking (c) standing (d) deficient (e) beneficial

The word most nearly opposite in meaning to *ponderous* is (a), *delicate.*

Use the following strategies when taking a test on antonyms.

▶ **Strategies**

1. *Look at the word, think of its meaning, and think "not," or the opposite of the word.* If you try to read the choices before you establish the meaning of the word, you may get confused.

2. *Eliminate words that are synonyms, are different parts of speech, or are obviously wrong.* Also eliminate words that may be associated with a word but are not antonyms.

3. *Consider all of the choices before deciding which one is the best possible answer.* Do not choose the first answer that appears to be correct; there may be another answer that is more appropriate.

4. *Remember that many words have more than one meaning.* If you do not realize that *frame* can mean "to construct," "to conceive," or "to arrange for a purpose," you may miss a test item.

5. *Use your knowledge of prefixes, suffixes, and Greek and Latin roots to help you understand the meaning of unfamiliar words.* Refer to Unit 11, "Building Vocabulary."

Assignment 1 Antonym Questions

On your paper, write the letter of the word that is most nearly opposite in meaning to the capitalized word. Use a dictionary, if necessary, to check your choices after you have finished.

SAMPLE LEGIBLE: (a) illegal (b) illegitimate (c) ineligible (d) legless (e) unreadable

ANSWER (e)

1. OBSTRUCT: (a) demand (b) clear (c) purchase (d) employ (e) frustrate
2. ENLIGHTEN: (a) lessen (b) mystify (c) fester (d) melt (e) handicap
3. FUNDAMENTAL: (a) doubtful (b) unreligious (c) affable (d) negligent (e) nonessential
4. FLAGRANT: (a) clandestine (b) lawless (c) soothing (d) revengeful (e) dedicated
5. REVENUE: (a) contract (b) delegation (c) account (d) expense (e) calendar
6. MEDIOCRITY: (a) truth (b) farce (c) distinction (d) monotony (e) wisdom
7. ACQUIT: (a) convict (b) deliberate (c) pledge (d) surround (e) distend
8. EQUABLE: (a) certain (b) liberal (c) unflappable (d) unsteady (e) reversible
9. MITIGATE: (a) unshackle (b) circumstantial (c) flatter (d) classify (e) intensify
10. INGENUOUS: (a) stupid (b) clumsy (c) sly (d) shy (e) cute

Sentence-Completion Questions

Sentence-completion test items require you to supply a missing word or words that fit in the context of a sentence. Sentence-completion items require only an understanding of the words in the sentence and in the answer choices. Your skill in determining meaning from context is very important. (See pages 476–477.)

Study the following example.

A ⟋?⟍ person is one who ⟋?⟍ the motives and virtues of others.

(a) trustworthy . . questions (b) skeptical . . believes (c) critical . . endorses (d) cynical . . scorns (e) jealous . . leads

Only (d) makes sense in both blanks and fits the sense of the sentence.

Follow these strategies for taking sentence-completion tests.

▶ **Strategies**

1. *Read the sentence and analyze its structure and its probable meaning.* The sentence may present a contrast, offer reasons, or give a definition.
2. *Look for context clues.* The correct choice may be based on logic, tone, grammar, or word choice.
3. *Look for transitional words that may signal a reason or an example.* Those words include *because, since, but,* and *if.*
4. *Eliminate as many wrong answers as you can.*
5. *Insert your choice in the answer blank, and read the sentence to make sure that your answer makes sense.* In a sentence that has two blanks, make sure that both answers make sense.

Assignment 2 **Sentence-Completion Questions**

On your paper, write the letter of the word or words that best fits the meaning of the sentence as a whole.

SAMPLE The audience considered the dancer's performance to be ⟋?⟍, but the newspaper critic cited several ⟋?⟍.
(a) awkward . . falls (b) graceful . . jumps (c) powerful . . awards (d) flawless . . mistakes (e) listless . . missteps

ANSWER (d)

1. When she dropped the vase, it shattered on the tile floor, sending glass ⟋?⟍ everywhere.
(a) fractions (b) segments (c) globules (d) shreds (e) shards
2. A person who does not relish opera will probably not ⟋?⟍ the skill of an accomplished mezzo-soprano.
(a) bask in (b) audit (c) appreciate (d) relinquish (e) require
3. Most wild animals will ⟋?⟍ a person only if they cannot run away or if they must ⟋?⟍ their young.
(a) assault . . shield (b) attack . . defend (c) charge . . sacrifice
(d) peruse . . instruct (e) attend to . . evacuate

4. In the 1840s, women who __?__ in factories frequently worked __?__ twelve-hour days with only a half-hour break for lunch.
   (a) toiled . . irksome (b) labored . . grueling (c) sweated . . distorted (d) frolicked . . demanding (e) sewed . . luxurious
5. Benjamin Franklin is a(n) __?__ of a self-made man who __?__ his fortune in the printing business and was then able to retire to pursue other interests.
   (a) sample . . squandered (b) model . . fell into (c) instance . . harvested (d) example . . acquired (e) exception . . received
6. Isaac Asimov can truly be called a(n) __?__ writer, for he has __?__ over three hundred books.
   (a) prolific . . written (b) lethargic . . produced (c) tardy . . published (d) greedy . . sold (e) expansive . . printed
7. Psychologists say that "Type A" personalities tend to be nonstop workers who are competitive, aggressive, and impatient; by contrast, "Type B" personalities are relaxed, __?__, and __?__.
   (a) intelligent . . thin (b) easygoing . . imperturbable (c) colorless . . pessimistic (d) economical . . wise (e) giddy . . blunt
8. Leah exhibited her __?__ in archery by hitting the center of the target __?__.
   (a) prowess . . consistently (b) potential . . considerately (c) inadequacy . . unfailingly (d) technique . . angrily (e) effort . . erroneously
9. Some creatures move with __?__ swiftness: A running cheetah can reach the speed of 70 miles per hour, and a duck hawk in a dive can __?__ the speed of 180 miles per hour.
   (a) astonishing . . attempt (b) staggering . . extort (c) crass . . gain (d) torpid . . reach (e) amazing . . attain
10. A mother gently __?__ her small daughter to be quiet and __?__ until the dinner party was over.
    (a) harangued . . cautious (b) admonished . . well mannered (c) nurtured . . solicitous (d) instructed . . explicit (e) importuned . . apocalyptic

Analogy Questions

Analogy questions challenge your ability to understand the relationship between two words and your ability to recognize a similar or parallel relationship between two other words. When taking an analogy test, establish first the relationship that exists between the two capitalized words. Then, from the list of choices that follows, select the pair of words that has a relationship similar or parallel to that of the capitalized words. Here is a sample analogy.

SYMPHONY : COMPOSER ::   (a) poet : poem   (b) music : dancer
(c) law : lawyer   (d) editor : city   (e) novel : writer

Use the following strategies to answer analogy questions.

▶ **Strategies**

1. *When reading an analogy, substitute "is to" for the single colon and "as" for the double colon.* Read the sample analogy this way: "SYMPHONY is to COMPOSER as *poet* is to *poem*" and so forth.

2. *Determine the relationship between the capitalized pair of words.* (See below for some common types of relationships.)

3. *Try each pair of terms to see if it has the same relationship.* Formulate a sentence that contains the capitalized words and expresses their relationship. For example, "A SYMPHONY is created by a COMPOSER." Then substitute the word-pair choices in your sentence: "A *poet* is created by a *poem*."

4. *Eliminate the word pairs that have different relationships.*

5. *Check for grammatical patterns.* If the capitalized words are a noun/adjective pair, then the answer must be a noun/adjective pair.

6. *Select the word pair that most closely duplicates the relationship.*

Look again at the sample analogy. The relationship of the capitalized pair of words is one of an artistic product and its creator. Eliminate (a) because, while the pair *poet : poem* expresses the relationship, the order of artistic creation and creator is reversed. Eliminate (b) because *music* is not created by a *dancer*. Eliminate (c) because *lawyers* do not create *law;* they administer it. Eliminate (d) because an editor is not created by a *city*. The correct choice is (e), *novel : writer*.

Common Relationships of Analogy Word Pairs

Relationship	Example
Synonym	slender : thin (same meaning)
Antonym	sick : healthy (opposite meaning)
Part of a whole class	table : furniture (a kind of furniture)
Part of a whole item	leg : table (a part of a table)
Member of same class	cherry : grape (both are fruits)
Size	mound : hill (a hill is a large mound)
Cause/effect	carelessness : accident (causes accidents)
Time sequence	infancy : maturity (youth before age)
Object/purpose	silo : storage (a silo stores grain)
Tool/user	lariat : cowboy (a cowboy uses a lariat)
Action/object	weighing : scales (uses scales)
Degree	adoration : love (degrees of affection)

Assignment 3 **Analogy Questions**

On your paper, write the letter of the pair of words that best expresses a relationship similar to that expressed by the capitalized pair of words.

SAMPLE   CONFLAGRATION : FLAME ::   (a) hose : water
        (b) fire : ash   (c) hurricane : breeze   (d) log : kindling
        (e) mishap : catastrophe

ANSWER   (c)

1. FROG : POND ::   (a) cow : pasture   (b) dog : junkyard
   (c) tree : jungle   (d) ocean : whale   (e) princess : dungeon
2. WHEAT : GRAIN ::   (a) peas : beans   (b) carpet : rug
   (c) pamphlet : words   (d) yogurt : dairy product   (e) fowl : chicken
3. LANE : BOULEVARD ::   (a) book : library   (b)
house : penthouse   (c) stream : river   (d) cottage : garden
   (e) pasture : building
4. HIDE : COW ::   (a) paint : wall   (b) pig : bristle
   (c) coat : person   (d) shell : crab   (e) hat : head
5. HORS D'OEUVRE : MAIN COURSE ::   (a) precipitation : rain
   (b) epilogue : novel   (c) prehensile : tail   (d) orator : oration
   (e) overture : opera
6. PERFORMANCE : APPLAUSE ::   (a) brave : medal   (b)
galleon : treasure   (c) cultivation : harvest   (d) dread : anxiety
   (e) July : May
7. ANTHROPOLOGY : HUMANS ::   (a) alchemy : science
   (b) archeology : architecture   (c) theology : religion
   (d) earth : geology   (e) psychology : childhood
8. CYCLONE : WIND ::   (a) apple : gravity   (b) nut : pecan   (c)
azure : depression   (d) buzzard : eagle   (e) chamois : leather
9. PEGASUS : HORSE ::   (a) Medusa : snake   (b) Babe : blue
   (c) Pluto : constellation   (d) Cyclops : man   (e) centaur : nymph
10. OMINOUS : PROMISING ::   (a) audacious : inquisitive
   (b) repugnant : pleasing   (c) servile : pleasant
   (d) flowering : odiferous   (e) conspicuous : impoverished

Reading-Comprehension Questions

Reading-comprehension questions test your ability to understand what is directly or indirectly stated in a passage. They may also test your ability to interpret and to analyze what you read. Reading-comprehension passages vary in length, but they always contain all of the information that you need to answer the accompanying questions.

Follow these strategies when answering reading-comprehension test items.

▶ **Strategies**

1. *Read the passage, asking yourself, "What is the main idea?"* Also be alert for reasons, supportive examples, and summary statements, which will help you to grasp the focus of the passage.

2. *Read the questions first if the passage is long or is on an unfamiliar subject.* For example, if the passage is on astronomy, about which you may know little, reading the questions first may help you to follow the information more easily and to find important points.

3. *Read the questions that follow the passage.* Do not reread the passage for each question, or you will not finish the test.

4. *Read all the answers, and select the best answer.* Select your answer solely on the basis of what is in the passage, not on your personal knowledge or opinion.

5. *If you cannot answer a question, go on to the next one.* Do not allow a difficult question to distract you from other questions.

Answers to Eliminate

Kind of Answer	Characteristic
Incorrect	Contradicts statements in the reading
Not relevant	May be true but does not answer the question
Incomplete	Focuses on only *part* of the information when an answer is sought that covers *all* the information
Too general	Makes generalizations that go beyond the reading
External	Facts or ideas *may* be correct but are not in the reading
Reverse order	Answer *would* be correct if the order of some information items were reversed

Study the following passage and its questions.

(hyŏo-rīs′tĭks)   Much of people's thinking seems to be based on *heuristics*, which are mental shortcuts or rules of thumb. Suppose, for example, that you are about to leave home in the morning but cannot find your watch. You might search for the watch in every possible location, room by room. But to obtain the same outcome more quickly, you are likely to search first in the places where your past experience suggests the watch might be; this approach is a heuristic. Similarly, in deciding which political candidates to vote for, your rule of thumb might be to support all those in a particular party rather than research the views of each individual. People use heuristics like these because they are easy and frequently work well. But heuristics can also bias cognitive processes and cause errors. For example, many of those who vote for everyone on a particular party's election ticket may later be chagrined to discover that they got the president they wanted, but they also got a local sheriff whose views they despise.

Which of the following is most likely to illustrate the concept of a heuristic?
(a) Going out on a date for the first time
(b) Obtaining a passport
(c) Arguing with a neighbor
(d) Packing for a business trip
(e) Graduating from high school and moving into an apartment

The previous passage is an extended definition of the concept of a *heuristic*. The central idea of a heuristic is that it is a mental shortcut that is developed by repeatedly performing a task.

If you read through the choices, you can eliminate (a), (b), and (e) because they are first-time experiences. Eliminate (c) because even though many arguments may have occurred, there are no mental shortcuts involved in the act of arguing—no task is being accomplished. The correct choice is (d). A person who has previously packed for a trip will accomplish the task more quickly than a person packing for the first time.

Assignment 4 — Reading-Comprehension Questions

Read the passage that follows. On your paper, write the letter of the best answer for each question.

> The end of World War II ushered in a period of growth and prosperity in the United States. An affluent society thrived in a period of booming productivity.
>
> As America's productivity grew by leaps and bounds in the postwar years, so did its appetite for goods and services. In the affluent postwar years, middle-class Americans could afford to satisfy desires for a home or a car that they had to defer during the Depression and the war. If they lacked the cash to buy what they wanted, they borrowed the money. Credit to support the nation's shopping spree grew from over $8 billion worth of short- and intermediate-term loans in 1946 to $127 billion in 1970. Here was the economic basis of the consumer culture.
>
> As Americans consumed goods and services, they were using up the world's resources. Consumption of crude petroleum soared 118 percent from 1946 to 1970, but domestic production increased only 97 percent. The extra oil had to be imported. Electricity use jumped too, from 270 billion kilowatt-hours to 1.6 trillion. By the mid-1960s the United States, with only 5 percent of the world's population, produced and consumed over one third of the world's goods and services.

1. The main idea of the passage is that
   (a) the population growth in the United States was commensurate with growth of manufacturing after World War II.
   (b) after World War II, the United States prospered and consumed more goods, services, and natural resources.
   (c) middle-class Americans bought more items on credit.
   (d) the term "affluent society" was coined to describe the people of the United States after World War II.
   (e) people bought more homes and cars and used more oil and electricity after World War II.

2. According to the passage, the economic foundation of the affluent society was
   (a) credit. (b) cash. (c) oil. (d) desire. (e) the baby boom.
3. Before World War II, Americans
   (a) used more natural resources.
   (b) used more oil but less electricity.
   (c) used fewer natural resources.
   (d) used the same amount of natural resources.
   (e) used more credit and fewer resources.
4. By the mid-1960s, the United States
   (a) used over half of the world's goods and services.
   (b) used most of the world's goods and services.
   (c) made and used over a third of the world's goods and services.
   (d) made and used most of the world's goods and services.
   (e) made and used a proportionate share of the world's goods.
5. From reading the passage, one can infer that
   (a) Americans had more comforts and luxuries after World War II.
   (b) an affluent society is one in which people have cars.
   (c) in order for a society to grow, it must import oil.
   (d) American social values declined after World War II.
   (e) Americans spent over $100 billion on a shopping spree.

Tests of Standard Written English

The SAT also has a section called the Test of Standard Written English (TSWE). Rather than being used as a college admission test, however, the TSWE is used to determine which English courses you should take after you have gained admission to a college. The test questions, which cover your knowledge of grammar, usage, mechanics, and logical word choice, focus on your ability to recognize errors in standard written English.

Reference Point:
page 616

Sentence Correction   These test questions require you to choose the best way of stating an underlined portion of a sentence. There may be an error in logic or in sentence structure. If more than one answer seems correct, choose the one that is most effective in the context. In this kind of test, choice (A) is always the same as the underlined portion and means "Make no change."
Study the following sample test item.

<u>While listening to opera and eating grapes,</u> the telephone rang twenty times, but I did not hear it.
(A) While listening to opera and eating grapes,
(B) In the course of listening to opera and eating grapes,
(C) While I listened to opera and was eating grapes,
(D) While I listened to opera and ate grapes,
(E)   As I was listening to the opera and had eaten grapes,

Use the following strategies to answer sentence-correction test questions.

▶ **Strategies**

1. *Read the entire sentence, and study the underlined portion to determine if it is incorrect.*
2. *If there is an error, read all of the choices and pick the one that best corrects the sentence error.*
3. *Write (A) if there is no error.*

If you read the sample sentence critically, you probably noticed that the introductory clause modifies *telephone* rather than *I*. The correct answer is (D).

Reference Point: *pages 667–669*

Assignment 5 **Sentence Correction**

On your paper, write the letter that indicates the best correction for the underlined part of each sentence. If the original sentence is correct, write (A).

SAMPLE   A shrew is the <u>tiniest and the most</u> numerous mammal.
       (A) tiniest and the most
       (B) tiniest and it is the most
       (C) tiniest, and the most
       (D) tiniest; it is the most
       (E) tiniest: it is the most

ANSWER   (A)

1. Napoleon may have wanted <u>fame, he certainly sought</u> power.
       (A) fame, he certainly sought
       (B) fame; he certainly sought
       (C) fame, he, certainly sought
       (D) "fame," he certainly sought
       (E) fame, Napoleon certainly sought

2. <u>Having a good friend is when you know you are liked and accepted as you are.</u>
       (A) Having a good friend is when you know you are liked and accepted as you are.
       (B) A good friend is a person who likes you and a person who accepts you as you are.
       (C) One is a good friend who likes you and accepts you as you are.
       (D) A good friend will like people and accept them as you are.
       (E) A good friend likes and accepts you as you are.

3. Duties of the shift supervisor will include <u>dispatching freight, maintenance of time cards, and you should resolve employee disputes.</u>

(A) dispatching freight, maintenance of time cards, and you should resolve employee disputes.

(B) the dispatch of freight, the maintenance of time cards, and you should resolve employee disputes.

(C) dispatching freight, maintaining time cards, and you should resolve employee disputes.

(D) dispatching freight, maintaining time cards, and resolving employee disputes.

(E) dispatch of freight, maintenance of time cards, and resolve of employee disputes.

4. Marissa is an orator of great skill and who wants to be an attorney.

(A) is an orator of great skill and who wants to be an attorney.

(B) is skillful as an orator, but who wants to be an attorney.

(C) is a skillful orator who wants to be an attorney.

(D) , who wants to be an attorney, as an orator has great skill.

(E) is one whom is skilled as an orator and she wants to be an attorney.

5. Hopefully, you can get another job before your next car payment is due.

(A) Hopefully, you can get another job

(B) I hope that you can get another job

(C) Another job will appear hopefully

(D) Another job will hopefully appear

(E) In hopes that you can get another job

6. The Smiths seem more concerned about property values than their neighbors.

(A) about property values than their neighbors.

(B) for property values than their neighbors.

(C) over property values than their neighbors.

(D) with property values than their neighbors.

(E) about property values than about their neighbors.

7. The worried businessman feared that his partners were cutting his throat behind his back.

(A) that his partners were cutting his throat behind his back.

(B) that his throat was being cut behind his back by his partners.

(C) that behind his back his throat was being cut by his partners.

(D) that his partners were covertly taking advantage of him.

(E) covertly that his partners were taking advantage of him.

8. Having escaped his leash, I watched as my dog ran down the street after the mail carrier.

(A) Having escaped his leash, I watched as my dog ran down the street after the mail carrier.

(B) I watched as my dog, having escaped his leash, ran down the street after the mail carrier.

   (C) I watched as my dog ran down the street after the mail carrier, having escaped his leash.

   (D) Having escaped his leash, the mail carrier was run after by my dog as I watched down the street.

   (E) As I was watching, my dog escaped his leash and ran after the mail carrier down the street.

9. The quarterback was distraught to discover that he had failed <u>to break the state record for passing by a few feet.</u>

   (A) to break the state record for passing by a few feet.

   (B) to break, by a few feet, the state's record for passing.

   (C) by a few feet to break the state record for passing.

   (D) by passing the state record by a few feet.

   (E) to have broken the state's passing record by a few feet.

10. <u>I could feel the hum of the dentist's drill in my mouth three inches below my knees.</u>

   (A) I could feel the hum of the dentist's drill in my mouth three inches below my knees.

   (B) I could feel the hum of the dentist's drill three inches below my knees in my mouth.

   (C) Three inches below my knees, I could feel the hum of the dentist's drill in my mouth.

   (D) The dentist's drill in my mouth made a humming that I could feel three inches below my knees.

   (E) In my mouth, three inches below my knees, I could feel the hum of the dentist's drill.

Error Identification   These test items require you to identify writing that does not follow the conventions of standard usage. They test your knowledge of subject-verb agreement, pronoun-antecedent agreement, correct use of modifiers, correct case of pronouns, and so forth. Error-identification test items follow the format shown here.

Each man <u>should give</u> copies of <u>their</u> forms to Elizabeth, <u>Skip,</u> and <u>me.</u>
          A   B   C   D

<u>No error.</u>
  E

▶ **Strategies**

  1. *Read the sentence for meaning.*

  2. *Look carefully at each lettered part and decide if it is correct.* Sometimes a sentence will have no error. No sentence ever has more than one error.

  3. *If there is no error, write (E).*

    Look again at the sample sentence. If you follow the strategies, you will see that (B) is incorrect and should be *his.*

On your paper, write the letter of the error in each sentence. Write (e) if there is no error.

SAMPLE   Leave us not grant the award solely for the candidate's looks.
          A   B   C   D

No error.
    E

ANSWER   (A)

1. Who is the tallest, Blair or I? No error.
   A B   C   D   E

2. You can tell he's a good player by how well he throws. No error.
       A   B   C   D   E

3. The capital of the state is a lot further from here than she thinks.
       A   B   C   D

No error.
   E

4. We wanted to visit the South last year; however, mother wanted to
                         A   B   C

see relatives who live in Seattle. No error.
            D   E

5. The children's playroom looks like it usually does; let's clean it be-
       A   B   C D

fore our guests arrive. No error.
                          E

6. It's an award that should be given to the person that deserves it the
   A   B   C

most. No error.
 D   E

7. Laura asked, "May we watch the film version of
              A B

"Romeo and Juliet," please?" No error.
        C   D   E

8. "Even if twenty five of you object," Tom shouted, "the schedule
            A   B   C

will not be changed!" No error.
            D   E

9. Most of the student's paper was well-written, but the paper that
                A   B

she wrote on November 13 is even better. No error.
                      C   D   E

10. The catalogue lists the company's address as follows: DCA Manu-
                             A   B

facturing, 11104 Davis Drive, Whittier, CA, 99603. No error.
              C   D   E

Standardized Tests of Writing Ability

Standardized tests of writing ability ask you to write a short essay on a certain topic. The results of these tests may be used to predict your performance in writing courses, to diagnose your writing problems, to measure your growth as a writer, or to assess your school's writing program.

Unlike classroom essay tests, you usually have less than an hour, sometimes less than a half hour, in which to complete the essay. Because you do not have time for much revision, your thoughts must be very well organized *before* you begin to write. Use these strategies when writing a short essay.

Like the essays that you write in your classes, standardized writing tests measure your ability to generate and organize ideas; to use supporting detail; and to use correct grammar, usage, and punctuation.

▶ Strategies

1. *Carefully read the directions and the test question so you know what is being asked for.* (See Essay Questions, pages 446–447.)
2. *Use prewriting techniques, such as clustering and outlining, to plan and organize your answer.*
3. *As you write, glance back at your cluster or rough outline* to make sure that you are staying on the topic.
4. *Proofread your essay for errors* in spelling, usage, and punctuation.

Assignment 7 Test of Writing Ability

On your paper, answer one of the following essay questions. Allow thirty minutes for planning, writing, and proofreading. Follow the preceding strategies.

1. *Evaluation:* Do you think that women's professional sports should get as much broadcast coverage as men's professional sports do? Why or why not?
2. *Analysis:* Think of a controversial television program, either an entertainment program or a documentary program, that evoked a strong response in you. Relate the content of the program and explain why you think that the program should have or should not have been censored.
3. *Problem—Solution:* You are applying for a job that involves supervising others, settling disputes and problems, and meeting deadlines. As part of the job application form, you are asked to describe a problem that you have had and the steps that you took to solve it. Write the answer that you would use for the job application.

Listening and Speaking

You engage in public speaking every time you talk with your friends, speak in class, address a school assembly, or make a report to a committee. Whatever your speaking situation, and whether you are addressing friends or strangers, your objective is to convey a clear message to your listeners. In this unit, you will study and apply principles that will help you to speak more effectively in public. You will also practice strategies for listening during speeches and interviews. Finally, you will learn to conduct an interview and to be interviewed.

Preparing Your Speech

Speeches may vary from formal to informal, depending on the occasion, the purpose, and the audience. The President's State of the Union Address is a formal speech. The report given by your ski club treasurer is an informal speech. A speech may also be either prepared or **impromptu.** For example, before delivering a speech about the life of Chaucer to your class, you would need to do research, organize your speech, and rehearse it. On the other hand, if your teacher asked you to describe a character from Chaucer's *The Canterbury Tales*, you would speak on the spur of the moment, giving an impromptu speech.

As in writing, your overall purpose in giving a speech may be to inform, to persuade, or to entertain your listeners. Sometimes you may combine purposes in a single speech, as you would if you wanted to inform your listeners about an issue and persuade them to support your position on that issue.

When you give an informative speech, your purpose is to explain, to define, to report, to describe, or to demonstrate. For example, when you explain the problems associated with the destruction of the ozone layer, your purpose is to inform your listeners.

Your purpose in giving a persuasive speech is to form or change your listeners' attitudes or opinions. You may also want your audience to take some action. For example, when you suggest that your listeners refrain from using products that contain chlorofluorocarbons — which damage the ozone layer — your purpose is to persuade.

As in preparing a written report, the key to giving a successful speech is careful planning. Plan and prepare your speech one step at a time, following this procedure.

Reference Point: *pages 372–427*

▶ **Procedure**

1. *Select and limit your subject.* Choose a subject that you can discuss within your time limit. Shakespeare is too broad a subject, but a description of your favorite Shakespearean heroine would be manageable in a half-hour talk.

2. *Decide on your general and specific purposes for making the speech.* The **general purpose** of your speech is to inform, to persuade, to entertain, or perhaps a combination of these purposes. Your **specific purpose** is a more exact statement of what you want your listeners to know, to feel, to think, or to do. In a talk about your experiences as an exchange student, for example, your general purposes might be to inform, to persuade, and to entertain. Your specific purpose might be to encourage your listeners to participate in the exchange-student program at your school.

3. *Analyze your audience in relation to your topic and purpose.* Think about your listeners' interests, backgrounds, attitudes, and age group. Decide how you want your speech to affect your audience. For example, persuading athletic coaches that your school should climininate competitive sports would probably be a lost cause. You would do better to try to persuade parents and administrators to support your position. Adjust your speech to your audience's familiarity with your topic, defining new vocabulary and explaining basic concepts if necessary.

4. *Prepare a thesis statement* that in clear, specific language tells your audience exactly what you are going to talk about. For example, your thesis statement might be "Becoming an exchange student can enrich your life in many unexpected ways."

Reference Point: *pages 46–47*

Assignment 1 **Limiting Subjects and Determining Purpose**

On your paper, list a speech topic for three of the following subjects. Keeping your intended audience in mind, write a general purpose and a specific purpose for each. Save your paper.

SAMPLE The environment
ANSWER Recycling
To persuade
To inspire my audience to participate in recycling programs

1. Ecology
2. Latin America
3. Politics
4. Literature
5. Cooking
6. Films
7. The Grand Canyon
8. Nuclear energy
9. Jane Austen

Developing a Thesis Statement

On your paper, write an appropriate thesis statement for each of the three speech topics that you chose in Assignment 1.

SAMPLE   Recycling

ANSWER   One of the ways that we can all help to clean up the environment is to recycle newspapers and containers.

Gathering Information

Gather the information that you need to meet your specific purpose and to support your thesis statement. You may use information that is based on your own knowledge, observations, and experiences. You can also consult a variety of references such as books, magazines, and newspapers. Use library resources — the card catalog and appropriate indexes. Remember to record bibliographical information about your sources. Finally, you can interview people with special knowledge of your topic.

Reference Point: pages 383–391

Depending on your topic, purpose, and audience, the material that you present in your speech may be facts, opinions, or opinions sup-ported by facts. Be sure to distinguish fact from opinion and to use each appropriately *(pages 234–235)*.

The following kinds of information may be appropriate for your speech.

Explanations. Explain unfamiliar concepts. Tell what something is, how it functions, or why it happens.

Definitions. Define unfamiliar or difficult words for your listeners.

Examples and illustrations. Give examples, which represent gen-eral categories, or illustrations — extended and detailed examples.

Statistics. Use statistics — facts in the form of numbers — sparingly, so that they will interest your listeners and add authority to your speech.

Quotations. Cite statements, exactly as originally spoken or writ-ten, to add variety and impact to your speech.

Anecdotes. Use a brief account of an incident to amuse, inspire, or enlighten your audience. Be sure that your anecdotes relate directly to the ideas in your speech and that they are appropriate for your audi-ence and the occasion.

Reference Point: pages 394–397

Take notes on the information that you find. Using note cards, place one piece of information on each card. Label the cards with sub-ject headings, and indicate the source of the information.

Gathering Information

Step 1: Choose a subject for a ten-minute speech to your English class. On your paper, write a limited topic and a thesis statement.

Step 2: Using appropriate references, gather information about your topic. *Step 3:* Prepare and label note cards for several of the kinds of information listed on page 464. Include only information that is clearly related to your topic. Save your paper and your note cards.

Organizing Your Speech

Organize your material into a speech that has an introduction, a body, and a conclusion. Read over the note cards that you made when you did research on your topic. Group the cards according to subject, and underline key words and phrases. Note statistics and quotations that back up your ideas. Because the body of a speech contains most of the material, you should develop that part first.

The Body of Your Speech

To prepare the body of your speech, choose a pattern of organization that will help your listeners to understand your ideas and your supporting information.

Use **chronological order** when your topic includes a set of steps or a time sequence. Use **spatial order** when your topic involves physical or geographical relationships. Use **order of importance** when you can rank your information from most to least important or from least to most important.

Reference Point: *pages 36–38*

Next, using your thesis statement as a starting point, make a rough or a topic outline that includes your main headings and important subheadings. Eliminate irrelevant details.

Reference Point: *pages 46–51*

The Introduction to Your Speech

In your introduction, prepare your listeners for the ideas that you are going to present. Follow these guidelines.

▶ **Strategies**

1. *Create interest in your topic and explain why it is important.* To arouse your listeners' interest, you might begin your speech with a rhetorical question, a quotation, a startling statement, a moving or humorous anecdote, or some little-known information.

2. *Establish a good relationship with your audience.* Develop rapport with your listeners, and lead them into the body of your speech. Make your listeners feel that they have a stake in your message and that you and they have common interests.

3. *Present your thesis statement.* Tell your audience exactly what your speech is going to be about.

4. *Indicate how your speech is organized.* Cue your listeners to the pattern or patterns of organization that you are using. For example, if your topic were the causes of World War I, you might cue

your use of order of importance and chronological order by saying, "The major causes of World War I date back to the early nineteenth century."

5. *Use material in your introduction that relates directly to what you will say in the rest of your speech.*

The Conclusion of Your Speech

Your conclusion should sum up your speech and leave a strong impression in your listeners' minds. Conclude an informative speech with a summary of major points that will help your listeners to understand and to remember the information. The conclusion of a persuasive speech gives you a last chance to influence your audience's opinions and actions. End a persuasive speech with a restatement of your position, a striking statistic, a challenging question, or a call for action.

Assignment 4 **Organizing Your Speech**

Step 1: Using your note cards, your limited topic, and your thesis statement from Assignment 3 on page 464, make a rough outline of the points that you want to emphasize. *Step 2:* Choose an appropriate method for organizing your speech. Then make a topic outline with main headings, subheadings, and supporting details. *Step 3:* Write the points that you want to cover in your introduction and your conclusion. Save your papers.

Preparing to Deliver Your Speech

Although it's possible to read a speech from a prepared manuscript, it's preferable to speak extemporaneously. When you give an **extemporaneous** speech, you prepare your topic in advance and then deliver the speech without notes or with simple note cards. By using note cards instead of reading your speech, you will be able to speak more naturally and to maintain eye contact with your listeners. You will also be able to adjust your speech to the reactions that you sense in your audience, and you will not distract your listeners with shuffling papers.

Using Note Cards   Use your note cards as a guide, not as a crutch, as you deliver your speech. Record just enough information to jog your memory.

Prepare a card for each main heading in your outline, including its subheadings and supporting material. Except for material that you must present in exact form, such as quotations and statistics, write only key words and phrases on the cards. Include names, dates, and other important information. You may want to use different colored inks for main ideas, subheadings, and supporting material. Write on only one side of your note cards, and don't crowd your notes. Write clearly so that you will be able to read the cards at a glance, and number them to keep your information in order.

The Wording of Your Speech   Unlike a reader, who can pause to absorb ideas and reread passages, a listener must be able to understand a speech immediately. Therefore, the language that you use in your speech must be clear, precise, and appropriate.

As you plan the key words and phrases for your note cards, consider your **style** — how you use language. Spoken style is more forceful, less formal, and more personal than is written style. Spoken style usually uses simpler vocabulary and sentence structure, and it clarifies by means of signals, transitional words, repetition, and summary. Use the following strategies as you prepare your speech.

▶ **Strategies**

1. *Use short sentences.* Avoid complexity and vagueness. You may use partial sentences occasionally to achieve a special effect. For example, you might say, "More electives, more learning!"
2. *Choose familiar, concrete, specific words.* Say *cat* rather than *feline*; *exit* rather than *means of egress*; *generous* rather than *nice*.
3. *Use commands, exclamations, and questions to stimulate interest.*
4. *Use parallel structure to add rhythm to your speech.* For example, you might list parallel items: "You can maintain your health by eating properly, by sleeping eight hours a night, and by exercising daily."
5. *Insert signals — key words or phrases — to alert your listeners to what is coming.* These may be signals of purpose, background information, key points, or supporting material.
6. *Use transitional words and phrases* — such as *however, on the other hand, finally,* and *most important* — to establish connections between your basic ideas and your supporting material.
7. *Repeat and summarize your main points frequently.*
8. *Avoid generalizations or statements that include every member of a category or every occurrence of an event.* Avoid making assertions with such words as *all, always, none,* and *never.*
9. *Choose vivid words that will create images in your listeners' minds.* Invoke the five senses to make your language more lively. For example, if you were describing a beach, you might say, "The hot sand seemed to shimmer in the hazy sunshine."
10. *Eliminate jargon or special expressions that are limited to one profession or area of interest.* While it would be appropriate to use specialized music terms if you were talking with a group of music students, you would need to eliminate or to define those terms if you were speaking to a different audience.

11. *Avoid clichés — trite expressions that have lost their impact.* Replace expressions such as "nice," "like a fifth wheel," "as sly as a fox," and "last but not least" with more meaningful words and phrases.

Reference Point: *pages 66–68*

Unity, Coherence, and Conciseness As you prepare your speech, keep in mind unity, coherence, and conciseness. To achieve unity in your speech, include only information that supports your thesis statement and that fulfills your specific purpose. Your speech will be coherent if you present your ideas in a logical order, keeping related ideas together. If you make your speech concise, using as few words as possible, your audience will understand and remember your message, and you will find it easier to cover all your material within your time limit.

Assignment 5 **Making Note Cards**

Using the materials that you prepared in Assignment 4, make note cards with which to deliver your extemporaneous speech. As you create your notes, think about effective wording and the unity, the coherence, and the conciseness of your presentation.

Delivering Your Speech

Although you're almost ready to face your audience, you still need to make a few final preparations. These preparations will help you to improve the content and the delivery of your speech. They will also help you to be more relaxed during your presentation.

Final Preparations

Having prepared your note cards, you are now ready to plan visual aids for your speech. You will also need to rehearse your speech, to become familiar with the setting, and to concentrate on the manner of your delivery.

Using Visual Aids Use appropriate visual aids — materials such as scale models, slides, maps, sketches, photographs, charts, and posters — to make your speech more interesting and easier to understand. Organize your materials, and decide exactly how you'll use the visual aids in your speech. Be sure that your visual aids are large enough for everyone in the audience to see. Practice with the materials so that you'll be able to manage them skillfully.

Rehearsing Your Speech You will give your speech with more ease, confidence, and authority if you rehearse it well. Using your note cards, practice your speech aloud until you are very familiar with the content and fluent in your delivery. Use a tape recorder or video camera if they are available, or ask family members and friends to listen and comment.

Becoming Familiar with Your Setting If possible, find out in advance about the place where you will deliver your speech. It will help you to know whether the room is large or small; whether there will be a desk, a lectern, or a microphone; and whether the setting lends itself to the visual aids that you plan to use. For example, if you plan to show slides, you'll need to find out if a slide projector and screen are available and how and when to get them. You would also need to know whether the slides have to be arranged in a "carousel" or other container.

Presenting Your Speech

Your delivery will affect your listeners' response to your speech. How well your listeners concentrate on the content and how well they understand your main points depend to some extent on your voice, posture, gestures, facial expression, and use of eye contact. Here are some strategies for presenting your speech effectively.

▶ **Strategies**

1. *Vary the rate, volume, pitch, and tone of your voice.* Speak slowly and clearly, at a volume that is audible to everyone in the room. Pause for emphasis, to signal a transition, or to allow your listeners time to absorb information.
2. *Be aware of your posture and your gestures.* Stand straight but not stiffly, without leaning on a desk or a lectern. Don't sway back and forth or from side to side. Gesture and move about in a natural, relaxed way.
3. *Be aware of your facial expression.* Think about your topic, and let yourself react naturally so that your facial expression will reflect the emotions that you feel as you speak — concern, surprise, delight, puzzlement, determination, and so forth.
4. *Make eye contact with your audience.* Look at your listeners, not at the back wall, the floor, or the ceiling. Let your eyes move from face to face, establishing personal contact.

Evaluating a Speech Use the following checklist to evaluate the speeches that you hear and to assess your own speeches during the rehearsal stage.

Evaluation Checklist

	Strong	Average	Needs Improvement
Topic			
Introduction			
Body			
Conclusion			
Organization			
Wording			
Visual Aids			
Voice			
Facial Expression			
Eye Contact			
Gestures and Posture			

Assignment 1 **Rehearsing and Evaluating Your Speech**

Rehearse your speech using the materials that you prepared in the previous Assignments. Use a tape recorder, or rehearse in front of family or friends. Make any needed improvements in your notes and delivery. Then use the Evaluation Checklist to assess your speech.

Assignment 2 **Delivering Your Speech**

Review the strategies on page 469, and deliver your ten-minute speech to your English class.

Effective Listening

Whether you are listening to a speech, participating in a conversation, conducting an interview, or being interviewed, you need to be an active rather than a passive listener. Active listeners evaluate what they hear. Passive listeners, on the other hand, have difficulty concentrating and may not be able to distinguish fact from fiction, dependable information from slick sales talk, or digressions from supporting examples. Following these guidelines will help you to become an active listener.

▶ Strategies

1. *Think about your purpose in attending the speech or interview.* Ask yourself what you hope to learn from it.
2. *Learn what you can in advance about the speaker, the topic of the*

speech, or the purpose of the interview. This will help you to understand the speaker's point of view and will heighten your interest. It may also help you to formulate some questions in advance.

3. *Make sure that you arrive on time,* with your note-taking materials ready.

4. *Clear your mind of other concerns* so that you can concentrate. Maintain a positive and interested attitude.

5. *Listen for signals that cue the speaker's purpose or a change of direction.*

6. *Be alert to main ideas and supporting details.*

7. *Pay attention to summaries that restate the purpose, a main idea, or other important information.*

8. *Listen to take notes.* Taking brief but complete notes will enable you to understand and to remember a speaker's purpose. Be sure to take notes when you are interviewing someone.

9. *Wait until the scheduled question-and-answer period to ask questions.* Interrupting the speaker may irritate that person and distract other members of the audience.

10. *Ask directly to have something explained or restated.* You might say, for example, "Would you please explain what you meant by . . ."

11. *Ask for more information or for suggestions for further study or action.*

<hr>

Assignment **Taking Notes on a Speech**

Attend a public speech, or listen to a speech on radio or television. Take notes on the speaker's important points. On your paper, write a brief summary of the speech.

Interviewing and Being Interviewed

Interviews usually fall into two categories: formal and informal. Conversations with friends or similar spontaneous dialogues in which there is direct questioning are examples of informal interviews. A formal interview, on the other hand, is a scheduled event. You may conduct a formal interview to get evidence for a persuasive essay or to gather information for a report or a personal decision. You may be interviewed when you apply for a job or for admission to college. Good speaking and listening skills are needed when you conduct an interview as well as when you are the person being interviewed.

Being the Interviewer

While an informal interview is often unplanned, a formal interview requires preparation. The following strategies will help you to prepare a formal interview and to conduct it.

▶ **Strategies**

1. *Call the person you wish to interview to make an appointment.* Arrange for a mutually convenient time and place to meet.

2. *Find out as much as you can about your topic and about the person you plan to interview.*

3. *Prepare a list of questions for the interview.* Ask open-ended questions that allow your subject to expand on the topic. Ask spontaneous questions as they occur to you.

4. *Arrive on time and dress appropriately.*

5. *Adopt a courteous and respectful manner.*

6. *Take note-taking materials or a tape recorder.* Ask your subject for permission to use the tape recorder and to use quotations from the interview. Check your quotations for accuracy.

7. *Keep the interview on track.* You can be open to useful and interesting digressions, but don't allow the interview to wander too far from the topic.

8. *End on a courteous note and thank the person for his or her time.* Offer to send the person a copy of the interview after you have written it up.

Writing Up Your Interview Review your written notes or those that you've transcribed from a tape. Delete irrelevant or distracting information. Then arrange your notes in a logical order. Use chronological order, for example, if your interview subject related events in a sequence. Use order of importance if the person described events from most to least important or vice versa.

You may present your interview information as a question-and-answer dialogue or as a narrative in which you relate the information indirectly. In a narrative presentation, you may include direct quotations. In both of the following examples, the information is organized chronologically.

QUESTION How did you first become interested in a career in journalism?

ANSWER I took a fascinating and very challenging journalism course in high school, and I also wrote articles for the school paper.

QUESTION When did you get your first job as a journalist?

ANSWER While I was in college, I took a part-time job covering sports for a small local newspaper. I loved it because I got to attend all the games and then got paid to write about them!

NARRATIVE Mercedes Quiroga, a reporter for our city's largest newspaper, first became interested in a career in journalism after taking a "fascinating and very challenging" course in journalism during high school. Having written articles for her high school paper, she began to earn money as a journalist while she was attending college. She had a job covering sports for a small local paper. She said that she "loved it" because she "got to attend all the games and then got paid to write about them."

Assignment 1 **Conducting a Formal Interview**

Contact someone in your community who is an expert in a field that interests you, and arrange for an interview. Prepare the interview and conduct it. Then write it up, using a logical order, in either dialogue or narrative form.

Being the Person Interviewed

When you are being interviewed, you need to practice a high level of listening and speaking skills. You may be interviewed formally or informally, sharing your special knowledge of a subject. For example, if you are a foreign-film buff, your friends might ask you about the latest films, actors, directors, and so forth. If you are planning to attend college, you might have an interview in which a college-admissions representative will ask you about your interests, background, and academic goals. You will also need to prepare for a job interview.

Preparing for a College Interview

While many colleges and universities do not require formal interviews, some colleges encourage students who live nearby to come in to the admissions office for an interview. Students who do not live near the college may be interviewed by alumni of the college.

Once you have made a list of the colleges that you might like to attend, use these guidelines to prepare for an interview.

▶ **Strategies**

1. *Write or call the admissions office to find out about the procedures.* Some colleges encourage students to drop in. Others require appointments.

2. *Familiarize yourself with materials about the college before the interview.* Most colleges send out information packets and course

catalogues on request. You might also find information in your guidance counselor's office or in the library. Knowing something about the college will help you to speak confidently.

3. *Prepare a list of questions.* These questions might concern your academic interests, the scholarship aid available, or campus life. Review your questions a number of times so that you can bring them up naturally during the interview. The interviewer will evaluate the kinds of questions that you ask as well as how you answer questions.

4. *Dress appropriately for the interview.*

5. *Listen carefully to the questions, and answer them as directly as possible.*

6. *Try to be relaxed, but don't be too casual.* Remember that you are trying to make the best impression possible.

7. *Don't interrupt the interviewer,* and avoid talking too fast or too much.

8. *Be prepared to talk about yourself.* While you will have many questions about the school, the interviewer will want to know about you and why you are interested in this particular college. Discuss your educational goals and how the school can help you to fulfill them. Most interviewers will try to find out what makes you different from other applicants. Talk about your extracurricular interests enthusiastically. Most important, be yourself.

9. *Don't make jokes at your own or others' expense.* Never belittle your abilities.

10. *Be aware of when the interview has come to an end.* Don't continue the conversation once the interview is over. Thank the interviewer for his or her time and leave.

11. *Limit yourself to two interviews a day.* You may be visiting several colleges in a short time, but it will be difficult for you to do your best at each interview if you are feeling rushed.

12. *Write a brief thank-you note to the interviewer.*

Assignment 2 Preparing for a College Interview

Choose a college that you are interested in attending. *Step 1:* Do some research about that school and then, on your paper, write ten questions that you might ask an interviewer. *Step 2:* Write ten more questions that an interviewer might ask you. Write possible answers to those questions. Save your papers.

Assignment 3 Role-Playing a College Interview

Working with another student in your English class, role-play a college interview. Use the questions and answers that you prepared for Assignment 2. Take turns being the applicant and the interviewer. Ask a third student to evaluate the applicant's performance. Videotape the role plays if possible.

Preparing for a Job Interview

When you interview for a job, you will have two main objectives. First, of course, you'll want to make a good impression on your prospective employer; second, you'll want to get information about the job and the organization. Many of the strategies that you use when you conduct a formal interview *(page 472)* or when you have a college interview *(pages 473–474)* are appropriate for a job interview as well.

▶ **Strategies**

1. *Find out about the place where you are applying for a job.* Read articles about it; interview people who work there.
2. *Think about the kinds of questions that the employer might ask.* For example, if you were applying for a job in a bank, the employer might ask you about your math skills. Be prepared to answer difficult questions such as "What do you like most and least about yourself?" Write out questions and possible answers.
3. *Make a list of questions to ask the interviewer.* The employer will want to assess your interest in the job. Prepare thoughtful questions about the way a company or an organization operates. Ask about the responsibilities that the job would entail.
4. *Line up three references.* Ask three adults who know you well and who would speak highly of you and your abilities to serve as references. Take their names, addresses, and daytime telephone numbers to the interview.
5. *Rehearse the interview with family members or friends.* They can ask you questions from the list that you have prepared, and you can try to respond as you would to a prospective employer.

Assignment 4 **Asking and Answering Questions**

Check the newspaper for a job that interests you. On your paper, make a list of questions that an employer might ask you if you were to apply for the job. Write possible answers to the questions. Save your paper.

Assignment 5 **Role-Playing a Job Interview**

Working with another student in your English class, role-play the questions and answers that you each wrote for Assignment 4. Take turns being the employer and the prospective employee. Ask a third student to evaluate the performance of the job applicant. Videotape the role plays if possible.

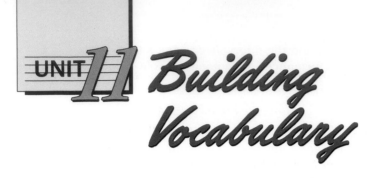

UNIT 11 Building Vocabulary

Learning how to praise, persuade, negotiate, criticize, or explain means learning how to express your thoughts and ideas with precision. By choosing the right words, you can command the attention of your reader or listener. At the same time, you can increase your comprehension of what other people are saying or writing by recognizing the words they use. In this unit you will discover how to build your vocabulary; this discovery will help you to succeed as a writer, a speaker, and a listener.

How to Learn New Words

In your notebook, make a list of words from your reading and listening that you want to include in your vocabulary. Look up the definitions of these words in a dictionary, and add the meanings to your list. Study these words and their meanings frequently. Try to use at least one of these words every day in your writing or in your conversation. When you encounter these words, study the context in which they are used. Observing context will make it easier for you to incorporate these words into your own writing and speech.

As you become more competent and confident in your use of new words, you will find that your list becomes an invaluable vocabulary resource. Add to your list and continue to use it in building your vocabulary.

Using Context to Get Meaning

When you encounter an unfamiliar word in your reading, you may be able to determine its meaning by examining the **context,** the passage in which the word appears. The following strategies suggest ways in which context can help you to determine meaning.

1. *Use the general sense of the passage along with your own knowledge and experience* to infer a meaning.
2. *Look for synonyms or restated definitions* of the unfamiliar word.
3. *Look for examples in the passage that may further explain or describe the unfamiliar word.*
4. *Notice whether the unfamiliar word is compared or contrasted with a familiar word or idea.* If so, use that known idea to help you to infer a meaning.

Assignment | **Context**

Read the following paragraph, paying special attention to the words in italic type. Write those words in your notebook. Beside each word write the meaning that you think the word has in the paragraph. Then find each word in a dictionary and compare your definition to the definition in the dictionary. Correct your definition if necessary. Write an original sentence for each word, using context clues to help define the word.

A young American boy who *aspired* to join the army during the Civil War found himself in a *quandary*. Army regulations *mandated* that recruits be eighteen years old or older. Hence, his dilemma — to enlist he would have to lie about his age, and lying, in the mind of this *virtuous* boy, was nothing short of a moral *transgression*. To avoid this *ignominy*, he contrived a scheme. On a scrap of paper he wrote the number *18* and tucked it in the sole of his shoe. Then, when asked if he were over eighteen, he answered with sufficient *veracity*, "Yes."

Getting Meanings from Word Parts

Thousands of English words have been formed by the combination of word parts — roots, prefixes, and suffixes. By learning the meanings of these words parts, you can often determine the meanings of unfamiliar words.

Roots Many words in the English vocabulary have Latin or Greek roots. Recognizing a single **root**, the central or basic element of a word, is the first step you can take in figuring out the meanings of a number of English words. For example, you may recognize the common root *-magn-* (meaning "great," "grand," or "large") in the words *magnifi-*

cent, magnify, and *magnitude.* In the sentence "All agreed that the contribution was a magnanimous gesture on his part," you can use your knowledge of the root *-magn-* to conclude that *magnanimous* means "grand" or "generous."

Keep in mind that two different word roots can have the same meaning even if they have different origins. For example, in the following list of roots, the Latin root *-circ-* and the Greek root *-cycl-* both mean "circle"; the Latin root *-aqua-* and the Greek root *-hydr-* both mean "water"; and the Latin root *-equ-* and the Greek root *-iso-* both mean "equal."

The hyphens before and after each root in the following lists indicate that the root may appear at the beginning, in the middle, or at the end of a word.

The spelling of the root may change slightly when it becomes part of an English word. For example, the spelling of the root *-jur-* changes in the word *justify.* Alternate spellings are shown in parentheses.

Common Latin Roots

ROOT	MEANING(S)	EXAMPLES
-ag- (-act-)	do, drive, lead	agent, action
-am- (-amic-)	love, friend	amorous, amicable
-aqua-	water	aquarium, aquatic
-cent-	hundred	centimeter, century
-circ-	circle	circus, circulate
-equ-	equal	equidistant, equation
-jur- (-jus-)	law, justice	jury, justify
-rupt-	break	abrupt, interrupt
-seq- (-sec-)	follow	sequel, consecutive
-sol-	alone	isolate, solitude

Common Greek Roots

ROOT	MEANING(S)	EXAMPLES
-cycl-	circle	bicycle, cyclone
-hydr-	water	hydraulic, hydroplane
-iso-	equal	isosceles, isotope
-micro-	small	microbe, microscope
-morph-	form	amorphous, metamorphosis
-neo-	new	Neolithic, neophyte
-nom-	divide	astronomy, binomial
-proto-	first	protocol, prototype
-soph-	wise	philosophy, sophisticated
-zo-	animal	zoology, protozoan

Prefixes and Suffixes   A **prefix** is a word part with a distinct meaning of its own that is placed before a word or a root to create a new word. When you add a prefix to a base word or a root, the spelling of the word does not change.

A **suffix** is a word part with a distinct meaning of its own that is placed at the end of a word or a root to change the function and, sometimes, the meaning of the word. When you add a suffix to a base word or a root, the spelling of the word may change. Two or more suffixes may be added to a base word to make another word; for example, *coincidentally* is made up of *coincident* plus *-al* plus *-ly*.

The following is an example of a step-by-step approach to determining the meaning of the word *egregious* by examining the meanings of its prefix, root, and suffix. By knowing that *-e-* means "out of," that *-greg-* means "flock," and that the adjective suffix *-ious* means "full of," you can figure out that the meaning of *egregious* is "out of the flock." In the sentence "Despite stellar performances by the actors, her play failed miserably because of egregious directing," you can use the context to determine that the precise definition of *egregious* is "outstandingly bad."

Prefixes

PREFIX	MEANING(S)	EXAMPLES
ambi- (amphi-)	both, around	ambiguous, amphibious
bi- (bin-)	two, twice	bicycle, binary
contra-	against, opposite	contradict, contrary
hyper-	over, beyond	hyperbole, hypersensitive
inter-	between, among	intercede, intermission
intra-	in, within	intramural, intravenous
intro-	in, inward	introspective, introvert
retro-	back, backward	retroactive, retrospect
super-	above, over	superfluous, superimpose

Suffixes

These suffixes make verbs out of nouns or adjectives:

SUFFIX	MEANING(S)	EXAMPLES
-ate	make, apply, do	fascinate, radiate
-en	cause to be, become	brighten, lengthen
-fy	make, form into	amplify, qualify

These suffixes make nouns out of verbs or adjectives:

SUFFIX	MEANING(S)	EXAMPLES
-ee	recipient of action, in condition of	addressee, employee
-ian	of or belonging to, skilled in	civilian, physician
-ion	result of act or process, state of being	evolution, adhesion
-ment	result of act or process, state of being	advertisement, environment

These suffixes make adjectives out of nouns or verbs:

SUFFIX	MEANING(S)	EXAMPLES
-able (-ible)	inclined to, capable of	adaptable, responsible
-ic	of, pertaining to, characteristic of	angelic, scenic
-ish	suggesting, like	impish, stylish
-less	lacking, without	aimless, sleepless

This suffix makes adverbs out of adjectives:

SUFFIX	MEANING	EXAMPLES
-ly	in a way that is	carefully, joyously

Assignment Roots, Prefixes, and Suffixes

Choose one root, one prefix, and one suffix from the lists on pages 478–479. For each of these three word parts, write three words not found in these lists that contain the part. Write these nine words in your notebook; then write an original sentence for each of the nine words.

How to Choose the Best Word

To be sure that you express yourself accurately and convincingly, you need to learn about *synonyms* and about the difference between *denotation* and *connotation*.

Synonyms

With a vocabulary of more than 700,000 words, the English language is rich in synonyms. Although many words have similar definitions, few words have exactly the same meaning. There is often some slight difference in meaning that makes one word more appropriate than another in your writing or speaking. These differences are called **shades of meaning.** Recognizing shades of meaning can help you to make correct word choices.

Notice the shades of meaning that differentiate the words in the following sets of synonyms.

complex — complicated, intricate, involved, tangled, knotty
opinion — view, sentiment, feeling, impression, belief

Now look carefully at the word *courage* and three of its synonyms.

Courage means strength that can be used to face danger with confidence and bravery. *Fortitude* stresses strength of mind to endure pain and adversity. *Mettle* emphasizes the capacity to rise to a challenge. *Tenacity* stresses persistence in resisting adversity.

The American Heritage Dictionary of the English Language
Second College Edition

As a skilled writer and speaker, you need to be aware of shades of meaning and to use the synonym that will precisely convey your thoughts and ideas. Most dictionaries list synonyms for certain entry words *(page 481).*

Assignment 1 Synonyms

Choose five words from the following list and write them in your note-book. Use a dictionary or a thesaurus to find at least two synonyms for each word. Write the synonyms next to the words. Then, for each set of synonyms, write a sentence using one of the synonyms. Make sure that your sentences show the correct use of the synonyms in context.

1. surfeit
2. tenable
3. dour

4. lampoon
5. vestige
6. wrest

7. irascible
8. precept
9. mundane

Denotation and Connotation

Many words have a denotative meaning and a connotative meaning. **Denotation** refers to the definitions listed in a dictionary. **Connotation** refers to the ideas and feelings associated with words. These ideas and feelings can be neutral, positive, or negative. In the following examples, note the more positive connotation of the word *conscientious* when compared with the connotation of the word *meticulous*.

Few employees are as **conscientious** about their work as Elena is.

Brett is a **meticulous** dresser who spends most of his salary on designer clothes.

Also, the same word can have different connotations in different contexts, such as the word *worried* in the following sentences.

George **worried** and fretted about everything.

Mr. White was **worried** because his son had not come home.

Make sure that you know the connotations of the words you use.

Using the Dictionary

If you wish to find the meaning, the pronunciation, or other infor-mation about a word, you need to know how to use a dictionary.

Entry Words   An **entry word** in a dictionary is the word that is being defined. The entry word shows, in boldface type, the correct spelling of the word, alternate spellings when applicable, and the inflected forms of nouns and verbs when these forms of the word cause irregular spelling. These spellings are divided into syllables by dots or hyphens to show you where to divide a word at the end of a line of writing. The entry itself contains information about the word, including pronunciation, part(s) of speech, and definitions.

> ma·tric·u·late (mə-trĭk′yə-lāt′) *tr. & intr.v.* -lat·ed, -lat·ing, -lates. To admit or be admitted into a group, esp. a college or university; enroll. — *n.* A matriculant. [Med. Lat. *matriculare, matriculat-*, to matriculate < LLat. *matricula*, list < *matrix*, list. — see MATRIX.] — ma·tric′u·la′tion *n.*

Pronunciations   The pronunciation usually follows the entry word and appears within brackets, parentheses, or bars. Light and heavy accent marks show which syllables are stressed. Most dictionaries contain a complete pronunciation key near the front of the dictionary and a shorter key on each page or each pair of pages.

> **haute cui·sine**   (ōt′ kwĭ-zēn′) *n.* **1.** Elaborate or skillfully prepared cuisine. **2.** The food prepared in the style of haute cuisine. [Fr. : *haute*, high + *cuisine*, cooking.]

Parts of Speech   Dictionaries identify the part or parts of speech of a word. Most dictionaries identify all the different parts of speech under a single entry word. A few dictionaries provide separate entries when a word is used as more than one part of speech.

Definitions   The most important information in a dictionary is the definitions of words. When an entry word has multiple definitions, each definition is indicated with a number or a letter or both. Read all of the definitions before selecting one that is appropriate to the context in which the word is being used.

> **hel·ter-skel·ter**   (hĕl′tər-skĕl′tər) *adv.* **1.** In disorderly haste; pell-mell. **2.** Haphazardly. — *adj.* **1.** Carelessly hurried and confused. **2.** Haphazard. — *n.* Turmoil; confusion. [Orig. unknown.]

Labels   When appropriate, dictionary entries include usage labels, such as *Nonstandard, Informal,* or *Slang.* Such labels are a guide to the correct use of words.

Reference Point:
pages 616–618

> **nerd** also **nurd**   (nûrd) *n. Slang.* A socially inept, foolish, or ineffectual person. [Prob. alteration of NUT.]

Etymologies   The **etymology** of a word is its origin and historical development. It is usually given in brackets or parentheses after the pronunciation or at the end of the entry. The following is the etymology for the words *Homo sapiens.*

> [NLat. *Homo sapiens*, specific name: *Homo*, genus name (< Lat. *homo*, man) + Lat. *sapiens*, pr. part. of *sapere*, to be wise.]

Undefined Related Forms   Many entry words have related forms made by adding suffixes. When the meaning of these words is obvious, they are simply listed at the end of the entry without definitions. These forms usually show syllable divisions, stress marks, and parts of speech.

> **sa·ga·cious**   (sə-gā′shəs) *adj.* Possessing or showing sound judgment and keen perception; wise [< Lat. *sagax, sagac-,* quick-witted.] — **sa·ga′ cious·ly** *adv.* — **sa·ga′cious·ness** *n.*

Synonyms Because the English language abounds with synonyms, dictionaries often list them for an entry word and explain their connotations. Some dictionaries also list antonyms. The following is a list of synonyms for the word *but*.

> *Synonyms: but, however, still, yet, nevertheless*. Each of these words introduces a statement in opposition to what precedes it. *But*, which notes but does not stress the opposition, is the most widely applicable: *He was ill, but he kept the appointment*. In the same example, *however* would soften the contrast between the two elements. *Still, yet*, and *nevertheless*, in the same example, emphasize contrast.

Usage Notes When a definition or a usage label is not sufficient to clarify a problem of usage, some dictionaries provide usage notes. The following is a usage note for the word *esquire*.

> *Usage:* The term *Esquire*, and its abbreviation *Esq.*, traditionally reserved for men, is now sometimes used in correspondence addressed to women, especially female attorneys: *Jane Roe, Esq.*

Homographs In most dictionaries, homographs are listed as separate entry words and are identified by superscripts. Read all the definitions of each entry to find the meaning that is appropriate to the context of the word.

> ruck[1] (rŭk) *n.* **1.** A large number mixed together; jumble. **2.** The multitude of ordinary people. [ME *ruke.*]

> ruck[2] (rŭk) *v.* **rucked, ruck·ing, rucks.** — *tr.* **1.** To make a fold in; crease. **2.** To disturb or ruffle; irritate. — *intr.* **1.** To become creased. **2.** To become irritated. — *n.* A crease or pucker, as in cloth. [Ult. < ON *hrukka*, wrinkle.]

Using a Thesaurus

A **thesaurus** is a collection of synonyms. Unlike dictionaries, which are always organized alphabetically, thesauruses can be organized in a variety of ways.

One kind of thesaurus lists groups of synonyms under very general categories, such as "Freedom" and "Liberation." Since the categories and the words within them are not alphabetically arranged, this kind of thesaurus provides a complete index to guide the user to the appropriate group of synonyms.

The following excerpts from *Roget's International Thesaurus* show the wealth of material from which you can choose when you are looking for a certain word. The left-hand column shows an excerpt taken from the text of the thesaurus. The right-hand column shows an excerpt taken from the index of the thesaurus.

762.12 **INDEPENDENT, free lance; individualist,** rugged individualist; free spirit; **liberal,** libertarian, latitudinarian; libertine, freethinker; free trader; **nonpartisan,** neutral, mugwump; isolationist; nonaligned nation; third world, third force.

independent

    n. free lance 762.12
       neutral 806.4
       nonpartisan 744.28
    adj. free 762.21
       neutral 806.7
       nonpartisan 744.28
       proud 905.8
       self-helpful 785.23
       strong-willed 624.15
       unrelated 10.5
       voluntary 622.7
       wealthy 837.13

The excerpt from the text of the thesaurus shows only one group of synonyms for the noun *independent.* The list of synonyms in the right-hand column shows that there are three synonym groups for the noun, as well as nine for the adjective.

Other thesauruses arrange groups of synonyms under a main word similar to the entry word in a dictionary. The main words are listed alphabetically. Sometimes each synonym of the main word is also included in the alphabetical list. For the synonyms, the information given is only a cross-reference to the main entry.

independent *adjective*

1. Free from the influence, guidance, or control of others.
2. Having political independence.
3. Able to support oneself financially.

1. **Syns:** self-contained, self-reliant, self-sufficient.
2. FREE *adjective.*
3. **Syns:** self-sufficient, self-supporting.

Some thesauruses give definitions for each synonym group, but some do not. To choose a word that is best for your purpose, you must carefully consider the shades of meaning and the different connotations of each word. If you are not sure of the differences in meaning or usage among the synonyms, consult a dictionary.

Assignment 2   Improving Your Vocabulary

Step 1: From the following list, choose ten words that are not already part of your everyday vocabulary. *Step 2:* Write the words in your notebook, leaving two or three blank lines for a definition and a sentence. *Step 3:* Look up each word in your dictionary to learn its meaning and pronunciation. *Step 4:* In your notebook, write a brief definition and a sentence using the word. *Step 5:* Study the words from time to time, and use them in your speaking and writing whenever appropriate. *Step 6:* When you have learned these words, make a new list and study them in the same way.

1.	arcane	11.	livid
2.	bilk	12.	mecca
3.	collusion	13.	nabob
4.	deplore	14.	obviate
5.	edict	15.	placid
6.	finite	16.	redress
7.	gist	17.	surly
8.	hiatus	18.	trek
9.	impute	19.	vindicate
10.	jubilee	20.	writhe

UNIT 12 Spelling Skills

How to Study Spelling Words

Use the following procedure to study words that you wish to learn how to spell.

▶ **Procedure**

1. *Look at the word and study its letters.*
2. *Pronounce the word to yourself,* and think about the sounds of the letters.
3. *Write the word,* and think about difficult letter combinations.
4. *Check your spelling* to make sure that it is correct.
5. *Study the word* until you have memorized its spelling.
6. *Know what the word means* so that you can be certain that you are spelling the word you need. It is easy to be misled by words that are spelled or are pronounced similarly.

Spelling Rules

Making Nouns Plural

The following rules will help you to form the plurals of nouns when you write.

Rule S 1   Form the plural of most common nouns and proper nouns by adding -s to the singular.

alibi	omelet	Celt	Paquette
alibis	omelets	the Celts	the Paquettes

Rule S 2   Form the plural of common nouns and proper nouns that end with s, x, z, ch, or sh by adding -es.

abyss	crutch	tax	Ruiz
abysses	crutches	taxes	the Ruizes

Rule S 3 Form the plural of a common noun that ends with *y* preceded by a consonant by changing the *y* to *i* and adding -*es*.

commodity	intricacy	observatory	promontory
commodities	intricacies	observatories	promontories

Rule S 4 Form the plural of a common noun that ends with *y* preceded by a vowel by adding -*s*.

buoy	fray	replay	valley
buoys	frays	replays	valleys

Rule S 5 Form the plural of most proper nouns that end with *y* by adding -*s*.

David and Rachael Lindsay	Stacy
the Lindsays	the two Stacys

Rule S 6 Form the plural of most common nouns that end with *f* or *fe* by changing the *f* to *v* and adding -*es*.

loaf	thief	wolf
loaves	thieves	wolves

EXCEPTIONS	reef	spoof	waif
	reefs	spoofs	waifs

Rule S 7 Form the plural of common nouns that end with *ff* by adding -*s*.

bluff	cuff	sheriff	staff
bluffs	cuffs	sheriffs	staffs

Rule S 8 Form the plural of common nouns that end with *o* preceded by a vowel by adding -*s*.

cameo	kazoo	radio	scenario
cameos	kazoos	radios	scenarios

Rule S 9 Form the plural of common nouns that end with *o* preceded by a consonant in one of two ways: for some nouns, add -*s*; for others, add -*es*. For a few nouns, either -*s* or -*es* is correct (check a dictionary).

dynamo	innuendo	memento
dynamos	innuendoes	mementos (mementoes)

Rule S 10 Form the plural of a letter, a symbol, a number, or a word that is printed in italic type (underlined) for special attention by adding an apostrophe and -*s* (*'s*). Do not underline (italicize) the plural ending.

Reference Point: *pages 737–738*

J	*20*	*yes*	*
J's	*20*'s	*yes*'s	*'s

Rule S 11 Certain common nouns change their form when they are plural.

crisis	die	mouse	tooth
crises	dice	mice	teeth

Rule

S 12

Some common nouns and many proper nouns have the same form for both singular and plural.

aircraft   chassis   species   Portuguese

Rule

S 13

Form the plural of a compound noun that is written as one word by changing the last word in the compound to its plural form. Form the plural of a compound noun that is hyphenated or written as two or more words by making the most important word plural.

onlooker	stagehand	hanger-on	bill of sale
on**lookers**	stage**hands**	**hangers**-on	**bills** of sale

Summary: Forming Noun Plurals

Noun Ending	Change or Add	Noun	Plural
s, x, z, ch, sh	Add *-es*	arch	arches
Consonant + *y*	Change *y* to *i*, add *-es*	city	cities
Vowel + *y*	Add *-s*	play	plays
f or *fe*	Change *f* to *v*, add *-es*	wolf	wolves
ff	Add *-s*	cliff	cliffs
Vowel + *o*	Add *-s*	radio	radios
Consonant + *o*	Add *-s* or *-es*	piano	pianos
		tomato	tomatoes

Some nouns form their plurals in irregular ways that cannot easily be predicted. Always consult a dictionary if you are not sure of how a word should be spelled.

Special Cases

Noun Ending	Change or Add	Noun	Plural
Proper nouns — end in *y* or *o*	Add *-s*	Cary Chicano	two Carys Chicanos
Plural of letters, symbols, or numbers	Add *-'s*	*J*	*J*'s
Words that change their form	Change base word	mouse	mice
Words that remain the same	Change nothing	chassis	chassis
Compound words written as one word	Add *-s*	sidewalk	sidewalks
Compound words written as two words or hyphenated	Make most important word plural	mother-in-law	mothers-in-law

Adding Endings

The following rules will help you to remember how to spell words when you add endings other than the plural (*-s* and *-es*).

Doubling the Final Consonant

The final consonant is *not* doubled when adding an ending that begins with a consonant, as in *slimness*. The final consonant is *sometimes* doubled when adding an ending that begins with a vowel.

Rule S 14   Double the final consonant when adding an ending to a one-syllable word that ends with a single consonant preceded by a single vowel.

flip	hot	peg	skim
flipping	hottest	pegged	skimmed

Rule S 15   Double the final consonant when adding an ending to a word that has more than one syllable, that ends with a single consonant preceded by a single vowel, and that has the primary stress on the last syllable.

allot	prefer	refer	regret
allotted	preferred	referring	regrettable

Rule S 16   To words that end in *c* preceded by a single vowel, do not double the *c*. Instead, add *-k* before endings that begin with *e* or *i* to keep the hard *c* sound.

mimic	picnic	shellac
mimicking	picnicking	shellacked

Doubling Final Consonants

Use the following questions to decide whether to double the final consonant when you add an ending. If you answer yes to any *three* of the questions, double the final consonant of the word before you add the ending.

1. Does the ending begin with a vowel?
2. Does the word end with one consonant preceded by one vowel?
3. Does the word have only one syllable?
4. Does the word have more than one syllable, and is the most stress on the last syllable?

Dropping the Final e

Rule S 17   When adding an ending that begins with a consonant to most words that end with silent *e*, keep the final *e*.

blithe	contrite	loathe
blithely	contriteness	loathesome

EXCEPTIONS	argue	true
	argument	truly

Rule
S 18
When adding an ending that begins with a vowel to most words that end with silent *e*, drop the final *e*.

contrive	cringe	disparage
contrivance	cringing	disparaging

EXCEPTIONS

dye	mile	singe
dyeing	mileage	singeing

Rule
S 19
When adding an ending that begins with *a* (as in *-able*) or *o* (as in *-ous*) to most words that end with *ce* or *ge*, keep the final *e* to preserve the soft sound of the *c* or the *g*.

advantage	enforce	notice
advantageous	enforceable	noticeable

EXCEPTION   mortgage   mortgagor

Changing the Final *y* to *i*

Rule
S 20
For most words that end with *y* preceded by a consonant, change the *y* to *i* before adding any ending except *-ing*.

deny	study	vary
deniable	studied	variable
denying	studying	varying

EXCEPTION   wry   wryly

Rule
S 21
For most words that end with *y* preceded by a vowel, do not change the *y* to *i* before adding an ending.

alloy	enjoy	journey
alloyed	enjoyable	journeying

EXCEPTIONS

day	gay
daily	gaily

Assignment **Adding Endings**

On your paper, combine the base word and the ending in parentheses to form a single, correctly spelled word. Then write a sentence using each.

SAMPLE   teaspoonful (plural)
ANSWER   teaspoonfuls   Louis used only three teaspoonfuls of milk on his cereal.

1. codify *(-ing)*
2. collate *(-ed)*
3. colony *(-al)*
4. convey *(-ed)*
5. courtesy (plural)
6. crescendo (plural)
7. double-header (plural)
8. guide *(-ance)*
9. handful (plural)
10. harmony *(-ous)*
11. head of state (plural)
12. industry *(-ous)*

13. leaf (plural)
14. notice *(-able)*
15. passer-by (plural)

16. polite *(-ness)*
17. reflex (plural)
18. tradesman (plural)

Spelling Patterns

The *ie/ei* Pattern

The following rules will help you to decide whether to spell a word with *ie* or with *ei*.

Rule S 22 Use *ie* if the vowel combination has a long *e* sound (as in *fiend*) unless the letter *c* immediately precedes the pair of vowels.

chief	liege	siege
grieve	shield	perceive

EXCEPTIONS leisure   neither

Rule S 23 Use *ei* after *c* or when the sound is not long *e* (as in *height*).

receipt   foreign   sleight   meiosis

EXCEPTIONS efficient   lie   species

Rule S 24 If the vowel combination has a long *a* sound (as in *beige*), use *ei*.

feint   neighbor   veil   weight

Rule S 25 If the two vowels are pronounced separately in the word, spell them in the order of their pronunciation.

biennial   diet   piety   reimburse

The "Seed" Sound Pattern

The "seed" ending sound has three spellings: *-sede*, *-ceed*, and *-cede*. The spelling *s-e-e-d* does not occur as a suffix in any word, except those formed from the word *seed*.

1. Only one word ends in *-sede*: *supersede*.
2. Three words end in *-ceed*: *exceed*, *proceed*, and *succeed*.
3. All other such words end in *-cede*: *accede*, *intercede*, and *secede* are some examples.

Assignment **Spelling Patterns**

With a classmate, take turns testing each other on *ie/ei* words and "seed" words. If you misspell a word, write it down, study it, and ask your partner to test you on it again.

Pronunciation and Spelling

Certain kinds of pronunciation errors commonly cause spelling problems. Always check a dictionary for the pronunciation of words that you are unsure of, paying special attention to each of the letters that spell the sounds.

Extra Sounds or Omitted Sounds   Words are often misspelled because they are pronounced with extra sounds or with sounds left out. Study the words in the following list. Pay special attention to the underlined letters to make sure that you neither add nor omit sounds when you spell or pronounce these words.

different	leverage	surprise	representative
foliage	recognize	temperament	history

Transposed Letters   Sometimes people write letters in the wrong order because they pronounce them or think of them in the wrong order. Such errors often occur in the words in the following list. Pay special attention to the underlined letters to make sure that you pronounce and spell them in the correct order.

amateur	irrelevant	prevalent	tragedy
hundred	pervade	realtor	unanimous

Homophones and Commonly Confused Words   Words that have the same pronunciation but different origins, spellings, and meanings are called **homophones.** Some other sets of words are not homophones, but they are similar enough in sound and spelling to create confusion. Learn the spellings and meanings of the words in the following list so that you will use them correctly in your writing.

Reference Point: pages 671–689

acclamation, acclimation	envelop, envelope
aesthetic, ascetic	flaunt, flout
air, heir	hew, hue
callous, callus	ingenious, ingenuous
chili, chilly	knead, need
cite, sight, site	later, latter
cooperation, corporation	stationary, stationery
discus, discuss	verses, versus

Assignment   Homophones and Commonly Confused Words

On your paper, write five sentences, each of which uses a pair of homophones or commonly confused words. Select the words for the sentences from the preceding list.

Other Spelling Aids

Use the following strategies to improve your spelling.

▶ **Strategies**

1. *Keep a list of troublesome words.* Study your list frequently, and use the words in your writing.
2. *Create your own memory aids,* called mnemonic (nĭ-MŎN'ĭk) devices, for difficult words. For example:

   Something that is **extraordinary** is *extra ordinary*.
   An **island** *is land*.
   There is an *ache* in **moustache**.

3. *Think carefully about how words sound and look.*
4. *Always consult a dictionary if you are unsure of a spelling.*

Alternate Spellings of Sounds

If you do not know how to spell a word, you may have difficulty locating it in a dictionary. You may have to guess the spelling or check possible spellings until you find the correct one. Some sounds can be spelled in more than one way. The following list suggests where to look if a word is not spelled the way you expect.

Word Sounds and Spellings	
Consonant Sounds	**Alternate Spellings**
f, as in *f*east	*ph,* as in *ph*ysical
j, as in *j*ustice	*g,* as in *g*enerate
k, as in *k*eep	*c, ch,* or *qu,* as in *c*onfirm, *ch*rome, and *qu*ay
n, as in *n*est	*gn, kn,* or *pn,* as in *gn*arl, *kn*ow, and *pn*eumonia
r, as in *r*ight	*wr,* as in *wr*ath
s, as in *s*ip	*c* or *ps,* as in *c*ircus and *ps*ychiatrist
Vowel Sounds	**Alternate Spellings**
a, as in *a*che	*ei,* as in *ei*ghteen
e, as in *e*ver	*ae, oe,* and *u,* as in *ae*sthetic, *Oe*dipus, and b*u*rial
i, as in *i*dea	*ai* or *ei,* as in *ai*sle and *ei*der
o, as in n*o*	*eau* or *ew,* as in bur*eau* and s*ew*
oo, as in b*oo*t	*ieu, eu,* or *ou,* as in ad*ieu,* man*eu*ver, and l*ou*ver
u, as in *u*rban	*e* or *ea,* as in *e*rmine and *ea*rly

Some sounds are especially confusing because they may have many different letter combinations to represent them. These sounds may be located anywhere within a word. Two such examples follow.

SOUND	ALTERNATE SPELLINGS	
sh, as in *sh*ip	*ce*, as in o*ce*an	*sch*, as in *sch*ist
	ch, as in *ch*andelier	*se*, as in nau*se*ous
	ci, as in spe*ci*al	*si*, as in pen*si*on
	psh, as in *psh*aw	*ss*, as in ti*ss*ue
	s, as in *s*ugar	*ti*, as in na*ti*on
	sc, as in con*sc*ience	
ch, as in *ch*ip	*c*, as in *c*ello	*ti*, as in ques*ti*on
	cz, as in *Cz*ech	*tu*, as in den*tu*re
	tch, as in la*tch*	

Assignment Correcting Misspellings

Choose ten words that you often misspell. List them on your paper, and create a mnemonic device for each word. When you have mastered the correct spelling, use each word as often as you can in your writing.

Frequently Misspelled Words and Problem Endings

Certain words are misspelled so often that they are considered problem words. You have studied some difficult words earlier in this unit. The following lists include more words for you to master.

Frequently Misspelled Words

academically	ecstasy	inoculate	phenomenon	severely
accessible	embarrass	intellectual	prominent	suppress
accumulation	exhibition	iridescent	questionnaire	suspicion
aggressive	exhilarate	irritable	rehearsal	ukulele
apparatus	exhilaration	laboratory	reminisce	vacillate
buoyancy	foresee	livelihood	requisition	vengeance
clientele	hemorrhage	miscellaneous	rhythm	vicious
conscientious	hypocrisy	mucilage	ridiculous	
coupon	incessant	ordinarily	schism	
criticism	inevitable	parallel	scissors	
curriculum	inimitable	pastime	sergeant	

Some word endings are easily confused. To avoid misspellings, make sure that you are using the correct ending. The lists that follow include some words with easily confused endings. To learn the correct ending, pronounce the word, stressing the final sound.

Words with Confusing Endings

-able	-ible	-ance	-ence
accountable	audible	acceptance	absence
appreciable	collapsible	admittance	confidence
changeable	compatible	allowance	consistence
despicable	deductible	balance	dependence
indispensable	eligible	clearance	excellence
indisputable	flexible	insurance	experience
negotiable	permissible	intolerance	interference
noticeable	plausible	maintenance	negligence
predictable	reversible	resistance	occurrence
reputable	sensible	variance	subsistence

-ant	-ent	-ise	-ize
abundant	competent	advertise	authorize
accountant	consistent	advise	cauterize
attendant	dependent	comprise	hospitalize
defendant	different	despise	mobilize
hesitant	equivalent	devise	ostracize
ignorant	independent	disguise	randomize
intolerant	patient	exercise	realize
pleasant	persistent	improvise	sympathize
reluctant	respondent	revise	tranquilize
tenant	transparent	surprise	transistorize

Assignment **Improving Your Spelling and Proofreading**

On your paper, rewrite these paragraphs. Correct the spelling errors.

Edgar Rice Burroughs did not seem destinned for sucess. His grades were medeocre. He was not a contientious student, and he took frequent abcences from school in search of adventure.

After Burroughs graduated from what he refered to as "a polite reform school," he had jobs rangeing from soldier to policemen to clerk to cowboy. Bourroughs was often fired for incompetance. His failures depressed and embaressed him and weighed heavilly on his mind. Sometimes, to sleep at night, he liked to imagine superheros who were confident, competant, and could do everything right.

In his thirties Edgar Rice Burroughs submited some of his "bedtime stories" to a publisher. The stories were published. A book he wrote, however, was rejected by every majer publisher in the United States before it was finaly published. The book, *Tarzan of the Apes*, has sold over 25 million copies. Burroughs wrote more than sixty other books during his livetime.

UNIT 13 Letters and Forms

Just as there are customary methods for taking tests and doing research reports, there are also correct procedures to follow for writing letters and completing forms. The guidelines in this unit will help you to master the clear and correct communication that is as important in the business world as it is in school.

Writing Business Letters

In this unit you will learn how to write standard business letters: the order letter, the request letter, the adjustment letter, the commendation letter, and the opinion letter. In addition, you will learn how to write a letter applying for a job and how to write a résumé.

In writing these letters, you will follow the steps of the writing process: prewriting, drafting, revising, proofreading, and publishing. Planning the content and organization of your letter will ensure that you have included all of the essential information. Revising for specific details and accurate wording will help you to get a prompt response.

The business letter on the next page contains all the information necessary to the person who will receive it.

The Format of a Business Letter

The first thing to notice about a business letter is the way it is arranged. The format of a business letter clearly distinguishes it from personal correspondence. As you read the following strategies for correct business letter format, refer to the letter on page 497.

▶ Strategies

1. *Use unlined white paper measuring 8½ inches by 11 inches.*
2. *Type your letter if possible.* Otherwise, use black or blue ink.
3. *Leave ample margins on all sides of your letter.*
4. *Check to see that the heading and the inside address are complete and accurate.* The **heading** is your address and the date. Spell out

the name of your state, or abbreviate it by using the Postal Service abbreviation and ZIP Code.

Reference Point: *page 707*

The **inside address** is the name and address of the person or organization to whom you are writing. Include such titles as *Dr.*, *Mr.*, or *Ms.* with a person's name. In the last line of the inside address, use the same form for the state as you used in the heading.

1560 Bloomingdale Avenue
Chicago, Illinois 60622
June 20, 19--

Ms. Marian Stevens
Director of Admissions
Huntington University
3500 Calumet Avenue
Chicago, Illinois 60616

Dear Ms. Stevens:

On behalf of Wayne High School's senior class, I would like to invite you, as director of admissions of Huntington University, to participate in our College Night. This important activity will be held in the Wayne Gymnasium from 6:00 P.M. to 9:00 P.M., September 25.

It has been traditional for the senior class to hold this popular activity early in the year so that students will have an opportunity to hear more about the colleges and universities in our area. We would be pleased if you could give a ten minute talk and then be on hand to answer students' questions about Huntington.

In order to complete our plans, we hope to receive your response to our invitation by August 15. We would also like you to be our guest at a reception for speakers, officers of the senior class, and the Wayne High School administration directly following College Night.

Thank you very much.

Sincerely yours,

Juan Lopez

Juan Lopez
Senior Class President

5. *Use an appropriate salutation, or greeting.* Capitalize the first word and all the nouns in the **salutation.** Place a colon after the salutation. Use *Dear Sir, Dear Madam,* or *Dear Sir or Madam* when addressing someone whose name you do not know.

6. *Include in the body of the letter all the information necessary to achieve your purpose.* The **body** consists of the paragraphs that

state your business. In typing your letter, use single spacing. Leave an extra line of space between the salutation and the first paragraph and between all other paragraphs.

7. *Avoid slang and contractions.* Do not write in a tone that is too casual.

8. *Avoid using clichés and wordy expressions in an effort to sound formal and businesslike.* Note the substitutions in the following examples.

AVOID	USE
in the amount of	for
enclosed please find	enclosed is
herein enclosed	enclosed
at the earliest possible date	as early as possible
at the present time	now
I wish to express my gratitude	thank you
in accordance with your request	as you requested
as per your request	as you requested
It is incumbent upon us to	We need to

9. *Do not end your letter with a participial phrase, such as "Thanking you in advance" or "Hoping to hear from you soon."*

10. *Do not forget the complimentary close.* Capitalize only the first word of the complimentary close. Place a comma at the end of the close. *Yours truly, Very truly yours, Sincerely yours*, and *Yours sincerely* are acceptable complimentary closes.

11. *Be sure to sign your name.* Write your full name below the complimentary close. If your letter is handwritten, print your name under your signature. If it is typed, type your name under your signature.

12. *Proofread your letter carefully for errors in typing, spelling, usage, and punctuation.*   If you find errors, rewrite or retype it.

Styles of Business Letters

The two styles of business letters are the block style and the modified block style. In the **block style,** all parts of the letter start at the left margin. Paragraphs are not indented. Use the block style only when you are typing a letter. The letter on page 497 is written in block style.

In the **modified block style,** place the heading, the complimentary close, and the signature to the right. You may either indent paragraphs or start them at the left margin, as in the block style. You may use the modified block style for either handwritten or typed letters.

Kinds of Business Letters

The most common types of business letters that you will write are the request letter, the order letter, and the adjustment letter. The commendation letter and the opinion letter are forms that you may use less frequently. The job application letter and the résumé are important documents when you are applying for a job.

The Request Letter

Write a request, or inquiry, letter when you need information on a specific subject or when you need a brochure or a catalogue. You might also use this format when you are asking for someone's services, as in the letter on page 497. Like all business letters, the request letter should be brief, but it should also contain all the necessary information.

When writing a request letter, follow these strategies.

▶ **Strategies**

1. *Make your requests reasonable and specific.* For example, do not request from the National Park Service all available information on parks. Instead, ask for information about one or two particular parks.
2. *Offer to pay for printed material if you are not certain that it is free.*
3. *Allow sufficient time for your request to be filled.* If you need information for a class report, for example, write at least three weeks before your report is due.

The Order Letter

When ordering merchandise through the mail, you must sometimes write an order letter. Make sure that your letter contains complete and accurate information about quantity, size, color, cost, and catalogue number.

When writing an order letter, follow these strategies.

▶ **Strategies**

1. *Give the source of the advertisement or the catalogue year, season, or number from which you are ordering.*
2. *Double-check your arithmetic.* Also, make sure that you have included postage and handling costs if necessary.
3. *Explain how you intend to pay for the merchandise.* Do not send cash through the mail. Use a money order or a check instead.
4. *Explain if you must have the merchandise by a certain date.*
5. *Type or write the word* Enclosure *in the bottom left corner of your letter if you have enclosed a check or a money order.*

The Adjustment Letter

Write an adjustment letter whenever an order that you place is not filled correctly or when merchandise that you purchase is defective.

Explain the problem courteously and suggest a solution.

When writing an adjustment letter, follow these strategies.

▶ **Strategies**

1. *State the problem accurately and clearly in the first paragraph of your letter.*
2. *Suggest a solution.* Ask politely for a refund or a replacement.
3. *Keep a copy of your letter until the adjustment that you request has been made.*

The Commendation Letter

Have you ever had the experience of being impressed by the generous actions of an individual or a group? This is the time to write a letter of commendation. In this type of letter, you are able to show your appreciation to a person, a group of people, or an organization. For example, suppose that you hear about an individual who has single-handedly saved a park from being turned into a shopping mall. To express your appreciation and admiration for this action, you might write the person a letter, praising his or her actions.

Follow these strategies when writing a commendation letter.

▶ **Strategies**

1. *Establish your purpose in writing to the individual, group, or organization.*
2. *Explain how the actions of the person or group have influenced you in a positive manner.* Praise these actions and activities.
3. *Suggest that the good work of the group or individual be continued* as you end on a note of encouragement.

Assignment 1 **Writing a Business Letter**

Step 1: Choose one of the kinds of business letters — request, order, adjustment, or commendation — that you would like to write. Make some notes on what you plan to say and how you will organize it.
Step 2: On an unlined sheet of paper, write or type your letter in modified block style. Make sure that you have the correct address of the person, the group, or the organization you are writing to. *Step 3:* Revise and proofread your letter. *Step 4:* Address an envelope. Mail your letter.

An Opinion Letter

Occasionally, there may be local or national issues on which you wish to express your opinion. One effective way to express an opinion is to write a letter to a newspaper, a national magazine, a television or radio network, or an elected official, such as a mayor or a senator.

Your letter of opinion will be more likely to achieve the result that you wish if you maintain a reasonable tone throughout. Anger, sarcasm, and accusations offend readers and will diminish your persuasiveness. If your letter is restrained, logical, courteous, and tactful, you may persuade others to accept your opinion.

Read the opinion letter that follows and then study the strategies for writing one.

454 Tulane Avenue
Odessa, Texas 79765
April 20, 19--

The Honorable Lucy Perkins
Mayor of the City of Odessa
City Hall
Odessa, Texas 79765

Dear Mayor Perkins:

I am writing in response to a recent proposal that developers build a new shopping mall in the three-block area stretching from Ridgecrest to Stillwood streets. Because of a rash of construction of new homes in the area, developers are, for the first time, eager to buy this city land at a low price, construct a two-story mall, and then rent space to merchants. I do not think the city should accept this offer.

Within the last ten years, two new malls have been built to serve city residents. A third mall seems unnecessary and would be, perhaps, a threat to the city's economy. According to an article in The Register, managers of the two existing malls have complained recently about a large drop in business. A third mall with a whole new set of stores could pose a serious threat to the existing stores. That same article suggests that the malls have become more of a meeting place than a buying place.

What the city really needs rather than another shopping mall is a large municipal swimming pool. A recent editorial in The Register suggested the construction of an Olympic-sized pool with accompanying bathhouse and surrounding park area. Memberships could be issued or daily admission could be charged to use the facilities so that, eventually, the pool could become profitable. A swimming pool would provide a good recreational facility for all residents and would greatly enhance the appeal of living in our city.

Respectfully,

Lee Bok

Lee Bok

Use the following strategies to write an effective opinion letter.

▶ **Strategies**

1. *Write promptly.* Editors often will not publish letters on subjects that are no longer current.
2. *Remember to keep your letter brief.* Many newspapers and magazines prefer letters to be two hundred words or less.
3. *Use the salutation* To the Editor: *in letters to newspapers and magazines.*
4. *Address your query or suggestion to the public official who is best able to respond to it.* For example, do not write to the governor about matters that pertain only to your community, and do not write to your mayor about an issue to be decided in the United States Senate.
5. *Begin your letter by giving a brief summary of the situation or issue about which you are writing.* Then state your opinion briefly and clearly.
6. *Support your opinion with logical and factual statements.* Once you have made your point, do not wander from it.

Reference Point:
pages 230–236

7. *Conclude your letter by summarizing your main points or, when appropriate, by suggesting a course of action that you think should be followed.*
8. *Sign your letter.* Also include your address and telephone number so that the newspaper can verify that you wrote the letter.

Forms of Address When writing to elected officials, use conventional forms of address. Consult the following chart.

Person and Address	Salutation
The President The President The White House Washington, DC 20500	Dear Mr. President: Sir:
United States Senator or Representative The Honorable Justin Hale The United States Senate (or House of Representatives) Washington, DC 20510	Dear Senator (or Representative) Hale: Dear Sir (or Madam):
Governor The Honorable Clyde Doyle Governor of Utah Salt Lake City, UT 84100	Dear Governor Doyle: Dear Sir (or Madam):

Person and Address (continued)	Salutation (continued)
State Senator or Legislator The Honorable Mary O'Brien The State Senate (or The General Assembly) Richmond, VA 21900	Dear Senator O'Brien (or Represenative) O'Brien: Dear Madam (or Sir):
State Legislator The Honorable Cesar Ruiz The General Assembly Richmond, VA 21900	Dear Representative Ruiz: Dear Mr. Ruiz: Dear Sir (or Madam):
Mayor The Honorable Lynn Venable Mayor of Toledo City Hall Toledo, OH 54301	Dear Mayor Venable: Dear Madam (or Mr.) Mayor:

Assignment 2 Writing an Opinion Letter

Using the following information, write a letter of opinion in modified block style. Add additional details if necessary. Then revise and proof read your letter.

Every morning for the past two years, you have followed the antics of *Julie*, a cartoon strip that appears in *The Tampa Gazette*. You enjoy this cartoon very much and personally identify with the way Julie handles things. However, the new feature editor for the *Gazette* has dropped Julie and replaced her with the activities of a platypus named "Horace." You are upset by this change and feel that *Julie* is a much better cartoon strip than *Horace*. After doing some research, you find out that *Julie* is being run in other newspapers in other communities. Write to Mr. Paul LePage, Feature Editor, *The Tampa Gazette*, 10 Lee Road, Orlando, FL 32810. Suggest that Julie be returned to her readers as soon as possible.

Assignment 3 Writing a Letter to a Magazine

Look through a magazine that you enjoy reading. Choose an article that causes you to have a strong opposing reaction to what the writer is saying. Write a letter to the editor of the magazine in which you offer arguments against the main points in the article.

The Job Application Letter

When applying for a job, you need to write a letter of application and a résumé. Both are necessary to give a prospective employer an accurate impression of you and your qualifications.

The purpose of an application letter is to get an appointment for an interview. Study this letter of application. Notice how it uses the strategies that follow.

69 Buick Street
New Orleans, LA 70126
May 26, 19--

Ms. Jessie Ramirez
Director
Underwater World
1603 Castle Street
New Orleans, LA 70127

Dear Ms. Ramirez:

I am responding to your May 25 advertisement in the Sun Times for a summer assistant at the aquarium. I would like to be considered for that position.

I understand from your advertisement that you need an assistant to feed the fish and clean the tanks. You will note from my enclosed résumé that I have worked part-time in a tropical fish store and have been a summer volunteer at an animal park in New Orleans. Through these two posts, I have become familiar with fish and animal care.

I believe that my background, interests, and experience qualify me for the position advertised: furthermore, I am hoping to pursue a career in marine biology. I would be pleased to meet with you for an interview at your convenience. My home phone number is 555-2073, and I can be reached there any afternoon after 3:30.

Thank you for your consideration.

Very truly yours,

Nicholas Grazzi

▶ **Strategies**

1. *State what position you are seeking in the first paragraph and tell how you learned of it.* Do not merely say that you are interested in any position that happens to be open.

2. *Make a brief reference in the second paragraph to whatever experience you have that qualifies you for the job.* This information need not be presented in detail here. You will be more explicit in your résumé *(pages 505–506).*

3. *Express confidence in your ability to do the job, but do not boast.*

4. *Conclude by stating courteously that you would like to have a*

personal interview at the employer's convenience. Tell where and when you can be reached to arrange an appointment.

5. *Read your letter aloud for tone to make sure that you do not sound arrogant, flippant, or too casual.* If you wish, have a family member or a teacher read your letter.

6. *Include additional information about yourself in an attached résumé.*

Writing a Résumé

With your letter of application, enclose a résumé. A **résumé,** sometimes called a data sheet, is a summary of your qualifications. Its purpose is to present your qualifications in a clear, well-organized manner. A résumé is also an opportunity for you to make a statement about yourself as a potential employee. Include the following information in your résumé: position wanted, experience, education, personal interests and special skills, and references.

Begin work on your résumé before you start applying for a job. You need time to collect all the data and to organize, draft, and revise your résumé until it represents your best effort. Spelling, grammar, or punctuation errors on a résumé would probably make a bad first impression on a potential employer. In contrast, a neat, organized résumé reflects well on your diligence and enterprise. An early start will also allow you time to contact those persons whom you wish to use as references. Study the résumé to accompany the job application letter *(page 506)*.

Use the following strategies when writing a résumé.

▶ **Strategies**

1. *Type your résumé.* It should be neat and free of errors.

2. *Limit your résumé to one or two pages.*

3. *List your most recent work experience first.* Include the dates that you were employed, the places where you were employed, and the responsibilities that you had.

4. *Include information about any special skills, talents, awards, or interests.* This information should show that you have stayed with an activity, that you are well-rounded, or that you are achievement-oriented.

5. *Do not include personal data such as age, height, weight, religion, and so forth.*

6. *List two, preferably three, references, with an address or telephone number for each.* One of your references should be a character reference, someone who knows you well. Do not include family members or friends your own age. Do not list anyone without first obtaining his or her permission.

```
                         Nicholas A. Grazzi
                           69 Buick Street
                        New Orleans, LA 70126
                        Telephone: 555-0888


    POSITION WANTED              Aquarium assistant

    EXPERIENCE                   Tanya's Fish Tank,
                                 September-March 19--.
                                 Fed fish; cleaned tanks;
                                 assisted customers in
                                 finding appropriate fish

                                 New Orleans Animal Park,
                                 June-September 19--.  Worked
                                 as volunteer; fed animals;
                                 cleaned animals' cages

    EDUCATION                    Will graduate with honors
                                 from Lafayette High School,
                                 June 6, 19--

    SKILLS AND INTERESTS         SKILLS
                                 Have driver's license
                                 Speak French
                                 Have life-saving certificate
                                 Have scuba-diving
                                 certification

                                 INTERESTS
                                 Member of Varsity Tennis Team
                                 Collector of tropical fish
                                 Member of Hikers
                                 International

                                 AWARD
                                 First-place trophy winner in
                                 city-wide tennis competition

    REFERENCES                   Ms. Tanya DuBois
                                 Tanya's Fish Tank
                                 22 Buchanan Street
                                 New Orleans, LA 70122

                                 Mr. Arnold Stein
                                 New Orleans Animal Park
                                 470 Bristol Place
                                 New Orleans, LA 70114
```

Assignment 4 Writing an Application Letter

Write a letter of application in response to the following advertisement. Study the strategies for writing a letter of application on page 504. Supply all information needed. Remember that the purpose of a letter of application is to get an interview. Include a separate résumé.

Filling Out Forms

You are familiar with such school forms as registration cards and schedules. You may also be familiar with forms in the business world, such as job applications or order blanks. Here are some strategies for filling out most forms.

▶ Strategies

1. *When you know that you will be filling out a form, bring such information as the names and addresses of personal references, your driver's license, and your social security card.*
2. *Carry both a pencil and a pen.* Either may be required.
3. *Read carefully through all directions before filling out the form.* Check whether printing or writing is called for.
4. *Make sure that your handwriting or printing is clear and legible.*
5. *Give complete answers and check your figures if numbers are involved.*
6. *Be sure to shade in the correct boxes when filling out a test form.*
7. *Proofread the form for errors in facts and spelling.*
8. *Note any incomplete answers, and submit the missing information as soon as possible.*

Assignment 1 | Applying to College

Imagine that you are a senior at Somerset High School in San Jose, California about to fill out the following portion of a college application form. You want to study English as a part-time student. On your paper, write the answers to the questions that follow.

SOMERSET COUNTY COMMUNITY COLLEGE
Application for Admission

Academic Program Codes

| Business Admin. | BA | Criminal Justice | CJ |
| Computer Science | CS | English | EN |

(1) Name _____

(2) Social Security # _____

(3) Mailing address _____

(4) Place of birth _____

(5) Date of birth _____

(6) High school attended_____

(7) Year graduated_____

(8) High school location: City:_____ (9) State _____

(10) Program to which you are applying (use codes):_____

(11) Status: Freshman (F) Transfer (T) Cond. Ed. (C)_____

(12) Will you attend SCCC full time (FT), part-time days (PD), or
    part-time evenings (PE)?_____

---

1. What should you write on line 6 of the application?
2. What belongs on line 10?
3. What should be written on line 11?
4. What should you put on line 12?

Assignment 2 | Filling Out an Information Form

Study the application for driver education classes. On your paper, write
the answers to the questions that follow the application.

O'Hara's Driving School

(1) **Name** (last, first, middle)_____

(2) **Address** (number, street, city, state, ZIP) _____

_____

(3) **Telephone** _____

(4) **Date of birth**_____

(5) **Name of school** _____

(6) **Grade in school**_____

(7) **Date of learner's permit** _____

(8) **Parent's/guardian's signature**_____

(9) **Applicant's signature** _____

---

1. How should you fill out line 1?
2. What should you write on line 3?

3. What should you write on line 8?
4. On what line should you sign your name?

Filling Out a Registration Form

Imagine that you want to be in a long-distance bicycle race. You rode in the same race last year on June 16, 1988, finishing in tenth place. The entry fee is $3.00. Your bicycle is a silver-and-blue Panther Racer. Study the registration form. On your paper, write the answers to the questions that follow the application.

Registration Form

             (1) **Date** _____

(2) **Name** _____

(3) **Address** _____

(4) **Telephone** _____ (5) **Age** _____

(6) **Date of Birth** _____

(7) **Height** _____ (8) **Weight** _____ (9) **Sex (M/F)** _____

(10) **Make of bicycle** _____

(11) **Have you ridden in this race before? Yes** _____ **No** _____

(12) **If yes, write date and order of finish** _____

(13) **Entry fee (please enclose) and form of payment** _____

(14) **Signature** _____

(15) **If under 18, signature of parent or guardian**

_____

---

1. What should you write on line 10?
2. Which is the best information to give on line 11?
3. How should you complete line 12?
4. Where and how should you state that you are paying with a $3.00 money order?

UNIT 14 Using a Word Processor

Word Processing in the Working World

Nearly every profession in the modern world depends on computer technology. Car mechanics generate printed diagnostics. Executives travel with laptop computers. Journalists can instantaneously send words to publishers across oceans and continents. The computer age is here, but the revolution has only begun.

If you have access to a personal computer, use it as a tool for all stages of the writing process, and you'll soon see its advantages. A word processor can nearly match the fast pace of thought, and the more you use one, the faster you'll type. Because your writing is electronically stored on a magnetic disk, you can repeatedly retrieve it, revise it, correct it, and print out a neat, clean product without copying words over and over. Because the text is fluid and easily changed, you can experiment with both content and appearance. Additionally, your computer can link you with vast sources of information, as close as the neighboring terminal, as far as the farthest state. Learning to use a word processor can improve your writing *now* and ensure the computer literacy you'll need *later*. As with any tool, the more skilled you become, the more your process — and your product — will improve.

Assignment Conduct an Interview

Using the following questions as a starting point, interview *(pages 471–475)* an adult who uses word processing professionally. As this person discusses his or her profession, pursue other questions that seem relevant. Either take careful notes or use a tape recorder.

1. What kind of computer or word processor do you use? What software do you use?
2. How do you and others in your profession use a computer or word processor? What kinds of documents do you generate?
3. How were these jobs done before word processors were available?
4. What are the advantages of the word processor to your profession?
5. What are the disadvantages of the word processor as a tool?

6. What new developments in the computer industry will directly impact your profession?

Prewriting with a Word Processor

Give up your notion that a word processor is just a fancy typewriter, used to transform your handwritten product to a printed one. Instead, think of it as a writing tool that's valuable from the very earliest stages of prewriting. Special programs called **invention software** prompt prewriting responses, but any word processor will allow you to experiment with language and ideas. Try some of the following techniques, and develop some of your own. Always save and print out your prewriting. Underline words or phrases that are seeds of drafts to come.

Freewriting and Invisible Writing   If writing is mental athletics, freewriting on the word processor can be your warm-up exercise. Limber your fingers and your imagination, and put yourself in the writing mood with a three-minute flow of ideas. **Invisible writing** is blind freewriting. Simply turn down the brightness control on your monitor. This can be liberating because you won't be distracted by what you've just written.

Electronic Writer's Notebook   Label a disk "Notebook" and create your own storehouse of freewriting, ideas for topics, favorite quotations, and writing scraps. You can transfer from this storehouse directly to a draft without retyping. Occasionally, read your notebook to get ideas or inspiration. On the word processor, you can easily add more material between the lines or between the pages.

Writing Letters   Many writers use correspondence as a prewriting exercise to explore topics, to express concerns, and to experiment with language. Write a letter to the editor of your school or local newspaper, a famous person you admire, or a friend who has graduated and moved away. Whether you mail them or not, letters give you an audience for your ideas.

Electronic Survey   Use the word processor to conduct a survey, gather ideas, or collect examples to support or test a thesis. Type a question onto your screen and ask a variety of people to enter responses. Special software called **electronic mail** can send your survey to another school for additional, more varied responses. For example, if your topic is the television viewing habits of teen-agers in your school, you can conduct an electronic survey by asking, "List your three favorite TV shows and beside each, write a reason for this choice." A question-naire with multiple-choice questions can translate into statistics such as "Of 100 teen-agers surveyed, 87 live in homes with more than two TVs."

Electronic Dialogues   Trade monitors or keyboards with another writer so that you are viewing each other's words as you type. You can create a dialogue by typing and responding on the screens. Debate two sides of a hot issue as prewriting for a student council speech. Assume the roles of two characters from literature to create a scene that didn't occur but could have. To begin a piece of writing, freewrite about your subject as your partner asks prompting questions. Here, notice that topics for paragraphs emerge as the writer answers questions about his interview.

```
I interviewed my aunt who works as a chef in a large
restaurant.

She has to revise and proofread the menu every day.  They
use a desktop publishing program.  She even has a file of
graphics that she can just zap onto the menu where she
wants.  It's amazing.

No.  She even keeps her recipes on a disk and changes
them if she creates variations.  When she's cooking, she
just calls the recipe up on the screen.
```

```
Come on, how can a chef use a computer?
Is that all?
Anything else?
```

Online Searches for Information   A **modem** is a device that connects two or more computers by telephone line. With a modem and special software, you can access vast amounts of printed information. The *Readers' Guide to Periodical Literature*, back issues of the *New York Times*, or articles from major magazines can appear on your screen. Check with your librarian to find out what's available to you.

Assignment   Prewriting

Step 1: Transcribe the notes or the tape recording that you made in the Assignment on page 510 by entering them into the word processor. As you type, add your own comments about the interview. Include direct quotations to add strength and authority to your draft later, and be sure to use quotation marks. *Step 2:* Save this transcription as "Interview" and print it out. *Step 3:* Underline phrases or passages that you like and make notes about possible organization for an essay explaining how a certain profession uses computers.

Drafting with a Word Processor

As you become more skilled with a word processor, drafting on the screen will become second nature, and you'll appreciate the time that it saves. As you draft, forget about correctness and style — those will come later. Double- or triple-space your drafts for easier reading and marking.

Transferring Text   One of the sheer joys of using a word processor is the ability to move text, as if it were fluid, from one file to another. Pour a little of your freewriting into an opening paragraph. Spice a conclusion with a splash from your favorite poem, stored in your writer's notebook. If you finally admit that your favorite paragraph is irrelevant to your thesis statement, don't pour it down the drain. Transfer it to your notebook disk for safekeeping. It may become a main ingredient in a future piece of writing.

Internal Notes   As you draft, don't try to do too much at one time. When new ideas occur to you, don't develop them completely; instead, leave yourself notes to guide your revision later. Inserting these notes in all capital letters in brackets makes them easy to find and delete as you revise.

Alternate Versions   You can create different versions of any file simply by changing your original draft and giving the file a new name. Experiment with voice by shifting the *I* in a poem to *you*, saving it with a different name, and printing it out. If you can't decide between two opening sentences, print out two versions of your first paragraph. Read both aloud to get a sense of which is stronger.

▶ **Strategies**

1. *Save your work about every twenty minutes.* In case of a power or computer failure or an unexpected exit from your program, only the writing you've saved will be stored on your disk. For added security, back up your work onto another disk.
2. *Print hard copies often.* Leave each work session with a current printout so that you can write when you're away from the computer. A hard copy lets you see the entire piece of writing as your audience will see it.
3. *Keep your files well-organized.* Make sure that the names of the files you save provide enough information for future identification. When an assignment is complete, delete unnecessary files but not your final copy.

Reference Point:
page 206

Step 1: Using the word processor, outline an expository essay based on the Assignment on page 512. Imagine that you are writing for an issue of a student magazine devoted to the theme of technology in the professions. *Step 2:* On the word processor, draft your essay. Transfer chunks from your interview transcription directly into your draft. Include several internal notes. Save the draft and print out a hard copy.

Revising with a Word Processor

When you see a neat, clean draft roll out of your printer, resist all temptation to hand it to your audience. For most writers, this is when the real work begins. Rough writing that looks slick is still rough writing.

Mark up your draft by hand. When it gets messy, revise on the computer, save, and print again. Revising will seem like a smooth evolution, occurring in a flow of changes rather than in distinct drafts. Some writers do most of their revising on paper; others can work from the screen. Experiment with both methods to find what works best for you. Try some of these suggestions as you shape and reshape your writing.

Cut and Paste Use this technique to experiment with organization. On the screen, insert a [RETURN] after each sentence in your paragraph. Do *not* save this version. Use the [MOVE] command to rearrange the sentences into various orders. You can also print out this cut-up version and use scissors to separate the sentences. Try several possibilities and see the effects of different methods of organizing. Be open to surprises.

Gathering Responses Print out several hard copies and ask several readers to mark up your draft at the same time. Readers can also call up your file and type comments in all capital letters in brackets. You can easily delete these comments later.

Electronic Thesaurus If your software has an electronic thesaurus, you can quickly choose alternatives to weak or overused words. Always be wary of quick solutions, however. The computer cannot think, make judgments, or appreciate the subtlety of connotation *(page 481)*.

Style Analysis Programs Style analysis programs can make useful observations about weaknesses in your draft. They can count words by categories, calculate sentence lengths, identify redundant expressions, or list vague words. These programs are useful but limited, and they certainly cannot replace a critical reader.

```
File: Chef                          Redundant Expressions

The following expressions are redundant:

    Using a word processor is easy and simple...(line 8)

    Her first initial reaction to my...         (line 78)

    every day, new and different specials... (line 144)

File: Chef                          Clichés

This file contains the following clichés:

    cool as a cucumber              line 32

    easy as pie                     line 122
```

Assignment   **Revising**

Step 1: Using your internal notes as guides, revise your draft from the Assignment on page 514, save it, and print four triple-spaced copies. *Step 2:* Give three of these hard copies to three readers. Ask them to write comments on your draft, addressing content, clarity, word choice, and sentence structure. *Step 3:* Compare the comments on the hard copies. Do the readers make similar comments? Which comments do you agree with? Disagree with? *Step 4:* Mark up the fourth hard copy yourself, choosing from your readers' suggestions and adding revisions of your own. *Step 5:* Use this version to revise your file. Save your revision.

Proofreading with a Word Processor

Have you ever copied over a page to correct errors, only to discover that you've carelessly made new ones? This can never happen with a word processor. A corrected error stays corrected, and new ones cannot accidentally occur. Your proofreading goal, therefore, should be mechanically perfect writing.

Begin proofreading on the screen, using the cursor to look at each letter, each word, and each punctuation mark from beginning to end. Always do a final proofreading from a hard copy. The technology offers some help, but no machine can replace a critical mind and a sharp eye for detail.

Search and Replace All word processors offer a [SEARCH/REPLACE] function that will locate a certain character or pattern of characters throughout a file. This function can help in proofreading. For example, if you confuse *lose* and *loose*, search for these words and double-check them. Search for semicolons, quotation marks, commas, or apostrophes if they give you trouble. Search for and replace a misspelled word throughout a file without the danger of skipping one occurrence.

Proofreading Checklist By this time, you probably notice that you repeat particular errors. A personalized, stored checklist, therefore, can make your proofreading much more efficient. You can access and add to this file with every assignment. A personal checklist might include questions like "Have I replaced *should of* and *could of* with *should have* and *could have?*" and techniques like "Search for *it's* (it is) and *its* (possessive)."

Spelling Checkers Spelling checkers are programs that identify words in your file that don't appear in an electronic dictionary. Like style checkers, their accuracy is limited because they cannot think. For example, a spelling checker won't know the difference between *cite*, *site*, and *sight*, and it won't question "a ward processor." Always use a dictionary — and your head — to check spelling and usage.

Assignment Proofreading

Step 1: Proofread your essay with a partner. As you read from a hard copy, your partner should move the cursor through your file, checking for errors in spelling, usage, mechanics, and grammar and inserting an asterisk (*) into the file beside each error. *Step 2:* Repeat the exercise, switching roles and proofreading your partner's file. *Step 3:* Use the [SEARCH] function to locate all asterisks. As you make corrections, delete the asterisks. Save and print out a final copy.

Publishing with a Word Processor

Until the computer age, variations in print were beyond the individual writer. This is no longer so. With a word processor, you have a potential printing press sitting on your desk.

Formatting The arrangement of words on the printed page is called **formatting.** It includes spacing, pagination, type styles, centering, indenting, and columns. Formatting can enhance the meaning you convey. For example, a writer can capture the feeling of a live interview by using type style to distinguish between the two voices.

Type Sizes and Fonts   Experiment with type sizes, measured in **points** or **pitch,** in your text and titles. The various typefaces are called **fonts.** There are hundreds of fonts available, each with a different look and feeling. Use one font consistently throughout a piece of writing, but try several, choosing the one you like best.

> This is 10-point Helvetica type.
>
> This is 12-point Palatino type.
>
> This is 14-point Times type.

Graphics   If your computer and your software offer graphics, you can create charts, tables, graphs, diagrams, and even illustrations. Devices called **scanners** copy photographs or printed illustrations onto a computer disk. Collections of ready-made graphics are available on files called **clip art.**

Desktop Publishing   Writers can be their own publishers with software called **desktop publishing.** These programs allow you to integrate and arrange text and graphics in any variety of ways for newspapers, programs, magazines, and posters. The samples here were created with desktop publishing programs and printed on **laser printers,** printers that produce typeset quality print and graphics.

Like the pen and the typewriter before it, the word processor continues to evolve to meet more writing needs. Monitors are supplementing paper and pencil on children's school desks. Vast libraries of books, films, art, and music reside on disks rather than library shelves. Color monitors produce realistic, three-dimensional graphics. Word processors of tomorrow will even talk and listen in various languages. We cannot even imagine the writing tools of the twenty-first century. Practice using a word processor now — you'll want to be ready.

Assignment Publishing

Step 1: Look at several magazine articles based on interviews. Notice how publishers use type size and style, fonts, spacing, and graphics to enhance meaning. *Step 2:* Experiment with the visual dimension of your essay from the Assignment on page 516. Reformat your essay as a magazine article, and print two single-spaced final copies. *Step 3:* Send one copy of your article to the person you interviewed, accompanied by a word-processed cover letter expressing your thanks for the information and the perspective.

Grammar, Usage, *and* Mechanics

CONTENTS

The English Language:
Culture and History

What is the most complex, most useful, most important, most mystifying, most entertaining invention in the history of the human race? The space shuttle? The wheel? Television? The printing press? The microchip? All wrong! None of these others could have come into existence if people had not first invented language.

There is no way to know when language was first used by humans. It is possible, however, to make some reasonable assumptions about language. For instance, there is evidence that people were able to make stone tools at the beginning of the Paleolithic Age (or Old Stone Age) about one million years ago. Therefore it seems possible that Stone Age peoples had some rudimentary language, for considerable cooperation is necessary for making tools and for teaching tool-making skills to younger generations.

As languages are compared, it becomes clear that many of them are related to one another and can be grouped in families. Languages are always changing, and as groups of people who speak the same language move apart, variations in their speech will occur. Each group will develop a different dialect that has particular characteristics of pronunciation, vocabulary, and grammatical structure. If the speech of these groups becomes unintelligible to the others, then new, distinct languages are identified. For example, Spanish, French, Italian, and Portuguese are all descended from Latin, the official language of the Roman Empire. English, German, Danish, Swedish, and Dutch come from a single, unwritten Germanic language.

The Indo-European Family

One of the largest language families in the world is the **Indo-European** family, which includes many of the languages spoken between western Europe and central India. It was spoken over 5000 years ago, and though it was never written down, scholars have figured out what it must have been like by comparing the written and spoken languages descended from it.

No one knows exactly where Indo-European was first spoken. It probably began somewhere between eastern Europe and southern Russia. The words shared by the different

Indo-European languages offer an idea of what the original Indo-European culture was like and indicate the kind of region the people came from. For example, there are common words for *winter* and *snow*, for such northern trees as *oak*, *beech*, and *pine*, and for *bear*, *wolf*, and *beaver*. There are no common Indo-European words for *palm*, *bamboo*, and *rice*, nor for *elephant*, *tiger*, *camel*, or *monkey*. Thus the people who originally spoke Indo-European probably came from a northern, temperate climate. There is no common word for *sea* or *ocean*, so the first Indo-European speakers probably lived in an inland area.

From studying their vocabulary, scholars learned that the Indo-Europeans kept horses, dogs, and other domestic animals. They planted crops and mined for copper, gold, and silver. Families and social structures were highly organized within systems of laws and religious beliefs. Poetry, song, and gift-giving were all important elements of early Indo-European culture. While life in the complex world of the late twentieth century may seem more advanced or complicated, we can tell from their language that the people who spoke Indo-European were not much different from people today. They were not ignorant, simple, or primitive.

From their original homeland, the Indo-European peoples migrated westward throughout Europe, and southward and eastward as far as central India. Their culture and language traveled with them, changing over time, but still influencing the development of their dialects, which eventually became new languages.

The Birth of English

English was first spoken on the island of Britain, when Angles, Saxons, and Jutes, members of Germanic-speaking tribes across the North Sea from Britain, began to raid the coasts of Britain about A.D. 449. The Anglo-Saxons called their language *Englisc* (pronounced like *English*), which means "the language of the Angles." Today the term **Old English** refers to the English used by the Anglo-Saxons from about 450 to 1100.

The literature of the earliest Anglo-Saxons was oral. It was memorized and passed on by word of mouth from one generation to the next. The Anglo-Saxons did have an ancient Germanic alphabet of letters called **runes.** *Rune* meant "secret," "mystery," or "secret writing," and the alphabet was

ᚠ ᚢ ᚦ ᚠ ᚱ ᚺ ᚷ ᚹ ᚾ ᛁ ᛁ ᛝ ᛋ ᚲ ᛦ ᛂ ᛏ
f u th o r k g w h n i y ēo p eo s t

ᛒ ᛖ ᛗ ᛚ ᛝ ᛞ ᚫ ᚪ ᛠ ᛁᛟ ᚳ ᚷ ᛣ ᛋ
b e m l ng ē d ā æ y ea io c g cw s

Old English Futhork

used for magical, ritualistic, and religious purposes. The name of the runic alphabet, *futhork*, was formed from the first six letters. Each letter had a special meaning or symbolic function as well as standing for a sound. Many Old English runic inscriptions have survived on coins, rings, weapons, burial stones, and carved stone crosses.

The Anglo-Saxons began to keep more extensive written records after they were converted to Christianity in the seventh and eighth centuries. Christian missionaries brought the Bible, a book rich with expressive Latin, Greek, and Hebrew words. Christianity opened the doors of literacy for the Anglo-Saxon people. Their schools and monasteries were the foundation of the culture upon which the English language has grown and prospered. Writing and reading were taught in schools attached to monasteries and churches. The language of the Church was Latin; therefore, education was in Latin as well. When scribes began to write in Old English, they used the Roman alphabet that they had first learned for writing Latin, borrowing a few runic letters as well.

> Ælfred cyning hateð gretan Wærferð biscep his wordum luflice ond freondlice.
>
> "King Alfred commands Bishop Werferth (to be) greeted (with) his words (in a) loving and friendly (way)."

From a letter written by King Alfred to Werferth, the bishop of Worcester, in the year 871

Middle English and the Norman Conquest

In 1066 the French duke of Normandy, William, attacked Britain — beginning a period of upheaval that would have lasting effects on the English language. The Anglo-Saxon aristocracy was replaced by French-speaking Normans. English no longer had a place in the government of England. Laws were written in Latin and French, and for three hundred years French was the primary language of the nobility of England. English was the language of the lower classes.

When English gradually began to reappear in written literature, it was quite different from Old English. Many of the Old English word endings were lost, and spelling was changed under the influence of French scribes. One very important development was the increase in the English vocabulary as writers and speakers borrowed many words from Latin and French. With this extensive vocabulary, the English were able to discuss the world around them with flair and sophistication. Thus began the tradition of heavy borrowing from other languages that gives the language its richness and fluidity today.

English gradually crept back up the social scale, and by the end of the fifteenth century, a national English literature had developed. English was once again the language of all social classes. The English language — and its speakers — went through enormous change during this period from 1100 to 1500, the period of **Middle English.** They had lived under French rule and absorbed much that was French into their lives, along with much that was Roman. At the end of it, the people of Britain were, once again, masters in their own land. Not only would their language never be overwhelmed again, but it would grow to include speakers in every land in the world.

The Beginnings of Modern English

Language does not change over a short period of time without dramatic change in social mobility. That is exactly what happened next in London. The population of the city in 1500 was 75,000. By 1650, it had grown to 450,000. These new city dwellers developed different grammatical structures from the dialects that they had left behind in the rural areas. Verb endings that had come from religious writing, such as *-eth* (He walketh home) changed to *-s* or *-es* (He walks home). Noun plurals previously formed with *-n* or *-en*, such as *children, housen* (houses), and *shoon* (shoes), changed to *-s* or *-es*, and today only a few such irregular plurals exist in the language. *Thee, thou,* and *ye* were retained only in religious writings, replaced by the simpler pronoun *you.*

Middle English scribes, like the Old English scribes before them, wrote and spelled according to their own dialects. In the late fifteenth century, however, printing was brought to England, and standardization came with it. William Caxton, the first English printer, set up a press in Westminster near London in 1476. Caxton recognized the advantages of printing his books in a single dialect. The dialect that he and other early English printers adopted was the dialect of London and Westminster, the center of the English government and of the book-buying public. As education spread and as printed books made learning available to more and more people, this dialect became the basis of a standard written English used by everyone, no matter what dialect they spoke. This form of early modern English is the source of the standard English written and spoken by the first settlers from Britain who sailed to North America.

Renaissance Print Shop

Usage and Authority in the Age of Reason

The eighteenth century is called the "Age of Reason" because the rise of scientific thought led to a strong sense of order and logic as an ideal. Philosophy, literature, and the arts were affected by this new attitude just as much as the development of science was. In this desire to establish a systematic approach to ideas, even the English language was subjected to a new scrutiny.

The notion of "correctness" as an ideal became much more important than before, and this ideal went beyond the simple fact that speech needs to be understood by both speakers and listeners. Even among educated speakers and writers, there was considerable variation. Eighteenth-century grammarians set out to eliminate this variation by using logic, but often their logic was misapplied. Another method was to force English grammar into the more regular or settled usage of Latin, although what is right or regular in one language may not be in another. The result of these grammarians' good intentions is our current irregular and confusing grammatical structure and spelling system.

The first great English lexicographer, or dictionary writer, was Samuel Johnson (1709–1784). In order to preserve the purity of the language, Dr. Johnson set out to write a dictionary based on what he considered to be the best English writers. In the course of his work, he discovered that language change is irresistible, and when he published his dictionary in 1755 he stated, "I have only failed in an attempt which no human powers have hitherto completed." Johnson's dictionary was so well received, however, that it became the ultimate authority on the language for many. Even today people think of "the dictionary" as containing some sort of absolute truth.

Samuel Johnson (1709–1784)

The Beginnings of American English

At the time when Samuel Johnson's dictionary was published, considerable numbers of European settlers were established in the Americas. About two thirds of them were English. Twenty years later, in 1775, the first shots would be fired signaling the beginning of the American Revolution.

These settlers' language had already begun to change with the influence of new words borrowed from the American Indians *(squash, chipmunk, totem)*, as well as from other trading partners from many different countries *(bayou, cookie, canyon)*. John Witherspoon wrote of many "Americanisms" that he had heard while serving a term as a visiting college president near the end of the eighteenth century. He mentioned *can't, don't,* the word *mad* for *angry,* and *bamboozle* for *swindle.* Thomas Jefferson coined *belittle, cent,* and *dollar.*

Throughout the 1800s, the Scots-Irish, the Scandinavians, the Germans, other Europeans, and finally the Slavs and the Italians immigrated — many seeking freedom from religious persecution. The dialects of American English began to form, with the Eastern New England and Southern dialect regions remaining closely tied to the speech patterns of England. Meanwhile, the Scots-Irish moved on to Pennsylvania and then south and westward into West Virginia, the Carolinas, and Georgia. Some went farther west to Tennessee and beyond. The Scots-Irish influenced what was to become the South Midland dialect region.

Another group of people moved from Pennsylvania to Ohio, Indiana, and Illinois, influencing the distinct but similar North Midland dialect region. Germans and Scandinavians moved to Michigan, Wisconsin, and then farther west. Their Inland Northern dialect came to be the accepted dialect of educated speakers across the country and is now recognized as standard English. It is typical of the speech of broadcasters today on national radio and television.

Principal Dialect Regions of the United States

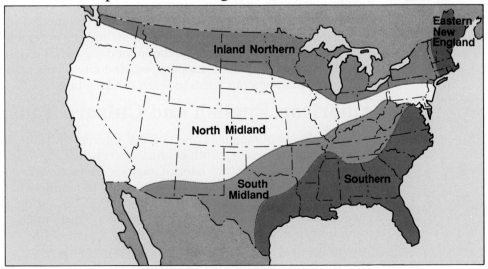

Language and Culture

At first the various immigrant groups tended to stay together, finding comfort and support among those who shared their ethnic heritage and religious beliefs. Education was associated with the church or synagogue, and teaching was in the native language, not English. Family and religion were the institutions supporting the first language of the immigrants, and for them the association was total.

Yet the pattern of language assimilation of these various language groups and cultures into American English was a powerful force in the history of the United States. However comfortable these immigrants' culture and language, they were drawn to and absorbed by the common culture and language of their adopted country. The conditions of early settlement life led to the necessity of a common language. It also led to dialect leveling. This explains why American English speakers have been thought of as a single dialect group, unlike English speakers in Britain, whose dialects, from their earliest history, are very distinct.

Free public education in urban school systems helped to further the influence of English. In the mid-1800s, the United States Commissioner of Education urged recruitment of children to the free public schools. In order to attract students in some midwestern cities, a bilingual program offered instruction in the students' first language. By the 1890s urban public schools offered primary instruction in English.

Adult immigrants learned English largely through their own intense motivation. In the cities labor groups worked together, providing interpreters to help the newcomers deal with the transportation system, sanitation, and the common necessities of daily life. Indeed, the immediate needs of personal safety and economic support required city dwellers, as well as the pioneers out west, to learn the language.

Hester Street in New York City, 1900

American English and Culture Today

The effects of language and cultural interdependence in the eighteenth and nineteenth centuries were different from those of today—a century later. Language helps to define a community, whether it is a small community of people who share their heritage or the larger community of the nation. Because there is a common language in the United States, communication has been possible in every aspect of life. Communication makes participatory government possible, from the level of local schools and town meetings to national policy and international interaction.

Immigrants who shared a native language and ethnic heritage struggled together to make new lives. Families tended to live in island-like communities. They knew what to expect in the routine of daily life and supported one another as they learned to function in a new language and a new culture. These groups were small and their immigration gradual, compared with the huge influx of newcomers since the passage of the Immigration Act of 1965.

Mexican Hispanics have always been part of the population of the Southwest and California because that region was, until 1848, part of Mexico. During the last twenty-five years, however, their numbers have grown by millions. Puerto Ricans, who are United States nationals, have arrived in large numbers, as have Hispanics from Central and South American countries.

Southeast Asians numbering in the millions have also arrived during this brief period. At present, two thirds of the world's immigrants come to the United States.

As a result we live in a vastly more pluralistic society today. The English language — and the culture of the United States — is changing as it reflects the ethnic heritage of representatives from virtually every nation in the world. Clear communication is basic to living in harmony, and it is broader than the words and sentences themselves.

It is useful to be aware of the signals coming from body language, along with the flow of English speech. These signals are so much a part of language and culture that most people are not even aware of them in themselves. They are embedded in cultural experience and are learned as every child learns its first language. Further, the signals are very commonly transferred to a second language, where they may be totally unexpected. Gestures such as pointing, nodding, head movements, and a touch of the hand send different messages in the context of different languages. Distance between speakers, voice quality, and posture are important. The eyes send powerful signals in glancing, staring, glaring, and in direct eye contact, downcast eyes, or complete eye avoidance. Behavior in language is strongly affected by the relationship of the speakers, and it has to do with age, gender, family, social class, and economic power.

All behavior associated with language affects communication. If any behavior is misinterpreted, then the listener or the speaker misunderstands the other's intent. A sense of "communicative flexibility" can make interactions with strangers positive and productive. The less shared background, the more explicit everything must be.

International English

The dramatic growth of English in the United States is matched by its rapid growth throughout the world. It has become the first language of the air, the sea, international trade, and diplomacy. English has become a common denominator in Third World countries, where previously the multiplicity of dialects precluded communication within a given country.

Today 750 million people worldwide speak English — one fourth of the world's population. For at least 350 million, it is a first language. It has a rich vocabulary enlarged by thousands of borrowings from other languages. It has a flexibility unequaled by any other language because words can freely move into the position of many parts of speech. It has many forms beyond the standard dialects of the speakers who share it as a first language. English has made communication possible among all the peoples of the world, and every speaker makes a contribution to its greatness.

Three Concentric Circles of English

Inner Circle
English is the native language and the basis of the culture.

Outer Circle
English is the official language used by non-native speakers in educational, commercial, and trade institutions.

Expanding Circle
English is used in foreign language contexts by non-native speakers.

Native speakers: 350 million
Non-native speakers: 400 million+
Total: 750 million to one billion

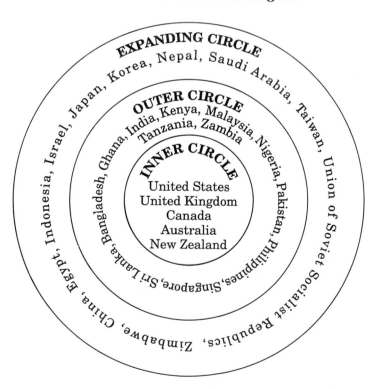

EXPANDING CIRCLE
Indonesia, Israel, Japan, Korea, Nepal, Saudi Arabia, Taiwan, Union of Soviet Socialist Republics, Zimbabwe, China, Egypt,

OUTER CIRCLE
Bangladesh, Ghana, India, Kenya, Malaysia, Nigeria, Pakistan, Philippines, Singapore, Sri Lanka, Tanzania, Zambia

INNER CIRCLE
United States
United Kingdom
Canada
Australia
New Zealand

English Language Activities

Choose one or more of these activities.

Borrowed Words

Words borrowed from other languages often abound in association with a particular aspect of life, such as business, law, and the arts. Using your library resources, find and list ten words in the stated categories that were borrowed from each of the following languages: *Spanish*, cowboys; *French*, society and wealth; *Dutch*, the sea; *Italian*, music; *Chinese*, food; and *Latin*, law.

Standardizing English

Research and prepare a short report on Samuel Johnson's influence on the spelling and grammar of modern English. Explain why Johnson wanted to standardize the spelling and usage of English, and discuss what degree of success he had. Cite some examples of current spellings and usage rules to support your case.

Creating New Words

Use a dictionary to find the meanings of the Greek and Latin word parts in the following list. Then create ten plausible words and give their meanings. Examples are *telebook*, meaning "a book sent electronically," and *astrocraft*, meaning "spacecraft."

-chron-	-mit- / -mis-
-circ- / -cycl-	-proto-
-cred-	-rupt-
-graph- / -gram-	-scrib- / -script-
-jud-	-sens- / -sent-

English and Citizenship

Write a persuasive essay on why a basic knowledge of English should or should not be required for United States citizenship. Explain exactly what an applicant must know in order to pass the citizenship test.

Immigrants' Experiences

Interview an adult immigrant to the United States. Write an account of the problems that the person encountered in adjusting to the language and culture. How might people in the community have helped?

International English

Research the nature of English usage in one of the countries listed in the Outer Circle in the diagram "Three Concentric Circles of English" on page 528. Write a two- or three-page essay describing spoken English within the country and its use in international communication.

UNIT 15 Grammar

When you study grammar, you study the underpinnings or the framework of writing. This unit covers the forms and the functions of the eight parts of speech, how to use these basic units to build phrases and clauses, and how to combine these word groups to construct clear, complete, smoothly flowing sentences. Understanding the basic structure of the English language will help you to use it more easily and more effectively in your writing.

As you work on building with words, you will also be learning about a period in history famous for both its artistic and architectural constructions and its masterpieces built of words. That period is *the Renaissance*, a time when new worlds were discovered and explored, when art and science flourished, and when the individual was regarded with increased respect.

In England theater was at the heart of the Renaissance. During the Elizabethan Age, appreciative audiences for the plays of Shakespeare and other dramatists ranged from ordinary people to Queen Elizabeth herself. Note the reference to theater within the selection shown here. Note also that although some conventions of grammar were different in the Renaissance, Shakespeare's sentences are still clear today, whether we read them or watch a performance.

*T*o-morrow, and to-morrow, and to-morrow,
Creeps in this petty pace from day to day,
To the last syllable of recorded time;
And all our yesterdays have lighted fools
The way to dusty death. Out, out, brief candle!
Life's but a walking shadow, a poor player,
That struts and frets his hour upon the stage,
And then is heard no more. It is a tale
Told by an idiot, full of sound and fury,
Signifying nothing.

William Shakespeare *(1564–1616)*
from *Macbeth*

← *The future*

← *Great verbs!*

Responding to Literature

Macbeth gives his famous "Tomorrow" speech upon hearing of the death of his wife. His words are colored by his mood. Think about the description of life that you might give if you were grieving, angry, optimistic about the future, or satisfied with some recent accomplishment. Choose two contrasting moods and list vivid nouns, verbs, and adjectives for a "definition" of life colored by those moods. Use phrases and clauses to record some ideas for dramatic metaphors. Save this prewriting to use later in your own poem.

Parts of Speech

The eight parts of speech are nouns, pronouns, verbs, adjectives, adverbs, prepositions, conjunctions, and interjections.

Nouns

A **noun** names a person, a place, a thing, or an idea.

PERSONS	merchant	explorer	William Shakespeare
PLACES	Florence	palace	Flanders
THINGS	motet	Mona Lisa	caravel
IDEAS	humanism	scientific method	conquest

Dates and days of the week are also classified as nouns.

A.D. 1500   Friday   November 29, 1455

Changes in Noun Form

Number   A noun is either singular or plural. A **singular noun** refers to only one person, place, thing, or idea and a **plural noun** to more than one. Adding -s or -es to the singular noun is the usual way of forming the plural; however, English has many irregular plurals.

Reference Point: pages 486–488

SINGULAR	prince	medium
PLURAL	princes (regular)	media (irregular)

Possessive Form   Although in the past English nouns had many forms, in modern English nouns change their form only in the possessive. To form the possessive of a singular noun or of a plural noun that does not end in -s, add -'s to the nominative form.

(mĕd′ə-chē)

NOMINATIVE	pope	Erasmus	Medici
POSSESSIVE	pope's	Erasmus's	Medici's

The **pope's** see is Rome.
Erasmus's most famous work is *The Praise of Folly*.
Giovanni di Bicci de' **Medici's** descendants were powerful figures in the history of Italy.

To form the possessive case of a plural noun that ends in -s, add the apostrophe only.

(dōj′əz)

NOMINATIVE	explorers	doges
POSSESSIVE	explorers'	doges'

Explorers' lives were difficult in the fifteenth century.
The **doges'** palace in Venice faces the Grand Canal.

Common and Proper Nouns

A **common noun** names a class of people, places, things, or ideas. Do not capitalize a common noun unless it begins a sentence. A **proper noun** gives the name or title of a particular person, place, thing, or idea, and it always begins with a capital letter.

COMMON NOUN   Often **palaces** were built in **cities**.
PROPER NOUN   The **Pitti Palace** commands a hillside in **Florence.**

Compound Nouns

A **compound noun** consists of two or more words used together to form a single noun. There are four kinds of compound nouns. One kind is formed by joining two or more words: *stonework.* A second kind consists of words joined by hyphens: *city-state.* A third kind consists of two words that are often used together: *sea level.* The fourth kind is a proper noun that consists of more than one word: *Loire River.*

Collective Nouns

A **collective noun** refers to a *group* of people, places, things, or ideas. These nouns are singular in form and may take singular or plural verbs.

A **swarm** of new ideas enticed the Renaissance mind.
A **society** was formed to oversee the maintenance of the park.

Concrete and Abstract Nouns

Concrete nouns refer to material things, to people, or to places. Some concrete nouns name things that you can perceive with your senses: *architecture, music, manuscripts.* Other concrete nouns name things that can be measured or perceived only with the aid of technical devices. Although you cannot see a proton, *proton* is a concrete noun because it names a material substance. In the following sentences, the nouns in boldface type are concrete.

If you work for the government, you will meet **politicians.**
Renaissance **scholars** and **artists** throughout **Europe** studied the **literature** and **art** of ancient **Greece** and **Rome.**

The central Renaissance **country** was **Italy,** and the quintessential Renaissance **city** was fifteenth-century **Florence.**

Abstract nouns name ideas, qualities, emotions, or attitudes.

Scholars consider **naturalism** and the **pursuit** of **beauty** to be important Renaissance **characteristics.**

Galileo Galilei defended the **freedom** to pursue **truth.**
The change in the itinerary created **agitation** among the tourists.
Pollution is a major **concern** of the citizens.

Exercise 1 Kinds of Nouns

? Critical Thinking:

What are the four kinds of compound nouns?

On your paper, rewrite each of the following sentences, replacing each blank with the kind of noun noted in parentheses. Underline the nouns that you use.

SAMPLE The Hundred Years' War is an __?__ (abstract) of the kinds of conflicts fought by __?__ (proper) during the Renaissance.

ANSWER The Hundred Years' War is an example of the kinds of conflicts fought by Europeans during the Renaissance.

1. Between 1337 and 1453, England and France were two __?__ (common) at war over the region of southwestern France.
2. That area of __?__ (proper) was called "Guienne," and it was held as a fiefdom under English __?__ (abstract).
3. When France tried to bring __?__ (proper) under its rule, a __?__ (collective) of inhabitants decided they would resist the French.
4. The local inhabitants protested France's __?__ (abstract) because they preferred a __?__ (common) who was distant to one who was close by and could collect taxes.
5. The invading English, whose longbows were a strong __?__ (abstract) over the heavy armor worn by the French __?__ (concrete), found themselves winning many __?__ (concrete).
6. Despite all these __?__ (abstract), England could not destroy the resistance in France, even as the French saw each __?__ (collective) of cattle dwindling and each __?__ (collective) suffering.
7. Eventually, the __?__ (common) of Guienne decided to rally to the French, even though their __?__ (concrete), Charles VII, was a weak __?__ (common).
8. The new __?__ (abstract) of patriotism in France was embodied by Joan of Arc, who led an __?__ (common) for __?__ (proper; compound).
9. The international __?__ (common) had ended, but a __?__ (compound) broke out in England between the __?__ (collective) supporting Henry VI and the party led by Richard, Duke of York.
10. Centuries later, this __?__ (abstract) in English history from 1453 to 1485 became known as the "War of the Roses" because the symbols of the warring factions were __?__ (concrete).

Using Nouns Effectively

In writing, you usually need to use both concrete nouns and abstract nouns. Abstract nouns are necessary in most forms of writing. However, if you link them with details and examples that include concrete nouns, your writing will be clearer and more interesting.

Read the following paragraph from the *Decameron* by Italian Renaissance writer Giovanni Boccaccio. Notice how Boccaccio uses concrete nouns to describe the scene. The concrete nouns are in italic type.

The *place* was somewhere on a little *mountain,* at some distance away from our *roads,* full of various *shrubs* and *plants* with rich, green *foliage* — most pleasant to look at; at the *top* there was a country *mansion* with a beautiful large inner *courtyard* with open *collonades, halls,* and *bedrooms,* all of them beautiful in themselves and decorated with cheerful and interesting *paintings;* it was surrounded by *meadows* and marvelous *gardens,* with *wells* of fresh *water.* ... And the *group* discovered, to their delight, that the entire *palace* had been cleaned and the *beds* made in the *bedchambers,* and that fresh *flowers* and *rushes* had been strewn everywhere.

Giovanni Boccaccio *(1313–1375)*
from the *Decameron*

Boccaccio relies on concrete nouns to evoke a certain feeling about the place that he describes. *Mansion, courtyard, collonades,* and *palace* convey a sense of the regal. *Shrubs, plants, meadows, gardens, flowers,* and *rushes* create a sense of the natural lushness of the scene. Note that Boccaccio does not completely avoid abstract nouns; *delight* is abstract.

In your own writing, use concrete nouns to make ideas and impressions more vivid and interesting.

Exercise 2　Identifying Nouns

On your paper, write the nouns used in each sentence. Label each noun *Proper, Collective, Concrete,* or *Abstract.*

SAMPLE　The love of books during the Renaissance was embodied in the literary quest of many writers.

ANSWER　love — Abstract; books — Concrete; Renaissance — Proper; quest — Abstract; writers — Concrete

? Critical Thinking:

What makes a noun collective?

1. Some knowledge of the beliefs of Latin and Greek writers and philosophers can help us understand the progress of western civilization.
2. For years, scholars ignored the works of these authors.
3. During the Renaissance, an Italian writer named Francesco Petrarch became curious about ancient manuscripts.
4. Petrarch and a group of writers who shared his interest began to search libraries throughout Italy for the forgotten treasures.
5. Lawyers read the old books with great zeal in preparation for their cases.
6. This research revived an interest in the life of ancient Rome.
7. Poets began to imitate the forms used by ancient Roman authors such as Catullus and Horace.
8. Petrarch wrote a series of famous sonnets dedicated to a woman named "Laura."
9. Another writer of the Italian Renaissance, Giovanni Boccaccio, wrote a book called the *Decameron.*

10. For centuries, other writers borrowed many of the plots from Boccaccio's book for their own creations.

Pronouns

A **pronoun** is a word that is used in place of a noun. A pronoun
identifies persons, places, things, or ideas without renaming them. The
noun that a pronoun replaces is the **antecedent** of that pronoun. There
are seven kinds of pronouns: personal, demonstrative, reflexive, intensive, interrogative, relative, and indefinite.

Personal Pronouns

Personal pronouns require different forms to express person, number, and gender. **Person** refers to the relationship between the speaker
or writer (first person), the individual or thing spoken to (second person), and the individual or thing spoken about (third person). The
number of a personal pronoun indicates whether the antecedent is singular or plural. The **gender** of a personal pronoun indicates whether the
antecedent is masculine, feminine, or neuter.

> Tricia and Annette will not soon forget Machiavelli's *The Prince*, for **it**
> greatly astonished **them**. [*It* replaces *The Prince*, and *them* replaces
> *Tricia and Annette.*]

> Critics who try to interpret *The Prince* are perplexed because **they** find
> inconsistencies and contradictions. [*They* replaces *critics.*]

Possessive Pronouns

Possessive pronouns are personal pronouns that show ownership or
belonging.

> Copies of *The Courtier* have arrived at the bookstore, and we can pick up
> **ours** at any time. [*Ours* replaces *copies.*]

> Georgina is doing **her** term paper on Sir Francis Bacon. [*Her* refers to
> *Georgina.*]

The following chart shows the common personal pronouns; the
possessive pronouns are in parentheses.

Personal Pronouns		
	Singular	**Plural**
First Person	I, me (my, mine)	we, us (our, ours)
Second Person	you (your, yours)	you (your, yours)
Third Person	he, him (his) she, her (her, hers) it (its)	they, them (their, theirs)

Demonstrative Pronouns

Demonstrative pronouns specify the individual or the group that is being referred to. The demonstrative pronouns are *this, that, these,* and *those.*

> **This** is a more interesting collection of Florentine paper than **that.**
> **These** are the antique editions of Montaigne's *Essais;* **those** are the modern editions.

Reflexive Pronouns

Reflexive pronouns indicate that people or things perform actions to, for, or on behalf of themselves. To form a reflexive pronoun, add the suffix *-self* or *-selves* to the personal pronouns.

Reflexive Pronouns	
First Person	myself, ourselves
Second Person	yourself, yourselves
Third Person	himself, herself, itself, oneself, themselves

> Cervantes's Don Quixote convinces **himself** that the world is like the romances that he reads. He rides out to find adventure for **himself.**

Intensive Pronouns

Intensive pronouns are the same words as the reflexive pronouns, but they draw special attention to a person or a thing mentioned in the sentence. Intensive pronouns usually come immediately after the nouns or pronouns that they intensify.

> Don Quixote chases his dream until the dream **itself** becomes reality.
> [The pronoun *itself* draws special attention to the word *dream.*]
> Cervantes **himself** believed that the world could be a better place.
> [The pronoun *himself* draws special attention to the word *Cervantes.*]

Interrogative Pronouns

Interrogative pronouns introduce questions. The most frequently used interrogative pronouns are *who, whom, which, what,* and *whose.*

> **Who** sailed to eastern Canada in 1497? John Cabot, of course.
> We have biographies of many explorers. **Which** would you like to read?
> **Whose** is this *Renaissance Reader?*

Relative Pronouns

Relative pronouns introduce adjective clauses *(pages 588–589),* which modify nouns and pronouns. The relative pronouns are *who, whom, whose, which,* and *that.*

Sir Thomas More's home in Chelsea, **which** was known as the "Great House," was a center of political and scholarly inquiry. [*Home* is the antecedent of *which.*]

We read some writings by More **that** were commissioned by Henry VIII. [*Writings* is the antecedent of *that.*]

Erasmus, **whose** *The Praise of Folly* is well known, was a member of More's circle. [*Erasmus* is the antecedent of *whose.*]

Indefinite Pronouns

Indefinite pronouns refer to people, places, or things in general. Often you can use these pronouns without antecedents. The following chart contains commonly used indefinite pronouns.

Indefinite Pronouns			
all	either	most	other
another	enough	much	others
any	everybody	neither	plenty
anybody	everyone	nobody	several
anyone	everything	none	some
anything	few	no one	somebody
both	many	nothing	someone
each	more	one	something

Margaret More Roper's learning astonished **everyone!** **Few** thought women capable of intellectual endeavors.

Anyone with an interest in political science should read More's *Utopia.*

For a time Henry VIII respected **none** of his statesmen more than he did Lord Chancellor Thomas More.

Exercise 3 **Pronouns**

? Critical Thinking:

When does *which* introduce an adjective clause, and when does *that*?

On your paper, write the following sentences, replacing the blanks with suitable pronouns. Use the kind of pronoun indicated in parentheses. Underline the pronouns that you use.

SAMPLE Nicholas Copernicus __?__ (intensive) did not think of his contributions as revolutionary, but __?__ (personal) were.

ANSWER Nicholas Copernicus <u>himself</u> did not think of his contributions as revolutionary, but <u>they</u> were.

1. Copernicus, __?__ (relative) we credit with starting a revolution in astronomy, was born in Poland.
2. __?__ (personal) was interested in mathematically describing the movements of the sun, the moon, and the stars.
3. The consequences of __?__ (possessive) discovering that the center of the universe is not Earth but the sun were far reaching.
4. __?__ (interrogative) would have thought his decision would transform our understanding of __?__ (possessive) place in the universe?

5. The problem __?__ (relative) Copernicus faced was explaining the movement of the planets across the sky.
6. Unfortunately, __?__ (indefinite) except Copernicus __?__ (intensive) thought that the old hypothesis, __?__ (relative) stated that Earth was the center of the universe, was wrong.
7. Copernicus noticed that the "wandering stars," as the Greeks called __?__ (personal), did not remain fixed in relation to the other stars in the sky.
8. __?__ (demonstrative) inspired him to hunt through ancient texts for an explanation of the strange, wandering stars.
9. __?__ (interrogative) of the ancient theories was the one __?__ (relative) Copernicus used?
10. The system __?__ (relative) Aristarchus of Samos had suggested in the third century B.C. was rejected by ancient astronomers because __?__ (indefinite) could find any evidence to support __?__ (personal).
11. Copernicus found __?__ (reflexive) attempting to describe mathematically the system __?__ (relative) Aristarchus of Samos had developed to explain the planetary motion that __?__ (personal) saw.
12. __?__ (demonstrative) had been rejected by ancient astronomers because __?__ (indefinite) believed that the theory was mathematically superior to any of the theories __?__ (relative) stressed Earth's importance.
13. Copernicus, __?__ (relative) spent enormous amounts of time calculating the movement of Earth in space, found __?__ (reflexive) with a theory that __?__ (personal) believed.
14. __?__ (indefinite) __?__ (relative) respected Copernicus were nonetheless slow to adopt __?__ (possessive) new calculations.
15. Almost __?__ (indefinite) thought that Copernicus's theory described the motions of the planets any more accurately than Ptolemy's older theory, __?__ (relative) placed Earth at the center of the universe.

Exercise 4 Using Pronouns in Writing

The following paragraphs need pronouns in order to make them read more smoothly and less repetitiously. On your paper, rewrite the entire passage, replacing nouns with pronouns where suitable. Use any of the kinds of pronouns studied in this section. Underline the pronouns in your rewritten paragraphs.

Critical Thinking:
Which sentences can be combined with the help of a relative pronoun?

SAMPLE   The Medicis belonged to an Italian family. The Medici family was very powerful in Florence for three centuries.

ANSWER   The Medicis belonged to an Italian family that was very powerful in Florence for three centuries.

The Medicis, although the Medicis were poor in the beginning, soon established the Medicis as merchants and bankers. Through marriage the Medicis became affiliated with the most important families of Europe, and the affiliation between the Medicis and the most important families of Europe produced three popes and two queens. The popes and the queens played a major role in the Renaissance. Although the Florentines had adopted a democratic constitution, the democratic constitution was a sham. The Medicis found that the Medicis were able to control the government, although the Medicis often held no official governmental position.

The first important member of the Medicis was Giovanni di Bicci de' Medici. Giovanni di Bicci de' Medici lived from 1360 to 1429; Giovanni di Bicci de' Medici's sons founded the two branches of the Medici family. Giovanni di Bicci de' Medici's elder son, Cosimo de' Medici, was the first Medici of the Medici family to rule Florence. The heirs of Giovanni di Bicci de' Medici's younger son, Lorenzo de' Medici, became grand dukes. Those grand dukes are the grand dukes who ruled Tuscany for many years. In addition to being powerful in Italian government and finance, the Medicis were also notable patrons of the arts. The Medicis helped to make Florence a haven for artists. These artists in turn made Florence famous internationally for Florence's culture.

Verbs

A **verb** is a word that expresses an action or a state of being. There are three kinds of verbs: action verbs, linking verbs, and auxiliary verbs.

Action Verbs

An **action verb** describes the behavior or action of someone or something. Action verbs may express physical actions or mental activities.

Hans Holbein **painted** a famous portrait of Thomas More. [*Painted* refers to a physical action.]

Henry VIII **ordered** Thomas More beheaded for treason. [*Ordered* refers to a physical action.]

More **believed** that he should serve God first and the king second. [*Believed* refers to a mental activity.]

Linking Verbs

A **linking verb** connects a noun or a pronoun with a word or words that identify or describe the noun or pronoun *(pages 575–577)*. Many linking verbs are verbs of being, which you form from the word *be*.

William Roper, More's son-in-law, **was** the *first* of many to write a biography of this remarkable man. [The word *first* identifies William Roper.]
English politics **was** *turbulent* during the time of the Reformation. [The word *turbulent* describes English politics.]

There are several linking verbs in addition to *be*.

appear	grow	seem	stay
become	look	smell	taste
feel	remain	sound	turn

Anne Boleyn **grew** *impatient* as she waited for Thomas More to recognize her as Henry VIII's lawful wife and queen. [*Grew* links the adjective *impatient* to *Anne Boleyn.*]

This tale **sounds** *fictitious*, but it **is** *true*. [*Sounds* links the adjective *fictitious* to *tale*; *is* links the adjective *true* to *it.*]

Some verbs can be either action verbs or linking verbs, depending on their use in a sentence.

ACTION   More **remained** at the king's court no longer.
LINKING   Henry VIII **remained** determined to divorce his present wife.

Exercise 5 | Distinguishing Action Verbs and Linking Verbs

On your paper, write the verbs in the following sentences. Label each verb *Action* or *Linking*.

? **Critical Thinking:**

What verbs can be either action verbs or linking verbs?

SAMPLE   Although Christopher Columbus was Italian, he lived many years in Portugal.

ANSWER   was — Linking; lived — Action

1. Christopher Columbus, an Italian, married a Portuguese woman and joined the Portuguese Navy.
2. At first his plan for exploring the ocean looked possible to the Portuguese king.
3. The king, however, eventually rejected Columbus's plan; it also sounded unfeasible to the Florentines and the Venetians.
4. After eight years the Spanish monarchs Ferdinand V and Isabella I gave Columbus the necessary financial backing.
5. Ironically, Henry VII of England grew interested in Columbus's plans soon after Spain had funded the voyage.
6. On April 17, 1492, Columbus signed an agreement that gave to Spain any land that he discovered during his exploration.
7. Little knowledge of geography existed at the time of Columbus's voyage; maps outlined less than one fourth of Earth's surface.
8. On October 12, 1492, Columbus's patience paid off, and his three ships reached Watling Island in the Bahamas.
9. Columbus's voyage greatly influenced people's ideas about the shape of Earth, and these ideas grew more popular in succeeding years.
10. After Columbus returned with evidence of newly discovered lands, Spain made him an admiral and governor general of the new lands.
11. The next year, he sailed with seventeen ships to Puerto Rico and became leader of a colony in Hispaniola.

12. When Columbus explored Venezuela five years later, he tasted fresh water and realized that this land was a continent.
13. Columbus remained governor of Hispaniola for several years before he returned to Spain.
14. By a freak of fortune, Amerigo Vespucci, a merchant who visited the lands discovered by Columbus and wrote accounts of his adventures, became in the public's eyes the discoverer of the American continents.
15. England and France soon followed Spain's lead and initiated their own voyages across the Atlantic Ocean; soon the battle for possession of the American continents became a heated one.

Auxiliary Verbs

Sometimes a verb needs the help of another verb, called an **auxiliary verb** or a **helping verb.** The verb that it helps is called the **main verb.** Together, a main verb and an auxiliary verb form a **verb phrase.** A verb phrase may have more than one auxiliary verb. Common auxiliary verbs appear in the following list.

am, are, be, been, is, was, were	may, might
can, could	must
do, does, did	shall, should
have, has, had	will, would

In the following sentences, the auxiliary verbs are in italic type, and the main verbs are in boldface type. Like any other adverbs, *still* and *not* are not part of the verb phrase.

Thomas More *must have* **known** that the king *would* not **let** him simply resign his post.
He *was* probably **waiting** to be arrested.

Exercise 6 Distinguishing Auxiliary Verbs from Main Verbs

? Critical Thinking:

Can a verb phrase have more than one auxiliary verb?

On your paper, write the verb phrases in the following sentences. Underline the auxiliary verbs once and the main verbs twice.

SAMPLE   The madrigal can be considered two different forms of music, although both forms did begin in Italy.

ANSWER   can be considered; did begin

1. Fourteenth-century madrigal performers would sing with three voices as background and one voice for the melody.
2. Madrigals of the sixteenth century should sound completely different from those of the fourteenth century.
3. These later madrigals might seem unrelated because they adapted the fourteenth-century form rather loosely.
4. Giovanni Gabrielli and Orlando di Lasso were composing classic madrigals during the Renaissance.

5. Orlando di Lasso, a Dutch composer, is often named as the Renaissance composer who must be studied.
6. Di Lasso could work as choirmaster as well as singer, and he had published his first books of madrigals by 1555.
7. Because of the quality of di Lasso's music, he should receive credit for his contribution to Flemish music.
8. Claudio Monteverdi, who should stand with Lasso as a madrigal specialist, must also be considered as a great figure in the history of opera.
9. Monteverdi's first opera, *Orfeo*, which is not often seen these days, is still mentioned in any study of opera.
10. His opera *The Coronation of Poppaea* was written in 1642, and students should know that the work was completed the year before Monteverdi's death.

Exercise 7 **Supplying Auxiliary Verbs**

On your paper, rewrite the following sentences, replacing each blank with an auxiliary verb. Underline the auxiliary verbs once and the main verbs twice.

? Critical Thinking:

What are the common auxiliary verbs?

SAMPLE   The Medici grand duke __?__ asked Galileo Galilei, a professor in Padua, Italy, to return to his native Florence.

ANSWER   The Medici grand duke <u>had</u> <u>asked</u> Galileo Galilei, a professor in Padua, Italy, to return to his native Florence.

1. Galileo's mind was such that he __?__ construct an effective telescope after having only heard that one existed.
2. When he used his new telescope to explore the sky, Galileo discovered that celestial bodies, which __?__ thought to be smooth, had mountains.
3. __?__ the discovery of the moon's ruggedness convince Galileo to write a book called *The Message of the Stars?*
4. Galileo __?__ told that his findings contradicted the traditional view that Earth and celestial bodies were very different.
5. Galileo __?__ also __?__ remembered as a student of mechanics who had great mathematical skills.
6. He __?__ decided to tackle the problem of explaining the movement of falling and thrown bodies.
7. His theory differed from that of the Greek philosopher Aristotle, who __?__ lived some eighteen hundred years earlier.

8. Because his contemporaries thought that Galileo __?__ not __?__ tampered with Aristotle's beliefs, the scientist's ideas met with furious opposition.

9. Although the Renaissance __?__ seem enlightened compared with the centuries before it, suspicion of new ideas was still rampant.

10. Ignoring the disapproval he __?__ __?__ noticed, Galileo continued to experiment.

11. Strange as it __?__ seem to today's students, experimentation was not common in Galileo's day.

12. Although previous scientists __?__ __?__ checked their theories against reality, few did.

13. Galileo, who __?__ been instrumental in explaining Copernicus's theories, __?__ finally called by Church authorities to answer for his beliefs.

14. He __?__ told that if he __?__ not stop his discussions of the Copernican system, he __?__ __?__ sent to jail.

15. Galileo __?__ __?__ decided that his beliefs __?__ __?__ taught anyway, because he persisted in championing Copernicus.

16. Galileo __?__ __?__ been able to continue teaching if his teachings __?__ been less threatening to the important powers of the age.

17. Finally, the man who __?__ __?__ __?__ considered a precious resource in nearly any other culture __?__ condemned and told that he __?__ renounce all his beliefs.

18. Galileo, who probably __?__ __?__ explained the important scientific problems of his day, __?__ finally silenced; even so, his contributions __?__ still remembered for their brilliance and scope.

Characteristics of Verbs

Verbs have several characteristics that you need to understand in order to use them correctly.

Transitive Verbs and Intransitive Verbs

All action verbs are either transitive or intransitive. A **transitive verb** directs its action toward someone or something, which is called the **object of the verb** (*pages 572–573*).

> verb ┌─── obj. ───┐
> King Henry VIII **married** *Catherine of Aragon* shortly after his accession in 1509. [*Catherine of Aragon* is the object of the verb *married*. *Married* is transitive.]

> verb ┌─ obj.─┐ ┌─── obj. ───┐
> Henry VIII **executed** *Anne Boleyn* and *Catherine Howard* in 1536 and 1542, respectively. [*Anne Boleyn* and *Catherine Howard* are the objects of the verb *executed*. *Executed* is transitive.]

The performer of the action of an **intransitive verb** does not direct that action toward anyone or anything. In other words, an intransitive verb does not have a receiver of the action. Some action verbs, such as *go*, are intransitive. All linking verbs are intransitive.

Although Mary Stuart **knew** about her cousin Elizabeth Tudor's attitudes, she **behaved** as if she did not. [The verbs *knew* and *behaved* do not have objects. They are intransitive.]

The Tudors **seem** larger than life. [*Seem* is a linking verb. It is intransitive.]

Many verbs can be either transitive or intransitive, depending on whether there is a receiver of the action.

TRANSITIVE **Study** Sir Francis Bacon's *Essays* tonight. [The object of *study* is *Essays.*]

INTRANSITIVE Renaissance scribes copied manuscripts and **studied.** [*Studied* has no object.]

Exercise 8 | **Distinguishing Transitive and Intransitive Verbs**

On your paper, copy each verb or verb phrase and label it *Transitive* or *Intransitive.*

Critical Thinking:
Does the verb have a receiver of its action?

SAMPLE   Francisco Pizarro, the Spanish conquistador, was the conqueror of Peru.

ANSWER   was — Intransitive

1. Francisco Pizarro traveled the world as an explorer.
2. In 1524, with Diego de Almagro, Pizarro searched the coasts of Ecuador and Peru for the famous Inca Empire.
3. In 1532 Pizarro was the guest of the Incan emperor, Atahualpa.
4. Pizarro offered Atahualpa friendship and then overthrew the Peruvian ruler.
5. Pizarro's actions toward Atahualpa seem underhanded to students today.

6. When the mountain town of Cuzco fell, Pizarro's conquest was complete.
7. Pizarro successfully defended Cuzco when the new Incan emperor, Manco Capac, fought back.
8. Pizarro wanted Chile under his rule, so he promised Diego de Almagro territory and money in return for its acquisition.
9. When Pizarro cheated him out of the promised territory, Almagro was furious.
10. Almagro seized the town of Cuzco, but his attempt at revenge eventually failed.
11. Almagro's followers, who hated Pizarro for his treachery, later deposed the explorer.

12. Although Pizarro had been a conquistador of resourcefulness and cunning, his greed and ambition overshadowed his admirable qualities.
13. Pizarro's brothers suffered similar fates because of greed.
14. Juan Pizarro died in an attack against the Incan fortress Sacsahusman, and Gonzalo was ousted as governor of Quito, Ecuador, in 1539, by the Spanish viceroy in 1541.
15. Hernando Pizarro, Francisco's half brother, tried to curry favor for his family at the Spanish court but found himself imprisoned instead.

Active Voice and Passive Voice   A verb is in the **active voice** when the subject performs the action of the verb. The active voice is generally a more effective way to express action.

> The *Medici* **governed** Florence for generations.

A verb is in the **passive voice** when the subject receives the action of the verb. Use the passive voice only when you want to emphasize the receiver of the action, or when the person or thing performing the action is unknown, or occasionally when there is no other way to write the sentence. Overuse of the passive voice is tedious and weakens your writing.

Rule   To form the passive voice, use a form of the verb *be* and the past participle of the main verb.

> Florence **was governed** by the Medici for generations. [Emphasizes the subject, *Florence*.]

Only transitive verbs *(page 544)* can be changed into the passive voice. Intransitive verbs cannot be in the passive voice because they do not have receivers of action. When a verb in the active voice is changed to the passive voice, its direct object becomes the subject of the sentence, and the subject becomes the object of the preposition *by*.

ACTIVE VOICE   Machiavelli **used** *Cesare Borgia* as the model for the ruler in *The Prince*.

PASSIVE VOICE   *Cesare Borgia* **was used** by *Machiavelli* as the model for the ruler in *The Prince*.

Exercise 9   **Active and Passive Voice**

? Critical Thinking:
What becomes the subject of a sentence in the passive voice?

For each verb listed, write a sentence using the verb in the active voice. Then rewrite the sentence, changing the verb to the passive voice.

SAMPLE   travel
ANSWER   Vasco da Gama traveled the southwestern coast of India.
The southwestern coast of India was traveled by Vasco da Gama.

1. explore	6. see
2. navigate	7. speak
3. urge	8. end
4. reach	9. greet
5. visit	10. prepare

Changes in Verb Form   An important characteristic of the verb is that the way it is used determines its form. A verb form changes in order to agree in person and number with its subject. It also changes to express tense and mood. The basic forms of a verb are its **principal parts.** (For an explanation of the rules governing changes in verb form, see pages 620–622.)

Exercise 10   Identifying Characteristics of Verbs

Step 1: On your paper, write the verb or verb phrase in each of the following sentences. *Step 2:* Label it *Action* or *Linking*. *Step 3:* If the verb is an action verb, label it *Transitive* or *Intransitive*. *Step 4:* If the sentence is in the passive voice, label it *Passive.*

? **Critical Thinking:** When is a verb intransitive?

SAMPLE   For fourteen years Niccolo Machiavelli was employed by the Florentine government as a minor official.

ANSWER   was employed — Action, Transitive, Passive

1. Machiavelli was an original thinker.
2. He spent his childhood in the Italian city of Florence.
3. The government employed Machiavelli as secretary of defense.
4. Through diplomatic missions, Machiavelli was introduced to powerful world leaders such as Cesare Borgia.
5. As defense secretary, Machiavelli became well known for his role in planning a citizens' militia.
6. Machiavelli was dismissed from his official position by the Medici family in 1512.
7. After his dismissal, Machiavelli suffered a brief imprisonment.
8. Machiavelli appeared undaunted by his experience and retired to his country estate.
9. Once he was in the country, Machiavelli wrote his famous books on politics.
10. Machiavelli's reputation was gained by the ideas that he discussed in *The Prince.*
11. To most scholars, Machiavelli's contributions to history are the views of power and leadership that were outlined by him in *The Prince.*
12. *The Prince,* a tract that has remained controversial, is based on the theory that success in political action is paramount.
13. The term *Machiavellian* now refers to someone who can justify dishonest methods as a means to an end.

14. The result of such tactics was seen by Machiavelli as necessary for the peace of the country; in other words, the successful ruler must be ruthless.

15. Many rulers since Machiavelli's time have pointed to Machiavelli's precepts as justification for ruthless methods.

Using Verbs Effectively

Verbs can make the difference between an ordinary piece of writing and one that stirs the reader's imagination. For this reason, good writers use verbs that tell how something happened. Consider the verb *fought* and a more specific verb in the following example.

Don Quixote **fought** a windmill.
Don Quixote **tilted** at a windmill.

When we read the verb *tilted*, we form a definite image of Don Quixote thrusting his lance at the windmill.

The following extract is from the novel *Don Quixote*, written by Miguel de Cervantes between 1605 and 1615. Note how Cervantes uses specific verbs to describe the action.

> This said, [Don Quixote] *clapped* spurs to his horse Rozinante, without giving ear to his squire Sancho, who *bawled* out to him, and *assured* him that they were windmills, and no giants. But he was so fully possessed with a strong conceit of the contrary, that he did not so much as hear his squire's outcry, nor was he sensible of what they were, although he was already very near them. . . . [C]overing himself with his shield, and couching his lance, he *rushed* with Rozinante's utmost speed upon the first windmill he could come at, and, running his lance into the sail, the wind *whirled* about with such swiftness, that the rapidity of the motion presently broke the lance into shivers, and *hurled* away both knight and horse along with it.

Miguel de Cervantes *(1547–1616)*
from *Don Quixote*

With the verb *bawled*, Cervantes tells us how Sancho sounded. The verbs *rushed*, *whirled*, and *hurled* depict the action more specifically and vividly than would the verbs *rode*, *moved*, and *pushed*. In your own writing, use verbs that show the reader how an action occurs.

Exercise 11 Using Verbs Effectively

? Critical Thinking:
Is each verb specific and vivid?

The passage that follows contains ineffective verbs. On your paper, rewrite the passage so that the verbs are more effective. Underline all the verbs that you add to the paragraphs.

SAMPLE The people of Europe had very few industries during the Renaissance.

ANSWER The people of Europe developed very few industries during the Renaissance.

Most people during the Renaissance were farmers, even in northern Italy, where there was some industry. The people in industry were clothmakers, shoemakers, and armor makers. Those who made these items still used their hands and simple tools, although some used power-driven machines. Water mills and windmills made grain; some pumps in mines used water mills.

The most common of the forms of mass manufacturing was the *putting-out* system. In this method, employers gave raw materials to workers, who made finished goods at home. The employee's pay was on a piecework basis; he or she was the producer, and the employer came and got the finished items, which would then be sold. The wages of these workers, even though their children and their wives usually worked too, were very low. Home workers used vegetables from garden plots around their cottages to make up for their low wages.

There were very few large-scale businesses during the Renaissance. Enterprises that used many workers under one roof, the way a modern factory would, were rare. There were some of these factories after the mid-fifteenth century. Such businesses were primarily forges or printers that made books after the invention of the movable-type printing press.

Adjectives

An **adjective** is a word that modifies a noun or a pronoun. To modify means to change; an adjective modifies a word by describing or limiting it. In some sentences, nouns and certain pronouns are used as adjectives. In such cases, consider them adjectives. Adjectives answer the question *Which? What kind?* or *How many?*

> **WHICH?** Charles V ruled several **European** *countries*. [Which countries? *European* countries.]
>
> **WHAT KIND?** As Holy Roman emperor and king of Spain, Charles had **extraordinary** *power*. [What kind of power? *Extraordinary* power.]
>
> **HOW MANY?** Charles's empire had **numerous** financial *problems*, however. [How many problems? *Numerous.*]

Articles

The most frequently used adjectives are the articles *a*, *an*, and *the*. *A* and *an* are **indefinite articles** because they do not specify a particular person, place, thing, or idea. *The* is called the **definite article** because it always specifies a particular person, place, thing, or idea.

INDEFINITE   Ferdinand and Isabella cooperated in **a** *plan* for peace and prosperity in Spain.

DEFINITE   Ferdinand is famous for **the** foreign policy *decisions* that he made.

Placement of Adjectives

Adjectives usually appear directly before the nouns or pronouns that they modify. Sometimes a comma separates adjectives from the words that they modify.

Isabella's influence led to the **popular** *conquest* of Granada and the **momentous** *discovery* of the Americas.

Aloof and **clever,** *Ferdinand* was praised by Machiavelli in *The Prince.*

Adjectives may follow linking verbs and modify the subjects *(pages 566–567)* of sentences.

Gresham's Law remains **useful** to monetary experts today. [*Remains* is a linking verb.]

Sometimes adjectives follow the words that they modify and are separated from them by commas.

Sir Thomas Gresham, **successful** and **influential,** advised Queen Elizabeth I on her loans.

Proper Adjectives

A **proper adjective** is an adjective formed from a proper noun. Proper adjectives are usually capitalized.

To create many proper adjectives, you use the suffixes *-n, -an, -ian, -ese, -ish,* or *-al,* changing the spelling of the noun as needed.

PROPER NOUN	PROPER ADJECTIVE
Florence	Florentine
Flanders	Flemish

Sometimes the proper noun is used unchanged as a proper adjective.

Last evening we saw a **Monteverdi** *opera.*

The **London** *stage* was a lively place in **Elizabethan** *times.*

Nouns Used as Adjectives

Some words that usually function as nouns can function as adjectives without changing form, as in the following examples.

The office contained **mahogany** *paneling* and tables with **glass** *tops*.

The invention of the **jet** *airplane* has diminished the need for

passenger *trains* but **freight** *trains* have had an increase in business.

Possessive Nouns   **Possessive nouns** are nouns that show possession or ownership; they function as adjectives because they modify nouns or pronouns. (For rules on the spelling of singular possessives and plural possessives, see pages 728–729.)

The **tunnel's** *lights* suddenly went out, plunging us into darkness.

Everyone admired the **actor's** *costumes*.

Pronouns Used as Adjectives

A pronoun functions as an adjective when it modifies a noun or a pronoun. Indefinite pronouns, demonstrative pronouns, interrogative pronouns, the relative pronoun *whose,* and the possessive pronouns in the following chart may serve as adjectives.

Possessive Pronouns Used as Adjectives		
	Singular	Plural
First Person	my	our
Second Person	your	your
Third Person	his, her	its, their

Your *map* of the United States ultimately owes **its** *existence* to Amerigo Vespucci, the Italian explorer who first applied the name *continent* to the Americas. [Note that the possessive pronoun *its* is spelled without an apostrophe.]

The words in the preceding chart are called *possessive pronouns* in this textbook, but some people call them *pronominal adjectives.*

The following chart contains examples of the other kinds of pronouns that can function as adjectives.

Other Pronouns Used as Adjectives	
Indefinite	few, many, several, some
Demonstrative	that, this, these, those
Interrogative	what, which, whose
Relative	whose

Few *families* are more famous than the Medicis, **whose** *members* included monarchs, statesmen, and popes as well as beggars, thieves, and murderers.

I wonder **which** family *member* was considered most brilliant.

Exercise 12 Adjectives

Critical Thinking:

What other parts of speech can function as adjectives?

On your paper, write the adjectives in the following passage. Next to each adjective, write the word or words that it modifies.

SAMPLE   The Renaissance artist enjoyed filling the canvases of his magnificent paintings with beautiful women.

ANSWER   The — artist; Renaissance — artist; the — canvases; his — paintings; magnificent — paintings; beautiful — women

(1) Raphael, an important Renaissance painter, was born in the flourishing Italian town of Urbino in 1483. (2) During his early years, he studied with the influential artist Perugino. (3) Perugino's influence can be seen in one of Raphael's first masterpieces, *Marriage of the Virgin.*

(4) In 1504 young Raphael went to live in Florence, where he studied the incomparable paintings of Leonardo da Vinci. (5) Leonardo's glorious figures and balanced compositions had a strong impact on Raphael.

(6) Four years later Pope Julius II invited Raphael to join a group of renowned artists working in Rome. (7) The pope, ambitious and forward looking, wanted to rebuild the ancient city with the finest workmanship available. (8) One of Raphael's monumental tasks was to complete a group of frescoes in the Vatican quarters of the pope. (9) Confident and assured, the artist created some brilliant scenes on the arched walls and curved ceilings of these private rooms. (10) A striking example is *School of Athens*, a wall painting that covers an entire side of one chamber. (11) A careful examination of this work reveals not only several leading Greek philosophers, but a small portrait of the artist himself. (12) A seated figure in the foreground is thought to be the legendary Michelangelo.

(13) The succeeding pope, Leo X, was so happy with Raphael that he treated the artist royally. (14) Raphael lived in a splendid palace, wore expensive clothes, and had numerous servants. (15) The great artist, cultured and generous, attracted a large following of loyal students and created a highly organized painting workshop.

(16) Raphael fell in love with a lovely woman named Margherita Luti, whom he immortalized in many radiant pictures. (17) In *La Fornarina* she wears an elegant bracelet with the telling words *Raphael Urbinas* on it. (18) Some scholars believe he painted the comely Margherita's face into the popular *Sistine Madonna.*

Using Adjectives Effectively

Adjectives provide the means for creating a mood or a lasting impression of a person, a place, or a thing. To create a mood, use adjectives that appeal to the senses. Examples of such adjectives include *white*, *black*, *gigantic*, *minuscule*, *tepid*, and *frigid*. However, you can also use adjectives that refer to emotional states and abstract qualities. *Innocent*, *angry*, *confusing*, and *hopeful* are examples of such adjectives.

The following passage is a somewhat humorous description of himself that Cervantes wrote in the prologue to his *Three Exemplary Novels*. Notice how Cervantes uses mainly adjectives that appeal to the sense of sight since he wants us to "see" him. Some of these adjectives are in italic type.

> This man you see here with the *aquiline* countenance, the *chestnut* hair, the *smooth*, *untroubled* brow, the *bright* eyes, the *hooked* yet *well-proportioned* nose, the *silvery* beard that less than a score of years ago was *golden*, the *big* mustache, the *small* mouth, the teeth that are scarcely worth mentioning (there are but half a dozen of them altogether, in *bad* condition and very badly placed, no two of them corresponding to another pair), the body of *medium* height, neither *tall* nor *short*, the *high* complexion that is *fair* rather than *dark*, the slightly *stooping* shoulders, and the somewhat *heavy* build — this, I may tell you, is the author of *La Galatea* and *Don Quixote de la Mancha* ... as well as other works that are straying about in these parts — without the owner's name, likely as not.

Most of Cervantes's adjectives appeal to the senses: *aquiline*, *chestnut*, *hooked*, *big*, *small*, *fair*, *stooping*, and so on. *Untroubled*, on the other hand, refers to an abstract quality.

In your writing, use adjectives that appeal to the senses and those that refer to emotional states or abstract qualities.

Exercise 13 Using Adjectives Effectively

The paragraphs that follow need adjectives to make them more descriptive. Rewrite the paragraphs, using adjectives to make the setting more vivid. Underline the adjectives in your rewritten paragraphs.

SAMPLE   Sailors returned to Spain and told tales about the land that they had seen.

ANSWER   <u>Excited</u> sailors returned to Spain and told <u>fascinating</u> tales about the <u>beautiful, new</u> land that they had seen.

Vasco Nuñez de Balboa lived in the port of Moguer on the coast of Spain. In 1501 ships stopped there before heading west to explore the Americas. Captains took aboard supplies, and they also hired sailors. Balboa joined one expedition. Like other explorers, he hoped to find wealth and fame in the Americas.

Balboa's party sailed to the coast of South America, where they spent days exploring. The sailors marveled at the land. However,

? Critical Thinking:
What adjectives can appeal to the senses?

they had to settle on the island of Hispaniola, which was the Spanish base in the Americas. There Balboa tried to make a living by raising pigs.

By 1510 Balboa had returned to the mainland of South America. He led a group of settlers to a site on the Gulf of Uraba, where he established the town of Darién. Balboa befriended Indians in the area and was soon rewarded for his efforts. His guides told him about a sea on the other side of the isthmus. He also learned about a land of riches farther south. These reports referred to the Inca Empire in Peru.

Balboa set out with a group of Spaniards and Indians across the isthmus. From the peak of a mountain, he looked down on an ocean. It stretched to the horizon. Balboa was the first European to see the eastern shore of the Pacific Ocean.

Adverbs

Like adjectives, adverbs are modifiers. An **adverb** is a word that modifies a verb, an adjective, or another adverb. An adverb answers one of five questions about the word or phrase that it modifies: *How? When? Where? How often?* or *To what extent?*

HOW? Ferdinand Magellan *persisted* **courageously** in his search for a passage from the Atlantic to the Pacific.

WHEN? Magellan found the strait and **eventually** *reached* his goal, the Philippines.

WHERE? He *died* **there,** falling short of circumnavigating the globe.

HOW OFTEN? **Sometimes** Magellan's sailors *had deserted* him.

TO WHAT EXTENT? Magellan seemed **entirely** *devoted* to his quest.

Adverbs such as *rather, really, certainly, indeed,* and *truly* are adverbs of extent and are used for emphasis.

Leonardo da Vinci was a **truly** *remarkable* man in both the breadth and the depth of his interests. [To what extent was Leonardo da Vinci remarkable? *Truly* remarkable.]

The words *not* and *never* are adverbs. They tell *to what extent* (not at all) and *when* (never).

Leonardo da Vinci *is* **not** easily *categorized.*

He **never** *finished* his painting *Battle of Anghiari.*

Noun or Adverb? Many sentences contain words that, while customarily nouns, sometimes function as adverbs. Such adverbs usually tell *when* or *where*.

Yesterday I *found* a book on da Vinci at the library.

Adverbs That Modify Verbs

Adverbs often modify verbs. An adverb does not have to appear next to the verb that it modifies. Notice the different positions of the adverb *gradually* in the following sentences.

BEGINNING **Gradually**, Renaissance ideals *influenced* all of Europe.

MIDDLE Renaissance ideals **gradually** *influenced* all of Europe.

END Renaissance ideals *influenced* all of Europe **gradually**.

Adverbs That Modify Adjectives

Adverbs may modify adjectives. An adverb usually comes directly before the adjective that it modifies.

In spite of da Vinci's **very** *numerous* writings and art works, we have

comparatively *little* information about Leonardo the man.

The Mona Lisa always draws an **enormously** *varied* audience.

Adverbs That Modify Other Adverbs

Adverbs can modify other adverbs. Such adverbs usually precede the adverbs that they modify.

Da Vinci is fascinating because he imagined **so** *accurately* solutions to a variety of problems. [*So* emphasizes *accurately*.]

Da Vinci performed **extremely** *brilliantly* with little formal education.

Exercise 14 | Identifying Adverbs

On your paper, write the adverbs in the following paragraphs. Next to each adverb, write the verb, adjective, or adverb that it modifies.

SAMPLE Titian is certainly considered a brilliantly talented giant of the High Renaissance.

ANSWER certainly — is considered; brilliantly — talented

(1) Tiziano Vecelli (Titian) studied diligently under the guidance of several masters. (2) Of these, Giorgione was possibly most influential. (3) From him Titian first learned to use vibrant color as an instrument of a rather romantic approach to portraiture.

Critical Thinking:
What parts of speech can adverbs modify?

(4) This influence can be seen quite clearly in Titian's remarkable painting *A Man in Blue.* (5) Here, the rendering of the subject's sensuous silk sleeve greatly enhances the visual poetry of the painting.

(6) Titian usually worked in Venice and in 1516 was aptly named the official painter of the Venetian state. (7) He was a productive artist who often worked very hard on several paintings simultaneously. (8) Sometimes this approach made him slightly late in delivering a commissioned work, but his finished pieces were worth the wait.

(9) One of Titian's really dedicated fans was Charles V. (10) The emperor so admired Titian's work that he would not allow any other artist to paint his portrait. (11) *Portrait of Charles V with His Dog* is one of the most opulently painted masterpieces that resulted from this highly beneficial relationship. (12) Other well-placed persons also came eagerly to Titian's door. (13) Dukes and kings from many parts of Europe were always flattered to have their portraits done by Titian.

(14) Clearly, Titian loved the grand and dazzling life of Venice in this period. (15) The artist lived magnificently in a fine house nearby and traveled occasionally to accept commissions. (16) He produced truly splendid altarpieces, beautifully expressed religious paintings, and many works with mythological themes. (17) Although Titian was ardently admired during his time, he was not universally respected: Michelangelo, for one, thought that the artist drew carelessly. (18) Today, students carefully note both Titian's prodigious talent and his relatively few flaws.

Exercise 15   Effective Use of Adverbs

? Critical Thinking:

What questions can adverbs answer?

The following paragraphs need adverbs to make them more descriptive. Rewrite the paragraphs. Underline the adverbs in your rewritten paragraphs. For variety, use adverbs that modify verbs, adjectives, and other adverbs.

SAMPLE   Many explorers sailed from Europe to North America in the 1500s.

ANSWER   Many explorers courageously sailed from Europe to North America in the 1500s.

Jacques Cartier grew up in a French seaport and studied navigation in Dieppe. He was respected in his profession. Some historians believe that Cartier sailed to Newfoundland with a fishing fleet in the early 1500s. He may have traveled to the Americas in the 1520s with Giovanni da Verrazano of Italy. He went to North America in 1534 at the request of King Francis I of France. The king hoped that Cartier would find gold and other riches on this expedition.

Cartier and his crew landed in what is Canada today. They met some Iroquois and were able to befriend them. In a true test of this friendship, the head of the Iroquois nation sent his two sons back to France with Cartier. The Iroquois told the French about precious metals that they could find farther north.

The king sent Cartier on a second expedition. The explorer reached the Gaspé Peninsula and pushed on into a large gulf. From the gulf Cartier discovered the mouth of a wide river. Since it was the feast day of Saint Lawrence, he named both the gulf and the river after this saint. The explorers sailed up the river until they came to a mountain. This would become the site for the city of Montreal.

Prepositions

A **preposition** is a word that establishes a relationship between a noun or a pronoun and another word in a sentence.

Vasco da Gama was the discoverer **of** the sea *route* **from** western *Europe* **to** *India*. [The preposition *of* relates *route* to *discoverer*. The preposition *from* relates *Europe* to *route*. The preposition *to* relates *India* to *route*.]

The following list contains frequently used prepositions.

along	beyond	off	to
among	by	on	toward
around	despite	onto	under
at	down	out	underneath
before	during	outside	until
behind	except	over	up
below	for	past	upon
beneath	from	since	with
beside	in	through	within
besides	near	till	without
between	of		

A **compound preposition** is a preposition that consists of more than one word.

Aside from scant *information* on his birth and education, little is known of da Gama's early life.

Frequently used compound prepositions are in the following list.

according to	in addition to	on account of
aside from	in front of	out of
as of	in place of	prior to
as well as	in regard to	with regard to
because of	in spite of	with respect to
by means of	instead of	

A preposition is usually followed by a noun or a pronoun, which is called the **object of the preposition.** The preposition, the object, and the modifiers of that object together form a **prepositional phrase.**

Some scholars have wondered whether Shakespeare really wrote all
 prep.   obj.
of those numerous **plays.** [The prepositional phrase consists of the preposition *of*, the modifiers *those* and *numerous*, and the object, *plays.*]

In some sentences, particularly interrogative sentences, the preposition follows the object.

 obj.   prep.
Whom are you siding **with** in the controversy over who wrote Shakespeare's plays? [**Think:** With whom are you siding?]

A prepositional phrase functions as an adjective if it modifies a noun or a pronoun. A prepositional phrase functions as an adverb if it modifies a verb, an adjective, or another adverb.

USED AS AN ADJECTIVE   Shakespeare's sonnets are a *sequence* **of 154 poems.**

USED AS AN ADVERB   These poems *are written* **in the Elizabethan (or Shakespearean) sonnet form.**

Some words function either as prepositions or as adverbs according to their use in a sentence.

 prep.
PREPOSITION   Hamlet first sees his father's ghost walking **outside the**
 obj.
castle at Elsinore.

 adv.
ADVERB   The guards who are **outside** with Hamlet are terrified.

Exercise 16 Prepositional Phrases

? Critical Thinking:

What is a compound preposition?

On your paper, list the prepositional phrases in the following sentences. Underline the prepositions once and the objects of the prepositions twice.

SAMPLE   The term *utopia*, which was first used by Thomas More, refers to any imaginary place with ideal political, social, and economic conditions.

ANSWER   by Thomas More; to any imaginary place; with ideal political, social, and economic conditions

1. Thomas More was born in London and went to Oxford University.
2. He embarked on a legal career in 1494 and for several years was an undersheriff of the city.

3. More soon came to the attention of King Henry VIII.
4. He fulfilled a number of duties for the king from 1518 to 1529.
5. Prior to his years in service to the king, More had written *Utopia*, an influential book about justice and equality.
6. This book, which discusses More's views on government, is written partly in the form of a dialogue.
7. In the book a Portuguese sailor named Raphael Hythlodaye travels along to North America with Amerigo Vespucci.
8. Hythlodaye recounts tales of his travels through many wild lands.
9. On the island of Utopia, Hythlodaye discovers an ideal society where the divisions between rich and poor do not exist.
10. Those who live in More's Utopia are concerned for the health and happiness of their fellow human beings.

Conjunctions

A **conjunction** is a word that connects words or groups of words. There are three kinds of conjunctions: coordinating conjunctions, correlative conjunctions, and subordinating conjunctions.

Coordinating Conjunctions

A **coordinating conjunction** connects individual words or groups of words that perform the same function in a sentence. The coordinating conjunctions are *and, but, for, nor, or,* and *yet.* (For a complete explanation of phrases and clauses, see pages 578–603.)

> Shylock in *The Merchant of Venice* is accused, arrested, **and** then saved by his daughter Portia. [connects words]
>
> King Lear, hoping to divest himself of responsibilities **but** not expecting to be stripped of all of his powers, gives up his throne. [connects phrases]
>
> Romeo and Juliet cannot openly express their love, **nor** can they live without each other. [connects clauses]

Exercise 17 Combining Sentences: Conjunctions

On your paper, combine each pair of sentences into one sentence using the coordinating conjunction in parentheses. Rewrite the sentence so that the conjunction connects the sentence parts indicated. Underline the conjunction in the new sentence.

? **Critical Thinking:**
How is a phrase different from a clause?

SAMPLE   Jan Vermeer was born in 1632 in Delft, Holland. Little else is known about him. (*but;* clauses)

ANSWER   Jan Vermeer was born in 1632 in Delft, Holland, <u>but</u> little else is known about him.

1. Jan Vermeer has been mistaken for a painter named Vermeer from Utrecht. He has been mistaken for a Vermeer from Haarlem. (*and;* phrases)

2. Jan Vermeer completed only forty paintings in his lifetime. He was a painstaking artist. (*for;* clauses)

3. Vermeer married in his hometown. He painted in his hometown. He died in his hometown. (*and;* words)

4. When Vermeer died at the age of forty-three, his widow was left with only paintings. She was also left with debts. (*and;* words)

5. The paintings quickly passed out of the family's hands. His wife could not survive without selling them. (*for;* clauses)

6. In the next 150 years, little was heard about Vermeer. Art dealers found it more advantageous to attribute his work to better-known artists. (*for;* clauses)

7. It took a French writer twenty-four years to research Vermeer. In 1866 he published three articles about the artist whom he called "The Sphinx of Delft." (*but;* clauses)

8. You can see a Vermeer at the Frick Collection in New York City. You can see a fine example of his work at the National Gallery in London. (*or;* phrases)

9. Vermeer's paintings show quiet scenes of domestic life. They have a radiant quality of an immortal nature. (*yet;* clauses)

10. Vermeer's works are admired for their incandescent light. They are also admired for their control of space. (*and;* phrases)

11. One of Vermeer's paintings is *The Artist in His Studio. Fame and the Artist* is another name for the painting. (*or;* phrases)

12. Adolf Hitler bought this painting many years after the artist's death for a sum equivalent to $660,000 in today's currency. It was still a bargain. (*yet;* clauses)

13. The painting was among those hidden as World War II drew to an end. Soldiers from General Patton's Third Army discovered it in a salt mine near Salzburg in 1945. (*but;* clauses)

14. The painting did not legitimately belong to Hitler. It didn't belong to the United States. (*nor;* clauses)

15. The picture is now in the Kunsthistorisches Museum in Vienna. It is a prized possession there. (*and;* clauses)

Correlative Conjunctions

A **correlative conjunction** is a conjunction that consists of two or more words that function together. Like coordinating conjunctions, correlative conjunctions connect words that perform equal functions in a sentence. The following list contains correlative conjunctions.

both . . . and   neither . . . nor
either . . . or   not only . . . but (also)
whether . . . or

Michelangelo **both** painted **and** sculpted. [connects words]
Not only did Michelangelo paint and sculpt, **but** he **also** produced quite creditable poetry. [connects clauses]

On your paper, combine each pair of sentences into one sentence using a correlative conjunction. Underline the conjunction that you use.

Critical Thinking:

What can correlative conjunctions connect?

SAMPLE   Henry the Navigator was not English. Henry was not Spanish.
ANSWER   Henry the Navigator was <u>neither</u> English <u>nor</u> Spanish.

1. Henry was a Portuguese prince. He was a student of mathematics.
2. Henry's older brothers wanted to be worthy of knighthood. Henry himself wanted to be worthy of knighthood.
3. They took over a town in Morocco. They fought with valor.
4. Henry governed the town. He sent out exploring parties along the African coast.
5. In Henry's time Europeans did not know much about the Atlantic Ocean. They did not sail far out into it.
6. He was interested in trade routes. He was interested in geography.
7. Henry established a school for navigation that brought mapmakers together. It brought navigators together.
8. Henry welcomed astronomers if they came from Portugal. Henry welcomed astronomers if they did not come from Portugal.
9. Shipbuilders made many advances in their knowledge. Instrument makers made many advances in their knowledge.
10. The astrolabe did not exist before Henry's school was started. The caravel did not exist before Henry's school was started.
11. Henry raised money for expeditions. Henry planned routes for expeditions.
12. Henry sent out forty expeditions. He may have sent out fifty expeditions.
13. Portuguese explorers sailed into the Atlantic Ocean. They sailed along the coast of Africa.
14. He did not sail on any of these voyages. He did not ever see the lands he helped others to reach.
15. Henry's navigational knowledge opened the way for the later explorations of Vasco da Gama. Henry's navigational knowledge opened the way for the later explorations of Bartholomeu Dias.

Subordinating Conjunctions

A **subordinating conjunction** introduces a subordinate clause *(pages 588–589)*, which is a clause that cannot stand by itself as a complete sentence. The subordinating conjunction connects the subordinate clause to an independent clause, which *can* stand by itself.

```
                    ──── sub. clause ────────────────
Although Shakespeare and Milton are perhaps better known,
```

```
                    ──── indep. clause ───────────────
Edmund Spenser was also one of England's greatest poets.  [The subordi-
nating conjunction although introduces the subordinate clause and con-
nects it to the independent clause.]
```

Subordinating conjunctions usually express relationships of time, manner, cause, condition, comparison, or purpose.

TIME	after, as, as long as, as soon as, before, since, until, when, whenever, while
MANNER	as, as if, as though
CAUSE	because
CONDITION	although, as long as, even if, even though, if, provided that, though, unless, while
COMPARISON	as, than
PURPOSE	in order that, so that, that

——————— sub. clause ———————
If you read Spenser's *The Faerie Queene*, you will enter a world in which fantasy and reality mirror one another. [*If* expresses condition.]

——————— sub. clause ———————
When you read *The Faerie Queene*, use a companion book to explain its allusions and the language. [*When* expresses time.]

Conjunction or Preposition? Certain words can function as either conjunctions or prepositions. However, there are two important differences between a word used as a preposition and one used as a conjunction. First, a preposition always has an object, and a conjunction never has one.

PREPOSITION **Before** *me* is a book of Renaissance poetry. [The pronoun *me* is the object of the preposition *before.*]

CONJUNCTION **Before** we read it, we should learn something about Renaissance poets' use of myth and allegory. [*Before* has no object. Instead, it introduces the subordinate clause *Before we read it.*]

Second, a preposition introduces a prepositional phrase. A conjunction, on the other hand, connects words or groups of words.

——————— prep. phrase ———————
PREPOSITION **After** much preparation, Renaissance poets made classical allusions with ease. [*After* introduces the prepositional phrase *After much preparation.*]

CONJUNCTION Spenser's literary career flourished **after** Sir Walter Raleigh presented him to Queen Elizabeth I. [*After* connects the subordinate clause *after Sir Walter Raleigh presented him to Queen Elizabeth I* to the preceding independent clause.]

Conjunctive Adverbs

A **conjunctive adverb** is an adverb that functions somewhat like a coordinating conjunction because it usually connects independent clauses *(pages 587–588)*. A semicolon precedes the conjunctive adverb, and a comma usually follows it.

CONJUNCTIVE ADVERB   The poetry and drama of the English Renaissance are glorious; **nevertheless,** they are enjoyed by relatively few modern readers.

COORDINATING CONJUNCTION   The poetry and drama of the English Renaissance are glorious, **but** they are enjoyed by relatively few modern readers.

The following list contains frequently used conjunctive adverbs.

also	furthermore	later	still
besides	however	moreover	then
consequently	indeed	nevertheless	therefore
finally	instead	otherwise	thus

Exercise 19 | **Combining Sentences: Conjunctions, Adverbs**

On your paper, rewrite the following paragraphs, combining sentences by using conjunctions and conjunctive adverbs whenever appropriate to connect ideas and to provide variety. You may make other changes so that the passage reads smoothly. Underline the conjunctions and the conjunctive adverbs that you use.

**? Critical
Thinking:**

What punctuation precedes
a conjunctive
adverb?

SAMPLE   Ferdinand Magellan was born in about 1480 in Portugal. His parents were well-to-do. They were of the nobility.

ANSWER   Ferdinand Magellan was born in about 1480 in Portugal. His parents were well-to-do; moreover, they were of the nobility.

Europeans knew little of Earth's geography in the 1400s. Few had ever left their own continent to see what the rest of the world was like. The voyages of Christopher Columbus changed that. Vasco da Gama's expeditions helped. Magellan was intrigued by the news of these voyages. He, too, became interested in navigation. He became interested in exploration. The lure of finding wealth was great. The challenge of adventure on the high seas was enticing. The challenge of adventure in new lands was enticing.

Magellan was ambitious. He was intelligent. He was somewhat ruthless. He made several sea voyages with different Portuguese fleets in the early 1500s. These took him to faraway places such as India. He went to Malaysia. He learned about the Spice Islands from the letters of a friend.

Magellan was determined to go to the Spice Islands. He thought that he could get there by sailing around the tip of South America. It seemed to him that this would be a shorter route than going around the tip of Africa and across the Indian Ocean. King Manuel I of Portugal would not agree to Magellan's proposal. A few years later, Magellan got the king of Spain to support the trip. King Charles I insisted that Magellan take mostly Spanish sailors on this voyage.

The expedition began on September 20, 1519. It left from Spain. Magellan had five ships. He led 241 sailors. They sailed to Brazil. They spent the winter in what is now Argentina. Trouble broke out. One ship's crew rebelled. Magellan put down the mutiny. On October 18, 1520, the expedition found a passage around the tip of the continent. The strait became known as the Strait of Magellan. By the time the fleet had sailed through it, another ship's crew had mutinied. That ship returned to Spain. Magellan called the calm waters he saw the "Pacific Ocean". The word *pacific* means "peaceful." His journey back was not peaceful. It took ninety-eight days to cross the Pacific. The sailors got sick. They had no food. Their water wasn't clean. Many died. Magellan was killed in a battle in the Philippines.

Interjections

An **interjection** is an exclamatory word or phrase that can stand by itself, although it may also appear in a sentence. Many interjections express strong emotions. They are followed by exclamation marks.

Oh! Giotto's frescoes are exquisite!

When an interjection appears within a sentence, you should set it off with a comma or commas.

So, you didn't find what you were looking for at the Vatican Museum.
My, these della Robbia reproductions are truly excellent!

Exercise 20 | Interjections

❓ **Critical Thinking:**
How may an interjection be punctuated?

On your paper, write an interjection for each blank of the following paragraph. Choose the interjections from the following list, and use each only once. Be sure to punctuate the interjections correctly and to add capital letters if necessary.

of course	good grief	say	oh
my goodness	indeed	well	alas

SAMPLE   __?__ The wives of Henry VIII had a difficult time.
ANSWER   My goodness! The wives of Henry VIII had a difficult time.

__?__ did Henry VIII really have six wives? __?__ he did! He had to establish a new religion to divorce Catherine of Aragon, his first wife. Later, he beheaded Anne Boleyn, his second bride. __?__ Jane Seymour (number three) __?__ died in childbirth. Henry next married Anne of Cleves, a woman whom he had never met. This marriage didn't work out either. __?__ how could it? Henry then had Catherine Howard executed; however, his sixth wife, Catherine Parr, outlived him. __?__ good for her!

Avoiding Common Writing Problems

In every writing situation, you need to choose different parts of speech. Try to select vivid verbs, nouns, adverbs, and adjectives that help involve your readers in your topic. To help your readers, you will need to use all parts of speech correctly.

Writing Assignments

Parts of Speech in a Magazine Article As a staff writer for *Pen and Quill* magazine, you will write an article about the Renaissance artist Benvenuto Cellini. *Step 1:* Select from and then organize the prewriting notes below.

> **Prewriting Notes**
> Benvenuto Cellini (1500–1571) — Italian goldsmith, sculptor, writer
> wrote *Autobiography*, an exaggerated, lively account of his adventures
>   in Rome, Florence, Paris
> *Perseus*, one of his well-known sculptures, in Loggia de Lanzi
>   in Florence, Italy
> one surviving work as goldsmith — gold and silver saltcellar
> commissioned to do *Nymph of Fontainebleau*, a bronze relief, for King
>   Francis I of France
> Michelangelo wrote to Cellini, "I have known you all these years as the
>   greatest goldsmith of whom the world has ever heard."
> Cellini worked on *Perseus* for nine years and was never paid.
> made delicate gold cup shaped like a seashell — decorated with pearls
>   and enamel
> Cellini's work popular with popes, princes, kings

Step 2: Write your article, using vivid language that will interest your readers. *Step 3:* Revise your article, checking for effective, clear, and concise word choices. *Step 4:* Proofread your article, paying particular attention to parts of speech. *Step 5:* Submit a clean copy of your article to your school publication.

Reference Point:
pages 89–92

A Personal Narrative Imagine that you are living during the Renaissance. Whom or what would you choose to be? Think of real or imaginary artists, explorers, writers, musicians, rulers, or scientists. Then complete this sentence: "I would most like to be — ." Freewrite to gather details. Select and organize notes for a personal narrative as if you were that person. In several paragraphs, describe one significant event or experience. As you revise, check for paragraph unity. Proofread your narrative, giving particular attention to parts of speech. Make a clean copy and include it in a class notebook entitled *Renaissance Narratives*.

Reference Point:
pages 154–183

Sentence Structure

Four Sentence Purposes

A **sentence** is a group of words that has a subject and a predicate and that expresses a complete thought. It describes an action or states the condition of a person, a place, or a thing. There are four categories of sentences: declarative, interrogative, imperative, or exclamatory.

A **declarative sentence** makes a statement and ends with a period. An **interrogative sentence** asks a question and ends with a question mark. An **exclamatory sentence** shows strong feeling and ends with an exclamation point. An **imperative sentence** gives an order or makes a request. A mild command or request ends with a period, but a strong command or request ends with an exclamation point. Some imperative sentences take the form of questions but are actually mild commands or polite requests. Such sentences end with periods.

DECLARATIVE	El Greco was the pupil of the painter Titian.
INTERROGATIVE	Who was the first Holy Roman emperor?
EXCLAMATORY	The Renaissance produced such beautiful art!
IMPERATIVE	See the basilica when you are in Rome.
	Don't touch that masterpiece!
	Will you please hand me that copy of *Don Quixote*.

<hr>

Exercise 1 **Sentence Purpose**

? Critical Thinking:
Does the sentence make a statement, ask a question, give an order or request, or show strong feeling?

On your paper, write sentences in which you use the following groups of words and add appropriate punctuation. Label each sentence *Declarative*, *Interrogative*, *Imperative*, or *Exclamatory*.

SAMPLE Have you read
ANSWER Have you read Leonardo da Vinci's study of bird flight? — Interrogative

1. Don't you think
2. into the air
3. how magnificently
4. observations about birds
5. a bird's wing
6. would it be possible
7. the flight of
8. against the air
9. could be lifted
10. could a person

Subjects and Predicates

Simple Subjects

The **simple subject** is the noun or pronoun that names the person, place, thing, or idea that the sentence is about. The simple subject does not include modifiers. The complete subject *(pages 568–569)* consists of the simple subject and its modifiers. In this book the term *subject* refers to the simple subject. In the following sentences, the simple subject is in boldface type.

> **Leonardo da Vinci** was the first modern anatomist.
> The **foundations** of modern anatomical study were laid by Andreas Vesalius.
> What were the outstanding **contributions** of Paracelsus?

The simple subject of an imperative sentence is always *you.* Often, *you* is understood rather than stated.

> Be sure to read about Renaissance medicine in your history book.
> [**Think:** *You* be sure.]

Compound Subjects   A **compound subject** is a simple subject that consists of two or more nouns or pronouns of equal rank. The term compound subject refers to a compound *simple* subject.

> An **interest** in fame, a **concern** for life on Earth, and a **desire** to revive classical civilization were marks of the Renaissance. [*Interest, concern,* and *desire* form the compound subject.]

Simple Predicates

The **simple predicate** is the verb or verb phrase that describes the action or states the condition of the subject. The simple predicate does not include modifiers and words that complete the meaning of the verb. Therefore, it does not include adverbs such as *not* or *never.* The complete predicate *(page 569)* includes all such modifiers and complements *(page 572).* It does include adverbs such as *not* and *never.* In this book the term *predicate* refers to the simple predicate. In the following sentences, the simple predicate is in boldface type.

> By the end of the fifteenth century, the *influence* [subj.] of the Renaissance
> **had been felt** [pred.] in Spain.

> The *Renaissance* [subj.] **did** [pred.] not **reach** [pred.] Germany until about 1500.

> How **do** [pred.] *scholars* [subj.] **view** [pred.] the Renaissance in these countries?

Compound Predicates   A **compound predicate** is a simple predicate that consists of two or more verbs or verb phrases of equal rank. The term *compound predicate* refers to a compound *simple* predicate.

> Christopher Columbus **led** his crew on one expedition after another and finally **reached** the Far East by sailing west. [*Led* and *reached* form the compound predicate.]

Exercise 2 | Identifying Subjects and Predicates

? Critical Thinking:

What is included in a simple subject and a simple predicate?

Write the simple subject and the simple predicate of each sentence. Underline each simple subject once and each simple predicate twice.

SAMPLE Hernando Cortés, a sixteenth-century Spanish conquistador, claimed Cuba and Mexico for the king of Spain.

ANSWER Hernando Cortés claimed

(1) Diego Velásquez, the Spanish governor of Cuba, heard that a wealthy Aztec empire existed in Mexico. (2) The governor asked Hernando Cortés to lead an expedition there. (3) Cortés and his followers would befriend the Aztecs, develop trade with them, and claim Mexico for the king of Spain. (4) Before the expedition's departure, Velásquez became suspicious of Cortés's loyalty. (5) Velásquez, questioning Cortés's motives, removed him from command of the expedition. (6) Ignoring the governor's directive, Cortés completed preparations and sailed for Mexico in February 1519. (7) The expedition of approximately six hundred daring Spanish adventurers sailed in a fleet of eleven ships. (8) Making several stops en route to Mexico, Cortés added interpreters to his expedition. (9) These newcomers spoke the language of the Mayas and the Aztecs.

(10) Cortés's fleet landed in Vera Cruz on the east coast of Mexico and established its base there. (11) Cortés then burned his ships, thereby eliminating any possibility of turning back. (12) The expedition began its long march inland to the Aztec capital at Tenochtitlán. (13) Along the way thousands of people from many tribes joined Cortés's forces. (14) Those Spaniards once loyal to Velásquez were won over to Cortés's cause. (15) The Aztec emperor Montezuma, a superstitious ruler, feared the revenge of the god Quetzalcoatl. (16) As a sign of humility to the god, he sent gifts of gold to the strangers. (17) Unfortunately, the gifts only whetted Cortés's appetite for more gold. (18) Montezuma then welcomed the strangers to his island capital on Lake Texoco and gave them shelter in one of his palaces. (19) In return for this kindness, Cortés and his soldiers took their host prisoner claiming Mexico for the king of Spain. (20) Hernando Cortés then proclaimed himself the governor and captain general of Mexico.

Complete Subjects and Complete Predicates

The **complete subject** consists of the simple subject and all the words that modify it or identify it.

|───────────── complete subject ─────────────|
Columbus's *estimate*, that the voyage would be 2400 nautical miles, was doubted by the Portuguese. [*Estimate* is the simple subject.]

———————complete subject———————
Planning to ask France's Charles VIII for funds, *Columbus* was persuaded by Queen Isabella to undertake his expedition for Spain instead. [*Columbus* is the simple subject.]

The **complete predicate** consists of the simple predicate and all the words that modify it or complete its meaning.

———————complete predicate———————
Sir Francis Drake, an English explorer, *sailed* **around the world in a voyage lasting from 1577 to 1580.** [*Sailed* is the simple predicate.]

———————complete predicate———————
Superior ships and equipment *ensured* **Drake's victories over Spain.** [*Ensured* is the simple predicate.]

———————complete predicate———————
Drake *defeated* **the Spanish Armada and then** *destroyed* **its remnants.** [Included in the complete predicate is the compound simple predicate *defeated* and *destroyed.*]

Placement of Subjects and Predicates

Subjects and predicates may be arranged in a variety of ways in sentences. The placement of the subject and the predicate often depends on the purpose of the sentence. In the examples that follow, the complete subjects are underlined once and the complete predicates twice.

DECLARATIVE SENTENCES
Vasco Nuñcz de Balboa, a Spanish planter, soldier, and explorer, discovered the Pacific Ocean in 1513. [The subject precedes the predicate.]

In Panama City stands a statue in honor of Balboa, discoverer of the Pacific. [The sentence has inverted word order; that is, the subject follows the predicate.]

Because they competed for the discovery of new passages and territories, Spain and England, who were great powers, were also great enemies. [The subject is between the two parts of the predicate.]

INTERROGATIVE SENTENCE
How did Balboa plot his voyage? [**Think:** Balboa did plot.]

IMPERATIVE SENTENCE
Compare the feats of Balboa, Columbus, and Magellan. [**Think:** You compare. The entire imperative sentence is the complete predicate because the subject, *you*, is understood.]

EXCLAMATORY SENTENCES
Vasco da Gama's accomplishment was actually greater than Columbus's!

On your paper, combine each pair of sentences into one sentence by joining their subjects. Underline the complete subject in your new sentence. Label the simple subjects *subj*. You may make other changes so that the passage reads smoothly.

SAMPLE   Mary Stuart reigned briefly as queen of England in the sixteenth century. Elizabeth Tudor, Mary's cousin, reigned as queen of England too.

ANSWER   Both Mary Stuart and Elizabeth Tudor, Mary's cousin, reigned as queens of England in the sixteenth century.

1. King James of Scotland was Mary Stuart's father. Mary of Guise, his French wife, was her mother.
2. King Henry of France was Mary's great-uncle. King Henry's sister was also Mary's relative.
3. King Henry influenced Mary's upbringing while she was in the royal court. Catherine de' Medici, his wife, also influenced Mary.
4. Their eldest son Francis was at one time Mary's husband. Henry Stuart was also Mary's husband.
5. Upon King Henry's death, Francis became the reigning monarch of France. Mary also became the reigning monarch of France.
6. "Queen of Scotland" was one of Mary's titles. "Queen of France" was Mary's title too.
7. When Mary returned to Scotland, the religious powers were changing. The political climate was likewise changing.
8. The Catholic Church had proclaimed itself the official church of Scotland. The Protestant church made the same proclamation.
9. When the throne in England became vacant, Mary Stuart claimed to be the legitimate queen of England. Elizabeth Tudor made the same claim.
10. Would Mary Stuart become queen of England? Would Elizabeth Tudor become queen of England?
11. Mary plotted to take the throne away from Elizabeth Tudor. Some of the Catholic nobility also plotted to take the throne away from Elizabeth.
12. Elizabeth's retaliation against Mary's plot to overthrow her was strong. Public reaction was equally strong.
13. By 1565 the Protestants of Scotland had aligned themselves against Mary. Elizabeth I of England was aligned against Mary too.
14. After her escape from prison in 1568, Mary fought against the Scottish nobility. A small army of her supporters also fought against the Scottish nobility.
15. Mary was defeated and was forced to flee Scotland. Her supporters were also forced to flee.

On your paper, combine each pair of sentences into one sentence by joining their predicates. Label the simple predicates *pred*.

SAMPLE   John Cabot discovered the Maritime Provinces of Canada. He also found a fishing area now known as the Grand Banks.

                                    pred.

ANSWER   John Cabot discovered the Maritime Provinces of Canada and

           pred.

found a fishing area now known as the Grand Banks.

1. John Cabot's family lived in Genoa, Italy, when he was born. The family later moved to Venice.
2. As an adult, Cabot worked as a merchant and mapmaker. He sailed regularly between Venice and ports in Egypt.
3. Cabot took Italian goods to merchants in Egypt. There, he traded the goods for exotic spices from the Far East.
4. In 1492 he heard about Christopher Columbus's voyage for Isabella and Ferdinand of Spain. He thought that Columbus had found a new route to Asia.
5. Cabot pondered Columbus's route. He decided that there was a route still shorter than the one that Columbus had taken.
6. Cabot had read Marco Polo's description of the wealth in Asia. He had heard reports of westward voyages made by sailors looking for new fishing grounds.
7. Cabot dreamed of making his own voyage to Asia. He hoped to bring back jewels and spices.
8. Cabot's request for permission to sail was refused by both Portugal and Spain. It was granted by Henry VII of England.
9. Cabot promised the king one fifth of the riches he hoped to find in Asia. He also agreed to repay money he had borrowed for the voyage from English merchants.
10. In May 1497, Cabot sailed from the English port of Bristol. He headed west.
11. On June 24 he reached either Newfoundland or an island off the coast of Nova Scotia. Cabot claimed the land for the king of England.
12. He commanded a ship called the *Matthew*. He had a crew of eighteen sailors, including his three sons.
13. His crew was excited by the wealth of fish off the coast of Newfoundland. They caught fish by lowering a basket into the sea.
14. Cabot did not gather the jewels and the spices that he had expected. He found the fishing area that is now called the Grand Banks instead.
15. Cabot thought that he had landed in Asia. He reported his accomplishment to the English court upon his return home.

Complements

A **complement** is a word or a group of words that completes the meaning of a verb in a sentence or a clause *(page 587)*. Complements are always part of the complete predicate.

> Rembrandt's self-portraits *are* **fascinating.** [The self-portraits are *what? Fascinating. Fascinating* is a complement.]
>
> They *reveal* **his personality.** [They reveal *what? His personality. His personality* is a complement.]

If the preceding sentences did not have complements, their meaning would be incomplete.

> Rembrandt's self-portraits are [Are *what?*]
> They reveal [Reveal *what?*]

This section covers three types of complements: objects, objective complements, and subject complements.

Objects

Objects are nouns or pronouns that follow action verbs in the active voice *(page 546)*. There are two kinds of objects: direct objects and indirect objects.

Direct Objects   A **direct object** is a noun or a pronoun that follows an action verb in the active voice and receives the action of the verb. It answers the question *What?* or *Whom?* Verbs that take direct objects are called transitive verbs *(pages 544–545)*. Modifiers are not part of the object.

> Rembrandt also *painted* **portraits** of his wife, his neighbors, and wealthy patrons. [Painted *what? Portraits.*]
>
> He *married* **Saskia van Uylenburgh** in 1634. [Married *whom? Saskia van Uylenburgh.*]

Indirect Objects   An **indirect object** is a noun or a pronoun that names the person or thing to whom or for whom an action is performed. An indirect object follows an action verb in the active voice. In most cases an indirect object is used with a direct object. The indirect object comes immediately after the verb and before the direct object.

>   I.O. D.O.   D.O.
> Rembrandt's late self-portraits *show* **me** his *sadness* and *discouragement.* [**Think:** The self-portraits show *to* me his sadness and discouragement.]
>
>   I.O. D.O.
> Will you *bring* **me** your *book* on Rembrandt when you come? [**Think:** Will you bring *to* me your book?]

Compound Objects Like subjects and predicates, objects may be compound. A **compound object** consists of two or more objects that complete the same predicate.

COMPOUND DIRECT OBJECT	D.O. Rembrandt painted group **portraits** and D.O. biblical **scenes.**
COMPOUND INDIRECT OBJECT	I.O. I.O. The museum guide showed **Paulette** and **me** the famous *Night Watch* by Rembrandt.

Exercise 5 Subjects, Predicates, and Objects

On your paper, copy the following sentences. In each sentence underline the simple subject once and the simple predicate twice. Write *D.O.* over each direct object and *I.O.* over each indirect object.

SAMPLE   Queen Elizabeth I ruled England from 1558 until her death in 1603.

ANSWER   Queen Elizabeth I <u>ruled</u> D.O. England from 1558 until her death in 1603.

> **Critical Thinking:**
> Which object answers to or for what or whom?

1. Tutors taught the young Elizabeth French and Italian.
2. The future queen had inherited red hair and pale eyes from her father, King Henry VIII.
3. A great orator like her father, the queen delivered effective speeches to beggars as well as to diplomats.
4. She had also acquired Henry's fondness for music, art, and literature.
5. Many scholars give Elizabeth credit for the way she ruled.
6. She welcomed the greatest English poets, musicians, writers, and scholars of the time to her court.
7. Elizabeth brought England a period of relative peace and prosperity.
8. The majority of the people of England gave Elizabeth their love and loyalty.
9. Poets, such as Edmund Spenser, composed masterpieces in the queen's honor.
10. During Elizabeth's reign Shakespeare provided both the nobility and the poor entertainment such as *Romeo and Juliet* and *A Midsummer Night's Dream.*
11. However, not everyone in England enjoyed the growth and energy of Elizabeth's rule.
12. Queen Elizabeth established Protestantism as the official religion for her subjects.
13. Protestant authorities in Elizabeth's government imprisoned many Catholic writers and intellectuals.

14. Protestant forces in Scotland, France, and the Netherlands sought military support and financial aid from Elizabeth.
15. Overall, the Elizabethan Age provided the country a climate of artistic and intellectual opportunity that has rarely been equaled.

Objective Complements An **objective complement** is a noun or an adjective that follows a direct object and explains, identifies, or describes that object. Only certain verbs take objective complements: *make, find, think, elect, choose, appoint, name, consider, call,* and synonyms of these verbs.

NOUN AS OBJECTIVE COMPLEMENT

D.O.   O.C.
The board of directors has appointed *Dr. Chang* **curator**. [*Curator* is the objective complement of the verb phrase *has appointed*. It identifies the direct object, *Dr. Chang*.]

ADJECTIVE AS OBJECTIVE COMPLEMENT

D.O.   O.C.
They considered his *credentials* **excellent**. [*Excellent* is the objective complement of the verb *considered*. It describes the direct object, *credentials*.]

A sentence may have a compound objective complement, which consists of two or more objective complements.

┌──D.O.──┐   O.C.
The board has appointed *Dr. Chang* the **curator** of the gallery and the **coordinator** of the Rembrandt exhibit. [The nouns *curator* and *coordinator* are objective complements.]

Exercise 6 **Identifying Objects and Objective Complements**

? Critical Thinking:
Which words complete the meaning of the direct object?

On your paper, write the direct objects, indirect objects, and objective complements in the following sentences. Label each word that you write *Direct object, Indirect object,* or *Objective complement.*

SAMPLE Historians call Peter Paul Rubens the greatest Flemish painter of the seventeenth century.

ANSWER Peter Paul Rubens — Direct object; painter — Objective complement

1. Critics consider Peter Paul Rubens's baroque-style paintings vivid and dynamic.
2. Viewers throughout the centuries have found his hunting and biblical scenes, portraits, and landscapes colorful, exciting, and inventive.
3. Rubens also enjoyed success as a diplomat and made several official trips to England, France, and Spain.
4. Rubens's mother made him an apprentice to several local Flemish painters when he was only ten years old.

5. In 1600, having learned the basics of painting, Rubens moved to Italy and continued his art studies there.
6. In Italy the duke of Mantua, Vincenzo Gonzaga, gave Rubens a job as a court painter.
7. The duke also named Rubens curator of the Gonzaga Gallery, which housed the duke's collection of great art works.
8. The duke's collection of Italian sculpture and paintings caught Rubens's attention.
9. The young artist thought the duke's art collection brilliant.
10. The duke later gave Rubens an appointment to the diplomatic mission to Spain.
11. Rubens took King Philip III of Spain costly presents from the duke of Mantua.
12. Several aristocratic families and churches commissioned Rubens to create important paintings for them.
13. King Charles I of England designated the artist a knight because of his fine work as a diplomat.
14. Did the painter Rubens consider the diplomatic life challenging?
15. Rubens found the countryside around his estate near Brussels beautiful and worthy of being captured on canvas.
16. Rubens also considered stories from mythology good sources for his paintings.
17. In 1622 Marie de' Medici appointed him painter of the important events of her life.
18. He gave her twenty-four large and dramatic paintings.

Subject Complements

A **subject complement** is a word that comes after a linking verb and identifies or describes the subject of a sentence or a clause *(page 587)*. Subject complements often follow forms of the verb *be*. Some other verbs that may take subject complements are in the list that follows.

appear	look	sound	feel	seem	taste
become	remain	stay	grow	smell	turn

There are two kinds of subject complements: predicate nominatives and predicate adjectives.

Predicate Nominatives   A **predicate nominative** is a noun or a pronoun that follows a linking verb and identifies the subject of the sentence.

P.N.
Amerigo Vespucci was an Italian **explorer** who sailed to the Americas. [*Explorer* identifies the subject, *Amerigo Vespucci.*]

P.N.
Amerigo is the **source** of the name of the American continents. [*Source* identifies the subject, *Amerigo.*]

P.N.   P.N.

Vespucci was chief **navigator** and **mapmaker** for a Spanish trading company in the early 1500s. [The sentence has a compound predicate nominative, *navigator* and *mapmaker*. Both identify *Vespucci*.]

Predicate Adjectives   A **predicate adjective** is an adjective that follows a linking verb and modifies the subject of the sentence.

Vespucci's *voyages* are not very **well known.** [The predicate adjective, *well known*, modifies the subject, *voyages*.]

Columbus's *voyages*, which occurred earlier, are much more **famous.** [The predicate adjective, *famous*, modifies the subject, *voyages*.]

Many *people* are **surprised** and **disappointed** to find out where the name *America* comes from. [The sentence has a compound predicate adjective, *surprised* and *disappointed*.]

In some sentences the predicate adjective precedes the verb or verb phrase.

Fortunate is the *person* whose name lives on through history. [The predicate adjective, *fortunate*, modifies the subject, *person*.]

Exercise 7 Distinguishing Subject Complements

Critical Thinking:

Which word or words identify or describe the subjects?

On your paper, list the subject complements in the following sentences. Label each complement *Predicate nominative* or *Predicate adjective*.

SAMPLE   Edmund Spenser was a poet of the Elizabethan Age.
ANSWER   poet — Predicate nominative

1. Details of Edmund Spenser's birth and early life remain unclear.
2. London was definitely his place of birth; the date, probably about 1552, is less certain.
3. Also obscure are the details about his schooling.
4. He was, however, a student at Cambridge University, earning a master's degree in 1576.
5. At Cambridge, Gabriel Harvey and Sir Philip Sidney were friendly to Spenser.
6. Both men appeared eager to help the budding poet.
7. Spenser's first major poem, published in 1579, was *The Shephearde's Calender.*
8. His epic poem, *The Faerie Queene*, is a masterpiece of English literature.
9. *The Faerie Queene* remained unfinished at the time of Spenser's death in 1599.
10. The poem is both an adventure and an allegory.

11. Many of the descriptive passages seem extremely florid to today's readers.
12. Some of the symbolic characters in the poem are holiness, friendliness, justice, and evil.
13. The heroine of the poem is a queen named "Gloriana".
14. The poem's setting is a mythical land invented by Spenser.
15. Spenser was thankful for Sir Walter Raleigh's help in publishing the first three books of *The Faerie Queene.*

The Writing Connection

Varying Types of Sentences

As a writer, you have the opportunity to choose among different kinds of sentences to create variety in your writing. A combination of simple, compound, complex, and compound-complex sentences allows you to express complicated ideas smoothly and without distracting repetition. In addition, when it is appropriate for your writing situation, you can also choose sentences with different purposes. For instance, you might use declarative and interrogative sentences in an interview, a few exclamatory sentences in a review, or imperative sentences in a set of directions. Whatever you are writing, take advantage of the full range of sentences that is available to you, but be sure to construct and punctuate them correctly.

Reference Point:
pages 71–87

Writing Assignment

An Essay Test Question Read the following essay question.

Reference Point:
pages 446–447

> The term *Renaissance man* or *Renaissance woman* refers to a person with diverse interests and expertise in many areas. He or she excels in athletics, the arts, science, philosophy, language, and politics. Briefly compare and contrast yourself with this ideal.

To answer the essay question, freewrite your ideas. Then select the notes that you wish to use and organize them logically. Write a brief essay, using as many kinds of sentences as are appropriate to your message, tone, and purpose. As you revise, check for sentence variety. Read your revision aloud to see whether it flows smoothly and whether sentence variety has made the rhythm of your essay interesting but not choppy. Be sure that your sentences are not so long that you lose your train of thought before you come to the end. Next, check your draft to make sure that all sentences are correctly constructed and punctuated. Finally, proofread your essay and make a clean copy for your teacher.

Phrases and Clauses

Different types and uses of phrases and clauses can help you vary sentence structure in your writing. This section explains the functions of both phrases and clauses.

Phrases

A **phrase** is a group of related words that functions as a single part of speech but lacks a subject, a predicate, or both. This section deals with three common kinds of phrases: prepositional phrases, appositive phrases, and verbal phrases.

Prepositional Phrases

A **prepositional phrase** consists of a preposition and its object, including any modifiers of that object. In the following sentences, the prepositional phrases are in boldface type.

> Flemish artists **of the fifteenth century** liked to paint scenes **with rich textures and reflections in mirrors.** [The second prepositional phrase has a compound object of the preposition, *textures* and *reflections*. In addition, the prepositional phrase *in mirrors* modifies *reflections.*]

> **Which artist** are you thinking **of?** [**Think:** Of which artist are you thinking?]

Prepositional Phrases Used as Adjectives A prepositional phrase that modifies a noun or a pronoun functions as an adjective. Such a phrase is sometimes called an **adjective phrase.**

> MODIFIES NOUN   The round, convex *mirrors* **in these paintings** reflect things in miniature.

> MODIFIES PRONOUN   *One* **of these paintings** is a van Eyck portrait.

Prepositional Phrases Used as Adverbs A prepositional phrase functions as an adverb if it modifies a verb, an adjective, or another adverb. This kind of prepositional phrase is sometimes called an **adverb phrase.**

> MODIFIES VERB   The Dutch and Flemish portraitists *painted* lace, velvet, and brocade **with great skill.**

MODIFIES ADJECTIVE   They were *curious* **about reflections** too.

MODIFIES ADVERB   They painted various textures *down* **to the smallest detail.**

A prepositional phrase can modify the object in another prepositional phrase.

There is a mirror in the *middle* **of the** *portrait* by Jan van Eyck.

Appositives and Appositive Phrases

An **appositive** is a noun or a pronoun placed near another noun or pronoun to explain it or identify it.

The Italian *explorer,* **Giovanni da Verrazano,** was employed by King Francis I of France.

Will *we* **tourists** get a chance to see the Verrazano-Narrows Bridge?

Verrazano, **navigator and pirate,** visited New York harbor in 1524. [The sentence has a compound appositive, *navigator* and *pirate.*]

Appositive Phrases   Like an appositive, an **appositive phrase** explains or identifies a noun or a pronoun. It includes all the words or phrases that modify an appositive.

The Verrazano-Narrows Bridge, **a beautiful sight,** connects Brooklyn and Staten Island.

Even *we* **native New Yorkers** did not know who Verrazano was.

A successful enterprise, Verrazano's *expedition* of 1524 explored the North American coast.

Essential and Nonessential Appositives   An **essential appositive** or an **essential appositive phrase** is an appositive that is necessary to the meaning of the sentence. This kind of appositive should not be separated from the rest of the sentence with a comma.

New York City's *landmark* **the Verrazano-Narrows Bridge** is longer than the nearby George Washington Bridge. [New York City has more than one landmark. The appositive is necessary to identify which landmark.]

A **nonessential appositive** or a **nonessential appositive phrase** is an appositive that is not necessary to the meaning of the sentence. Such an appositive should be set off with a comma or commas.

───── appositive phrase ─────
The Verrazano-Narrows Bridge, **a New York City landmark,** is longer than the nearby George Washington Bridge. [The appositive is not necessary to identify the bridge being discussed.]

Exercise 1 **Prepositional and Appositive Phrases**

**? Critical
Thinking:**

How can I use a phrase to identify the noun?

Number your paper from 1 to 15. Next to each number, write a prepositional or an appositive phrase to complete the sentence. Use the kind of phrase that is indicated.

SAMPLE The Renaissance, (1) (appositive phrase), brought changes (2) (prepositional phrase) as well as in large ones.

ANSWER 1. a time of great originality
2. in small things

Our most common table utensil, (1) (appositive phrase), first appeared in the sixteenth century. Before that, people ate with the "utensils" everyone had at hand, (2) (appositive phrase). Diners simply sat around a big bowl or platter and pulled from it chunks (3) (prepositional phrase). The only artificial aid, (4) (appositive phrase), was used for slicing or spearing choice morsels. Since few hosts could afford a whole set of knives, guests usually brought their own knives (5) (prepositional phrase).

The third member of the table trio, (6) (appositive phrase), began to be used widely around the same time as forks and knives did. Spoons, which were set (7) (prepositional phrase) with the other utensils, were most useful (8) (prepositional phrase). Earlier, such dishes were sopped up (9) (prepositional phrase). As an alternative, the guests might pass a single, large spoon (10) (prepositional phrase). Even with individual spoons, most diners still ate soups or stews (11) (prepositional phrase), taking turns. Individual bowls, like individual knives, were affordable only (12) (prepositional phrase).

Even the highest levels of society, (13) (appositive phrase), were slow to adopt such implements. Centuries passed before the modern table setting — (14) (appositive phrase) — filtered down to ordinary people. Even today, we still eat sandwiches and many other foods the old-fashioned way — (15) (prepositional phrase).

Verbals

Verbals are verb forms that function as nouns, adjectives, or adverbs but retain some of the properties of verbs. For instance, they express action or being, and they may take complements. There are three kinds of verbals: participles, gerunds, and infinitives.

Participles A **participle** is a verb form that can function as an adjective while still keeping some of the properties of a verb. It expresses action or being, and it may take a complement.

Annoyed, *Pablo* missed the **guided** *tour* through Rembrandt's house in Amsterdam. [Both *annoyed* and *guided* are participles.]

There are two kinds of participles: present participles and past participles. They are two of the four principal parts of a verb. (For a complete explanation of the principal parts of verbs, see pages 620–622.)

To form a present participle, add *-ing* to the infinitive form of a verb.

Did he finally figure out those **puzzling** *directions?* [*Puzzling* is a present participle that consists of the verb *puzzle* and the ending, *-ing.*]

To form a past participle, first determine whether the verb is regular or irregular *(pages 620–622)*.

1. *Regular verbs.* To form the past participle of a regular verb, add either *-d* or *-ed* to the infinitive form of the verb.

INFINITIVE	PAST PARTICIPLE
exhaust	exhausted

2. *Irregular verbs.* To form the past participle of an irregular verb, use a special form of the verb. (See pages 621–622 for a list of past participles of commonly used irregular verbs.)

INFINITIVE	PAST PARTICIPLE
freeze	frozen
tear	torn

As you recall, besides functioning as adjectives, present participles and past participles can form part of a verb phrase. When a participle functions as a verb, it is not a verbal. This section deals with present participles and past participles that function as adjectives. (For an explanation of participles used as verbs, see pages 620–622.)

A participle used as an adjective may have one or more auxiliary verbs. The auxiliary verb and the participle function as a unit to modify a noun or a pronoun.

Having been lost, *Pablo* vowed never to drive in Amsterdam again without a map. [*Having* and *been* are the auxiliary verbs, and *lost* is the participle.]

Participial Phrases A **participial phrase** consists of a participle and its modifiers and complements. The participial phrase functions as an adjective to modify a noun or a pronoun. Both present participles and past participles may be used to form participial phrases.

There is *Pablo* **waiting in line** to see Rembrandt's house.

Exasperated by his difficulty finding the house, *Pablo* was almost ready to leave without seeing it.

Having finally seen the small museum, *Pablo* felt that his perseverance had been worthwhile.

Notice that in the preceding sentences, the participial phrases are near the words that they modify. If they were placed differently, the meaning of the sentence could change or become unclear.

Having finally seen the small museum, his perseverance had been worthwhile to Pablo.

(For an explanation of the correct placement of participial phrases, see page 668.)

Another kind of phrase that is formed with participles is the absolute phrase. An **absolute phrase** modifies the entire independent clause *(pages 587–588)* of the sentence; it does not have a direct grammatical connection with any single word in the independent clause. An absolute phrase contains both a participle and the noun or pronoun that is modified by the participle. Consequently, the phrase is "absolute," or complete within itself.

The museum being full of Rembrandt's works and other belongings, Pablo spent a long time there. [The absolute phrase modifies the entire independent clause by telling why Pablo spent a long time there.]

Exercise 2 Combining Sentences Using Participial Phrases

? Critical Thinking:
How can I change one sentence into a participial phrase?

On your paper, combine each of the following pairs of sentences by rewriting one sentence as a participial phrase. Underline the participial phrases in your sentences. You may use absolute phrases.

SAMPLE   We are accustomed to modern comforts. Most of us would dislike many aspects of Renaissance life.

ANSWER   Being accustomed to modern comforts, most of us would dislike many aspects of Renaissance life.

1. The house of a poor peasant was a rough wooden structure with a thatched roof. Such a dwelling was more hut than house.
2. The house consisted of a single room. This room served as living room, kitchen, and bedroom for the whole family.
3. Houses had few furnishings. They usually consisted of a bench or two, a table, perhaps a cupboard, and a few pots and pans.
4. Feather mattresses had not yet reached the masses. The bed often was no more than a pile of straw on the packed-dirt floor.

5. Candles were luxuries. The only light after sunset came from the fire on the brick hearth.
6. The house of a middle-class farmer or artisan might have several rooms. It provided privacy unknown to the peasant.
7. The floor was inset tile. Wooden floors did not become popular until later.
8. The windows might have the newly available glass. Thus they improved on the crude shutters of the peasant's hovel.
9. The house would look rather bare to us. The furniture was better but not much more plentiful than in poorer homes.
10. Nightfall might or might not bring candlelight. It depended on the owner's willingness to spend money.
11. We have heard of the wealth of families like the Medicis. We might expect their dwellings to be luxurious even by today's standards.
12. True, these palaces had many rooms, countless candles, great art, and fine furniture. The furniture included down mattresses.
13. However, they were limited like all other homes by their times. They would seem uncomfortable to people today.
14. The only heat came from very inefficient fireplaces. This left even palaces bitterly cold in winter.
15. Consider all of this. Would you trade central heating for a chance to meet Michelangelo?

Gerunds   A **gerund** is a verbal that ends in *-ing* and functions as a noun while keeping some of the properties of a verb. It expresses action or being, and it may take a complement such as a direct object or an indirect object.

USED AS SUBJECT
Reading was not a widespread skill during the Renaissance.

USED AS DIRECT OBJECT
Don't forget **exploring** when you think of Renaissance achievements.

USED AS INDIRECT OBJECT
Historians give **printing** credit for changing Renaissance life.

USED AS OBJECT OF PREPOSITION
Many lessons in **drawing** can be learned from the sketchbooks of Leonardo da Vinci.

USED AS PREDICATE NOMINATIVE
The way most Renaissance people spent their time was **working.**

USED AS APPOSITIVE
My favorite pastime, **reading,** is how I learned about the Renaissance.

Be sure that you can distinguish between gerunds and participles. They are identical in form, but participles can function as adjectives, while gerunds always function as nouns.

Gerund Phrases A **gerund phrase** consists of a gerund and its modifiers and complements.

┌──────gerund phrase──────┐
The pushing of the crowd all but prevented us from **buying our tickets**

┌──────gerund phrase──────┐
to the Rembrandt exhibit.

Like a gerund, a gerund phrase may perform as a noun.

USED AS SUBJECT
Taking photographs is not permitted at the Rembrandt exhibit.

USED AS DIRECT OBJECT
Notice how Rembrandt emphasized **depicting textures in both light and shadow.**

USED AS INDIRECT OBJECT
He also gave **illustrating biblical stories** a high priority.

USED AS OBJECT OF PREPOSITION
Rembrandt was extraordinarily skilled at **revealing the personalities of his subjects.**

USED AS PREDICATE NOMINATIVE
A way to increase your appreciation of a Rembrandt painting is **stepping back and looking from a distance.**

USED AS APPOSITIVE
This experience, **seeing so many Rembrandts in one exhibit,** is a rare opportunity.

Exercise 3 | Combining Sentences Using Gerund Phrases

**? Critical
? Thinking:**
What functions does a gerund phrase perform?

On your paper, combine each of the following pairs of sentences, using gerund phrases. Underline each gerund phrase and label it *Subject, Direct object, Indirect object, Object of a preposition, Predicate nominative,* or *Appositive.*

SAMPLE In Renaissance times, people traveled the European countryside. It was a slow, difficult, and dangerous endeavor.

ANSWER Traveling the European countryside in Renaissance times was a slow, difficult, and dangerous endeavor. — Subject

1. Until about 1500, land travelers had only two options. They walked or rode horseback.
2. Only the wealthy rode horseback. Only they could afford it.
3. Most people had no alternative. They went on foot.
4. People covered twenty or thirty miles a day by horse. Any more than that was unusual, except in emergencies.
5. Some covered nearly as much ground on foot. It was not uncommon for a good walker.

6. In the 1500s, a third travel option became available. People could go by coach.
7. Most people still made their journeys on foot. They preferred it to the slow and miserably uncomfortable early coaches.
8. People met danger on the rough, trail-like roads. It was something every traveler expected in those days.
9. Some people were robbed by bandits. This was at least as common as flat tires or other car problems today.
10. Travelers grouped together whenever possible. It was their best defense against "highway robbery."
11. Hostels or inns were built along the main roads. Even kings gave this high priority.
12. People stayed at these inns. It was better than a night in the forest, but hardly a pleasant experience.
13. People slept in the same shed as the animals. This was more the rule than the exception.
14. Some people had an actual bed. This did not guarantee a good night's sleep.
15. People faced such hardship. It was not unusual then but simply part of normal life.

Infinitives   An **infinitive** is a verbal that consists of the first principal part *(pages 620–621)* of the verb. The word *to* usually, though not always, precedes the infinitive. An infinitive may function as a noun, an adjective, or an adverb. Like a participle and a gerund, an infinitive has some of the characteristics of a verb. It expresses action or being and may take a complement.

NOUN FUNCTION
To explore was one of the goals of Renaissance monarchs. [subject]
Because they could claim the lands they discovered, Renaissance monarchs wanted **to explore.** [direct object]
The purpose of many expeditions was **to explore** and **to conquer.** [predicate nominative]

ADJECTIVE FUNCTION
Many navigators went to various Renaissance monarchs seeking a

chance **to explore.** [What kind of chance? The chance to explore.]

ADVERB FUNCTION

Finding gold was another goal of those who *went* **to explore.** [Why did the people go? They went *to explore.*]

Being robbed by pirates was a risk for treasure-laden ships that were too

slow **to escape.** [To what extent were the ships slow? They were too slow *to escape.*]

You may form an infinitive with one or more auxiliary verbs and a past participle. Such infinitives indicate the time of the action.

The *place* **to have been** in the 1400s was the city of Florence.

Much of the *art* **to be studied** in our Renaissance art class is still in Florence today.

Note: Do not confuse infinitives and prepositional phrases. *To* followed by a verb is an infinitive; but *to* followed by a noun or a pronoun is a prepositional phrase.

Infinitive Phrases   An **infinitive phrase** consists of an infinitive and its modifiers and complements. An infinitive phrase can function as a noun, an adjective, or an adverb.

NOUN FUNCTION   **To visit the city of Florence** is my dream.

ADJECTIVE FUNCTION   Florence is the best *place* **to get the "flavor" of the Italian Renaissance.** [Which place? The place *to get the flavor of the Italian Renaissance.*]

ADVERB FUNCTION   Many tourists *come* **to see the art treasures of Florence.** [Why do the tourists come? They come *to see the art treasures of Florence.*]

Sometimes an infinitive phrase may be used without the word *to*.

Will you help **plan my trip to Florence?** [**Think:** help *to* plan my trip to Florence.]
My parents' travel agent helped **choose our itinerary.** [**Think:** helped *to* choose our itinerary.]

Exercise 4   Combining Sentences Using Infinitives

? Critical Thinking:

What functions can an infinitive phrase perform?

On your paper, combine each of the following sets of sentences, using at least one infinitive phrase. Underline the infinitive phrases.

SAMPLE   People have always welcomed a good story. It entertained them.

ANSWER   People have always welcomed a good story to entertain them.

1. Today we have television, movies, books, and other media. They provide us with stories.
2. Someone writes these books and scripts. It is someone's job.
3. During the Renaissance most people, even kings and queens, did not read stories or anything else. They did not know how.

4. Courts often hired storytellers. The storytellers entertained the royal family and their court.
5. In general, priests could read. They were the only ones so able, although the language they used was Latin.
6. Perhaps the new interest in learning in the Renaissance inspired Giovanni Boccaccio. He began his great *Decameron* in 1350.
7. Not only was the *Decameron* a book of stories rather than a priestly text, but Boccaccio made a landmark decision. He used everyday Italian instead of Latin.
8. The tale begins with ten young aristocrats fleeing the city of Florence. They are escaping the plague of 1348.
9. Like most wealthy city dwellers in plague years, the group travels to a country estate. They wait out the epidemic.
10. They pass the long days and nights. They decide that each of them must tell ten stories — a total of one hundred.
11. The stories' natural style and down-to-earth content persuaded readers. They snapped up copies as fast as they could be printed.
12. Boccaccio's success may have influenced England's Geoffrey Chaucer. He tried something similar with his *Canterbury Tales*.
13. Chaucer's storytellers were people who had gathered together from all walks of life. They were making a pilgrimage.
14. Like Boccaccio, Chaucer wrote in the common language of his country, and he carefully selected each tale. The tale fit the personality of the storyteller.
15. He intended a long work like the *Decameron*, but his health did not allow him. He did not complete all of the intended tales.

Clauses

A **clause** is a group of related words that contains both a subject and a predicate. There are two kinds of clauses: independent clauses and subordinate clauses.

Independent Clauses

An **independent clause** can stand by itself as a sentence. The following sentence contains two independent clauses, which are in boldface type. Notice that each clause has a subject and a predicate and that each could be a separate sentence. The subject is underlined once, and the predicate is underlined twice.

> **Albrecht Dürer is best known as a painter and printmaker,** but **he was also an author and scholar.**

A comma and the coordinating conjunction *but* join the clauses in the preceding sentence. *But* is not part of either clause. Rather, it coordinates, or connects, the independent clauses. The other coordinating conjunctions are *and, or, nor, for,* and *yet.*

You can also join independent clauses with either a semicolon alone or a semicolon and a conjunctive adverb *(pages 562–563)*.

> Dürer's diary, letters, and memoirs of his family survive today; scholars know more about him than about many other Renaissance artists. [semicolon]

> Dürer's diary, letters, and memoirs of his family survive today; **therefore,** scholars know more about him than about many other Renaissance artists. [semicolon and conjunctive adverb]

Subordinate Clauses

A clause that cannot stand by itself is a **subordinate clause.** This kind of clause is sometimes called a **dependent clause.** Although a subordinate clause has both a subject and a predicate, it cannot stand by itself because it does not express a complete thought. In the following examples, the subjects are underlined once, and the predicates are underlined twice.

> Which is one of Dürer's self-portraits
> While he was painting in the Alps
> Although his prints are more famous

Notice that the preceding subordinate clauses begin with the words *which, while,* and *although. Which* is a relative pronoun *(pages 537–538)*, and *while* and *although* are subordinating conjunctions *(pages 561–562)*. Many subordinate clauses begin with either a relative pronoun or a subordinating conjunction. Such introductory words are part of the subordinate clause, and they join the subordinate clause to an independent clause.

> ┌──── indep. clause ────┐ ┌──── sub. clause ────┐
> Most critics admire this 1500 painting, **which** is one of Dürer's
> self-portraits.

> ┌──── indep. clause ────┐ ┌──── sub. clause ────┐
> Dürer kept a travel diary **while** he was painting in the Alps.

> ┌──── sub. clause ────┐ ┌──── indep. clause ────┐
> **Although** his prints are more famous, Dürer was one of the first artists to
> paint water colors from nature.

Adjective Clauses A subordinate clause functions as an adjective if it modifies a noun or a pronoun. Such clauses are called **adjective clauses.** Most adjective clauses begin with a relative pronoun such as *that, which, who, whom,* and *whose.*

> ┌──── adj. clause ────┐
> Many of the *paintings* **that** Dürer did early in his career are self-portraits. [Which paintings? The paintings *that Dürer did early in his career.*]

adj. clause

I can't think of an *artist* **whose** prints are more famous than Dürer's. [Which artist? The artist *whose prints are more famous than Dürer's.*]

You may also begin adjective clauses with relative adverbs. Some of the relative adverbs are *after, before, since, when,* and *where.*

adj. clause

The *years* **since** Dürer first experimented with etching have brought many changes in printmaking. [Which years? The years *since Dürer first experimented with etching.*]

Sometimes the introductory word in an adjective clause is implied.

The *woodcuts* **Dürer did** are often of religious scenes. [**Think:** woodcuts *that* Dürer did.]

Essential and Nonessential Clauses An adjective clause that is necessary to identify a noun or a pronoun is an **essential clause.** An essential clause is not separated from the rest of the sentence by commas.

ESSENTIAL CLAUSE

adj. clause

Dürer wrote *books* **that** deal with perspective, geometry, the theory of art, and civil defense. [The clause is essential in order to identify the books.]

A nonessential clause is an adjective clause that is not necessary to identify a noun or a pronoun. It is set off by commas.

NONESSENTIAL CLAUSE

adj. clause

Praying Hands, **which** was engraved in 1508, was a study for a church altarpiece. [The clause is nonessential because without it, the reader would still know which painting is being discussed.]

Exercise 5 Combining Sentences Using Adjective Clauses

On your paper, combine the following sets of sentences by writing one or more of the sentences as adjective clauses. Underline the adjective clauses in your rewritten sentences.

Critical Thinking: How are adjective clauses used in a sentence?

SAMPLE   Renaissance education was vastly different from our system. It definitely was not for everyone or even for most people. Our system tries to reach all potential students.

ANSWER   Renaissance education, which definitely was not for everyone or even for most people, was vastly different from our system, which tries to reach all potential students.

1. The Italian city of Florence was the wellspring of the Renaissance. It had as good an educational system as any other in Europe.

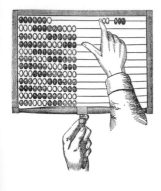

2. In the 1340s a study was made of Florentine schools. There were about ten thousand students in the system.

3. These ten thousand students all were boys. They represented about ten percent of the city's population. This was a very high figure for the time.

4. They learned basic reading and writing skills. These skills would enable them to do most of the ordinary jobs in Florence's complex society.

5. Of the ten thousand there were only about one thousand lucky ones. They went on to the higher education. This education was needed for the complicated and profitable merchant life.

6. These one thousand learned arithmetic, bookkeeping, and how to use the abacus. The abacus was the computer of its day.

7. When they were about eighteen years old, a final five hundred were chosen. They would go to the university. There, they would study Latin and other skills needed for professions such as the law.

8. In all cases, rote learning was the main teaching method. It required a great deal of repetition and memorization.

9. Often, the teacher simply read aloud from a book. This was perhaps natural before the invention of printing. There was rarely more than one copy of any book available.

10. Girls were not part of this system. They did receive some education. It was aimed mainly at making them good homemakers.

11. Most girls learned "feminine" skills and a few learned basic literacy. The former included sewing, weaving, and dancing. The latter was helpful in running a large household.

12. A very few girls received a more formal education. It required private tutors. Such girls probably did not number more than a dozen in a century.

13. Florence was the richest city of its time. It had a great need for educated people. They could run its elaborate commerce and plot its tricky state policies.

14. Other Italian cities promoted education somewhat less. These cities trailed Florence but were far ahead of the rest of Europe.

15. France and England had not yet begun their Renaissance. In those countries, even the highest nobles had almost no formal learning. Their Renaissance would begin in the next century.

16. Even young children were treated like small adults in these countries. They went to work in the fields at a young age. They would labor there all their lives.

17. A few were more fortunate. They were apprenticed to craftspeople such as blacksmiths or millers. These people taught them a trade in return for work.

18. Of course, the people of these countries were products of their time and place. They might have wondered why they needed more education. They had always done without it before.

Adverb Clauses   A subordinate clause functions as an adverb when it modifies a verb, an adjective, or another adverb. Such clauses are called **adverb clauses.**

MODIFIES VERB

The Spaniards *called* Domenikos Theotokopoulus "El Greco" **because he** —adj. clause

came from Greece.

MODIFIES ADJECTIVE

I'm *sure* **that El Greco's famous landscape is of Toledo, Spain.** — adv. clause —

MODIFIES ADVERB

For my research paper, I studied the influence of the style called "manner-

ism" on El Greco's painting more *thoroughly* **than the teacher had** —adv. clause—

expected.

An adverb clause always begins with a subordinating conjunction *(pages 561–562)*, which is a word that shows the relationship between the subordinate clause and the independent clause. (A list of frequently used subordinating conjunctions is on page 562.) Adverb clauses tell *how, when, where, to what extent,* and *why.* In the following examples, the subordinating conjunctions are in boldface type.

HOW

El Greco sometimes *painted* **as though** he were religiously inspired. —adv. clause —

WHEN

— adv. clause—
While he lived in Toledo, El Greco *painted* many portraits.

WHERE

I *will meet* you **where** the El Greco portraits are displayed. — adv. clause —

TO WHAT EXTENT

I find El Greco so *fascinating* **that** I am going to do my paper about him. —adv. clause —

WHY

—adv. clause—
Because they are distorted in color and form, some of his figures *have* an unearthly appearance.

Elliptical Clauses An **elliptical clause** is an adverb clause in which part of the clause is omitted. Even though the clause is incomplete, its meaning is clear; therefore, it is still classified as a clause.

adv. clause
Miriam knows *more* about El Greco **than I.** [**Think:** Miriam knows more than I know. *Than I* modifies *more.*]

adv. clause
While visiting Spain, she *had* a chance to see many El Greco originals. [**Think:** while she was visiting Spain.]

Exercise 6 Combining Sentences Using Adverb Clauses

Critical Thinking:
Which sentences can be changed into adverb clauses?

On your paper, combine the following sets of sentences by rewriting one or more of the sentences as an adverb clause. Underline the adverb clauses.

SAMPLE Everyone recognizes the development of the printing press as a great Renaissance breakthrough. Not much attention is given to advances in paper making.

ANSWER While everyone recognizes the development of the printing press as a great Renaissance breakthrough, not much attention is given to advances in paper making.

1. Suppose that paper had not been invented. The printing press would have been like a car without gasoline.
2. Paper's predecessor, parchment, was both beautiful and strong. These qualities made it ideal for important manuscripts.
3. Parchment was also expensive. It was made of sheepskin.
4. Besides, parchment's surface was very uneven. It was useless for the early printing presses.
5. Paper was cheap and smooth. It was a more logical material for large quantities of printed matter.
6. Paper making was already reasonably advanced. Then the first printing presses came along.
7. Basically, early paper making involved pounding cloth rags in a solution of water and chemicals. The fibers were tightly bound together.
8. The mixture was pressed to the desired thickness. Then it was dried into a flat sheet.
9. Almost any cloth fiber was suitable for this process. Rags and other such low-cost materials produced a very long-lasting paper.
10. Today's quickly degraded, wood-pulp paper might have been invented first. We would have few books from the last century, let alone from the Renaissance.
11. Paper mills required water both as an ingredient and for power. They were invariably built beside rivers.

12. Furthermore, the water had to be pure and clear. It would not discolor or otherwise harm the paper.
13. For this reason, mills were located upstream of towns. At these locations there was less risk of pollution.
14. Today, the mill would be considered the polluter. The situation would be reversed.
15. The printing industry boomed in the late Renaissance. Demand for raw materials for paper making exceeded the supply.

Noun Clauses   A subordinate clause that functions as a noun is called a **noun clause.**   A noun clause may function as a subject, a predicate nominative, a direct object, an indirect object, an object of a preposition, or an appositive.

SUBJECT

───── noun clause ─────

How the invention of gunpowder changed Renaissance life is the topic of today's lecture.

PREDICATE NOMINATIVE

───── noun clause ─────

The turning point was **when cannon became powerful enough to destroy the protective walls around cities.**

DIRECT OBJECT

───── noun clause ─────

City dwellers found **that their stone walls no longer protected them from their enemies.**

INDIRECT OBJECT

───── noun clause ─────

The walls did not give **whoever lived within the city** better protection than they did to those who moved outside to the new "suburbs."

OBJECT OF A PREPOSITION

───── noun clause ─────

Victory in a war now went to **whichever side had better artillery.**

APPOSITIVE

───── noun clause ─────

Larger cannon required larger and stronger gun carriages, **whatever could support the tremendous weight.**

You may introduce a noun clause with a relative pronoun or a subordinating conjunction.

RELATIVE PRONOUNS
who, whom, whose, which, what, whoever, whomever, whatever, whichever

SUBORDINATING CONJUNCTIONS
how, that, when, where, whether, why

Sometimes you may construct a noun clause without using an introductory word.

Did you know **improvements in gun carriages led to improvements in road building?** [**Think:** know *that* improvements in gun carriages caused improvements in road building.]

One particular kind of noun clause is the **infinitive clause.** It consists of an infinitive that has a subject. If the subject of the infinitive is a pronoun, that pronoun is in the objective case *(pages 653–654)* as if it were the direct object of the preceding verb. However, it is not; the entire infinitive clause serves as the direct object of the preceding verb.

They built **roads to be wider and stronger.** [*Roads* is the subject of the infinitive.]

They designed **them to support the weight of the heavier wagons and artillery.** [*Them* is the subject of the infinitive.]

Renaissance engineers developed **pavement to serve this purpose.**

Thus gunpowder caused **Renaissance engineers to build the first paved roads.**

Exercise 7 Noun Clauses

On your paper, copy each of the following sentences and underline each noun clause. Then write how the noun clause is used in the sentence.

Critical Thinking:
Which clause is functioning as a noun?

SAMPLE   What did most of the work in Renaissance society was horse-power, in the literal sense of the word.

ANSWER   What did most of the work of Renaissance society was horse-power, in the literal sense of the word. (subject)

1. Horses and oxen were what powered the Renaissance.
2. How important these animals were is obvious from an analysis of energy use in Renaissance times.
3. In terms of energy expended, animal power accounted for over half of what was done.
4. As for the next greatest energy source, you can guess what it was.

5. What part wood played is indicated by the fact that its burning made up twenty-five percent of the entire energy picture of Renaissance Europe.
6. Water mills accounted for the largest part of what remains of this energy picture.
7. Since people worked very hard during the Renaissance, let's see what their energy contributed.
8. What human beings did amounted to about one twentieth of the total energy output.
9. What animals did, by comparison, represents about ten times the work put out by their human masters.
10. Before we start thinking of Renaissance people as lazy, consider how much stronger animals are.
11. Compared with horsepower, the average person can do only about one twelfth of what a horse can do.
12. Match up the figures from the Renaissance and see how people and animals compared regarding work.
13. Did you know that people in the Renaissance seem to have worked considerably harder than their animals?
14. What remains of the energy picture besides animal power, wood-burning, water mills, and human work is insignificant.
15. However, one other energy source did provide power in a somewhat unpredictable way; think of a windmill or a sailboat and you will guess that this energy source was the wind.

Sentences Classified by Structure

Sentences are classified according to the number and kinds of clauses that they contain. The four kinds of sentences are simple, compound, complex, and compound-complex.

Simple Sentences   A sentence containing one independent clause and no subordinate clauses is a **simple sentence.** It may have any number of phrases, and it may have a compound subject, a compound predicate, or both. However, it has only one clause.

> Biblical stories, classical scenes, and portraits were all popular subjects for painting during the Renaissance.
> Renaissance artists studied Greek and Roman statuary, taking much of their inspiration from it.

Compound Sentences   A sentence consisting of two or more independent clauses but no subordinate clauses is a **compound sentence.** The independent clauses are usually joined with a comma and one of the coordinating conjunctions: *and, but, nor, or, for,* or *yet.*

> Giotto painted many church frescoes, **but** he was also an architect.

Independent clauses may also be joined with a semicolon or with a semicolon and a conjunctive adverb such as *nonetheless, consequently,* or *still (pages 562–563).* A comma usually follows the conjunctive adverb.

┌────────────────────indep. clause────────────────────┐
His figures are not painted in the flat, decorative medieval manner;

┌──────────────indep. clause──────────────┐
they are solid and natural looking.

┌──────────────────────indep. clause──────────────────────┐
Giotto is the first important Italian painter to break away from the medie-

┌───────────────────────indep. clause───────────────────────┐
val style; **consequently,** he is sometimes called the "first Renaissance

artist."

Complex Sentences   A sentence consisting of one independent clause and one or more subordinate clauses is a **complex sentence.**

┌──────────────sub. clause──────────────┐ ┌──────────indep. clause──────────┐
Although they have been damaged by time, some of Giotto's frescoes can

still be seen in Florence today.

┌indep. clause₁┐ ┌──────────────sub. clause──────────────┐ ┌──
The frescoes, which are painted directly into plaster walls, are badly in

┌──────indep. clause──────┐
need of restoration. [The sentence contains one independent clause: *The frescoes are badly in need of restoration.* That clause contains a subordinate clause: *which are painted directly on plaster walls.*]

Compound-Complex Sentences   A sentence consisting of two or more independent clauses and one or more subordinate clauses is a **compound-complex sentence.**

┌──────────────────sub. clause──────────────────┐ ┌──
While many of Giotto's later works are well known, it is not certain that he

┌──────────indep. clause──────────┐ ┌──────────indep. clause──────────┐
worked on the frescoes in Assisi, and much about his early life is also

unknown.

┌──────────────sub. clause──────────────┐ ┌──────────indep. clause──────────┐
Though he was born into poverty, Giotto became successful as an artist,

┌─────indep. clause──────────────────────────────────────┐
┌──────────────sub. clause──────────────┐
and his work, which greatly influenced later Renaissance painters, is still

prized today. [The second independent clause, *his work is still prized today,* is interrupted by the subordinate clause *which greatly influenced later Renaissance artists.*]

┌──────────────┐
│ **Exercise 8** │ **Sentence Combining: Sentence Classification**
└──────────────┘
Each of the following items consists of a set of sentences. Combine each set to make one sentence, and write that sentence on your paper.

Label the sentences that you write *Simple, Compound, Complex,* or *Compound-Complex.*

SAMPLE Most of us today take running water, and plenty of it, for granted. People in the Renaissance could not and did not.

ANSWER Most of us today take running water, and plenty of it, for granted, but people in the Renaissance could not and did not. — Compound

1. Even the smallest village had its nearby stream, river, or other water supply. Otherwise, the village would not have existed.
2. Availability of water is one thing. Access to it is another. Getting enough water during the Renaissance usually meant hard work.
3. Someone in each family had to carry water. He or she made as many trips as necessary with buckets or jars.
4. Large riverside cities went through the same process. They did it on a much larger scale.
5. For example, Paris at one time had some thirty thousand professional water carriers. Their job was to haul water from the Seine River.
6. A carrier might deliver sixty buckets of water, two at a time, to the fifth floor of a building. There were no elevators. The pay was pocket change.
7. Even worse, from our point of view, was the quality of the water. It was polluted at best. At the worst, it was deadly.
8. London's Thames River was equally filthy. Water from it was sent through wooden pipes three times a week to private houses. There it stagnated in storage tanks.
9. Segovia, Spain, was luckier. It had repaired an old Roman aqueduct. Its supply of clean water was the envy of visitors.
10. Venice had an unusual water system. This city is surrounded by water. Unfortunately, all of it is salt water.
11. Visitors often commented on Venice's many wells. They were not wells, however, but cisterns.
12. Each cistern was a huge ceramic bowl. It was set in the earth and filled with fine sand. It had a hollow shaft in the middle.
13. Rainwater seeped down through the sand. The sand helped to purify it. It was later drawn up through the shaft.
14. Despite its cisterns, Venice often had to bring in fresh water by barge. The cisterns ran dry in droughts. They became fouled with salt water during storms.
15. Some towns on high riverbanks raised their water with pumps. The pumps, in turn, were driven by water wheels in the current. Water was being used to get water.
16. Cities near mountains had snow melt or snow itself. Someone had to fetch the snow from the peaks. This form of water was used mainly to cool the midsummer drinks of the rich.

17. Perhaps sailors had the worst lot. Barreled shipboard water almost always went bad. No one could find a way to save it.
18. Water was harder to get in the Renaissance than now. People used less of it. They probably didn't think much about this fact.
19. Most people considered bathing positively unhealthy. They avoided it as long as possible. This, for many people, meant all winter.
20. The modern custom of watering a lawn might have amused people of the Renaissance. Grass, in Renaissance times, was a weed. No one would water a weed.

Writing Complete Sentences

A **complete sentence** is a group of words that has at least one subject and one predicate and that expresses a complete thought. You should use complete sentences in your writing. Two common errors in writing are the use of sentence fragments and run-on sentences. In this section you will learn how to recognize and correct both kinds of errors.

Avoiding Sentence Fragments

A **sentence fragment** is a group of words that lacks a subject or a predicate or that does not express a complete thought.

COMPLETE SENTENCE
Harriet planned to visit Florence on her trip to Italy.

FRAGMENT
Harriet planned. **To visit Florence on her trip to Italy.** [The second group of words lacks a subject and a predicate.]

FRAGMENT
Harriet, planning to visit Florence on her trip to Italy. [The group of words lacks a predicate.]

If the sentence fragment is a phrase, you can correct it by combining the fragment with a related sentence.

FRAGMENT
During her stay. She would like to see Michelangelo's *David*.

COMPLETE SENTENCE

┌── prep. phrase ──┐
During her stay, she would like to see Michelangelo's *David*.

FRAGMENT
Florence is the home of the Uffizi Gallery. **One of the world's great art museums.**

COMPLETE SENTENCE ┌── appositive phrase ──┐
Florence is the home of the Uffizi Gallery, **one of the world's great art museums.**

FRAGMENT

To see the Renaissance frescoes and sculpture. That is what Harriet wants to do.

COMPLETE SENTENCE

Harriet wants **to see the Renaissance frescoes and sculpture.** [infin. phrase]

FRAGMENT

Harriet should also visit the cathedral. **Located in the heart of the city.**

COMPLETE SENTENCE

She should visit the cathedral, **located in the heart of the city.** [participial phrase]

FRAGMENT

Climbing to the top of the cathedral. That requires great energy.

COMPLETE SENTENCE

Climbing to the top of the cathedral requires great energy. [gerund phrase]

If the sentence fragment is a subordinate clause used without an independent clause, combine the fragment with a related sentence.

FRAGMENT

Many famous Renaissance artists worked on the Duomo. **Which features a dome designed by Brunelleschi.**

COMPLETE SENTENCE

Many famous Renaissance artists worked on the Duomo, **which features a dome designed by Brunelleschi.** [sub. clause]

FRAGMENT

Before she leaves Florence. Harriet should be sure to see the bronze baptistry doors by Ghiberti.

COMPLETE SENTENCE

Before she leaves Florence, Harriet should be sure to see the bronze baptistry doors by Ghiberti. [subordinate clause]

Some sentence fragments require additions or rewording.

FRAGMENT

The Renaissance, leaving its mark on Florence.

COMPLETE SENTENCE

The Renaissance left its mark on Florence.

FRAGMENT

The city, which is a mecca for art lovers.

COMPLETE SENTENCE

The city is a mecca for art lovers.

The following paragraphs contain sentence fragments. On your paper, rewrite the paragraphs, eliminating the sentence fragments.

SAMPLE   Some Renaissance art patrons gained immortality. Not for who they were, but for who gathered around them.

ANSWER   Some Renaissance art patrons gained immortality not for who they were, but for who gathered around them.

Isabella d'Este was one of the greatest. Renaissance patrons of the arts. Born in 1474. To the noblest family of Ferrara, Italy. As a girl, she was instructed. By some of Italy's greatest teachers. To have received such an education then. That was extremely unusual for a girl. By the time she married, at 16. She already was recognized as a cultured woman. During her life. Isabella displayed great diplomatic skill. This skill she applied in the service of her city. Helping to keep it one of the most powerful in Italy.

Yet Isabella's name would long ago have faded into oblivion. Except for one thing: She attracted to her court the greatest geniuses of the Renaissance. To have her portrait done by both Leonardo da Vinci and Titian. That was a kind of immortality in itself. Appearing, and sometimes living, at her court. There were many other outstanding artists, musicians, and writers. By all accounts, her intelligence and taste. They were as responsible for this gathering of greatness as her wealth and power.

Isabella gave her respect and her patronage. To such people as Leonardo. Through them, she gained a name. That still echoes down the centuries. You are reading about her, after all. More than 500 years after she was born.

Avoiding Run-On Sentences

A **run-on sentence** consists of two or more separate sentences written as one sentence. In some run-on sentences, only a comma separates the two sentences; in others there is no punctuation at all.

RUN-ON   Northern Renaissance artists painted many interior scenes with tile floors, doing so allowed them to experiment with perspective. [A comma by itself cannot connect two independent clauses. Such an error is often called a "common splice."]

RUN-ON   Northern Renaissance artists painted many interior scenes with tile floors doing so allowed them to experiment with perspective. [The sentences are run together without punctuation or a conjunction.]

CORRECT   Northern Renaissance artists painted many interior scenes with tile floors, for doing so allowed them to experiment with perspective. [A comma and the coordinating conjunction *for* connect the two clauses.]

There are several ways to correct run-on sentences. Read the following run-on sentence. Then study the five ways in which you can correct that sentence.

RUN-ON SENTENCE   Holland became prosperous during the Renaissance, Dutch paintings show comfortably furnished homes.

1. Separate the run-on sentence into two or more sentences.

   CORRECT   Holland became prosperous during the Renaissance. Dutch paintings show comfortably furnished homes.

2. Join the independent clauses with a comma and a coordinating conjunction *(page 559)*.

   CORRECT   Holland became prosperous during the Renaissance, **and** Dutch paintings show comfortably furnished homes.

3. Join the independent clauses with a semicolon.

   CORRECT   Holland became prosperous during the Renaissance; Dutch paintings show comfortably furnished homes.

4. Turn one of the independent clauses into a subordinate clause, and add a subordinating conjunction *(pages 561–562)* or a relative pronoun *(pages 537–538)*.

   CORRECT   **Because** Holland became prosperous during the Renaissance, Dutch paintings show comfortably furnished homes.

5. Join the independent clauses with a semicolon and a conjunctive adverb such as *also, thus, therefore, however, otherwise, instead,* or *finally (pages 562–563)*.

   CORRECT   Holland became prosperous during the Renaissance; **therefore,** Dutch paintings show comfortably furnished homes.

Exercise 10 Eliminating Run-On Sentences

The following paragraphs contain numerous run-on sentences. On your paper, rewrite the paragraphs, correcting each of the run-on sentences.

Critical Thinking:
How can I create separate sentences?

SAMPLE   A polymath is someone with knowledge or skill in many different areas the Renaissance is famous for such people.

ANSWER   A polymath is someone with knowledge or skill in many different areas, and the Renaissance is famous for such people.

Leonardo da Vinci was perhaps the most extraordinary mind of all time, almost no field of art or science was beyond the scope of his learning. Yet many other Renaissance men and women amaze us almost as much as Leonardo their talents and interests were so wide ranging. One of these many-sided geniuses was Benvenuto Cellini he was born a mason's son in 1500, during the height of the Italian Renaissance.

Cellini became the premier goldsmith of the age he was also a sculptor of great talent. This combination of skills is not surprising, the two fields have much in common. Many sculptors work in metal, a good goldsmith must have artistic talent. The surprising thing is Cellini's other career he was a *condottiere*, a commander of mercenary soldiers. His services were sought by numerous powerful leaders they were fighting the frequent intercity wars of the period. Cellini did not restrict himself to being a soldier he was also a cannon maker, an explosives expert, and a fortification designer.

We know more about Cellini than most people of his time, he revealed himself in his fascinating *Autobiography*. It shows him as a brash, brawling, extroverted man he was not above singing his own praises. Typically, Cellini was skilled as a writer he was skilled in all his other pursuits. The book amounts to an inside look at the Renaissance anyone interested in the era should read it.

The Writing Connection

Eliminating Sentence Fragments and Run-On Sentences

Whether you are writing a biography, a brochure, or a business letter, your sentences should always express complete thoughts. Incomplete sentences present your ideas in a fragmented or disconnected fashion. Run-on sentences are confusing because they do not tell your reader where one distinct idea ends and another begins. Readers often lose track of the message if the "signposts" provided by correctly punctuated complete sentences are missing or jumbled.

Don't worry if your prewriting or first drafts contain fragments or run-on sentences. At these stages, you are still determining what your ideas are and how best to express them. However, to make sure that your audience will understand your writing, you should revise it to eliminate fragments and run-on sentences. Correcting these errors will give your writing clarity and coherence.

Writing Assignment

A Plaque Inscription *Step 1:* To write your own plaque inscription, select one of the following topics or another of your choice.

- a plaque to honor a real or imaginary Renaissance writer, ruler, or artist
- a plaque to commemorate a real or invented historical event of the Renaissance
- a plaque to identify a real or imaginary Renaissance site or building

Step 2: To gather details, list words or phrases associated with your topic. You may wish to use some of the material in this unit for reference. *Step 3:* Turn your notes into complete sentences to create your plaque inscription. Refer to the previous exercise for form and style. *Step 4:* As you revise your writing, check to be certain that your tone and style suit your purpose and audience. Pay particular attention to sentence structure. Make your inscription as clear and concise as possible. *Step 5:* Proofread your inscription and make a clean copy. *Step 6:* Post it on a class bulletin board of inscriptions commemorating Renaissance people and achievements.

Parts of Speech (pages 532–565)

A. Identifying Specific Kinds of Nouns On your paper, write the nouns in italic type in each sentence. Label each noun *Common, Proper, Compound, Collective, Possessive, Concrete,* or *Abstract.* Some nouns may fall into more than one category.

1. Although many think that Shakespeare had a mysterious *life,* it was actually well documented, considering the times in which he lived.
2. The *documentation* of *Shakespeare's* life consists mainly of every-day items such as business *letters* and property records.
3. However, the importance of *Shakespeare* was not in the way he lived his life but in what he produced.
4. In fewer than twenty-five years, the *playwright* wrote thirty-eight plays.
5. His *home town* was Stratford-on-Avon, where a *crowd* of tourists can often be seen trying to find the *house* in which Shakespeare was born.
6. *Stratford-on-Avon,* a picturesque farming *village,* was an important *connection* for the playwright throughout his life.
7. Shakespeare's *father* was a leather worker who provided a comfortable life for his *family* and was a member of the *town council.*
8. Since the *children* of those involved in city government received free tuition, Shakespeare was able to join a *class* at the local *grammar school.*
9. As a *student,* Shakespeare probably studied the classics; however, he did not go on to attend a *university.*

B. Identifying Pronouns On your paper, write the pronouns in the following sentences. Then label each *Personal, Demonstrative, Reflexive, Intensive, Interrogative, Relative,* or *Indefinite.*

10. Shakespeare, who studied Latin in school, later taught himself French.
11. Although he did not know the classics as well as certain playwrights of his day, Shakespeare probably thought that his knowledge was sufficient.
12. One who reads Shakespeare's plays cannot fail to realize that he or she is reading the work of a master.
13. Not everyone believes that Shakespeare himself had much to do with the writing of the plays we attribute to him.
14. Shakespeare's general knowledge of legal matters often makes lawyers who read his works believe that Shakespeare himself had been a lawyer.

15. Shakespeare must have decided for himself that his worldly knowledge, which encompassed everything from ships to botany to war, was more important than classical schooling.
16. That is a copy of Shakespeare's first published play; I promised to give it to my cousin, who is reading Shakespeare for the first time.

C. Verb Phrases   On your paper, write the verb phrases in the following sentences, underlining the auxiliary verbs once and the main verbs twice. Label the verb phrases *Action* or *Linking*.   Then label the action verbs *Transitive* or *Intransitive.*

17. At the beginning of his career in the theater, Shakespeare was residing in the town of Stratford.
18. By 1592 Shakespeare was traveling back and forth between London and his home in Stratford.
19. The troupe in which Shakespeare worked as an actor must have provided regional tours as well as work in London.
20. Shakespeare may also have begun his career as a playwright during these early years.
21. Shakespeare's practical knowledge of the theater must have grown because of his experience as a stage manager.
22. Did Shakespeare really play the ghost in *Hamlet* and the servant Adam in *As You Like It?*
23. You should know that during 1592, after the plague had hit London and the theaters, Shakespeare was working, but as a poet not as a playwright.

D. Modifiers   *Step 1:* On your paper, write the adjectives and adverbs in the following sentences. *Step 2:* Label each *Adjective* or *Adverb.*
Step 3: Write the word or words that each modifies.

24. Shakespeare met many members of royalty through his theater work.
25. Shakespearean scholars now believe that the writer dedicated several early poems to a patron.
26. A young earl was flatteringly portrayed in two poems.
27. By 1597 Shakespeare had truly arrived; he bought New Place, one of the very largest houses in Stratford.
28. His interests had gradually changed almost entirely from acting to writing.
29. By his late forties, Shakespeare was living exclusively in retirement in his palatial house.
30. His friends often described the playwright as being gentle and self-effacing.
31. When he died at a relatively early age, he remembered his theater colleagues in his will.
32. The Elizabethan Age of drama may never be equalled; Shakespeare was not the only timeless playwright of that era.

Sentence Structure (pages 566–577)

A. Writing Sentences On your paper, write four sentences for each of the following word groups. Make the first sentence in each group declarative, the second interrogative, the third imperative, and the fourth exclamatory. The first one has been done for you as a model.

1. of the Renaissance

   There was a new awakening of curiosity and study during the time of the Renaissance.
   What were the achievements of the Renaissance?
   Tell me the major achievements of the Renaissance.
   Bravo to the scholars, artists, and explorers of the Renaissance!

2. exploring unknown lands
3. who discovered the Americas
4. painting and sculpture
5. around the sun
6. the path
7. move faster
8. time it took
9. about the planets
10. worked with
11. tried to find
12. artists and artisans
13. a time of learning
14. great works of art

B. Combining Sentences Using Compound Subjects On your paper, combine each pair of sentences by making the two simple subjects into a compound subject. Underline the compound subjects that you write.

15. Johannes Kepler made important advances in astronomy. Tycho Brahe did, too.
16. Kepler's father was a poor man who moved to the city of Weil, Germany, before Kepler's birth. His mother was also poor.
17. Science fascinated Kepler when he attended school. Mathematics fascinated him as well.
18. Political persecution in Germany was one reason Kepler moved to Czechoslovakia in 1599. An invitation from a friend was another.
19. Tycho Brahe studied the planets and made observations about them. So did his assistant Kepler.
20. The planet Mars was visible in the night sky. The stars were also visible in the night sky.
21. Brahe tried to determine the exact orbit of Mars. So did Kepler.
22. Circles had been considered by earlier astronomers trying to describe the paths the planets took around the sun. Combinations of circles had also been considered.

23. Brahe's observations could be confirmed only by an elliptical orbit. Kepler's observations could too.
24. Telescopes were studied by Kepler to see how curved glass reflected light. Eyeglasses were similarly studied.
25. The laws of planetary motion were a discovery of Kepler's. So were improved lenses for telescopes.
26. Tycho Brahe served as imperial mathematician to Rudolph II of the Holy Roman Empire. Johannes Kepler did too.
27. Kepler was one of the great astronomers of all time. Galileo was also a great astronomer.

C. Subjects, Predicates, and Objects   *Step 1:* Copy the following sentences on your paper. *Step 2:* Underline the simple subjects once and the simple predicates twice. *Step 3:* Write *D.O.* over the direct objects and *I.O.* over the indirect objects.

28. Christopher Columbus first asked King John II of Portugal to finance the explorer's voyage to the Indies.
29. Columbus requested many privileges as well as financial support from the king.
30. The king refused Columbus's requests.
31. So Columbus visited Queen Isabella and King Ferdinand in the kingdom of Granada in Spain.
32. He requested ships and sailors for a voyage to the Spice Islands of the East Indies.
33. Columbus received permission from the queen to search for a new, shorter route to the Indies.
34. Isabella and her councilors offered the explorer three boats and a crew of sailors.
35. The royal couple saw in Columbus's voyage an opportunity to extend Christianity to a new land.
36. What other benefits would a shorter sea route to the East Indies bring?

D. Distinguishing Complements   On your paper, list the complements in the following paragraph. Label each complement *Direct object, Indirect object, Objective complement, Predicate nominative,* or *Predicate adjective.*

(37) The Spanish fought the Moors in Granada in a ten-year war. (38) The Moors were Muslims who had settled in Spain during the eighth century. (39) The center of Moorish wealth and culture was Granada. (40) By the late 1200s, the Moors had lost their land and made Granada their last stronghold in Spain. (41) Isabella and Ferdinand were determined to drive out the remaining Moors. (42) The royal couple considered nearby Santa Fe their headquarters and remained a force there until Granada fell. (43) During this long war, Isabella built the soldiers a hospital close to the battleground. (44) The Spaniards finally routed the Moors and drove them out of Spain.

Phrases and Clauses (pages 578–603)

A. Identifying Phrases On your paper, write the italicized phrase or phrases in italic type in each sentence. Then label each phrase *Prepositional, Appositive, Participial, Gerund,* or *Infinitive.*

1. *Comparing the Renaissance to the ages that preceded it,* we see an age of enlightenment, achievement, and fresh ideas.
2. *To view the Renaissance this way* may distort reality.
3. After all, the groundwork for the Renaissance was laid in the preceding centuries, *the so-called Dark Ages.*
4. *Based on this fact,* the name *Dark Ages* is no longer considered a true reflection of those pre-Renaissance times.
5. Besides, the Renaissance was not *without its own problems.*

B. Identifying Verbal Phrases On your paper, write the verbal phrase or phrases for each sentence. Then label each phrase *Participial, Gerund,* or *Infinitive.*

6. Looking back at the Renaissance, we can single out the major developments and events of the period.
7. The ability of Renaissance artists to create great sculpture and painting remains impressive today.
8. Discovering the American continents was the culmination of many other great voyages of exploration.
9. Gutenberg's development of the printing press, giving everyone access to books, revolutionized education.
10. Having access to books and other printed material also had tremendous political repercussions.
11. In England, the writing of poetry and drama reached a high point in Shakespeare's plays and sonnets.
12. The rise of cities, leading to modern Paris, London, and Rome, began in the Renaissance.
13. Discoveries in astronomy gave educated people, and eventually everyone, a new way to look at the universe.

C. Independent and Subordinate Clauses On your paper, write the following clauses and label each one *Independent* or *Subordinate.* Capitalize and punctuate the independent clauses correctly.

14. the Renaissance voyages of discovery did not come out of nowhere
15. they could not have happened without the magnetic compass
16. which was invented as early as the eleventh century
17. neither did voyagers such as Columbus prove that the world is round
18. that idea was widely accepted by educated people long before the year 1492
19. having been calculated by Greek mathematicians in ancient times

D. Adjective and Adverb Clauses   *Step 1:* On your paper, write the adjective and adverb clauses in the following sentences and label them *Adjective* or *Adverb*.   *Step 2:* Underline the subordinating conjunction that introduces each clause.   *Step 3:* Beside each clause write the word or phrase that it modifies.

20. *Renaissance,* which means "rebirth," aptly describes the age.
21. The Renaissance was a time when many old ideas were rediscovered by writers and scholars.
22. Some of the most important of these ideas were ones that had originated in ancient times.
23. Many of those ideas had been forgotten until inquisitive minds sought them out.
24. For example, Renaissance sculpture started where the ancient Greeks had left off.
25. As you probably know, it was the Chinese who actually invented gunpowder.
26. Similarly, although Europe refined the process, printing came from China, where it had been developed centuries earlier.

E. Classifying Sentences   *Step 1:* On your paper, copy the sentences in the following paragraph.   *Step 2:* Underline each independent clause. *Step 3:* Put brackets around each subordinate clause.   *Step 4:* Label each sentence *Simple, Compound, Complex,* or *Compound-Complex.*

   Someone who has broad interests is often called a "Renaissance man" or a "Renaissance woman." People today sometimes think that the men and women of the Renaissance did everything or knew everything. Of course, there were geniuses like Leonardo da Vinci, but we must remember that the average person was deeply ignorant. This person was sure that the world was flat. He or she also feared witchcraft, dreaded the evil eye, and had other similar superstitions. Even the educated minority held many ideas that most people reject today. For example, there were many nobles who held astrologers in high esteem, and almost everyone believed that mice could grow from grains of wheat.

F. Revising a Paragraph for Correct Sentence Structure   On your paper, rewrite the following paragraph, correcting every fragment and run-on sentence.

   It would be difficult today. To be a Renaissance man or woman. Our world is more complicated, there is so much to learn. The field of science shows. The problem a person would face in becoming a Renaissance man or woman. Scientists today study for many years, even then they master only a single branch of the field. New developments occur daily, even mastery over a single specialty takes constant study. Just to keep up with them. Where is the time? For a second career such as architecture? By comparison, a person of Renaissance times. Could learn almost all. That was known about the world.

The Meaning of Words: Denotation and Connotation

"When *I* use a word," Humpty Dumpty said, in rather a scornful tone, "it means just what I choose it to mean — neither more nor less."

"The question is," said Alice, "whether you *can* make words mean so many different things."

"The question is," said Humpty Dumpty, "which is to be master — that's all."

Lewis Carroll *(1832–1898)*
from *Through the Looking-Glass*

This conversation between Alice and Humpty Dumpty highlights a basic feature of language — words mean what people want them to mean. That is to say, the meanings of words are determined by the context in which people use them. Humpty Dumpty's problem is that no one else knows what meaning he gives to some words. For example, he says that by *glory* he means "a nice knock-down argument," and by *impenetrability* he means "we've had enough of that subject." Neither of these words has these meanings for anyone else, and thus they do not convey Humpty Dumpty's meaning to Alice or to the reader. We must share a general understanding about words in order to communicate.

One might even say that words have no meaning at all until they are used in a context that allows someone to understand them. For example, the following phrases give some idea of the range of senses the word *board* can have: *an oak board, a chess board, room and board, passengers on board a ship, fall overboard, the school board, a board game, the Atlantic seaboard, to board up the windows, to board a ship,* and *to board at school.* Thus *board* by itself has several potential meanings, but only in context does it take on a specific meaning.

If words have no inherent meaning, then where do dictionary definitions come from? **Lexicographers,** as dictionary writers are called, do not simply make up words or meanings to put into dictionaries. They collect many examples of each word as it is actually used by people in their everyday speech and writing.

Many words have just one meaning, but many others, especially words that have been in the language for a long time, have developed a number of distinct senses, or **denotations.** It is the lexicographer's task to identify and list the denotations of any word in a dictionary. A lexicographer cannot easily include the connotations of a word — the suggested implications, ideas, or emotions that it evokes.

Often a longer or Latin-derived word will carry stronger connotations than a shorter, more common one. For instance, *conflagration* suggests something more extensive than *fire; amicable* is more restrained or formal than *friendly.* Sometimes **euphemisms** replace common terms, enhancing the connotation or softening a negative connotation. An example is *sales associate* for *retail clerk.*

The **meaning** of a word consists of particular notions that are associated with it at any given time. For example, in 1634 English speakers used the borrowed Latin word *candor* to mean "brilliant whiteness." It had other associations, such as "innocence," "kindness," and "integrity" all of which became obsolete by 1725. Today *candor* means "frankness of expression" and "impartiality," and we might associate the word with such notions as *attitude in transmitted information or opinion, good, fair, democratic,* and *true.* If you were to read a passage written in 1700 in which *candor* meant "innocence" with your understanding of today's meaning of the word, then you would misunderstand the author's point.

The meanings of words are constantly changing, as are the associations — both negative and positive — that we give to individual words. Therefore, it pays to be aware of both the denotations and the connotations of words. Alice is right in questioning whether Humpty Dumpty can use words to mean whatever he wants them to mean, ignoring the history of meaning that each word has. Humpty Dumpty is also right, however. If we are not masters of our own language, then our language can be used by others to master us.

Vocabulary Activities

Word Associations with Euphemisms   List five terms and one euphemism commonly used in place of each term. Indicate the associations that each term calls to your mind. Do the same for each euphemism. For example, *retreat* is commonly replaced by the euphemism *orderly withdrawal* in the military. *Retreat* may call to mind *giving up, unpatriotic, cowardly,* and *uncontrolled. Orderly withdrawal* may call to mind *controlled maneuver, sensible,* and *lifesaving.* Discuss your list with a partner to find out whether you share the associations.

Influential Connotations   Bring to class two examples of newspaper editorials or magazine articles that exemplify the writer's use of connotations to slant the writing. Explain how certain words are avoided and others are cleverly used to achieve the writer's goal.

The Literature Connection

For centuries visitors have thronged to Florence, Italy, to see the Renaissance art and architecture and to find and express in writing the spirit of that age. The American novelist Henry James made many trips to Italy in the 1800s and finally settled on one piece of architecture as "the soul" of Renaissance Florence.

Guided Reading   Read the following passage several times and think about how James put it together. Notice how phrases and clauses are layered upon one another, almost as though James were constructing a tower himself.

*B*ut perhaps the best image of . . . what I have called temperate joy, in the Florentine impression and genius, is the bell-tower of Giotto, which rises beside the Cathedral. No beholder of it will have forgotten how straight and slender it stands there, how strangely rich in the common street, plated with coloured marble patterns, and yet so far from simple or severe in design. . . . Nothing can be imagined at once more lightly and more pointedly fanciful; it might have been handed over to the city, as it stands, by some Oriental genie tired of too much detail. Yet for all that suggestion it seems of no particular time — not grey and hoary like a Gothic steeple, not cracked and de-spoiled like a Greek temple; its marbles shining so little less freshly than when they were laid together, and the sunset lighting up its cornice with such a friendly radi-ance, that you come at last to regard it simply as the graceful, indestructible soul of the place made visible.

Henry James *(1843–1916)*
from *Italian Hours*

Find the negative words here, and explain their effect.

What are some adjective phrases that James uses?

Describe the bell tower in your own words.

Writing Applications

A Description   Reread James's description of the bell tower, and note how many times he describes it by saying what it *isn't*. Brainstorm to think of a subject for description that you could write about "in reverse" or in terms of negatives. List or cluster phrases and clauses to express those negatives. Use vivid nouns and adjectives. If possible, express some of your negatives as metaphors. Then turn your prewriting into a free-verse poem or a prose description.

A Travel Essay The selection on the previous page focuses on a building in Italy that Henry James saw as a representation or a symbol of a particular time and place. Brainstorm to think of a structure or a scene that symbolizes a particular time or place to you. Then write a brief descriptive essay as though you were a traveler there. Explain why you chose that symbol to represent that place. Use descriptive phrases and clauses. Finally, put your travel essay into a folder and share it with your classmates.

Enrichment Connections

Choose one or more of these activities to do on your own or as a group.

Fine Arts

An Oral Report Do library or museum research to study three or four Renaissance portraits — for example Leonardo's Mona Lisa or a portrait by Rembrandt. Look carefully at the paintings. Consider these questions: Does the artist seem to be trying to flatter the sitter or to reveal his or her personality? What does the person seem to be like? How do the costume and the background contribute to the effect? Prepare an oral report on the portraits, using concrete nouns and vivid adjectives.

A Biographical Sketch In the Writing Connection on page 577, you explored the idea of the *Renaissance man or woman*. Do research to expand your knowledge of the term. Then choose a person — real or from a literary work — who you think fits your expanded definition. Write a brief biographical sketch

Across the Curriculum

Social Studies Do library research on one of the major explorers or expeditions of the Renaissance. Use the information that you find as the basis for a first-person account of part of an expedition. You might write the journal of a sailor on a voyage with Sir Francis Drake, a free-verse poem about first sighting land from Columbus's ship, or a letter from someone who circumnavigated the globe with Magellan. Be sure to use transitional adverbs to make the sequence of events clear. Post your account on the class bulletin board.

explaining why your subject should be considered a Renaissance man or woman. As you revise, use phrases and clauses to help you turn short, choppy sentences into longer, smoother ones. Contribute your writing to a class portfolio of sketches.

CELEBRATING
DIVERSITY

Arna Bontemps

How might a "Renaissance" be an awakening? How might it mark a culture's success in finding a voice or in celebrating an identity?

The definition of the word renaissance is "a movement or period of vigorous artistic and intellectual activity." The Harlem Renaissance, which took place in the 1920s, marks an intellectual awakening of the African-American community, specifically in Harlem in New York City. The poems that follow were written by one poet of the Harlem Renaissance and illustrate the diversity of expression of the period. As you read, notice the careful use of language, and look up any words that you do not understand. When you have finished, choose one or more of the suggested activities that follow the poems. These activities may broaden your understanding of the meaning of *renaissance*.

Nocturne of the Wharves

All night they whine upon their ropes and boom
against the dock with helpless prows:
these little ships that are too worn for sailing
front the wharf but do not rest at all.
Tugging at the dim gray wharf they think   5
no doubt of China and of bright Bombay,
and they remember islands of the East,
Formosa and the mountains of Japan.
They think of cities ruined by the sea
and they are restless, sleeping at the wharf.   10

Tugging at the dim gray wharf they think
no less of Africa. An east wind blows
and salt spray sweeps the unattended decks.
Shouts of dead men break upon the night.
The captain calls his crew and they respond—   15
the little ships are dreaming—land is near.
But mist comes up to dim the copper coast,
mist dissembles images of the trees.
The captain and his men alike are lost
and their shouts go down in the rising sound of waves. 20
Ah little ships, I know your weariness!
I know the sea-green shadows of your dream.
For I have loved the cities of the sea,
and desolations of the old days I
have loved: I was a wanderer like you   25
and I have broken down before the wind.

Arna Bontemps (1902–1973)

Reconnaissance

After the cloud embankments,
the lamentation of wind
and the starry descent into time,
we came to the flashing waters and shaded our eyes
from the glare.   5

Alone with the shore and the harbor,
the stems of the cocoanut trees,
the fronds of silence and hushed music,
we cried for new revelation
and waited for miracles to rise.   10

Where elements touch and merge,
where shadows swoon like outcasts on the sand
and the tried moment waits, its courage gone—
there were we

in latitudes where storms are born.   15

Arna Bontemps (1902–1973)

A Black Man Talks of Reaping

I have sown beside all waters in my day.
I planted deep, within my heart the fear
that wind or fowl would take the grain away.
I planted safe against this stark, lean year.

I scattered seed enough to plant the land   5
in rows from Canada to Mexico
but for my reaping only what the hand
can hold at once is all that I can show.

Yet what I sowed and what the orchard yields
my brother's sons are gathering stalk and root;   10
small wonder then my children glean in fields
they have not sown, and feed on bitter fruit.

Arna Bontemps (1902–1973)

How does the title "Reconnaissance" capture the meaning of that poem? Where is the poem taking place? What scene is set in the first stanza of "Nocture of the Wharves"? What are the little ships dreaming about in the second stanza? Why does the speaker identify with the little ships? Why is the speaker bitter in "A Black Man Talks of Reaping"?

Changing Places

What kind of place would you pick for personal reconnaissance? What dreams would the little ships be having if you had written "Nocturne of the Wharves"? What country would they "think no less of"? How would you feel if, like the speaker in "A Black Man Talks of Reaping," you could not finally benefit from something you had worked hard to create? What images would you use to illustrate your frustration and bitterness? Try to locate yourself mentally and emotionally in these poems, and retain your orientation as you do one or more of the activities that follow.

WRITING

Bitter Fruit   "A Black Man Talks of Reaping" may be seen as a historical poem evoking the bitterness of a slave or a poor tenant farmer. The speaker has worked hard for a landowner but isn't allowed to enjoy the fruits of his labor. The poem may also be seen as the lament of a people who have helped to build a country but are denied full participation in it. Although most of us have not suffered in this magnitude, we have perhaps felt something of what the speaker feels. Perhaps you have trained hard for a sports team and been cut at the last minute; perhaps you have worked long and hard on a friend's campaign for student council only to be ignored by the person after the election. Do prewriting to generate ideas and details, and then write a first-person narrative, a short story, or a poem about a situation in which you have "sown but not reaped." Conversely, you may have been in or can imagine a situation in which you have "reaped but not sown"—have benefited from someone else's labor. You might want to write about this kind of situation instead. You may want to publish a class anthology of these first-person narratives, short stories, and poems.

Borrowed Words   As is often the case in English, the word *renaissance* has been borrowed in its entirety from the French. The literal meaning is "rebirth." Look up the word *renaissance* in a dictionary. Note all of the different ways in which this word has been interpreted. Choose one of the various definitions and write a new definition for the Harlem Renaissance or any other kind of renaissance.

CRITICAL THINKING

Analogies   The poems presented here use a number of words that either can be easily confused or have multiple meanings. To help you understand the various meanings of these words, create analogies using the words that follow or other words from the poems. For information on analogies, see pages 439–441.

embankment	lamentation
desolations	latitudes
dissemble	stark
revelation	reconnaissance

WRITING

Oasis   "Reconnaissance," like many poems, can be read in different ways. One interpretation is that it describes a place of respite from war, an island for *non*military reconnaissance, a place for "miracles to rise." If you could escape from the "war" of your world, where would you go for rest and recreation? Even if your oasis is imaginary, what landscape do you see? Use brainstorming or clustering to generate images of a peaceful place, and then write a poem or a descriptive essay about it. Share your writing with a classmate and discuss the differences between your peaceful places.

DID YOU KNOW?   The Harlem Renaissance gave to the United States and to the world such renowned musicians as Duke Ellington, Louis Armstrong, and Bessie Smith. Among the artists were sculptor Meta Warrick Fuller and illustrator Aaron Douglas. James Van Der Zee, the great Harlem photographer, specialized in portraits of the most famous members of the Harlem Renaissance.

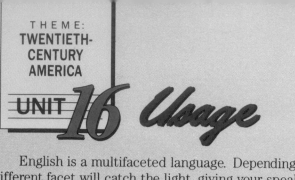

English is a multifaceted language. Depending on the level of usage, a different facet will catch the light, giving your speaking and your writing a distinctive character. You may use colloquial language or slang when you write to a friend—or ceremonial language when you write your student council bylaws. This unit reviews standard English usage, which is the facet of our language that you use most often in your writing. Refer to the appropriate section in the following pages whenever you are unsure about a point of usage. You will quickly find the tools that you need to polish your writing to just the right degree.

The *United States in the twentieth century* has experienced unparalleled change in most aspects of its social, political, and economic life. As you review contemporary standard English usage, you will also review some of the events and people that have made this period so critical to both United States and world history. The selection shown here is a great poet's effort to put the nation's past into perspective and to suggest the shape of the future. Read the poem aloud several times. Then focus your attention on the paradoxes, or apparent contradictions, in the poem. Notice how the poet deftly uses everyday language and conventional sentence structure to convey complex ideas.

The Gift Outright

*T*he land was ours before we were the land's.
She was our land more than a hundred years
Before we were her people. She was ours
In Massachusetts, in Virginia,
5 But we were England's, still colonials,
Possessing what we still were unpossessed by,
Possessed by what we now no more possessed.
Something we were withholding made us weak
Until we found out that it was ourselves
10 We were withholding from our land of living,
And forthwith found salvation in surrender.
Such as we were we gave ourselves outright
(The deed of gift was many deeds of war)
To the land vaguely realizing westward,
15 But still unstoried, artless, unenhanced,
Such as she was, such as she would become.

Robert Frost *(1874–1963)*

*Contra-
diction
here.
One in
line 11
too.*

*Possess
used as
a verb
and an
adjective?*

Responding to Literature

Robert Frost once described "The Gift Outright," which was written in 1942, as "a history of the United States in sixteen lines." What does his *use* of English tell you about his view of the country's past, present, and future? In responding to the poem, ask yourself questions such as these: Does he play with words? Which words does he repeat and to what effect? Which verb does he use most often? Is the language of the poem ornate and artificial, or is it "plain spoken"? Which words have figurative meaning? Which word seems most important and why? Then try to synthesize all your thoughts and impressions into a statement of the poem's main idea, including what it implies about the future. Save your response in your writer's notebook.

Levels of Usage

The English language is dynamic. It is constantly changing, gaining new words and phrases as well as losing some expressions as they fall into disuse. Moreover, English embraces different types and levels of usage that are employed by different groups of people in a variety of circumstances. These sometimes-overlapping types of usage range from that found in particular occupations or professions — **jargon** — to that used in particular locales or by particular ethnic groups — **dialect.** There is also **colloquial** English, which is used in everyday conversation, and **ceremonial** English, which is used only on important occasions. **Slang** is language that is used briefly by cliques or by certain age groups, and **archaic** language is English that is no longer used at all.

There is, however, one type of usage that is generally considered correct and appropriate for most writing and speaking situations. It is called **standard English.** While it is true that some of today's slang may become part of standard English in the future and that some current usage may become obsolete, it is also true that this level of English is recognized as standard today. It is the language that you will need to use in school, in most business and employment situations, and in addressing people whom you don't know well.

This section covers current, standard English. You will find that following the rules of standard usage will help you to write exactly what you mean in a way that will be readily understood and respected by a wide variety of readers.

Whenever you speak or write, you need to decide what level of usage is appropriate to your message and your audience. Generally, you will use **informal English** in conversation and in writing personal letters to friends or notes to your family. Written, informal English is characterized by the sentence structure and vocabulary typical of conversation and by more relaxed standards of usage than those of formal English. Informal English includes contractions as well as some colloquial expressions and slang.

Formal English is the standard English that is used for serious speaking occasions and most writing. It is composed of words, expressions, grammar, and standards of usage found in formal essays, scholarly writing, and speeches made on significant occasions. It is the type of usage that you are reading now, and it is employed throughout this book. Formal English uses extensive vocabulary, few contractions, and almost no slang. You should use formal English for most of your school work, during personal interviews for college or employment, and in the letters requesting such interviews. In many other situations, such as business presentations, community committee meetings, and letters to the editor, the use of formal English will help to insure that your message is understood and that it is received with respect.

There are several kinds of usage that are suitable only in special writing circumstances. Ceremonial language is one example. You would not use the language found on an engraved wedding invitation, for example, in a term paper for history class. Slang and colloquial expressions are also appropriate only in very informal writing or when used for special effect in creative writing or dialogue. Dialect, too, can make an impact in those special situations, but dialect is difficult to write well and should be used sparingly.

Jargon is another type of usage that should be avoided in most writing situations. It employs the special words used by people in a particular field of work or activity. Such occupational language can be an efficient, precise means of communication for specialists. When specialists write or speak to a wider audience, however, they must adjust their language, being careful not to bewilder the reader or listener. At its worst, jargon can be inflated and pretentious.

JARGON   The position afforded much interface, impacting on management objectives.

JARGON   Our big people need to get into the paint and hit the boards if we're going to shut down their transition game.

Overly formal language or the use of long, "difficult" words and lengthy, very complex sentence structure should also be avoided. Some writers think that inflated language makes a good impression, but in reality the reverse is true. **Verbosity,** or wordiness, is a related pitfall. It is the practice of saying something in the most complicated way possible. **Redundancy** also adds unnecessary words. It is the practice of saying or writing the same thing in several different ways to no purpose. Redundancy usually occurs because of carelessness or ignorance.

INFLATED VERBOSITY   Having articulated his well-considered opinion to everyone gathered in the audience to listen, the author reiterated his message and fielded questions adroitly and with acuity.

(ə-kyoo′ĭ-tē)

REDUNDANCY   In my opinion I think that the author expressed her theme and view of the world in what she was saying in her book.

Be careful to eliminate redundancy and verbosity from your writing. Use concrete words. Never avoid a short, simple word just because it is common. Repeat an idea in a phrase or sentence only when the idea is made clearer by the repetition. Be careful, too, not to use overly formal language in an effort to impress your reader.

Nonstandard English is composed of words, expressions, and grammatical constructions that are not generally accepted as correct. Nonstandard English should not normally be used to communicate with a general audience and is inappropriate in almost every writing situation.

To communicate effectively, you should learn to recognize the levels of English usage and to employ them appropriately. The way you speak and write says a great deal about you. Even though you may wish to use slang with your friends or speak colloquially with your family, you will also find it necessary to use formal, standard English. The more familiar and comfortable you are with this level of usage, the easier it will be for you to write it when it is important to do so.

Exercise Scope of Usage

? Critical Thinking:

What words or phrases are unnecessary?

On your paper, rewrite each of the following sentences in clear, formal English, removing jargon, redundancy, and verbosity.

SAMPLE   People were resolved, despite any and all obstacles, to insist emphatically on fulfilling their resolve to survive the Great Depression.

ANSWER   People were resolved, despite all obstacles, to survive the Great Depression.

1. The day Herbert Hoover became President of these glorious United States, his optimistic, sanguine inaugural address was hopeful.
2. Most listeners agreed with this seasoned, practical politician who had considerable experience in politics.
3. Hoover, like millions of other North Americans, believed that the bubble of success, that fragile, shimmering creation everyone loves and thinks is indestructible (even though it bursts so easily) would never burst.
4. Unfortunately, economic patterns that have their own cyclical inevitability can result in an economic catastrophe that few would have foretold or prophesied.
5. A stock market crash of unparalleled, never-experienced-before severity and depth occurred just approximately about eight months after Hoover's optimistic, hopeful inauguration speech.
6. The crash occurred on "Black Thursday," October 29, 1929, with the most dire and unprognosticated results.
7. One of the most terrible, dreadful consequences of the crash was that workers lost their jobs, with the tragic result that by 1932 twelve million people were unemployed.
8. It was as a result or consequence of the crash that the populace of the United States experienced in their consciousness for the first time the tragedy of large numbers of homeless people.
9. More than a million homeless people wandered the roads of the great country we call the "United States" or settled in shantytowns made out of decrepit, old, probably torn as well, packing cartons and car bodies that had long been ignored.
10. In the summer of 1932, a "Bonus Army" that was made up of twelve thousand World War I veterans who had no jobs and were unemployed, marched on Washington with the hopes and aspirations of persuading Congress to make a veterans' bonus appropriation.

Avoiding Verbosity and Redundancy in Your Writing

To convey your message efficiently and effectively, your writing should be clear and concise. Redundancy and verbosity may confuse or distract your audience. It is not unusual to find wordiness or repetition in freewriting or first drafts. There, they are part of the process of sorting through your thoughts. However, it is important to eliminate redundancy and verbosity when you are revising.

Reference Point:
pages 80–83

Writing Assignments

A Sports Column As you read the following first draft of a sports column from 1982, look for redundancy and verbosity.

> At long last, justice has finally been done. Jim Thorpe's Olympic gold medals have now been returned and restored to him — tragically almost thirty years after his death about three decades ago. Jim Thorpe may have been, in the opinion of many people, just possibly the greatest all-around athlete ever. He was the first athlete ever in history to win both the pentathlon and the decathlon in one Olympics, a feat which he accomplished in the Games of 1912.
>
> Initially the first success of this American Indian athlete was at a small, little Indian Industrial School which he led to national fame in football. Then, not long after his triumph at the Olympics, because of the meager, small salary he once got for playing baseball, Thorpe lost his gold medals. In the opinion of those in charge of such things at the time, this money made him a professional — not an amateur — athlete. The International Olympic Committee has finally in its wisdom seen fit to reconsider and to reinstate the name of Jim Thorpe in the roster of the champions of 1912.

Now rewrite the column, revising it to eliminate redundancy and verbosity. Be sure that you retain the meaning of the column.

A Playbill As the publicity director for a theatrical production, you must write a short description of the play's setting for the playbill to be distributed to the audience. *Step 1:* Choose a play or movie that you have seen, and jot down notes about the setting. *Step 2:* Select and organize the elements that you wish to include. *Step 3:* Write a short description — about four or five lines — including details that show how the play's setting affects the action or impact of the play. *Step 4:* Revise, checking for redundancy and verbosity. *Step 5:* Proofread your description and post it on the class bulletin board.

Reference Points:
*pages 120–148,
165, 288–289,
and 298–300*

Your ability to communicate increases dramatically with your ability to use verbs correctly. By changing the form of a verb, you can express its tense, the number and the person of its subject, its voice, and its mood.

Principal Parts of Verbs

The four basic forms of a verb, called the **principal parts,** are the infinitive, the present participle, the past, and the past participle. By using these forms alone or with auxiliary verbs, you can express the various tenses of a verb.

The infinitive and the present participle are formed in the same way for all verbs. The **infinitive** is the basic verb form that appears in the dictionary. The word *to* usually precedes the infinitive in a sentence; in some sentences, however, the word *to* is understood but not stated.

INFINITIVE   Two years is a long time *to* **train** for a mission.

Knowing that we will one day go into space will make us all **train** willingly. [*to* is understood before *train*]

The **present participle** is always a combination of the infinitive and *-ing;* it is used in a sentence with a form of the verb *be* as an auxiliary verb.

PRESENT
PARTICIPLE   The crew *is* **training** to prepare for any emergency.

Regular Verbs

Verbs are considered regular or irregular depending on how their past and past participle forms are constructed. You form the past and the past participle of any regular verb by adding *-d* or *-ed* to the infinitive. In a sentence, the past participle takes a form of the verb *have* as an auxiliary verb.

PAST   The astronaut **trained** in weightless conditions to simulate space flight.

PAST
PARTICIPLE   She *has* **trained** for a long time to prepare for this day.

Here are the principal parts of two regular verbs. The auxiliary verbs in parentheses remind you that the correct form of the verb *be* is used with the present participle and the correct form of the verb *have* is used with the past participle. The third-person singular form of each auxiliary verb is shown in the chart.

Principal Parts			
Infinitive	**Present Participle**	**Past**	**Past Participle**
offer	(is) offering	offered	(has) offered
contribute	(is) contributing	contributed	(has) contributed

Irregular Verbs

Irregular verbs are considered irregular because they do not follow the standard rules for forming their past and past participle. Like regular verbs, however, they do use a form of the auxiliary verb *be* with the present participle and a form of the auxiliary verb *have* with the past participle. The following sentences show the correct use of the principal parts of the irregular verb *wear*.

INFINITIVE   In the twenties many girls begged their parents to let them **wear** short skirts. [*to* is understood before *wear*]

PRESENT PARTICIPLE   Flappers *were* **wearing** the latest styles.

PAST   They **wore** long ropes of beads with their short, fringed dresses.

PAST PARTICIPLE   Some flappers *had* **worn** their hair short for years.

Although no standard rules govern the formation of the past and the past participle of irregular verbs, you should have little trouble mastering their usage. You have probably already developed a good sense of what is correct by what sounds correct. Memorize the principal parts of verbs that you use frequently, and consult your dictionary for those that you do not use as often. The following list contains many irregular verbs and should serve as a useful reference. The third-person singular forms of the auxiliary verbs are shown in parentheses.

Infinitive	Present Participle	Past	Past Participle
be	(is) being	was	(has) been
become	(is) becoming	became	(has) become
begin	(is) beginning	began	(has) begun
bite	(is) biting	bit	(has) bitten
blow	(is) blowing	blew	(has) blown
burst	(is) bursting	burst	(has) burst
catch	(is) catching	caught	(has) caught
choose	(is) choosing	chose	(has) chosen
come	(is) coming	came	(has) come
dive	(is) diving	dived, dove	(has) dived
do	(is) doing	did	(has) done

draw	(is) drawing	drew	(has) drawn
drive	(is) driving	drove	(has) driven
eat	(is) eating	ate	(has) eaten
fall	(is) falling	fell	(has) fallen
find	(is) finding	found	(has) found
fling	(is) flinging	flung	(has) flung
fly	(is) flying	flew	(has) flown
get	(is) getting	got	(has) gotten
give	(is) giving	gave	(has) given
go	(is) going	went	(has) gone
grow	(is) growing	grew	(has) grown
have	(is) having	had	(has) had
know	(is) knowing	knew	(has) known
lay	(is) laying	laid	(has) laid
lead	(is) leading	led	(has) led
leave	(is) leaving	left	(has) left
lie	(is) lying	lay	(has) lain
lose	(is) losing	lost	(has) lost
ride	(is) riding	rode	(has) ridden
ring	(is) ringing	rang	(has) rung
rise	(is) rising	rose	(has) risen
say	(is) saying	said	(has) said
set	(is) setting	set	(has) set
sit	(is) sitting	sat	(has) sat
speak	(is) speaking	spoke	(has) spoken
swear	(is) swearing	swore	(has) sworn
swim	(is) swimming	swam	(has) swum
tear	(is) tearing	tore	(has) torn
tell	(is) telling	told	(has) told
throw	(is) throwing	threw	(has) thrown
wear	(is) wearing	wore	(has) worn
write	(is) writing	wrote	(has) written

Exercise 1 Irregular Verbs

? **Critical Thinking:**

How are the principal parts of irregular verbs formed?

On your paper, write the form of the verb in parentheses that correctly completes each sentence. Do not use auxiliary verbs other than those already given in the sentences.

SAMPLE The 1929 stock market crash __?__ investors off guard. (catch)
ANSWER caught

1. Herbert Hoover was President during the Great Depression, which also __?__ known as "Hoover's Depression." (become)
2. Farmers had __?__ money, and too many people were buying on credit. (lose)
3. Hoover asked Congress to pass laws that would help the country before it __?__ itself apart. (tear)
4. Hoover __?__ the way in supporting public works and conservation programs that would provide jobs. (lead)

5. The Hoover administration __?__ us 800 public buildings and helped states build about 37,000 miles of major highways. (give)
6. It __?__ a major hand in adding three million acres to national parks and enlarged the national forests. (have)
7. The Hoover administration also __?__ us the Hoover Dam on the Colorado River. (leave)
8. Hoover had __?__ public life in 1914, supervising the production and distribution of food for North American soldiers and civilians during World War I. (chose)
9. He had __?__ to the highest office in the land by winning the largest majority of electoral votes ever received by a candidate until that time. (rise)
10. Hoover __?__ that disarmament was important and signed an agreement with Great Britain and Japan to limit the number of fighting ships. (know)

Verb Tense

You use the various forms of a verb to show whether an action or a condition takes place in the present, took place in the past, or will take place in the future. The forms of a verb that express time are called **tenses.** To form tenses, you combine the principal parts with auxiliary verbs. The six English tenses — three simple and three perfect — are present, past, future, present perfect, past perfect, and future perfect.

To **conjugate** a verb is to list all of the forms for its six tenses. The conjugation of a verb also shows how the verb forms change for the first person, the second person, and the third person and for the singular and the plural. The following conjugation continues on page 624.

Conjugation of the Regular Verb *Walk*	
Singular	**Plural**
Present Tense I walk you walk he/she/it walks	we walk you walk they walk
Past Tense I walked you walked he/she/it walked	we walked you walked they walked
Future Tense I will (shall) walk you will walk he/she/it will walk	we will (shall) walk you will walk they will walk

Conjugation of the Regular Verb *Walk* (continued)	
Singular	**Plural**
Present Perfect Tense I have walked you have walked he/she/it has walked	we have walked you have walked they have walked
Past Perfect Tense I had walked you had walked he/she/it had walked	we had walked you had walked they had walked
Future Perfect Tense I will (shall) have walked you will have walked he/she/it will have walked	we will (shall) have walked you will have walked they will have walked

The Six Tenses of Verbs

Present Tense   To form the present tense of a verb, use its infinitive. To form the third-person singular, you usually add *-s* or *-es* to the infinitive.

Rule

U 1

Use the present tense to show an action that takes place now, to show an action that is repeated regularly, or to show a condition that is true at any time.

My grandfather **tells** stories about World War II.
He **tells** a different one every time the family gets together.
He says that **telling** these stories makes him nostalgic.
[**Think:** *Telling* the stories always makes him nostalgic.]

Rule

U 2

Use the present tense in statements about literary works or other works of art.

In *The Grapes of Wrath*, the Joad family **loses** its farm.

Rule

U 3

Use the present tense occasionally to describe past events with special immediacy. When the present tense is used for this effect, it is called the *historical present*.

During the Great Depression, many farm families **become** migrant workers.

In informal communication, you can use the present tense to describe future action if you include a word or a phrase that clearly indicates that the action will occur in the future.

We **study** *The Grapes of Wrath* next week.

Past Tense   To form the past tense of a regular verb, add *-d* or *-ed* to the infinitive.   To avoid confusion, memorize the principal parts of irregular verbs.

Rule	Use the past tense to express action that occurred in the past and was completed entirely in the past.
U 4

I **took** *The Grapes of Wrath* out of the library.

Future Tense   To form the future tense, combine *will* or *shall* with the infinitive form of the main verb.

Rule	Use the future tense to describe action that will occur in the future.
U 5	I **will take** it to school with me tomorrow.

Present Perfect Tense   To form the present perfect tense, use *has* or *have* with the past participle of the main verb.

Rule	Use the present perfect tense to describe action that was completed either in the recent past or at an indefinite time in the past.
U 6

I **have** just **read** *The Grapes of Wrath.*

Past Perfect Tense   To form the past perfect tense, use *had* with the past participle of the main verb.

Rule	Use the past perfect tense to describe an action that was completed by a certain time in the past or before another action was completed.
U 7

       past perf.   past
I **had read** the whole book before I **realized** that I could have waited until the end of the week.

Future Perfect Tense   To form the future perfect tense, use *will have* or *shall have* with the past participle of the main verb.

Rule	Use the future perfect tense to describe a future action that will be completed before another future action will be completed.
U 8

I **will have finished** my book review before the rest of the class begins.

Exercise 2 | **Verb Tense: Choosing Verb Tense**

On your paper, write the required form of the verb in parentheses to complete each sentence correctly.

SAMPLE   World War I __?__ on November 11, 1918.   (*end* — past)
ANSWER   ended

1. The headlines on January 8, 1918, __?__ the following: "Wilson __?__ of Fourteen Points to Congress." (*say* — past; *speak* — present)

? **Critical Thinking:**

Which tense uses two auxiliary verbs?

2. Before becoming President, Woodrow Wilson __?__ a scholar, a teacher, and a university president. (*be* — past perfect)

3. He __?__ his Fourteen Points outlining a peace plan even before World War I ended. (*write* — past perfect)

4. Thus, the Fourteen Points __?__ the basis for a peace settlement. (*become* — past)

5. World leaders __?__ the peace conference at the palace of Versailles in January 1919, and delegates from twenty-seven nations __?__. (*hold* — past; *attend* — past)

6. Wilson __?__ an immediate triumph by forcing plans for a League of Nations into the peace treaty. (*score* — past)

7. Starting in Ohio, he __?__ eight thousand miles and __?__ thirty-seven speeches in favor of the treaty in twenty-two days. (*ride* — past; *make* — past)

8. Although his supporters __?__ themselves out on his behalf, the Senate __?__ to ratify the Versailles Treaty. (*wear* — past; *fail* — past)

9. When twenty-five nations __?__ charter members of the League, which __?__ for the first time on January 10, 1920, people all over the world __?__ that the time for world peace __?__. (*become* — past; *meet* — past; *say* — past; *come* — past perfect)

10. Eventually twenty-one more nations __?__ the League, and prospects for peace __?__ even better; however, by the late 1930s, nations __?__ to withdraw from the League. (*join* — past perfect; *seem* — past; *begin* — past perfect)

Tenses of Infinitives and Participles

Infinitives *(page 585)* and participles *(page 581)* have two tenses: the present and the perfect.

	INFINITIVE	PARTICIPLE
PRESENT	to walk	walking
PERFECT	to have walked	having walked

Rule U 9   Use infinitives and participles in the present tense to express action that occurs at the same time as that of the main verb.

PRESENT   I wanted **to walk** in the Freedom March.

Walking with my brother, I saw hundreds of other people joining the March.

Rule U 10   Use infinitives and participles in the perfect tense to express action that takes place before the action of the main verb.

PERFECT   **To have walked** in the Freedom March made me feel proud.

Having walked so far, I was glad when we finally reached the Lincoln Memorial.

The Progressive, Emphatic, and Modal Forms

The Progressive Form   To form the progressive, use the appropriate tense of the verb *be* with the present participle of the main verb.

Rule   Use the progressive form of a verb to describe continuing action.

U 11   PRESENT PROGRESSIVE
They **are walking** to protest discrimination.

PAST PROGRESSIVE
They **were walking** to the Lincoln Memorial.

FUTURE PROGRESSIVE
They **will be walking** for the next two hours.

PRESENT PERFECT PROGRESSIVE
They **have been walking** for two hours.

PAST PERFECT PROGRESSIVE
They **had been walking** for two hours.

FUTURE PERFECT PROGRESSIVE
They **will have been walking** for two hours by the time everyone gathers at the Memorial.

When communicating informally, you can use the present progressive tense to express future action. Be sure to include a word or a phrase that indicates the future.

She said, "We **are walking** in the March regardless of the weather."

The Emphatic Form   To use the emphatic form, use the present or the past tense of the verb *do* with the infinitive form of the main verb.

Rule   Use the emphatic form to add emphasis or force to the present and past tenses of a verb.

U 12
PRESENT EMPHATIC
We **do walk** to show our support for civil rights.

PAST EMPHATIC
We **did walk** in the famous March on Washington.

The Modal Form   Modals are the auxiliary verbs *can, could, do, did, may, might, must, shall, should, will,* and *would*. Modals are used with main verbs to add emphasis or to provide shades of meaning.

Rule   Use *can* (present tense) and *could* (past tense) to express ability to perform the action of the main verb.

U 13
We **can** still **audition** for tickets for *Our Town*. We **could have gotten** better seats if we had bought them yesterday.

Rule

U 14

Use *do* (present tense) and *did* (past tense) to make negative statements and to ask questions.

We **do** *not* **like** standing in line.
Did you **buy** your tickets yesterday?

Rule

U 15

Use *may* to mean "have permission to" or to express a possibility.

The director said that we **may get** small parts in *Our Town*.
We **may be** late for the tryouts if we don't hurry.

Rule

U 16

Use *might* to express a possibility that is somewhat less likely than one expressed by *may*.

There is always a chance that the rehearsal **might be canceled.**

Rule

U 17

Use *must* to convey the idea that the action of the main verb is required or to suggest a possible explanation.

You **must be** on time for the tryouts.
You **must be** a very good actress to have the lead in *Our Town*.

Rule

U 18

Use *should* to suggest that something ought to happen or that, although something ought to happen, it may not.

You **should audition** for the stage manager. [**Think:** You ought to audition.]
You **should be** at the tryouts by now. [**Think:** You should be, but you aren't.]

Rule

U 19

Use *would* to express actions that were repeated in the past or to show that you disapproved of an action in the past.

In the winter we **would have** rehearsal every day. [repeated action]
We were always late. Well, we **would leave** everything until the last minute! [disapproval]

Exercise 3 **Choosing the Correct Form and Tense of Verbs**

Critical Thinking:

Which verb ending indicates continuing action?

On your paper, write the following sentences, correcting all errors in the use of verbs. Underline the corrected verb forms. If a sentence has no errors, write *Correct*.

SAMPLE To win their rights to an education was an accomplishment that women were proud of.

ANSWER To <u>have won</u> their rights to an education was an accomplishment that women were proud of.

1. Having disciplined herself to read and study, Abigail Adams, the wife of President John Adams, deplored the fact that female learning was ridiculed and that girls were denied a rigorous education.

2. Many colonial towns had so-called "dame schools," kept by women who taught young girls and boys to read and write.
3. Fighting the New York legislature for permission to have started a school, Emma Willard went on to have made education history.
4. Public opinion about education for girls shifts back and forth until after the Civil War.
5. Some people will say that the state of women's education was a national disgrace.
6. This opinion was substantiated by European visitors who constantly commented about the uneducated women in the United States.
7. By the 1830s most states had a program of primary public education and the call went out to young men: We are asking you to become teachers.
8. Because women will have taught for half or a third of the salary demanded by men, those who hired teachers now looked for women to handle the jobs.
9. Now, the thinking went, women did have schools of their own to prepare them for the teaching profession.
10. In case you will wonder, that is how many women's colleges began.

Sequence of Tenses

In most sentences, you use verbs that are in the same tense because the time periods described are the same. In some situations, however, you need to use verbs in different tenses to show a difference in time. You can show this difference in time effectively by changing not only the forms of the verbs but also the relationship of one verb to another.

Consistency of Tenses When two or more actions take place at the same time, you should use verbs that are in the same tense, particularly when you write compound sentences and sentences with compound predicates. Also, remember to use the same verb tense throughout a paragraph unless the meaning of the paragraph requires that you shift tense.

Rule
───
U 20
Use verbs in the same tense to describe actions occurring at the same time.

INCORRECT Hugh **bought** [past] the *Our Town* tickets, while the rest of
us **park** [pres.] the car.

CORRECT Hugh **bought** [past] the *Our Town* tickets, while the rest of
us **parked** [past] the car.

Shifts in Tense If you need to show a shift from one time period to another, be sure to indicate accurately the relationship between the tenses. By changing forms and tenses, you can express precisely the time sequence that is required.

Rule
U 21 If two actions occurred at different times in the past, use the past perfect tense for the earlier action and the past tense for the later one. To emphasize the closeness in time of two events, however, use the past tense for both.

earlier   later
past perf.   past

Jackie Robinson **had played** college football before he **entered** professional baseball. [actions that occurred at different times in the past]

earlier   later
past   past

Robinson **broke** the color line in baseball and **made** it easier for other black athletes to enter professional sports. [past actions that were close in time]

Rule
U 22 If two actions occur in the present but one began in the past, use the present perfect tense for the earlier action and the present tense for the later one.

earlier   later
pres. perf.   pres.

Because she **has been rehearsing** all afternoon, Meg **feels** a sense of accomplishment.

Rule
U 23 If two actions will occur in the future, use the future perfect tense for the action that will take place earlier and the future tense for the action that will occur later.

earlier
future perf.

Because we **will have been rehearsing** *Our Town* for several

later
future

weeks, we **will be** ready for opening night.

Exercise 4 Shifts in Tense

? Critical Thinking:

When do you use more than one tense in a sentence?

On your paper, write each sentence, using the correct verb in parentheses. Underline the verb or verb phrase that you use.

SAMPLE We have been studying the presidency of Theodore Roosevelt and (know, knew) many facts about him.

ANSWER We have been studying the presidency of Theodore Roosevelt and <u>know</u> many facts about him.

1. Roosevelt had been Vice President for only six months when President McKinley (had been, was) assassinated in September 1901.

2. Roosevelt had become so popular that millions of North Americans affectionately (called, had called) him "Teddy."
3. After a cartoonist drew him with a bear cub, toymakers (had begun, began) making stuffed animals called "teddy bears."
4. Roosevelt had always respected the environment, so during his presidency he (had proposed, proposed) legislation to protect the nation's forests and other natural resources.
5. The policy of Roosevelt's predecessors had resulted in colossal waste because it (is, had been) based on the idea that natural resources were inexhaustible.
6. As a result, forests had been cut without thought of future timber needs or erosion, and cattle ranchers and sheepherders (were allowed, had been allowed) to overgraze grasslands.
7. Roosevelt supported legislation providing federal aid to irrigation projects and more than tripled the area of the national forests; as a result, he (will make, made) the cause of conservation popular.
8. By the time Roosevelt (was, had been) elected President, business monopolies or *trusts* had already become large and powerful; increasingly, people (had blamed, blamed) the trusts for rising prices.
9. After he (had signed, signed) a treaty for the construction of the Panama Canal, Roosevelt (says, said) that that act was his "proudest accomplishment."
10. After scholars have praised Roosevelt's conservation and trust-busting activities, they also (mention, mentioned) his promotion of the Pure Food and Drug Act.

Mood

In addition to tense and voice, verbs also express mood. Although you use the indicative mood more frequently, the effective use of the imperative mood and the subjunctive mood will enhance your writing.

The Indicative and the Imperative Moods

Rule
U 24
Use the indicative mood to make a statement of fact or to ask a question.

Pop art sometimes **copies** ordinary objects.
Did you **go** to the pop-art retrospective?

Rule
U 25
Use the imperative mood to make a request or to give a command.

In the imperative mood, the subject of the sentence is often understood rather than stated. Use of the imperative mood adds directness and emphasis to your writing.

Look at the soft sculptures as well as the paintings.
Notice how much this pop-art painting resembles a comic strip.

The Subjunctive Mood

Of the three moods, the subjunctive mood is the most infrequently used in conversation and in informal writing. It is primarily used in formal communications, especially in diplomatic statements and in parliamentary procedure. You also use the subjunctive mood, however, to make doubtful, wishful, or conditional statements; to express something that is contrary to fact; or to ask, insist, order, request, or propose in a respectful manner.

You can use verbs in the subjunctive mood in the present tense and in the past tense.

PRESENT SUBJUNCTIVE

If the truth **be known,** I am to be congratulated on my pop-art sculpture.

PAST SUBJUNCTIVE

If the truth **were known,** I should have been congratulated on my pop-art sculpture.

The most commonly used verb in the subjunctive mood is the verb *be*, used as a linking verb or as an auxiliary verb. Study the differences between the indicative mood and the subjunctive mood in this partial conjugation of the verb *be*.

Indicative		Subjunctive	
Present			
I am	we are	(if) I be	(if) we be
you are	you are	(if) you be	(if) you be
he/she/it is	they are	(if) he/she/it be	(if) they be
Past			
I was	we were	(if) I were	(if) we were
you were	you were	(if) you were	(if) you were
he/she/it was	they were	(if) he/she/it were	(if) they were

Rule

U 26

Use *be* for the present subjunctive of the verb *be* regardless of its subject.

Mrs. Ng asks that her class **be** polite at the pop-art exhibit.
She asks that her students **be** respectful of the other visitors.

Rule

U 27

Use *were* for the past subjunctive of the verb *be* regardless of its subject.

If Rosa **were** here, she wouldn't have made fun of those soup-can paintings.
If Rob and Akiko **were** here, they would have enjoyed seeing the giant comic strips.

Rule

U 28

To form the present subjunctive of verbs other than *be*, use the infinitive form of the verb regardless of its subject.

Professor Fernandez insists that the class **study** op art as well as pop art.

Rule

U 29

To form the past subjunctive of verbs other than *be*, use *had* as an auxiliary verb with the past participle of the main verb.

If I **had known** more about pop art, I would have gone to the exhibit earlier.

Had I **gone** earlier, I would have had more time to enjoy it.

Rule

U 30

To express something that is not true or that you doubt will ever be true, use a verb in the subjunctive mood in a clause that begins with such words as *if*, *as if*, *as though*, or *that*.

He regarded a soup can as though it **were** art!

Notice that something that is contrary to fact is often expressed as a wish or a condition.

I wish that I **were going** to the pop-art exhibit. [I am not going.]
If I **were** you, I would read the catalogue before viewing the exhibit. [I am not you; this statement is contrary to fact.]

Rule

U 31

Use the subjunctive mood in clauses beginning with *that* and in clauses following verbs that (1) make requests, such as *ask, prefer,* and *request;* that (2) make demands, such as *demand, determine, insist, order,* and *require;* and that (3) make proposals, such as *move, propose, recommend,* and *suggest.*

These clauses often appear in formal usage, particularly in standard expressions used in parliamentary procedure.

Morris recommended that this session of the Student Council **be** postponed.

Exercise 5 Mood

On your paper, write each verb or verb phrase. Then label each one *Indicative, Imperative,* or *Subjunctive.*

SAMPLE   If I were a Supreme Court justice, I would vote for the decision.

ANSWER   were — Subjunctive; would vote — Indicative

1. Had the 1896 Supreme Court decision in the case of *Plessy* v. *Ferguson* been different, the history of black people in the United States would have been different too.

? Critical Thinking:

Which mood expresses a wish?

2. In that decision the court ruled that a state law providing for "separate but equal facilities" for black and white people be upheld.

3. This decision was the law of the land until the famous case of *Brown* v. *Board of Education of Topeka* in May 1954, when the Supreme Court ordered that integration of public schools be carried out "with all deliberate speed."

4. One reason this case was brought to the Supreme Court was that black people who had fought for their country in World War II were demanding that their country treat them and their children as first-class citizens.

5. Read the Fourteenth Amendment to the Constitution of the United States and you will see that it guarantees equal protection under the law to all citizens.

6. Some northern and western states did pass legislation outlawing discrimination; had the laws been obeyed, black people would not have faced discrimination in buying homes and seeking jobs.

7. In fact, the laws were often ignored, and so the National Association for the Advancement of Colored People (NAACP), which led the legal battle against segregation, insisted that discrimination cases be taken to court.

8. Consider some Supreme Court decisions that attacked the problem of segregation.

9. In 1946 the Supreme Court declared a Virginia law requiring segregation on interstate buses invalid, and two years later the court ordered that agreements to prevent real estate owners from selling their property to minority groups be declared unlawful.

10. The stage for *Brown* v. *Board of Education of Topeka* had been set by a series of Supreme Court decisions requiring that black students be admitted to then all-white state colleges.

The Writing Connection

Using Consistent Verb Tenses in Your Writing

Used correctly, the different verb tenses convey a precise sense of time. They indicate whether something occurred or existed in the past, the present, or the future as well as variations of those times, such as the distant past and the immediate past. Verb tenses also show the relationship between ongoing events and those that have been completed. Therefore, you must choose carefully among the different tenses to express your exact meaning. Errors in verb-tense usage can distract or confuse your audience.

Writing Assignments

An Eyewitness Account Imagine that you are a witness to the historic Freedom March in Washington, D.C., in 1963 and that you have been asked to write an account of your first-hand observations. *Step 1:* Read the following prewriting notes and select the ones you wish to use.

Reference Point:
pages 154–183

> **PREWRITING NOTES**
> organized to protest racial inequality
> 200,000 blacks and whites marched
> Leaders of the march hoped to urge Congress to pass a civil rights bill
>   that would prohibit segregation.
> Marchers sang a freedom song, "We Shall Overcome."
> Who led the march? — Dr. Martin Luther King, Jr.
> At the base of the Lincoln Memorial, Dr. King gave his famous "I have
>   a dream" speech.

Step 2: Organize your notes logically. You may wish to "create" some additional, concrete details that will give your account more impact, such as how you felt or what someone near you said. Add these details to your notes. *Step 3:* Write your account in the present tense. Use other verb tenses where they are appropriate to convey your precise meaning. Try to give your audience a sense of immediacy so that your readers will feel as though they are actually witnessing the march. *Step 4:* Revise your piece, making your writing as vivid and concrete as possible. Be sure to check carefully for consistency of tense. *Step 5:* Proofread your account, and make a clean copy for your teacher.

A Newspaper Column A newspaper column is usually more personal than a news article. The columnist often expresses his or her view in a personal style. To write such a column giving your opinion, first select one of the following twentieth-century topics or one of your own choosing: the most interesting public figure, the most significant political change or event, the most influential work of art or literature, or the most important scientific advance. Be sure that you have an opinion about the topic and some evidence to support it. Ask yourself questions as a way of gathering details. Then write a short newspaper column, clearly stating your opinion and giving reasons to support it. Ask a classmate to read what you have written and to comment on both content and usage. Next, revise your draft with your classmate's comments in mind. Pay particular attention to consistency of tense. Finally, proofread your column and prepare a neat copy to submit to your school newspaper or to a special-edition class newspaper.

Reference Point:
*pages 230–231,
234–236, and
254–259*

Subject-Verb Agreement

Singular and Plural Subjects and Verbs

Rule   A subject and its verb must agree in number.

U 32   You can change the forms of nouns, pronouns, and verbs to express number. If the subject is singular, the form of the verb should be singular. If the subject is plural, the form of the verb should be plural.

> **SINGULAR**   *Grandma Moses* **was** a primitive painter who lived on farms all her life.
>
> **PLURAL**   Her *paintings* **are** scenes of rural life.

Verb Phrases

For a verb phrase to agree with its subject, the auxiliary verb must agree in number with the subject.

> **SINGULAR**   *Marianne* **has tried** some primitive landscapes.
>
> **PLURAL**   *Marianne and I* **have taken** art lessons together.

Intervening Words and Phrases

Sometimes, words and phrases come between a subject and its verb. Such intervening words or phrases do not change the number of the subject, and, as always, the verb must agree in number with the subject. Be sure to make the verb agree in number with the subject of the sentence, not with some word in the intervening phrase.

> **SINGULAR**   *Grandma Moses*, a latecomer to oils, **was** seventy-six years old when she created her first painting. [**Think:** Grandma Moses *was.*]
>
> **PLURAL**   The *critics* viewing her one-artist show in 1940 **were impressed** with her naive realism. [**Think:** critics *were.*]

Inverted Word Order

In some sentences, especially questions or sentences beginning with *Here* or *There*, you may have difficulty locating the subject because the verb comes before the subject. By mentally rearranging the sentence in its normal subject-verb order, you can find the subject and make the verb agree with it in number.

> **SINGULAR**   In the landscape **is** a peaceful *farm*. [**Think:** farm *is.*]
>
> **PLURAL**   There **are** many *scenes* of farm life. [**Think:** scenes *are.*]

SINGULAR   **Is** Uncle George or Aunt Susan meeting us at the exhibit?
[**Think:** Aunt Susan *is.*]

PLURAL   Here **are** a *painting* and an *embroidery* done by Grandma
Moses. [**Think:** a painting and an embroidery *are.*]

Exercise 1 Locating Subjects and Verbs

On your paper, write the verb form in each sentence that agrees in number with the subject of the sentence. Label each verb or verb phrase
Singular or *Plural*.

SAMPLE   An announcement about an electric motor developed by a
group of California scientists (has been, have been) made.
ANSWER   has been — Singular

1. Researchers at the University of California at Berkeley (have constructed, has constructed) an electric motor the width of a human
hair.
2. Amazingly, the rotor in the device (measure, measures) only sixty
microns; a human hair is seventy to one hundred microns thick.
3. Scientists here and at other research centers (has, have) also created gears with teeth the size of blood cells.
4. These devices, small and light enough to be inhaled, (has been,
have been) classified as machines because of their moving parts.
5. At least a hundred times larger than these (is, are) the next smallest devices, according to researchers at the University of
California.
6. One possible application that scientists envision for the future (includes, include) scissors or perhaps electric buzz saws for delicate
microsurgery.
7. There (is, are) other possibilities too; one machine that scientists
dream about (travels, travel) through arteries.
8. The possibility of developing armies of "gnat robots" (are, is)
something that engineers at the Massachusetts Institute of Technology (are talking, is talking) about.
9. Still experimental (is, are) the actual construction of such tiny
moving parts.
10. The actual uses for a new technology always (remains, remain)
speculative for a while, but in the future (lies, lie) a vast array of
amazing new machines.

Critical
Thinking:
Can *here* or
there ever be
the subject of
a sentence?

Determining the Number of the Subject

In some sentences, you may find it troublesome to determine the
number of the subject. To avoid confusion, pay special attention to the
types of subjects shown on the following pages.

Subject-Verb Agreement   637

Compound Subjects

A **compound subject** *(page 567)* is composed of two or more subjects that are connected by *and, or, nor, either . . . or,* or *neither . . . nor.* A compound subject may take a singular or a plural verb, depending on (1) which conjunction is used and (2) whether the words in the compound subject are singular or plural.

Rule
───
U 33

Use a plural verb with most compound subjects connected by *and.*

PLURAL   The *Prime Minister* and the *President* **have attended** the Yalta Conference.

Rule
───
U 34

Use a singular verb with a compound subject that refers to one person or one thing or to something that is generally considered as a unit — that is, plural in form but singular in meaning.

SINGULAR   The well-known *historian and lecturer* **is addressing** our twentieth-century history class tomorrow. [The author and lecturer are the same person.]

Rule
───
U 35

Use a singular verb with a compound subject that is composed of singular nouns or pronouns connected by *or* or *nor.*

SINGULAR   Either my *father* or my *uncle* **has** my grandfather's World War II medals.

Rule
───
U 36

Use a plural verb with a compound subject that is composed of plural nouns or pronouns connected by *or* or *nor.*

PLURAL   Neither the *medals* nor Grandfather's other war *mementos* **have been discarded.**

Rule
───
U 37

When a compound subject is composed of a singular subject and a plural subject connected by *or* or *nor,* use a verb that agrees in number with the subject that is closer to the verb in the sentence.

SINGULAR   Neither the *medals* nor the *uniform* **is** in our attic.

PLURAL   Neither my *grandfather* nor his *sons* **remember** where these war mementos are.

In following this rule, you may discover that some sentences sound awkward. In that case, rephrase the sentence.

The *medals* **are** not in our attic, and neither **is** the *uniform.*

Rule
───
U 38

When the subject is both affirmative and negative, use a verb form that agrees in number with the affirmative part of the subject.

My *uncles,* not *I,* **are going** to search for Grandfather's war souvenirs.

Indefinite Pronouns as Subjects

Indefinite pronouns *(page 538)* are pronouns that refer to people or things in general. Some indefinite pronouns are always singular and, therefore, always take singular verbs. The following chart gives examples of singular indefinite pronouns.

Singular Indefinite Pronouns	
anybody	neither
anyone	nobody
anything	no one
each	nothing
either	one
everybody	other
everyone	somebody
everything	someone
much	something

SINGULAR   Almost *everybody* **takes** snapshots.

Some indefinite pronouns are always plural and, therefore, always take plural verbs. The most common are *both, few, many,* and *several.*

PLURAL   *Many* **take** photography more seriously.

The indefinite pronouns *all, any, enough, more, most, none, plenty,* and *some* may be singular or plural, depending upon their antecedents *(page 536).*

SINGULAR   *Most* of the photography by Ansel Adams **is** landscapes. [The indefinite pronoun refers to *photography;* it is singular and takes the singular verb *is.*]

PLURAL   *Most* of Adams's photographs **are** of the West. [*Most* refers to *photographs;* it is plural and takes the plural verb *are.*]

Sometimes, an indefinite pronoun refers to a word that is understood rather than stated.

Even though some had gone, *most* **were** still at the Ansel Adams exhibit when we arrived. [The listener or reader would know that the pronouns refer to *viewers.*]

Exercise 2   Agreement of Subjects and Predicates

On your paper, write the subject of each of the following sentences. Then write the verb form in parentheses that agrees with the subject. Finally, state whether the subject and the verb are singular or plural.

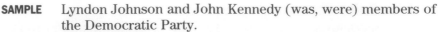

? Critical Thinking:

How do you determine whether an indefinite pronoun is singular or plural?

SAMPLE   Lyndon Johnson and John Kennedy (was, were) members of the Democratic Party.

ANSWER   Lyndon Johnson and John Kennedy — were — plural

1. Both partisans and foes (has, have) problems assessing the career of Lyndon Baines Johnson, for he was a complicated man.

2. Johnson lived for politics; in fact, most of his adult life (was, were) spent in politics.

3. In 1948 this popular and capable senator and loyal party member (were, was) chosen as majority leader of the Senate, the youngest ever selected majority leader by either party.

4. When hardly anyone else (was, were) thinking about space exploration, Johnson sponsored the law that established the National Aeronautics and Space Administration (NASA); soon everyone (was, were) thinking about space.

5. The first civil rights bill in more than eighty years (was, were) passed thanks to the efforts of Lyndon Johnson.

6. Johnson announced his candidacy for the presidency a week before the 1960 nominating convention, but most of the votes on the first ballot (was, were) cast in favor of Senator John F. Kennedy.

7. For his vice-presidential nominee, Kennedy chose Johnson. "Johnson, he said, "(has, have) demonstrated on many occasions his brilliant qualifications for the leadership we require today."

8. One hour and thirty-nine minutes after President Kennedy was assassinated, both Mrs. Johnson and Mrs. Kennedy (was, were) at Johnson's side when he took the oath of office aboard the presidential jet at Love Field, near Dallas.

9. Today much of the federal budget (goes, go) to help citizens participating in programs begun by Lyndon Johnson.

10. Johnson's heart and soul (was, were) invested in creating what he called the "Great Society."

Collective Nouns as Subjects

A **collective noun** *(page 533)* is a word that names a group of people or a collection of objects that is singular in form and may be either singular or plural in meaning. Examples include *committee, crowd, fleet, jury,* and *team.*

Rule

U 39   If a collective noun refers to a group as a whole, use a singular verb.

     SINGULAR   The *committee* **convenes** at noon. [The committee is thought of as a whole.]

Rule

U 40   If a collective noun refers to individual members or parts of a group, use a plural verb.

     PLURAL   The *committee* **debate** the merits of the civil rights bill. [The members of the committee are acting as individuals.]

Nouns with Plural Form

Nouns such as *economics, mathematics, measles,* and *news* are plural in form but singular in meaning. Although they end in *s,* they refer to a single thing or to a unit and, therefore, take a singular verb. (Notice that removing the *s* does not make a singular noun; for instance, *measle* is not the singular form of *measles.*)

SINGULAR   *Aeronautics* **is** an important area of study for future astronauts.

Other nouns, such as *clothes, congratulations, pliers,* and *scissors,* end in *s* and take a plural verb although they refer to one thing.

PLURAL   The *scissors* **are floating** in the weightless atmosphere of the space capsule.

Some nouns, such as *athletics, dramatics,* and *politics,* end in *s* but may be singular or plural, depending upon their meaning in the sentence. Use your dictionary to find out whether a noun that ends in *s* takes a singular or a plural verb.

SINGULAR   In her interview, Helen Hayes said that *dramatics* **has** always **been** important in her life. [*dramatics* is the practice of acting]

PLURAL   His *dramatics* on the court **bring** the tennis player bad publicity. [*dramatics* are instances of dramatic behavior]

Exercise 3 **Agreement of Subjects and Predicates**

On your paper, write the verb that correctly completes each sentence.

SAMPLE   A team of people working together as one often (accomplish, accomplishes) more than a single person can.
ANSWER   accomplishes

? Critical Thinking:

Is a noun ending in *s* always plural?

1. The women's liberation movement (have gone, has gone) through many stages.
2. That is natural, for even a group of people with similar goals (do, does) not always speak with one voice.
3. The changing politics of the women's movement (makes, make) fascinating reading.
4. One woman says that her family (was, were) often in disagreement about feminism and had interesting debates among themselves.
5. The Congress, too, (has, have) often been in bitter disagreement about legislation for women's rights.
6. Feminists have learned that a political action committee (is, are) effective in winning congressional support.
7. Congress (has, have) passed many laws to promote equal rights for women.
8. The public (seems, seem) to support the idea of equal pay for equal work.

9. The public (is, are) often in disagreement about other aspects of the role of women in society, however.
10. Economics (is, are) a critical factor in the further advancement of the women's movement.

Titles and Names as Subjects

Titles of individual books, stories, plays, movies, television programs, musical compositions, and magazines take the singular form of the verb, even though the titles may contain plural words. The name of a country or of an organization also takes a singular verb when it refers to an entire country or group. (See pages 712 and 737 for rules regarding capitalization and underlining, or italics, for titles.)

SINGULAR   Hemingway's *A Farewell to Arms* **was made** into a movie.

SINGULAR   The United Nations often **sends** peace-keeping forces into troubled areas.

Words of Amount and Time

Rule
——
U 41   Use singular verbs with words and phrases that refer to single units: fractions, measurements, amounts of money, weights, volumes, or intervals of time when the interval refers to a specific unit.

SINGULAR   *Two hundred meters* **was** the length of Jesse Owens's record-setting run.

Rule
——
U 42   Use a plural verb when the amount or the time is considered to be a number of separate units.

PLURAL   *Four gold medals* **were** won by Jesse Owens.

When you use *the number* or *the variety* as a subject, you usually use a singular verb. When you use *a number* or *a variety* as a subject, you usually use a plural verb.

SINGULAR   *The number* of Olympic medals won by this black American **was** a severe disappointment to Adolf Hitler.

PLURAL   *A number* of medals **were** won by other black athletes.

Exercise 4   **Agreement: Titles, Names, Amounts, and Time**

Critical Thinking:
Does the title of an organization use a singular or a plural verb?

On your paper, write the verb that correctly completes each sentence.

SAMPLE   *The New York Times* (has, have) printed many stories about Harry S. Truman.
ANSWER   has

1. When Harry S. Truman became President upon the death of President Franklin Roosevelt, the United States (was, were) still at war.

2. The United Nations (was, were) still in the process of being organized.
3. An estimated one billion dollars (was, were) saved as a result of Truman's investigations of waste and inefficiency in defense spending.
4. Eight years (is, are) a long time to be President, and Truman's years in office (was, were) eventful ones.
5. Only four weeks of his term (was, were) gone when Germany surrendered, and the war in Europe was over.
6. After the war, millions of dollars (was, were) approved by Congress to help to rebuild Europe through the Marshall Plan.
7. *Headlines*, a television series, (was, were) in agreement with most political analysts when it declared that Truman would lose the 1948 election.
8. *The London Times* (was, were) not alone in predicting that the Republican candidate, New York governor Thomas E. Dewey, would be a sure winner.
9. (Was, Were) the Organization of American States (OAS) in existence during Truman's term of office?
10. Truman's *Year of Decisions*, which he wrote after leaving office on January 19, 1953, (discuss, discusses) his presidency and (is, are) a valuable resource for historians.

Sentences with Predicate Nominatives

Using a predicate nominative *(page 575)* can confuse subject-verb agreement when the subject and the predicate nominative differ in number.

Rule

U 43

Use a verb that agrees in number with the subject, not with the predicate nominative.

> **INCORRECT** *Flowers* **is** one of Georgia O'Keeffe's favorite subjects.
>
> subj.   P.N.
> **CORRECT** *Flowers* **are** one of Georgia O'Keeffe's favorite subjects. [plural subject; singular predicate nominative]

Exercise 5 **Sentences with Predicate Nominatives**

On your paper, write the verb in parentheses that agrees with the subject.

SAMPLE The four World War II allies (was, were) the force that controlled Berlin.

ANSWER were

1. The Truman Doctrine (is, are) one of Harry Truman's most important legacies.

Critical Thinking:
Does the predicate nominative affect the number of the verb?

2. Isolationism and avoidance of worldwide responsibility (was, were) an old United States policy that the Truman Doctrine helped to change.
3. After World War II, the USSR and its neighboring states (were, was) a force to be reckoned with.
4. According to the allied peace terms, Berlin (was, were) now two cities controlled by the United States, Britain, France, and the USSR.
5. The Berlin Air Lift (was, were) supplies for over two million people; these supplies were flown to the German capital on Truman's orders.
6. Truman was interested in Korea, whose fate (was, were) conflict and war between forces in the north and forces in the south.
7. The Security Council of the United Nations decided that the North Koreans (was, were) the aggressor and called on UN members to aid South Korea.
8. Two days later President Truman acted upon his belief that American soldiers (was, were) the solution and ordered American military forces into action.
9. Military, naval, and medical units (was, were) the response of other member nations of the UN.
10. The UN forces (was, were) the responsibility of General Douglas MacArthur.

Agreement in Adjective Clauses

When a relative pronoun, such as *who, which,* or *that,* is the subject of an adjective clause *(page 588),* decide whether the verb of the adjective clause should be singular or plural by finding the antecedent *(pages 537–538)* of the relative pronoun.

Rule
_____
U 44

The verb of an adjective clause and the antecedent of the relative pronoun must agree in number.

> SINGULAR *Willie Mays, who* **was** one of baseball's greatest center fielders, was known for his "basket catch." [*Who* refers to *Willie Mays,* the singular antecedent.]

> PLURAL Other baseball *center fielders who* **have achieved** fame include Joe DiMaggio, Duke Snider, and Mickey Mantle. [*Who* refers to *center fielders,* the plural antecedent.]

Rule
_____
U 45

When an adjective clause follows the term *one of those,* use a plural verb in the clause.

> PLURAL Joe DiMaggio is *one of those who* **are** still talked about today.

Exercise 6 Agreement in Adjective Clauses

On your paper, write the verb form in parentheses that agrees with the subject. Then identify the subject of the clause and its antecedent.

? Critical Thinking:

When does a relative pronoun use a plural verb?

SAMPLE   Dwight D. Eisenhower, who (was, were) one of the most popular men in the country, became President in 1953.

ANSWER   was — who — Dwight D. Eisenhower

1. In 1948 Eisenhower had said that lifetime professional soldiers were people who (was, were) not good choices for political office.
2. By 1952, however, Republicans, who (was, were) urging him to run for President, finally prevailed.
3. That successful election was one of those that (shows, show) how personal popularity can win elections.
4. The new President, who (was, were) used to delegating authority in the army, directed that information and opinions come to him only "through channels."
5. At Eisenhower's urging, Congress, which at that time (was, were) controlled by the Republicans, extended the Social Security Act to ten million more people and increased its benefits.
6. He pushed Congress to enact a program of health insurance, which (was, were) to be partially underwritten by the federal government, but he could not get the measure passed.
7. His first order of business was one of those tasks that (is, are) often promised in campaigns but rarely fulfilled: balancing the budget.
8. By 1956 the federal budget, which (is, are) often a battleground for Congress and the President, showed its first surplus in eight years.
9. The accomplishment of building the St. Lawrence Seaway with Canada was one of those projects that (was, were) attempted earlier but (was, were) not successful until the Eisenhower administration.
10. During Eisenhower's first term, the United States economy, which (tends, tend) to rise and fall in cycles, reached new peaks of prosperity.

Every and *Many a*

As adjectives, *every* and *many a* (or *many an*) emphasize separateness when they modify subjects. *Every teacher* means "every single teacher," not "all teachers"; *many a teacher* means that each teacher is separate from all the other teachers.

Rule

U 46

Use a singular verb with a single subject or a compound subject modified by *every, many a,* or *many an.*

Every "flapper" and "sheik" **was** learning the Charleston.

In the twenties, *many a* college student **was** doing a dance called the "Varsity Drag."

? Critical Thinking:

Which adjective can make a compound subject singular?

On your paper, rewrite each sentence, correcting all errors in subject-verb agreement by changing the form of the verb. Underline the correct verb form in each new sentence. If a sentence contains no errors, write *Correct* on your paper.

SAMPLE   Many a challenge were faced by the United States during the Eisenhower years.

ANSWER   Many a challenge <u>was</u> faced by the United States during the Eisenhower years.

1. Two major attempts to reduce the President's power was made during Eisenhower's first term.
2. The Bricker amendment, named after Senator John W. Bricker of Ohio, was designed to limit the President's treaty-making powers.
3. There was many senators in favor of the amendment, but in the end it failed by a single-vote margin.
4. One of the nation's biggest problems during the Eisenhower years were the wild accusations of Senator Joseph R. McCarthy.
5. McCarthy accused many patriotic people of being communists, and many a senator were afraid to challenge him.
6. McCarthy's attack against libraries was one of those maneuvers that were frightening to people who defend free speech.
7. Not all of the news during the Eisenhower years was bad; with the help of leaders in Congress, for example, the Civil Rights Acts of 1957 and 1960, guaranteeing blacks the right to vote, was passed.
8. *The Cold War Years* are one of those titles that sounds right for a book about this era.
9. Launching of the first *Sputnik* in 1957 and putting the first man in space were an immediate psychological victory for the Soviets and spurred North American moves into space.
10. Near the end of Eisenhower's second term, many citizens was in favor of more social programs. Such programs were the loser, people believed, because so much money were going into defense.

The Writing Connection

Making Subjects and Verbs Agree in Your Writing

To make your writing clear and easy to follow, you should take special care with subject-verb agreement. The subject of a verb may be either singular or plural, and it may be in the first, second, or third person. Be sure to select the verb form that agrees with its subject in number and person.

Writing Assignment

A Publicity Flier You and your friends are planning a Golden Oldies Costume Party to raise money for charity, and you have been asked to write a publicity flier to distribute at school. You want to attract the interest — and attendance — of as many students as possible.

First, choose a "time" for your party from the following list. Select one with which you are familiar from your studies, your reading, or the media.

The Roaring Twenties	The Fabulous Fifties
World War II Era	The Sixties

Next, brainstorm with several of your classmates, pooling what you know about the period. Use clustering for details about popular music, dress, lifestyle, famous people, and slang expressions. Then, on your own, look over your prewriting notes and decide which details would be most useful for the decorations, entertainment, refreshments, and activities of your costume party. Also select details for suggested costumes. Now write your flier, using vivid language to appeal to your schoolmates. Before you revise, ask a classmate for comments on both the content and the usage of your draft. With your classmate's comments in mind, revise your advertisement, making sure that you have used correct subject-verb agreement. Finally, proofread your flier and "distribute" it to your classmates by adding it to the class bulletin board.

Reference Point:
pages 13–15

Using Pronouns

Pronoun Antecedents

All pronouns, whether they are personal *(page 536)*, indefinite *(page 538)*, relative *(page 537)*, reflexive *(page 537)*, or intensive *(page 537)*, must agree with their antecedents in number, gender, and person *(page 536)*.

Agreement in Number

Rule
U 47
Use a singular pronoun to refer to or to replace a singular antecedent; use a plural pronoun to refer to or to replace a plural antecedent.

Singular Pronouns	Plural Pronouns
I, me, my, mine you, your, yours she, her, hers he, him, his it, its	we, us, our, ours you, your, yours they, them, their, theirs

SINGULAR   *Jack* said that **he** would take **his** camera.

PLURAL   Jack's *friends* said that **they** would take **their** cameras.

Rule
—
U 48   Use a plural pronoun to refer to or to replace two or more singular antecedents joined by *and;* use a singular pronoun to refer to or to replace two or more singular antecedents joined by *or* or *nor.*

Jack and Franco went to see the exhibit by Ansel Adams, **their** favorite photographer.

Neither *Jack nor Franco* wants **his** own photos to look like Adams's.

Indefinite Pronouns as Antecedents   The following indefinite pronouns are singular in meaning. Use singular pronouns to refer to or to replace them.

Singular Indefinite Pronouns			
anybody	everybody	nobody	somebody
anyone	everyone	no one	someone
anything	everything	nothing	something
each	much	one	
either	neither	other	

SINGULAR   *Each* of the women had **her** own opinion about the Ansel Adams landscapes.

In sentences where the intended meaning of a singular indefinite pronoun is plural, use a plural pronoun to refer to or to replace the antecedent. For example, it is not sensible to use a singular pronoun in the following sentence.

UNCLEAR   When *everybody* arrived at the exhibit, **he or she** bought a ticket and went inside.

Because the antecedent *everybody* really means *all* and not *each person* individually, you should use a plural pronoun or, preferably, rewrite the sentence to avoid the awkward construction.

CLEAR   When *everybody* arrived at the exhibit, **they** bought tickets and went inside.

BETTER   When *all* of the people arrived at the exhibit, **they** bought tickets and went inside.

Some indefinite pronouns, such as *several, both, few,* and *many,* are plural in meaning; use plural pronouns to refer to or to replace them.

PLURAL   *Several* of the students tried taking **their** own landscape photographs.

Some indefinite pronouns, such as *any, enough, more, most, none, plenty,* and *some,* can be either singular or plural. Use either singular or plural pronouns to refer to or to replace them, depending on the meaning of the sentence.

SINGULAR   *All* of the color in this print has lost **its** vibrancy. [*All* refers to *color,* which is singular; *its* refers to *all.*]

PLURAL   *All* of the photographs in this gallery have the western wilderness as **their** subject. [*All* refers to *photographs,* which is plural; *their* refers to *all.*]

Collective Nouns as Antecedents   When an antecedent is a collective noun *(page 533),* you must first determine whether the collective noun is singular or plural in meaning. If it is singular, use a singular pronoun to refer to or to replace it; if it is plural, use a plural pronoun.

SINGULAR   The photography *class* voted to change **its** meeting time. [The meeting time is for the entire class as a unit.]

PLURAL   The photography *class* voted to do **their** landscape photos on **their** own time. [The class voted for individual photo taking.]

Exercise 1   Agreement in Number

On your paper, write the pronoun in parentheses that agrees with the antecedent in each sentence. Then write the antecedent.

SAMPLE   The nation suffered during (its, their) worst economic depression in the 1930s.

ANSWER   its — nation

1. In 1929 the stock market dropped to (their, its) lowest point in years.

? Critical Thinking:

What is an antecedent?

2. The rich person and the poor person alike had (his, their) future determined by the stock-market crash.
3. Many people lost (his or her, their) jobs in the 1930s.
4. None of the local governments across the nation could collect much of (its, their) taxes.
5. In the 1920s, hardly any of the leading companies realized that an oversupply of (their, its) products existed.
6. Because of competition, some of the producers lowered (his or her, their) prices below the actual cost of production.
7. In 1932 everybody turned (his or her, their) attention to the newly elected President, Franklin Roosevelt.
8. Much of his vision of the ideal government still has (its, their) appeal today.
9. The Congress used (its, their) power to create economic reform.
10. Roosevelt and other statesmen used (his, their) influence to create the New Deal.

Agreement in Gender

The gender *(page 536)* of a pronoun is either masculine, feminine, or neuter. The masculine pronouns are *he, him,* and *his;* the feminine pronouns are *she, her,* and *hers;* and the neuter pronouns, those refering to neither masculine nor feminine antecedents, are *it* and *its.*

Rule
U 49

Use a pronoun that agrees in gender with its antecedent.

MASCULINE   *Martin Luther King, Jr.,* motivated **his** followers to take action.

FEMININE   *Flannery O'Connor* based **her** stories on her own experience.

NEUTER   The *poetry* of Robert Frost and Emily Dickinson still has **its** appeal today.

Sometimes it is unclear whether the gender of a singular antecedent is masculine or feminine. If a neuter pronoun will not work, you can use the phrase *his or her* to show that the antecedent could be either masculine or feminine. This construction, however, is often awkward. If possible, rewrite the sentence so that the antecedent and all words that refer to it or replace it are plural. Sometimes you can repeat the noun that is the antecedent.

AWKWARD   A test *pilot* must have confidence in **his or her** skills.

BETTER   Test *pilots* must have confidence in **their** skills.

Agreement in Person

Pronouns are in either the first person, the second person, or the third person *(page 536)*.

Rule   Use a pronoun that agrees in person with its antecedent.

U 50

FIRST PERSON   *I* will read *The Great Gatsby* before **my** brother does.

SECOND PERSON   Will *you* read *The Great Gatsby* before **your** brother does?

THIRD PERSON   *Annette* will read *The Great Gatsby* before **her** brother does.

When the indefinite pronoun *one* is an antecedent, use a third-person singular pronoun to refer to it or to replace it, or repeat the indefinite pronoun.

One often feels that **he or she** is suffering along with the characters in *The Grapes of Wrath.*

One often feels that **one** is suffering along with the characters in *The Grapes of Wrath.*

Note: In general, do not use *he* to represent both *he* and *she*. You should either repeat the noun or pronoun that is the antecedent or rewrite the sentence to make both the antecedent and the pronoun plural.

Exercise 2   **Pronoun Agreement**

On your paper, write the pronoun or pronoun phrase in parentheses that correctly completes each sentence. Then identify the gender, number, and person of the pronoun or pronouns.

SAMPLE   Women can be proud of (her, their) role in the history of jazz.
ANSWER   their — feminine; plural; third person

1. The ancestors of black Americans brought African musical traditions with (him, them) to the United States.
2. American folk music had (his, its) influence on jazz too.
3. Black American musicians listened to many different kinds of music and slowly blended (it, them).
4. When one listens to jazz, (one, he) is listening to a truly American musical form.
5. In the early 1900s, a typical jazz musician spent (his, his or her) life in the South.

? Critical Thinking:
What pronouns are used when the gender of the antecedent is unknown?

6. Later on, many musicians brought (one's, their) instruments to northern cities.
7. New Orleans and Kansas City certainly had (its, their) influences on jazz.
8. In 1922 Louis Armstrong moved to Chicago, taking his experiences in New Orleans with (it, him).
9. Other musicians took New Orleans jazz rhythms with (him, them) to New York City.
10. One can sometimes hear the influence of many different kinds of music, from regional to classical, when (he, he or she) listens to modern jazz.

Agreement of Reflexive and Intensive Pronouns

Reflexive and intensive pronouns *(page 537)*, formed by adding either *-self* or *-selves* to personal pronouns, must also agree with their antecedents in number, gender, and person. Reflexive and intensive pronouns are always used with antecedents; do not use them alone to replace a noun or a personal pronoun.

    INCORRECT For the first time, *Robert and I* are flying the plane by **itself.**

    INCORRECT For the first time, Robert and **myself** are flying the plane.

    CORRECT For the first time, *Robert and I* are flying the plane by **ourselves.**

(For more information on correct usage of reflexive and intensive pronouns, see the Usage Notes on pages 680, 683, and 686.)

Exercise 3 **Pronoun Agreement**

? **Critical Thinking:**

Can a reflexive or intensive pronoun replace a subject?

On your paper, write the pronoun in parentheses that correctly completes each sentence.

SAMPLE   John asked (us, ourselves) what we knew about the history of television.

ANSWER   us

1. Many inventors found (ourselves, themselves) imagining how television might work.
2. Vladimir Zworykin (themselves, himself) made a TV in the 1920s.
3. (Himself, He) created a device called an "iconoscope."
4. RCA and NBC began an experimental TV station for (itself, themselves) in 1930.
5. The station (itself, themselves) was in New York City.
6. (It, Itself) continued in operation until 1933.
7. In 1939, during the World's Fair (it, itself), commercial broadcasts began in New York City.

8. (Themselves, They) ceased during World War II, however.
9. My friends and I consider (themselves, ourselves) lucky to live in the age of television.
10. Fran and (he, himself) like situation comedies and variety shows best.

Pronoun Case

To show the grammatical use of a pronoun in a sentence, you change its form, or case. The three cases are nominative, objective, and possessive.

Personal Pronouns by Case		
Case	Singular	Plural
Nominative	I you he, she, it	we you they
Objective	me you him, her, it	us you them
Possessive*	my, mine your, yours his, her, hers, its	our, ours your, yours their, theirs

*The words *my, your, his, her, its, our,* and *their* are sometimes called pronominal adjectives *(page 551).*

Pronouns in the Nominative Case

Rule
U 51
Use the nominative case when a pronoun acts as a subject *(page 566)*, as a predicate nominative *(page 575)*, or as an appositive to a subject or to a predicate nominative *(page 579)*.

SUBJECT
I would like to know who founded the Photo-Secession group in the early 1900s.

PREDICATE NOMINATIVE
It was **he,** Alfred Stieglitz, the man who also started the magazine *Camera Work.*

APPOSITIVE TO A SUBJECT

The couple, Georgia O'Keeffe and **he,** promoted modern art in their galleries. [**Think:** Georgia O'Keeffe and he promoted.]

APPOSITIVE TO A PREDICATE NOMINATIVE

They were the ones, Stieglitz and **she,** who promoted modern art.
[**Think:** They are Stieglitz and she.]

Pronouns in the Objective Case

Rule

U 52

Use the objective case when a pronoun acts as a direct object *(page 572)*, as an indirect object *(page 572)*, as an object of a preposition *(page 558)*, as a subject or object of an infinitive clause *(page 594)*, as an appositive to a direct or an indirect object *(page 572)*, or as an appositive to an object of a preposition *(page 579)*.

DIRECT OBJECT
Mara helped **her** with information on Georgia O'Keeffe.

INDIRECT OBJECT
She lent **her** a book of O'Keeffe's paintings.

OBJECT OF A PREPOSITION
Nancy gave it back to **her** after her class.

SUBJECT OF AN INFINITIVE CLAUSE
Mr. Chen told **them** to see him after school.

OBJECT OF AN INFINITIVE CLAUSE
Mr. Chen wanted me to tell **them** about the new O'Keeffe exhibit.

APPOSITIVE TO A DIRECT OBJECT
Mr. Chen drove the girls, Mara and **her,** to the exhibit.

APPOSITIVE TO AN INDIRECT OBJECT
He told them, Mara and **her,** all about O'Keeffe's life.

APPOSITIVE TO AN OBJECT OF A PREPOSITION
Mr. Chen wanted to discuss the paintings with both of them, Mara and **her.**

Exercise 4 **Nominative and Objective Case Pronouns**

Critical Thinking:

When are pronouns used in the nominative case?

On your paper, write the pronouns in parentheses that correctly complete each sentence. Beside each pronoun write whether it is in the nominative or the objective case.

SAMPLE The class and (me, I) visited Hoover Dam.
ANSWER I — nominative

1. My friends, Jack and (her, she), learned that Hoover Dam is one of the highest dams in the world.
2. The guide showed (we, us) students a picture of President Hoover.
3. The dam is named after (he, him).
4. The guide said, "This is (him, he)."

5. Jan asked either (him, he) or the assistant why the dam was built.
6. The guide told us, the class and (me, I), that the dam was completed in 1936.
7. Andy told Jan and (me, I) that Hoover Dam is 726 feet high and 1244 feet long.
8. My partners, Rosa and (he, him), said that the dam supplies electricity to cities in the Pacific Southwest.
9. The guide told (we, us) future engineers, Roberto and (I, me), that the dam stores billions of gallons of water.
10. These are my classmates, Roberto and (her, she), who accompanied (I, me) on the trip to Hoover Dam.

Pronouns in the Possessive Case

Possessive pronouns show to whom or to what something belongs. They do not include apostrophes.

Rule
U 53
Use the possessive pronouns *mine, yours, his, hers, its, ours,* and *theirs* to refer to or to replace nouns.

You can use these possessive pronouns in the same way that you would use nouns. These pronouns can function as subjects, predicate nominatives, direct objects, indirect objects, objects of prepositions, or appositives.

SUBJECT
Hers was the first television in the neighborhood.

PREDICATE NOMINATIVE
The house that everyone wanted to visit was **hers.**

DIRECT OBJECT
After hearing that Uncle Gustav already had a TV, my grandmother went out and bought **hers.**

INDIRECT OBJECT
The neighbors gave **hers** a rave review.

OBJECT OF A PREPOSITION
Later in the fifties, the Goldbergs got the first of **theirs.**

APPOSITIVE
Now the neighborhood could choose from two televisions, **hers** and **theirs.**

Rule
U 54
Use the possessive pronouns* *my, your, his, her, its, our,* and *their* to modify nouns.

My grandmother still has **her** first television set.

*These possessive pronouns are sometimes called pronominal adjectives *(page 551).*

Rule Use a possessive pronoun to modify a gerund.

U 55 **Gerunds** *(page 583)* are *-ing* forms of verbs that are used as nouns. Because they function as nouns, use the possessive forms of nouns and pronouns to modify them.

> **Your** studying is more important than any television show! [*Your* is used instead of *you* because it modifies *studying* — it is *your studying* that is important.]

Exercise 5 Possessive Pronouns

? **Critical Thinking:**
Do possessive pronouns ever have apostrophes?

On your paper, write the pronoun in parentheses that correctly completes each sentence. Indicate the person, the number, and the case of each pronoun.

SAMPLE (Mine, My) report was about President Kennedy.

ANSWER My — first person; singular; possessive case

1. (He, His) was an important, but short, presidency.
2. (Yours, Your) report told of Kennedy's heroism in World War II.
3. It was so well done, the class gave (your, yours) a standing ovation.
4. After reading (our, ours) report about Kennedy's stand on civil rights, Joan wrote (her, hers).
5. (Theirs, Their) reports told of Kennedy's early political career as a member of Congress and senator.
6. (You, Your) telling of how President Kennedy began the Peace Corps was inspiring.
7. (Him, His) dealing with the Soviets showed resolve and strength.
8. (Your, You're) report told of the President's tragic assassination in Dallas in 1963.
9. (He, His) was the story of the youngest man ever elected President and the youngest ever to die in office.
10. (Mine, My) report discussed (his', his) personal charm and courage.

Compound Constructions with Pronouns

It is sometimes troublesome to choose the correct case for pronouns in compound constructions, such as compound subjects or compound objects of a preposition. To determine which case you should use, say the sentence to yourself, leaving out the conjunction and the noun or the other pronoun in the compound construction. When you have determined how the pronoun functions by itself, you can decide whether to use the nominative case or the objective case.

> Dad and **they** were Brooklyn Dodger fans. [**Think:** They were Brooklyn Dodger fans.]

> Between **you** and **me,** I don't think that Dad ever forgave the Dodgers for moving to Los Angeles. [Because *you* and *me* are compound objects of the preposition *between,* use a pronoun in the objective case, *me.*]

On your paper, rewrite each sentence, correcting errors in pronoun usage. Underline the corrections that you make. If a sentence contains no errors, write *Correct* on your paper.

? **Critical**
Thinking:
How does the
pronoun func-
tion in the
sentence?

SAMPLE   Randy and them enjoyed the United States bicentennial
              celebration.

ANSWER   Randy and they enjoyed the United States bicentennial
              celebration.

1. Between you and I, I enjoy fireworks on special occasions.
2. Everyone present at the celebration, the performers and us, felt pride and excitement that day.
3. They and we knew that the United States was born in 1776.
4. In 1976, our neighbors and we celebrated the nation's two-hundredth birthday.
5. The parade of tall ships impressed the tourists and I.
6. They and I listened to politicians speak and watched fireworks.
7. The celebrations were for them and us.
8. The Constitution of the United States is very important to you and I.
9. Special educational television shows about the Constitution impressed my friends and me.
10. They and I learned a great deal about the freedoms of speech, assembly, and religion that the Constitution guarantees.

Who and Whom

You can use the forms of the word *who* either as interrogative pronouns *(page 537)* or as relative pronouns *(page 537)*. As is true of other pronouns, the way that you use the pronoun determines which case or form of the word you should choose. *Who* and *whoever* are in the nominative case; *whom* and *whomever* are in the objective case; *whose* is in the possessive case.

Who and Whom as Interrogative Pronouns   *Who* and *whom* are interrogative pronouns when they introduce questions. To determine whether to use *who* (the nominative case) or *whom* (the objective case), simply turn the question into a statement.

Rule   Use *who* when an interrogative pronoun acts as a subject or as a
──────   predicate nominative. Use *whom* when an interrogative pronoun acts
U 56   either as an object of a verb or as an object of a preposition.

        NOMINATIVE   **Who** were the movie stars of the 1920s? [*Who* is the
                     subject of the verb *were.*]

        OBJECTIVE   By **whom** was the biography of Clara Bow written?
                     [*Whom* is the object of the preposition *by.*]

If the interrogative pronoun *who* or *whom* is followed by an interrupting phrase, such as *do you think*, you can mentally rearrange the sentence, leaving out the interrupting phrase, to determine the use of the pronoun in the sentence and which form of the pronoun to use.

Who *do you think* was the most romantic star of the twenties? [**Think:** Who was the most romantic star? *Who* is the subject.]

In informal writing and in conversation, *who* is often used to ask a question, regardless of whether the nominative or the objective case is needed. In formal usage, however, you should follow the rules for using the nominative case, *who*, and the objective case, *whom*.

INFORMAL **Who** do you plan to take to the Twenties Film Festival?

FORMAL **Whom** will Professor O'Hara take to the festival?

Who and Whom as Relative Pronouns   When forms of the word *who* introduce subordinate clauses *(page 588)*, they are relative pronouns. Decide the correct form of the word by its use in the subordinate clause, not by its use in the main clause.

Rule
—
U 57

Use *who* or *whoever* when a relative pronoun is the subject of the subordinate clause; use *whom* or *whomever* when a relative pronoun is an object within the subordinate clause.

Clara Bow, **who** *was called the "It Girl" in the twenties*, does not look glamorous to us today. [*Who* is the subject of the clause *who was called the "It Girl" in the twenties*.]

Rudolf Valentino, **whom** many people *adored*, is another twenties star who looks out of date today. [*Whom* is the direct object of *adored*.]

Exercise 7   Using *Who* and *Whom*

Critical Thinking:
Can *whom* ever be a subject?

On your paper, write the pronoun that is correct in formal usage. Then indicate how the pronoun is used in the sentence.

SAMPLE   (Who, Whom) knows about the history of the American film industry?

ANSWER   Who — subject

1. In 1872 Eadweard Muybridge, (who, whom) was an English photographer, photographed running horses.
2. Muybridge, (who, whom) used twenty-four cameras, took twenty-four still pictures to make the horses appear to run.
3. In 1889 George Eastman, for (who, whom) the Eastman Kodak Company is named, developed celluloid film.
4. Later that year Thomas Edison, (who, whom) was a famous inventor, developed the kinetoscope.

5. Edison, (who, whom) most students remember as the inventor of the electric light bulb, created devices to photograph and show a series of moving pictures.
6. In 1903 Edwin Porter, (who, whom) worked for the Edison company, directed the first movie with a real story.
7. For (who, whom) did Porter make *The Great Train Robbery?*
8. (Who, Whom) do you think became one of the first movie stars?
9. (Whoever, Whomever) opened the first motion picture theater in Los Angeles in 1902 had great foresight.
10. In 1907 *The Great Train Robbery* was shown to (whoever, whomever) was willing to pay five cents to see it.
11. (Who, Whom) do you think opened the first nickelodeon?
12. Audiences were loyal to (whoever, whomever) they enjoyed in the movies.
13. Louis B. Mayer, Samuel Goldwyn, and others, for (who, whom) large film studios were later named, began the movie industry in Los Angeles.
14. D. W. Griffith, (who, whom) you may have studied, was a director (who, whom) learned to use close-ups, flashbacks, and fade-outs.
15. Success seemed to come to (whoever, whomever) worked hard at creating movies and (whoever, whomever) audiences enjoyed.

Pronouns with Appositives

The pronouns *we* and *us* are often used with appositives, as in *we engineers* or *us students*. Because an appositive explains or renames the word to which it is in apposition, you must first determine how the phrase is used in the sentence. If the phrase is a subject or a predicate nominative, use the nominative case of the pronoun; if the phrase is an object, use the objective case.

As another way to determine which case to use, say the sentence to yourself without the appositive.

NOMINATIVE **We** engineers studied the construction of the Hoover Dam.
[**Think:** **We** studied. Because *we* and *engineers* are subjects, *we* is in the nominative case.]

OBJECTIVE A special tour of the dam will be given for **us** students.
[**Think:** A special tour for **us**. Because *us* and *students* are objects of the preposition *for*, *us* is in the objective case.]

Exercise 8 **Pronouns in Appositive Phrases**

On your paper, write the pronoun in parentheses that correctly completes each of the following sentences. Then write its case.

? **Critical Thinking:**
Can *us* ever be a subject?

SAMPLE (We, Us) students read novels by Ernest Hemingway.
ANSWER We — nominative

1. For (we, us) twentieth-century readers, Hemingway is an important writer.
2. That he won a Nobel Prize was not a surprise to (we, us) students.
3. Many of the short stories in the collection *In Our Time* are admired by (we, us) readers.
4. The greatest admirers of Hemingway's novel *A Farewell to Arms* are (we, us) World War I history buffs.
5. (We, Us) students also found *For Whom the Bell Tolls* a fascinating tale of the Spanish Civil War.
6. For all of (we, us) readers, Hemingway's humanity shines through in these commentaries about human struggle.
7. (We, Us) Hemingway fans find his writing style to be refreshingly simple and unique.
8. His modern style of understatement impresses (we, us) students.
9. Although Hemingway's style is concise, his descriptions make (we, us) readers feel his characters' underlying deep emotions.
10. Among those who defend his courage and independence are (we, us) Hemingway enthusiasts.

Pronouns in Comparisons

In some comparisons using *than* or *as,* part of the phrase or clause is not stated, but merely implied. To choose the correct pronoun, mentally supply the missing words to determine how the pronoun is used. Because the case of the pronoun used in an incomplete comparison can alter your intended meaning, make your choice carefully. In the following examples, notice the change in meaning according to the choice of pronoun.

NOMINATIVE   I admire Charlie Chaplin as much as **he.** [**Think:** as much as *he does.* Use the nominative-case pronoun because *he* is the subject of the implied clause, *he does.*]

OBJECTIVE   I admire Charlie Chaplin as much as **him.** [**Think:** as much as *I admire him.* Use the objective-case pronoun, *him,* because the intended meaning makes *him* the object of the verb *admire* in the implied clause *I admire him.*]

Exercise 9 | Pronouns in Comparisons

Critical Thinking:

How should the comparison be completed?

On your paper, write the pronoun in parentheses that correctly completes each sentence.

SAMPLE   When speaking of Babe Didrikson, many people say that there was no greater woman athlete than (she, her).

ANSWER   she

1. Most of Babe Didrikson's fans said that no one could play golf as well as (she, her).

2. She also competed in baseball, basketball, football, pocket billiards, tennis, boxing, and swimming; can you name anyone who played as many sports as (she, her)?

3. When she competed against other great female javelin throwers in the 1932 Olympics, Babe Didrikson was better than (they, them) and set a world record.

4. At that Olympics, no eighty-meter hurdler was better than (she, her); Didrikson set the world record in that sport too.

5. When the Amateur Athletic Union named Babe Didrikson and others to its All-America woman's basketball team, the AAU was saying that no one plays basketball better than (they, them).

6. Babe Didrikson was married to wrestler George Zaharias and had no greater fan than (he, him).

7. When Babe Didrikson had a winning streak of seventeen, no woman golfer had ever won as many tournaments in a row as (she, her).

8. She went on to win the Tam O'Shanter All-America tournament too, and people said that no one had made as spectacular a recovery from illness as (she, her).

9. However, Babe Didrikson died two years later at the age of forty-two, and few athletes were missed as much as (she, her).

10. According to the Associated Press award, no woman athlete of the first half of the twentieth century was more outstanding than (she, her).

Clear Pronoun Reference

To avoid confusing your listeners or readers, be certain that the pronouns you use refer clearly to their antecedents. If you find an unclear reference, rephrase the sentence.

Rule
U 58
Avoid using a pronoun that could refer to more than one antecedent.

UNCLEAR   Kennedy picked Johnson to be his running mate because **he** was a good politician. [Who was a good politician? The antecedent of *he* is unclear.]

CLEAR   Kennedy picked Johnson to be his running mate because Johnson was a good politician.

Rule
U 59
Avoid using the pronouns *it, they, you,* or *your* without a clear antecedent in formal usage.

The following example shows how you can usually replace the pronoun with a noun to eliminate confusion.

UNCLEAR   I forgot my costume and my lines for the play. When the director heard about **it,** she was furious. [What is *it?* The pronoun has no clear antecedent.]

CLEAR   I forgot my costume and my lines for the play. When the director heard about my irresponsibility, she was furious.

Rule
U 60
Do not use the pronoun *your* in place of an article (*a, an,* or *the*) if
possession is not involved.

AVOID   Many of **your** astronauts have been training for years.

USE   Many astronauts have been training for years.

Rule
U 61
Avoid using *which, it, this,* and *that* to refer to ideas that are not
clearly stated.

The following example demonstrates how you can avoid making
such general references.

GENERAL   We toured the Kennedy Space Center, but we didn't see any astronauts, **which** was quite disappointing. [The pronoun *which*
has no clear antecedent.]

CLEAR   We toured the Kennedy Space Center, but we were quite disappointed because we didn't see any astronauts.

Exercise 10   Clear Pronoun Reference

**? Critical
Thinking:**
Is there a pro-
noun that
could have
more than one
antecedent?

On your paper, rewrite the following sentences, making certain that all
pronoun references are clear and accurate. If a sentence is correct,
write *Correct.*

SAMPLE   Robert Frost was one of your greatest American poets.
ANSWER   Robert Frost was one of the greatest American poets.

1. Robert Frost and his father came from New England, but he grew
up in San Francisco.
2. Frost's father died when he was very young.
3. As a young man, Frost worked on the farm and in shoe shops; he
found it a beneficial experience.
4. Frost attended both Dartmouth College and Harvard University,
but he soon discovered that it wasn't what he wanted.
5. Frost and his wife wanted a quiet life. Although his family disapproved, they moved to England.
6. He and his wife bought a house in the country and lived there,
which was excellent for writing poetry.
7. When Frost returned to the United States, he found that he had
become very famous, which was quite sudden.
8. He won the Pulitzer Prize and a Congressional Gold Medal, but
they say that he never let it change his simple way of life.
9. Frost lectured at various colleges and continued to write, which
was what he loved to do best.
10. Frost attended President John F. Kennedy's inauguration and read
one of his poems, which was a great honor.

The Writing Connection

Using Clear Pronoun Reference in Your Writing

When you use pronouns to replace nouns, you add variety to your word choice. Pronouns can also help you combine short sentences into longer ones to vary the length and structure of your sentences. If they are used carelessly or incorrectly, however, pronouns can confuse your audience. Therefore, you must always make it clear what the antecedent of each pronoun is by following the guidelines for clear pronoun reference.

Reference Point:
pages 71–87

Writing Assignments

A Biography As an editorial assistant in a publishing company, you are writing a short biography of F. Scott Fitzgerald for a book jacket. Read the following prewriting notes. Select those you wish to use, organize them logically, and then write a brief paragraph.

Reference Point:
pages 154–183

F. Scott Fitzgerald (1896–1940) wrote novels and short stories.
Famous novels — *The Great Gatsby, Tender Is the Night*
educated at private schools and Princeton University
The theme of his writing was often the conflict between material success and moral choices.
Fitzgerald's work reflects the jazz age of the 1920s, commentary on World War I, the 1929 stock-market crash
writing often based on his own personal experiences
Fitzgerald and his wife Zelda lived in Paris in the early 1920s.
Who was Fitzgerald's famous editor? — Maxwell Perkins, at Charles Scribner's Sons
first novel — *This Side of Paradise*, published 1920
Fitzgerald also worked in advertising and screenwriting

An Editorial You are the editor of a local newspaper. You are going to write an editorial that is lighter than usual. Your editorial will answer the question: What household appliance has had the most influence on the United States in this century?

First, freewrite to gather ideas about the effects of different appliances, such as dishwashers, vacuum cleaners, washing machines, or microwaves. Then select one to write about. Cubing or clustering will help you gather more details and different perspectives on your topic. Decide on a tone that is suitable to the level of seriousness of your editorial. As you write your draft, keep your tone consistent. Next, revise your editorial. Pay particular attention to clear pronoun reference. Finally, proofread your editorial and prepare a clean copy to submit to your school newspaper or to post on a classroom bulletin board.

Modifiers in Comparisons

By using different forms of adjectives and adverbs, you can compare two or more persons or things. The three degrees of comparison are *positive, comparative*, and *superlative*.

The Three Degrees of Comparison

You use a modifier in the positive degree to assign some quality to a person, a thing, an action, or an idea. You use a modifier in the comparative degree to compare a person, a thing, an action, or an idea with another one. You use a modifier in the superlative degree to compare a person, a thing, an action, or an idea with at least two others.

ADJECTIVES

POSITIVE	The line at that gas station is **long.**
COMPARATIVE	During the energy crisis, lines at gas stations were **longer.**
SUPERLATIVE	They were the **longest** lines that I have ever seen.

ADVERBS

POSITIVE	Today the lines move **quickly.**
COMPARATIVE	This line moves **more quickly** than that one.
SUPERLATIVE	Of all the lines, the self-serve line moves the **most quickly.**

Using Comparisons Correctly

Rule

U 62

Add the suffix -*er* to form the comparative and the suffix -*est* to form the superlative of modifiers with one or two syllables.

Reference Point:
pages 489–490

In some cases, to form the comparative modifier correctly, you must drop a final *e*, double a final consonant, or change a final *y* to *i* before adding the suffix.

Modifiers		
Positive	**Comparative**	**Superlative**
short	shorter	shortest
funny	funnier	funniest

Rule

U 63

Use *more* to show the comparative degree and *most* to show the superlative degree in three instances: with all three-syllable words, with two-syllable words that would otherwise be difficult to pronounce, and with adverbs ending in -*ly.*

Modifiers Using *More* and *Most*

Positive	Comparative	Superlative
serious	more serious	most serious
dreadful	more dreadful	most dreadful
restfully	more restfully	most restfully

Rule

U 64 Use *less* and *least* to form the comparative and the superlative degrees of comparisons showing less.

Comparisons Using *Less* and *Least*

Positive	Comparative	Superlative
humorous	less humorous	least humorous
hopeful	less hopeful	least hopeful
ambitiously	less ambitiously	least ambitiously

Remember, also, that some modifiers are irregular and do not form comparisons in a standard way. You should memorize them to be able to use them correctly.

Irregular Comparisons

Positive	Comparative	Superlative
good	better	best
well	better	best
many	more	most
much	more	most
little	less	least
bad	worse	worst
ill	worse	worst
far	farther*	farthest
far	further	furthest

Rule

U 65 Avoid double comparisons. Use either the word *more* or *most* or else the appropriate suffix; do not combine the two.

INCORRECT I think that Charlie Chaplin was the **most funniest** actor who ever lived.

CORRECT I think that Charlie Chaplin was the **funniest** actor who ever lived.

Rule

U 66 Avoid incomplete comparisons by clearly indicating the things being compared.

When you compare one member of a group with the rest of the group, you can avoid being unclear or misleading by using the comparative degree and the word *other* or *else.*

UNCLEAR   *The Little Tramp* is *more popular* **than any** movie in the film festival. [This sentence says either that *The Little Tramp* is more popular than any movie in the festival including itself, or that it is not included in the festival and is more popular than the movies that are included.]

CLEAR   *The Little Tramp* is *more popular* **than any other** movie in the film festival. [*The Little Tramp* is the most popular movie in the festival.]

Rule   Use the words *as . . . as* or *as . . . as . . . than* to complete a com-
——
U 67   pound comparison.

A compound comparison really makes two statements by using both the positive and the comparative degrees of a modifier. The positive degree shows that the things being compared are at least equal or similar; the comparative degree shows that they may, in fact, be different. Because you would still have a complete sentence if you removed the second, or parenthetical, part of the comparison, use commas to set off the parenthetical part from the rest of the sentence.

Watching the space shuttle land was **as** exciting **as,** if not *more exciting* **than,** watching it take off.

Watching the space shuttle land was **as** exciting **as** watching it take off, if not *more exciting.*

Rule   Avoid making comparisons that are illogical because of missing or
——
U 68   faulty elements or because no comparison can be made.

To avoid having your reader or listener misunderstand your meaning, rephrase the comparison to include all of the important words.

ILLOGICAL   Elizabeth writes computer programs that are **as complicated as** Francine. [Computer programs cannot be compared to Francine. Elizabeth can write programs; she cannot write Francine.]

LOGICAL   Elizabeth writes computer programs that are **as complicated as** Francine's. [**Think:** Elizabeth's programs are as complicated as Francine's programs.]

Certain adjectives, such as *perfect, unique, dead, round, full,* and *empty,* do not have a comparative or superlative degree because they express an absolute condition. Because logically nothing can be "more perfect" or "more empty," use the forms *more nearly* or *most nearly* when you use these words in comparisons.

It was the **most nearly perfect** launch that I have ever seen.

Exercise 1 | Using Comparisons Correctly

On your paper, write the correct form of the modifier given in parentheses. Identify the degree of comparison of each correct modifier.

SAMPLE   Franklin Delano Roosevelt's presidency lasted (longer, more long) than twelve years.

ANSWER   longer — comparative

1. He began law school in 1904 but soon thought that he would be (happier, more happier) as a politician.
2. As a New York State senator, Roosevelt was (as successful if not more successful than; as successful as, if not more successful than,) many experienced politicians.
3. In 1913 Roosevelt was appointed to a (powerful, most powerful) position as assistant secretary of the navy.
4. In August of 1921, Roosevelt became crippled by polio; this was the (worse, worst) setback of his life.
5. By exercising with special equipment, Roosevelt made his arms and shoulders (more powerful, most powerful) than before.
6. As governor of New York, Roosevelt devised a (better, best) plan than the previous governor's to help the unemployed.
7. When he became President in 1933, Roosevelt's popularity was much (greater than the former President, greater than the former President's).

8. During Roosevelt's presidency, the government controlled businesses (more strongly, most strongly) than before.
9. Within his first three months in office, Roosevelt went (more far, further) than any previous President in direct action to help the country out of its economic depression.
10. One of Roosevelt's programs supplied funds for building (more better, better) roads, schools, and bridges.

Placement of Phrases and Clauses

Rule   Place modifying phrases and clauses as close as possible to the
────   words that they modify.
U 69

     Misplacement of phrases and clauses can create unclear and unintentionally humorous sentences. To avoid misplacing modifiers, identify the word to be modified and place the modifying phrase or clause as close as possible to that word, while retaining your meaning.

> **UNCLEAR**   Mrs. Santos decided to support Roosevelt's bid for reelection, **persuaded by his famous fireside chats.** [The phrase *persuaded by his famous fireside chats* appears to be modifying *reelection,* thereby distorting the meaning of the sentence.]

CLEAR Mrs. Santos, **persuaded by his famous fireside chats,** decided to support Roosevelt's bid for reelection.

CLEAR **Persuaded by his famous fireside chats,** *Mrs. Santos* decided to support Roosevelt's bid for reelection.

Notice in the following example that improper placement of the modifying phrase can alter the meaning of the sentence. As you revise your sentences, check to be certain that your intended meaning is still clear.

UNCLEAR **Marching in the bicentennial parade,** a dog walked in front of me. [Who was marching in the parade?]

CLEAR **Marching in the bicentennial parade,** *I* noticed a dog in front of me. [Meaning: I was marching in the parade when I noticed the dog in front of me.]

CLEAR **In front of me,** I noticed a *dog* **marching in the bicentennial parade.** [Meaning: The dog was marching in the parade.]

Rule

U 70 To avoid dangling modifiers, provide an antecedent for every modifying phrase or clause to modify.

A **dangling modifier** is a modifying phrase or clause that does not clearly or logically modify any word in the sentence; a dangling modifier can make a sentence unclear or unintentionally humorous.

UNCLEAR **After finishing your juice,** the bottle must be recycled. [Who or what is finishing the juice?]

CLEAR **After finishing your juice,** you must recycle the bottle. [The adverb phrase *after finishing your juice* now modifies the verb phrase *must recycle.*]

You can also correct a dangling phrase by changing the phrase to a subordinate clause.

CLEAR **After you finish your juice,** the bottle must be recycled.

In current usage some dangling modifiers have become accepted as part of idiomatic expressions. These are usually such present and past participles as *allowing for, based on, considering, concerning, failing, generally speaking, granting, judging, owing to,* and so forth.

Judging from the cover, the magazine is about computers.
According to available information, our school will be getting six new computers.
Generally speaking, the computer science department at our school is very good.

You can determine whether an expression is acceptable even though it may seem to be a dangling modifier by asking yourself these questions: "Does the reader expect a word for the phrase to modify, or is the phrase or clause common enough to be considered an idiom? Is the meaning of the sentence clear?"

Exercise 2 Placement of Phrases and Clauses

On your paper, rewrite each of the following sentences, eliminating all misplaced or dangling modifiers.

? Critical Thinking:
Is the modifying phrase near the word(s) that it modifies?

SAMPLE   Henry Ford revolutionized industry in the United States using assembly lines.

ANSWER   Using assembly lines, Henry Ford revolutionized industry in the United States.

1. Henry Ford's first gasoline engine was built at the age of thirty.
2. Supported on bicycle wheels, Ford constructed his first car.
3. His first automobile is on exhibition in Michigan, completed in 1896.
4. Ford built the inexpensive "Model T" convinced that everyone should own an automobile.
5. Produced on an assembly line, Henry Ford made cars inexpensively.
6. As they moved along a conveyor belt, each worker performed a separate task in assembling the cars.
7. Inexpensive to manufacture, the price of the Model T was only $260 in 1925.
8. Model T's were seen all over, affordable to people with modest incomes.
9. Few people owned cars before the introduction of the Model T, although they are a common possession today.
10. Half of the automobiles in the United States were Fords between 1917 and 1927.
11. Ford decided to share the company's profits with his employees, encouraged by his success.
12. Located in Willow Run, Michigan, he set up the world's largest aircraft assembly plant.
13. Ford donated a great deal of money, along with his son, Edsel, to the charitable Ford Foundation.
14. Wishing to commemorate human progress in the fields of science and technology, the Henry Ford museum was established.

Using Modifying Phrases and Clauses in Your Writing

You can use modifying phrases and clauses to add variety to the length and structure of your sentences and to make your writing flow more smoothly. As you are drafting, try combining brief items from your prewriting notes into complex sentences. During revising, you can combine short, choppy sentences into longer, smoother ones. Either way, you must always be careful to place those phrases and clauses correctly so that the meaning of your sentence is clear. Misplaced or dangling modifiers are often misleading and can confuse your reader.

Reference Point:
pages 71–87

Writing Assignments

A Press Release An announcement to the media about a newsworthy event or product is called a "press release." It is similar to an advertisement because it reflects the point of view and the interests of the person or organization issuing the release. *Step 1:* To write a press release announcing the first available models of a twentieth-century invention, select one of the following topics or one of your own choice.

> a radio
> a personal computer
> a tape recorder
> an air conditioner
> a helicopter
> a vacuum cleaner

Step 2: Cluster to gather details about the invention. Then refer to your clustering notes as you freewrite about why people would want to buy one of these "newfangled" products. *Step 3:* Write your press release, using descriptive, persuasive language. Remember that your audience has never heard of your product before. If necessary to make your draft flow smoothly, combine short, descriptive phrases and clauses into longer, smoother sentences. *Step 4:* Revise your press release, making certain that modifying phrases and clauses are correctly placed and that your sentences are logical. *Step 5:* Read your press release aloud to a classmate. Ask your classmate whether your draft is clear, flows smoothly, and is convincing. *Step 6:* With your classmate's comments in mind, make any needed revisions. *Step 7:* Proofread your press release and make a clean copy. Submit it to a class portfolio of press releases.

A *Who's Who* Article To write a brief article about yourself for a *Who's Who of the Twentieth Century,* first brainstorm for ideas. Try to imagine what readers might want to know about you. Jot down notes on your current interests, goals, hobbies, and accomplishments or describe yourself as you would like to be in ten years. Write your article. Where desirable, combine several items from your prewriting notes into complex or compound sentences. As you revise, tighten up your description. Combine short, choppy sentences into longer, smoother ones. Be sure to place phrases and clauses correctly. Proofread your article and make a clean copy for your teacher.

Usage Notes

The following pages contain an alphabetical list of words and phrases that often present usage problems. Each entry describes correct usage, and most entries include examples. Cross-references help you to locate related information.

a lot, alot *A lot* means "a great number or amount" and is always two words; avoid using *a lot* in formal usage. *Alot* is not a word.

a while, awhile *While* is a noun and can be preceded by *for a* or *in a* to make a prepositional phrase. *Awhile* is an adverb; do not use *for* or *in* before *awhile.*

My grandmother had to wait **awhile** before she could afford a television. She saved her money **for a while** and then bought one.

accept, except *Accept* is a verb that means "to agree" or "to receive." *Except* is a preposition that means "leaving out" or "but."

She did not want to **accept** a loan to buy a television.
My father complained that all his friends had televisions **except** him.

adapt, adopt *Adapt* means "to change or adjust" or "to make more suitable." *Adopt* means "to take or accept."

During the Great Depression, many families had to **adapt** to a lower standard of living.
During World War II, some families temporarily **adopted** children from the war zone.

advice, advise *Advice* is a noun that means "helpful suggestion or opinion." *Advise* is a verb that means "to give or offer counsel."

In the twenties, many people were **advised** to play the stock market. Unfortunately, many followed that **advice** and lost their money in the crash.

affect, effect   *Affect* is a verb that means "to influence." *Effect* can be a verb that means "to bring about or achieve" or a noun that means "result."

Everyone was **affected** directly or indirectly by the Great Depression.
The "bank holiday" **effected** a change in their style of life. [verb meaning "brought about"]
The **effects** of the flood were far reaching. [noun meaning "results"]

ain't   *Ain't* is nonstandard. Do not use it.

all ready, already   *All ready* functions as a compound adjective that means "entirely ready" or "prepared." *Already* is an adverb that means "before some specified time" or "previously." Do not confuse the two.

The troops were **all ready** to be sent to the front, but World War II was **already** over!

all right, alright   *All right* means "satisfactory," "unhurt," "correct," or "yes, very well." *Alright* is an incorrect spelling; do not use it.

The first thing the soldier did was let his family know he was **all right**.
All right, we will throw a welcome-home party for him.

all the farther, as far as   *All the farther* should not be used for *as far as*.

One hundred twenty feet was **as far as** the first airplane could fly. [not *all the farther*]

all together, altogether   *All together* means "in a group." *Altogether* means "completely" or "thoroughly."

My aunts and uncles went **all together** on their first airplane flight because they were afraid to go separately.
They are **altogether** too nervous to be good travelers.

almost, most   Do not confuse the adverb *almost* with the adjective *most*.

adj.   adv.
Most students have **almost** finished *For Whom the Bell Tolls*.

although, though   Both of these conjunctions mean "in spite of the fact." In conversation, *though* can be used as an adverb to mean "however." Avoid this usage in written English.

David has read other books by Hemingway, **although** (or *though*) they haven't been assigned. [conjunction]
He didn't want to read the short stories, **though**, because he prefers novels. [adverb]

among, between   Use *among* for comparisons involving groups of persons or things.   Use *between* when only two items are being considered at a time.

My favorite **among** Hemingway's short stories is "The Snows of Kilimanjaro."

There was a big difference **between** the original story and the movie version.

amount, number   Use *amount* with a noun that names something that can be measured or weighed.   Use *number* to refer to things that can be counted.

A substantial **amount** of money was lost in the stock-market crash.

A substantial **number** of people suffered financial ruin.

and / or   *And / or* means "either *and* or *or*."   It is confusing and should be avoided.

anxious, eager   Both words can mean "strongly desirous," but you should use *anxious* to suggest concern or worry.

During the Great Depression, Abigail was **anxious** to get a job to help support her family.

Pablo was **eager** to begin his exciting new job as an assistant to a film director.

any more, anymore   These terms are not interchangeable.   The phrase *any more* describes quantity; *any* is an adverb modifying the adjective *more*.   *Anymore* is an adverb meaning "at present" or "from now on."

Are there **any more** stories by Hemingway that you especially like?

He's not my favorite writer **anymore.**

anywhere, everywhere, nowhere   Do not use in a plural form: *anywheres, everywheres, nowheres.*

appraise, apprise   *Appraise* means "to evaluate"; *apprise* means "to inform."

Having **appraised** the World War I helmet, the antique dealer **apprised** its owner that it was worth fifty dollars.

apt, liable, likely   In informal usage, these words are often used interchangeably.   In formal usage, only *apt* and *likely* are interchangeable, meaning "tending to" or "inclined to be."   Use *liable* to suggest the probability of a harmful, unfortunate, or negative event or to show exposure to legal action.

Robert was **apt** to try anything new. [or *likely*]

His mother said that he was **liable** to get hurt flying in one of those new-fangled airplanes.

What's more, the airline was not **liable** if the plane crashed.

as, like In formal usage, *like* is most often used as a preposition to introduce a prepositional phrase. *As* is most often used as a conjunction to introduce a subordinate clause.

> Juan, who wants to be a baseball player, runs **like** Jackie Robinson. [prepositional phrase]
>
> Juan, who wants to be a baseball player, runs **as** Jackie Robinson did. [subordinate clause]

In informal usage, *like* is sometimes used as a conjunction. Avoid using *like* as a conjunction in formal usage in place of *as*, *as if*, or *as though*.

> AVOID Juan feels **like** he can steal a base at any time.
>
> USE Juan feels **as though** he can steal a base at any time.

as far as, all the farther See *all the farther, as far as.*

author Do not use *author* as a verb. Books are *written*, not *authored*.

bad, badly *Bad* is always an adjective, and *badly* is always an adverb. Use *bad* following a linking verb.

> When the Dodgers moved away from Brooklyn, my uncle felt so **bad** that he cried.
>
> He felt that the team had treated him **badly.**

because, on account of *On account of* means "because of" or "due to." The phrase functions as a preposition and takes an object. Do not use *on account of* instead of *because* to introduce a subordinate clause.

> The production of *Our Town* was postponed **on account of** the storm.
>
> The production of *Our Town* was postponed **because** the electricity went out. [not *on account of*]

being as, being as how, being that Do not use these expressions for *since* or *because.*

> **Since** he had broken his leg, Aaron could not perform in *Our Town.* [not *Being as*]
>
> **Because** he couldn't perform, Aaron was made assistant to the director. [not *Being that*]

beside, besides *Beside* means "next to." *Besides* means "in addition to."

> At the exhibit, Andrew Wyeth's paintings were hung **beside** his son Jamie's.
>
> **Besides** Andrew Wyeth's still lifes, the exhibit also featured his portraits.

between, among See *among, between.*

between you and me Never use the nominative case *I* as the object of a preposition. *Between* is a preposition.

> **Between you and me,** I prefer the landscapes. [not *between you and I*]

borrow, lend, loan   A person *borrows from* and *lends to* another person. *Loan* is a noun meaning "that which is lent" or "the act of lending." You may also use *loan* as a verb, but *lend* is preferred.

> Pia **borrowed** a book on Andrew Wyeth from Louise. [verb]
> Louise **lent** (or *loaned*) Pia the book. [verb]
> The **loan** of the book gave Pia a preview of what she would see at the exhibit. [noun]

both, either, neither   When used to modify compound elements, place *both, either,* and *neither* just before the compound construction. The elements in the compound construction should be parallel or similar in form.

> INCORRECT   Rachel intends **both** to be a pilot and an astronaut.
> CORRECT   Rachel intends to be **both** a pilot and an astronaut.

bring, take   Use *bring* when you mean "to carry to." Use *take* when you mean "to carry away."

> **Bring** your tape of *The Wizard of Oz* when you come to my house. Remember to **take** it with you when you go home.

bust, busted   Do not use these words as verbs to substitute for *break* or *burst.* The verbs *bust* and *busted* are nonstandard.

> The stock-market crash was described as a **burst** balloon. [not *busted*]

can, may   See "Modals," page 627.

cannot (can't) help but   In standard English, use *cannot (can't) help* followed by a gerund.

> My little sister **can't help** wishing that she could see *The Wizard of Oz* every day. [not *can't help but wish*]

can't hardly, can't scarcely   Avoid these terms; they are double negatives.

> I **can hardly** believe how much she loves that movie! [not *can't hardly*]

compare to, compare with   Use *compare to* when pointing out similarities; use *compare with* when pointing out similarities and differences.

> Because of his "basket catch," he's been **compared to** Willie Mays. **Compared with** Mays, however, he's a poor hitter and base runner.

consensus of opinion   Because *consensus* means "group or collective opinion," this phrase is redundant. Use only the word *consensus.*

credible, creditable, credulous   *Credible* means "believable" or "worthy of belief." *Creditable* means "worthy of commendation." *Credulous* always applies to people and means "willing to believe" or "gullible."

Although it is not a **credible** story, people still get involved in *The Wizard of Oz.*
It is more than a **creditable** job; the movie is a classic.
Very young children are **credulous;** they believe the story could happen.

Exercise 1 Correct Usage

? Critical Thinking:

Which word or phrase is appropriate?

On your paper, write the word or phrase in parentheses that correctly completes each sentences.

SAMPLE Woodrow Wilson was (altogether, all together) one of the finest Presidents the United States has ever had.

ANSWER altogether

1. As a freshman at Princeton University, Woodrow Wilson (already, all ready) had an interest in public speaking.
2. (Being as how, Since) Wilson wanted a career in public life, he began law school in 1879.
3. After practicing law for a short time, Wilson found that he had no interest in being a lawyer (any more, anymore).
4. (Eager, Anxious) to become a college teacher, Wilson studied history at Johns Hopkins University.
5. In 1902 the trustees of Princeton University reached a (consensus of opinion, consensus), making Wilson the university president.
6. Wilson (affected, effected) many changes within the college.
7. In 1910, on the (advice, advise) of James Smith, Jr., Wilson ran for the office of governor of New Jersey.
8. In 1912 the Democratic Party searched (between, among) its members for a strong candidate for President.
9. In his first term as President, Wilson worked (both to improve, to improve both) banking and trade laws.
10. Wilson acted (like, as if) a world government were possible and believed strongly in the League of Nations as a body to promote world peace (and / or, and to) avoid war.

data is, data are *Data* is the plural form of the Latin *datum.* In formal English it should be followed by a plural verb. In informal English a singular verb may be used.

differ from, differ with Things (or persons) *differ from* each other if they are physically dissimilar. When persons *differ with* each other, they are in disagreement.

Microwave ovens **differ from** conventional ovens.
I **differ with** my mother over whether we need a microwave.

different from, different than Use *different from.* Use the idiom *different than* only to introduce a subordinate clause.

My ideas about the benefits of frozen dinners are **different from** hers.
[not *different than*]

My ideas about the benefits of frozen dinners are **different than** hers are.

disinterested, uninterested   *Disinterested* implies a lack of self-interest; it is synonymous with *unbiased* or *impartial*.   *Uninterested* implies a lack of any interest.

In spite of my pleading, my father is **uninterested** in buying a microwave, while my mother is a **disinterested** bystander.

double negative   A double negative is the use of two negatives where one is sufficient.   Avoid using *not* or contractions with *-n't* with words such as *no, none, never,* and *nothing.*   (See also *can't hardly, can't scarcely.*)

When my grandmother was young, she did**n't** have a television.   [not *no television*]

double subject   Do not use a noun and a pronoun together as a single subject.

INCORRECT   My **grandmother she** listened to the radio instead.
CORRECT   My **grandmother** listened to the radio instead.
CORRECT   **She** listened to the radio instead.

each and every   *Each and every* is redundant.   Use either *each* or *every.*

eager, anxious   See *anxious, eager.*

effect, affect   See *affect, effect.*

e.g., i.e.   *E.g.* stands for the Latin words *exempli gratia,* meaning roughly "an example for free."   *E.g.* means "for example" in English.   *I.e.* stands for the Latin words *id est,* meaning "that is," and should be used to cite an equivalent.   Use both sparingly.

either, both, neither   See *both, either, neither.*

eminent, imminent   *Eminent* means "prominent" or "outstanding in some way."   *Imminent* means "about to occur."

Many an **eminent** statesman predicted that World War II was **imminent.**

et al.   This is a Latin abbreviation for *et alii* and means "and others" (persons, not things).   It is used most often in footnotes to refer to other members of a team of authors.

etc.   This Latin abbreviation for *et cetera* means "and other things," "and so forth."   Avoid using *etc.* in formal writing; use *and so forth* instead.   Do not use *and etc.;* it is redundant.

every day, everyday   *Every day* means "each day."   *Everyday* is an adjective meaning "ordinary."

At the turn of the century, women wore hats and gloves **every day.**
Their **everyday** clothes look formal and uncomfortable to us.

every one, everyone *Every one* refers to each person or thing in a group and is usually followed by *of*. *Everyone* means "everybody, every person."

Every one of us watched the shuttle launch on television.
Everyone watched the shuttle launch on television.

everywhere, anywhere, nowhere See *anywhere, everywhere, nowhere*.

except, accept See *accept, except*.

explicit, implicit These adjectives are antonyms. *Explicit* refers to something that is directly stated. *Implicit* refers to something that is not directly stated.

The antiwar protesters were **explicit** in their demands.
Implicit in these commercials is the suggestion that if you use the product you will be happy.

famous, infamous, noted, notorious *Famous* means "renowned or celebrated." *Infamous* means "of evil fame or repute." *Noted* means "celebrated." *Notorious* means "known widely and regarded unfavorably."

The **famous** (or *noted*) politician wrote a spy story.
In it, the **notorious** (or *infamous*) double agent was finally caught and punished.

farther, further These two words are not interchangeable. *Farther* means "more distant in space." *Further* means "more distant in time or degree," or "additional."

The double agent was **farther** from his home than anyone realized.
He had penetrated **further** into the government than anyone suspected.
The novel explored his motives **further.**

fewer, less Use *fewer* to refer to things that you can count individually. Use *less* to refer to quantities that you cannot count and to amounts of time, money, or distance when the amount is a single quantity.

There are **fewer** companies polluting the harbor than there were last year.
There is **less** pollution in the harbor.
If we all work together, it will take **less** than two hours to clean up the park.

figuratively, literally *Figuratively* and *literally* are antonyms. An expression that uses a metaphor to represent a fact is figurative; an expression that states a fact is literal.

Variety was speaking **figuratively** in its headline "Wall Street Lays an Egg."
What it meant **literally** was that the stock market had had a disaster.

first, firstly; second, secondly Use *first* and *second*, not *firstly* and *secondly* to mean "in the first (or second) place."

First, we must alert people to the need for a clean environment. [not *Firstly*]

formally, formerly These two words sometimes sound alike but have distinct spellings and meanings. *Formally* means "in a formal or official manner." *Formerly* means "previously" or "at an earlier time."

The environmentalist spoke **formally** to the committee.
Formerly, she had been too shy to speak in front of formal groups.

former, latter Of two things or persons named sequentially, the first is the *former;* the second is the *latter.*

Individually and as a couple, Georgia O'Keeffe and Alfred Stieglitz were important to modern art. The **former** (O'Keeffe) was a painter, while the **latter** (Stieglitz) was a photographer and gallery owner.

further, farther See *farther, further.*

good, well *Good* is an adjective. *Well* can be an adverb or a predicate adjective meaning "satisfactory" or "in good health." The opposite of feeling sick is feeling *well.*

Hemingway is a **good** writer.
He writes **well.**
In his story "A Day's Wait," the boy does not feel **well.**

got, have *Got* is the past tense of the verb *get.* It means "obtained." Avoid using *got* with or in place of *have.* Also avoid using *don't got* in place of *don't have.*

I **have** to read "The Snows of Kilimanjaro" today. [not *I got to*]
I **don't have** any other homework. [not *I don't got*]

had ought, hadn't ought Avoid using *had* and *hadn't* with *ought.* Instead, use *ought,* which is usually followed by the preposition *to.*

You **ought** to recycle those old newspapers. [not *had ought*]
He **ought not** to throw recyclable bottles away. [not *hadn't ought*]

half a Use *a half* or *half a(n).* Do not use *a half a(n).*

We can take the cans and bottles to the recycling center in **a half** hour. [not *a half an hour*]

hanged, hung *Hanged* and *hung* are alternate forms of the past tense and past participle of the verb *hang.* Use *hanged* when referring to death by hanging. Use *hung* in all other cases.

In the old westerns, thieves were sometimes **hanged** for their crimes.
I **hung** my Andrew Wyeth print in the living room.

have, got See *got, have.*

have, of *Have* and *of* sound similar in rapid speech, but they are different parts of speech. *Have* is a verb; *of* is a preposition. Be careful
to say and write *have* when completing a verb phrase, especially
after the helping verbs *should, would,* and *could. Of* is not a verb.

> We should **have** been more careful to protect the environment. [not
> *should of*]

hisself, theirselves *Hisself* and *theirselves* are both nonstandard forms.
Do not use them. *Himself* and *themselves* are the correct forms for
reflexive and intensive pronouns.

hung, hanged See *hanged, hung.*

i.e., e.g. See *e.g., i.e.*

imminent, eminent See *eminent, imminent.*

implicit, explicit See *explicit, implicit.*

imply, infer *Imply* means "to hint at" or "to suggest." *Infer* means "to
reach a conclusion based on evidence or deduction." These words
are not interchangeable.

> I **implied** in my remarks that we students could raise more money with a
> recycling drive than a car wash.
> I **inferred** from the applause that the audience supported my suggestion.

in, into Use *in* to mean "within" and *into* to suggest movement toward
the inside from the outside.

> Ruth walked **into** the antique-car museum without knowing what to
> expect.
> While she was **in** the museum, she was amazed at how beautiful the old
> cars were.

Exercise 2 **Correct Usage**

**? Critical
Thinking:**
Which word or
phrase is ap-
propriate in
formal
English?

On your paper, write the word or phrase in parentheses that completes
each sentence correctly.

SAMPLE The first radios looked different (from, than) those of today.
ANSWER from

1. The first commercial broadcasting station (into, in) the United
   States was established in 1920.
2. Early radio programs included dramas, newscasts, comedies, variety shows, (and so forth, etc.)
3. Many musicians, (i.e., e.g.) Benny Goodman, gained popularity
   through radio broadcasts.
4. Radio programs (literally, figuratively) helped to boost the popularity of dance band music in the 1930s.

5. Some people are (disinterested, uninterested) in hearing old radio programs, but I find them fascinating.
6. In recording a radio drama, some producers used a microphone that (hung, hanged) from the ceiling.
7. Radio dramas often used music to (infer, imply) a change of mood.
8. Radio dramas were different (from, than) television dramas because the audience had to imagine the action in a radio show.
9. With the advent of television, there were (less, fewer) radio dramas on the air than there had been (formally, formerly).
10. When radio shows weren't doing (good, well) in the 1950s, program directors designed broadcasts that suited most people's (every day, everyday) schedules.

individual, person   Use *individual* to distinguish one person from a larger group. Do not use *individual* generally in place of *person*.

> Supporters of civil rights believe that all **persons** should be treated as **individuals.**

ingenious, ingenuous   *Ingenious* means "clever"; *ingenuous* means "naive."

> It took a series of **ingenious** inventors to create the airplane that we know today.
> At the turn of the century, was it **ingenuous** to believe that human beings could fly?

irregardless, regardless   Do not use *irregardless;* it is nonstandard. Use *regardless* instead.

> I still like Broadway musicals, **regardless** of what you say.

its, it's   *Its* is a possessive pronoun; *it's* is the contraction for *it is*.

> During World War II, the nation mobilized **its** resources for the war effort.
> **It's** easy to see why so many women took factory jobs during the war.

judicial, judicious   *Judicial* means "of or pertaining to a court of law." *Judicious* means "having or showing good judgment."

> In the fifties, it took **judicial** proceedings to integrate some schools.
> The civil rights movement was **judicious** in its tactics; it practiced nonviolence.

just exactly   This phrase is redundant. Use either *just* or *exactly*

> It takes me **just** four minutes to make dinner in my microwave.
> It takes **exactly** four minutes.

kind of, sort of   In most writing do not use these colloquial forms to mean "somewhat." See also *these kinds, this kind.*

> Unfortunately, the middle of my microwaved dinner is still **somewhat** cold. [not *kind of* or *sort of*]

latter, former See *former, latter*.

lay, lie *Lay* is a transitive verb that means "to put or to place something somewhere." It always takes a direct object. *Lie* is an intransitive verb that means "to be in or to assume a reclining position." It does not take a direct object. (See page 621 for the principal parts of these irregular verbs.)

Someday there may be robots that can clean, cook, and **lay** the table but never need to **lie** down to rest.

learn, teach Do not use these words interchangeably. To *learn* is "to receive knowledge" or "to acquire knowledge." *Teach* means "to give knowledge."

I will **learn** to use the computer quickly if Janice **teaches** me.

leave, let *Leave* means "to go away" or "to abandon." *Let* means "to permit" or "to allow."

Please **let** me **leave** my copy of *A Farewell to Arms* in your locker.

less, fewer See *fewer, less*.

liable, apt, likely See *apt, liable, likely*.

lie, lay See *lay, lie*.

like, as See *as, like*.

likely, apt, liable See *apt, liable, likely*.

likewise *Likewise* is an adverb that means "similarly." Do not use it as a conjunction to mean "and" or "together with."

President Kennedy's quick wit, **together with** his good humor, made his press conferences fun to watch. [not *likewise*]

literally, figuratively See *figuratively, literally*.

loan, borrow, lend See *borrow, lend, loan*.

many, much Use the adjective *many* to describe things that you can count (pencils, people). Use the adjective *much* to describe things that you cannot count (gas, truth, strength). When used as indefinite pronouns, *much* is singular and *many* is plural.

Many volunteered for the armed services during World War I.
Much was written about their heroism.

may, can See *can, may*.

may, might See "Modals," page 627.

may be, maybe In the term *may be*, *may* is an auxiliary that indicates possibility. (See "Modals," page 627.) The adverb *maybe* means "perhaps."

Donna **may be** able to try out for *The Glass Menagerie.*
Maybe Donna will try out for the play.

more than one This phrase, although plural in meaning, takes a singular verb.

More than one girl wants the part of Laura.

most, almost See *almost, most.*

much, many See *many, much.*

myself, yourself Do not use a reflexive pronoun in place of *I, me,* or *you.*

INCORRECT My brother and **myself** are trying out for the role of the gentleman caller.

CORRECT My brother and **I** are trying out for the role of the gentleman caller.

neither, both, either See *both, either, neither.*

nohow, noway *Nohow* and *noway* are nonstandard. Avoid using them. You can, however, use *no way* correctly as two words.

INCORRECT **Noway** can Laura break out of her glass menagerie.

CORRECT There is **no way** that Laura can break out of her glass menagerie.

noted, notorious, famous, infamous See *famous, infamous, noted, notorious.*

nothing like, nowhere near In formal English, use *nothing like* to mean "not at all like"; use *nowhere near* to mean "not anywhere near."

Today's videos are **nothing like** the first silent movies. [formal]
The video store is **nowhere near** my house. [formal]
That silent movie was **nowhere near** as difficult to follow as I had thought it would be. [informal]

nowhere, anywhere, everywhere See *anywhere, everywhere, nowhere.*

of, have See *have, of.*

off, off of *Of* is unnecessary. Do not use *off* or *off of* in place of *from.*

Imagine how surprised people were to see this new invention, the vacuum cleaner, just lift dirt **off** the floor. [not *off of*]
My grandmother bought her vacuum **from** a door-to-door salesperson. [not *off*]

only To avoid confusion, place *only* before the element that it modifies. The placement of *only* can dramatically affect the meaning of your sentence.

Only the wizard of Oz gave the scarecrow a diploma.
The wizard of Oz **only** gave the scarecrow a diploma.
The wizard of Oz gave **only** the scarecrow a diploma.
The wizard of Oz gave the scarecrow **only** a diploma.

on to, onto   In the phrase *on to, on* is an adverb and *to* is a preposition. *Onto* is a preposition that means "to a position on" or "upon."

After Dorothy met the scarecrow, they went **on** to Oz.
Dorothy's house fell **onto** the wicked witch.

outside, outside of   Use *outside of* only when *outside* is a noun and *of* is a preposition.

They had to wait **outside** the gates of Oz. [not *outside of*]
In the movie, what color was the **outside of** the city of Oz?

passed, past   *Passed* is the past tense of the verb *pass,* which means "to move on or ahead; to proceed." *Past* is an adjective that means "no longer current," "over," or "before the present"; a noun that means "a time earlier than the present"; an adverb that means "so as to go beyond"; and a preposition that means "beyond, after."

The Freedom March **passed** through the streets of the capital. [verb]
It was larger than any **past** marches. [adjective]
The marchers wanted to put discrimination in the **past.** [noun]
They marched **past** by the hundreds. [adverb]
They were not **past** caring about liberty and justice for all. [preposition]

people, persons   Use *persons* when referring to a relatively small, specific group. Use *people* when referring to a large group in a collective sense.

Three **persons** (or *people*) represented our group in the march.
Even **people** who had been pessimistic about the march were thrilled by Dr. King's speech. [not *persons*]

persecute, prosecute   To *persecute* people is to harass, oppress, or otherwise mistreat them. To *prosecute* is to bring a court action.

Civil rights activists were often **persecuted** in those days.
Some were even arrested and **prosecuted** for protesting segregation.

person, individual   See *individual, person.*

Exercise 3 **Correct Usage**

❓ Critical Thinking:
Which word or phrase follows formal, standard usage?

On your paper, write the word or phrase in parentheses that correctly completes each sentence.

SAMPLE   Before World War II, (less, fewer) women worked (outside of, outside) the home.
ANSWER   fewer; outside

1. When World War II began, (many, much) new job opportunities became available to women.
2. In 1942, because of a shortage of workers, more than one crop (was, were) lost.
3. Thousands of women, (likewise, together with) many youngsters, helped to save the harvest.
4. At first, many people (only thought, thought) women should do (only clerical, clerical) or domestic work.
5. (Regardless, Irregardless) of this belief, women went on to perform the same demanding jobs that men had performed.
6. In the 1940s, the New York Stock Exchange hired (it's, its) first female clerk.
7. As reporters and editors, women also (lent, loaned) their talents to the field of journalism.
8. In the (past, passed), women had never been allowed to perform such heavy work as (laying, lying) bricks.
9. Many women (learned, taught) (off of, from) experts how to weld and assemble machine parts; they earned the nickname "Rosie the Riveter."
10. Before World War II, fourteen million women held jobs; at the end of the war, (most, almost) twenty million women were working.

precede, proceed   *Precede* means "to exist or come before in time." *Proceed* means "to go forward or onward."

John Kennedy **preceded** Lyndon Johnson as President, but Johnson **proceeded** with many of Kennedy's policies.

provided, providing   In formal usage use *provided* as a conjunction meaning "on the condition that" or "if."

I will call you tomorrow **provided** I don't see you this evening. [not *providing*]

raise, rise   *Raise* is a regular transitive verb that means "to lift"; it always takes a direct object. *Rise* is an irregular intransitive verb that means "to move upward." See page 622 for the principal parts of the irregular verb *rise*.

You **raise** an interesting question about the stock-market crash.
Does a small **rise** in the Dow-Jones average have any significance?

real, really   *Real* is an adjective; *really* is an adverb.

It is **really** fortunate that there are now safeguards against another stock-market crash. [not *real*]

That is a **real** relief!

reason is because, reason is that   *Reason is because* is redundant. Use *reason is that* or simply *because*.

INCORRECT	The **reason** that many people lost money **is because** they had bought stock on credit.
CORRECT	The **reason** that many people lost money **is that** they had bought stock on credit.

refer back *Refer back* is redundant. Use *refer.*

I **refer** to yesterday's lecture on the Depression. [not *refer back*]

regardless, irregardless See *irregardless, regardless.*

regretful, regrettable *Regretful* means "full of sorrow or regret." *Regrettable* means "deserving regret or sorrow."

Many people were **regretful** about Jim Thorpe's being disqualified from the Olympics.
Taking away his gold medals was a **regrettable** decision.

respectfully, respectively *Respectfully* means "showing respect or esteem." *Respectively* means "each in the order indicated."

My grandparents always speak **respectfully** of President Roosevelt.
They say that he saw them through the Depression and the war, **respectively.**

rise, raise See *raise, rise.*

said, says, goes, went *Said* is the past tense of the verb *say; says* is a present-tense form. Do not use *says* for *said.* Also, do not use *goes* or *went* for *said.*

Gary called and **said,** "Do you have a copy of Robert Frost's poems?" [not *says* or *goes*]

second, secondly; first, firstly See *first, firstly; second, secondly*

seldom ever *Seldom ever* is redundant. Use only *seldom.*

-self, -selves The suffix *-self* is singular; *-selves* is plural. Be sure to use the correct suffix to form a reflexive pronoun.

SINGULAR   *myself, yourself, himself, herself*

PLURAL   *ourselves, yourselves, themselves*

set, sit *Set* is a transitive verb that means "to place something." *Sit* is an intransitive verb that means "to rest in an upright position"; *sit* does not take a direct object.

The civil rights demonstrators were told to **sit** down at the whites-only lunch counter.
The waiter would not **set** silverware or dishes in front of them.

slow, slowly *Slow* is an adjective that can be used as an adverb in informal speech, especially in commands or for emphasis. *Slowly* is an adverb; it is preferred in formal usage.

The process of cleaning up the environment is **slow.** [predicate adjective]
Progress is made **slowly.** [adverb]
It's as though someone said, "Go **slow!**" [adverb; informal]

so, so that   Both can be used to mean "in order that." However, use *so* only in informal speech or writing. *So* is also used as an explanatory or superlative qualifier of adjectives and adverbs.

Flappers bobbed their hair **so that** they would be chic. [or informally, *so*]   (shĕk)
They were **so** excited about their new Model T that they all tried to climb in at once.

some time, sometime, sometimes   When you use two words, *some* is an adjective modifying *time.* *Sometime* can be an adverb that means "at an indefinite time." *Sometimes* is an adverb that means "occasionally, now and then."

       adj. noun
It takes **some time** to learn the Charleston.

               adv.
Would you teach me **sometime?**

  adv.
Sometimes I wish that I had lived in the Roaring Twenties.

sort of, kind of   See *kind of, sort of.*

supposed to, used to   *Supposed to* means "expected to" or "required to." *Used to* means "accustomed to, familiar with." Be sure to spell *supposed* and *used* with a final -*d*.

At the turn of the century, ladies were **supposed to** wear a hat and gloves in public. [not *suppose to*]
Today people are not **used to** dressing so formally. [not *use to*]

Used to can also reflect a customary action in the past.

They **used to** dress for dinner every evening.

sure, surely   *Sure* is an adjective meaning "certain" or "dependable." *Surely* is an adverb meaning "certainly, without doubt."

In the twenties, many people were **sure** that prosperity would continue.

The stock-market crash **surely** took them by surprise.

take, bring   See *bring, take.*

teach, learn   See *learn, teach.*

than, then   Use *than* as a conjunction in a comparison. Use *then* as an adverb to show a sequence of time or events. Do not use either one as a conjunction between two independent clauses.

He thinks that *The Sun Also Rises* is better **than** *A Farewell to Arms.*
I'm almost finished with the former; **then** I will read the latter.

that, which, who Use *that* as a relative pronoun to introduce essential clauses *(page 589)* that refer to things or to collective nouns referring to people. Because it introduces an essential clause, do not use a comma before *that*.

The airplane **that** first flew at Kitty Hawk is now in a museum.

Use *which* as a relative pronoun to introduce nonessential clauses *(page 589)* that refer to things or to groups of persons. Always use a comma before *which* when it introduces a nonessential clause.

Kitty Hawk, **which** was the site of the first successful airplane flight, is in North Carolina.

Use *who* or *whom* as a relative pronoun to introduce essential and nonessential clauses that refer to persons. Use a comma before *who* or *whom* when it introduces a nonessential clause.

The brother **who** was injured in a test flight was Orville.
The Wright brothers, **who** built the first successful airplane, had previously built bicycles.

that there, this here Do not use either construction. Use only *this* or *that*.

In what year did the Wright brothers fly **that** airplane? [not *that there*]

theirselves, hisself See *hisself, theirselves*.

then, than See *than, then*.

these kinds, this kind Use *this* or *that* to modify the singular nouns *kind, sort*, and *type*. Use *these* and *those* to modify the plural nouns *kinds, sorts*, and *types*. Use the singular form of these nouns when the object of the preposition is singular; use the plural form when the object of the preposition is plural.

This kind of model airplane is easy to construct.

These kinds of models are more difficult.

though, although See *although, though*.

till, until Both words are acceptable. *Until* is preferred as the first word in a sentence. Do not use *til* or *'til*.

Until the Nineteenth Amendment passed in 1920, women did not have the right to vote in national elections.

toward, towards Both mean "in the direction of" or "approaching," but *toward* is preferred. *Towards* is the British form.

try and, try to Use *try to* instead of *try and*.

Please **try to** keep the environment clean. [not *try and*]

uninterested, disinterested   See *disinterested, uninterested.*

used to, supposed to   See *supposed to, used to.*

very   Use *very* only sparingly. Overuse diminishes its effect.

way, ways   Do not use *ways* when referring to distance.

> During the Great Depression, people were willing to travel a long **way** to find work.   [not *ways*]

well, good   See *good, well.*

where . . . at   Do not use *at* after *where.*

> **Where** is the stock exchange located?   [not *Where is it at?*]

which, that, who   See *that, which, who.*

who, whom   See pages 657–658.

-wise   Avoid using *-wise* on the end of a word to mean "with reference to" or "concerning."

> AVOID   **Businesswise,** many people did well in the twenties.
>
> USE   Many people did well in business in the twenties.

would have   Do not use *would have* instead of *had* in clauses that begin with *if.*

> **If** they **had** not borrowed money to buy stocks, they would not have lost so much in the crash.   [not *if they would have*]

yourself, myself   See *myself, yourself.*

Exercise 4   Correct Usage

On your paper, write the word or phrase in parentheses that correctly completes each sentence.

? **Critical Thinking:**
Which word or phrase is correct in standard usage?

SAMPLE   In the beginning of the twentieth century, women began to move (toward, towards) being legally equal with men.

ANSWER   toward

1. For (some time, sometime), the women's movement had made no progress in gaining the right to vote.
2. In the early 1900s, women's clubs became (real, really) popular.
3. From 1900 to 1920, the number of working, middle-class women continued to (raise, rise).
4. Many of the club members (proceeded, preceded) to fight for improvements in working conditions for women.
5. Women's clubs were responsible for organizing the first kindergartens, which gave mothers more freedom (then, than) ever before.
6. Harriet Stanton Blatch was the woman (that, which, who) founded the Women's Political Union.

7. In 1910 and 1911, women won the right to vote in Washington and California, (respectfully, respectively).
8. Women wanted Congress to pass a constitutional amendment (so, so that) women all over the country could vote.
9. Many women (surely, sure) celebrated when the Nineteenth Amendment, (that, which) gave women the right to vote, became part of the United States Constitution.
10. Without the efforts (that, which) millions of women across the nation made, women (would have, would of) waited much longer for the right to vote.

The Writing Connection

Correct Usage in Your Writing

Reference Points:
pages 87–89 and pages 498–505

Knowing how to write standard, formal English is important for a number of reasons. In certain writing situations, such as letters of application or of complaint, you will want to be certain that you are taken seriously. If you use an inappropriate level of formality or nonstandard usage, you may distract, offend, or even unintentionally amuse your reader. In any of these cases, you will not be making the impression that you wish to make.

Therefore, it is worthwhile to check carefully for correct usage when you are revising your writing. Then you can make sure that your meaning will be understood and that your message will make the best possible impression.

Writing Assignments

Reference Point:
pages 355–365

An Arts Review As an arts reporter for a local television station, you are writing a review for the late news. *Step 1:* Select one of the following topics or another of your choice. Then narrow your topic to a particular arts "event."

a current movie or television program
a concert, such as jazz, classical, or folk
a dramatic play or musical
a museum exhibition of paintings or sculpture

Step 2: Cluster to gather real or invented details about the event that you are reviewing. *Step 3:* Write a short review. State your opinion of the arts event and give reasons to support your reaction. *Step 4:* Revise your review, checking for paragraph unity. Make sure that your details support your opinion. Pay particular attention to correct usage. *Step 5:* Proofread your review and make a clean copy for your teacher.

A Radio Interview To write an interview with a prominent public figure of the twentieth century, first freewrite names of real or invented interview subjects. Choose one person. To gather details, think about what questions a radio audience would want to ask your subject and how the person would be likely to respond. Jot down questions and invent plausible answers. Next, turn your notes into a question-and-answer dialogue, using at least four of the following word pairs.

Reference Point:
pages 471–474

advice / advise	famous / noted / notorious	persecute / prosecute
appraise / apprise	formally / formerly	precede / proceed
borrow / lend / loan	imply / infer	raise / rise
eminent / imminent	passed / past	sure / surely

When you revise your interview, read it aloud, checking for appropriate tone and style. Then read it over silently to check for correct usage and mechanics. Proofread your dialogue and prepare a clean copy. Finally, perform your interview with a classmate or post it on the bulletin board. Ask for responses from your teacher and your class.

Levels of Usage   *(pages 616–619)*

Formal and Informal English   The following sentences contain examples of informal English, such as slang and colloquial expressions, as well as nonstandard English. On your paper, revise each sentence, using more formal English where necessary, and correcting nonstandard usage when it appears.

1. Turns out scientists are like trying to find out why we love those thrill machines called roller coasters.
2. Me and my friends could sure tell them a thing or two about riding on them roller coasters.
3. I been reading that some intellectual types think that we riders crave thrills and more thrills, and that's why we like to ride the old roller coaster.
4. They have this idea that when people get on a roller coaster, it's kinda like they're into this daring situation, you know?
5. So when you finish the ride and nothing bad happens, you get this real blast because you've lived through it.
6. It's like you had been skiing down a totally awesome hill, and you finally make it.
7. Some science people are actually like studying types they call "thrill seekers," people who seem to get off on like intense experiences.
8. One guy says that a lot of people might take a ride once but that's it, forget it, never again for them.
9. Then you got the thrill lovers who can't stay away from things like roller coasters; I mean they wouldn't do nothing but that all day, irregardless of the time and money they spent.
10. Now get this — being into thrills is all in the brain, and that's the honest-to-goodness truth.
11. Here's the thing — a lot of people are so cool and laid back that they don't freak out over most things, so they can take extra exciting things.
12. There are like these nerves in the brain that get stimulated when something totally exciting happens, and some people are set off more easily than others.
13. Once you have that special thing going, whatever, you know you like probably have some extra chemical called "monoamine oxidase" (whew!) that gets you worked up.
14. Another thing that turns you on when you ride a roller coaster is that you ain't thinking of nothing but that ride, like you're really concentrating.

Using Verbs   (pages 620–635)

A. Verb Tense   On your paper, write the form of the verb named in parentheses for each sentence.

1. The fact that buried garbage causes groundwater pollution is one reason that more cities soon __?__ incinerators. (*use* — future)
2. By converting waste to energy, one incinerating plant is producing steam that __?__ five hundred buildings. (*heat* — present)
3. At present more than two hundred communities in the United States __?__ incinerators. (*construct* — present perfect)
4. Some critics of incinerators __?__ that no level of risk __?__ acceptable, and they __?__ that massive efforts to recycle and reduce garbage are preferable to incinerators. (*believe* — present; *be* — present; *argue* — present)
5. Critics also __?__ that burning without airborne emissions __?__ toxic pollutants to concentrate in the ash; these critics do not believe that burning garbage __?__ safe ever. (*state* — present perfect; *cause* — present; *be* — future)

B. Progressive, Emphatic, and Modal Forms of Verbs   On your paper, write the form of the verb specified in parentheses.

6. Supporters of incineration __?__ out for some time that the new incinerators are unlike the old models and __?__ many safety features. (*point* — present perfect progressive; *contain* — emphatic)
7. According to law, most incinerators being designed in the United States __?__ "mass burn" technology; burners using this technique __?__ virtually everything and remove toxic chemicals from the exhaust. (*use* — modal; *incinerate* — modal)
8. By the time you read this, a new incinerator __?__ thousands of tons of garbage. (*burn* — future perfect progressive)
9. A spokesperson for the company that operates the new incinerator says that scientists __?__ on a better system for the future, but that the company __?__ the plant with the most advanced technology available at the time. (*work* — present progressive; *build* — emphatic)
10. Because we __?__ out of landfill areas, incineration __?__ our only viable method for disposing of garbage. (*run* — present progressive; *be* — modal)

C. Shifts in Tense   Rewrite the following paragraph, correcting all errors in verb tense. Underline the changes that you make.

Over the years, medical research makes many advances in the treatment of heart disease. Every day, researchers will have been exploring new, more effective techniques. Open-heart surgery, which is performed first in 1952, had saved many thousands of lives. By the year 2000, surgeons will use lasers during heart surgery for many years.

Subject-Verb Agreement   (pages 636–647)

A. Collective Nouns, Indefinite Pronouns, and Nouns with Plural Form as Subjects   On your paper, write the subject of each sentence. Then write the verb or verb phrase in parentheses that agrees with the subject.

1. A group (admires, admire) several quilts because the objects are hung on a museum wall.
2. Not everybody (see, sees) the beauty of quilts as clearly if the objects are casually thrown onto a bed.
3. Old clothes, too, (is, are) admired as treasured and rare objects when they hang in antique shops today.
4. In fact, of the objects we treasure today, many (was made, were made) for simple home use or for simple adornment.
5. We admire these things because in our increasingly mechanized, assembly-line world, nothing (is, are) more prized than the unique, handmade object.
6. All the old "folk art" we admire (were, was) once a contemporary expression of people's lifestyle.
7. Much of this "folk art" (was, were) based on traditional or commercial forms.
8. Plenty of American furniture (were, was) orginally modeled after English Chippendale, for example, but soon acquired its own characteristics.
9. The audience for all kinds of folk art (is growing, are growing).
10. A group of collectors (is, are) often in disagreement over the worth of any particular object.
11. The economics of collecting folk art (varies, vary), but anyone who (loves, love) these objects can enjoy collecting just for the pleasure it brings.
12. A wise family (cherishes, cherish) its collection of heirlooms and humble treasures.

B. Correcting Errors in Subject-Verb Agreement   On your paper, rewrite the following paragraph, changing the form of the verb if it does not agree with the subject. Underline the corrected verbs and verb phrases.

   The job of air controller is one of those positions that is often cited as being highly stressful. Neither air controllers nor the Federal Aviation Administration believe that the current air control system is working. They feel that something needs to be done about the present system. Every air controller monitors flight-pattern changes on flight strips and then radios planes about them. There's problems with this system because of possible human error. Many an emergency cause breakdowns in communication. Economics is one factor determining the future of this career, and politics are another.

Using Pronouns   (pages 647–663)

A. Pronoun Antecedents   On your paper, rewrite the following sentences, supplying the kind of pronoun named in parentheses. Make sure that the pronoun agrees with its antecedent. Underline the pronoun.

1. Irving Berlin wrote many songs glorifying the United States even though the composer __?__ was a Russian immigrant. (intensive)
2. Berlin said that __?__ liked to write patriotic songs. (personal)
3. "White Christmas" and "Alexander's Ragtime Band" have earned __?__ composer many fans. (personal possessive)
4. Everybody has __?__ own feelings about "God Bless America." (personal possessive)
5. I __?__ have heard some recordings of Berlin's Broadway musicals. (intensive)
6. Teresa and I enjoy listening to records of __?__ favorite composer, Irving Berlin. (personal possessive)
7. Karen said that __?__ knew that Berlin's first big hit was "Alexander's Ragtime Band." (personal)
8. Karen gave __?__ credit for knowing that the song was first heard by the public in 1911. (reflexive)
9. After everyone listened to Karen speak, __?__ realized that she knew a lot about Irving Berlin and his music. (personal)
10. The United States government awarded Berlin some of __?__ most distinguished civic medals. (possessive)
11. Irving Berlin Fan Club members had __?__ own ideas about the composer's contributions. (personal possessive)
12. Each of the women who attended the concert last week had __?__ own reactions to Berlin's music. (personal possessive)

B. Pronoun Case   On your paper, rewrite this paragraph, using the correct pronouns in parentheses. Underline the pronouns that you use.

(We, Us) fans of popular twentieth-century music think that George Gershwin was a wonderful composer. (Him, He) and his brother Ira wrote many famous songs and musicals. Modern, harmonic ideas were of great interest to Ira and (he, him). (Who, Whom) do you think wrote the words to the Gershwin songs? Ira's clever lyrics are a large part of these songs for (we, us) Gershwin fans. For (who, whom) were Gershwin's songs written? (Them, They) were written for the American public, not for music critics. (Whoever, Whomever) heard George Gershwin's songs, however, seemed to enjoy them. Perhaps Gershwin's most memorable work is *Rhapsody in Blue*, for its opening notes are unforgettable to (whoever, whomever) has heard them. And (who, whom) could forget the wonderful Gershwin opera *Porgy and Bess*? Many people including (we, us) believe *Porgy and Bess* to be one of the greatest works of American music.

Using Modifiers   (pages 664–671)

A. Modifiers in Comparisons   On your paper, complete each sentence, using the form of the modifier named in parentheses. Underline the modifier that you use.

1. Hawaii has a __?__ climate than that of the continental United States. (*warm* — comparative)
2. During the mid-twentieth century, __?__ congressional bills than ever before supported statehood for Hawaii. (*much* — comparative)
3. By 1959 members of Congress became __?__ than they had ever been about admitting Hawaii to the Union. (*serious* — comparative)
4. People living in Hawaii had __?__ hope of gaining statehood in the early 1900s. (*little* — comparative)
5. Politically, the __?__ thing that could have happened for Hawaiians occurred in 1959: Congress voted to accept Hawaii into the Union. (*good* — superlative)
6. Before gaining statehood, Hawaiians were in a much __?__ political position than they were afterwards. (*bad* — comparative)
7. They could not vote for the United States President or their own governor, and their member of Congress was __?__ than the other members. (*powerful* — comparative)
8. The __?__ action the Hawaiian member of Congress could take was to introduce bills; he was not allowed to vote for them. (*much* — superlative)
9. Since statehood the economy of Hawaii has become one of the __?__ economies in the United States. (*explosive* — superlative)
10. Hawaii has become __?__ than it has ever been before. (*prosperous* — comparative)

B. Using Comparisons Correctly   On your paper, rewrite the following paragraph, making comparisons clear and complete and eliminating misplaced or dangling modifiers and double comparisons.

Alaska is the most largest state in the United States, but it has less fewer people than any other state. Alaskans have to dress more warmly than just about anyone in the United States in winter. Surviving an Alaskan winter can be as difficult as Siberia. For only about two cents an acre, for which he was severely criticized, Secretary of State William Seward bought Alaska from Russia in 1867. Americans thought that Seward's purchase of the region was the most worse deal ever made. People soon found Alaska to be rich in oil, minerals, timber, and fish proving Seward's critics to be wrong. In 1958 Congress voted to make Alaska the most newest state in the United States. Proclaiming it the forty-ninth state, Alaskans were welcomed into the Union by President Eisenhower in 1959. Today, Alaska is more richer than it has ever been. Finding it a wonderful summer vacationland, Alaska is visited by many tourists every summer.

Usage Notes   (pages 671–691)

A. Correct Usage   On your paper, rewrite each sentence, correcting usage errors and replacing informal English with formal language.

1. On account of he could create characters without uttering a word, Charlie Chaplin became very famous as a silent movie actor.
2. Beside his being an actor, Chaplin was a brilliant director.
3. The tramp he had a mustache and carried a cane.
4. Some critics can't hardly believe how inspired some of Chaplin's work was.
5. Chaplin made his movie plots credulous.
6. Compared to other comedians of his time, Chaplin is usually considered the funniest.
7. Each and every film of Chaplin's early years was a success.
8. In the early 1900s, Chaplin made short films, i.e., *The Pawn Shop*.
9. Often people were literally walking on air after a Chaplin film.
10. *Modern Times, The Great Dictator,* and *The Gold Rush* are some of his most notorious, best-loved films.
11. Persons around the world loved his films.
12. His movies were skillfully conceived and ingenuously constructed to be both funny and heart-wrenching.
13. Comic relief was often just exactly what audiences needed during the hard times of the Great Depression.
14. Chaplin's films often tried to learn people by example to be kind and compassionate.
15. More than one of his films were about a serious subject.

B. Revising for Correct Usage   The following paragraph contains many examples of informal or incorrect usage. Read the paragraph. Then revise it, correcting all usage errors. Make sure that you use all verbs, pronouns, and modifiers correctly.

Critics have went that the Marx brothers were one of the few real zany comedic acts in American history. The trio of Groucho, Chico, and Harpo seldom ever behaved normally on film or on stage. They acted insultingly and childishly so they could surprise their audiences. The Marx brothers sometime used pantomime to amuse people. Harpo was suppose to be unable to speak, although in real life he sure could. Films such as *Duck Soup, Animal Crackers,* and *A Night at the Opera* created a circus-like affect on film. Audiences of the 1930s and 1940s were always anxious to see the comedians' newest film. At the time, the Marx brothers were the wildest act anywhere. The brothers used their musical talents to get laughs; they were actually good musicians though. Every one loved Harpo's harp playing, Chico's piano playing, and Groucho's singing of humorous songs.

Dialects of American English

The more you study the English language, the more you discover the wide variation in English grammar, pronunciation, vocabulary, and even spelling. Yet nearly everyone grows up being uncomfortable about using the language correctly. Just what is this "correct English" that we are supposed to have learned?

The standard English that you are studying in school is the most acceptable form for written English, but what about the language that you *hear* people using every day? It may not be the same in pronunciation, vocabulary, or grammatical form, but those differences do not add up to "bad" English. They define the speaker's **dialect.** Social class and education also influence one's speech. The language that you use with your friends may not be suitable for talking with your employer, with your parents' friends, or for being interviewed on national television. The reverse is also true; your friends would think it odd if you talked to them the way you do to your teachers, your employers, or your elders. Thus, you have a **social style** in your language; the level of formality in your speech depends on the social situation in which you find yourself.

The notion of what is usually meant today by "correct English" was established during the eighteenth century — the "Age of Reason." In the United States, John Adams proposed that an American English Academy be established by Congress "for refining, correcting, improving, and ascertaining the English language." Thomas Jefferson was asked to lead the movement; however, he effectively pre-empted the effort when he noted the rapidly changing nature of the English language to meet the needs of American English speakers. How could his own generation have met those needs if the language had been "fixed" in the year 1000 or 1500? As a result of this openness to change, English has accepted thousands of borrowed words representing virtually every language in the world. Its evolution in the United States is a result of the adoption and melding over time of elements of the languages of wave after wave of settlers and immigrants.

The first waves of settlers in North America brought their English dialects along with them. Those who stayed in the Northeast retained many of the pronunciation characteristics of the London dialect — and it persists today. Eastern New England speakers drop the *r* sound in *far* and *barn (fah, bahn)* and sometimes add an *r* sound to words ending in vowels *(area / arears).* The Southern dialect has also tended to remain stable. Dialect difference in grammatical structure is exemplified by the use of a plural form of the pronoun *you.* *You-all* or *y'all* has been a useful form for Southern speakers for about two hundred years. The influence of the Scots-Irish vocabulary is evident in Appalachia, for whom a *wishbone* is a *pulleybone,* and a *faucet* is a *spicket* or *spigot.*

The next waves of settlers — in the main, Germans and Scandinavians — moved on to Pennsylvania and then farther north. In time, five major American English dialects developed: Eastern New England, Inland Northern, North Midland, South Midland, and Southern. The **Eastern New England** dialect region includes Maine, New Hampshire, most of Vermont, Massachusetts, Rhode Island, and Connecticut. **Inland Northern** begins at about the eastern border of New York State and extends across the Great Lakes and west to the Pacific. **North Midland** begins at the east coast of New Jersey and Delaware, moves westward through Pennsylvania, Ohio, and Illinois, and then broadens to encompass most of the western half of the country. **South Midland** is a diagonal band that begins in West Virginia, moves through Kentucky and Tennessee, and then continues southwest across parts of Oklahoma and Texas. The **Southern** dialect region is restricted to the southeastern part of the country and extends from Virginia approximately diagonally to eastern Texas. You might wish to trace these regions on a map of the United States and identify your own dialect region.

The speech characteristics of the Inland Northern dialect have come to be accepted as standard English. It is the speech of broadcasters on national radio and TV. Standard English is important because better jobs and better pay are available to those who speak it. Dialects have their very special place as well because they reflect people's varied backgrounds, values, and special bonds with family and friends.

Vocabulary Activities

Dialect Differences   What are the characteristics of your dialect? Do you drop particular sounds in words, such as dropping the *r* sound at the ends of words, or the final consonant in words like *desk* or the *g* in *reading?* How do you pronounce *bake, pie, greasy, white, path, fog, Tuesday, poor, marry, Mary, merry,* and *oil?* What do you call a worm used as bait for fishing, a frying pan, athletic shoes, and firewood? Use your library's resources to compare your list with other dialects. Use a dictionary to check the pronunciation of these words in standard English.

Social Style   List several words with special meanings that you use only with your family because everyone shares an understanding of them. Write a brief essay that compares the development of these special words in your "family dialect" with the way that any dialect develops.

The Literature Connection

This unit provides you with a review of standard English usage. Refer to specific sections as usage questions arise for you, including questions about when it's appropriate to incorporate slang, jargon, dialects, and even nonstandard English into your writing and speaking.

Guided Reading   In 1960 John Steinbeck set out with his dog, Charley, to experience firsthand the cultural wealth of his nation. As you read, notice Steinbeck's mixed feelings about the loss of regional speech and the fact that change keeps language alive.

*O*ne of my purposes was to listen, to hear speech, accent, speech rhythms, overtones and emphasis. For speech is so much more than words and sentences. . . . It seemed to me that regional speech is in the process of disappearing, not gone but going. Forty years of radio and twenty years of television must have this impact. Communications must destroy localness, by a slow, inevitable process. . . .

To what extent has Steinbeck's 1960 prediction come true?

I who love words and the endless possibility of words am saddened by this inevitability. For with local accent will disappear local tempo. The idioms, the figures of speech that make language rich and full of the poetry of place and time must go. And in their place will be a national speech, wrapped and packaged, standard and tasteless. . . .

What other cultural aspects of *localness* are disappearing?

Even while I protest the assembly-line production of our food, our songs, our language, and eventually our souls, I know that it was a rare home that baked good bread in the old days. . . . It is the nature of a man as he grows older, a small bridge in time, to protest against change, particularly change for the better. . . . The sad ones are those who waste their energy in trying to hold it back, for they can only feel bitterness in loss and no joy in gain.

Analyze Steinbeck's usage in this passage — its level, correctness, and unique or pleasing characteristics.

John Steinbeck *(1902–1968)*
from *Travels with Charley*

Writing Applications

Writing About Your World   Steinbeck discovered that the United States is made up of hundreds of little worlds that reflect the nation while remaining unique. Explore the little world that you inhabit. Look at the signs on the streets and roads; read the local newspapers, magazines, and flyers; and talk with people from different walks of life. *Listen* carefully to what people say and how they sound. Then write a short essay or a story about your world, focusing on the way people *use* language.

Writing About Change   Change in language, as Steinbeck says, is inevitable. What do you think the future holds for English in the United States? What effect will mass communications, for example, or the need to solve global problems have on its evolution? Will English sound the same throughout the country, or will there still be local ways of saying things? Write a short expository essay or a story about your views. Be sure to include *reasons* for your predictions.

Enrichment Connections

Choose one or more of these activities to do on your own or as a group.

Keeping Tabs on the Language

Every day you hear or read unintentional abuses of standard English, such as a newscaster who reports that "*Less* and *less* people are registering to vote." Clip these "bloopers" or write them down and bring them to class to discuss. Consider keeping a "Dubious Distinction" notebook for the most flagrant abuses. You also might write a polite letter to some offender who shows a disregard for the language.

A Poem

"The Gift Outright" focuses on the complex relationship of the land, its people, and its history. Read over your notes for *Responding to Literature* on page 615, and reread the poem several times, jotting down additional thoughts about this relationship. Then write a short poem about the future of the United States. Develop the idea of "the gift." What will become of the "unstoried, artless, unenhanced" land of Frost?

Speaking and Listening

The Sound of Idioms   Idioms, such as *boggle the mind, lame duck,* and *shoot the breeze,* can add zest to your speech and writing when used appropriately. Brainstorm to come up with a list of idiomatic expressions, and do some research to discover their meaning and origin. Then write a short telephone dialogue in which you use some of these idioms. Consider the comic possibilities of one person taking an idiom literally.

CELEBRATING DIVERSITY

How do you use language to express your feelings about things that are really important to you? Do you ever prepare what you're going to say in advance, to make sure you convey your meaning exactly? Do you ever polish and repolish a piece of writing, such as a letter to someone you care about or a journal entry meant for you alone?

Poetry is the most "polished" of all literary genres. While at first glance it may seem that poetic conventions—such as meter and stanza patterns—inhibit the writer's freedom, poets also have the advantage of choosing their own patterns and manipulating them to suit their purposes. Thus, *usage* in poetry is often quite different from that of any other writing. As you read the poems that follow, note the strong feelings expressed by the poets. Also notice how the usage of each poem—including word choice and word order—contributes to its overall effect. Then work on one or more of the activities that follow the selection. Working on them may give you a new insight into how to choose and use words most effectively.

If Blue Doesn't Exist

If blue doesn't exist,
throw yourself into greens,
into thick pines of the green
that absorbed
the deep blue   5
your eye disavows.

If blue doesn't exist,
bloom in vermillions;
in rubies,
in forbidden poppies,   10
in burning rosebushes,
suns of sand,
foam and chaos.

If blue doesn't exist,
give yourself to black pollen of oblivion,   15
tomb or shadow;
burn in the color of night
clouding your pupil,
in the out-dated trench
or the grave   20
marked with only R.I.P.

If blue doesn't exist
sink into white
into jasmine that can't blot out
your denial of blue,   25
infinity,
open sky.
Or in the prayers
of your never ending
troubled longing for blue,   30
for pure blue . . .

                 Delia Quiñónez *(1946-   )*

The Earth Recovered

This is the earth recovered
where now we sing brand new songs.
Awakened by a nocturnal rain
that chatters on about renovations,
the fresh foliage that sprouts   5
bright green, gives us a vista of promise
with every drop that falls.

This is a new song
I had wanted that we sing together.

Fast is the flight, yes,   10
and burying the dead
has meant rescuing life
giving it new color.

Vidaluz Meneses *(1944-   )*

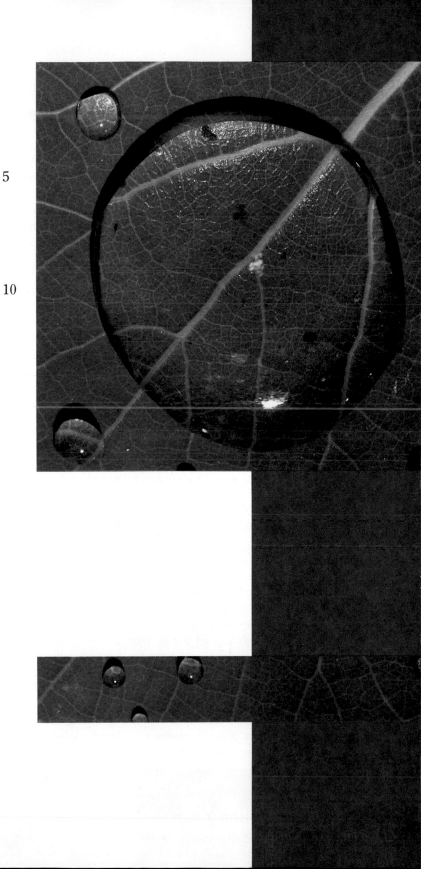

Taking Another Look

After reading the first poem over several times, what do you think the repeated phrase "If blue doesn't exist" means? In general terms, what do the other colors represent? What associations, mood, or atmosphere is created by the colors and other evocative words of each stanza? What is your opinion of the unusual way the poet uses colors? Now look at the more traditional way color is used in "The Earth Recovered" What does *green* represent? What brings fresh foliage? How are the songs and the colors related? What is the symbolic meaning of *new color* in the last line?

Changing Places

The poets featured here come from different countries and backgrounds (Meneses from Nicaragua and Quiñónez from Guatemala), but the difference between their world and yours doesn't prevent you from actively responding to their poems. Literature has that power— to express both the limitless variety and the fundamental unity of human experience. How does your cultural experience affect the way you see something as ordinary as the color blue or spring? What images and associations would you use to write about them? How has being a resident of this country influenced your associations? How has living in your particular part of the country colored your perspective? How has being a member of your family influenced how you *see* and feel about things? Keep these questions in mind as you work on one or more of the following activities.

LANGUAGE

Colorful Language   Working in a group, look through both poems for words related specifically or by association to color. List the words, including such color-suggestive examples as *poppies* and *rubies* as well as color names such as *vermillions*. Next have different members of your group collect other color-related words from sources that present a spectrum of choices, such as a box of crayons, an artist's paint catalogue, a brochure for wall paint, or a make-up advertisement. Don't forget the "noncolors," black, white, and gray. Discuss how the word chosen to represent the color differs for different purposes.

Then work together to create two short pieces of writing that use the same basic colors for contrasting purposes. Word choice will make all the difference. For example, you might use black, white, and gray for an ad for velvet and lace evening gowns and for a description of a crumbling mansion on a dark and lonely night. On the other hand, you might use yellows, oranges, and reds for an ad for summer fruits and for a description of a fire raging through a city. Refer to your group's palette of colors to select exactly the right words for your purpose.

WRITING

Poetic Polish Choose the topic of spring or the color blue, and freewrite or cluster to explore your associations with it. What do you see, hear, feel, taste, smell? What people, places, events do you associate with your topic? Then draft a poem that expresses your unique perspective. Experiment with new and unusual ways to use the words and phrases that you collected in your prewriting. Try out different rhythms, stanza patterns, and word orders. Finally, polish your poem and share it with your classmates.

WRITING

If . . . Then The poem "If Blue Doesn't Exist" exhorts readers to take a particular course of action if they fail to find what they are searching for, represented by *blue*. When you haven't found the "blue" in your life, what have you done instead? What have you learned from these experiences? Write a brief essay in which you address this common human predicament. Employ the formal usage suitable to an essay.

Skill WORKSHOP

Wealth in Words These poets—and consequently, their translators—use rich, specific words, some of which may be new to you. Choose five words that are new to you or that are used in a way that surprises you. Analyze their spelling and structure by answering these questions, using a dictionary if necessary. How is the word pronounced? How many syllables does it have? Which syllable is accented? What part of speech is the word? If it is a noun, what is its plural? Are there any silent letters in the word? If so, what are they?

UNIT 17 Mechanics

When you take notes on a lecture or from a book, you want to save time and space. You might abbreviate the names of people and places, or you might use symbols in place of words.

While your own individual notes help you to recall key concepts, you must follow guidelines for mechanics when you present these notes in formal writing. For example, if you write a research paper or an essay, you use appropriate abbreviations, capitalization, punctuation, italics, and numbers to convey your ideas clearly. In this way your readers will fully comprehend your thoughts and your opinions.

As you study mechanics in this unit, you'll be reading about *colleges and universities*. The selection shown here highlights the value of a good education. As you read, consider how the author uses mechanics to show two characters discussing a young man's future schooling.

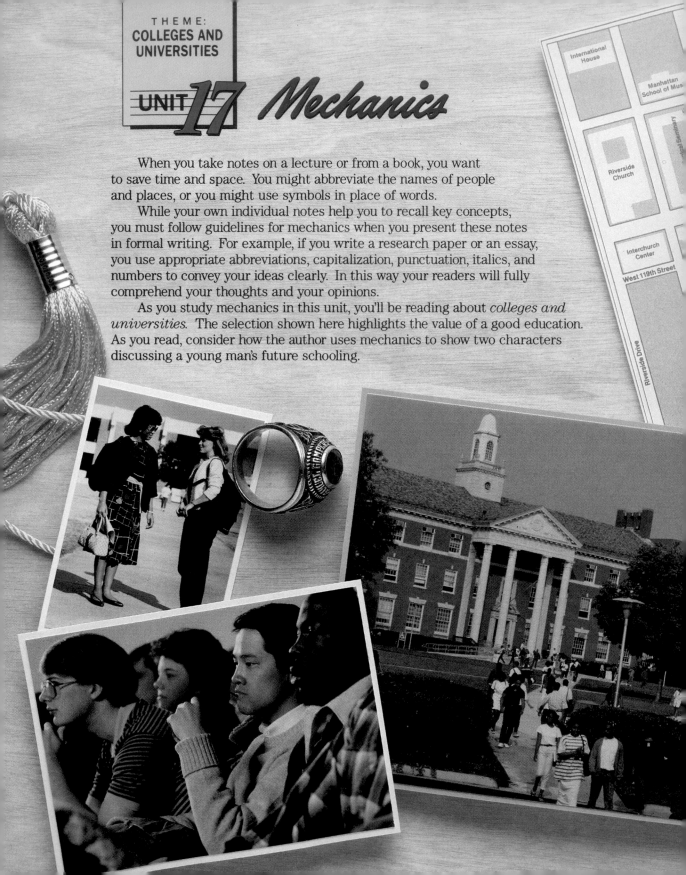

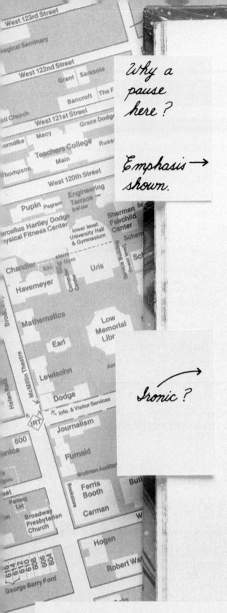

Why a pause here?

*Emphasis →
shown.*

Ironic? →

"Well," said Mr. Riley, "there's no greater advantage you can give him than a good education. Not," he added, with polite significance—"not that a man can't be an excellent miller and farmer, and a shrewd sensible fellow into the bargain, without much help from the schoolmaster."

"I believe you," said Mr. Tulliver, winking, and turning his head to one side, "but that's where it is. I don't *mean* Tom to be a miller and farmer.... I shall give Tom an eddication an' put him to a business, as he may make a nest for himself, an' not want to push me out o' mine." ...

Mr. Riley ... had no private understanding with the Rev. Walter Stelling; on the contrary he knew very little of that M.A. and his acquirements—not quite enough perhaps to warrant so strong a recommendation of him as he had given to his friend Tulliver. But he believed Mr. Stelling to be an excellent classic, for Gadsby had said so, and Gadsby's first cousin was an Oxford tutor; which was better ground for the belief even than his own immediate observation would have been, for though Mr. Riley had received a tincture of the classics at the great Mudport Free School, and had a sense of understanding Latin generally, his comprehension of any particular Latin was not ready. Doubtless there remained a subtle aroma from his juvenile contract with the *De Senectute* and the Fourth Book of the *Aeneid,* but it had ceased to be distinctly recognisable as classical, and was only perceived in the higher finish and force of his auctioneering style. Then, Stelling was an Oxford man, and the Oxford men were always—no, no it was the Cambridge men who were always good mathematicians. But a man who had had a university education could teach anything he liked; especially a man like Stelling....

George Eliot (Mary Anne Evans) *(1819–1880)*
from *The Mill on the Floss*

Responding to Literature

The two characters in this selection share opinions on education; Mr. Riley believes that someone with a university degree can teach anything, and Mr. Tulliver believes that education will get Tom into business. How do you feel about education? Freewrite about colleges, vocational training, your own school plans, and the advantages and the disadvantages of higher education. Include ideas, opinions, and experiences, and try to use quotations, school names, specific degrees, and so on. Save your notes in your writer's notebook for later use.

Abbreviations

Abbreviations are shortened forms of words that can be used to save time and space. For example, postal abbreviations make it easier to address an envelope or fill out a form. Common abbreviations such as *CD*, *TV*, and *NATO* are fast and informal ways to get a message across, if they are familiar to your readers. Abbreviations save space in tables and graphs, making them easy to read. Considerate writers, however, rarely use abbreviations in formal writing.

Rule Use standard abbreviations for certain titles preceding and following
─────
M 1 a person's name.

Dr. Juan Gomez	Henry Ford **III**	Mia Alberti, **Ph.D.**
Mr. John Holt	**Ms.** Toni Morrison	Armand Rhue, **D.D.S.**

Use abbreviations such as *Rev.* (Reverend), *St.* (Saint), and *Dr.* only if they appear with a person's name. Spell them out in the absence of a person's name.

> **INCORRECT** Nadia Schanda was, at twenty-two, the youngest **prof.** in the English department.

> **CORRECT** Nadia Schanda was, at twenty-two, the youngest **professor** in the English department.

In informal situations, the abbreviations for academic degrees, such as *B.A.*, *M.A.*, and *Ph.D.*, may be used without a person's name.

> I think a **Ph.D.** and two **M.D.'s** teach the medical ethics course.

Civil, military, and religious titles are spelled out when they are used with the last name alone but may be abbreviated when used with a full name. The spelled-out form is preferable, however, in all cases where space is not a problem.

General Grant	**Gen.** Ulysses S. Grant
Reverend King	**Rev.** Martin Luther King, Jr.

Note: Given names should not be abbreviated.

> **INCORRECT** **Chas.** James's economics class is his largest.

> **CORRECT** **Charles** James's economics class is his largest.

Capitalizing Title Abbreviations. Capitalize the abbreviation of a personal or official title when it precedes a person's name.

> "When is the term paper due, **Dr.** Wendel?" asked the student.

Capitalize the abbreviations *Sr.* and *Jr.* as well as those for academic degrees or honors that follow a person's name.

| Sharon Ellis, **J.D.** | Shahini Chand, **L.L.D.** |
| Andrew Meo, **M.B.A.** | Daryl Jones, **B.Ch.E.** |

Punctuating Title Abbreviations. Use a period after abbreviations for titles that precede and follow a person's name. If an abbreviation occurs at the end of a sentence, and if the abbreviation itself contains periods, no additional period is necessary. Do, however, place commas, semicolons, question marks, and exclamation points after the period following an abbreviation.

Kathy first got her **M.A.T.** and later went back to school for her **D.Ed.**
Is your economics professor Lester Hart, **Jr.?**

Use a comma to set off *Jr., Sr.,* and the abbreviations of academic degrees when these follow a person's name.

Lella Benigni, **R.N., Ph.D.,** will become dean of the school of nursing.

To form the plural of an abbreviation with periods, add an apostrophe and an *s.*

B.A.'s   Ph.D.'s

Rule

M 2

Use standard abbreviations for the names of organizations, agencies, and certain people that are well known by their initials.

ORGANIZATIONS AND AGENCIES   **FBI, YMCA, AFL-CIO, AMA, OPEC**

PEOPLE   **FDR, JFK, LBJ**

These abbreviations may be pronounced as individual letters (*CIA, NFL*) or as words (acronyms such as *NATO, PAC,* and *SCORE*). These are acceptable in most writing as long as they are familiar. If you think that the abbreviation may not be familiar to your reader, you can spell out the full term at its first appearance, indicate its abbreviation in parentheses, and use the abbreviation from then on.

Punctuation of Initials. When initials are used to abbreviate three or more words, they are usually written without periods.

To form the plural of an abbreviation that contains no periods, add a lower-case *s* without an apostrophe.

YMCAs   SATs

Rule

M 3

Use standard abbreviations for dates and times of day that include numbers.

44 B.C. (before Christ)
seventh century B.C.
A.D. 1215 (*anno Domini,* in the year of the Lord)
second century A.D.
7:15 A.M. (*ante meridiem,* before noon)
2:14 P.M. (*post meridiem,* after noon)

Notice that B.C. is placed after the number of the year, and A.D. is placed before the number of the year. Both B.C. and A.D. are placed after centuries expressed in words.

Do not use A.M. and P.M. as substitutes for the words *morning, afternoon,* or *evening.*

INCORRECT	Orientation for incoming freshmen will begin on the A.M. of September 12, 1990.
CORRECT	Orientation for incoming freshmen will begin on the **morning** of September 12, 1990.

Do not use A.M. or P.M. with numbers written as words.

INCORRECT	nine A.M.
CORRECT	nine o'clock in the morning *or* 9 A.M.

Rule   Do not abbreviate days of the week, the months, or standard units of
─────
M 4   time such as *second, minute, hour,* or *year* in formal writing.

Capitalizing Initials. The capitalized abbreviations A.M., P.M., B.C., and A.D. are often typeset as small capitals. When hand-writing, typewriting, and word-processing, capitalize B.C. and A.D.; for A.M. and P.M., choose either capital or lower-case letters and be consistent.

Rule   Spell out units of measurement in formal writing.
─────
M 5 | INCORRECT | The Scholastic Aptitude Test is three **hrs** long. |
|---|---|
| CORRECT | The Scholastic Aptitude Test is three **hours** long. |

Long phrases that are repeated frequently, such as *miles per hour (mph), cycles per second (cps),* and *revolutions per minute (rpm),* may be abbreviated in a text once the full term is spelled out and the abbreviation is identified in parentheses. These abbreviations need not be punctuated with periods.

Note: Units of measure and weight may be abbreviated in technical or informal writing when they are accompanied by a numeral; do not abbreviate units of measurement when they follow a number expressed in words. When using these abbreviations, do not use periods, except in the case of *gal.,* to show that you mean *gallon* (not *gal*), and *in.,* to show that you are writing the abbreviation of *inch,* not the word *in.* The following abbreviations for units of weight and measure are commonly used in tables, and in scientific and technical writing.

Traditional Measurements					
in.	inch(es)	tsp	teaspoon(s)	pt	pint(s)
ft	foot, feet	tbsp	tablespoon(s)	qt	quart(s)
yd	yard(s)	oz	ounce(s)	gal.	gallon(s)
mi	mile(s)	lb	pound(s)	F	Fahrenheit

Metric Measurements					
mm	millimeter(s)	km	kilometer(s)	L	liter(s)
cm	centimeter(s)	g	gram(s)	C	Celsius
m	meter(s)	kg	kilogram(s)		

Rule

M 6

Spell out geographical names and points of the compass in formal writing. Spell out words such as *street, avenue,* and *boulevard.*

Nevada (*not* Nev. or NV)   **southwest** of campus (*not* SW)

First **Avenue** (*not* Ave.)   **Mount** Lassen (*not* Mt.)

EXCEPTIONS The abbreviations *N., S., W.,* and *E.,* as well as *NW, NE, SE,* and *SW,* may be used in addresses before or after the street name. The word *Saint* is often abbreviated when it is used in the names of cities.

328 G Street **NE**	**St.** Louis	1306 Bates Avenue **SW**
2367 **E.** Elm Street	**St.** Tropez	47 **W.** Park Avenue

U.S.S.R. (or *USSR*) is an acceptable abbreviation for *Soviet Union,* as is *D.C.* for *District of Columbia* in the phrase *Washington, D.C.*

Use the two-letter Postal Service abbreviations only with ZIP Codes in addresses. Do not use them in formal writing.

Alabama	AL	Montana	MT
Alaska	AK	Nebraska	NE
Arizona	AZ	Nevada	NV
Arkansas	AR	New Hampshire	NH
California	CA	New Jersey	NJ
Colorado	CO	New Mexico	NM
Connecticut	CT	New York	NY
Delaware	DE	North Carolina	NC
District of Columbia	DC	North Dakota	ND
Florida	FL	Ohio	OH
Georgia	GA	Oklahoma	OK
Guam	GU	Oregon	OR
Hawaii	HI	Pennsylvania	PA
Idaho	ID	Puerto Rico	PR
Illinois	IL	Rhode Island	RI
Indiana	IN	South Carolina	SC
Iowa	IA	South Dakota	SD
Kansas	KS	Tennessee	TN
Kentucky	KY	Texas	TX
Louisiana	LA	Utah	UT
Maine	ME	Vermont	VT
Maryland	MD	Virginia	VA
Massachusetts	MA	Virgin Islands	VI
Michigan	MI	Washington	WA
Minnesota	MN	West Virginia	WV
Mississippi	MS	Wisconsin	WI
Missouri	MO	Wyoming	WY

Note that there is no comma between the state abbreviation and the ZIP Code.

Claremont, **CA 91711**   Princeton, **NJ 08540**

Rule
M 7
Spell out the names of academic subjects and the labels for the parts of books.

political science [*not* poli. sci.]   economics [*not* econ.]
page [*not* p.]   volume [*not* vol.]

Reference Points:
*pages 387–392
and 405–410*

Abbreviations that designate parts of books are acceptable only in citing references in a research paper.

Rule
M 8
Use common Latin abbreviations for source citations and for comments in parentheses. Use periods with these abbreviations.

e.g.   for example *(exempli gratia)*   **cf.**   compare *(confer)*
et al. and others *(et alii)*   **i.e.**   that is *(id est)*
etc.   and so forth *(et cetera)*   **N.B.**   note well *(nota bene)*

Rule
M 9
Spell out the word equivalents of symbols such as &, %, =, +, and ¢ in formal writing.

The number of Ph.D. degrees conferred increased by 519 **percent** between 1950 and 1984.

The ampersand (&) is not used in formal writing except in the name of a company that requires it.

Gibbs **&** Chavez   BT&D

The dollar symbol ($) is acceptable in all types of writing but only when it precedes amounts expressed in numerals. Do not use the symbol as a substitute for the words *money* or *dollars*.

The cost is over **ten thousand dollars.** [*not* ten thousand $]
The cost is over **$10,000.** [*not* $ ten thousand]

Exercise Abbreviations

**Critical
Thinking:**
What abbreviations are acceptable in formal writing?

On your paper, rewrite the following sentences to correct the faulty use of abbreviations. If no corrections are needed, write *Correct.*

SAMPLE   James Wilson jr. has completed 50% of the work needed to earn his degree.
ANSWER   James Wilson, Jr., has completed 50 percent of the work needed to earn his degree.

1. Most undergraduates take fifteen hrs. of classes each week.
2. The University of Al-Azhar in Cairo was founded about 970 a.d.
3. The first university in the U.S., Harvard U., was founded in the A.D. seventeenth century.

708   Unit 17   Mechanics

4. I'm not sure whether Capt. Samuels teaches Eng. comp. or psych.
5. The new library building takes up 80% of the ground allotted to the old one but will contain two thousand more sq. ft.
6. Admiral John Cranston, Sr., gave the commencement address at 1:25 P.M.
7. On his college application, Bruce printed his mailing address: 407 Sanders Road, Pittsburgh, PA 15216.
8. The textbook, which is at least 3 in. thick, cost only four $.
9. Freshmen cannot take the calculus class taught by Prof. Kiran Raj, junior, in the classroom at 17 N. Ash Street.
10. Three B.A.'s and three Ph.D.'s will speak at the 8:15 p.m. lectures about J.F.K. at the two Y.M.C.A.s nw. of the campus.

The Writing Connection

Using Abbreviations in Your Writing

In most writing situations, you decide when abbreviations are appropriate. For example, in a letter to a college dean, you would use standard abbreviations in the heading and inside address but not in the body. Think about your writing purpose and your audience before you use abbreviations.

Reference Point:
pages 24–26

Writing Assignments

Description for a College Guide Below are prewriting notes for a description of a college for a college guide. Some abbreviations in these notes are incorrect. You will write a description of Gallaudet College for *Gordon's Guide to Colleges. Step 1:* First, select from and then organize the following prewriting notes.

PREWRITING NOTES
Gallaudet Col. — located in Washington, DC
offers deaf students BA & MA degrees in liberal arts
1864 — authorized by the US Congress to give college degrees
named for Thom. Hopkins Gallaudet, pioneer in educating the deaf
also features preschool, adult ed. program, research programs
enrollment of over two thous. students; over 250 teachers

Step 2: Write a short description that will be useful to students interested in Gallaudet College. Use only standard abbreviations that are appropriate in formal writing. *Step 3:* Revise your description, checking for paragraph unity. *Step 4:* Proofread, checking the use of abbreviations. *Step 5:* Make a clean copy and give it to a classmate to read for clarity and correct use of abbreviations. Then file your description in your writer's portfolio.

Capitalization

In English, capital letters indicate the beginning of a sentence and proper nouns *(page 533)*.

Capitalization in Sentences

Rule M 10   Capitalize the first word of a sentence and the first word of a direct quotation that is a complete sentence.

> **Fewer** than one million students graduate from colleges in the United States each year.

> Denise said, "**If** I take summer courses, I can graduate early."

Interrupted Quotations.   If a quoted sentence is interrupted by an expression such as *Lucy said*, begin the second part of the quotation with a lower-case letter.

> "Linda is living on campus," said Jules, "**but** I am living at home."

If the second part of an interrupted quotation is a new sentence, begin it with a capital letter.

> "I hope that I hear from some schools this week," said Sarah. "**I** mailed my applications well before the deadlines."

Rule M 11   Capitalize the first word of each line of a poem if that is how the poet wrote it.

> **The** sentencing goes blithely on its way,
> **And** takes the playfully objected rhyme
> **As** surely as it keeps the stroke and time
> **In** having its undeviable say.
> > Robert Frost, "In a Poem"

Many modern poets do not capitalize the first word of each line of poetry. When you copy a poem, follow the style of the poet.

> > **beauty** is a shell
> > **from** the sea
> > **where** she rules triumphant
> > > William Carlos Williams, "Song"

Proper Nouns

Rule M 12   Capitalize people's names and their initials. If a last name begins with *Mc*, *O'*, or *St.*, capitalize the next letter as well. If a last name begins with *Mac*, *de*, *D'*, *la*, *le*, *van*, or *von*, use capitalization according to individual family preference.

> J. **O'**Shea   Hernando **de** Soto   Robert **La Roche**

Personal and Official Titles. Capitalize a personal or an official title or its abbreviation when it precedes a person's name. Capitalize a title when it is used as a name in direct address *(page 718).* Capitalize the names and abbreviations of academic degrees or honors that follow a person's name. Capitalize the abbreviations *Sr.* and *Jr.*

Dean Simpson	**Superintendent** Rossi
Eleanor Brock, **M.D.**	**Governor** Ralston
David Oleson, **Jr.**	Pedro Costas, **Ph.D.**

What time will the exam start, **Professor?**

BUT   Dr. Rose became a full **professor** this year.

Do not capitalize a title that follows or substitutes for a person's name unless it is the title of a head of a national government. Do not capitalize prepositions, conjunctions, and articles that are parts of titles unless one begins a sentence.

TITLE BEFORE NAME	TITLE FOLLOWING NAME
Professor Fischer	Walter Fischer, **professor**
President Wilson	Woodrow Wilson, **President**

The **president** of the college will address the freshman class at four o'clock this afternoon.

Gods of Mythology. Capitalize the names of gods and goddesses of mythology, but do not capitalize the word *god* or *goddess.*

Aurora was the Roman **goddess** of the dawn.

Rule
M 13
Capitalize the names of particular places, such as continents, countries, cities, parks, and rivers.

Bering Strait	Erie Avenue	Iceland	Ohio
Cooper River	Fairmont Park	Kalamazoo	Paraguay

Compass Points. Capitalize compass points that refer to specific geographic regions. Do not capitalize compass points that simply indicate directions or general regions.

We spent our semester break in the **Southwest.**
We traveled **west,** then **southwest** to reach our destination.

Heavenly Bodies. Capitalize the names of planets, stars, and constellations. Do not capitalize *sun* and *moon.* Capitalize *Earth* when referring to the planet; do not use the article *the* with *Earth.* Do not capitalize *earth* when you use it to refer to the land surface as opposed to the oceans, or to mean "soil." The article *the* may be used with *earth.*

Andromeda	Neptune	Sirius	Aquarius

We compared the moon rocks with rocks from **Earth.**

BUT   We brought the samples of **earth** that we had collected back to the lab.

Rule
M 14   Capitalize the names of nationalities, peoples, and languages.

Asian   Melanesian   Finnish

Rule
M 15   Capitalize the names of days, months, holidays, and special events. Do not capitalize the name of a season unless it is part of a proper noun.

Tuesday   August   spring   Memorial Day

Rule
M 16   Capitalize the names of historical events and specific historical periods, awards, and documents. Do not capitalize the names of centuries or general historical periods.

the Middle Ages   the Nobel Prize   the Treaty of Versailles

BUT   twentieth-century poetry   the gilded age

Rule
M 17   Capitalize the first, the last, and all other important words in the titles of books, newspapers, poems, television programs, musical works, paintings, and so forth. (See also pages 642, 737.) Capitalize a conjunction, an article, or a preposition only when it is the first or the last word in a title or when a conjunction or a preposition has five or more letters.

*A Man **Without** a Country*   "Singin' **in the** Rain"

Rule
M 18   Capitalize the name of a school subject that is a language or that is followed by a course number. Capitalize a proper adjective in the name of a school subject.

Latin   science   **French** literature
Biology II   history   **American** history

Rule
M 19   Capitalize the names of structures and the names of organizations, such as businesses, religions, government bodies, clubs, and schools. Capitalize a word such as *school* or *club* only when it is part of a proper noun.

Holmes Hall   House of Representatives
Taoism   Gordon's Bookstore
the Museum of Fine Arts   The Chess Association

the Broadcasters' **Club**   **BUT**   a broadcasters' **club**

Avila **College**   **BUT**   a technical **college**

Rule
M 20   Capitalize trade names. Do not capitalize a common noun that follows a trade name.

Tree-Ripe fruit juice   **Lyle** lamps

Rule
M 21   Capitalize the names of trains, ships, airplanes, rockets, and spacecraft *(page 737)*.

the *Lake Shore Limited*   *Viking II*

Other Uses of Capitalization

Rule

M 22

Capitalize most proper adjectives *(page 550).* Use a lower-case letter for a proper adjective that is in common usage.

Queen Anne's lace	**Persian** cat	**Gordian** knot
BUT **oxford** shoes	**roman** numeral	**india** ink

If you are not sure whether to capitalize a proper adjective, consult your dictionary.

Rule

M 23

Capitalize the pronoun *I.*

Elka and **I** will be attending the same college.

Avoiding Unnecessary Capitalization

Capitalization should not be used for emphasis. Although advertising often uses capital letters to call attention to certain words, you should avoid unnecessary capitalization in your formal writing. Use a dictionary as a guide to capitalization in any special situations that you encounter.

Rule

M 24

Do not capitalize common nouns used in place of proper nouns.

Yuko has chosen a **college.**
Yuko has chosen **Cornell College.**

Rule

M 25

Do not capitalize the names of relationships unless they form part of proper names or replace proper names.

My **uncle** went to Augustana College in Illinois.
We called **Uncle** Keith last night.
My **father** went to Augustana College in South Dakota.
I want to go to **Father's** school.

Exercise **Capitalization**

On your paper, rewrite each sentence, using capitalization correctly. Use your dictionary if you need help. If no corrections are needed in a sentence, write *Correct.*

? Critical Thinking: When is a person's title capitalized?

SAMPLE The quadrangle at my college is named sumner park after the School's founder.

ANSWER The quadrangle at my college is named Sumner Park after the school's founder.

1. A representative of the national institutes of health turned over the first shovelful of Earth for the new science lab.
2. the math professor is an arab who was raised as a muslim in paris.
3. Mia, an art student, will sail to england on the *queen elizabeth* II, travel to france for the cannes film festival, go to turkey to study byzantine mosaics, and then fly home on the *concorde.*

4. One of the poems that professor Grant assigns in american poetry 1 is langston hughes's "Afro-American fragment," which begins with the following lines: "so long, / so far away / is Africa."
5. Di is taking russian literature 202 and history 109 this semester.
6. A united states Senator spoke at the Bates College graduation ceremony in may; the College President welcomed her.
7. Astronomers at many universities are studying the relationship between Earth and the other planets in our solar system.
8. After the Spring Term, Ben will travel South with uncle Bill to visit a factory that uses Space Age technology.
9. "in Greek mythology, the goddess Persephone was believed to bring Spring every year," said professor Stern. "the Sun was supposedly pulled across the sky by helios, the Sun God."
10. The French Professor always signs his letters Michael W. Gomez, sr., Ph.d., Instructor.

The Writing Connection

Using Capitalization in Your Writing

Every sentence in your writing begins with a capital letter. Sometimes you also need to capitalize nouns. For example, on a registration form, you would capitalize your name and the proper nouns in your address. You might write *Spanish I* as one course for which you are registering. When you proofread, be sure that your capitalization is appropriate for your writing situation.

Reference Point:
pages 98–106

Writing Assignments

Reference Point:
pages 12–13

A Course Description To write a description for a college catalogue, you will invent a dream course. *Step 1:* Make an interest inventory of your favorite school subjects or subjects that interest you. *Step 2:* Team up with a classmate whose favorite subject is the same as or similar to yours. Brainstorm with your classmate to invent the details of the course: what it might cover, how the classes might be conducted, what special projects the students might be involved in, and so on. *Step 3:* With your partner write a brief overview of the course. Include the name of the professor who teaches the course, when and where classes are held, some of the books and the articles that are required reading, and why students should take the course. *Step 4:* Revise your description, checking for complete, clear information. *Step 5:* Proofread your description, paying special attention to capitalization. *Step 6:* Post your course description on the class bulletin board, or contribute it to a class notebook of dream courses.

A College Profile Imagine that you are planning to continue your education after high school. Freewrite your impressions of an actual — or imagined — visit to a college or university, a junior college, a nursing school, a technical institute, a vocational school, a police academy, or another post-secondary educational or training institution. List the school's name and location and the date on which you visited. Then cluster notes around main topics such as impressions of students, graduation requirements, athletic facilities, admissions interview, dining halls, course offerings, library, and lab/shop/computer rooms. Check to see that your notes include correct capitalization. Save your notes in your writing portfolio, or use them to write a short college profile.

Reference Point: *pages 11–12*

Punctuation

Punctuation marks show when to stop, when to pause, and when to pay special attention to a particular part of a sentence.

Periods, Question Marks, and Exclamation Points

The Period

Rule

M 26 Use a period at the end of a declarative sentence, a mild command, or a polite question.

Vocational education combines general education and training.
Visit the program at the university.
Dorothea, would you please hand me the course catalogue.

The Question Mark

Rule

M 27 Use a question mark at the end of an interrogative sentence.

Does that vocational education program train students in trade?

Rule

M 28 Use a question mark after a question that is not a complete sentence.

The course? Economics of farming.

Rule

M 29 Use a question mark to express a doubt about what comes before it.

References to apprenticeship, the forerunner of vocational education, date back to the time of Hammurabi (1792?–1750? B.C.).

The Exclamation Point

Rule
M 30
Use an exclamation point at the end of a sentence that expresses strong feeling or a forceful command or after a strong interjection or other exclamatory expression.

Watch out!
Don't drop the football!
Congratulations! You are the new freshman class president.

Note: Use exclamation points infrequently. Express strong feeling through precise word choice and good sentence structure, rather than through the use of exclamation points.

| Exercise 1 | End Punctuation

Critical Thinking:
What does end punctuation indicate?

On your paper, write each sentence, supplying the correct punctuation.

SAMPLE Imagine In the colonial period, all college students studied Greek and Latin

ANSWER Imagine! In the colonial period, all college students studied Greek and Latin.

1. Many people who came to this country in search of religious freedom founded small church colleges
2. Did you know that land was put aside for schools in new territories
3. Were you aware how remarkable the University of Virginia was during Thomas Jefferson's time
4. What a breakthrough All students were free to take any course that was offered
5. Among the first institutions established for women were the Troy Female Seminary in Troy, New York, and Mount Holyoke College in South Hadley, Massachusetts
6. Wow Oberlin College was really revolutionary
7. Why It was the first college to admit black students and the first to become coeducational
8. Would you please find out the dates when black students and women were admitted to Oberlin College
9. After Michigan was admitted to the Union, its legislature acted to recharter the University of Michigan as a state university
10. Stop interrupting I was saying that a major development in the nineteenth century was the improvement of higher education

Commas

Commas in Series

Rule
M 31
Use commas to separate three or more words, phrases, or clauses in a series. Use a comma after each item except the last. Do not use

commas to separate pairs of nouns that are thought of as a single item or as a unit.

Besides books, the university bookstore sells **paper, pens, pencils, art supplies, office supplies, sweatshirts,** and **mugs.**

College students today finance their studies through **grants, scholarships, loans,** and **co-op or work-study programs.**

Most schools help prospective students plan their costs by providing guidelines for expenses such as **tuition and fees, room and board, books, transportation,** and **other expenses.**

Do not use commas to separate items in a series if all of them are joined by conjunctions.

Community colleges are often called "junior colleges" **or** "commuter colleges" **or** "two-year colleges."

Adjectives. Use commas to separate two or more adjectives preceding and modifying the same noun if they are coordinate in thought. Adjectives are coordinate in thought if the word *and* inserted between them does not change the meaning of the sentence.

The professor was a **tall, elegant, silver-haired** man.

If the last adjective before the noun is considered part of the noun, do not put a comma before it.

Classes began on a **clear, warm September** day.

If one of the adjectives in the series has a modifier, do not put a comma before the adjective.

The communication arts classes are in the **dark red** brick building next to the library. [*Dark* modifies *red.*]

Other Modifiers. Use commas to separate three or more modifiers in a series.

He answered the question **quietly, cautiously,** and **slowly.**

Phrases and Clauses. Use commas to separate three or more phrases or clauses in a series unless they are joined by conjunctions.

A college education **prepares you for a professional career, raises your cultural awareness,** and **makes you a better citizen.** [phrases]
I visited six colleges, I applied to five, and **I was accepted at three.** [clauses]
I turned down Reed and **I turned down Rice** and **I will attend Pomona.** [clauses joined by conjunctions; no commas]

Commas After Introductory Expressions

Rule   Use a comma to show a pause after an introductory word or phrase.
___
M 32   *Prepositional Phrases.* Use a comma after an introductory prepositional phrase *(page 578)* of four or more words.

> **Before the first lecture,** the professor gave us the syllabus.

Participial Phrases. Use a comma after an introductory participial phrase *(pages 581–582).*

> **Fearing that he was late for the exam,** Li ran to class.

Adverb Clauses. Use a comma after an introductory adverb clause *(pages 591–592)* regardless of its length.

> **Before she left the dorm,** Sandra watered her plants.

Interjections. Use a comma to separate *yes, no,* and other interjections such as *oh* and *well* from the rest of the sentence.

> **Yes,** Sheila is eligible for the athletic scholarship.
> **Well,** I think that we should try to arrive early in the day.

Commas to Separate Sentence Parts

Rule   Use a comma before a coordinating conjunction *(page 559)* that joins
___
M 33   the independent clauses of a compound sentence.

> In Harvard's first century, 70 percent of its graduates went into the ministry, **but** today the percentage is much lower.
>
> Limited college curriculum has given way to thousands of course offerings, **and** giant universities exist side by side with smaller colleges across the country.

Rule   Use a comma or a pair of commas to set off words of direct address
___
M 34   and parenthetical expressions within a sentence.

> **Frank,** may I borrow your French book?
> The French vocabulary exam, **incidentally,** is this Friday.

Rule   Use a comma or a pair of commas to set off a nonessential apposi-
___
M 35   tive *(page 580).* Do not set off an essential appositive *(page 579).* Treat an abbreviated title or a degree following a name as a nonessential appositive.

> **NONESSENTIAL**
> Ruth's sister, **Sonia,** begins graduate school the day that Ruth begins college. [Ruth has only one sister.]
>
> Isaac Asimov, **author of both scholarly and science-fiction books,** was the speaker at our first college convocation.
>
> Wilma Sarkin, **D.D.,** teaches a course in religion and ethics.

ESSENTIAL

My cousin **Tony** is studying Japanese language and literature.
[I have more than one cousin.]

The exchange student **Yukiko Funaka** will speak at the convocation. [There is more than one exchange student.]

Rule
___
M 36

Use a comma or a pair of commas to set off a nonessential phrase or a nonessential clause *(page 589)* from the rest of the sentence. Do not set off an essential phrase or an essential clause *(page 589)*.

NONESSENTIAL

Gould Hall, **built by the river,** is a favorite dormitory with sophomores. [Gould Hall is a favorite.]

The students, **who found the new material difficult,** met in study groups. [All of the students found the material difficult.]

ESSENTIAL

The dormitory **built by the river** is a favorite with sophomores. [Only this dormitory is their favorite.]

The students **who found the new material difficult** met in study groups. [Only the students who found the new material difficult met in study groups.]

Rule
___
M 37

Use commas before and after the year when it is used with the month and the day in a sentence. Do not use commas when only the month and the year are given.

Joanne moved into her new apartment on **July 7, 1989,** and she plans to stay there until she graduates from college.

Stuart visited several colleges in Boston in **September 1990.**

Rule
___
M 38

Use commas before and after the name of a state, a province, or a country when it is used with the name of a city. Do not use commas between a state and its ZIP Code.

Michigan State University is in **East Lansing, Michigan.**

Craig checked the address on his application: Office of Admissions, University of Wyoming, **Laramie, WY 82071.**

Rule
___
M 39

Use a comma after the greeting, or salutation, of a social letter and after the complimentary close of any letter.

Dear Roseanna,   Sincerely yours,   Yours truly,

Exercise 2 **Commas**

On your paper, rewrite the following sentences, adding or deleting commas where necessary.

SAMPLE   Yes Norma plans to major in oceanography next year.
ANSWER   Yes, Norma plans to major in oceanography next year.

? Critical Thinking:
What makes an appositive, a phrase, or a clause nonessential?

1. People go to college to develop an interest, that they already have to develop new skills and to prepare for careers.
2. Most students after all are looking for more than just a degree.
3. In general college graduates earn more money than high school graduates and that is a consideration for many students.
4. Confronted with the hundreds of colleges in the United States one is hard pressed to find the most appropriate one.
5. Marion Walker and Mark Beach authors of *Making It in College* advise minority students to attend universities that are large and heterogeneous and mirror the real world.
6. Almost all colleges require an application a high school transcript letters of recommendation and test scores.
7. The Scholastic Aptitude Test a three-hour examination tests a student's knowledge and ability to reason.
8. The Achievement Tests which are not required by all schools test a student's ability in math language and social studies.
9. The personal statement that you write with your application should be neat specific concrete and honest.
10. Kate who was feeling the pressure of application deadlines wrote *Kate Malloy B.A.* every time she felt like quitting.

Commas to Prevent Misreading

Rule

M 40

Use a comma to separate sentence parts that might otherwise be read together in a confusing manner. It is often better to rewrite the sentence if you can.

Later, former class presidents will gather for a photograph.
In step one, two questions are answered.

Repeated Words. Use a comma to separate most words that are repeated. Rewrite sentences to avoid repeating words whenever possible.

What references I **found, found** their way into my term paper.

Rule

M 41

Use a comma to separate a date from a number written in numerals.

In **1984, 1103** graduates received degrees in optometry.

Avoiding the Overuse and Misuse of Commas

Rule

M 42

Do not separate a subject from its verb with a comma.

INCORRECT The number of students from other countries studying at North American colleges, has greatly increased in this century.

CORRECT The number of students from other countries studying at North American colleges has greatly increased in this century.

Rule Do not separate a verb or a preposition from its object with a comma.

M 43 **INCORRECT** To prepare for the exam, I reread, all my lecture notes.

CORRECT To prepare for the exam, I reread all my lecture notes.

Exercise 3 **Using Commas Correctly**

Rewrite the following sentences, using commas correctly. If a sentence needs no changes, write *Correct.*

SAMPLE Students with different educational goals, can go to different institutions of higher learning.

ANSWER Students with different educational goals can go to different institutions of higher learning.

Critical Thinking: How can commas help to prevent confusion?

1. Because of, increased competition for, places at four-year colleges, many students apply to, community or junior colleges.
2. In the past few years, attendance at two-year colleges, has increased dramatically.
3. A student who attends a two-year college, may receive an Associate of Arts degree.
4. After year two three out of four students know better what they want out of college.
5. A university has, an undergraduate division that confers bachelor's degrees and, a graduate division that is made up of graduate and professional schools.
6. A college may be a separate institution specializing in, a single branch, of knowledge.
7. Schools in the United States, must be accredited.
8. The American Medical Association, for example, accredits, medical schools.
9. In 1984, 1,380,011 people received degrees from, community colleges, liberal arts colleges, and universities.
10. The question is is a community college, a four-year college, or a university the right place for, you?

Semicolons

Semicolons are used to connect independent clauses and to clarify meaning in sentences that contain a number of commas.

Rule Use a semicolon to connect independent clauses.

M 44 *Without a Coordinating Conjunction.* Use a semicolon in a compound sentence to connect closely related independent clauses that are not joined by a coordinating conjunction.

There are about 1200 proprietary institutions of post-secondary education; they were founded as profit-making institutions.

With a Conjunctive Adverb or an Explanatory Expression. Use a semicolon to connect independent clauses that are joined by a conjunctive adverb *(pages 562–563)* or by an explanatory expression. Use a comma after the conjunctive adverb or the explanatory expression.

> The number of proprietary institutions increased rapidly in the '70s and early '80s; **however,** it did not continue its rapid ascent after 1984.

> Most proprietary institutions provide vocational training; **in addition,** many business corporations provide their own comparable training programs.

Rule   Use a semicolon to clarify meaning in a sentence that contains sev-
M 45   eral commas.

Independent Clauses. Use a semicolon to clarify and separate independent clauses that have several commas within them, even when a coordinating conjunction is used.

> I have studied the works of Ralph Waldo Emerson, a neighbor of one of my ancestors; and I would also like to study the works of Henry David Thoreau, Louisa May Alcott, and Bronson Alcott.

Items in a Series. Use semicolons to separate items in a series if those items have internal commas. The semicolons make it clear how many items are in the series.

> UNCLEAR   At my college interview were Ms. Stone, the dean of admissions, Mr. Amory, the dean of men, and Mr. Ita, the head of the art department. [three or five people?]

> CLEAR   At my college interview were Ms. Stone, the dean of admissions; Mr. Amory, the dean of men; and Mr. Ita, the head of the art department. [three people]

Exercise 4   Semicolons

? Critical Thinking:

How can a semicolon prevent confusion?

On your paper, write each sentence, adding or deleting semicolons as necessary. You may need to replace commas with semicolons to make some sentences clearer.

SAMPLE   At the end of the nineteenth century, scientific schools in the United States were poor, therefore, they were not respected in Europe.

ANSWER   At the end of the nineteenth century, scientific schools in the United States were poor; therefore, they were not respected in Europe.

1. The oldest European university, the University of Bologna in Italy, was founded in about 1100, however, it had existed as a law school since 890.

2. The first universities were founded to serve the professions, therefore, they taught law, medicine, and theology.

3. The lyceum movement; the first large-scale effort to provide adult education; began during Andrew Jackson's presidency.
4. People who had voted for tax-supported schools were now demanding colleges, indeed, the existing church-supported colleges were not able to meet the growing need.
5. Congressman Justin Morrill of Vermont was greatly interested in education, in fact, he introduced a bill providing that proceeds from the sale of public lands be used to establish colleges.
6. Because agriculture was changing; new methods had to be developed to meet new conditions in the West.
7. The need for Congressman Morrill's bill was obvious, however, President Buchanan vetoed it; Congressman Morrill persisted, a new bill became law in 1862.
8. At this time most colleges and universities in the United States had poor equipment, libraries, and other facilities, and their faculties were ill-trained, mistreated, and overworked.
9. There were no first-rate graduate schools in law, medicine, or the liberal arts, consequently, people seeking the best training in these fields went to Europe.
10. By 1900, however, three technical schools had been founded in the United States; the Massachusetts Institute of Technology in Cambridge, Massachusetts, the California Institute of Technology in Pasadena, California, and Purdue University in West Lafayette, Indiana.

Colons

Rule
M 46

Use a colon to introduce an explanatory phrase or a list of items that completes a sentence. The part of a sentence before a list may contain a demonstrative word such as *these* or *those* or an expression such as *the following* or *as follows*.

The instructions that we received ahead of time about the ACT tests told us what to do: **arrive early and line up at the auditorium door.**

The ACT tests cover **these** four academic areas: **English, mathematics, social studies, and natural sciences.**

Do not use a colon to introduce a list that immediately follows a verb or a preposition.

To score well on the ACT test, students must demonstrate knowledge, problem-solving ability, and reasoning ability. [*not* must demonstrate:]
The ACT prepares reports on each student's test for the student, the high school, and the colleges to which the student has applied. [*not* for:]

Rule

M 47 Use a colon to separate two independent clauses when the second clause explains or completes the first sentence.

I know why I'm feeling so good today: I think that I did well on the ACT test.

Rule

M 48 Use a colon to introduce a direct quotation if the sentence does not contain a verb that indicates that someone is speaking, such as *answered* or *declared*.

When we finished the ACT test, the monitor **gave us this advice:** "Treat yourselves to something special!"

Do not use a colon before an indirect question or an indirect quotation.

INCORRECT   We wondered: whether we could ever forget those tests.

CORRECT   We wondered whether we could ever forget those tests.

Rule

M 49 Use a colon to separate the hour and the minutes in an expression of time, the chapter and the verse in a Biblical reference, the title and the subtitle of a book, and the volume and the page number of a book or a magazine reference.

3:22 P.M.   *College Board Achievement Test*: English Literature
Genesis 12:2   *Mountaineering Monthly* 6:72

Rule

M 50 Use a colon after the salutation of a business letter.

Dear Dean Statler: Dear Ms. Fortuna:

Exercise 5   Colons

? Critical Thinking:

When can a colon introduce a direct quotation?

Some of the sentences that follow need colons. On your paper, write the sentences, supplying or deleting colons where needed. You may have to replace other punctuation with colons in some sentences. If a sentence is correct as it is, write *Correct*.

SAMPLE   An important requirement for college is money, if students cannot get it from some source, they cannot attend.

ANSWER   An important requirement for college is money: if students cannot get it from some source, they cannot attend.

1. In 1987 the $261 billion the United States spent on education included the following forms of financial aid for college students grants, loans, and work-study jobs.
2. The guidance counselor began her discussion of loans with these words "If you receive a low-interest government loan, you must repay principal plus interest."
3. The intent of the Guaranteed Student Loan Program (GSLP) is: to help students from lower- and middle-income families finance their educations with low-interest loans in their own names.

4. The approximately eight thousand domestic institutions that qualify for participation in the GSLP must meet these two requirements that they obtain certification by the Office of Education and that they agree with rules set forth by the commissioner of the United States Office of Education.

5. Make a note of the following two programs administered by colleges and universities the National Direct Student Loan, now known as the Perkins Loan Program, and the College Work Study Program.

6. Financial need isn't always the only consideration for receiving financial aid athletic ability, academic excellence, musical talent, artistic ability, and an interest in the health professions are also qualifying conditions.

7. Loan payments begin six months after you complete your studies you must pay at least fifty dollars every month until the loan has been repaid.

8. Funds to students also come from private organizations; foundations, clubs, and community organizations.

9. Tom, who included a reference from the Bible, Corinthians 2,1, in his college application, also included the following personal and academic references his high school principal and his family doctor.

10. Dear Ms. Greenfield
I am writing to confirm our appointment to discuss financial aid on Friday, February 2, at 1030 A.M. Incidentally, thank you for the article from *Newsweek* (6, 80).
Sincerely,
Tony DiPalma

Quotation Marks

Rule
M 51

Use quotation marks to show that you are writing the exact words that someone said, thought, or wrote. Use quotation marks at both the beginning and the end of the quotation.

Eliza asked, **"How is the college year divided?"**
Vic said, **"It depends on what system a college uses."**

Do not use quotation marks around an indirect quotation, a retelling in other words of what another person said, thought, or wrote.

Vic said that it depends on what system a college uses.

Long Quotations. When you are copying a quotation of five or more lines (in a research paper, for example), set it off from the rest of your paper by indenting it ten spaces from the left margin. Double-space the quotation if you are typing. Do not use quotation marks with a quotation that is set off in this way.

Reference Point: *pages 406–407*

Dialogue. When you are writing a dialogue, begin a new paragraph and use a separate set of quotation marks each time the speaker changes.

> **"Is Lewis and Clark College on the semester system?"** Miako asked.
>
> **"No,"** replied Kathy. **"Its calendar consists of three eleven-week terms."**

In a dialogue where one speaker is speaking for more than one paragraph, use opening quotation marks at the beginning of each paragraph, but use end quotation marks only at the end of the last paragraph or when words such as *he said* interrupt the speech.

> **"College** calendars commonly follow the two-semester system, " **explained** the counselor. **"The** most common system divides the calendar into two semesters of sixteen weeks each. The first semester begins in August or September, the second in January or early February, ending the year in May.
>
> **"Most** schools also hold a six- to eight-week summer session. By attending school all year, students may graduate in three years instead of **four."**

Rule
——
M 52

Use quotation marks to set off the title of a short story, an article, an essay, a short poem, or a song. Use them also to set off the title of any piece that forms part of a larger work such as the following: a single television show that is part of a series, a chapter of a book, a section of a newspaper, or a feature in a magazine. (See also page 712.)

> Dr. Chen assigned Browning's poem **"My Last Duchess."**
>
> Please rehearse **"The Impossible Dream,"** the second song in the show.
>
> The sixth and final episode, entitled **"Today's Environment,"** was informative.
>
> Luke always reads the **"Hints for Hikers"** column in *Wilderness* magazine.

Rule
——
M 53

Use quotation marks to set off words used in unexpected ways, such as nicknames, slang, technical terms, or unusual expressions.

> The rather staid president of my university was known as **"Bulldog"** in college.
>
> Our physics professor explained that the bottom of a hydroplane is designed so that the boat **"planes"** on the surface of the water.

Note: The preceding rule is for informal usage only. Avoid quotation marks used for these purposes unless such usage is necessary to create a desired effect.

Rule

M 54   Use quotation marks to set off a word that defines another word.

I use the word *calculating* to mean **"shrewd."**

Other Punctuation with Quotation Marks

The following rules will help you to determine where and how to use single quotation marks, commas, periods, colons, semicolons, question marks, and exclamation points with quotation marks.

Rule

M 55   Use single quotation marks around a quotation or a title that occurs within a longer quoted passage.

"Watch the episode called **'The Industrial Revolution'** at eight o'clock tonight," said Mr. Creiger.

Rule

M 56   Place a comma or a period inside closing quotation marks.

"Tour the library early**,**" said Professor Bey, "so that when you begin research, you'll know where to find sources**.**"

Rule

M 57   Place a semicolon or a colon outside closing quotation marks.

The librarian announced, "The library will close in five minutes"**;** consequently, we gathered our books and left.

Now I remember why I carefully read the article "How to Improve Your Memory"**:** I didn't want to forget any of the details.

Rule

M 58   Place a question mark or an exclamation point inside the closing quotation marks if it applies only to the material quoted. If it applies to the entire sentence, place it outside the quotation marks. If both the quotation and the sentence require a question mark or an exclamation point, put the end mark inside the closing quotation marks.

Loren wondered, "Did I miss the appointment?" [The quotation itself is a question.]

Did Alicia say, "I'm going to the bookstore"? [The entire sentence, not the quotation, is a question.]

How did you answer the question "What are your goals for college?" [Both the quotation and the sentence are questions.]

Avoiding the Misuse of Quotation Marks

Rule

M 59   Avoid the overuse of quotation marks for slang, jargon, or technical terms.

Beth and I bought these "totally awesome" jumpsuits at this "radical" boutique where we absolutely "ran amuck!"

Rule

M 60   Avoid the use of quotation marks for emphasis. Such use tends to imply *so-called* and may create the opposite of the intended effect.

Come to a get-acquainted "tea" for "new" students and meet some of our "talented" and "intelligent" faculty members.

On your paper, rewrite each sentence, adding or deleting quotation marks as needed. Be sure to use capitalization, other punctuation, and paragraphing correctly. If a sentence needs no changes, write *Correct* on your paper.

SAMPLE   Are you enjoying your courses asked Bonnie.
ANSWER   "Are you enjoying your courses?" asked Bonnie.

1. One of the short stories we read for American literature was J. D. Salinger's For Esmé — with Love and Squalor.
2. I had read an article about Salinger in the Book Review section of *The Morning Standard.*
3. Ernest Hemingway was, in some ways, the opposite of Salinger because while Salinger is private, Hemingway led a public life.
4. What is the English assignment George asked. I don't know. I missed class too, Emily replied.
5. Grace announced to our medieval history class Today we are going to look at manuscripts in the Pierpont Morgan Library; consequently, everyone left the building for the bus stop.
6. I don't know why I decided to write a report on the essay Reconstruction in the South: perhaps I thought it would be easy.
7. Did Cynthia ask Did Dan enjoy the poetry reading last night?
8. Did you ever read Robert Frost's poem Stopping by Woods on a Snowy Evening? Mr. Watson asked.
9. Dwayne began his anthropology paper with the following quotation: "People who lived long ago, like people of today, asked questions about things around them. Because they did not have scientific answers, they explained natural phenomena with stories we call myths. Myths are powerful stories that reveal some underlying truth about our experience of the world."
10. While I watched Beverly Bubbles Sills singing Annie Laurie on TV, I read an article called How to Take Exams from last month's issue of *Modern Living*, Grace said.

The Apostrophe

Possessives

Rule   Use an apostrophe to show possession.

M 61   *Singular and Plural Nouns.* Use an apostrophe and an *s* (*'s*) to form the possessive of a singular noun, even if it ends in *s*, *x*, or *z*. Use an apostrophe and an *s* to form the possessive of a plural noun that does not end in *s*.

Plural Nouns Ending in s. Use an apostrophe alone to form the possessive of a plural noun that ends in *s*.

the students' exams   the colleges' rivalry

Ancient Classical Names Ending in s. Use an apostrophe alone to form the possessive of ancient classical names that end in *s*.

Socrates' dialogues   Hippocrates' oath

Joint Ownership. Use the possessive form of only the last person's name when a thing is jointly owned.

Dr. Wu and Dr. Ornstein's book on economic theory

Separate Ownership. Use the possessive form of each name when two or more people are named as owners of separate but similar items.

Wallace Stevens's and T. S. Eliot's poetry

Expressions Ending in s. Use an apostrophe alone to form the possessive of most expresssions that end in *s* or the sound of *s*.

for goodness' sake   three years' work

Compound Nouns. Change the last word of a compound noun *(page 533)* to the possessive form.

the passer-by's comment   the bellboys' uniforms

Contractions

Rule   Use an apostrophe to replace letters or numbers in a contraction.

M 62   I **can't** wait until semester break.
Were the students of the '60s quite different from us?

Plural Forms

Rule   Use an apostrophe and an s *('s)* to form the plural of letters, numbers, symbols, and words that you are referring to as words or symbols *(page 738)*.

M 63

Do not underline (italicize) the *'s* when forming these plurals.

There are three *s*'s in *dissatisfied*.
The vote received twenty-five *yea*'s and three *nay*'s.

Note: The plurals of abbreviations that do not include periods are formed by adding only *s*.

I took the **SATs** last Saturday.

BUT   The **SAT'**s on the poster were faded. [Referring to the letters, not to the test]

Although names of years are written with numerals, they also usually function as words and should be treated as such.

My grandmother told stories about her college days in the early **1900s**.

BUT   The *1990*'s were blurred in Chapter 2 and Chapter 17. [Referring to the numerals, not to the year.]

Avoiding the Misuse of Apostrophes

Rule

M 64

Do not use the apostrophe to form the plurals of nouns. The plural of a noun is generally formed by adding *s* or *es*, as in *books, families, tomatoes,* and *atlases.* (See page 532.)

> INCORRECT   Fortunately, we finished our **essay's** on time.
>
> CORRECT   Fortunately, we finished our **essays** on time.

Rule

M 65

Do not add an apostrophe or *'s* to possessive personal pronouns: *mine, yours, his, hers, its, ours, theirs.* They already show ownership.

> Are these lecture notes **yours?**

In addition, do not confuse possessive forms of personal pronouns with contractions.

> The cat washed **its** face. [*not* it's]

Exercise 7   Apostrophes

Critical Thinking:

Which plurals need apostrophes?

On your paper, rewrite each sentence, adding or deleting apostrophes as necessary. Be sure also to use underlining (to indicate italic type) correctly. If a sentence needs no apostrophe, write *Correct.*

SAMPLE   The colleges new library opened last week.
ANSWER   The college's new library opened last week.

1. The history of libraries parallels the history of writing.
2. People who didnt have paper kept records on a variety of materials.
3. Six thousand years ago people wrote their as, bs, and cs, so to speak, on bone, stone, clay, and wood.
4. The 700,000 papyrus scrolls in the Alexandria, Egypt, library represented many years work.
5. When the library was destroyed, copies of Sophocles's and Thucydides's manuscripts may have been lost.
6. Every bookworms favorite friend, paper, was invented by the Chinese in about A.D. 105; however, the art of paper making took a thousand years' to reach Europe.
7. Gale had to research a paper comparing Faulkners and Hemingways styles; the librarian directed her to several sources.

8. Did I mention my sister-in-laws problem locating material on Robert Wilsons and Philip Glasss opera *Einstein on the Beach?*
9. Its clear that my cousin has made up her mind to join the WACs.
10. Were libraries contents affected in the 70s and 80s when many mens and womens colleges became coeducational?

Hyphens, Dashes, Slashes, and Ellipsis Points

The Hyphen

Rule

M 66

Use a hyphen to divide a word at the end of a line. Do not divide a word of one syllable, such as *washed* or *grieve*. Do not divide any word so that one letter stands by itself.

Always divide a word between its syllables and in such a way that the reader will not be confused about its meaning or pronunciation.

INCORRECT   The dining hall serves an awful lot of **mash-ed** potatoes. [*Mashed* is a one-syllable word.]

CORRECT   The dining hall serves an awful lot of **mashed** potatoes.

INCORRECT   During semester break the weather was **a-bominable,** improving only when classes resumed. [The letter *a* stands by itself.]

CORRECT   During semester break the weather was **abominable,** improving only when classes resumed.

Prefixes and Suffixes. Divide a word with a prefix only after the prefix. Divide a word with a suffix only before the suffix.

Gita and Li told me that they attended an exciting **inter-national** conference for students last summer.

Students role-played officials of their respective **govern-ments** trying to resolve global conflicts.

Compound Words. Divide a compound word that is written as one word between the base words. Divide a hyphenated compound word at the hyphen.

Many students who attend Boston College commute by **street-car** or bus.

If I start typing my paper tonight, I should finish it **some-time** tomorrow.

Rule

M 67

Use a hyphen after the prefixes *all-*, *ex-*, and *self-*. Use a hyphen to separate any prefix from a proper noun or a proper adjective.

all-purpose	Neo-Platonism	**BUT**	neophyte
ex-president	pre-Alexandrian	**BUT**	preview
self-assured	intra-Asian	**BUT**	intrastate

Note: Do not use a hyphen between most other prefixes and their root words.

    entitle   predetermine   substandard

Rule
M 68

Use a hyphen after the prefix of a word that is spelled the same as another word but has a different origin and meaning (a homograph).

    re-collect   re-count   re-form
    recollect   recount   reform

Rule
M 69

Use a hyphen after the prefix of a word when the last letter of the prefix is a vowel and is the same as the first letter of the base word.

    de-escalate   pre-eminent   re-educate

Rule
M 70

Hyphenate compound adjectives when they precede the noun that they modify but not when they follow it. Do not hyphenate a compound adjective when its first word is an adverb that ends in *ly*.

The moderator introduced **up-to-date** issues.

The issues that the moderator introduced were **up to date.**

The **highly praised** course on early music filled up early on registration day.

Fractions. Hyphenate a fraction that is used as a modifier. Do not hyphenate a fraction that is used as a noun.

MODIFIER The soup was **two-thirds** water.
NOUN **One third** of the soup was vegetables.

Rule
M 71

Use a hyphen to separate compound numbers from twenty-one through ninety-nine.

forty-nine   seventy-three

BUT five hundred   ninety thousand

The Dash

Rule
M 72

Use a dash to show an interruption in a thought or in a statement. Use a second dash to end the interruption if the sentence continues.

"If we can just — "; suddenly he had another idea.

Someone — I think it's Barbara — will present her research project tomorrow.

Appositives and Parenthetical Expressions. Use dashes when appositives or parenthetical expressions have internal commas.

Many universities have multiple campuses — the State University of New York, for example, has over sixty — but most have only one.

Several universities — California State University, the State University of New York, and the University of Wisconsin, to name a few — have enrollments of over 100,000 students.

In typing, use two hyphens to represent a dash. Do not type a single hyphen to stand for a dash.

Note: Avoid the overuse of dashes in formal writing.

The Slash

Rule Use a slash to separate two words that function as one idea.

M 73 the **fast/slow** switch   a **true/false** test

When used between two words, the slash is not surrounded by extra space.

Note: Avoid using *and/or* or *he/she* constructions.

Rule Use a slash to show the ends of lines quoted from poetry or a play

M 74 written in verse when you are quoting them within a paragraph.

> Bill Turner's poem "University Curriculum" is a wry comment on the courses taught in some schools: "In this factory, where the axe-grinders **/** are whetted by degrees, **/** there are courses in log-rolling **/** and a shortage of trees."

Note: When it is used to separate lines of poetry, the slash is surrounded by space.

Ellipsis Points

Rule Use ellipsis points, a set of three spaced periods (. . .), to indicate an

M 75 omission or a pause in written or quoted material.

> Now the purpose of education **. . .** is to set up a current of understanding between the student and the things of the world in which he or she lives.
> Walter Prescott Webb, An Honest Preface

Other Punctuation Marks. If what precedes the ellipsis points is part of a complete sentence, use a period followed by three ellipsis points (. . . .). If what precedes the ellipsis points is not part of a complete sentence, use only the three ellipsis points, leaving a space before the first point (. . .). If what precedes the ellipsis points is part of a complete sentence ending with a question mark or an exclamation point, retain that mark before the three ellipsis points.

ORIGINAL PASSAGE

Pretty soon all twenty of us — our class — would be leaving. A core of my classmates had been together since kindergarten. I'd been there eight years. We twenty knew by bored heart the very weave of each other's socks. I thought, unfairly, of the Polyphemus moth crawling down the school's driveway. Now we'd go, too.
Annie Dillard, An American Childhood

Pretty soon all twenty of us . . . would be leaving. A core of my class-mates had been together since kindergarten. . . . We twenty knew by bored heart the very weave of each other's socks. . . . Now we'd go. . . .

Sentences and Paragraphs. Use a line of periods to show the omission of a stanza of poetry or of a paragraph from written material.

Exercise 8 Hyphens, Dashes, Slashes, Ellipsis Points

? Critical Thinking:

What are the rules for word division?

On your paper, copy the following sentences. Add hyphens, dashes, slashes, and ellipsis points where necessary.

SAMPLE   Jelissa is attending a four year college.
ANSWER   Jelissa is attending a four-year college.

1. Most guidance counselors divide higher educational institutions into two year colleges, four year colleges, and universities.
2. Students who attend two year colleges whether full time, part time, or at night usually come from the local area.
3. One student pointed out advantages of working while in school: not only do you get paid, but you can also work in the field that you're studying and gain self confidence as well.
4. Four year colleges we usually call them liberal arts colleges are often supported by private money.
5. Many university professors as students, administrators, and professors themselves will tell you spend only a small portion of their time with students.
6. Clearly, all purpose descriptions of higher education are impossible because there is so much variation within each category of school.
7. At all institutions and that means every one there are teachers who stand out and students who achieve more than is expected.
8. Sixty three of the ninety nine students in Sid's graduating class went to four year colleges, and twenty four, or two thirds, of the rest went to community junior colleges.
9. In English class we read John Holmes's poem "The Father," which begins this way: "Hearing his son and daughter Laugh, and talk of dances, theaters, Of their school, and friends, And books, Taking it all for granted, — He sighs a bit. . . ."
10. We spent one half of the term reading the work of four neorealist painters and studying several interAmerican movements.

Parentheses and Brackets

Parentheses

Rule

M 76

Use parentheses to enclose material that is not basic to the meaning of the sentence.

Kathleen is this year's coordinator of the AWS (Associated Women Students) tutorial program for disadvantaged youngsters.

Dr. Munck (physics) will serve on the tenure committee.

The Occidental College football team (known as the Tigers) has a long-standing rivalry with the Pomona College team.

If the parenthetical material forms a complete sentence within another sentence, do not use a capital letter or a period to mark the sentence inside the parentheses. If a question mark or an exclamation point is needed, include it.

American Samoa Community College (it is publicly controlled) is located in Pago Pago, Samoa.

After the closing parenthesis, use the punctuation that would be needed if the parenthetical material were not in the sentence. If the parenthesis ends the sentence, put the period *outside* the parenthesis.

Her most popular course is in the art of fine handwriting (*calligraphy*).

My favorite style is the *uncial*, a medieval (A.D. 400–800) hand used in Greek and Latin manuscripts.

If the parenthetical material is not inside another sentence, use capitalization and punctuation within the parentheses just as if the parentheses were not there.

The class examined some detailed photographs of Greek ruins. (They saw pictures of temples at Delphi.)

Brackets

Rule
___
M 77

Put brackets around any explanatory words or other information that you are adding to a quotation.

Tolstoy wrote, "The most powerful weapon of ignorance [**is**] the diffusion of printed matter." [In the original, a dash is used. The writer here inserted *is* to make a complete, clear sentence.]

___

Exercise 9 **Parentheses and Brackets**

On your paper, write the following sentences, using parentheses and brackets correctly.

SAMPLE Amy visited her sister her sister goes to Dartmouth last week in New Hampshire.

ANSWER Amy visited her sister (her sister goes to Dartmouth) last week in New Hampshire.

1. When Carol graduates, she hopes to work for the FDA Food and Drug Administration.
2. Many students apply to several colleges at the same time. Applying to four or five is not unusual.

 Critical Thinking:
What punctuation can go inside the closing parenthesis?

3. His favorite courses were in anthropology and sociology the social sciences.

4. Reading difficulties such as vocalization saying words in the mind with lip movement decreases reading efficiency and will affect a college student's progress.

5. As the dean wrote it was in the orientation handbook, "Think! Just because words are in a book doesn't mean that they're true."

6. Our college library has become a center for local cultural events. See the attached schedule for details about the fall program.

7. "We plan to surprise her with it an honorary degree at June commencement," President Nicholson said.

8. After you pass the administration building isn't it the first building on the left after you go through the north gate, turn left.

9. Most libraries use the Dewey decimal system. See pages 22–29 for details.

10. When I did research at the Library of Congress, I learned that it had the largest collection of incunabula books printed before 1501 in the United States.

The Writing Connection

Using Punctuation in Your Writing

Reference Point:
page 345

You will always use punctuation in all forms of writing. However, you may choose specific punctuation in certain situations. In a literary essay, for example, you might use quotation marks and slashes to quote lines of poetry. When you use the words of a famous literary critic, you might use ellipsis points and brackets.

Whether you write up an interview, fill out an application form, or write an acceptance letter, you must follow the punctuation rules that are appropriate for your purpose and audience.

Writing Assignments

Reference Point:
pages 46–106

An Essay for a College Application Imagine that you are applying to a college. As part of your application, you must write a short essay, which the admissions committee will read. Choose one of the following essay topics. Then freewrite to gather ideas. Select and organize notes to write a two-paragraph essay. As you revise, make certain that your style and tone are appropriate for a college application essay. Now proofread your essay, paying particular attention to punctuation. Share your essay with a partner and discuss its strengths and weaknesses. Then save it in your writing portfolio.

1. Describe the person you would most like to interview if you were given the opportunity. Explain your reasons briefly.
2. Describe the most difficult challenge you have faced to date.
3. What is the most influential work of literature that you have read? Briefly explain your choice.
4. If you could be an inanimate object, what would you choose to be? Explain why.

A Written College Tour As a volunteer guide, you give tours of your college campus and the surrounding community to prospective students and their families. To help new guides, you will write a typical tour. *Step 1:* Brainstorm a list of facts students want from a college tour or a community tour. Then make a cluster to gather details. *Step 2:* Write your tour, inventing information about college facilities and courses or the resources and points of interest in the community. Give at least five model questions and answers in the form of a dialogue. *Step 3:* As you revise your writing, check for consistent tone and style. *Step 4:* Proofread your writing, giving special attention to punctuation. *Step 5:* Make a clean copy and show it to another "tour guide" in your class. Discuss its strengths and weaknesses. Then contribute it to a class notebook entitled *College Tours*.

Using Italics and Numbers in Writing

Italics

In printed material, certain words and symbols are set in italic type (*slanted letters like these*). In handwriting and typing, you should underline such words and symbols according to the following rules.

Rule
M 78
Underline (italicize) the names or the titles of books, book-length poems, newspapers, magazines, periodicals, plays, movies, television series, paintings, trains, ships, aircraft, and so forth.

Underline (italicize) an article (*a, an, the*) that comes before a title only if it is part of the title. (See also page 712.)

The Portrait of a Lady	*Paradise Lost*
A Midsummer Night's Dream	*Twelfth Night*
the *Song of Roland*	*The Rake's Progress*

Rule

M 79

Underline (italicize) letters, numbers, symbols, and words when you are referring to them as words or symbols.

"A *12* next to a course title on your transcript means that you got an *A*," said Aiofe.

(prō´lĭ-gōm´ə-nŏn´)

Ryan noticed that *prolegomenon* was misspelled on the title page of his philosophy paper.

Rule

M 80

Underline (italicize) words from other languages if those words are not found in an English dictionary. Do not italicize foreign place names or currency.

"I decided, *am Ende*, to go to Dartmouth," said Karl.

BUT The new restaurant has a standard **à la carte** menu. [*A la carte* is commonly used in English.]

Underline (italicize) a word or phrase that you wish to emphasize. Avoid overuse of this device.

"After *hours* of reading," said an exhausted Tanya, "I finished the Economics 2 assignment."

Exercise 1 **Italics**

? Critical Thinking:

When should foreign words and phrases be underlined?

On your paper, copy the following sentences, underlining wherever italic type would be used.

SAMPLE All forms of media are used at Graham Junior College, from the Encyclopaedia Britannica to Sixty Minutes.

ANSWER All forms of media are used at Graham Junior College, from the Encyclopaedia Britannica to Sixty Minutes.

1. Art appreciation classes see slides of pictures such as Salvador Dali's Mona Lisa, a copy of the original with a moustache added.
2. Agatha Christie's famous mystery novel Murder on the Orient Express takes place on a famous train called the Orient Express.
3. Students of Southern politics would enjoy the film All the King's Men, which is about the life of Governor Huey Long.
4. When I edited my term paper, I changed the number 16 to 15 and corrected the word superfluous, which I had misspelled.
5. The television series Masterpiece Theatre dramatizes books — Brideshead Revisited, for example — that are on many reading lists.
6. Did Bill write a paper about the space shuttle Columbia?
7. When students in the play-production class saw a production of The Glass Menagerie, they saw how the theory that they had learned actually worked on stage.
8. Professor Chang suggested that some of us work with Samuel Coleridge's long poem The Rime of the Ancient Mariner and turn it into a play.

9. Although the speaker's words were not apropos to my situation per se, I considered them carefully.
10. Murray Kempton, a columnist for Newsday, also writes articles for The New York Review of Books.

Using Numbers in Writing

Rule
—
M 81

Spell out numbers of one hundred or lower and numbers that are rounded to hundreds and can be written in one or two words only.

Three years are usually required to earn a graduate degree in law or theology, and **four** years are required to earn one in medicine.

Over **one thousand** students participated in the Walk for Hunger.

BUT   Approximately 875 students completed the ten-mile walk.

Spell out common fractions with small denominations unless they are combined with a whole number and would be cumbersome to spell out.

Three quarters of those participating in the walk collected over $100 in pledges.

Note: Do not mix numerals and words when writing two or more numbers in the same category.

INCORRECT   **Two hundred** seniors and 125 doctoral students were awarded degrees on May 29.

CORRECT   **Two hundred** seniors and **one hundred twenty-five** doctoral students were awarded degrees on May 29.   [Words are used to describe the numbers of people; numerals are used in the date.]

Cardinal Numbers in Compounds.   Spell out cardinal numbers that occur in compounds with nouns or adjectives.

five-dollar tickets   twenty-pound turkey

Punctuation of Compound Numbers.   Hyphenate compound numbers from twenty-one through ninety-nine.

thirty-two   eighty-six   ninety-three

Ordinal Numbers.   Spell out ordinal numbers (*first, second, third,* and so forth) in your writing.   You may write the day of the month as an ordinal number preceding the month, but the month followed by an Arabic numeral is the preferred form.

first quarter   June 8
seventh grade   **eighth** of June

Rule M 82 Spell out any number that begins a sentence, or rewrite the sentence. (The word *and* is unnecessary in writing numbers including those numbers between one hundred and one hundred ten.)

INCORRECT 2020 four-year colleges operated in the United States in 1984.

CORRECT **Two thousand twenty** four-year colleges operated in the United States in 1984.

CORRECT In 1984 there were **2020** four-year colleges in the United States.

Rule M 83 Spell out an expression of time unless it is a specific time using A.M. or P.M. Use numerals and A.M. or P.M. in all technical writing.

Ruth usually leaves her dormitory at about **eight o'clock.**

BUT My computer printout was finished at 3:51 A.M.

Rule M 84 Use numerals to express dates, street numbers, room numbers, apartment numbers, telephone numbers, page numbers, and percentages. Spell out the word *percent*.

July **16, 1925**   pages **56–101**
122 San Gabriel Avenue   **10** percent

Dates. When you write a date, do not add *st, nd, rd,* or *th* to the numeral.

INCORRECT   May 5**th**, 1971   October 2**nd**
CORRECT   May **5**, 1971   October **2**

| Exercise 2 | **Numbers in Writing** |

Critical Thinking:
When should numbers be written as words?

On your paper, write the following sentences, correcting any errors in the writing of numbers. You may have to rewrite parts of some sentences. If a sentence contains no errors, write *Correct.*

SAMPLE Grinnell College, a 4-year liberal arts institution, is located in Grinnell, Iowa.

ANSWER Grinnell College, a four-year liberal arts institution, is located in Grinnell, Iowa.

1. The first day of orientation is August 31st.
2. Claire had to pay a 15-dollar late registration fee.
3. 231 freshmen live in that dormitory.
4. Al plans to take 2 semesters of math in his 3rd year of college.
5. Each roommate will have to pay 50% of the gas and electric bill.
6. Miguel finished his term paper at exactly four fifteen A.M.
7. Since Benito has been working in the college bookstore, he's unpacked at least five hundred boxes of supplies.

8. One hundred graduate students and 54 undergraduates signed the petition on April tenth.
9. My mother received her Master's Degree on June 10th, 1969, along with 80 other students, one of whom was my grandmother.
10. On the 6th day of May, Gwen has to take 3 tests, verify her nine forty-five A.M. appointment with her teacher in room 907, and deliver 1 of the 2 ten-dollar theater tickets.

The Writing Connection

Using Italics and Numbers in Your Writing

In certain writing situations, you will need to use italics and numbers. For example, if you submitted a reading list with your college application, you would underline book titles. In your formal essays, you might also use numbers in their correct forms to describe, for example, school sports activities or your winning second prize for a science experiment.

If your writing situation calls for italics and numbers, proofread carefully to be sure of using them correctly.

Reference Point: *pages 98–106*

Writing Assignments

A Brochure Suppose that as a college student you are writing a brochure for a college fair. To attract applicants who are interested in theater, you will describe your college's theater productions and its drama club. *Step 1:* Brainstorm for ideas about real or imagined theater productions. Then select from and organize your notes. *Step 2:* Write two paragraphs for the brochure. *Step 3:* Revise, replacing any dull or vague words with vivid, precise language. *Step 4:* Proofread, checking especially for the correct use of italics and numbers. *Step 5:* Make a clean copy of your paper and post it on the class bulletin board.

A Student Profile As part of your college application, you are asked to explain one of your interests. Choose one of the following topics or another topic. After you select and organize your notes, write a short profile of your activities. As you revise, combine some short sentences. Proofread your profile, checking your use of italics and numbers. Then file it in your portfolio.

1. team or intramural sports
2. school newspaper or literary magazine
3. community service or volunteer work
4. student government
5. travel experiences
6. hobbies

Abbreviations (pages 704–709)

A. Titles, Organizations, Place Names   On your paper, rewrite the following sentences to correct the faulty use of abbreviations.

1. Is the newly dedicated quantum physics building on Grand Ave. or 6th St.?
2. Ari will be leaving on Wednesday for an interview at Blue Mt. Coll. in Blue Mt., Miss.
3. The panel members who were discussing the proposed site of the new toxic waste dump consisted of Geraldine Madden, who used to be my dr., Rev. Kantor, and the Hon. Warren Jocelyn.
4. The seniors are going to NYC to see a B'way show and to Wash., D.C., to meet with Rep. Green and Sen. Nunn.
5. Noel and Ted gave a presentation on the Org. of Am. States for Profs. Ho and Bridges before their meeting with pres. Smythe in the adm. bldg.

B. Measurements, Dates, Time, and Symbols   On your paper, rewrite the following sentences, using abbreviations correctly.

6. Don't forget to bring ten $ to class on Fri. for art supplies & the new workbooks.
7. Consuela dropped a beaker containing ten fl. ozs. of solution and had to repeat the experiment.
8. We submitted the first part of the science project on Tues. & the second part during the first wk. of Apr.
9. Mister Boukydis discussed the period from the fifth century b.c. to 500 a.d.
10. Because the classroom measures less than three hundred sq. ft. and more than three quarters of the space is filled with furniture, there is little room for guests.

C. Proofreading Abbreviations   On your paper, rewrite the following paragraph, correcting the faulty use of abbreviations.

My friend Mister Wm. A. Davenport junior, who lives in CA, had a bk. published by a univ. press. He told me that univ. presses specialize in scholarly bks. Bill's prof., doctor Roberto E. Winters (we call him "dr." because he has a Doctor of Philosophy degree), helped him finish up his manuscript when Bill missed his Feb. deadline. That's why Bill wanted to spend several $ on a gift for him. When Bill found out that the prof. needed a mechanic to fix his car, he called his brother in LA and the two of them fixed it rt. away.

Capitalization   (pages 710–715)

A. Sentences and Proper Nouns   On your paper, rewrite the following sentences, using correct capitalization.

1. students in earth sciences 104 have seen pictures of earth taken from the moon.
2. Former presidents such as president jimmy carter often speak at university functions.
3. Carmela studied the renaissance during her junior year in italy.
4. professor st. james, chairperson of the french department, lives on west fork road, two blocks east of the library.
5. The king of the spring carnival is a czech who arrived at our school last september.
6. My father, Henry Gianni, jr., is the son of dean Henry Gianni, sr., and Roberta Gianni, m.d.
7. Brenda's paper about hermes, a greek god whom the romans called mercury, is due on the first day of spring.
8. Our drama class is writing a play called *the letter a,* based on nathaniel hawthorne's book *the scarlet letter.*
9. Denise Fairchild, rabbi, teaches a history of religion course along with rabbi Walter Goldstein, father Thomas Danaher, and the reverend Bradford Laker.
10. "did you meet my english professor?" June asked. "he's organizing a literary society called friends of henry james."

B. Proofreading for Capitalization   On your paper, rewrite the following paragraphs, correcting errors in capitalization.

high school Graduates all over the Country attend Vocational Schools, also known as Vocational technical schools. Students do not attend for four years or receive a b.a. Instead, they attend Schools such as the ace school for medical and dental assistants and receive a Certificate of completion, usually after two years of School. Cooking, Secretarial, Carpentry, plumbing, and Electrician certification are among the available Courses of Study. Often, students who have graduated from a Vocational School continue learning while they are employed as Apprentices or Assistants in their chosen fields. For instance, a student who studied how to be a Chef might try to get a Position in a large Hotel or resort kitchen where he or she could learn still more from experienced cooks. If you plan to attend such a School, make sure you know which of your skills you would like to develop. Then, consult your guidance Counselor to find out which schools would offer the best courses for your particular field.

"The commercial on the show *get working soon* advertised a School that taught Students to become Printers," uncle Bob told me. "As I found out," he added, "Their equipment was obsolete, so I couldn't get a job on my home-town paper, the *daily star.*"

Punctuation   (pages 715–737)

A. End Punctuation, Commas, and Apostrophes   On your paper, rewrite the following sentences, adding appropriate end punctuation, commas, and apostrophes.

1. Although students are supposed to go to school to learn 53 percent of the people questioned in the National Science Foundations poll agreed with the idea that scientists are dangerous because they know too much

2. That tall thin fellow with the light brown hair is not only our star basketball player but hes also attained a 4.0 average

3. Because Japan expects to be the first to build the worlds fastest computer dozens of United States universities budgets include research funds for "fifth generation" computers

4. Nyna its your letter of acceptance from Indiana University in Bloomington Indiana

5. Imagine During 1986 Japans schools produced twice as many science Ph.D.s as schools in the United States did

B. Quotation Marks, Semicolons, and Colons   On your paper, rewrite the following sentences, using quotation marks, semicolons, and colons correctly.

6. The first question on the science exam was: Why do stars "twinkle"?

7. Marjorie is writing a letter to the Op Ed section of the *River City Star.*

8. Ed is interested in genetic engineering in agriculture, therefore, he plans to attend agricultural college.

9. Charlotte started reading: *Progress or Stalemate A History of the Women's Movement* at 730 and was amazed to find herself still reading at 1200.

10. Types of vitamins include: fat-soluble and water-soluble, Professor Martin explained. Then he said, let me quote the American Council on Science and Health; Do not ingest either one in excessive amounts.

C. Proofreading for Punctuation   Rewrite the following paragraph, inserting needed punctuation.

   In the 90s many jobs will require information processing therefore students will need a liberal arts orientation to do the following gather information analyze it process it and store it. Will education be ongoing Emphatically yes said one consultant Take engineers she continued In five years 50 percent of what theyve learned goes into the computer in ten years itll be 90 percent. Theyll have to go back to school every ten years for new information to get replenished as it were and so will people in other fields.

Using Italics and Numbers   *(pages 737–741)*

A. Italics   On your paper, rewrite the following sentences, underlining the words that should be in italic type.

1. Students who wish to compare job prospects in various fields consult the Occupational Outlook Handbook.
2. Did you read the long poem Evangeline when you were in high school?
3. Spacecraft such as Apollo 11 are now pictured in history textbooks.
4. Does Our Times magazine have a summer intern program for students?
5. Those who study ancient civilizations study whatever paintings survived, such as the Egyptian wall painting known as The Grape Harvest.
6. Everyone in English Literature 102 looked forward to seeing the film Wuthering Heights, because they had all read the book.
7. LaToya hung a motto over her desk: nil desperandum.
8. Students who want to see nontraditional television drama should watch the series Channel Crossings tonight.
9. Students of railroading talk about the first run of the De Witt Clinton on the Mohawk & Hudson Railroad in 1831.
10. Fix the following errors on your paper: 46 should be 66, and the word illogical is misspelled.
11. Ian has been a reporter for two newspapers — The Boston Globe and The New York Times.
12. In this class we will read Hemingway's novel The Old Man and the Sea, which won a Pulitzer Prize, and we will also read a book of Hemingway's short stories called The Nick Adams Stories.
13. Tanya's parents are sailing to Puerto Rico and the Virgin Islands on the cruise ship Monica.
14. The French words bourgeois and chic have become part of the English language.

B. Using Numbers in Writing   On your paper, rewrite the following paragraphs correctly, using Arabic numberals or spelling out numbers.

Colleges and universities run on money. Where do they get it? The *Nineteen Eighty-Eight Information Please Almanac* lists the top 75 universities' endowment funds, which range from more than one hundred million dollars (University of Wisconsin) to $3,865.7 million (Harvard University). Wisconsin spends approximately $ six hundred million for about eighty percent of its operating expenses; Harvard wouldn't say how much it spent. For the academic year September first 1985 through May 30th, 1986, full professors in public colleges received an average of a little more than forty two thousand dollars; those in private colleges received an average of five thousand dollars more.

Task-Oriented Process Terms

As you enter college or the work force, you will have an increasing number of obligations that you are expected to carry out. Whether you are responsible for turning in your academic assignments on time, producing a product, or performing a service, you will be expected to accomplish these tasks in a dependable fashion. Acting responsibly means that you have learned to function with a minimum of guidance.

The first step in this process is to *formulate* — express in systematic terms — what you plan to do. Then you will *commit* — pledge — yourself to carrying out your responsibilities. You will be expected to perform your duties in a *conscientious* — thorough and painstaking — manner. Finally, you will be rewarded with appropriate acknowledgment in the form of grades if you are in school, or *remuneration* — payment — if you are in the work force.

These synonyms for common terms will appear regularly in material that you will *encounter* — meet — in everyday life, perhaps first in a personnel or college counseling office. This list of synonyms is not meant to suggest that you should express yourself with such a string of "big words" — indeed you would sound pretentious if you did. You can prepare yourself for the "language of life after high school," however, if you work at developing your vocabulary in systematic ways so that you will understand such terms when you hear them.

Accomplishing every task is a process, as you have already learned in working through the writing process. A task-oriented process requires successive stages of planning, analyzing requirements, carrying out the task, monitoring, and completing goals. You can give yourself a head start by learning the terminology used at each of these stages.

Planning Stage	
Get idea	*envision / conceive*
Discuss it	*illustrate, create* a *scenario, compare* to example from personal experience
Describe it	*sketch / outline / delineate / frame*
Request evaluation of it	make a *proposal / recommendation*
Evaluate it	*assess, appraise*

Planning Stage (continued)	
Analyze requirements	*plot / lay out / map out* plan for production write *specifications* for *production: work force, time,* and *cost*
Evaluate analysis	determine *feasibility, viability, impact enumerate resources forecast profitability* or *outcome*
Make decision to proceed	*authorize / commit*

Carrying Out the Task	
Review the requirements	*clarify, specify, elucidate*
Plan your time	*synchronize, sequence* your *schedule*
Do the work	*execute / discharge / perform* your duties
Solve problems	prepare for *contingencies, alternatives*

Monitoring Stage	
Guide	*advise, inspire, oversee, counsel, support, sustain*
Measure	*keep posted, analyze performance, render an account, report*
Correct	*revise, reorganize, rectify, realign, restore*

Completing Goals	
Payment	*compensation, remuneration, bonus, stipend, honorariums, fringe benefits*
Personal reward	*satisfaction, enrichment, edification, self-confidence, self-assurance*

Simple, clear, straightforward language is always advised, yet it is to your advantage to understand the kind of terminology in these task-oriented process charts. As you become comfortable with such terms, you will find occasion to use them yourself.

Vocabulary Activities

Understanding Process Terminology Make a list of the words in each chart that are unclear to you. Look up the definitions of the terms in a dictionary and then use each word in a sentence.

Planning Is the Key Choose a familiar process, such as holding a school dance, setting up a car-wash fund raiser, or cooking a meal for a group. Make a chart, breaking down the jobs into tasks, with appropriate "process" terminology.

The Literature Connection

Attending college can be a challenging, enlightening, and exciting experience. Many writers recall their own college memories in novels, stories, biographies, essays, and poems. In this selection from his autobiography, *Hunger of Memory*, Richard Rodriguez describes his first encounter with the term *minority student* and how he felt about being so identified.

Guided Reading   As you read, notice the author's use of mechanics in this passage. Consider how punctuation, capitalization, and italics help to convey the author's opinions about his education.

*I*n college one day a professor of English returned my term paper with this comment penciled just under the grade: 'Maybe the reason you feel Dickens's sense of alienation so acutely is because you are a minority student.' *Minority student*. It was the first time I had seen the expression; I remember sensing that it somehow referred to my race. Never before had a teacher suggested that my academic performance was linked to my racial identity. After class I reread the remark several times. Around me other students were talking and leaving. The professor remained in front of the room, collecting his papers and books. I was about to go up and question his note. But I didn't. I let the comment pass; thus I became implicated in the strange reform movement that followed.

Richard Rodriguez (1944–   )
from *Hunger of Memory*

How did the writer feel about being identified as a minority student? Why might he have hesitated to speak to the professor?

How has the writer used italics and punctuation for emphasis?

Writing Applications

A Journal Entry   Write an imaginary journal entry about your first day at college or at business or vocational school. Describe your feelings, impressions, and experiences. Include invented details about the

school, such as what it looks like, where it is located, what courses you plan to take, and so on. When you have finished writing your journal entry, proofread it for appropriate use of mechanics.

A Letter   Write a brief informal letter to a real or invented teacher. Your purpose for writing should be to thank this teacher for guiding you in a certain direction or for teaching you something that has been particularly valuable or useful. As you write, include specific details and use mechanics effectively to convey your thoughts. When you finish writing, proofread for appropriate mechanics.

Enrichment Connections

Choose one or more of these activities to do on your own or as a group.

Creative Writing

Dialogue   Invent two characters who have just started college or vocational school. Write appropriate dialogue for a skit or a play scene in which these characters discuss their feelings about education. For ideas, use your freewriting notes from *Responding to Literature* on page 703. You might also use the dialogue from *The Mill on the Floss* on that page as a model. Proofread your dialogue for effective mechanics.

A Song   Brainstorm real or invented details to create a school or college song. Write lyrics that will inspire loyalty and foster school spirit. Include facts about the school's history, its faculty, its unique qualities, and so on. Use appropriate mechanics to help rally your listeners. You might wish to set your song lyrics to music.

Across the Curriculum

Social Studies   Choose one college, university, or vocational school in or near your community. Then conduct research to find out when it was founded, who founded it, what courses and degrees are offered, who teaches there, what well-known graduates attended the institution, and so on. Use your notes to write a short research paper, a newspaper article, or a publicity brochure about the school, making certain to follow the guidelines for the appropriate use of mechanics.

CELEBRATING
DIVERSITY

If you had the chance to organize a ceremony honoring one person who has been a major influence on you, whom would you choose? What characteristics of that person do you admire? What sort of influence has he or she had on you?

Here is a speech by the novelist Ralph Ellison about his former teacher, Inman Page. Page, who had once been a slave, was the first African-American graduate of Brown University, which is in Providence, Rhode Island. As you read the speech, notice what Ellison remembers about Page. Also note what he has to say about the relationship between racial groups in the United States. Then choose one or more of the activities that follow the selection. Working on them may give you a new insight into pioneering achievements.

When confronted by such an unexpected situation as this, what does one say? It's not that I haven't been aware of Dr. Page's influence upon my life, for after all these many years he is apt to be conjured up by a wide variety of contacts and situations. And he was so dominant a figure during my school days that his voice and image are still evoked by certain passages of the Bible. I remember him in a context of ceremonies, in most of which he acted as the celebrant—but never in my wildest fantasies would I have anticipated my being called upon to play a role in a ceremony dedicated to his memory. Such a development would have seemed impossible because in my mind my relationship with Dr. Page has remained what it was back in the 1930s, which was that of a boy to a grand, dignified elder. In my scheme of things there remained between us a fixed hierarchal distance that had been dictated by age, accomplishment, and authority. So while I would have had no problem in imagining myself witnessing such a ceremony as this, the idea of my having an active role in it would have been in the realm of the impossible. And now that I find myself standing here, it is as though a preordained relationship has been violated, and as a result, my sense of time has begun leaping back and forth over the years in a way which assaults the logic of clock and calendar, and I am haunted by a sense of the uncanny.

And all the more so as I look at these portraits in which Richard Yarde depicted Dr. Page as he appeared when a student here at Brown. He was a much older man when I came to know him, but the dignified educator with whom I was familiar is prefigured in the portraits, especially in the cast of the eyes. This makes for a pleasant surprise, because during my school days it never occurred to me that Inman Page had ever been a *young* man. To me he was always lofty and enigmatic, a figure of authority and penetrating vision. Perhaps that is why I am haunted by a feeling that somehow Dr. Page must have prear-

ranged today's proceedings years ago, with the foreknowledge that at some predestined time and place they would culminate, at least for me, in a moment of astonishment and instruction. . . .

Thus we are gathered here today as the result of such linkages between ideals and personalities which were forged and began forming a chain of cause and effect more than a hundred years ago.

Which is to suggest that from the period of the Emancipation there has been transmitted throughout the Afro-American areas of this country a continuing influence that sprang from the early New England tradition of education. That tradition, which has contributed so much to this nation's vitality, was introduced into the areas of the South from which I spring by young graduates of New England colleges who went south to teach the newly freed slaves. I am, incidently, the grandson of a freedman—which would appear to be something of an irony of history. But despite the rapid acceleration of historical change in the United States, the period of slavery isn't so far in the past as it might seem. Inman Page, who was himself a slave and who left this campus at a time when the dismantling of the Reconstruction was well under way, was a bearer of that same tradition of New England education of which I speak. And through him its standards were imparted to many, many ex-slaves and their descendants. And since that transmitted tradition is still alive, I think it a good idea to keep this historical circumstance in mind when we hear glib talk of a "white culture" and a "black culture" in the United States. Because the truth of the matter is that between the two racial groups there has always been a constant exchange of cultural, of stylistic elements. Whether in the arts, in education, in athletics, or in certain conceptions and misconceptions of democratic justice, interchange, appropriation, and integration—not segregation—have been the constants of our developing nation. So at this particular moment of our history I think it very important that we keep in mind that the culture of the United States is a composite, pluralistic culture-of-cultures, and that all of its diverse elements have been to some extent inspirited by those ideals which were enshrined during the founding of this nation. In our embrace of these ideals we are one and yet many, and never more so than after they led to the Civil War, the Emancipation, and the Reconstruction. It was these ideals which inspired the many examples of personal courage such as can be seen in the life of Inman E. Page. For certainly his act of implanting the ideals of New England education out in the "Territory," that then young wild state of Oklahoma, called for both courage and a dedication to education. Because by the time he graduated from Brown the Reconstruction, which had promised full citizenship to the freedmen, was, as I've said, well on the way toward betrayal. It was a most pessimistic period for his people but he did his best, and therefore, thanks to Inman Page—and no matter how incongruously—I am here.

Ralph Ellison *(1914-   )*
from "Portrait of Inman Page:
A Dedication Speech"

Taking Another Look

What was Ellison's relationship with Page in the 1930s? Why does he feel strange participating in (rather than observing) a ceremony honoring Page? What does Ellison mean when he says it never occurred to him that Page had actually been young? How was the tradition of New England education introduced to newly freed slaves in the South? What aspect of "glib talk" about "white culture" and "black culture" does Ellison object to? What does he feel are the "constants of our developing nation"? Where was the "Territory"? Why was the era of Page's graduation from Brown a pessimistic time for his people? In what two ways is Inman Page responsible for Ellison's being "here"?

Changing Places

Can you imagine what it must have been like for a freed slave to attend a university in the North? If you had been in Page's position, what would you have looked forward to at Brown? What would you have feared? Once you had your degree, what career do you think you would have chosen? Would you have "given back" to your community—other freed slaves and their descendants—as Page did? Think about these questions as you work on one or more of the activities that follow.

WRITING

Ground-breaking Achievement   Imagine that you are breaking new ground by becoming the first of a particular group to belong to a particular organization. You might be the first girl on your high-school football team, the first male in a formerly all-women's college, the first student on the school board, the first United States resident on a bicycle tour of New Zealand, or the first of your race or ethnic group in a new school or club. Write a letter to your best friend either about your hopes or your fears regarding your first day or about the first day itself. Think carefully not only about how others would be likely to react to you but also about what might seem strange to you about your new environment and how you would react to it.

CRITICAL
THINKING

Chain of Influence   In his speech, Ellison acknowledges "linkages between ideals and personalities which were forged and began forming a chain of cause and effect more than a hundred years ago." In fact, his relationship with Dr. Page seems to be one of his most important "linkages." List at least ten "ideals and personalities" that have influenced your development as an individual. Consider each one as a cause, and then beside each, write about the effect the person or idea has had upon you. Such an exercise could spark a personal essay, such as those often requested by college admissions departments.

LANGUAGE

First of All . . .   In a group, brainstorm the language of "firsts." Collect as many words and phrases as you can that refer to being first and to the many meanings of *first*, such as *first in time, best,* and so forth. Include slang terms. Then check each term in the dictionary or use other sources to find out its origin. Note whether the term comes from a foreign language (many come from French) or from the jargon of a particular sport, group, or activity (such as vaudeville's *top banana*). Compile a list of *first* words and phrases and their origins; post it in your classroom.

SPEAKING and LISTENING

But Seriously, Folks . . .
Write a short speech honoring someone you know. It might be a serious speech to be given on a serious occasion, such as an awards ceremony, or a humorous speech to be given at a "roast." If necessary, do research to discover the significant achievements of the person whom you have chosen. Then deliver your speech to your class.

DID YOU KNOW?   Ralph Waldo Ellison was named for Ralph Waldo Emerson, whom his father admired, but the name was a source of both embarrassment and longing for Ellison. He was embarrassed to have been named for a white person, and yet part of him wanted to be a writer like the famed essayist.

Ellison was influenced by both African-American and other writers, among them Langston Hughes, Richard Wright, T. S. Eliot, Ezra Pound, Ernest Hemingway, and Gertrude Stein.

Appendix

A Sample Research Paper

The following pages show the complete sample research paper entitled "Micromachine Technology: The Small Revolution," portions of which appear at the end of Unit 7, Writing A Research Paper *(pages 372–433)*. The complete sample paper is presented here for easy reference as an example of research paper style, format, and documentation according to MLA guidelines. The last page of the sample paper, shown on page 759, is the Works Cited page.

Lavinia Washington

English 4

Mr. Martin

April 15, 19--

Micromachine Technology: The Small Revolution

In the 1970s and 1980s, computers changed the way people lived, worked, and entertained themselves. A spin-off of computer chip technology called "micromachine technology" promises equally impressive changes for the twenty-first century. Tiny sensors and miniscule motors, some no wider than a human hair, are already displaying potential uses that rival science fiction.

Background

Micromachine technology began in 1954 when researchers discovered that "it was possible to etch tiny valves, cantilevers, channels, and bridges into silicon" (Schlender). Because researchers had no use for their discovery, they did not pursue its development.

Micromachine technology got its next major boost in the 1970s. A scientist trying to develop an instrument for the National Aeronautics and Space Administration (NASA) needed to create a miniature valve--and could not. Although the deadline for NASA's project elapsed, the scientist continued to work on the problem. Finally, he succeeded. He created a valve that opened and shut in five thousandths of a second and let in ten billionths of a liter of gas (McDermott 90). Micromachine technology was born.

Technology

Today many laboratories make microparts, microsensors, and micromachines. All laboratories use very similar materials and processes.

Building Material

Like computer chips, micromachine devices are fabricated of silicon. The purity of silicon makes it an ideal building material for structures that cannot tolerate impurities, air bubbles, or other irregularities. Silicon is not only pure, but also it is stronger than stainless steel (Peterson and Barth 92).

Building Processes

A process known as photolithography is used to make microparts, such as valves. First, patterns for the parts are imprinted on silicon wafers. Then caustic chemicals etch away parts of the wafer to form three-dimensional shapes such as pits, pyramids, and walls. The cost to make each part is low because many parts are made at once in batches, just like computer chips (Angell, Terry, and Barth 44).

Since microparts are too small to assemble into a micromachine, another process is utilized to make devices that would normally require the assembly of several microparts. This process is called "sacrificial layering." Using this process, micromachines are built as completely assembled units. For example, to form a hub with a rotating arm, the whole assembly is constructed in layers of silicon separated by layers of silicon dioxide. When the assembly is completed, the sacrificed layers of silicon dioxide are etched away with acid, and the arm is free to move (Hoffer 80). Writer Andrew Pollack created an analogy of "a mechanic who builds a structure of alternating layers of metal and ice and then melts the ice, leaving only the metal" (C12).

Classification of Technology

Micromachine technology has two classifications: devices with moving parts and devices with nonmoving parts. Devices with nonmoving parts evolved first and are commonly used as sensors (Pollack C12).

Micromachines with moving parts are, for the most part, in the experimental stage. In fact, the definition of "micromachines" as tiny devices "distinguished as machines by their moving parts and their ability to do work" (Pollack C1) is relatively new. As recently as 1981, the term "micromachine" meant "microcomputer" in Tracy Kidder's Pulitzer Prize-winning book, The Soul of a New Machine (154-70). The ambiguity of the term decreased as the technology grew.

Microsensors

Microsensors perform a variety of tasks, including detecting heat, pressure, and sound (Schlender). They also measure vibration, liquid flow, chemical composition, infrared light, acceleration, and vacuum conditions (Peterson and Barth 93).

Uses in Medicine

In the field of medicine, microsensors are employed in a variety of products. For example, millions of microsensors are used each year in disposable blood pressure gauges (Schlender).

Microsensors in the form of microelectrodes greatly advanced the study of brain stimulation. With tips as small as one millionth of an inch in diameter, microelectrodes led the way to ground-breaking research by enabling scientists to study very small or very remote areas of the brain. For example, microscopic electrodes allow scientists to chart individual brain cell activity or to excite selected cells to prompt activity. In addition, tiny manipulators let scientists probe remote, previously inaccessible areas of the brain (Tether).

Uses in Auto Industry

The auto industry developed a host of sensor devices. One such device is a microsensor that mounts on a wheel and monitors a tire's air pressure. If the air pressure fluctuates dangerously, a warning signal is relayed to the driver (Smith). Auto makers also employ microsensors to control fuel injection devices. The sensors gauge the temperature and humidity of outdoor air and adjust the fuel mix accordingly (Smith).

In the future, auto makers plan to use microsensors that gauge the roughness of a roadway and then relay that information to a car's shock absorbers and springs, which will continually adjust the car's suspension to suit the road surfaces (Schlender).

Uses in Robotics

In the field of robotics, groups of microsensors let machines sense their environment with nearly human awareness. For example, tiny pressure sensors mounted on robots' fingertips are almost as sensitive as the nearly ten thousand sensors in a human fingertip (McDermott 91). In the future, tiny silicon microphones may provide robots with sound discrimination that rivals human hearing (Anderson).

Other Uses

Microsensors are invaluable in any product in which size is a factor. Other products that operate by using microsensors include hang-glider altimeters, gravity-force monitors in fighter jets, and air-tank pressure sensors for scuba divers (Schlender).

Micromachines and Micromotors

Unlike microsensors, micromachines with moving parts, such as micromotors, are still in the developmental stage. New Scientist magazine reports that "at least six laboratories in the United States are working on the micromotors with funding from the National Science Foundation" (Anderson).

Present Research and Development

Some laboratories are developing extremely small but functional micromachines. For example, Bell Laboratories created a microturbine six hundred microns in diameter--about the width of six human hairs. The eight blades of the turbine spin at a rate of four hundred revolutions per second, which is faster than many jet engines (Waldman). Researchers at the University of California at Berkeley developed an even smaller motor that is the diameter of a single human hair (Pollack C1). Their motor has gears that are so small that the "notched teeth . . . are about the size of a red blood cell" (Anderson). Sixty thousand of these motors could fit in one square inch of space (Marbach).

Working on such a small scale poses unusual problems for researchers. Some gears and other microparts are so small that they are in danger of being accidentally inhaled by a researcher (Pollack C1) or being blown off a laboratory table by the slightest breeze (Marbach). A researcher who was carrying a tiny microgear in a shoebox tripped--and dropped the shoebox. The lid bounced off and the tiny microgear catapulted out of the shoebox, never to be seen again (Hoffer 121).

Method of Propulsion

Because the motors are so small, standard methods of propulsion do not work; however, some unconventional methods do work. Because the motors are so small and their parts so close together, micromotors can run on the low voltage of electrostatic energy, commonly known as "static cling." Anyone who has combed a cat's fur and then used the charged comb to pick up lint or bits of paper has seen electrostatic energy in operation (Pollack C12).

Uses in Medicine

The National Science Foundation predicts the extensive use of micromachines in medicine (Anderson). Current plans call for mass producing micromachines for less than a penny each (Hoffer 79). A disposable machine that is the size of a fly speck can perform tasks that are not feasible with larger, more costly mechanisms.

Microtools used with remote controls would allow doctors to perform surgery from inside the body (Marbach). For example, micromachines placed inside fat-clogged arteries could scrub away built-up fat (Waldman).

Micromachines fabricated as tiny cutting tools will make delicate eye surgery possible (Pollack C1). In addition, micromachines with temperature sensors injected into tumors could fight cancer by using special freezing techniques (McDermott 90).

Micromachines used as "smart pills" could be "implanted or swallowed and would dispense precisely the right amount of medication through microscopic valves" (Pollack C1).

Uses in Industry

In industry micromachines could have a broad range of applications. Some applications are already under study; others are still the province of imagination.

One practical application under study is micropumps that pump cool air over computer chips to keep them from overheating. Large super-computers, especially, generate an enormous amount of heat. Micropumps could eliminate the danger of data loss from malfunctions caused by heat build-up.

In telecommunications, researchers hope that micromachines will be used for delicate alignment tasks, such as aligning lasers and straightening optical fibers (Anderson). At present, such tasks are difficult and expensive, if not impossible.

Micromachines have the potential to do for electronics what transistors did for radio. Micromachines could reduce large, cabinet-size devices to the size of a palm-size mechanism (McDermott 90).

In addition to working individually, micromachines could also be harnessed to work together. At the Massachusetts Institute of Technology (M.I.T.), researchers dream of developing swarms of "gnat robots" (Hoffer 121). "Instead of having one big, expensive robot to do a job, thousands of small, very simple robots will do the work" as a team (Marbach). Millions of gnat robots could be used to scrub barnacles off a ship. Airborne, they could act as roving security devices (Hoffer 121). Gnat robots could also be sent on troubleshooting missions to dangerous areas, such as inside a nuclear submarine, or they could work on space probes (Marbach).

The Future

There are still many unknowns to resolve before launching micromotors in commercial products. Problems include lubricating barely visible machines and understanding the effects of heat and vibration on tiny parts (Hoffer 121).

Technical problems seem relatively easy to overcome, however, considering that micromachine technology has already allowed scientists "to create axles finer than a strand of a spiderweb, cogs smaller than a grain of dirt, motors lighter than a fleck of dust" (Heppenheimer 78). Based on what micromachine technology has accomplished thus far, scientists believe that more wonders are possible.

> Some turn their vision toward even smaller wonders, forseeing computers a few hunderd thousandths of a inch wide, with their atomic-scale components assembled using molecular wrenches; others look forward to cell-size, submarinelike robots that could be injected into the bloodstream to clean out cholesterol deposits or destroy viruses. (Heppenheimer 78).

Computer scientist Rodney Brooks believes that the first applications of micromachine robots, however, will be for "very mundane things" (Heppenheinmer 84). Other scientists agree, pointing out that in the computer industry, microprocessors are used in everyday products such as microwave ovens (Hoffer 121). Developers know, however, that even humble products can be incredibly profitable. Analysts estimate that sales from micromachine technology will exceed $1 billion within a few years (Schlender).

Thus, although micromachine technology is now found in devices as humble as blood pressure gauges, the future of the technology seems anything but humble. In fact, its future applications may well rival science-fiction fantasy.

Works Cited

Anderson, Ian. "Motors No Wider Than a Human Hair." New Scientist 1 Sept. 1988: 44.

Angell, James B., Stephen C. Terry, and Phillip Barth. "Silicon Micro-mechanical Devices." Scientific American Apr. 1988: 44-55.

Heppenheimer, T. A. "Microbots." Discover Mar. 1989: 78+.

Hoffer, William. "Micro Machines." Popular Mechanics July 1988: 79+.

Kidder, Tracy. The Soul of a New Machine. New York: Avon, 1981.

Marbach, William D. "A Small World Grows Tinier." Newsweek 30 Nov. 1987: 65.

McDermott, Jeanne. "The Coming Age of Micromachines." Popular Science June 1984: 87-91

Peterson, Kurt E., and Phillip Barth. "Design Engineering." McGraw-Hill Yearbook of Science and Technology. New York: McGraw, 1988.

Pollack, Andrew. "New Generation of Tiny Motors Challenges Science to Find Uses." New York Times 26 July 1988, late ed.: C1+.

Schlender, Brenton R. "Microsensors Make Their Mark in a Wide Variety of Products." Wall Street Journal 21 Nov. 1986: 35.

Smith, Emily T., ed. "Thanks to 'Micromechanics,' Tires Can Check Their Own Air." Business Week 29 June 1987: 105.

Tether, J. Edward. "Brain: Brain Research." Encyclopedia Americana. 1987 ed.

Waldman, Peter. "'Micromachines' Made from Silicon Crystals." Wall Street Journal 1 Apr. 1988: 13.

Documentation Styles

Many systems of documentation exist for citing sources in a piece of writing. Unit 7, Writing a Research Paper, presents the Modern Language Association (MLA) documentation style as one way to cite sources in a research paper *(pages 405–408)*. This appendix presents you with information on two other commonly used styles of documentation: the *Chicago Manual* style and the American Psychological Association (APA) style. Use the style of documentation that your teacher recommends. Follow your teacher's recommendations also for your title page, page headings, and other formatting decisions.

Chicago Manual Style

The Chicago Manual of Style, published by the University of Chicago Press, presents information on several styles of documentation, but the style most commonly called *Chicago Manual* is a note-bibliography system. It requires the use of either footnotes or endnotes along with a bibliography.

▶ Procedure

1. To cite a source within a research paper, insert a *superscript* — a raised number — in the text.

   "By 1982, 28 percent of the 80 million households in the United States subscribed to a cable television service."[1]

   A superscript is raised one-half space above the line of text and immediately follows, with no intervening space, the material that is identified in the accompanying note. The best placement of the superscript is at the end of a sentence or, if necessary for clarity, at the end of a clause. The number follows all punctuation except the dash.

2. The superscript refers to a note that provides information about the source. The note may appear either at the bottom of the page of the research paper *(footnote)* or at the end of the paper *(endnote)* in a section with all other notes. Footnotes and endnotes are usually numbered consecutively within a paper.

   1. John Tydeman et al., *Teletext and Videotex in the United States* (New York: McGraw-Hill, 1982), 111.

   The content of a note may vary depending on the kind of source being documented. The preceding note (for a book with more than three authors) contains the author's full name, *et al.* to indicate that there are other authors, the title of the book, the publisher's city, the name of the publication, the date of publication, and the page number on which the cited information appears.

3. Once a source has been cited fully in a note, subsequent references to the same source may be abbreviated. For example, a second reference to the source in item two could be abbreviated to include the author's last name (followed by et al.), a short version of the title, and the page number being referred to.

> 2. Tydeman et al., *Teletext*, 111.

4. In addition to notes within the paper, a bibliography of all sources appears at the end of the research paper.

The following chart contains examples of superscripts and their accompanying notes in *Chicago Manual* style. (Sentences without quotation marks are paraphrases.)

Chicago Manual Style Citations and Notes

Book	Citation	Authors Ornstein and Thompson state that in each of our brains "the number of possible interconnections between these cells is greater than the number of atoms in the universe."[1]
	Note	1. Robert Ornstein and Richard F. Thompson, *The Amazing Brain* (Boston: Houghton Mifflin, 1986), 21.
Reference Book	Citation	The same silicon-chip technology that made computers possible has made a new technology possible.[4]
	Note	4. Walter McDermott, "Silicon," *Science Encyclopedia*, 1989 ed.
Magazine Article	Citation	"At Bell Labs researchers have designed a motor that will weigh just .013 ounce."[1]
	Note	1. T. A. Heppenheimer, "Microbots," *Discover*, Mar. 1989, 81.

Newspaper Article	Citation	In fact, the definition of "micromachines" as tiny devices "distinguished as machines by their moving parts and their ability to do work"[1] is relatively new.
	Note	1. Andrew Pollack, "New Generation of Tiny Motors Challenges Science to Find Uses," *New York Times*, 26 July 1988, late ed., C1.
Collected Work	Citation	Pigeons are diligent messengers. In one eight-hour workday, a messenger pigeon can fly three hundred miles without stopping to eat or drink.[2]
	Note	2. Tony Soper, "Pigeons and People," in *Animal Stories: Tame and Wild*, eds. Gilbert Phelps and John Phelps (New York: Sterling, 1985), 164.

A bibliography page for the preceding sources would appear at the end of a research paper, as follows. Note that the sources are listed alphabetically by the author's last name. Also notice the style of indentation. The first line of each reference begins at the left margin; succeeding lines are indented *five* spaces.

Bibliography

Heppenheimer, T. A. "Microbots." Discover, Mar. 1989, 78, 80–84.

McDermott, Walter. "Silicon." Science Encyclopedia, 1989 ed.

Ornstein, Robert, and Richard F. Thompson. The Amazing Brain. Boston: Houghton Mifflin, 1986.

Pollack, Andrew. "New Generation of Tiny Motors Challenges Science to Find Uses." New York Times, 26 July 1988, late ed., C1, C12.

Soper, Tony. "Pigeons and People." In Animal Stories: Tame and Wild. Eds. Gilbert Phelps and John Phelps. New York: Sterling, 1985.

American Psychological Association (APA) Style

The American Psychological Association (APA) documentation style, presented in its *Publication Manual,* is similar to the MLA style in its use of parenthetical notations. The APA style, however, is an author-date system. It focuses on the date of publication in addition to the author's last name in a citation. APA does not require footnotes or endnotes but does require a list at the end of the paper that gives complete bibliographic information on each source. APA documentation is used most often in the sciences. (Note: The author-date system is also one of the styles covered in the *Chicago Manual.*)

▶ **Procedure**

1. For a paraphrase, a citation consists of the author's last name and the date of publication in parentheses, inserted at the end of the sentence but before final punctuation. A comma separates the author's name and the date.

   The same silicon-chip technology that made computers possible has made a new technology possible (**McDermott, 1989**).

2. If the author's name is used in the paraphrase, list only the date of publication in parentheses immediately after the author's name, for example, . . . *as Stuart (1990) states,* . . . . If both the author's name and the date appear, a parenthetical citation is not necessary.

3. If a book or an article has no author, an abbreviated version of the title takes the place of the author's name, for example, (**"Technology," 1989**).

4. If a quotation is used, the page number must be provided in addition to the author's name and the date of publication. (See the third example in the following chart.)

5. If the author's name is mentioned in conjunction with a quotation, the date appears immediately after the author's name and the page number appears at the end of the quotation. (See the first example in the following chart.)

6. A reference list of all sources appears at the end of the research paper.

The following chart contains examples of parenthetical citations in APA style. (Sentences without quotation marks are paraphrases.)

American Psychological Association (APA) Style Citations	
Book	Authors Ornstein and Thompson (1984) state that in each of our brains "the number of possible interconnections between these cells is greater than the number of atoms in the universe" (**p. 21**).
Reference Book	The same silicon-chip technology that made computers possible has made a new technology possible (**McDermott, 1989**).
Magazine Article	"At Bell Labs researchers have designed a motor that will weigh just .013 ounce" (**Heppenheimer, 1989, p. 81**).
Newspaper Article	In fact, the definition of "micromachines" as tiny devices "distinguished as machines by their moving parts and their ability to do work" (**Pollack, 1988, p. C–1**) is relatively new.
Collected Work	Pigeons are diligent messengers. In one eight-hour workday, a messenger pigeon can fly three hundred miles without stopping to eat or drink (**Soper, 1985**).

A list of references for the preceding sources would appear at the end of a research paper, as follows. Note that the entries are in alphabetical order according to the author's last name. Also notice the style of indentation. The first line of each reference begins at the left margin; succeeding lines are indented *three* spaces.

As you examine the references, note these points of style as well.

1. Initials only are used for authors' first and middle names.
2. In book titles and in article titles, only the first word of the title and the first word of the subtitle (if any), as well as proper names, are capitalized.
3. All major words in magazine and newspaper titles are capitalized.
4. Article titles do not appear within quotation marks.
5. The abbreviation *p.* or *pp.* precedes page numbers. Page numbers preceded by a letter show a dash between the letter and the number, as in the fourth entry that follows.

References

Heppenheimer, T. A. (1989, March). Microbots. Discover, pp. 78, 80–84.

McDermott, W. (1989). Silicon. Science Encyclopedia.

Ornstein, R., and R. F. Thompson. (1986). The Amazing Brain. Boston: Houghton.

Pollack, A. (1988, July 26). New generation of tiny motors challenges science to find uses. The New York Times, late ed., pp. C–1, C–12.

Soper, T. (1985). Pigeons and People. In G. Phelps and J. Phelps (Eds.), Animal Stories: Tame and Wild (p. 164). New York: Sterling. 1985.

Assignment **Practice with Documentation Styles**

Turn to Assignment 3 on pages 408–409 in your textbook. *Step 1:* Following the directions given, do items 1, 3, 4, 5, and 8. Use either *Chicago Manual* or APA documentation in place of MLA. *Step 2:* Create a bibliography page or a list of references for the same items, using the style that you chose in Step 1. *Step 3:* Work with a partner who used the other style of documentation and examine the differences and similarities in the two styles.

Applying Comparison and Contrast in Essay Tests

Explain the similarities and the differences between classical music and jazz. Compare and contrast writing with a word processor and writing with pen and paper. Describe the advantages and the disadvantages of credit cards.

Essay topics, or **prompts,** such as these may be common on social studies tests or on statewide examinations — situations in which you have a specified time limit for your writing. Although prewriting, drafting, revising, proofreading, and publishing will always help you produce good writing, sometimes you just don't have time to move carefully and slowly through the steps of the writing process.

When you need to finish an essay in a prescribed amount of time, you'll want to adapt what you've learned about the writing process. Applying comparison and contrast in timed writing means streamlining all the stages of your writing. You may be tempted to skip certain steps — to draft without prewriting, for example, or to publish without proofreading. If you master some strategies for speeding up the process rather than omitting steps, you'll write a much stronger essay, and consequently, earn a much higher grade.

▶ Strategies

1. *Read the prompt carefully and make sure you understand it completely.* Jot down or underline the important ideas.
2. *Plan your time.* Make a rough outline of the amount of time you'll spend on each stage of your writing, for example, Prewriting: 10 minutes. Allow time for revising and proofreading.
3. *Prewrite quickly but carefully.* An appropriate graphic organizer will focus and organize your ideas in one step.
4. *Devote most of your time to drafting.* Include as much specific detail as possible.
5. *As you revise, add additional details and examples if time permits.* Continue to think creatively about your topic, adding words and examples that will strengthen your argument.
6. *In consideration of your reader, proofread as carefully as possible.*

Prewriting To Compare and Contrast

Your writing prompt on a test will probably give you the major ideas for your writing, but you will still need to explore and focus your thoughts and organize them effectively — and you'll need to do these things quickly. Take a deep breath and relax; your skill in using the writing process will help you here. Begin by focusing all of your attention on the question at hand.

Understanding the Prompt

When you're writing timed essays for tests, you're usually given a writing topic, or *prompt.* Read it carefully, several times. If you fail to answer the question, or you don't answer it directly, all of your work will be in vain. As you read the prompt, underline key words or jot them down. Use these key words in your prewriting notes and in your thesis statement and/or topic sentences.

Suppose, for example, you found the following prompt on a state-wide examination.

> The only stores in your neighborhood are small, locally-owned shops: a drug store, a produce market, a hardware store and a gift shop. A huge supermarket chain proposes opening a new "super-store" on the same block. The town council has asked citizens to write letters expressing their views on the pros and cons of such a plan. In a letter to the council, discuss both sides of the proposal and state and support your own position.

As you read the prompt several times, you decide that the following words are important:

> supermarket chain, neighborhood
> write letters to town council
> "super-store" — both sides
> locally-owned shops
> state/support position

If you write these words on your paper or underline them in the prompt (if you're permitted to write on the paper), you'll notice that they tell you several important things. The words *opening new "super-store"* and *locally-owned shops* indicate that your discussion will involve the effects of the store on local merchants. The words *write letters, town council* help you to establish your format (a letter, probably more than one paragraph) and your audience (members of the town council). The words *both sides* and *state/support position* direct you to a persuasive purpose. Remaining focused on these ideas — and only these ideas — will help make your essay well-supported and coherent.

On your paper, write the most important words in the following prompts for essays that compare and contrast. Then write what these words tell you about the subject of your essay, your audience, and your purpose.

1. There are both positive and negative aspects to using credit cards in order to make purchases. Write an editorial essay for your school newspaper about the advantages and disadvantages of credit cards. Include and support your own opinion.

2. You work for a clothing store that sells clothing made of only natural fabrics — cotton, wool, linen, silk. Your manager has asked you to write some advertising copy for your local newspaper that compares and contrasts natural fabrics and synthetic fabrics and persuades the readers that natural fabrics are better.

3. Your music teacher has assigned you a research paper. You have chosen to write about classical music and jazz. Write a paper explaining the similarities and the differences between classical music and jazz.

Focusing and Organizing Your Ideas

Once you have analyzed your question or prompt and have located its main ideas, spend a few minutes focusing your own thoughts for your essay. As you've seen, your prompt often defines both your purpose and your audience *(pages 24–25)*. The sample prompt that asks for a position on the building of a new supermarket, for example, defines your audience as the members of your town council and your purpose as persuasion. However, if the prompt doesn't clearly indicate a purpose or an audience, decide on both before you begin to draft.

Many prompts ask you to express your ideas or to indicate your command of a subject by using comparison or contrast or both. When you compare, you show how two or more ideas or opinions are alike. When you contrast, you show how the ideas or opinions differ. Whenever possible, use both comparison and contrast for variety and strength. You may be asked to compare and contrast two things such as classical music and jazz, or you may be asked to discuss the advantages and the disadvantages of one thing, such as credit cards. Use comparison and contrast to persuade or simply to inform.

Brainstorming and clustering *(page 16)* can help you get started by allowing you to explore ideas. Charting *(page 17)* also gives you quick ways to generate ideas. Using the Five W's and How *(page 18)* can prompt a wealth of information, and making a time line *(pages 21–22)* can help generate and organize chronological ideas.

Comparing and Contrasting to Persuade

If you're asked to compare and contrast to persuade your audience to share your opinion, you'll want to present a coherent and effective argument. To prewrite for a comparison/contrast essay that persuades, establish your own position statement *(pages 230 and 247)*, and then generate ideas that address both sides of the issue. Keep in mind that balance is an important element in this kind of writing. You can provide balance in two ways.

- Group all of your information about one idea together, followed by all of your information about the second idea (AAA BBB).
- Every time you make a point about one idea, follow it with the corresponding point about the other idea (AB AB AB).

For the prompt on building a supermarket in the neighborhood, for example, you may decide that you do not support the new addition. To focus your ideas, you might use a graphic organizer like the following.

Viewpoint

| town should allow new supermarket to be built |

For
  convenience
  lower prices
  more tax dollars

Against
  will increase traffic
  streets less safe
  impersonal

Viewpoint

| town should rely on small, locally owned business |

For
  small businesses friendlier
  preserve small-town feelings
  products easy to find

Against
  no variety or competition
  higher prices
  often closed

My Choice

| The town should rely on small, locally-owned businesses. |

Practicing with graphic organizers every time you write will make using them more natural during a test. You can save a lot of time — and increase your chances for success — by quickly sketching and filling in such an organizer before you begin to draft.

Comparing and Contrasting to Inform

In certain types of tests, you're asked to show the examiner that you remember and understand a body of information that you've been studying. Sometimes, such an explanation involves the comparison and contrast of two ideas, events, people, or things. To prewrite for a comparison/contrast essay that explains or informs, you'll need a quick way to jot down similarities and differences. A Venn diagram (see the explanation and the example that follow), a chart *(page 17)*, or a list can be a particularly useful prewriting tool for this kind of comparison/contrast writing. Experiment with these prewriting techniques and others to see which ones work best for you in test situations.

Suppose, for example, that you are asked to compare and contrast the physical characteristics of African elephants and Asian elephants on a biology exam. One way to focus and organize your ideas quickly is to make a Venn diagram. On your paper, draw two overlapping circles, as in the example that follows. Label one circle *African* the other *Asian.* In the section of the diagram in which the two circles overlap, list the similarities between the two animals. In the two sections in which the circles do not overlap, list the differences. The result might be a Venn diagram like the one that follows.

Using a graphic organizer both focuses and organizes your ideas, saving steps when your writing is timed. You will discover that some graphic organizers work better for some subjects than others and that some work better for you than others. When you complete untimed writing assignments, experiment with a variety of graphic organizers. Then, when the clock is ticking, you'll feel confident using the ones that are most appropriate to your topic and your taste. If you use a variety of organizing tools, you'll relax and express your ideas clearly.

Here are several other kinds of graphic organizers that you might find useful when you compare and contrast.

Webbing Webbing may remind you of clustering *(pages 14–16)*. If you are comparing and contrasting African and Asian elephants, your web may look like the one that follows.

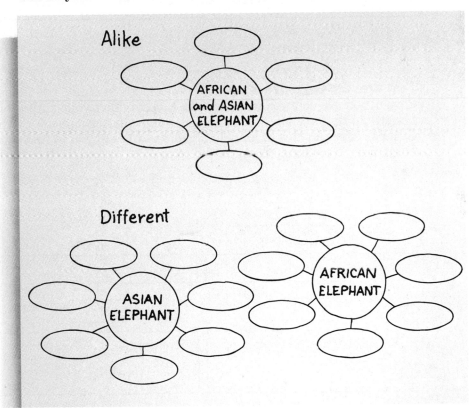

Charts or Lists Charting allows you to classify your ideas by dividing them into categories or logical parts. One type of chart is illustrated on page 17. A second type is a chart, seen below, that lists likenesses in the first column and differences in the next two columns.

Likenesses	Differences	
1.	1.	1.
2.	2.	2.
3.	3.	3.

Conclusion:

Other Graphic Organizers Several other kinds of charts can be useful when you are comparing and contrasting, whether your purpose is to inform or to persuade. Two examples follow. In Assignment 3, experiment with several types of graphic organizers to help you to find ways to organize information on your topic.

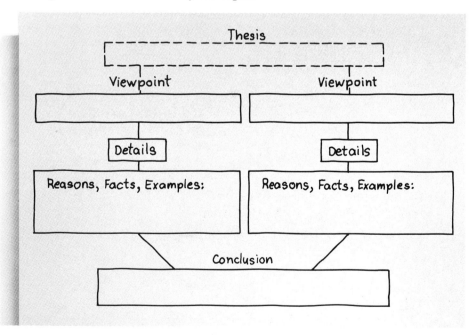

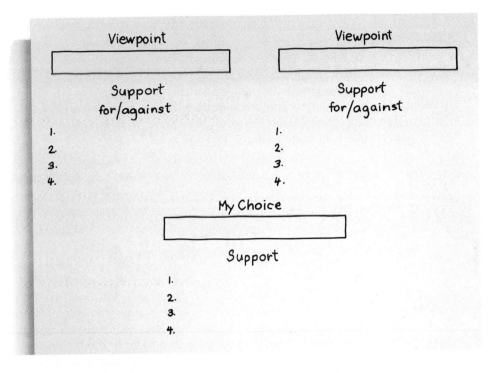

Viewpoint

Support
for/against

1.
2.
3.
4.

Viewpoint

Support
for/against

1.
2.
3.
4.

My Choice

Support

1.
2.
3.
4.

Assignment 2 Prewriting with Venn Diagrams

On your paper, write one of the following pairs of topics or another pair of your choice. Then make a Venn diagram that shows the major points of comparison and contrast between the elements of the pair. Since you are practicing for a timed test, do your prewriting as quickly as you can.

1. cooking with a microwave oven/cooking with a conventional oven
2. buying a new car/buying a used car

Assignment 3 Prewriting with Graphic Organizers

Choose one of the following writing prompts. Using clustering, a Venn diagram, a chart, a list, or another kind of graphic organizer, prewrite for an essay that will address the issues raised in the writing prompt you've chosen. Try to prewrite quickly.

1. Discuss the similarities and differences between swimming and jogging as means of staying fit.
2. Discuss the advantages and disadvantages of using standardized tests as college admissions criteria.
3. Compare and contrast two local restaurants.
4. Write an editorial for a music magazine comparing and contrasting two of your favorite musicians.

Step 1: Choose an essay topic or prompt — from a test you have recently taken in English or another subject, from a sample statewide examination, or from Assignments 1, 2, or 3 on the preceding pages.
Step 2: Using clustering, a Venn diagram, a chart or a list, or another type of graphic organizer, prewrite quickly for an essay on your chosen topic or prompt. *Step 3:* Discuss your prewriting with a partner or in a group, and save it in your writer's notebook.

Drafting

Drafting Your Comparison/Contrast Essay

Drafting your comparison/contrast essay should take up most of your limited test time. Budget one half to two thirds of the time available to you for drafting. If you have done effective prewriting, drafting your essay will be a smooth and efficient process. Consult your graphic organizer as you draft. Remember to include a topic sentence *(pages 40–42)* or a thesis statement *(pages 46–47)*, to support your ideas with elaboration and detailed body paragraphs *(pages 56–57)*, to balance your points, and to write an effective concluding paragraph *(page 58)*. Use appropriate transitional words and phrases, and include description and narrative anecdotes when they are relevant and helpful to the purpose of your essay. Because you may have only limited time for revising and proofreading, be more conscious of grammar and mechanics when you draft during a test than when you draft for an untimed assignment. Work quickly and carefully, with as much concentration as you can muster.

Assignment Drafting from a Graphic Organizer

Choose one of the following prompts and its graphic organizer. Expand the graphic organizer with your own ideas or adjust it to reflect your own opinion, and then draft a response to the prompt. Include as many examples and as much detail as you can.

1. Because of budget cuts, your school must eliminate one foreign language (either Latin or German) from its curriculum. Your principal has invited concerned students to express their opinions in writing. Write a short essay in which you discuss both choices and state your own opinion. (See page 775.)

Viewpoint	Viewpoint
Cut Latin	Cut German

Against

    84 students taking Latin
    Latin improves vocabulary
    Latin disciplines mind

For

    Latin is "dead" language
    Some Latin can be studied
      as part of English
    Preserves senior trip to
      Germany

Against

    Germany is industrial ally
    Seniors' German trip
      educational experience
    German is spoken language

For

    Only 32 students taking German
    Local college offers only
      French, Spanish, and Latin
    Latin helps study of English

My Choice

Our high school should eliminate Latin rather than German from its foreign language curriculum.

2. Part of your job in a small business is to arrange for speedy deliveries of important papers and letters within the city limits. Two kinds of delivery services are available to you: bicycle couriers and taxis. Your supervisor has asked you to write a memo explaining the advantages and disadvantages of each kind of service and to make a recommendation for your office.

Likenesses	Differences	
	Bicycles	**Taxis**
both are reliable	not affected by traffic	traffic can slow
deliver in 1 hour	$10.00 per delivery	$20.00 per delivery
pick up in office	no pollution	pollute air

Conclusion: Use bicycle couriers because they cost less and don't pollute.

Continuing Assignment **Draft a Comparison/Contrast Essay**

Step 1: Reread the prewriting that you did for the Continuing Assignment on page 774. *Step 2:* Draft an essay based on your prewriting. *Step 3:* Share your draft with a partner and discuss its strengths and weaknesses. Save your draft.

Revising Your Comparison/Contrast Essay

If you have kept to the tentative schedule that you made at the beginning of your test, you should have some time for revising. Revising in a timed situation, however, will be brief and independent, and you won't be making major, sweeping changes to your draft. Check to see how much time is available. Then ask yourself the following questions about your essay.

- Have I answered the prompt?
- Have I considered my audience and my purpose?
- Can I add other details, further elaboration, or more support for my ideas?
- Is there a balance among the ideas and opinions I am comparing or contrasting?
- Have I used effective transitional words or phrases?
- Have I supported my conclusion effectively?

Because you will not have time to recopy your essay, use arrows and circles to indicate information that has been added or rearranged. Make your revisions clearly and neatly. Your evaluator will know that your time was limited, but a messy, illegible essay will impress no one.

Assignment Revising on the Run

Here is a draft of an essay in response to the following prompt:

Your cousin Janet is getting married and is trying to decide whether to change her last name to that of her future husband. She has asked you to write a letter to give your advice. First, discuss the advantages and disadvantages of both options; then give your opinion.

Read the essay carefully and write it on your paper. Then revise the essay carefully but quickly. Use the questions and instructions above to guide your revision.

Dear Janet,

Congratulations on your upcoming wedding! I think that deciding what your name will be is a hard decision for a woman to make, for our names are really symbols of who we are.

If you take Carl's last name, you'll be giving the message, "Look, we are married now. We are a family." On tax forms, mortgages, bank accounts, and loans, your relationship will be clear to anyone who looks. You won't have to worry about what last name to give your children. Older relatives won't be confused about your intentions or how to address mail. Of course, you'll have to change all of your credit cards, driver's license, legal documents, and monogrammed towels but that should only take a few months!

If you keep your name, you'll be saying to the world, "Even though we are married, I am maintaining my independence." In writing, things will be complicated, and you'll probably have to do some constant explaining that you really are husband and wife. Conservative relatives may frown, and occasionally, you might get mail addressed to "Mr. and Mrs." just as if you'd kept your name.

> With love,
> Dana

Continuing Assignment **Revise a Comparison/Contrast Essay**

Step 1: Reread the draft of an essay that you wrote for the Continuing Assignment on page 775. *Step 2:* Revise the draft on the same paper, adding support, elaboration, and transitions as necessary. Be sure to mark your additions, deletions, and corrections legibly. *Step 3:* Share your revised essay with a partner and discuss its strengths and weaknesses. Save your revision.

Proofreading

Proofreading Your Comparison/Contrast Essay

Before you turn in your essay, proofread for correct sentence structure, usage, capitalization, punctuation, and spelling. Cross out mistakes neatly and make changes clearly and legibly. Whoever grades your test will appreciate your extra effort to make your writing easier to read.

The Grammar Connection

As you proofread your comparison/contrast essay, give special attention to this point.

Modifiers in Comparisons Make sure to use comparative modifiers when comparing two people, things, actions, or ideas and superlative modifiers when comparing more than two.

Reference Point: *pages 664–666*

When choosing between a dictionary and a thesaurus, remember that a dictionary offers ~~most~~ *more* kinds of information.

Proofreading Practice

Read the following paragraph from an essay comparing home-made spaghetti sauce and canned spaghetti sauce, and copy it onto your paper. As neatly as possible, make all necessary corrections in grammar, mechanics, usage, and spelling. Use symbols such as the ones on page 99, and be sure that your proofread draft is legible.

> Making spagetti sauce can be most expensive than canned sauce if your buying the ingredients fresh. a 5-quart batch cost about $12.00 as opposed to $10.00 for 5 quart jars. If you grow tomatoes, basil, oregano, parsly, and onions in your garden; however, the cost can go down to nearly nothing. Sauce from scratch takes longer, but jarred sauce wont fill your house with that sweet, rich smell.

Continuing Assignment Proofread Your Essay

Step 1: Reread the essay you revised for the Continuing Assignment on page 777. *Step 2:* As you reread, correct any grammar, usage, mechanics, or spelling errors neatly. *Step 3:* Exchange essays with a partner and check one another's proofreading.

Publishing

Publishing Your Comparison/Contrast Essay

Now you can relax and breathe a sigh of relief. Time has run out, and your essay is complete. You've used your knowledge of the subject and an abbreviated version of the writing process to produce a well-supported and clearly-stated essay. Maybe it's not perfect, but you can hand it in with confidence. Now your work is in the hands of your teacher or another evaluator. Pages 779–785 will give you some idea of the criteria they may use to grade your essay.

Continuing Assignment Publish a Comparison/Contrast Essay

Give the essay that you proofread for the Continuing Assignment above to your teacher. If possible, discuss the strengths and weaknesses of the essay with your teacher.

Evaluating Comparison/ Contrast Writing

One of the most common evaluation systems used for timed writing is holistic scoring, usually done by a group of evaluators. Each essay is read by at least two people, who score it — as a whole — from 1 (the lowest score) to 4 or 5 (the highest score). If the two evaluators give very different scores, a third reader mediates between them. Passing grades for statewide tests vary, but most students aim for a 3, 4, or 5 on such tests.

The essays that follow illustrate several responses to writing prompts for essays that compare and contrast. The first prompt served as the sample prompt for a persuasive essay in earlier sections of this unit (Understanding the Prompt, page 767). The second prompt illustrates the kind of question that may appear on a standardized writing exam. The score of each essay is indicated, and marginal commentary shows what factors make the "2" better than the "1," the "3" better than the "2," and the "4" better than the "3." The highest score for these essays is "4." Read the essays and the commentaries carefully.

Prompt There are both positive and negative aspects to using credit cards in order to make purchases. You are a writer for your school newspaper. Write an editorial essay for that newspaper about the advantages and disadvantages of credit cards. Be sure to state your own opinion. Support your position with convincing reasons.

Score 1

STRONG POINTS:
- Discusses one side fully
- Provides specific examples

WEAK POINTS:
- Fails to discuss disadvantages
- Not organized into clear paragraphs
- No transitions
- Contains irrelevant details
- Errors in spelling, usage, and mechanics

Credit cards are great. I can waltz into any old store in town, whip out a card, and buy what I want. I don't have to worry about getting money from my folks or spending my alowance. I have a friend who buys all her clothes herself when she goes shopping she just doesn't quit! Credit cards help you cash checks to. I can use my credit card as identification and in an emergency. My mother once got stuck in a bad snowstorm in chicago and had to stay overnight — she used her credit card to pay for dinner and a motel room. Credit cards help you buy big things, like computers, televisions, or airline tickets, too. Even if you don't have the money in your hand. I cant imagine life without a credit card. I don't even mine the bills that come in every month neither. My uncle keeps his credit cards in alphabetical order in a billfold we gave him for his birthday. I used my credit card to buy his present!

Score 2

STRONG POINTS:
- Includes introduction and conclusion
- Discusses both advantages and disadvantages
- Gives clear reasons
- Clearly organized paragraphs
- Uses transitions

WEAK POINTS:
- Few specific supporting details
- Includes several spelling, usage, and sentence structure errors
- Doesn't take a clear position

Credit cards have good and bad aspects. One good aspect is that major credit cards are convenient to use in most stores around the country. Another good aspect is that credit cards can be used like cash to make large or unplanned purchases. Like a VCR or a microwave oven. A third good aspect is that credit cards come in handy for emergencies when banks are closed or you don't have enough money with you. A fourth good aspect is that most credit cards can be used in foriegn countries. It's a good feeling to have one of these cards.

There are also bad aspects to using credit cards. Credit cards can be lost or stole and used by another person. Then you have to cancel tham and get new numbers. Another bad aspect is that credit cards make it too easy to make foolish decisions, like about what to buy in a store. My brother once bought a leather jacket that he can't really afford. Each person also has a different credit limit that they have to keep track of. You can't spend more money than your allowed. A fourth bad aspect is that credit card companies rip you off by charging a very high finance charge, which you have to pay every month. Some companies charge lots more than others do.

Using a credit card in restaurants, gas stations, supermarkets, and department stores has good and bad aspects. Consider these points before you apply for a credit card. You may decide it's not worth it to get one.

Score 3

STRONG POINTS:
- Includes strong introduction and conclusion
- Presents both good and bad points
- Gives specific examples
- Coherent paragraphs with transitions
- Takes a position

Using a credit card has both advantages and disadvantages. Before you rush to apply for a credit card, consider the good and bad aspects that are presented for you here.

Credit cards offer many advantages. First, a credit card teaches responsability. In order to have a credit card, you have to show that you can pay your bills promptly, and you can't go over your credit limit. Credit cards provide a great opportunity for learning to live on a budget. In addition, you have to learn to make sensable purchases with your credit card. If you go out on a shopping spree with your credit card, you'll eventually have to find a way to pay for what you bought.

A second advantage is that credit cards are required for many different reasons. For example, many stores and businesses ask for a credit card if you want to pay for something by writing a personal check. Also, you cannot rent a car unless you have a major credit card. Having a credit card also helps you to get a credit rating that can benefit you for the rest of your life as long as you are always careful to pay your bills.

A third advantage is that you can use credit cards for mail-order shopping from catalogues or to order items over the telephone. You just need to write your credit card number on mail-order forms or tell it to a salesperson. With a credit card, you can buy curtains, concert tickets, or a down jacket — without leaving home.

There are also disadvantages of having a credit card. Some people abuse their credit cards, chargeing too many purchases that they can't really afford to buy at the time. Since you can have many different credit cards, some people use each one up to the maximum limit and then start over with a new card. This is one easy way to get into trouble with debts.

A second disadvantage of having a credit card is that they can be stolen and then used again. Information can be copied from carbon slips from credit card purchases, or the cards themselves can be used if a thief forges the card owner's signature.

Finally, credit cards encourage people to spend, spend, spend. It is so easy to charge something, that enthusiastic customers often buy stuff they don't need on the spur of the moment without thinking. This can become a habit and cause you to be in debt for life.

Despite all that has been said here on the negative aspects of credit cards, it is clear that the vast majority of Americans want credit cards for buying different items, and most people can benefit from and enjoy their use. The advantages outweigh the disadvantages as long as the users are responsible and disciplined.

Score 4

To Charge or Not to Charge

When a credit card application arrives in the mail, you should carefully consider the pros and cons of filling it out. There are distinct advantages and disadvantages to using credit cards, and all of these will be discussed below.

One of the benefits of either a store credit card or a bank credit card is that people can meet their needs immediately even if they don't have the resources at the time. For example, if you need a pair of boots for winter but have to wait until you receive your paycheck from a part-time job, then you can still buy the boots with a credit card before the first big snowstorm of the year. If you suddenly remember an important birthday or anniversary in your family, you can buy a gift without worrying about having the cash in hand. In addition, a bank credit card will help you get a cash advance if you need money right away for an emergency.

Another bonus of credit cards is that they provide a record of expenses. A credit card slip, as well as a monthly statement, lists exactly what you bought, when you made the purchase, and where you shopped. This account of your purchases might help you stick to a budget or to help you understand your flexible expenses. As my brother said, "When I looked at my gas credit card, I realized how many times a week I bought gas. That's when I decided to trade in my gas guzzler for a newer compact that doesn't eat gas. Now I can save gas as well as keeping within a reasonable budget."

In addition, a third merit of the use of credit cards is convenience. For many consumers, the credit card saves time; if you happen to see something you want to buy, you don't have to go find a bank or an ATM machine first. In addition, a credit card allows you to take advantage of sales and special discounts even if you don't have the money at that moment. Some stores or banks make special offers or give discounts to their credit card holders only. A credit card also makes it convenient to use a check; in some cases, a store cashier will ask you to present a major credit card before he or she can accept your personal check or traveler's check. Rental car companies usually won't rent a car to anyone who can't produce a credit card. For those who travel on business, a credit card is a definite must.

On the other hand, using credit cards does have disadvantages. One drawback is that all credit card purchases actually cost more, once finance charges and interest payments are added on. When you pay with cash, you don't have to worry about any additional charges being tacked on later. The only way to avoid paying finance charges is to pay everything you owe by the due date, which necessitates paying every month. That can sometimes mean that a credit card is no more useful than using cash or checks.

Another negative aspect of credit cards is that they tend to lead to overspending. Many people do not know how the total amount they owe relates to their income. With a credit card, it is very easy to ignore the fact that you have no money saved up in a savings or checking account. My best friend, for example, had to take on a second part-time job to help her meet the expenses of a credit card bill. She owed a lot of money for a prom dress she bought at Fashion Boutique. If she had been using cash, she would have shopped more carefully, looking for a good bargain.

Another disadvantage is that you must agree to the terms of credit contracts before you can get a credit card. Many people don't carefully read their contracts or don't fully understand the terms of these contracts. Each credit card contract has a different finance charge, a different late payment charge, and a different payment schedule. You have to read these contracts thoroughly to find out about any special clauses or conditions.

Although it looks as if credit cards are here to stay, you should learn as much as you can about the pluses and minuses of shopping with credit. Using a credit card is a serious financial decision that should be carefully analyzed before you take risks with your money. If you do, however, having a credit card can help you be a responsible and disciplined shopper and a careful financial planner. They can make life easier and more fun — and that's their biggest advantage!

Prompt Before graduating from high school, all seniors have to decide what to do next with their lives. Think about what you want to do. Do you want to continue your education at a two-year or four-year college or get a job? In an essay, discuss each option, state your position, and support your position with convincing reasons.

Score 1

STRONG POINTS:
- States position clearly
- Provides reasons for position
- Gives specific examples

WEAK POINTS:
- Fails to discuss both options
- Offers few specific examples
- Contains errors in spelling and sentence structure

After graduating from Fremont High School, I plan to go to a state university to continue my education. I beleive that education is the key to success.

It is important to have a college degree if you want to have a good job in the future. Also, you have to have a bachelor's degree for most careers you need further education to be an architect, an engineer, a doctor, or a teacher, for example.

Going to college will give me a chance to study the subjects I like and to learn about new subjects they didn't teach at Fremont. Besides, I'm sure I'll need four years to decide on my career.

College will help me meet new friends and to learn about different cultures from international students I also hope to learn about different parts of the country by talking to other kids.

Score 2

STRONG POINTS:
- Discusses advantages and disadvantages of each option
- States a position clearly

There are pros and cons to continuing education or working after going to high school.

There are advantages to going to college. A college education prepares you for the future. You major in a subject that will later help you get a decent job. Going to college gives you a chance to learn responsability and become an adult.

There are disadvantages to going to college. A college

education is very expensive you'll probably have to take out huge loans to repay later.

Some advantages to working at a job after high school are you're able to earn a salery so that you can live on your own. You learn how to cooperate and work with others. You get to learn new skills.

Some clear disadvantages to working at a job after graduation are, you have to get up and go to sleep early. Starting to work at the age of eighteen limits the kinds of jobs you can apply for.

Having a job is the most satisfying option to take after graduation.

Score 3

After graduating from Roslindale High School, the seniors will attend college or get a job. Each option has positive and negative aspects.

One positive aspect of attending college is the opportunity to learn new subjects. A college education gives high-school students a chance to discover different areas that interest them.

A college education also improves your outlook for the future. White-collar proffessions require a college degree, and these jobs will pay higher wages.

A negative aspect is that a college education is expensive. Your bills could top $15,000 a year; that's more than $60,000 for a bachelor's degree!

Another negative aspect is the competition. You have to have good SAT scores, a decent record in high school, and reccommendations from teachers.

On the other hand, there are positive aspects to choosing to work at a job after high school. First, many employers will help pay for courses or training.

Second, a job provides you with real-life experience. You'll gain skills and knowledge that you can use even if you decide to go to college.

Third, working at a job means that you'll earn a salary. If you want to, you can save the money you earn for school later on.

There are also disadvantages to working after high school. First of all, it will be harder to advance in a job without a degree. Most good jobs today require more than a high-school diploma or GED.

Another disadvantage is that job opportunities will be limited. How many employers really want an inexperienced eighteen-year old to work for them?

In considering the options of attending college or working at a job after graduation from Roslindale High School, I feel that continuing my education is the best choice. With scholarships and loans available to me, I can afford a state university.

Score 4

STRONG POINTS:

- Includes strong introduction and conclusion
- Fully presents advantages and disadvantages of both options
- Gives facts, reasons, and statistics to support reasons
- Uses effective language and expression
- Uses a variety of transitions
- Uses sentence variety and a lively voice
- Relatively free of errors

In June our class at Marymount High School will celebrate the end of high school. Some of us will choose to continue our education, and others will choose to work. Either option has advantages and disadvantages.

One merit of attending college is that an education is insurance for the future. Not only do college students learn about different subjects, but they practice discipline. In addition, a college degree is the key to better-paying jobs with more responsibility.

Another bonus is that students delay making decisions about their future until they've explored different options. At college, a student's career interests continue to develop. Further, headhunters visit colleges to recruit seniors, giving students an excellent chance at landing a good job.

Attending college after high school does have drawbacks for some students. Most obviously, an education is a huge financial investment. Costs at a four-year private college are very high, and even a neighboring state university can be expensive.

Also, many students have difficulty choosing the right college, and high-school guidance counselors sometimes fail to give students realistic or helpful advice.

On the other hand, a job has some positive points. A high-school graduate can immediately begin to gain work experience and maturity. For example, if I were to accept a position as office manager, I would use a computer, purchase supplies, and learn new skills.

Another merit of working at a job is that it does not limit your opportunities for education at a later point, but may provide the necessary motivation. When students are ready or have saved money, they can always decide to continue their education. In fact, many employees at corporations are encouraged to take courses; some employers will help pay for training, conferences, seminars, and courses.

Students who work right after high school do face some obstacles, however. A worker with a high-school education will have limited employment opportunities.

After considering both the pros and cons of attending college or working after graduating, I favor continuing my education. My chances for a good job will increase considerably with a college degree.

Continuing Assignment | **Evaluate Your Comparison/Contrast Essay**

Work with a group of four or more classmates. Using the essays that you proofread for the continuing Assignment on page 778, exchange papers and score one another's essays. Try to explain to each student how he or she could raise the score.

Identifying Common Essay Techniques

Here are three essays illustrating some of the techniques that help you to produce good essays. As you'll see, these writers carefully considered their purposes, their audiences, and their own roles as writers as they wrote multiparagraph expository and persuasive essays. Their use of the writing process, especially their attention to revising and proofreading, resulted in strong, effective writing. Reading these essays and their annotations will alert you to the characteristics of good writing and will help you to produce it in your own essays and recognize it in the essays written by your friends and classmates.

Expository Writing That Describes

In this college admissions essay, the writer describes her greatest fear. Notice how she points out both the rational and irrational aspects of her fear, and how she uses humor to lighten a topic that might otherwise be chilling to some readers.

Living with Ophidiophobia

- The writer uses an ironical tone to open.

- Here, the irony continues as the writer admits the irrational nature of her fear.

- This paragraph elaborates on the writer's phobia.

My single greatest fear in life isn't being hit by a speeding train, getting a rare disease, or finding and losing a personal fortune. My fear is much simpler and more primitive — I am utterly afraid of snakes.

As I grew up in an urban area, my fear might well be regarded as quite irrational. Certainly there are few, if any, snakes to be found slithering along sidewalks or sunning themselves on the pavement. It is unlikely that I will ever encounter a slimy snake in a department store or office skyscraper; nevertheless, I still fear snakes.

This fear is seemingly easy to dismiss or conquer: I can attend an urban college and live in a city forever. Still, the fear grips me when I take a walk in the woods, visit a zoo, read a story about a snake, babysit for a child who plays with plastic toy snakes, or find myself watching a movie or television show that features snakes.

The roots of my deep fear can be traced to my first encounter with a snake when I visited some country cousins at the age of five. We were walking along a scenic path that wound around a pond. A large, long black snake that looked like a fat shoelace was calmly curled on a small pile of rocks in the sun. My cousins and I screamed all the way back home.

Another memorable incident occurred when I spent a week with my grandparents in Florida when I was twelve. As I prepared to dash into the inviting warm waters of the Gulf of Mexico, I screeched to a halt. Dozens of dead and dying eels writhed along the shore. To this day, I will only swim in a small, clear, chlorinated pool.

My most recent brush with a snake took place in southern California. Although I didn't actually see a single snake the whole time, our tour guide informed us that this was "rattler country" as we trudged up a rugged mountain path. He swung a huge pronged tool to "move the snakes out of the way." I practically tiptoed the whole way up and down the mountain so that I would be sure to hear that faint warning rattle like the rustle of leaves in a tree.

I definitely do not subscribe to the belief that "snakes are more afraid of you than you are of them." I also don't care if snakes are not slimy to the touch. I'm not going to touch one! If snakes are so wonderful, then why are they locked in cages in the reptile houses of zoos? Why do hikers in mountains or deserts carry snakebite kits and wear thick boots?

Although harmless snakes outnumber poisonous ones in the United States, I still won't take chances. Statistics don't matter if you trip on a copperhead or startle a Mojave rattlesnake. On the bright side, many snakebites merely cause paralysis, blindness, or tissue damage. As long as you don't live in Asia, Australia, or Africa, you probably won't die from a snakebite. Perhaps my snake phobia can be viewed in a positive light. I already know that in the future, after college, I will move to Ireland — a snakeless island.

Expository Writing That Narrates

The writer of the following essay explains to younger students how to apply for a part-time job. Notice how the writer uses a brief narrative to illustrate what can go wrong when a young job applicant isn't systematic about the application process.

Hunting for a Job

Would you like to earn extra spending money? Could you profit by some work experience? Do you need to acquire new skills? Perhaps you should consider taking a part-time job after school or during the school vacations. Before you rush out to knock on doors, however, prepare yourself to go about job-hunting systematically. I learned this lesson the hard way the first summer I tried to get a job.

I started my job hunt by going to places where my friends worked. In most of these places, I waited around just to find out that the positions were all filled. I only filled out one job application in a whole week of wandering around town. I never heard from the manager of that store, and later I realized that I would have hated working there anyway. I had given no consideration to what I might like to do or what I might be good at. After that, I looked in the newspaper, but most of the jobs I might qualify for wanted a résumé, and I didn't have one, so I didn't call or try for an interview. The whole summer went by before I finally realized what I had to do. You may profit by my experience!

First, determine your interests and skills. Do you like to work outdoors? Are you good at gardening chores or painting fences or houses? Would you prefer indoor work such as in an office or restaurant? Would you like to learn about catering, landscaping, or some other local business? Have you ever had a job that you enjoyed? Try to find a job in your community that would be suited to your abilities and interests.

After you have determined your interests and the skills that you already have, look for a job listing in the classified section of your local newspaper. Help-wanted advertisements describe the salary, hours, duties, and experience required for a particular job. Also, call local businesses to find out whether they need part-time help, or ask your school guidance counselor, friends, or family about employers who want to hire hardworking teens. You might also check to see if your community has a bulletin board where job openings are posted.

Next, put together a résumé if you don't have one already. Use a library reference or a textbook model to guide you. List your name, address, and telephone number; the position you want; your previous work experience; your education; special skills and interests; and personal references — people who are able to evaluate your strengths and weaknesses.

- This paragraph elaborates on the actual application procedure.

- In this paragraph, the writer points out the appropriate dress and response in an interview.

- This paragraph completes the detailed instructions.

- The conclusion restates the importance of the preceding steps.

Now apply for several jobs that interest you. You might contact employers by either letter or telephone to request an interview. When you apply for a job, you will write a letter of application to identify the job you want, your qualifications for the job, your interest in having an interview, and the telephone number where you can be reached. Send your résumé with your letter of application.

Once you've secured an interview for a job, you are halfway there. Dress neatly and appropriately for the interview, and answer all the prospective employers' questions politely and thoroughly. For example, don't say "I dunno" and shrug your shoulders if you aren't sure of an answer. Would you hire someone who appeared bored or stupid? Remember that you want to make a good impression and to show that you are the best person for this job.

During the job interview, you may be asked to fill out an application. Read the application form carefully, and give accurate, complete information. Write your answers neatly. After your interview, write a brief thank-you note to restate your interest in the job and to thank the interviewer for his or her time.

If you follow all these job-hunting tips, you should be able to find a part-time job that both interests you and gives you solid experience that you can draw from in the future. What's more, it shouldn't take you two months to find something! Good luck on your road to success!

Persuasive Writing That Describes

In this letter to a local business owner, the writer describes the benefits of supporting the high school yearbook. Notice how the writer begins with the most convincing reason — the advertising advantage to the businessman — and then proceeds to other motivating factors such as good customer relations and community pride.

Dear Mr. Bowman:

- The writer begins by stating her purpose.

- The writer states the most obvious benefit to the owner.

I am writing to ask you to place an advertisement in the Lewiston High School yearbook. Because you are a respected member of the local business community who supports many worthwhile causes, I am certain that you will appreciate the benefits of contributing to the yearbook.

One important reason to place an advertisement in our yearbook is to publicize your business. Nostalgia Nook is a great place to find old baseball cards and other sports memorabilia. Why not make sure that students and faculty know about your store? Your ad in the yearbook would reach many graduating students and their friends and relatives. As a matter of fact, last year's yearbook sales totaled more than 3500 copies; this year, we project sales of nearly 4000 copies.

- This paragraph contains the writer's second reason and elaborates on it with convincing details.

A second reason to support the yearbook is to acknowledge the good relationship between your store and Lewiston High School students. In the past, students have enjoyed shopping in Nostalgia Nook and buying cards and other memorabilia for their own collections as well as for those of friends and family members. Placing an advertisement in the yearbook to congratulate graduating seniors on their accomplishment is an excellent way to say "thank you" to some of your most loyal customers. In addition, an ad might help encourage new customers to come to your store and keep your current customers coming back in the future.

- An appeal to the owner's understanding of economic necessity.

A third reason for you to place an ad is that the yearbook especially needs your help now. Unfortunately, printing costs jumped by thirteen percent this year. According to Al Rosen of Rosen Printers, the cost of paper and ink has risen dramatically. If the staff doesn't sell an additional four pages of advertisements, then Lewiston High School might not have a yearbook at all.

- The writer continues with an appeal to community spirit.

You might also regard helping us as a way of joining with other business owners to show community spirit. In fact, the owners of businesses on your block — Krunchy Kones, Helen's Curtains, and Copies-While-U-Wait — have all pledged to place advertisements in the yearbook.

- Here the writer appeals to the business owner's good financial sense.

You may be pleasantly surprised at how little a yearbook advertisement costs, especially when compared with other types of advertising. A newspaper ad in the *Lewiston Ledger*, for example, runs more *per day, per column inch* than an average ad in our yearbook. If you call any local radio station for the price of one minute of air time (especially during peak hours), you'll find that it exceeds even the cost of newspaper advertising. Your Nostalgia Nook yearbook ad appears in a publication that nearly every student in Lewiston High School will see.

- To conclude, the writer encloses the necessary forms.

Placing an advertisment in our yearbook is a small expense for a successful business like Nostalgia Nook, but your support will go a long way toward helping us record precious memories of our high school years. I am enclosing a form and instructions for you to prepare your advertisement so that it is camera-ready. I urge you to submit your advertisment to the Lewiston High School yearbook staff as soon as possible.

Dictionary Plus

Analogies

An **analogy** is a correspondence, or similarity, between two things that are otherwise dissimilar. Analogy tests ask to you find the similarity between sets of otherwise dissimilar word pairs. You will be given a pair of words and will be asked to select another pair of words that has the same relationship. A sample test item follows.

Reference Point:
pages 451-453

NEGLIGENCE : ACCIDENT :: (A) supervision : oversight (B) grievance : complaint (C) fatigue : exertion (D) climate : humidity (E) gossip : innuendo

▶ ## Strategies

1. *Read the analogy, substituting "is to" for the single colon and "as" for the double colon.* "Negligence is to accident as what is to what?"
2. *Determine the relationship between the words in the given pair.* Negligence can lead to accidents; therefore, the relationship of the two words is one of cause and effect. Following are examples of this and other common relationships.

Relationship	Example
word/synonym	sagacious : astute
word/antonym	gauche : poised
class/member of class	reptile : lizard
member of same class	rattlesnake : copperhead
size	pebble : boulder
part/whole	brim : hat
cause/effect	negligence : accident
time sequence	primary : secondary
tool/user	rolling pin : baker
object/action	microscope : magnify
object/purpose	seat belt : safety
person or thing/characteristic	hurricane : windy
degree	intelligent : brilliant
object/material	tire : rubber
worker/creation	chef : soufflé
worker/workplace or field	Plato : philosophy
word/derived form	image : imagine

3. *Check for grammatical relationships.* If the capitalized words are a noun-adjective pair, then the answer must be a noun-adjective pair. Be careful not to eliminate a choice because one of its words can be more than one part of speech. In the example, *fatigue* in choice C and *gossip* in choice E can be either verbs or nouns; therefore, no choice can be eliminated.

4. *Eliminate the word pairs that have different relationships.* Choices A, D, and E can be eliminated. Choices D and E express thing/characteristic relationships. Choice A expresses the relationship of word/synonym.

5. *Try each remaining pair of words to see if it has the same relationship.* Choices B and C express cause/effect relationships. In choice C, however, the effect *(fatigue)* is listed before the cause *(exertion)*. Since the word pair you are trying to match lists cause first, choice B, *grievance: complaint,* is the correct answer. Watch for choices that express the desired relationship in reverse, and be sure to choose the answer that expresses the relationship in the correct order.

6. *Select the word pair that most closely duplicates the relationship.* No word pair in the example more closely duplicates the relationship than choice B does.

Reference Point: pages 436-442

Creating Your Own Analogies   Creating your own analogies can sharpen your writing and thinking skills, especially those involving comparison and contrast and determining relationships. Use strategies 2 and 3 to write your analogies and strategy 1 to check them. The Assignment that follows is a first step toward creating your own analogies.

Assignment 1 Analogies

Complete the following analogies.

1. CRANKY : BELLICOSE :: pop : __?__
2. PROFICIENT : ADEPT :: revenge : __?__
3. ROCK : ENDURING :: mayfly : __?__
4. IMPLICIT : EXPLICIT :: rebuke : __?__
5. VIRUS : ILLNESS :: gluttony : __?__

Using a Thesaurus

Reference Point: pages 483-484

A **thesaurus** is a book of synonyms. It may be organized alphabetically, like a dictionary, or it may use another organizing scheme.

One kind of thesaurus lists groups of synonyms under very general categories, such as "Silence" or "Sound." Since the categories and the words within them are not alphabetically arranged, this kind of thesaurus provides a complete index to guide the user to the appropriate group of synonyms.

The following excerpts from *Roget's International Thesaurus* show the wealth of material from which you can choose. The left-hand column shows an excerpt taken from the text of the thesaurus. The right-hand column shows an excerpt from the index of the thesaurus.

EXCERPT FROM TEXT

451.9 muffle, mute, dule, soften, deaden, cushion, baffle, damp, **dampen,** deafen; subdue, stop, tone down, **soft-pedal,** put on the soft pedal.

EXCERPT FROM INDEX

n. nose 256.7
  silencer 451.4

v. cover 228.19
  hush up 614.8
  mute 451.9
  silence 451.8

The excerpt from the text of the thesaurus shows only one group of synonyms for the verb *muffle*. The list from the index (on the right) shows that there are four synonym groups for the verb as well as two for the noun.

Other thesauruses arrange groups of synonyms under a main word similar to the entry word in a dictionary. The main words are listed alphabetically. Sometimes each synonym of the main word is also included in the alphabetical list. For the synonyms the information given is only a cross-reference to the main entry.

muffle   *verb*
1. To decrease or dull the sound of: *The trumpeter muffled his horn to give a blues quality to his playing.*

2. To hold (something requiring an outlet) in check.

1. **Syns:** dampen, deaden, mute, stifle.
   Near-ants: amplify, enhance, heighten, increase, magnify, reinforce, strengthen.

2. REPRESS.

Some thesauruses give definitions for each synonym group, but some do not. To choose a word that is best for your purpose, you must carefully consider the shades of meaning and the different connotations of each word. If you are not sure of the differences in meaning or usage among the synonyms, consult a dictionary.

Assignment 2 Using a Thesaurus

Look up each of the following words in a thesaurus. Then write a sentence using a more specific or vivid word that you find under that entry.

1. little   3. dark   5. guide   7. run   9. give
2. big   4. fair   6. neat   8. rest   10. push

Words with Multiple Meanings

Dad usually writes a *check* to pay for our groceries when we do our week's shopping.

The batter tried to *check* his swing, but he couldn't stop it in time.

"*Check!*" yelled Charelle. "I'm attacking your king, and you'll never figure out how to get him away!"

Skating quickly, Mick almost evaded Yuri, but Yuri *checked* him into the boards and gained control of the puck.

Reference Point: *pages 476-477*

Each of the sentences above uses the word *check* in a different way. In the first sentence, *check* is a noun meaning "a written order to a bank to pay the amount specified from funds on deposit." In the second sentence, it is a transitive verb meaning "to arrest the motion of abruptly." In the third it is an interjection indicating to a chess opponent that his or her king is in grave danger, and in the fourth it is a transitive verb meaning "to impede an opponent in control of the puck in ice hockey, either by using the body to block the opponent or by jabbing at the puck with the hockey stick." Altogether, *check* has fourteen meanings as a noun, two as an interjection, ten as a transitive verb, and eight as an intransitive verb. It also has other meanings as the phrasal verbs *check in* and *check out* and as the idiom *in check*. The clue to the meaning of *check* in each sentence is, of course, the word's context, or the passage in which the word appears. The following strategies suggest ways in which you can explore context for meaning.

▶ **Strategies**

1. *Use the general sense of the passage along with your own knowledge and experience to infer a meaning.* Experience probably tells you, for example, that Dad writes a bank draft rather than, say, a bill at a restaurant to pay for groceries.

2. *Look for synonyms or restated definitions of the unfamiliar word.* In the second example above, *stop* is a synonym for *check*.

3. *Look for examples in the passage that may further explain or describe the unfamiliar word.* In the third sentence, "I'm attacking your king" explains the interjection *check*.

4. *Notice whether the unfamiliar word is compared or contrasted with a familiar word or idea.* If so, use that known idea to help you to infer a meaning. In the fourth example above, *check* is contrasted with *evade*.

Assignment 3 | **Multiple-Meaning Words**

Reference Point: *pages 481-483*

Each of the words that follow has multiple meanings. Write at least three sentences for each word, illustrating a separate meaning in each sentence. Use a dictionary if you wish.

1. see   **3.** benefit   **5.** hand

2. close   **4.** duck   **6.** game

Dictionary

Pronunciation Key

Spelling	Symbol	Spelling	Symbol	Spelling	Symbol
pat	ă	judge	j	sauce	s
pay	ā	kick, cat	k	ship, dish	sh
care	âr	pique		tight, stopped	t
father	ä	lid, needle	l (nēd′l)	thin	th
bib	b	mum	m	this	*th*
church	ch	no, sudden	n (sŭd′n)	cut	cŭ
deed, milled	d	thing	ng	urge, term, firm	ûr
pet	č	pot, horrid	ŏ	word, heard	
bee	ē	toe, hoarse	ō	valve	v
fife, phase, rough	f	caught, paw, for	ô	with	w
				yes	y
gag	g	noise	oi	zebra, xylem	z
hat	h	took	o͞o	vision, pleasure, garage	zh
which	hw	boot	o͞o		
pit	ĭ	out	ou	about, item, edible gallop, circus	ə
pie, by	ī	pop	p		
pier	îr	roar	r	butter	ər

Example primary stress   secondary stress

dī′ə-lôg′

Abbreviation Key

Term	Label	Term	Label	Term	Label
adjective	*adj.*	interjection	*interj.*	pronoun	*pron.*
adverb	*adv.*	noun	*n.*	verb	*v.*
conjunction	*conj.*	preposition	*prep.*		

accede (ăk-sēd′) *intr. v.* **1.** To give one's assent. **2.** To arrive at or come into an office or dignity. **3.** To become a party to an agreement or treaty. *(491)*

accordant (ə-kôr′dnt) *adj.* In agreement or harmony; consonant. *(119)*

acuity (ə-kyo͞o′ĭ-tē) *n.* Acuteness of perception; keenness. *(617)*

adamant (ăd′ə-mənt, -mănt′) *n.* **1.** A legendary stone believed to be impenetrable. **2.** An extremely hard substance. — *adj.* Firm in purpose or opinion; unyielding. *(266)*

admonition (ăd′mə-nĭsh′ən) *n.* **1.** Mild or kind reproof. **2.** Cautionary advice or warning. *(118)*

adroit (ə-droit′) *adj.* **1.** Dexterous; deft. **2.** Skillful and adept under pressing conditions. *(617)*

aesthetic (ĕs-thĕt′ĭk) *adj.* **1.** Of or pertaining to the criticism of taste. **2. a.** Of or pertaining to the sense of the beautiful. **2. b.** Artistic. **3. a.** Having a love of beauty. **3. b.** *Informal.* In accordance with accepted notions of good taste. *(492)*

agapanthus (ăg′ə-păn′thəs) *n.* Any plant of the genus *Agapanthus*, which includes the African lily. *(133)*

amiable (ā′mē-ə-bəl) *adj.* **1.** Having a pleasant disposition; good-natured. **2.** Cordial; sociable; congenial. *(326)*

amicable (ăm′ĭ-kə-bəl) *adj.* Characterized by or showing friendliness; friendly. *(478)*

amorous (ăm′ər-əs) *adj.* **1.** Strongly attracted to love, especially sexual love. **2.** Indicative of love or sexual desire. **3.** Of or associated with love. **4.** In love; enamored. *(478)*

amorphous (ə-môr′fəs) *adj.* **1.** Without definite form; shapeless. **2.** Of no particular type; anomalous. **3.** Lacking organization; formless. **4.** Lacking distinct crystalline structure. *(478)*

anaerobe (ăn′ə-rōb′, ăn-âr′ōb′) *n.* A microorganism, as a bacterium, able to live in the absence of free oxygen. *(447)*

anthropomorphism (ăn′thrə-pə-môr′fĭz′əm) *n.* The attribution of human motivation, characteristics, or behavior to inanimate objects, animals, or natural phenomena. *(161)*

apocalyptic (ə-pŏk′ə-lĭp′tĭk) *adj.* Of or pertaining to a prophetic disclosure or revelation. *(451)*

appease (ə-pēz′) *tr. v.* **1.** To calm or pacify, especially by giving what is demanded; placate. **2.** To satisfy or relieve. *(42)*

appeasement (ə-pēz′mənt) *n.* **1. a.** The act of appeasing. **1. b.** The condition of being appeased. **2.** The policy of granting concessions to potential enemies to maintain peace. *(42)*

arbitrary (är′bĭ-trĕr′ē) *adj.* **1.** Determined by whim or impulse, not by reason or law. **2.** Based on or subject to individual judgment or discretion. **3.** Established by a court or judge rather than by a specific law or statute. **4.** Not limited by law; despotic. *(G3)*

arcane (är-kān′) *adj.* Known or understood only by a few; esoteric. *(485)*

archangel (ärk′ān′jəl) *n. Theology.* **1.** A celestial being next in rank above an angel. **2. archangels**. The eighth of the nine orders of angels. *(69)*

Argus (är′gəs) *n.* **1.** *Greek Myth.* A giant with a hundred eyes who was made guardian of Io and later slain by Hermes. **2.** An alert or watchful person; guardian. *(155)*

artificial intelligence *n.* **1. a.** The characteristics of a machine programmed to imitate human intelligence functions. **1. b.** Research in methods of such programming. **2.** Research in methods of programming designed to supplement human intellectual abilities. *(391)*

arum (ăr′əm, âr′-) *n.* **1.** Any of various plants of the genus *Arum*, having arrow-shaped leaves and small flowers on a spadix surrounded by or enclosed within a spathe. **2.** Also **arum lily**. Any of several plants related to the arum, such as the calla. *(133)*

ascertain (ăs′ər-tān′) *tr. v.* **1.** To discover through examination or experimentation. **2.** *Archaic.* To make certain and definite. *(698)*

ascetic (ə-sĕt′ĭk) *n.* A person who renounces the comforts of society and leads a life of austere self-discipline, especially as an act of religious devotion. — *adj.* Pertaining to or characteristic of an ascetic; self-denying; austere. *(119, 492)*

assail (ə-sāl′) *tr. v.* **1.** To attack with or as if with violent blows; assault. **2.** To attack verbally, as with ridicule or censure. *(F3)*

astrolabe (ăs′trə-lāb′) *n.* A medieval instrument used to determine the altitude of the sun or other celestial bodies. *(561)*

audacious (ô-dā′shəs) *adj.* **1.** Fearlessly daring; bold. **2.** Unrestrained by convention or propriety; insolent. *(453)*

autonomy (ô-tăn′ə-mē) *n.* **1.** The condition or quality of being self-governing. **2.** Self-government or the right of self-government; self-determination; independence. **3.** A self-governing state, community, or group. *(61)*

baroque (bə-rōk′) *adj.* **1.** Of, pertaining to, or characteristic of a style in art and architecture developed in Europe from about 1550 to 1700 and typified by elaborate and ornate scrolls, curves, and other symmetrical ornamentation. **2.** Of, pertaining to, or characteristic of a style of musical composition that flourished in Europe from about 1600 to 1750, marked by chromaticism, strict forms, and elaborate ornamentation. **3.** Ornate or flamboyant in style; richly ornamented. **4.** Irregular in shape. — *n.* The baroque style or period in art, architecture, or music. *(574)*

basilica (bə-sĭl′ĭ-kə) *n.* **1. a.** An oblong building of ancient Rome with a semicircular apse at one end, used as a court or place of assembly. **1. b.** A building of this design used as a Christian church. **2.** *Roman Catholic Church.* A church or cathedral accorded certain ceremonial rights by the pope. *(566)*

bilk (bĭlk) *tr. v.* **1.** To defraud, cheat, or swindle. **2.** To evade payment of. **3.** To thwart or frustrate. **4.** To elude. — *n.* **1.** One who cheats. **2.** A hoax or swindle. *(485)*

binary (bī′nə-rē) *adj.* **1.** Characterized by or composed of two different parts or components; twofold. **2.** Of or based on the number 2 or the binary numeration system. **3.** *Chemistry.* Consisting of or containing only molecules consisting of two kinds of atoms. **4.** Having two music sections or subjects. — *n.* Something that is binary, especially a binary star. *(479)*

binomial (bī-nō′mē-əl) *adj.* Consisting of or pertaining to two names or terms. — *n.* **1.** *Mathematics.* An expression consisting of two terms connected by a plus or minus sign. **2.** *Biology.* A taxonomic name in binomial nomenclature. *(478)*

biomedicine (bī′ō-mĕd′ĭ-sĭn) *n.* **1.** The branch of medical science dealing with the ability of humans to survive in and functionally cope with abnormally stressful environments and with the medical concerns of protectively modifying those environments. **2.** The study of medicine as it relates to all biological systems. *(373)*

bionic (bī-ăn′ĭk) *adj.* **1.** Consisting of or enhanced by or as if by electronic or mechanical devices or components. **2.** Of or relating to bionics. *(393)*

black hole *n.* A small celestial body with an intense gravitational field that is believed to be a collapsed star. *(387)*

blatant (blāt′nt) *adj.* **1.** Unpleasantly and often vulgarly loud and noisy. **2.** Completely and often offensively conspicuous; obvious. *(44)*

blithe (blīth, blīth) *adj.* **1.** Filled with gaiety; cheerful. **2.** Casual; carefree. *(489)*

bracken (brăk′ən) *n.* **1.** A fern, *Pteridium aquilinum*, having tough stems and branching, finely divided fronds. **2.** An area overgrown with bracken. **3.** A large, coarse fern. *(133)*

cadaverous (kə-dăv′ər-əs) *adj.* **1.** Suggestive of death; corpselike. **2. a.** Of corpselike pallor; pallid. **2. b.** Emaciated; gaunt. *(155)*

calibrate (kăl′ə-brāt′) *tr. v.* **1.** To check, adjust, or systematically standardize the graduations of a quantitative measuring instrument. **2.** To determine the caliber of (a tube). *(200)*

caravel *also* **caravelle** (kăr′ə-vĕl′) *n.* A small, light sailing ship of the kind used by the Spanish and Portuguese in the 15th and 16th centuries. *(532)*

carrel *also* **carrell** (kăr′əl) *n.* A nook near the stacks in a library, used for private study. *(247)*

celebrant (sĕl′ə-brənt) *n.* **1.** The priest officiating at the celebration of the Eucharist. **2.** A participant in a celebration. *(J2)*

celluloid (sĕl′yə-loid′) *n.* A colorless, flammable material made from nitrocellulose and camphor. *(658)*

centaur (sĕn′tôr′) *n. Greek Mythology.* One of a race of monsters having the head, arms, and trunk of a man and the body and legs of a horse. *(453)*

cerement (sĕr′ə-mənt, sîr′mənt) *n.* Cerecloth (cloth coated with wax, formerly used for wrapping the dead). *(319)*

chic (shēk) *adj.* **1.** Sophisticated; stylish. **2.** Dressed smartly and fashionably; modish. — *n.* **1.** Sophistication in dress and manner; elegance. **2.** Stylishness; fashionableness. *(687)*

chide (chīd) *tr. v.* **1.** To state one's disapproval to so as to correct or improve; scold; reprimand. **2.** To goad; impel. — *intr. v.* To express disapproval. *(336)*

circumstantial (sûr′kəm-stăn′shəl) *adj.* **1.** Of, pertaining to, or dependent upon circumstances. **2.** Of no primary significance; incidental. **3.** Complete and particular; full of detail. *(191)*

cistern (sĭs′tərn) *n.* A receptacle for holding water or other liquid, especially a tank for catching and storing rainwater. *(597)*

clandestine (klăn-dĕs′tĭn) *adj.* Concealed or kept secret, often for an illicit purpose. *(449)*

cockscomb (kŏks′kōm′) *n.* **1.** The comb of a rooster. **2.** The cap of a jester, decorated to resemble the comb of a rooster. **3.** Any of several plants of the genus *Celosia*, especially *C. argentea cristata*, having a showy crested or rolled flower cluster. **4.** Also **coxcomb.** A pretentious fop. *(367)*

collusion (kə-lōō′zhən) *n.* A secret agreement between two or more persons for a deceitful or fraudulent purpose. *(485)*

commensalism (kə-měn′sə-lĭz′əm) *n. Biology.* A relationship in which two or more organisms live in close association and in which one may derive some benefit but in which neither harms or is parasitic on the other. *(104)*

composite (kəm-pŏz′ĭt) *adj.* Made up of distinct components; compound. — *n.* **1.** A composite structure or entity. **2.** A complex material, such as wood or fiber glass, in which two or more distinct, structurally complementary substances, especially metals, ceramics, glasses, and polymers, combine to produce structural or functional properties not present in any individual component. **3.** A composite plant. *(J3)*

conductivity (kŏn′dŭk-tĭv′ĭ-tē) *n.* **1.** The ability or power to conduct or transmit. **2.** A measure of the ability of a material to conduct an electric charge, the reciprocal of resistivity. *(443)*

confront (kən-frŭnt′) *tr. v.* **1.** To come face to face with, especially with defiance or hostility. **2.** To bring face to face. **3.** To come up against; encounter. *(D4)*

congruity (kən-grōō′ĭ-tē, kŏn-) *n.* **1.** The quality or fact of being congruous (correspondent in character or kind; appropriate; harmonious). **2.** The quality or fact of being congruent (coinciding exactly when superimposed). **3.** A point of agreement. *(118)*

conjure (kŏn′jər, kən-jŏŏr′) *tr. v.* **1.** To call upon or entreat solemnly, especially by an oath. **2. a.** To summon (a spirit) by oath, incantation, or spell. **2. b.** To cause or effect by or as if by magic. **2. c.** To call to mind; evoke. — *intr. v.* **1.** To practice magic, especially legerdemain. **2.** *Obsolete.* To conspire. *(J2)*

constituent (kən-stĭch′ōō-ənt) *adj.* **1.** Serving as part of a whole; component. **2.** Empowered to elect or designate. **3.** Authorized to make or amend a constitution — *n.* **1.** Someone who authorizes another to represent him; client. **2.** A member of a group represented by an elected official. **3.** A constituent part; component. *(242)*

contrite (kən-trīt′, kŏn′trīt′) *adj.* **1.** Repentant for one's sins or inadequacies; penitent. **2.** Arising from contrition. *(489)*

convolute (kŏn′və-lōōt′) *adj.* Rolled or folded together with one part over another; coiled; twisted. — *intr. v. & tr. v.* To coil; twist. *(306)*

cornice (kôr′nĭs) *n.* **1.** *Architecture.* **1. a.** A horizontal molded projection that crowns or completes a building or wall. **1. b.** The uppermost part of an entablature. **2.** The molding at the top of the walls of a room, between the walls and ceiling. **3.** An ornamental horizontal molding or frame used to conceal rods, picture hooks, or other devices. — *tr. v.* To supply, decorate, or finish with or as if with a cornice. *(612)*

coxcomb (kŏks′kōm′) *n.* **1.** A conceited dandy; fop. **2.** *Obsolete.* A cap resembling a cockscomb, worn by a professional jester. **3.** **cockscomb** (sense 4) *(367)*

crescendo (krə-shĕn′dō) *n.* **1.** A gradual increase, especially in the volume or intensity of sound in a musical passage. **2.** A musical passage played in a crescendo. — *adj.* Gradually increasing in volume or intensity. — *adv.* With a crescendo. *(490)*

culminate (kŭl′mə-nāt′) *intr. v.* **1.** To reach the highest point or degree; climax. **2.** *Astronomy.* To reach the highest point above an observer's horizon. Used of stars and other celestial bodies. *(J2)*

cylindrical (sə-lĭn′drĭ-kəl) **cylindric** (-drĭk) *adj.* **1.** Having the shape of a cylinder, especially of a circular cylinder. **2.** Of or pertaining to a cylinder. *(200)*

decathlon (dĭ-kăth′lən, -lŏn′) *n.* An athletic contest in which each contestant participates in ten different track and field events. *(619)*

deciduous (dĭ-sĭj′ōō-əs) *adj.* **1.** Falling off or shed at a specific season or stage of growth. **2.** Shedding or losing foliage at the end of the growing season. **3.** Not lasting; temporary. *(141)*

deficit (dĕf′ĭ-sĭt) *n.* The amount by which something, as a sum of money, falls short of the required or expected amount; shortage. *(202)*

deplore (dĭ-plôr′, -plōr′) *tr. v.* **1.** To feel or express sorrow over. **2.** To feel or express regret about. **3.** To feel or express strong disapproval of; censure. *(485)*

derange (dĭ-rānj′) *tr. v.* **1.** To disturb the order or arrangement of. **2.** To disturb the normal condition or functioning of. **3.** To make insane. *(374)*

deride (dĭ-rīd′) *tr. v.* To speak of or treat with contemptuous mirth. *(329)*

deviate (dē′vē-āt′) *intr. v.* To turn or move increasingly away from a specified course or prescribed mode of behavior. — *tr. v.* To cause to turn aside or differ. — *n.*(–ĭt). A deviant. *(710)*

dialect (dī′ə-lĕkt′) *n.* **1. a.** A regional variety of a language distinguished by pronunciation, grammar, or vocabulary, especially a variety of speech differing from the standard literary language or speech pattern of the culture in which it exists. **1. b.** A variety of language that with other varieties constitutes a single language of which no single variety is standard. **2.** The language peculiar to an occupational group or a particular social class. **3.** The manner or style of expressing oneself in language or the arts. **4.** A language considered as part of a larger family of languages or a linguistic branch. *(698)*

disavow (dĭs′ə-vou′) *tr. v.* To disclaim knowledge of, responsibility for, or association with. *(I3)*

disparage (dĭ-spăr′ĭj) *tr. v.* **1.** To speak of as unimportant or small; belittle. **2.** To reduce in esteem or rank. *(490)*

dissemble (dĭ-sĕm′bəl) *tr. v.* **1.** To disguise or conceal behind a false appearance or semblance. **2.** To make a false show of; feign. — *intr. v.* To conceal one's real motives, nature, or feelings under a pretense. *(H2)*

doge (dōj) *n.* The elected chief magistrate of the former republics of Venice and Genoa. *(532)*

dour (do͞or, dour) *adj.* **1.** Marked by intractable sternness or harshness; forbidding. **2.** Silently ill-humored; gloomy. **3.** Sternly obstinate; unyielding. *(481)*

draft (drăft, dräft) **draught** *Chiefly British* (dräft) *n.* **1. a.** A current of air in an enclosed area. **1. b.** A device in a flue controlling the circulation of air. **2. a.** A pull or traction of a load. **2. b.** Something that is pulled or drawn. **2. c.** A team of animals used to pull or draw a load. **3. a.** A gulp, swallow, or inhalation.

3. b. The amount taken in by a single act of drinking or inhaling. **3. c.** A measured portion; dose. *(157)*

dreadnought (drĕd′nôt′) *n.* A heavily armed battleship. *(131)*

ecosystem (ĕk′ə-sĭs′təm, ē′kə-) *n.* An ecological community together with its physical environment, considered as a unit. *(394)*

edict (ē′dĭkt′) *n.* **1.** A decree or proclamation issued by an authority and having the force of law. **2.** A formal proclamation, command, or decree. *(485)*

eider (ī′dər) *n.* Any of several sea ducks of the genus *Somateria* and related genera, of northern regions, having soft, commercially valuable down and predominantly black and white plumage in the males. *(493)*

electromagnetism (ĭ-lĕk′trō-măg′nə-tĭz′əm) *n.* **1.** Magnetism arising from electric charge in motion. **2.** The physics of electricity and magnetism. *(430)*

elucidate (ĭ-lo͞o′sĭ-dāt′) *tr. v.* To make clear or plain; clarify. — *intr. v.* To give a clarification. *(747)*

embrown (ĕm-broun′) *tr. v.* **1.** To make brown or dusky. **2.** To darken. *(117, 134)*

emulate (ĕm′yə-lāt′) *tr. v.* **1.** To strive to equal or excel, especially through imitation. **2.** To compete with or rival successfully. **3.** *Computer Science.* To imitate one system with another so that both accept the same data, execute the same programs, and achieve the same results. *(155)*

enigmatic (ĕn′ĭg-măt′ĭk) *adj.* Of or resembling an enigma; puzzling. *(J2)*

enshrine (ĕn-shrīn′) **inshrine** (ĭn-shrīn′) *tr. v.* **1.** To enclose in or as if in a shrine. **2.** To cherish as sacred. *(J3)*

entrepreneur (ŏn′trə-prə-nûr′) *n.* A person who organizes, operates, and assumes the risk for a business venture. *(233)*

epiphany (ĭ-pĭf′ə-nē) *n.* **1. Epiphany.** A Christian festival held on January 6 in celebration of the manifestation of the divine nature of Christ to the Gentiles as represented by the Magi. **2.** A revelatory manifestation of a divine being. **3. a.** A sudden manifestation of the essence or meaning of something. **3. b.** A comprehension or perception of reality by means of a sudden intuitive realization. *(348)*

epitomize (ĭ-pĭt′ə-mīz′) *tr. v.* **1.** To make an epitome (a brief summary; abstract) of; sum up. **2.** To be a typical example of. *(182)*

equable (ĕk′wə-bəl, ē′kwə-) *adj.* **1. a.** Unvarying; steady. **1. b.** Free from extremes. **2.** Not easily disturbed; serene. *(449)*

estrange (ĭ-strānj′) *tr. v.* **1.** To remove from an accustomed place or relation. **2.** To alienate the affections of; make hostile or unsympathetic. *(443)*

evocative (ĭ-vŏk′ə-tĭv) *adj.* Tending or having the power to evoke (to call to mind or memory). *(274)*

exemplify (ĭg-zĕm′plə-fī′) *tr. v.* **1. a.** To illustrate by example. **1. b.** To serve as an example of. **2.** *Law.* To make a certified copy of (a document.) *(699)*

expansionism (ĭk-spăn′shə-nĭz′əm) *n.* The practice or policy of especially territorial or economic expansion by a nation. *(439)*

facsimile (făk-sĭm′ə-lē) *n.* **1.** An exact copy or reproduction, as of a document. **2. a.** A method of transmitting images or printed matter by electronic means. **2. b.** An image so transmitted. — *adj.* **1.** Of or used to produce facsimiles. **2.** Exactly reproduced; duplicate. *(262)*

fagot *also* **faggot** (făg′ət) *n.* **1.** A bundle of twigs, sticks, or branches bound together. **2.** A bundle of pieces of iron or steel to be welded or hammered into bars. — *tr. v.* **1.** To collect or bind into a fagot; bundle. **2.** To decorate with fagoting. *(117)*

fallacy (făl′ə-sē) *n.* **1.** A false notion. **2.** A statement or argument that is based on a false or invalid inference. **3.** Incorrectness of reasoning or belief; erroneousness. **4.** The quality of being deceptive. *(165)*

feasible (fē′zə-bəl) *adj.* **1.** Capable of being accomplished or brought about; possible. **2.** Capable of being utilized or dealt with successfully; suitable. **3.** Logical; likely. *(541)*

ferrule (fĕr′əl) *n.* **1.** A metal ring or cap placed around a pole or shaft for reinforcement or to prevent splitting. **2.** A bushing used to secure a pipe joint. — *tr. v.* To furnish with a ferrule. *(227)*

feudal (fyōōd′l) *adj.* **1.** Of, pertaining to, or characteristic of feudalism (a political and economic system of Europe from the ninth to about the fifteenth century, based on the rela-

tion of lord to vassal held on condition of homage and service). **2.** Of or pertaining to lands held in fee or to the holding of such lands. *(438)*

filament (fĭl′ə-mənt) *n.* **1.** A fine or thinly spun thread, fiber, or wire. **2.** A slender, threadlike appendage, part, or structure, such as the slender stalk of a stamen on which the anther is borne or a chainlike series of cells, as in some algae. *(67)*

filibuster (fĭl′ə-bŭs′tər) *n.* **1.** The use of obstructionist tactics, especially prolonged speechmaking, for the purpose of delaying legislative action. **2.** An instance of the use of obstructionist tactics. **3.** An adventurer who engages in a private military action in a foreign country. — *intr. v.* **1.** To use obstructionist tactics in a legislative body. **2.** To engage in a private military action in a foreign country. — *tr. v.* To use obstructionist tactics against (a measure, for example). *(241)*

finite (fī′nīt′) *adj.* **1. a.** Having bounds; limited. **1. b.** Existing, persisting, or enduring for a limited time only; impermanent. **2.** Being neither infinite nor infinitesimal. *(485)*

flagrant (flā′grənt) *adj.* **1.** Extremely or deliberately conspicuous; shocking. **2.** *Obsolete.* Flaming; blazing. *(449)*

florid (flôr′ĭd, flŏr′-) *adj.* **1.** Flushed with rosy color; ruddy. **2.** Heavily decorated or embellished; ornate. **3.** *Archaic.* Healthy; blooming. **4.** *Obsolete.* Abounding in or covered with flowers. *(577)*

florin (flôr′ĭn, flŏr′-) *n.* **1.** A former British coin worth two shillings. **2.** A guilder. **3. a.** A gold coin first issued at Florence, Italy, in 1252. **3. b.** Any of several former European gold coins similar to the Florentine florin. *(327)*

fluke (flōōk) *n.* **1.** The triangular blade at the end of either arm of an anchor, designed to catch in the ground. **2.** A barbed head, as on an arrow. **3.** One of the two horizontally flattened divisions of the tail of a whale or related animal. *(224)*

foliate (fō′lē-ĭt, -āt′) *adj.* **1.** Of or pertaining to leaves. **2.** Shaped like a leaf. *verb:* (-āt′) — *tr. v.* **1.** To hammer or cut (metal) into thin leaf or foil. **2. a.** To coat (glass, for example) with metal foil. **2. b.** To furnish or adorn with metal foil. **3.** To separate into thin layers. **4.** To decorate with foliage. **5.** To number the leaves of (a book, for example). — *intr. v.* **1.** To produce foliage. **2.** To split into thin layers. *(306)*

foxed (fŏkst) *adj.* Discolored with yellowish-brown stains, as an old book or print. *(133)*

fraternize (frăt′ər-nīz′) *intr. v.* **1.** To associate with others in a brotherly or congenial way. **2.** To mix intimately with the people of an enemy or alien group, often in violation of military law. *(118)*

freeze-dry (frēz′drī′) *tr. v.* To preserve (food, for example) by freeze-drying (rapid freezing and drying in a high vacuum). *(392)*

frond (frŏnd) *n.* **1.** The usually compound leaf of a fern. **2.** A large compound leaf of certain other plants, such as a palm. **3.** A leaflike thallus, as of a seaweed or lichen. *(H3)*

furze (fûrz) *n.* Gorse (any of several spiny, thickset shrubs of the genus *Ulex*, native to Europe, having fragrant yellow flowers). *(117)*

garrulous (găr′ə ləs, găr′yə-) *adj.* Habitually talkative, especially excessively so. *(327)*

gist (jĭst) *n.* **1.** The central idea of a matter; essence. **2.** *Law.* The grounds for action in a suit. *(485)*

glib (glĭb) *adj.* **1. a.** Performed with a natural, offhand ease. **1. b.** Showing little thought, preparation, or concern. **2.** Marked by a quickness or fluency that often suggests or stems from insincerity or deception. *(J3)*

glucose (glōō′kōs′) *n.* **1.** Dextrose (a sugar found in animal and plant tissue and derived synthetically from starch). **2.** A colorless to yellowish syrupy mixture of dextrose, maltose, and dextrins with about 20 per cent water, used in confectionery, alcoholic fermentation, tanning, and treating tobacco. *(410)*

haggard (hăg′ərd) *adj.* **1. a.** Appearing worn and exhausted; gaunt. **1. b.** Wild and unruly; uncontrolled. **2.** Wild and intractable. Used of a hawk in falconry. — *n.* An adult hawk captured for training. *(118, 126)*

half hitch *n.* A hitch made by looping a rope or strap around an object, and then back around itself, bringing the end of the rope through the loop. *(192)*

hallucination (hə-lōō′sə-nā′shən) *n.* **1. a.** False or distorted perception of objects or events with a compelling sense of their reality, usually as a product of mental disorder or as a response to a medication. **1. b.** The complex of material so perceived. **2.** A false or mistaken idea; delusion. *(F4)*

haute cuisine (ōt′ kwĭ-zēn′) *n.* **1.** Elaborate or skillfully prepared cuisine. **2.** The food prepared in the style of haute cuisine. *(482)*

heath (hēth) *n.* **1.** Any of various usually low-growing shrubs of the genus *Erica* and related genera, native to the Old World, having small evergreen leaves and small, urn-shaped pink or purplish flowers. **2.** An extensive tract of open, uncultivated land covered with herbage and low shrubs. *(117, 134)*

Hellene (hĕl′ēn′) **Hellenian** (hĕ-lē′nē-ən) *n.* A Greek. *(177)*

hiatus (hī-ā′təs) *n.* **1.** A gap or interruption in space, time, or continuity; break. **2.** A slight pause that occurs when two immediately adjacent vowels in consecutive syllables are pronounced, as in *reality* and *naive*. **3.** *Anatomy.* A separation, aperture, or fissure. *(485)*

hierarch (hī′ə-rärk′, hī′rärk′) *n.* **1.** One who occupies a position of authority in an ecclesiastical hierarchy. **2.** One who occupies a high position in a hierarchy. *(J2)*

hoary (hôr′ē, hōr′ē) *adj.* **1.** Gray or white with or as if with age. **2.** Covered with grayish hair or pubescence. **3.** Very old; ancient. *(612)*

honorarium (ŏn′ə-râr′ē-əm) *n.* A payment given to a professional person for services for which fees are not legally or traditionally required. *(747)*

hydraulic (hī-drô′lĭk) *adj.* **1.** Of, involving, moved, or operated by a fluid, especially water, under pressure. **2.** Setting and hardening under water, as Portland cement. *(478)*

hypermarket (hī′pər-mär′kĭt) *n. Chiefly British.* A very large commercial establishment that combines a department store and a supermarket. *(230)*

hypothesis (hī-pŏth′ĭ-sĭs) *n.* **1.** An explanation that accounts for a set of facts and that can be tested by further investigation; theory. **2.** Something that is taken to be true for the purpose of argument or investigation; assumption. *(G3)*

iconoscope (ī-kŏn′ə-skōp′) *n.* A television-camera tube equipped for rapid scanning of an information-storing, photoactive mosaic. *(652)*

ignominy (ĭg′nə-mĭn′ē, -mə-nē) *n.* **1.** Great personal dishonor or humiliation. **2.** Shameful or disgraceful action, conduct, or character. *(477)*

impel (ĭm-pĕl′) *tr. v.* **1.** To urge to action through moral pressure; compel. **2.** To drive forward; propel. *(167)*

imperceptible (ĭm′pər-sĕp′tə-bəl) *adj.* **1.** Not perceptible by the mind or senses. **2.** So subtle, slight, or gradual as to be barely perceptible. *(443)*

imperturbable (ĭm′pər-tûr′bə-bəl) *adj.* Unshakably calm and collected. *(323)*

impetus (ĭm′pĭ-təs) *n.* **1. a.** An impelling force; impulse. **1. b.** Something that incites; stimulus. **2.** The force or energy associated with a moving body. *(D4)*

impinge (ĭm-pĭnj′) *intr. v.* **1.** To collide or strike. **2.** To encroach; trespass. *(325)*

implacable (ĭm-plăk′ə-bəl, -plā′kə-) *adj.* Incapable of appeasement or mitigation; inexorable. *(152, 168)*

impressment (ĭm-prĕs′mənt) *n.* The act or policy of seizing people or property for public service or use. *(439)*

impute (ĭm-pyōōt′) *tr. v.* (a crime or fault) to another. **2.** To attribute to a cause or source. **3.** To attribute (wickedness or merit) to a person as transmitted by another. *(485)*

inception (ĭn-sĕp′shən) *n.* The beginning of something; commencement. *(287)*

incessant (ĭn-sĕs′ənt) *adj.* Continuing without respite or interruption; continuous. *(494)*

indulgence (ĭn-dŭl′jəns) *n.* **1.** The act of indulging or the state of being indulgent. **2.** Something indulged in. **3. a.** Something granted as a favor or privilege. **3. b.** Permission to extend the time of payment or performance. **4.** Liberal or lenient treatment; tolerance. **5.** *Roman Catholic Church.* The remission of punishment still due for a sin that has been sacramentally absolved. — *tr. v. Roman Catholic Church.* To attach an indulgence to. *(119)*

ingenuous (ĭn-jĕn′yōō-əs) *adj.* **1.** Without sophistication or worldliness; artless. **2.** Openly straightforward or frank; candid. **3.** *Obsolete.* Ingenious. *(449)*

inscrutable (ĭn-skrōō′tə-bəl) *adj.* Difficult to understand or fathom; enigmatic. *(152)*

irascible (ĭ-răs′ə-bəl, ī-răs′-) *adj.* **1.** Prone to outbursts of temper; easily angered. **2.** Characterized by or resulting from anger. *(481)*

isosceles (ī-sŏs′əlēz′) *adj.* Having two equal sides. *(478)*

isotope (ī′sə-tōp′) *n.* One of two or more atoms whose nuclei have the same number of protons but different numbers of neutrons. *(478)*

jasmine (jăz′mĭn) **jessamine** (jĕs′ə-mĭn) *n.* **1.** Any of several vines or shrubs of the genus *Jasminum*, especially *J. officinalis*, native to Asia, having fragrant white flowers used in making perfume. **2.** Any of several woody vines of the genus *Gelsemium*, especially *G. sempervirens*, of the southeastern United States, having fragrant yellow flowers. **3.** Any of several plants or shrubs having fragrant flowers. **4.** A light to brilliant yellow. *(I3)*

jubilee (jōō′bə-lē, jōō′bə-lē′) *n.* **1. a.** A special anniversary, especially a 50th anniversary. **1. b.** The celebration of such an anniversary. **2.** A season or occasion of joyful celebration. **3.** Jubilation; rejoicing. **4.** Often **Jubilee.** In the Old Testament, a year of rest to be observed by the Israelites every 50th year, during which slaves were to be set free, alienated property restored to the former owners, and the lands left untilled. **5.** *Roman Catholic Church.* A year during which plenary indulgence may be obtained by the performance of certain pious acts. *(485)*

laconic (lə-kŏn′ĭk) *adj.* Using or marked by the use of few words; terse; concise. *(141, 432)*

laggard (lăg′ərd) *n.* One that lags; straggler. — *adj.* Lagging or apt to lag. *(307)*

lamentation (lăm′ən-tā′shən) *n.* An act or instance of lamenting (mourning, grieving; regretting deeply). *(H3)*

lampoon (lăm-pōōn′) *n.* **1.** A broad satirical piece that uses ridicule to attack a person, group, or institution. **2.** A light, good-humored satire. — *tr. v.* To ridicule or satirize in a lampoon. *(481)*

latitudinarian (lăt′ĭ-tōōd′nâr′ē-ən, -tyōōd′-) *adj.* Favoring freedom of thought and behavior, especially in religion. — *n.* A latitudinarian person. *(484)*

Levant (lĭ-vănt′) *Geography.* Countries bordering on the E Mediterranean. *(131)*

leverage (lĕv′ər-ĭj, lē′vər-) *n.* **1. a.** The action of a lever. **1. b.** The mechanical advantage of a lever. **2.** Power to act effectively. **3.** The use of credit in order to improve one's speculative capacity. — *tr. v.* **1. a.** To provide (a company) with leverage. **1. b.** To supplement (money, for example) with leverage. **2.** To affect, as if by leverage. *(D4)*

lexicography (lĕk′sĭ-kŏg′rə-fē) *n.* The process or work of writing or compiling a dictionary. *(610)*

libation (lī-bā′shən) *n.* **a.** The pouring of a liquid offering as a religious ritual. **b.** The liquid poured. *(272)*

libertarian (lĭb′ər-târ′ē-ən) *n.* **1.** One who believes in freedom of action and thought. **2.** One who believes in free will. *(484)*

libertine (lĭb′ər-tēn′) *n.* **1.** One who acts without moral restraint; a dissolute person. **2.** One who defies established religious precepts. — *adj.* Morally unrestrained; dissolute. *(484)*

liege (lēj) *n.* **1.** A lord or sovereign in feudal law. **2.** A vassal or subject owing allegiance and services to a lord or sovereign under feudal law. **3.** A loyal subject to a monarch. — *adj.* **1. a.** Entitled to the loyalty and services of vassals or subjects. **1. b.** Bound to give such allegiance and services to a lord or monarch. **2.** Loyal; faithful. *(491)*

linguist (lĭng′gwĭst) *n.* **1.** A person who speaks several languages fluently. **2.** A specialist in linguistics. *(76)*

litany (lĭt′n-ē) *n.* **1.** A liturgical prayer consisting of phrases recited by a leader alternating with responses by the congregation. **2.** A repetitive or incantatory recital. *(324)*

litmus test (lĭt′məs tĕst) *n.* **1.** A test for chemical acidity using litmus paper. **2.** A test that uses a single indicator to prompt a decision. *(D4)*

livery (lĭv′ə-rē , lĭv′rē) *n.* **1.** The costume or insignia worn by the retainers of a feudal lord. **2.** A distinctive uniform worn by the male servants of a household. **3.** The distinctive dress worn by the members of a particular group. **4. a.** The boarding and care of horses for a fee. **b.** The hiring out of horses and carriages. **c.** A livery stable. *(155)*

livid (lĭv′ĭd) *adj.* **1.** Discolored, as from a bruise; black-and-blue. **2.** Ashen or pallid, as from anger. **3.** Extremely angry; furious. *(485)*

lotus *also* **lotos** (lō′təs) *n.* **1. a.** An aquatic plant, *Nelumbo nucifera*, native to southern Asia, having large leaves, fragrant, pinkish flowers, and a broad, rounded, perforated seed pod. **1. b.** Any of several plants similar or related to the lotus, as certain water lilies. **2.** A representation of any of various lotus plants in classical, usually Egyptian, sculpture, architecture, and art. **3.** Any of several leguminous plants of the genus *Lotus.* **4. a.** A small tree or shrub, *Zizyphus lotus*, of the Mediterranean region, the fruit of which is said to be that eaten by the lotus-eaters. **4. b.** The fruit of this tree. *(F1)*

lucid (lōō′sĭd) *adj.* **1.** Easily understood; intelligible. **2.** Mentally sound; sane. **3.** Translucent. *(443)*

lyceum (lī-sē′əm) *n.* **1.** A hall in which public lectures, concerts, and similar programs are presented. **2.** An organization sponsoring public programs and entertainment. *(723)*

madrigal (măd′rĭ-gəl) *n.* **1.** An unaccompanied vocal composition for two or three voices in simple harmony, following a strict poetic form, developed in Italy in the late 13th and early 14th centuries. **2.** A polyphonic part song, developed in Italy in the 16th century and very popular in England in the 16th and early 17th centuries, that is usually unaccompanied and features parts for four to six voices, using a secular text and sometimes an accompaniment by strings that either doubles or replaces one or more of the vocal parts. **3.** A lyric poem with a pastoral, idyllic, or amatory subject, developed from the lyrics of the 13th-century Italian madrigal. **4.** A part song. *(542)*

magisterial (măj′ĭ-stîr′ē-əl) *adj.* **1.** Of, pertaining to, or characteristic of a master or teacher; authoritative. **2.** Dogmatic; overbearing. **3.** Of or pertaining to a magistrate or his official functions. *(320)*

mandate (măn′dāt′) *n.* **1.** An authoritative command or instruction. **2.** The wishes of a political electorate, expressed by election re-

sults to its representatives in government. **3.
a.** A commission from the League of Nations
authorizing a nation to administer a territory.
3. b. A region under such administration. **4.**
Law. **4. a.** An order issued by a superior
court of law to a lower court. **4. b.** A contract by which an individual agrees to perform services for another without payment.
— *tr. v.* **1.** To assign (a territory, for example) to a specified nation under a mandate. **2.**
To make mandatory; require. *(477)*

matriculate (mə-trĭk′yə-lāt′) *intr. v. & tr. v.*
To admit or be admitted into a group, especially a college or university; enroll. — *n.* A
matriculant. *(481)*

mecca (mĕk′ə) *n.* **1. a.** A place that is regarded as the center of an activity or interest.
1. b. A goal to which adherents of a religious
faith or practice fervently aspire. **2.** A place
visited by many people. *(485)*

Medusa (mə-dōō′sə, -zə, -dyōō′-) *n.* **1.** *Greek
Mythology.* One of the three Gorgons. **2. medusa.** The tentacled, usually bell-shaped, free-
swimming sexual stage in the life cycle of a
coelenterate of the class Scyphozoa or
Hydrozoa. *(453)*

memento (mə-mĕn′tō) *n.* A reminder of the
past; keepsake. *(638)*

meson (mĕz′ŏn′, mē′zŏn′, mĕs′ŏn′, mē′sŏn′)
n. Any of several subatomic particles having
integral spins and masses generally intermedi-
ate between leptons and baryons. *(431)*

mettle (mĕt′l) *n.* **1.** Inherent quality of character and temperament. **2.** Courage and fortitude; spirit. *(480)*

microcircuit (mī′krō-sûr′kĭt) *n.* An electric
circuit consisting of miniaturized components.
(377)

micron *also* **mikron** (mī′krŏn′) *n.* A unit of
length equal to one-millionth (10^{-6}) of a
meter. *(411, 637)*

mitigate (mĭt′ĭgāt′) *intr. v. & tr. v.* To make
or become less severe or intense; moderate.
(449)

motet (mō-tĕt′) *n.* A polyphonic musical composition based on a text of a sacred nature
and usually sung without accompaniment.
(532)

mottle (mŏt′l) *tr. v.* To cover (a surface) with
spots or streaks of different shades or colors.
— *n.* **1.** A spot or blotch of color. **2.** A varie-
gated pattern, as on marble. *(133)*

mucilage (myōō′sə-lĭj) *n.* **1.** A sticky substance used as an adhesive. **2.** A gummy substance obtained from certain plants. *(494)*

mugwump (mŭg′wŭmp′) *n.* **1.** A Republican
who bolted his party in 1884, refusing to support James G. Blaine as candidate for the
U.S. presidency. **2.** A person who acts independently, especially in politics. *(484)*

multitudinous (mŭl′tĭ-tōōd′n-əs, -tyōōd′-) *adj.*
1. Very numerous; existing in great numbers.
2. Consisting of many parts. **3.** Crowded. *(55)*

mundane (mŭn′dān′, mŭn′dān′) *adj.* **1.** Of,
relating to, or typical of this world. **2.** Typical
of or concerned with the ordinary. *(481)*

mutualism (myōō′chōō-ə-lĭz′əm) *n.* An association, such as symbiosis, between two organisms. *(104)*

myriad (mĭr′ē-əd) *adj.* **1.** Constituting a very
large, indefinite number; innumerable. **2.**
Comprised of numerous diverse elements or
facets. — *n.* **1.** *Archaic.* Ten thousand. **2.** A
vast number. *(141)*

nabob (nā′bŏb′) *n.* **1.** A governor in India
under the Mogul Empire. **2.** A man of wealth
and prominence. *(485)*

Neolithic (nē′ə-lĭth′ĭk) *adj.* Of or denoting the
cultural period beginning around 10,000 B.C. in
the Middle East and later elsewhere and
characterized by the invention of farming and
the making of technically advanced stone
implements. *(478)*

neophyte (nē′ə-fīt′) *n.* **1.** A recent convert. **2.**
a. A newly ordained Roman Catholic priest.
2. b. A novice of a religious order. **3.** A be-
ginner; novice. *(478)*

newfangled (nōō′făng′gəld, nyōō′-) *adj.* **1.**
New; novel. **2.** Fond of novelty. *(673)*

nickelodeon (nĭk′ə-lō′dē-ən) *n.* **1.** An early
movie house charging an admission price of
five cents. **2. a.** A player piano. **2. b.** A juke
box. *(659)*

nocturnal (nŏk-tûr′nəl) *adj.* **1.** Of, pertaining
to, or occurring in the night. **2.** *Botany.* Having flowers that open during the night. **3.** *Zo-
ology.* Active at night, as certain animals.
(H2)

nocturne (nŏk′tûrn′) *n.* **1.** A painting of a
night scene. **2.** A romantic musical composition intended to suggest or evoke thoughts
and feelings of night. *(H2)*

oblivion (ə-blĭv′ē-ən) *n.* **1.** The quality or condition of being completely forgotten. **2.** An act or an instance of forgetting. **3.** Official overlooking of offenses. *(13)*

obscurity (ŏb-skyo͞or′ĭ-tē, əb-) *n.* **1.** Deficiency or absence of light; darkness. **2. a.** The quality or condition of being unknown. **2. b.** One that is obscure. *(118, 119)*

obviate (ŏb′vē-āt′) *tr. v.* To prevent by anticipating; make unnecessary. *(485)*

opacity (ō-păs′ĭ-tē) *n.* **1.** The quality or state of being opaque (impervious to the passage of light). **2.** Something that is opaque. **3.** Obscurity; impenetrability. *(117)*

orthodox (ôr′thə-dŏks′) *adj.* **1.** Adhering to the accepted or traditional and established faith, especially in religion. **2.** Adhering to the Christian faith as expressed in the early Christian ecumenical creeds. **3.** Adhering to what is commonly accepted, customary, or traditional. **4. Orthodox. 4. a.** Of, pertaining to, or designating any of the churches of the Eastern Orthodox Church. **4. b.** Of, pertaining to, or denoting Orthodox Judaism. — *n.* **1.** One that is orthodox. **2. Orthodox.** A member of an Eastern Orthodox Church. *(119)*

osprey (ŏs′prē, -prā) *n.* **1.** A fish-eating hawk, *Pandion haliaetus*, having plumage that is dark on the back and white below. **2.** A plume formerly used to trim women's hats. *(394)*

ostracize (ŏs′trə-sīz′) *tr. v.* **1.** To banish or exclude from a group; shun. **2.** To banish by ostracism, as in ancient Greece. *(495)*

pallid (păl′ĭd) *adj.* **1.** Having an abnormally pale or wan complexion. **2.** Lacking intensity of hue or luminousness. **3.** Lacking in radiance or vitality; dull. *(117, 134)*

papyrus (pə-pī′rəs) *n.* **1.** A tall aquatic sedge, *Cyperus papyrus*, of southern Europe and northern Africa. **2. a.** A paper made from the pith or the stems of the papyrus, used in antiquity as a writing material. **2. b.** A document written on this paper. *(74)*

parasitism (păr′ə-sĭ-tĭz′əm, -sī-) *n.* **1.** The characteristic behavior or mode of existence of a parasite. **2.** A diseased condition resulting from parasitic infestation. *(104)*

partisan (pär′tĭ-zən) *n.* **1.** A militant supporter of a party, cause, faction, person, or idea. **2.** A member of a detached, often unofficially organized body of fighters who attack or harass an enemy within occupied territory; guerrilla. — *adj.* **1.** Of, pertaining to, or characteristic of a partisan or partisans. **2.** Devoted to or biased in support of a single party or cause. *(157, 640)*

passe partout (păs pär-to͞o′) *n.* **1.** Something enabling one to pass or go everywhere, especially a master key. **2. a.** A mounting for a picture in which colored tape forms the frame. **b.** The tape so used. **3.** A mat used in mounting a picture. *(134)*

pavilion (pə-vĭl′yən) *n.* **1.** An ornate tent. **2. a.** A light, sometimes ornamental, roofed structure, used at parks or fairs for amusement or shelter. **2. b.** A usually temporary structure erected at a fair or show for use by an exhibitor. **3.** A building or other structure connected to a larger building; annex. **4.** One of a group of related buildings forming a complex, as of a hospital. **5.** The surface of a brilliant-cut gem that slants outward from girdle to culet. — *tr. v.* To shelter in or as if in a pavilion. *(123)*

pelt (pĕlt) *n.* **1.** The skin of an animal with the fur or hair still on it. **2.** A stripped animal skin ready for tanning. *(83)*

pentathlon (pĕn-tăth′lən, -lŏn′) *n.* An athletic contest consisting of five events for each participant, usually running, horseback riding, swimming, fencing, and pistol shooting. *(619)*

peruse (pə-ro͞oz′) *tr. v.* To read or examine, especially with great care. *(450)*

petulant (pĕch′ə-lənt) *adj.* **1.** Unreasonably irritable or ill-tempered; peevish. **2.** Contemptuous in speech or behavior. *(443)*

photolithography (fō′tō-lĭ-thŏg′rə-fē) *n.* A planographic printing process (printing from a smooth surface) using plates made according to a photographic image. *(399)*

placid (plăs′ĭd) *adj.* **1.** Having an undisturbed surface or aspect; outwardly calm or composed. **2.** Self-satisfied; complacent. *(485)*

pluralistic (plo͞or′əl-ĭs′tĭk) *adj.* Of or pertaining to pluralism, a condition of society in which numerous distinct ethnic, religious, or cultural groups coexist within one nation. *(J3)*

polymath (pŏl′ē-măth′) *n.* A person of great or varied learning. *(601)*

pre-empt (prē-ĕmpt′) *tr. v.* **1.** To gain possession of by prior right or opportunity, especially to settle on (public land) so as to obtain the right to buy before others. **2.** To appropriate, seize, or act for oneself before others. **3.** To be presented in place of; displace. **4.** To take precedence over. **5.** To gain a pre-eminent place in. — *intr. v.* To make a pre-emptive bid in bridge. *(443, 698)*

precept (prē′sĕpt′) *n.* **1.** A rule or principle imposing a particular standard of action or conduct. **2.** *Law.* A writ. *(481)*

prehensile (prē-hĕn′səl, -sīl′) *adj.* Adapted for seizing or holding, especially by wrapping around an object. *(453)*

preordain (prē′ôr-dān′) *tr. v.* To appoint, decree, or ordain in advance; foreordain. *(J2)*

prodigal (prŏd′ĭ-gəl) *adj.* **1.** Recklessly wasteful; extravagant. **2.** Profuse in giving; exceedingly abundant. **3.** Profuse; lavish. — *n.* A person given to luxury or extravagance. *(443)*

prodigious (prə-dĭj′əs) *adj.* **1.** Impressively great in size, force, or extent; enormous. **2.** Extraordinary; marvelous. **3.** Portentous; ominous. *(86)*

progenitor (prō-jĕn′ĭ-tər) *n.* **1.** A direct ancestor. **2.** An originator of a line of descent. *(417)*

prognosticate (prŏg-nŏs′tĭ-kāt′) *tr. v.* **1.**To predict, using present indications as a guide. **2.** To foreshadow; portend. *(618)*

prolegomenon (prō′lĭ-gŏm′ə-nŏn′, -nən) *n.* plural: **prolegomena** (-nə). A critical introduction. *(738)*

promontory (prŏm′ən-tôr′ē, -tōr′ē) *n.* **1.** A high ridge of land or rock jutting out into a sea or other expanse of water. **2.** *Anatomy.* A projecting bodily part. *(487)*

proponent (prə-pō′nənt) *n.* One who argues in support of something; advocate. *(249)*

protocol (prō′tə-kôl′ , -kōl, -kŏl′) *n.* **1.** The forms of ceremony and etiquette observed by diplomats and heads of state. **2.** The first copy of a treaty or other document prior to its ratification. **3.** A preliminary draft or record of a transaction. **4.** The plan for a medical or scientific experiment. — *intr. v.* To form or issue protocols. *(375, 478)*

prototype (prō′tə-tīp′) *n.* **1.** An original type, form, or instance that serves as a model on which later stages are based or judged. **2.** An early and typical example. **3.** *Biology.* A primitive or ancestral form or species. *(478)*

protozoan (prō′tə-zō′ən) **protozoon** (-ŏn′) *n.* Any of the single-celled, usually microscopic organisms of the phylum or subkingdom Protozoa, which includes the most primitive forms of animal life. *(478)*

provincial (prə-vĭn′shəl) *adj.* **1.** Of or pertaining to a province. **2.** Of or characteristic of people from the provinces; not fashionable or sophisticated. **3.** Limited in perspective; narrow and self-centered. — *n.* **1.** A native or inhabitant of the provinces. **2.** A person who has provincial ideas or habits. *(180)*

provisional (prə-vĭzh′ə-nəl) **provisionary** (-vĭzh′ə-nĕr′ē) *adj.* Provided for the time being, pending permanent arrangements. *(G3)*

prow (prou) *n.* **1.** The forward part of a ship's hull; bow. **2.** A projecting part similar in configuration to the prow of a ship, as the forward end of a ski. *(165)*

pungent (pŭn′jənt) *adj.* **1.** Affecting the organs of taste or smell with a sharp, acrid sensation. **2.** Penetrating; biting; caustic. **3.** Pointed. *(141)*

quintessence (kwĭn-tĕs′əns) *n.* **1.** The pure, highly concentrated essence of something. **2.** The purest or most typical instance. **3.** In ancient and medieval philosophy, the fifth and highest essence (after the four elements of earth, air, fire, and water), thought to be the substance of the heavenly bodies and latent in all things. *(533)*

radon (rā′dŏn) *n.* A colorless, radioactive, inert gaseous element formed by disintegration of radium. It is used as a radiation source in radiotherapy and to produce neutrons for research. *(379)*

ration (răsh′ən, rā′shən) *n.* **1.** A fixed portion, especially an amount of food allotted to persons in military service or to civilians in times of scarcity. **2. rations.** Food issued or available to members of a group. — *tr. v.* **1.** To supply with rations. **2.** To distribute as rations. **3.** To restrict to limited amounts. *(B3)*

reciprocity (rĕs′ə-prŏs′ĭ-tē) *n.* **1.** A reciprocal condition or relationship. **2.** A mutual or cooperative interchange of favors or privileges, especially the exchange of rights or privileges of trade between nations. *(119)*

reconnaissance *also* **reconnoissance** (rĭ-kŏn′ə-səns, -zəns) *n.* An inspection or exploration of an area, especially one made to gather military information. *(H3)*

redress (rĭ-drĕs′) *tr. v.* **1.** To set right; remedy or rectify. **2.** To make amends to. **3.** To make amends for. **4.** To adjust (a balance, for example). — *n.* (*also* rē′drĕs). **1.** Satisfaction or amends for wrong done. **2.** Correction or reformation. *(485)*

reiterate (rē-ĭt′ə-rāt′) *tr. v.* To say over again. *(617)*

remuneration (rĭ-myoo͞′nə-rā′shən) *n.* **1.** An act of remunerating. **2.** Something that remunerates; payment. *(747)*

renovate (rĕn′ə-vāt′) *tr. v.* **1.** To restore to an earlier condition, as by repairing or remodeling. **2.** To impart new vigor to; revive. *(14)*

repugnant (rĭ-pŭg′nənt) *adj.* **1.** Arousing disgust or aversion; offensive or repulsive. **2.** *Logic.* Contradictory; inconsistent. *(453)*

respondent (rĭ-spŏn′dənt) *adj.* **1.** Giving or given as an answer; responsive. **2.** *Law.* Being a defendant. — *n.* **1.** A person who responds. **2.** *Law.* A defendant, especially in divorce or equity cases. *(D3)*

retail (rē′tāl′) *n.* The sale of goods or commodities in small quantities to the consumer. — *adj.* Of, pertaining to, or engaged in the sale of goods or commodities at retail. — *tr. v.* **1.** To sell in small quantities directly to consumers. **2.** (*also* rĭ-tāl′). To tell and retell. — *intr. v.* To sell at retail. *(249)*

retrospective (rĕt′rə-spĕk′tĭv) *adj.* **1.** Looking back on, contemplating, or directed to the past. **2.** Looking or directed backward. **3.** Applying to or influencing the past; retroactive. **4.** Of or pertaining to a show exhibiting the work of an artist or school over a period of years. — *n.* A retrospective art exhibition. *(631)*

ruck[1] (rŭk) *n.* **1.** A large number mixed together; jumble. **2.** The multitude of ordinary people. *(483)*

ruck[2] (rŭk) *tr. v.* **1.** To make a fold in; crease. **2.** To disturb or ruffle; irritate. — *intr. v.* **1.** To become creased. **2.** To become irritated. — *n.* A crease or pucker, as in cloth. *(483)*

sagacious (sə-gā′shəs) *adj.* Possessing or showing sound judgment and keen perception; wise. *(366, 482)*

salver (săl′vər) *n.* A tray for serving food or drinks. *(328)*

sanguine (săng′gwĭn) *adj.* **1. a.** Of the color of blood; red. **1. b.** Ruddy. **2. a.** *Archaic.* Having blood as the dominant humor in terms of medieval physiology. **2. b.** Having the temperament and ruddy complexion formerly thought to be characteristic of a person dominated by this humor; passionate. **3.** Cheerfully confident; optimistic. *(618)*

schism (sĭz′əm, skĭz′-) *n.* **1. a.** A separation or division into factions, especially a formal breach of union within a Christian church. **1. b.** The offense of attempting to produce such a split. **2.** A body or sect that participates in or creates a schism. *(494)*

selsmograph (sīz′mə-grăf′) *n.* An instrument for automatically detecting and recording the intensity, direction, and duration of a movement of the ground, especially of an earthquake. *(218)*

sequester (sĭ-kwĕs′tər) *tr. v.* **1.** To remove or set apart; segregate. **2.** *Law.* To take temporary possession of (property) as security against legal claims. **3.** *Law.* To requisition and confiscate (enemy property). **4.** To cause to withdraw into seclusion. — *intr. v. Chemistry.* To undergo sequestration. *(370)*

servile (sûr′vəl, -vīl′) *adj.* **1.** Slavish in character or attitude; abjectly submissive. **2.** Of or suitable to a slave or servant. *(453)*

sharecrop (shâr′krŏp′) *intr. v.* To work as a sharecropper (a tenant farmer who gives a share of his crop to the landlord in lieu of rent). *(E2)*

shellac (shə-lăk′) *n.* **1.** A purified lac formed into thin yellow or orange flakes, often bleached white and widely used in varnishes, paints, stains, inks, and sealing wax, as a binder, and in phonograph records. **2.** A thin varnish made by dissolving flake shellac in denatured alcohol, used as a wood coating and sealer and for finishing floors. — *tr. v.* **1.** To apply shellac to. **2.** *Slang.* To defeat decisively. **3.** *Slang.* To administer blows to; batter mercilessly. — *intr. v.* To apply shellac. *(489)*

shoal (shōl) *n.* **1.** A place in a body of water where the water is particularly shallow. **2.** A sandy elevation of the bottom of a body of water, constituting a hazard to navigation; sandbank or sandbar. — *intr. v.* To become shallow. — *tr. v.* **1.** To make shallow. **2.** To come or sail into a shallower part of. — *adj.* Having little depth; shallow. *(151)*

sinew (sĭn′yoo) *n.* 1. A tendon. 2. Vigorous strength; muscular power. 3. Often **sinews**. The source or mainstay of vitality and strength. *(F4)*

sixpenny (sĭks′pə-nē) *adj.* 1. Valued at, selling for, or worth sixpence. 2. Of little worth; paltry. 3. (sĭks′pĕn′ē). Denoting a size of nails, generally two inches. *(328)*

skunk cabbage *n.* 1. An ill-smelling swamp plant, *Symplocarpus foetidus*, of eastern North America, having minute flowers enclosed in a mottled greenish or purplish spathe. 2. A plant, *Lysichitum americanum*, of western North America similar to skunk cabbage. *(192)*

solicitous (sə-lĭs′ĭ-təs) *adj.* 1. Concerned; attentive. 2. Full of desire; eager. 3. Anxious; worried. 4. Extremely careful; meticulous. 5. Expressing solicitude. *(301)*

spherical (sfĭr′ĭ-kəl, sfĕr′-) **spheric** (sfĭr′ĭk, sfĕr′-) *adj.* 1. **a.** Having the shape of a sphere; globular. 1. **b.** Having a shape approximating that of a sphere. 2. Of or pertaining to a sphere. 3. Of or pertaining to heavenly bodies; celestial. *(200)*

staphylococcus (stăf′ə-lō-kŏk′əs) *n.* Any of various Gram-positive, spherical parasitic bacteria of the genus *Staphylococcus*, occurring in grapelike clusters and causing boils, septicemia, and other infections. *(170)*

staunch (stônch, stänch) **stanch** (stänch, stănch) *adj.* 1. Firm and steadfast; true. 2. Having a strong or substantial construction or constitution. *(D4)*

stipend (stī′pĕnd′, -pənd) *n.* A fixed and regular payment, such as a salary for services rendered or an allowance. *(268)*

story (stôr′ē, stōr′ē) *n.* 1. The narration of an event or series of events, either true or fictitious. 2. A prose or verse narrative, usually fictional, intended to interest or amuse the hearer or reader; tale. 3. A short story. 4. The plot of a narrative or dramatic work. 5. A news article or broadcast. 6. An anecdote. 7. A lie. — *tr. v.* 1. To decorate with scenes representing historical or legendary events. 2. *Archaic.* To tell as a story. *(615)*

sublime (sə-blīm′) *adj.* 1. Characterized by nobility; majestic. 2. **a.** Of high spiritual, moral, or intellectual worth. 2. **b.** Not to be excelled; supreme. 3. Inspiring awe; impressive. 4. *Obsolete.* Of lofty appearance or bearing; haughty. 5. *Archaic.* Raised aloft; set high. — *n.* 1. Something that is sublime. 2. The ultimate example of something. *(118)*

subterfuge (sŭb′tər-fyooj′) *n.* A deceptive stratagem or device. *(226)*

succumb (sə-kŭm′) *intr. v.* 1. To yield or submit to an overpowering force or overwhelming desire; give in or give up. 2. To die. *(B2)*

superconductivity (soo′pər-kŏn′dŭk-tĭv′ĭtē) *n.* The flow of electric current without resistance in certain metals and alloys at temperatures near absolute zero. *(377)*

surfeit (sûr′fĭt) *tr. v.* To feed or supply to fullness or excess; satiate. — *intr. v. Archaic.* To overindulge. — *n.* 1. **a.** Overindulgence in food or drink. 1. **b.** The result of such overindulgence; satiety or disgust. 2. An excessive amount. *(481)*

surly (sûr′lē) *adj.* 1. Sullenly ill-humored; gruff. 2. *Obsolete.* Arrogant; domineering. *(485)*

swarthy (swôr′thē) *adj.* Having a dark complexion or color. *(119)*

symbiosis (sĭm′bē-ō′sĭs, -bī-) *n. Biology.* The relationship of two or more different organisms in a close association that may be but is not necessarily of benefit to each. *(104)*

synthesize (sĭn′thĭ-sīz′) *also* **synthetize** (-tīz′) *tr. v.* 1. To combine so as to form a new, complex product. 2. To produce by combining separate elements. — *intr. v.* To form a synthesis. *(D3)*

tariff (tăr′ĭf) *n.* 1. A list or system of duties imposed by a government on imported or exported goods. 2. A duty or duties imposed by a government on imported or exported goods. 3. Any schedule of prices or fees. — *tr. v.* To fix a duty or price on. *(242)*

teletext (tĕl′ə-tĕkst′) *n.* An electronic communication system in which printed information is broadcast by television signal to sets equipped with a decoder. *(409)*

tenable (tĕn′ə-bəl) *adj.* 1. Capable of being defended or sustained; logical. 2. Defensible from armed assault. *(481)*

tenacity (tə-năs′ĭ-tē) *n.* The condition or quality of being tenacious (holding or tending to hold firmly; persistent). *(480)*

threescore (thrē′skôr′, -skōr′) *adj.* Three times twenty; sixty. *(337)*

tincture (tĭngk′chər) *n.* **1.** A dyeing substance; pigment. **2.** An imparted color; stain; tint. **3.** A quality that colors, pervades, or distinguishes. **4.** A trace; vestige. **5.** A component of a substance extracted by means of a solvent. **6.** An alcohol solution of a nonvolatile medicine. **7.** A heraldic metal, color, or fur. — *tr. v.* **1.** To stain or tint with a color. **2.** To infuse, as with a quality; impregnate. *(703)*

torpid (tôr′pĭd) *adj.* **1.** Deprived of the power of motion or feeling; benumbed. **2.** Dormant; hibernating. **3.** Lethargic; apathetic. *(451)*

transship (trăns-shĭp′) **tranship** (trăn-shĭp′, trăns-) *tr. v.* To transfer from one vessel or vehicle to another for reshipment. — *intr. v.* To transfer cargo from one vessel or conveyance to another. *(131)*

trek (trĕk) *intr. v.* **1.** To make a slow or arduous journey. **2.** To travel by ox wagon in South Africa. — *n.* **1.** A journey or leg of a journey, especially when slow or difficult. **2.** A migration. **3.** A journey by ox wagon in South Africa. *(485)*

trenchant (trĕn′chənt) *adj.* **1.** Forceful and effective; vigorous. **2. a.** Extremely perceptive; incisive. **2. b.** Caustic; cutting. **3.** Distinct; clear-cut. *(431)*

trow (trō) *intr. v. Archaic.* To think; suppose. *(367)*

uncanny (ŭn-kăn′ē) *adj.* **1.** Exciting wonder and fear; inexplicable. **2.** So keen and perceptive as to seem preternatural. *(J2)*

unconscionable (ŭn-kŏn′shə-nə-bəl) *adj.* **1.** Not restrained by conscience; unscrupulous. **2.** Beyond prudence or reason; excessive. *(255)*

uncouth (ŭn-kōōth′) *adj.* **1.** Crude; unrefined. **2.** Awkward or clumsy; ungraceful. **3.** *Archaic.* Foreign; unfamiliar. *(54)*

unman (ŭn-măn′) *tr. v.* **1.** To cause to lose courage. **2.** To deprive of virility; emasculate. *(272)*

unmanned (ŭn-mănd′) *adj.* **1.** Without crew. **2.** *Obsolete.* Untrained. Used of a hawk. *(272)*

unpalatable (ŭn-păl′ə-tə-bəl) *adj.* **1.** Not pleasing to the taste. **2.** Not pleasant or agreeable. *(157)*

utopia (yōō-tō′pē-ə) *n.* **1. Utopia.** An ideally perfect place, especially in its socio-political aspects. **2.** An impractical, idealistic concept for social and political reform. *(558)*

veracity (və-răs′ĭ-tē) *n.* **1.** Adherence to the truth; truthfulness. **2.** Conformity to truth or fact; accuracy. **3.** Something that is true. *(477)*

vermilion (vər-mĭl′yən) *n.* **1.** A bright red mercuric sulfide used as a pigment. **2.** A vivid red to reddish orange. — *adj.* Of a vivid red to reddish orange. — *tr. v.* To color or dye vermilion. *(13)*

vestige (vĕs′tĭj) *n.* **1.** A visible trace, evidence, or sign of something that has once existed but exists or appears no more. **2.** *Biology.* A small, degenerate, or rudimentary organ or part existing in an organism as a usually nonfunctioning remnant of an organ or part fully developed and functional in a preceding generation or earlier developmental stage. *(481)*

viable (vī′ə-bəl) *adj.* **1.** Capable of living, as a newborn infant or fetus reaching a stage of development that will permit it to survive and develop under normal conditions. **2.** Capable of living, developing, or germinating under favorable conditions. **3.** Capable of success or continuing effectiveness; practicable. *(747)*

vindicate (vĭn′dĭ-kāt′) *tr. v.* **1.** To clear of accusation, blame, suspicion, or doubt with supporting arguments or proof. **2.** To justify or support. **3.** To justify or prove the worth of, especially in light of later developments. *(485)*

wattle (wŏt′l) *n.* **1. a.** Poles intertwined with twigs, reeds, or branches for use in construction, as of walls or fences. **1. b.** Materials thus used. **2.** A fleshy, often brightly colored fold of skin hanging from the neck or throat, characteristic of certain birds and some lizards. **3.** Any of various Australian trees or shrubs of the genus *Acacia.* — *tr. v.* **1.** To construct from wattle. **2.** To weave into wattle. *(133)*

wrest (rĕst) *tr. v.* **1.** To obtain by or as by pulling with violent twisting movements. **2.** To usurp forcefully. **3.** To extract by force, guile, or persistent effort; wring. **4. a.** To distort or twist the nature or meaning of. **4. b.** To divert to an improper use; misapply. —*n.* **1.** The action of wresting. **2.** A small tuning key for the pins of a harp or piano. *(481)*

writhe (rīth) *intr. v.* **1.** To twist or squirm, as in pain, struggle, or embarrassment. **2.** To move with a twisting or contorted motion. **3.** To suffer acutely. — *tr. v.* To cause to twist or squirm; contort. — *n.* An act or instance of writhing; contortion. *(485)*

yawp *also* **yaup** (yôp) *intr. v.* **1.** To utter a sharp cry; yelp. **2.** *Slang.* To talk loudly and stupidly. — *n.* **1.** A bark; yelp. **2.** *Slang.* Loud, stupid talk. *(375)*

yearn (yûrn) *intr. v.* **1.** To have a strong or deep desire; be filled with longing. **2.** To feel deep pity, sympathy, or tenderness. *(F3)*

Glossary of English Terms

As a convenient reference, this Glossary lists the key English instructional terms as they are defined in your textbook. The page references indicate the textbook pages on which these terms appear in boldface type accompanied by their definitions.

Absolute phrase A phrase that consists of a participle and the noun or the pronoun modified by the participle and that modifies an entire sentence *(p. 582)*

Abstract noun A noun that names a concept, a quality, an emotion, a condition, or an attitude *(p. 533)*

Action verb A verb that expresses the behavior or mental or physical action of someone or something *(p. 540)*

Active voice The voice of a transitive verb that shows the subject performing rather than receiving the action of the verb *(p. 546)*

Adjective A word that modifies a noun or a pronoun *(p. 549)*

Adjective clause A subordinate clause that modifies a noun or a pronoun *(p. 588)*

Adjective phrase A prepositional phrase that modifies a noun or a pronoun *(p. 578)*

Adverb A word that modifies a verb, an adjective, or another adverb *(p. 554)*

Adverb clause A subordinate clause that modifies a verb, an adjective, or another adverb *(p. 591)*

Adverb phrase A prepositional phrase that modifies a verb, an adjective, or another adverb *(p. 578)*

Alliteration A sound device in which initial sounds — usually consonant sounds — are repeated, for example, "The fair breeze blew, the white foam flew, / The furrow followed free" *(pp. 310, 335)*

Allusion A form of metaphorical comparison in which specific references are made to literature, history, or popular culture, creating an "inside joke" shared by the reader and the author *(p. 94)*

Analogy The similarity or correspondence in at least one respect of things that are otherwise dissimilar; the type of test question that measures one's ability to understand the relationship between two words and to recognize a parallel relationship between two other words *(pp. 32, 439)*

Analyzing The process of examining facts, details, or ideas by looking at the separate parts in order to get a better understanding of the whole; the counterpart of **synthesizing** *(pp. 17, 19, 442)*

Antecedent The noun that a pronoun refers to or replaces in a sentence *(p. 536)*

Appositive A noun or a pronoun placed near another noun or pronoun to explain or identify it *(p. 579)*

Appositive phrase An appositive and all the words or phrases that modify it *(p. 579)*

Archaic language Language that is no longer used in speaking and writing but may be encountered in reading *(p. 616)*

Argument A course of reasoning that is used, usually in a persuasive essay or speech, to demonstrate the truth or falsehood of something through the logical presentation and development of ideas *(p. 232)*

Associations The mental connections, including thoughts and feelings, that a person makes in response to a stimulus, for example, the image of an eagle in a poem *(p. 11)*

Assonance A sound device in which a vowel sound is repeated in words close to one another; for example, "mad as a hatter" *(p. 310)*

Authority An accepted source of knowledge or advice, which may be used as support in an argument *(p. 235)*

Auxiliary verb The verb that helps an action or a linking verb; sometimes called a **helping verb** (p. 542)

Begging the question The failure to provide genuine evidence in support of an argument (p. 254)

Block style The form of a typed business letter in which all parts start at the left margin and none of the paragraphs indent (p. 498)

Blurred sentence A sentence, usually compound, in which the relationship between or among the ideas is not clear (p. 79)

Body of a letter The paragraphs that state the writer's purpose (p. 497)

Call number The number in the upper-left corner of a library catalog card that identifies and helps to locate a book (p. 384)

Card catalog A file containing alphabetically arranged cards that tell what books are in the library and where to find them (p. 383)

Casual language The form of speaking or writing that is extremely informal, incorporating slang, sentence fragments, regional expressions and pronunciations, and contractions (p. 88)

Cause An event, a situation, or a condition that produces a result (p. 438)

Cause-and-effect relationship The relationship that exists between the cause of something and its effect; a formula for showing how one or more events or conditions bring about a result (pp. 33, 438)

Ceremonial language Language that is highly formal and is used only on important occasions (p. 616)

Characterization A writer's creation of characters in a literary work through representing their speech, appearance, behavior, thoughts, feelings, and so on (p. 334)

Characters The individuals who perform the actions or whose conflicts are presented in a fictional or nonfictional narrative or a play (p. 278)

Chronological order The arrangement of events according to the sequence in which they happen (pp. 36, 169, 282, 465)

Citation The acknowledgment of a source within the body of a report or essay (p. 405)

Class A group of items that share a common feature or features (p. 437)

Class name A word or phrase used to designate a group of items sharing a common feature or features (p. 437)

Classifying The process of sorting items that share a common feature into a group identified by a class name (pp. 34, 436)

Clause A group of related words that contains a subject and a predicate (p. 587)

Cliché An overused expression such as *make a mountain out of a molehill* (p. 93)

Climax The high point of the conflict in a fictional or nonfictional narrative or a play (pp. 168, 282)

Clip art The name of a computer file that contains ready-made or pre-programmed graphics (p. 517)

Closure The resolution achieved at the end of a paragraph or longer piece of writing by returning to the focusing or main idea (p. 44)

Coherence The clear and logical relation of parts in a sentence, a paragraph, or a longer piece of writing (p. 68)

Collective noun A noun that names a group or a collection of people, places, things, or ideas that are regarded as a unit (pp. 533, 640)

Colloquial language Informal language that is used appropriately in everyday conversation but not in formal writing and speaking (p. 616)

Common belief A value or an idea shared by most people, such as "Friends have a responsibility to stand by one another in times of need" (p. 235)

Common noun A word that refers to a class of people, places, things, or ideas (p. 533)

Comparison A statement that shows the similarities between two or more items; the act of comparing items (p. 30)

Complement A word or a group of words that completes the meaning of the predicate (p. 572)

Complete predicate A simple predicate and all the modifiers and other words that complete the meaning of the verb (p. 569)

Complete sentence A group of words that has at least one subject and one predicate and that expresses a complete thought (p. 598)

Complete subject The noun or the pronoun that states whom or what a sentence is about and all the words that modify it or identify it, excluding complements *(p. 568)*

Complex sentence A sentence consisting of one independent clause and one or more subordinate clauses *(p. 596)*

Compound-complex sentence A sentence that contains two or more independent clauses and one or more subordinate clauses *(p. 596)*

Compound noun A single noun that consists of two or more words joined together or consistently used together *(p. 533)*

Compound object Two or more objects that complete the same predicate *(p. 573)*

Compound predicate A simple predicate that consists of two or more verbs or verb phrases joined by a conjunction *(p. 567)*

Compound preposition A preposition that consists of more than one word, such as *in spite of,* and that expresses a relationship between a noun or a pronoun and another word in the sentence *(p. 557)*

Compound sentence A sentence consisting of two or more independent clauses but no subordinate clauses *(p. 595)*

Compound subject A simple subject consisting of two or more nouns or pronouns that are the subject of the same verb and that are connected by a conjunction such as *and, nor,* or *either . . . or (p. 567)*

Conciseness A quality of writing that is economical, that is, that states ideas directly and precisely *(p. 80)*

Concluding sentence The sentence that brings a paragraph to a close and returns the reader to the idea introduced in the topic sentence *(p. 39)*

Concrete noun A word that refers to a person, a place, or a thing that can be perceived through the senses or that can be measured or perceived with the aid of a device such as a telescope *(p. 533)*

Conflict The problem faced by the characters in a fictional or nonfictional narrative, a play, or a poem that may threaten their happiness or perhaps their lives *(pp. 168, 278)*

Conjugation A presentation of all the forms of the six tenses of a verb showing how each form of the verb changes for person and number *(p. 623)*

Conjunction A word or a phrase that connects individual words or groups of words *(p. 559)*

Conjunctive adverb A word that functions somewhat as a coordinating conjunction (for example, *consequently*), usually connecting independent clauses *(p. 562)*

Connotation The sum of the thoughts and feelings that a word suggests or evokes or of the cultural and personal associations that a person makes *(pp. 27, 91, 260, 481)*

Context The overall sense of the words and ideas in a reading selection, which can be used to figure out the meaning of an unfamiliar word *(p. 476)*

Contrast A statement that shows the differences between two or more items; the act of contrasting items *(p. 30)*

Convention A widely used and accepted literary device, such as the *aside* in drama; the standard practices followed when writing within a **genre** *(p. 348)*

Coordinating conjunction A word, such as *and, but, nor,* or *yet,* that connects words or groups of words that perform the same function in a sentence *(p. 559)*

Coordination The process of combining related elements (words, phrases, or clauses) of equal importance or value *(p. 72)*

Correlative conjunction Two or more words, such as *either . . . or, neither . . . nor,* or *not only . . . but (also),* that act together as a set and connect words that perform equal functions in a sentence *(p. 560)*

Critical thinking The ability to classify, analyze, interpret, and draw conclusions and inferences from acquired information *(p. 436)*

Dangling modifier A modifying word or phrase that does not clearly or sensibly modify any other word in the sentence *(p. 668)*

Declarative sentence A sentence that makes a statement and ends with a period *(p. 566)*

Deduce To reach a conclusion by reasoning; to infer from a general principle *(p. 240)*

Deductive reasoning The process of reasoning in which the conclusion follows necessarily from the premises *(p. 239)*

Definite article The adjective *the*, which always points out a particular item *(p. 549)*

Definition The meaning of a word, phrase, or expression that places a subject in a class and that tells how it differs from other members of its class *(pp. 34, 200)*

Demonstrative pronoun A pronoun, such as *this, that, these,* or *those,* that specifies which one or which group is referred to *(p. 537)*

Denotation The literal meaning or dictionary definition of a word as opposed to its connotative meaning *(pp. 91, 481, 611)*

Dependent or **subordinate clause** A clause that cannot stand by itself as a sentence *(p. 588)*

Desktop publishing A computer software program that allows users to integrate text and graphics for their own publications *(p. 517)*

Dialect A regional variety of a language distinguished from other varieties by pronunciation, vocabulary, or grammatical form; the five major American English dialects are Eastern New England, Inland Northern, North Midland, South Midland, and Southern *(pp. 616, 698)*

Dialogue A conversation between two or more characters in a narrative or a play *(pp. 173, 299, 335)*

Diction A writer's choice of words; one of the elements of a writer's style *(p. 335)*

Direct object A noun or a pronoun that receives the action of the verb and answers the question *What?* or *Whom? (p. 572)*

Direct quotation A presentation of the exact words that a person said, wrote, or thought *(p. 395)*

Documentation A writer's acknowledgment of his or her sources of information or of direct quotations, which appears either in the body or at the end of a paper *(pp. 345, 405)*

Double-entry log A log in which a reader records the facts and details of a piece of literature in one column and his or her emotional response to and interpretation of these facts and details in a second column *(p. 332)*

Dramatic irony A special form of irony in which the audience or the readers know something that the characters do not *(p. 335)*

Drawing a conclusion The process of looking carefully at all the facts and other evidence in order to arrive at a reasonable explanation *(p. 442)*

Effect Any result (event, situation, condition) brought about by a cause *(p. 438)*

Electronic mail The capability of some computers to link users in a network, allowing them to access one another's files and to send messages back and forth *(p. 511)*

Elegy A poem written in memory of a person who has died *(p. 368)*

Elliptical clause An adverb clause from which words are missing but whose meaning is nevertheless clear *(p. 592)*

Essential appositive or **essential appositive phrase** An appositive or an appositive phrase that is necessary to the meaning of a sentence and therefore is not set off with commas *(p. 569)*

Essential clause An adjective clause that is necessary to the meaning of a sentence and therefore is not set off with commas *(p. 589)*

Etymology The origin and the history of a word *(p. 482)*

Euphemism A word or expression that substitutes for an unpleasant or unflattering one, such as *sanitary engineer* for *garbage collector (p. 611)*

Example A specific case or instance that illustrates a class of things or that clarifies or supports a broad assertion *(p. 29)*

Exclamatory sentence A sentence that shows strong feeling and that usually ends with an exclamation point *(p. 566)*

Expert An accepted source of special knowledge or expertise, which may be used as support in an argument *(p. 235)*

Exposition The aspect of a narrative or a play that gives important information about the time and setting of the action and what preceded it, the characters' pasts and motives, the nature of the conflict, and so on; a piece of writing that explains, defines, or analyzes *(pp. 288, 299)*

Extemporaneous speech A speech that is prepared in advance but is delivered without the aid of notes *(p. 466)*

Fact A statement or piece of information whose truth can be proved through observing, calculating, experimenting, measuring, or researching *(p. 234)*

Fallacy A method of reasoning that violates the rules of logic *(p. 256)*

Falling action The period following the climax of a narrative or a play during which a resolution is or is not achieved *(p. 168)*

Figurative language Language that goes beyond the literal meaning of words to create new meanings and that requires interpreting through the imagination *(pp. 92, 335)*

First-person point of view The point of view in autobiographies and in narratives that uses the pronouns *I*, *me*, and *we* to stress the importance of the narrator's participation and authority *(pp. 162, 285)*

Flashback The interruption of the chronological flow of incidents in a narrative by an earlier incident *(pp. 283, 334)*

Focusing idea The main point about a topic, often reflected in the topic sentence of a paragraph *(pp. 22, 39)*

Font The term used to denote one of the many type styles, for example, *Times* *(p. 517)*

Foreshadowing A literary device in which some future event or condition is hinted at or prefigured *(p. 334)*

Form The arrangement of words, lines, or larger divisions in a poem; the **structure** or organization of a literary work *(pp. 308, 335)*

Formal language The level of language used for writing that serves a serious purpose and that typically involves relatively long and complex sentences and challenging vocabulary *(p. 87)*

Formatting The word-processing functions that allow the user to experiment with how his or her writing will appear on the printed page *(p. 516)*

Free-lance writing Writing that is done for a newspaper or other publication by a person who is not on the staff and often works independently *(p. 109)*

Gender One of the three categories (masculine, feminine, and neuter) into which pronouns are divided in English *(p. 536)*

Generalization A statement about an entire class of people, objects, events, and so on that is valid only if it has no exceptions *(p. 445)*

Genre A specific type or kind of literature, such as poetry, the short story, or the essay *(p. 331)*

Gerund A verbal that ends in *-ing* and that functions only as a noun *(pp. 583, 656)*

Gerund phrase A phrase consisting of a gerund, its modifiers, and its complements *(p. 584)*

Hasty generalization A generalization that is invalid because it has exceptions; a faulty conclusion based on too few experiences or facts *(p. 445)*

Heading The section of a letter, usually a business letter, that includes the writer's address and the date *(p. 496)*

Helping verb A verb, such as *do*, *can*, or *may*, that is used with an action or a linking verb; sometimes called an **auxiliary verb** *(p. 542)*

Homophone A word that has the same pronunciation as another word but a different spelling, origin, or meaning *(p. 492)*

Hyperbole An exaggeration that is used to make a strong point or to entertain *(p. 93)*

Hypothesis A tentative generalization, or assumption, based on one's observation and experience that can be proved or disproved through further investigation *(p. 237)*

Illustration An extended example *(p. 29)*

Image A word or group of words that appeal directly to the senses through concrete words and sensory details or to the imagination through similes and metaphors; an element in imaginative writing that can convey theme *(pp. 302, 335)*

Imperative sentence A sentence that gives an order or makes a request *(p. 566)*

Implied topic sentence A topic sentence that is not explicitly stated but is clear from the content of the writing *(p. 42)*

Impromptu speech A speech that is given without specific preparation; a spontaneous speech *(p. 462)*

Indefinite article One of two adjectives, *a* and *an*, that does not specify a particular person, place, thing, or idea *(p. 549)*

Indefinite pronoun A pronoun, such as *all*, *each*, or *none*, that refers to people, places, or things in general *(p. 538)*

Independent clause A clause that can stand by itself as a sentence *(p. 587)*

Indirect discourse A narrator's presentation or "paraphrase" of what a character or person says as opposed to dialogue or monologue *(p. 173)*

Indirect object A noun or a pronoun that names the person or thing *to* whom or *for* whom an action is performed *(p. 572)*

Indo-European language family An ancient language family that embraces many of the languages spoken today in the area between western Europe and central India *(p. 520)*

Inductive reasoning The process of reasoning in which a general conclusion is drawn from a set of specific experiences or observations *(p. 237)*

Infinitive A verbal that consists of the first principal part, or basic form, of the verb and is usually preceded by the word *to (pp. 585, 620)*

Infinitive clause A noun clause consisting of an infinitive that has a subject *(p. 594)*

Infinitive phrase A phrase consisting of an infinitive and its modifiers and complements *(p. 586)*

Informal language Language that is characterized by a conversational tone, colloquialisms, the use of first- and second-person pronouns, and perhaps slang; the level of usage that is generally appropriate when speaking with or writing to people with whom one is familiar *(pp. 88, 616)*

Informal outline A rough outline that consists of a numbered list of events in chronological order *(p. 169)*

Inside address The section of a letter, usually a business letter, that includes the name and possibly the title of the recipient of the letter and his or her address *(p. 497)*

Intensive pronoun A reflexive pronoun, such as *myself* or *yourself,* used to draw special attention to a noun in a sentence *(p. 537)*

Interest inventory A writer's list of the people, places, activities, things, and so on that he or she knows firsthand and finds exciting or provocative *(p. 158)*

Interior monologue A presentation of what is going on inside a character's mind, including feelings, thoughts, memories, reactions, or ob-servations; what a character thinks as opposed to what he or she says *(p. 289)*

Interjection An exclamatory word or phrase that can stand by itself or appear in a sentence and is usually followed by an exclamation point *(p. 564)*

Internal rhyme A sound device in which two words rhyme within a line of poetry, for example, "She wrote words that smote his too tender heart" *(p. 310)*

Interpreting The process of explaining or clarifying information, facts, examples, or evidence or the process of unfolding the meaning(s) of a piece of literature *(pp. 9, 442)*

Interrogative pronoun A pronoun, such as *what, who,* or *whose,* that introduces a question *(p. 537)*

Interrogative sentence A sentence that asks a question and ends with a question mark *(p. 566)*

Intransitive verb A verb whose action is not directed toward someone or something; a verb that does not take an object *(p. 544)*

Invalid conclusion A conclusion that is not consistent with the available evidence *(p. 442)*

Invention software Special word-processing programs that encourage the user to use his or her imagination by eliciting a response to various stimuli *(p. 511)*

Invisible writing A form of freewriting that involves turning down the brightness control on a computer screen and writing without the distraction of seeing what one has written *(p. 511)*

Irony A figure of speech in which one thing is said but something else, usually the opposite, is meant; a tone (which may pervade a work) that is characterized by a deliberate, though often subtle, contrast between apparent and intended meaning *(p. 335)*

Irrelevant details Details that distract, mislead, or confuse the reader because they are not sufficiently connected to the writer's topic *(p. 437)*

Jargon The specialized or technical language of a trade or a profession, which may be inappropriate in writing and speaking situations outside its original boundaries; sometimes used to refer to any wordy or overly formal language *(p. 616)*

Laser printer A printer that produces typeset quality print and graphics *(p. 517)*

Lexicographer A person who writes a dictionary *(p. 610)*

Line of reasoning The series of logical steps a writer takes to arrive at a conclusion or to defend an opinion *(p. 243)*

Linking verb A verb, such as *be*, that connects a noun or a pronoun with words that identify or describe the noun or the pronoun *(p. 540)*

Literal language Language that reflects the denotative meaning of words as opposed to the connotative or figurative meaning *(p. 92)*

Loaded words Words with highly positive or negative connotations whose use undermines the validity of an argument *(p. 255)*

Main heading One of the major headings in an outline that indicates a discrete idea and is numbered with a Roman numeral *(p. 50)*

Main idea The idea that controls the development of a paragraph or a longer piece of writing and gives it unity, usually contained in a thesis statement *(p. 437)*

Main verb The verb that is helped by an auxiliary or linking verb *(p. 542)*

Mapping A highly visual and creative form of outlining that results in a graphic representation of a writer's thinking and planning by showing the connection among facts, feelings, impressions, ideas, and so on *(pp. 48, 169)*

Meaning The significance of a word, including both its denotations and its connotations, that is determined, in part, by the context in which it is used *(p. 611)*

Member An item that shares a feature(s) with other items and belongs, along with them, to a class *(p. 436)*

Metaphor An implied comparison in which one thing (or group of things) is presented as if it were something else, usually something quite different; a form of figurative language *(pp. 93, 127, 309, 335)*

Middle English The form of English spoken and written during the period A.D. 1100 to 1500 *(p. 523)*

Modem A device that connects two or more computers through a telephone line, allowing users access to a variety of databases and software programs *(p. 512)*

Modified block style The written or typed form of a business letter in which the heading, the complimentary close, and the signature appear on the right *(p. 498)*

Modifier A word or group of words that adds to or limits the meaning of another word or group of words *(p. 130)*

Narrative A writing focus that is primarily concerned with telling a story *(p. 158)*

Narrator The person who tells a story; the narrator's voice may be that of a character or of another **persona** of the author *(p. 334)*

Nonessential appositive or **nonessential appositive phrase** An appositive or an appositive phrase that is not necessary to the meaning of the sentence and, therefore, is set off with commas *(p. 580)*

Nonessential clause An adjective clause that is not necessary to the meaning of a sentence and, therefore, is set off with commas *(p. 589)*

Nonprint resources Resource materials, such as compact discs, videotapes, and cassettes, carried by libraries in addition to printed materials *(p. 386)*

Nonstandard English Word choices and combinations that are incorrect for most speaking or writing situations but might be used to develop character or theme in a literary work *(p. 617)*

Noun A word that names a person, a place, a thing, or an idea *(p. 532)*

Noun clause A subordinate clause that functions as a noun in a sentence *(p. 593)*

Number The indication of whether a word, often a pronoun, refers to one (singular) or more than one (plural) person, place, thing, or idea *(p. 536)*

Object A noun or a pronoun that follows an action verb in the active voice and that receives or is affected by the action of the verb *(pp. 544, 572)*

Object of the preposition A noun or a pronoun that follows a preposition, although other words may intervene *(p. 558)*

Objective complement A noun or an adjective

that follows a direct object and explains, identifies, or describes that object *(p. 574)*

Old English The form of English used by the Anglo-Saxons from about A.D. 450 to 1100 *(p. 521)*

Omniscient point of view A kind of third-person point of view in which the narrator is "all-knowing," that is, can enter any of the characters' minds at any time and can freely comment on any aspect of the action or even the significance of the story *(p. 295)*

Onomatopoeia A sound device in which words such as *cuckoo* imitate the sounds that they denote *(pp. 310, 335)*

Opinion A personal thought, feeling, or judgment about a subject that cannot be proved but can be supported through reasoning *(p. 230)*

Order of importance The arrangement of details according to their significance *(pp. 38, 465)*

Paraphrase To restate the words of another person in one's own words; such a restatement *(pp. 345, 396)*

Participial phrase A phrase consisting of a participle and its modifiers and complements *(p. 581)*

Participle A verb form that functions as an adjective; it expresses action or state of being and may be followed by a complement *(p. 581)*

Passive voice The voice of a verb in which the subject receives rather than performs the action of the verb *(p. 546)*

Periodic sentence A sentence in which the main point is not presented until the end; a rhetorical strategy used to create suspense and to emphasize a point *(p. 83)*

Person The form a pronoun takes to distinguish between the speaker or writer (first person), the individual addressed (second person), and the individual or thing spoken or written about (third person) *(p. 536)*

Persona The speaker in a poem or the narrator in a story as distinguished from the poet or the storyteller; literally a mask *(pp. 26, 306, 334)*

Personal pronoun A kind of pronoun that

changes form to express person, number, and gender *(p. 536)*

Personification A form of comparison in which inanimate objects or ideas are given human characteristics, including thoughts, feelings, powers, or physical attributes; a form of figurative language *(pp. 93, 310, 335)*

Phrase A group of related words that functions as a single part of speech but that lacks a subject, a predicate, or both *(p. 578)*

Pitch Another word for **point;** the unit of measurement for type sizes *(p. 517)*

Plagiarism The act of using another person's words or ideas without acknowledgment *(p. 395)*

Plot The arrangement of actions, incidents, or events in a work of fiction *(pp. 278, 334)*

Plural noun A noun that names more than one person, place, thing, or idea *(p. 532)*

Point The unit of measurement for type sizes; also known as **pitch** *(p. 517)*

Point of view The perspective from which the narrator observes the subject; this perspective may be either first or third person and influences what the reader observes *(pp. 124, 285, 335)*

Possessive noun A noun that shows possession and answers the question *Whose?* or *Which? (p. 551)*

Possessive pronoun A personal pronoun that shows *to whom* or *to what* something belongs; also called a **pronominal adjective** *(p. 536)*

Predicate adjective An adjective that follows a linking verb and modifies the subject of the sentence *(p. 576)*

Predicate nominative A noun or a pronoun that follows a linking verb and that renames the subject of a sentence *(p. 575)*

Prefix A word part with a distinct meaning of its own that is added to the beginning of a base word or a root to make a new word *(p. 478)*

Preliminary position statement A sentence that summarizes the main position that will be supported in a persuasive paragraph or essay *(p. 230)*

Premises The first two statements of a syllogism which are assumed to be true and from which a conclusion necessarily follows (p. 240)

Preposition A word that expresses a relationship between a noun or a pronoun and another word in a sentence (p. 557)

Prepositional phrase A phrase consisting of a preposition, its object, and any modifiers of the object (pp. 558, 578)

Present participle One of the four principal parts of a verb; the participle is formed by adding the suffix -ing to the infinitive of a verb (p. 620)

Primary source The work about which one writes a literary or other type of essay and with which one supports and explains assertions (pp. 337, 344)

Principal part One of the four basic parts, or forms, of a verb: the infinitive, the present participle, the past, and the past participle (pp. 547, 620)

Pronoun A word that replaces or refers to a noun (p. 536)

Proper adjective An adjective, usually capitalized, that is formed from a proper noun (p. 550)

Proper noun The name or the title of a particular person, place, thing, or idea, usually beginning with a capital letter (p. 533)

Props The objects or furniture used in the production of a play (p. 300)

Rambling sentence A sentence that has too many phrases and clauses, making it difficult to read and understand (p. 78)

Rebuttal The act of refuting an opposing position with evidence and argumentation (p. 233)

Redundancy The needless repetition of an idea in the same or other words; an impediment to effective communication (p. 617)

Reflexive pronoun A pronoun formed with the suffixes -self or -selves, used to indicate that the subject acts to, for, or upon itself (p. 537)

Relative pronoun A pronoun, such as that, which, or whose, that introduces an adjective clause and tells which, what kind, or how many (p. 537)

Resolution A solution to a problem or an end to a conflict in a story, a poem, or other piece of writing (p. 282)

Résumé A summary of a person's qualifica-

tions for employment, including education and job histories (p. 505)

Rhyme scheme The pattern that rhyming words form in a poem; an element that contributes to the sound and sense of a poem (p. 310)

Rhythm A sound device created by the pattern of stressed and unstressed syllables in words and in lines of poetry (p. 310)

Rising action A series of actions that build in intensity or suspense to the climax (p. 168)

Root The central or basic element of a word (p. 477)

Rough outline An informal outline that consists of a numbered list of events in chronological order (pp. 49, 169)

Rune A letter from an ancient Germanic alphabet used by the Anglo-Saxons for magical, ritualistic, and religious purposes (p. 521)

Run-on sentence A faulty sentence consisting of two or more complete sentences written as if they were one sentence (p. 600)

Salutation The greeting of a letter (p. 497)

Scanner A device for copying photographs or printed illustrations onto a computer disk (p. 517)

Secondary source An essay, article, or book about a **primary source** that is used to support the central idea of a literary essay (pp. 337, 345)

Sentence A group of words that has a subject and a predicate and expresses a complete thought (p. 566)

Sentence fragment A group of words that either lacks a subject or a predicate or does not express a complete thought (p. 598)

Sentence outline An outline that includes headings written as complete sentences, used to organize prewriting notes for a research paper or another piece of writing (p. 398)

Set The constructed pieces, including furniture and props, that represent the setting of a play (p. 300)

Setting The time and the place — and often the atmosphere — of a literary work (pp. 165, 278, 334)

Shades of meaning The slight, subtle differences in meaning among synonyms, or words with similar **denotations** (p. 480)

Simile A direct comparison of two things using the word *like* or *as;* a form of figurative language *(pp. 93, 127, 309, 335)*

Simple predicate The verb or the verb phrase that describes the action or states the condition of the subject *(p. 567)*

Simple sentence A sentence made up of an independent clause but no subordinate clauses *(p. 595)*

Simple subject The noun or the pronoun that states whom or what the sentence is about *(p. 566)*

Singular noun A noun that names only one person, place, thing, or idea *(p. 532)*

Situation The event or the action taking place in a literary work or the condition of the speaker, the narrator, or the characters *(p. 334)*

Slang Informal, often nonstandard, language peculiar to a culture or subculture and characterized by spontaneity and transitoriness *(p. 616)*

Social style One's style of communication, including diction, tone of voice, and syntax, which varies with the social situation one is in *(p. 698)*

Spatial order The organization of details according to their location in space; used when a topic involves physical or geographical relationships *(pp. 37, 465)*

Speaker The person or the voice created by the poet to speak the words of a poem; the **persona** or mask of a poet *(p. 334)*

Stage business An action or a set of movements performed by an actor, often involving props *(p. 299)*

Stage directions The playwright's descriptions (usually enclosed in brackets) of various elements of a play, such as the character's movements or emotions, the set, props, or costuming *(pp. 300, 335)*

Stage right, stage left Terms that refer to the actors' right and left as they move onstage *(p. 300)*

Standard English The level of usage that is regarded as correct and appropriate for almost any speaking or writing situation *(p. 616)*

Stereotype A hasty generalization about all members of a specific group, such as a profession, a race, a gender, or a society *(p. 445)*

Structure The arrangement or the organization of a literary work, largely determined by the **conventions** of a given **genre** (for example, plays are usually organized into acts and scenes) *(p. 335)*

Style The qualities that distinguish one person's writing from another's, such as the approach toward a subject, the choice and use of words, and the construction of sentences *(pp. 87, 260, 335, 467)*

Subheadings The supporting details for the main headings of an outline, identified with capital letters *(p. 51)*

Subject complement A word that comes after a linking verb and identifies or describes the subject *(p. 575)*

Subordinate clause A group of words that has a subject and a predicate but cannot stand by itself as a complete sentence because it does not express a complete thought *(p. 588)*

Subordinating conjunction A word or phrase, such as *after, because,* or *even though,* that introduces a subordinate clause and connects it to an independent clause *(p. 561)*

Subordination The process of combining ideas of unequal importance, usually in a sentence, in such a way that their relative importance is evident *(p. 74)*

Suffix A word part with a distinct meaning of its own that is added to the end of a base word or a root *(p. 478)*

Summary A brief rewording of the important ideas in a reading selection, a film, a lecture, and so on *(p. 396)*

Supporting sentence A sentence that explains or otherwise develops what is stated in the topic sentence *(p. 39)*

Syllogism A set of three related statements — two premises and one conclusion — that tests the logic of a deductive argument *(p. 240)*

Symbol Something that stands for or represents something else; the meaning of a literary symbol is always conditioned by its context *(p. 335)*

Synthesizing The process of combining separate elements to form a logical and understandable whole; the counterpart of **analyzing** *(pp. 43, 56)*

Tense One of the six verb forms that expresses time *(p. 623)*

Theme The controlling idea or meaning of a literary work; a work may have several themes *(pp. 278, 335)*

Thesaurus A book of synonyms *(p. 483)*

Thesis statement In an essay, the topic sentence or other statement that tells the reader what the main idea is *(pp. 46, 141, 176, 211, 341, 379)*

Third-person point of view The perspective of a narrator who is an observer of the action and who uses the pronouns *he*, *she*, and *they* to refer to the characters *(pp. 162, 285)*

Time line A chronological list of important events in a person's life or in some other defined scope, such as a nation's history *(p. 158)*

Tone The narrator's or the speaker's tone of voice or attitude about the subject (including the characters and their actions in a story) or the audience, which may be ironic, serious, comic, satiric, and so on *(pp. 27, 124, 260, 306, 335)*

Topic outline An outline for a research report or other piece of writing in which the headings are written as single words, phrases, or clauses *(p. 50)*

Topic sentence The sentence that states the limited topic of the paragraph and its focusing idea *(pp. 39, 437)*

Transition A word or a phrase, such as *thus*, *while*, or *as soon as*, that helps readers to move with full understanding from one event or idea to the next *(p. 36)*

Transitive verb A verb that requires a direct object to complete its meaning; a verb that directs the action of the subject toward someone or something *(p. 544)*

Turning point The high point, or climax, of the action or the peak of the suspense in a narrative or a play *(p. 282)*

Unity The quality of a piece of writing in which the supporting sentences or paragraphs are clearly related to the topic sentence or the thesis statement *(pp. 39, 66)*

Valid conclusion A conclusion that follows logically from a convincing line of reasoning, whether inductive, deductive, or a combination of the two *(pp. 236, 442)*

Verb A word that expresses an action or a state of being *(p. 540)*

Verb phrase A phrase that consists of a main verb and one or more auxiliary verbs *(p. 542)*

Verbal A verb form (participle, gerund, and infinitive) that functions as a noun, an adjective, or an adverb *(p. 580)*

Verbosity Wordiness *(p. 617)*

Vertical file A file in which collections of miscellaneous printed materials are kept by libraries *(p. 386)*

Working source list A list of the sources to be used when writing a research report or other piece of writing *(p. 387)*

Works Cited A list of all sources and related publication information used in the preparation of a work, usually appearing at the end of a book or a paper *(p. 407)*

Index

placement of, 667–669; reducing, 80. *See also* type of clause.

cliché, 93, 295

climax, 168, 282

clip art, 517

closure, defined, 44

clustering, 14, 16

coherence, 36, 215; revising for, 67–68, 78–79

collective noun, 533, 640; in pronoun-antecedent agreement, 649

college application, 507–508

college interview, 473–474

colon, 723–724

comma, 147; with address or date, 719; with appositive, 718–719; with clauses, 718–719; with conjunctive adverb, 562; in direct address, 718; with independent clauses, 587, 595; interjection and, 564, 718; with introductory word or phrase, 314; in letter, 719; misuse of, 720–721; with nonessential element, 314, 718–719; after phrase, 718–719; to prevent misreading, 720; in series, 716–717; splice, 600

commendation letter, strategies for writing, 500

common noun, 533

comparison, 30–31; compound, 666; degrees of, 664; double, 665; illogical, 666; in descriptive writing, 127; incomplete, 665–666; modifiers in, 664–666; pronoun in, 660

comparison and contrast, 30–32, 766–785; in literary essay, 344

complement, 572–577; defined, 572; object as, 572–573; objective, 574; subject, 575–576

complete predicate, 568–569

complete subject, 568–569

complex sentence, 596

complimentary close, 498

compound comparison, 666

compound noun, 533

compound object, 573

compound predicate, 567–568

compound sentence, 595–596

compound subject, 567, 638

compound-complex sentence, 596

conciseness, revising for, 80–82

concluding paragraph, of essay, 58

concluding sentence, 39, 44–45, 140

conclusions: analyzing and interpreting, 442–443; validity of, 442

concrete noun, 533

conflict, 168, 279, 283, 289, 292, 293

conjunction, 559–564; adverb used as, 562–563; coordinating, 73, 559, 587, 595; correlative, 77, 560; defined, 559; misuse of, 100; preposition distinguished from, 562; subordinating, 75, 561–562, 591, 593

conjunctive adverb, 73, 562–563 with independent clauses, 588, 596

connotation, 27, 91, 481, 611

Conrad, Joseph, 150–152

context, 476–477

contraction, apostrophe in, 729

contrast, 30–31; in descriptive writing, 127

conventions, literary, 348, 361

Cooke, Alistair, 165

coordinating conjunction, 73, 559, 587, 595

coordination, 72

correlative conjunction, 77, 560

critical reading, 112–113

critical review, 355–365; audience and tone for, 355–356; drafting, 360–361; note taking for, 358; organizing, 359–360; planning, 358–360; prewriting, 355–359; proofreading, 364; publishing, 365; revising, 362–363

Critical Thinking

unit, *436–445;* analyzing, *17, 18, 19, 20, 24, 26, 64, 67, 69, 95, 113, 121, 122, 178, 179, 332, 333, 357, 442–443;* analyzing for fallacies, *256, 259;* cause and effect, *33, 34, 282, 283, 291;* classifying, *34, 35, 206, 336, 337, 398, 400, 436–437;* comparing, *30, 32, 93, 127;* contrasting, *30, 32, 127;* deductive reasoning, *239, 241;* defining, *35;* determining relationships, *13, 14, 15, 16, 17, 72, 74, 79, 121, 122, 216, 243, 245, 279, 438–441;* distinguishing among methods, *208, 209;* drawing conclusions, *442–443;* evaluating, *65, 87, 89, 144, 214, 215, 260, 261,*

Critical Thinking,   cont.

293, 311, 359, 378, 380, 381, 392, 393, 410, 412, 414, 416; evaluating opinions, *230, 231;* generalizing, *237, 238, 445;* in grammar, *534, 535, 538, 539, 541, 542, 543, 545, 546, 547, 548, 552, 553, 555, 556, 558, 559, 561, 563, 564, 566, 568, 570, 571, 573, 574, 576, 580, 582, 584, 586, 589, 592, 594, 597, 600, 601;* inductive reasoning, *237, 238;* interpreting, *9, 10, 336, 337, 359, 442–443;* in mechanics, *708, 713, 716, 719, 721, 722, 724, 728, 730, 734, 735, 738, 740;* organizing, *36, 37, 38, 48, 49, 50, 52, 132, 133, 169, 170, 204, 205, 344, 346, 398, 400;* predicting outcomes, *233, 234;* sequencing, *159, 282, 283, 360;* summarizing, *404;* synthesizing, *43, 56, 57;* in usage, *618, 622, 625, 628, 630, 633, 637, 640, 641, 642, 643, 645, 646, 649, 651, 652, 654, 656, 657, 658, 659, 660, 662, 667, 669, 676, 680, 684, 689*

from *Cry, the Beloved Country,* 133

cubing, 19–20

"Day-Long Day," F4

dangling modifier, 668–669

dash, 732–733

from *Decameron,* The, 535

declarative sentence, 566, 569

deductive reasoning, 239–241

definite article, 549–550

definition, 34–35

degrees of comparison, 664

demonstrative pronoun, 537, 551

denotation, 91, 481, 611

descriptive essay, 140–143; drafting, 140–143; structure of, 141–143

descriptive language, 129–131

descriptive paragraph, drafting, 137–140

descriptive writing, 120–148; audience for, 123–124; comparison and contrast in, 127; details in, 122, 124–129; discovering ideas for, 120; exploring ideas

quotation marks, 345, 725–728; misuse of, 727; other punctuation with, 296, 727; uses of, 725–727

radio program, citing as source, 390
rambling sentences, 78
Ratti, John, 307–308
reading, strategies for, 356–357
reading log, 332
reading-comprehension tests, 453–455
reasoning: chain of, 244; line of, 243; types of, 237–241
rebuttal, 244–245; defined, 233
"Reconnaissance," H3
reducing phrases and clauses, 80
redundancy, 617
reference works, 385–386; citing as source, 390
reflexive pronoun, 537; in pronoun-antecedent agreement, 652
relative adverb, 589
relative pronoun, 537, 551, 588, 593, 658
request letter, strategies for writing, 499
research paper, 372–433, 751–759; citations in, 405–408; documentation of, 405–408, 760–765, drafting, 402–408; headings for, 422; manuscript form of, 421–422; note taking for, 387–391; outline for, 398–399; plan for, 382–383; planning, 376–381; prewriting, 376–400; proofreading, 419–420; publishing, 421–423; researching for, 382–396; revising, 410–416; sample, 424–427; structure of, 402–404; thesis statement of, 379–380, 398; title of, 416; tone and style of, 414–416; topic of, 376–377; visual aids in, 403–404; Works Cited page, 407–408
resolution, 282

résumé: sample, 506; strategies for writing, 505
from *Return of the Native, The,* 117–119, 134–135
review. *See* critical review.
revising, 63–96; checklist for, 97, 853; for content, 144; for description, 144–145; for economy, 81–82; for emphasis, 83–84; for exposition, 214–217; for literary essay, 350–351; for narration, 178–180; peer review and, 64–65; for persuasion, 260–261; for poem, 311–313 purposes for, 66–68; of sentences, 71–86; for research paper, 410–419; for story, 293–296; strategies for, 63–64, 65, 66, 68; for style and tone, 87–95, 145–146, 295; for variety, 85–86; with word processor, 514–515; word choice in, 89–91
"River Skater," 306
Roberts, Robin, 55
Robinson, Marilynne, 318–320
Roget's International Thesaurus, 483–484
roots, 477–478
rough outline, 49–50
Rudolph, Wilma, C1
Rukeyser, Muriel, 301–302
run-on sentence, 100, 262, 600–601
runes, 521–522

salutation, 497
Sanchez, Ricardo, F3
Sasaura, Paul, 264–265
Scholastic Aptitude Test (SAT), 448, 456
from "Sculptor's Funeral, The," 127
secondary source, 337, 345
"seed" sound, 491
semicolon, 218; for clarification, 722; with conjunctive adverb, 562; with independent clauses, 588, 596, 721–722; with items in series, 722; sentence combining with, 73
sentence, 566–577; beginning of, 85–86; complete, 598; defined, 566; faulty, 77–79; length of, 86; parallel structure in, 77–78, 100; revising, 71–86; run-on,

100, 262, 600–601; structure of, 86, 595–596; types of, 566
sentence combining, 72–79, 216
sentence fragment. *See* fragment.
sentence length, 86
sentence order, 85–86
sentence outline, 53
sentence structure, 86, 595–596
sentence-completion tests, 449–450
sequence of tenses, 629–630
set, stage, 300
setting, 165, 278, 279, 283, 288, 298, 334
Shakespeare, William, 530–531
"Shaving," 271–277
short story, 278–297; characters in, 278, 279, 283, 289, 290–291; closing, 291–292; conflict in, 279, 283, 289, 292, 293; details in, 291; dialogue in, 289; drafting, 288–292; elements of, 278–279; events in, 291, 292; plan for, 281–286; plot in, 278, 282, 291; point of view in, 285–286, 294, 295; prewriting, 278–287; proofreading, 296–297; publishing, 297; revising, 293–296; setting in, 278, 279, 283, 288; theme of, 278, 292; tone of, 286, 295
simile, 93, 127, 309, 335
simple predicate, 567
simple sentence, 595
simple subject, 566–567
Singer, Isaac Bashevis, 129
situation, 334
from *Six Men,* 165
slang, 616, 617
slash, 345, 733
from *Small Town in Germany, A,* 123
Smith, Adam, 226
Smith, Stevie, 342
Snow, C. P., 163
from "Sonny's Blues," 444
sources, 337–338, 344–345; citing, 405–408; documenting, 405; evaluating, 392–393; lists of, 387–391; notes from, 394–396
spatial order, 37, 132–133, 204
speaker, 334
speech, 462–470; audience for, 462, 469; body of, 465; conclusion of, 466; delivering, 468–470; evaluation of, 468, 469–470; formality of, 462; information gathering for, 464;

verbosity, 617
vertical file, 386
viewpoints, 20
Villanueva, Tino, F4
vocabulary, 476–485; connotation and denotation, 481; context and, 476–477; dictionary and, 481–483; prefixes, roots, and suffixes, 477–480; strategies for learning, 477; synonyms, 480; thesaurus and, 483–484

The Vocabulary Connection
610–611, 698–699, 746–747

vocabulary tests, 448–452
voice, 546
van Lawick-Goodall, Jane, 161

Warner, Sylvia Townsend, 287
from *Way Things Work, The*, 200
Webb, Walter Prescott, 733

Welles, Winifred, 306
from *West with the Night*, 167, 168–169
Wharton, Edith, 443
"When You Are Old," 333
from *Who Pushed Humpty Dumpty?*, 201
who, whom, 657–658
from *Wilma*, C1
Willard, Nancy, 43
from "Will Diversity = Opportunity + Advancement for Blacks?" D2
"Word," 309
word choice, 81–82, 89–91, 216, 480–484; for speech, 467–468; in poetry, 309–310, 312; strategies for, 90–91
word division, 731
word processor, 510–517; drafting with, 513; electronic thesaurus for, 514; graphics for, 517; invention software for, 511; prewriting with, 511–512;

printers for, 517; proofreading with, 515–516; publishing with, 516–517; revising with, 514–515; spelling checker for, 516; style analysis programs for, 514–515
word usage, proofreading for, 102
working title, 164
writer's notebook, 8–10, 195–196; electronic, 511
writing: factors influencing, responses to, 109–112

The Writing Connection
565, 577, 602, 619, 634–635, 646–647, 663, 670–671, 690–691, 709, 714–715, 736–737, 741

writing contests, 109
"Written in the Sunset," F1

Yeats, William Butler, 333

Acknowledgments *(continued from page ii)*

From "Afro-American Fragment" by Langston Hughes in *Selected Poems of Langston Hughes*. Copyright © 1959 by Langston Hughes. Reprinted by permission of Alfred A. Knopf, Inc., and Harold Ober Associates, Inc.

From *The Amazing Brain* by Robert Ornstein and Richard F. Thompson. Copyright © 1984 by Robert Ornstein and Richard F. Thompson. Reprinted by permission of Houghton Mifflin Company and the Virginia Barber Literary Agency.

From *An American Childhood* by Annie Dillard. Copyright © 1987 by Annie Dillard. Reprinted by permission of Harper & Row, Publishers, Inc.

From *The American Heritage Dictionary* (Second Edition). Copyright © 1985 by Houghton Mifflin Company. Reprinted by permission of Houghton Mifflin Company.

From "Analyzing 'Araby' as Story and Discourse" by Sosnoski et al. in *James Joyce Quarterly*. Copyright © 1981 by the University of Tulsa. Reprinted by permission of *James Joyce Quarterly*, University of Tulsa.

From "Appetite" in *I Can't Stay Long* by Laurie Lee. Copyright © 1975 by Laurie Lee. Reprinted by permission of Andre Deutsch, Ltd.

"Araby" from *Dubliners* by James Joyce. Copyright ©1918 by B. W. Huebsch. Definitive text copyright © 1967 by The Estate of James Joyce. Reprinted by permission of Viking Penguin, a division of Penguin books USA, Inc., and Jonathan Cape, Ltd.

From "'Araby' and the 'Extended Simile'" (original title: "Joyce's 'Araby' and the 'Extended Simile'") by Ben L. Collins. In *James Joyce Quarterly*. Copyright © 1967 by the University of Tulsa. Reprinted by permission of *James Joyce Quarterly*, University of Tulsa.

From "The Author's Introduction" in *The Decameron* by Giovanni Boccaccio. Translated by Mark Musa and Peter E. Bondanella. Copyright © 1977 by W. W. Norton and Company, Inc. Reprinted by permission of W. W. Norton and Company, Inc.

From *Barrio Boy* by Ernesto Galarza. Reprinted by permission.

From *Blackberry Winter: My Earlier Years* by Margaret Mead. Copyright © 1972 by Margaret Mead. Reprinted by permission of William Morrow & Company, Inc.

"Boy with His Hair Cut Short" in *Waterlily Fire* by Muriel Rukeyser. Copyright © 1962 by Muriel Rukeyser. Reprinted by permission.

Excerpts from *A Brief History of Time* by Stephen W. Hawking, copyright © 1988 by Stephen W. Hawking, Interior Illustrations © 1988 by Ron Miller. Used by permission of Bantam Books, a division of Bantam, Doubleday, Dell Publishing group, Inc. and Writers House, Inc.

From "Churchill" by C. P. Snow. Copyright © 1963 by Cowles Magazine and Broadcasting, Inc. Reprinted by permission.

From *Cry, the Beloved Country* by Alan Paton. Copyright © 1948 by Alan Paton. Copyright © renewed 1976 by Alan Paton. Reprinted by permission of Charles Scribner's Sons, an imprint of Macmillan Publishing Company and Jonathan Cape, Ltd.

"Day-Long Day" from *Hay Otra Voz Poems* by Tino Villanueva. Copyright © 1972 by Tino Villanueva. Reprinted by permission of the author.

From *The Dining Room* by A. R. Gurney, Jr. copyright © 1981, 1982 by A. R. Gurney, Jr. Reprinted by permission.

Excerpts from *Dust Tracks On a Road* by Zora Neale Hurston. Copyright © 1942 by Zora Neale Hurston. Reprinted by permission of Harper Collins Publishers, Inc.

From "The Father" by John Holmes. Extensive efforts to locate the rights holder were unsuccessful. If the rights holder sees this notice, she or he should contact the School Division Permissions Department, Houghton Mifflin Company, One Beacon Street, Boston, MA 02108

From *Firebrat* by Nancy Willard. Copyright © 1988 by Nancy Willard. Reprinted by permission of Alfred A. Knopf, Inc.

From "Footfalls" by Wilbur Daniel Steele in *Introduction to the Short Story* edited by Robert W. Boynton and Maynard Mack. Copyright © 1929 by Wilbur Daniel Steele. Reprinted by permission of Harold Matson Company, Inc.

From *The Four-Minute Mile* by Roger Bannister. Reprinted by permission of Sir Roger Bannister.

From *Free to Choose* by Milton and Rose Friedman. Copyright © 1979, 1980 by Milton Friedman and Rose D. Friedman. Reprinted by permission of Harcourt Brace Jovanovich, Inc.

From *Freedom's Trail* (Teacher's Edition) by Bartlett, Keller and Carey. Copyright © 1981 by Houghton Mifflin Company. Reprinted by permission of Houghton Mifflin Company.

"From the North Terrace" by Rolfe Humphries in *Collected Poems of Rolfe Humphries* by Rolfe Humphries. Copyright © 1965 by Indiana University Press. Reprinted by permission of Indiana University Press.

From "The Garden Party" in *The Short Stories of Katherine Mansfield* by Katherine Mansfield. Copyright © 1922, 1937 by Alfred A. Knopf, Inc. Copyright © renewed 1950 by J. Middleton Murry. Reprinted by permission of Alfred A. Knopf.

"The Gift Outright" in *The Poetry of Robert Frost* by Robert Frost. Edited by Edward Connery Lathem. Copyright © 1942 by Robert Frost, and renewed 1970 by Leslie Frost Ballantine. Reprinted by permission of Henry Holt and Company, Inc., and Jonathan Cape, Ltd.

From "God Bless America" by John Oliver Killens from *The California Quarterly*. Copyright © 1952 by The California Quarterly.

From *Going Home* by Doris Lessing. Copyright © 1957, 1968 by Doris Lessing. Reprinted by permission.

From "A Good Long Sidewalk" from *Dancers on the Shore* by William Melvin Kelley (New York, NY: Doubleday, 1964).

"Good Work, Good Pay" by Art Buchwald. Copyright © 1989 by the *L.A. Times* Syndicate. Reprinted by permission of Art Buchwald.

From *Gorillas in the Mist* by Dian Fossey. Copyright © 1983 by Dian Fossey. Reprinted by permission of Houghton Mifflin Company and Hodder & Stoughton, Ltd.

From "The Great Mouse Plot" in *Boy: Tales of Childhood* by Roald Dahl. Copyright © 1984 by Roald Dahl. Reprinted by permission of Farrar, Straus & Giroux, Inc.

From *The Greeks* (revised edition, 1957) by H. D. F. Kitto. Copyright © 1951 by H. D. F. Kitto. Copyright © 1957 by the Estate of H. D. F. Kitto. Reprinted by permission of Penguin Books, Ltd.

From *The Habit of Being* by Flannery O'Connor. Edited by Sally Fitzgerald. Copyright © 1979 by Regina O'Connor. Reprinted by permission of Farrar, Straus & Giroux, Inc.

From *A History of the World* (revised edition) by Marvin Perry. Copyright © 1985, 1988 by Houghton Mifflin Company. Reprinted by permission of Houghton Mifflin Company.

From *An Honest Preface and Other Essays* by Walter Prescott Webb. Copyright © 1959 by Walter Prescott Webb. Copyright © renewed 1987 by Terrell Webb. Reprinted by permission of Houghton Mifflin Company.

From *Housekeeping* by Marilynne Robinson. Copyright © 1980 by Marilynne Robinson. Reprinted by permission of Farrar, Straus & Giroux, Inc., and the Ellen Levine Literary Agency.

From "Hunger in New York City" from *Going for the Rain: Poems* by Simon J. Ortiz. Reprinted by permission of the author.

"i yearn" by Richard Sanchez. Copyright © 1975 by Richard Sanchez.

"In a Poem" by Robert Frost in *The Poetry of Robert Frost* edited by Edward Connery Lathem. Copyright © 1942 by Robert Frost. Copyright © renewed 1970 by Leslie Frost Ballantine. Reprinted by permission of Henry Holt and Company.

"In Memory of W. B. Yeats": in *W. H. Auden: Collected Poems by W. H. Auden*. Edited by Edward Mendelson. Copyright © 1940 by W. H. Auden. Copyright © renewed 1968 by W. H. Auden. Reprinted by permission of Random House, Inc.

From *In the Shadow of Man* by Jane van Lawick-Goodall.

Copyright © 1971 by Hugo and Jane van Lawick-Goodall. Reprinted by permission of Houghton Mifflin Company.

From *Joyce's Dubliners: Substance, Vision and Art* by Warren Beck. Copyright © 1969 Duke University Press. Reprinted by permission of Duke University Press.

From *Joyce: The Man, the Work, the Reputation* by Marvin Magalaner and Richard M. Kain. Copyright © 1956 by New York University Press. Reprinted by permission of Marvin Magalaner.

From *The Labyrinth of Solitude; Life and Thought In Mexico* by Octavio Paz, translated by Lysander Kemp (New York, NY: Grove Press, 1961).

From *The Ladies of Missalonghi* by Colleen McCullough. Copyright © 1987 by Colleen Mc Cullough. Reprinted by permission of Harper & Row, Publishers, Inc. and Century Hutchinson, Ltd.

From *Lake Wobegon Days* by Garrison Keillor. Copyright © 1985 by Garrison Keillor. Reprinted by permission of Viking Penguin, a division of Penguin Books, USA, Inc., and Faber & Faber, Ltd.

From "The Little Shoemaker" by Isaac Bashevis Singer. Translated by Isaac Rosenfeld from *A Treasury of Yiddish Stories*, edited by Irving Howe and Eliezer Greenberg (New York, NY: Viking Penguin, 1954).

From *The Lives of a Cell* by Lewis Thomas. Copyright © 1974 by Lewis Thomas. All rights reserved. Reprinted by permission of Viking Penguin, a division of Penguin Books USA, Inc., and Oxford University Press. Originally appeared *in The New England Journal of Medicine.*

From "Look At all Those Roses" in *The Collected Stories of Elizabeth Bowen*. Copyright © 1959 by Elizabeth Bowen. Reprinted by permission of Alfred A. Knopf, Inc.

From *Lost in Translation: A Life in New Language* by Eva Hoffman. Copyright © 1989 by Eva Hoffman. Reprinted by permission of the publisher, E. P. Dutton, a division of Penguin Books USA, Inc.

From "Loveliest of Trees, the Cherry Now" in *The Collected Poems of A.E. Housman* by A.E. Housman. Copyright © 1939, 1940, 1965 by Holt, Rinehart and Winston. Copyright © 1967, 1968 by Robert E. Symons. Reprinted by permission of Henry Holt and Company, Inc.

"The Market Man" by John Ratti. Copyright © 1964 by *Harper's Magazine*. All rights reserved. Reprinted from January 1965 issue by special permission.

From *The Measure of the Universe* by Isaac Asimov. Copyright © 1983 by Isaac Asimov. Reprinted by permission of Harper & Row, Publishers, Inc.

From *Memoirs of Hector Berlioz: From 1803-1865* translated by Rachel and Eleanor Holmes, revised and annotated by Ernest Newman. Copyright © 1932 by Alfred A. Knopf, Inc. Copyright © 1960 by Vera Newman. Reprinted by permission of Alfred A. Knopf, Inc.

From "Microbots" by T. A. Heppenheimer in *Discover* magazine, March 1989. Reprinted by permission of Family Media, Inc.

From "Microsensors Make Their Mark in A Wide Variety of Products" by Brenton R. Schlender in the *Wall Street Journal*, November 21, 1986 issue. Reprinted by permission.

From *Midnight Sweets* by Bette Pesetsky. Copyright © 1988 by Bette Pesetsky. Reprinted by permission of Atheneum, an imprint of Macmillan Publishing Company, and Goodman Associates.

From "Mother Dear and Daddy" by Junius Edwards. Copyright © 1962 by John A. Williams.

From "Motors No Wider Than a Human Hair" by Ian Anderson in *New Scientist* magazine, September 1, 1988. Reprinted by permission of New Science Publications.

From "New Generation of Tiny Motors Challenges Science to Find Uses" by Andrew Pollack in *The New York Times*, July 26, 1988. Reprinted by permission of The New York Times Company.

"Not Waving but Drowning" in *Poems of Stevie Smith* by Stevie Smith. Copyright © 1972 by Stevie Smith. Reprinted by permission of New Directions Publishing Corporation.

From "On Summer" by Lorraine Hansberry from *Playbill Magazine*, June 1960 (New York, NY: Playbill Incorporated, 1960)

From *Out of Africa* by Isak Dinesen. Copyright © 1937, 1938 by Random House, Inc. Copyright © renewed 1965 by Rungstedlundfonden. Reprinted by permission of Random House, Inc.

From "The Passing" by Durango Mendoza. Copyright © 1981.

From *A People and A Nation* (Brief, second edition) by Norton et al. Copyright © 1988 by Houghton Mifflin Company. Reprinted by permission of Houghton Mifflin Company.

From "The Phoenix" in the *Cat's Cradle-Book* by Sylvia Townsend Warner. Copyright © 1940 by Sylvia Townsend Warner. Reprinted by permission of the Executors of the Sylvia Townsend Warner Estate.

From *Pilgrim at Tinker Creek* by Annie Dillard. Copyright © 1974 by Annie Dillard. Reprinted by permission of Harper & Row, Publishers, Inc. and Blanche C. Gregory, Inc.

From "Portrait of Inman Page: A Dedication Speech" from *Going to the Territory* by Ralph Ellison. Copyright © 1986 by Ralph Ellison. Originally appeared in *The Carleton Miscellany*, Vol. XVIII, No. 3, Winter 1980. Reprinted by permission of Carleton College, William Morris Agency, and Random House, Inc.

From "Prologue: To The Reader" in *Three Exemplary Novels by Miguel de Cervantes Saavedra*, translated by Samuel Putnam. Copyright © 1950 by The Viking Press. Copyright renewed © 1978 by Hilary Putnam. Reprinted by permission of Viking Penguin, a division of Penguin Books USA, Inc.

From *Psychology* by Bernstein et al. Copyright © 1988 by Houghton Mifflin Company. Reprinted by permission of Houghton Mifflin Company.

"Reconnaissance," "Nocturne of the Wharves," and "A Black Man Talks of Reaping" from *Personals* by Arna Bontemps. Copyright © 1963 by Arna Bontemps. Reprinted by permission of Harold Ober Incorporated.

"River Skater" in *Blossoming Antlers* by Winifred Welles. Copyright © 1933 by Winifred Welles. Reprinted by permission of Viking Penguin, Inc.

From *Roget's II: The New Thesaurus* (Expanded Edition). Copyright © 1988 by Houghton Mifflin Company. Adapted and reprinted by permission of Houghton Mifflin Company.

From *Roget's International Thesaurus* (Fourth Edition) revised by Robert L. Chapman. Copyright © 1911, 1977 by Harper & Row, Publishers, Inc. Reprinted by permission of Harper & Row, Publishers, Inc.

From "Scholars Track the Alphabet With New Precision" by John Noble Wilford, in *The New York Times*, November 8, 1988. Reprinted by permission of The New York Times Company.

From *Science and Human Values* by Jacob Bronowski. Copyright © 1956, 1965 by Jacob Bronowski. Reprinted by permission of Julian Messner, a Simon & Schuster division of Gulf & Western Corporation.

From "The Sculptor's Funeral" in *The Troll Garden* by Willa Sibert Cather. Copyright © 1905 by McClure, Phillips & Company. Reprinted by permission of Macmillan Publishing Company.

"Shaving" by Leslie Norris. First appeared in *Atlantic* magazine, April 1977. copyright © 1977 by Leslie Norris. Reprinted by permission of Gibbs Smith, Inc., and Seren Books.

"Si el azul no existe" ("If Blue Doesn't Exist") by Delia Quiñónez, translated by Pamela Carmell from *IXOK AMAR GO: Central American Women's Poetry for Peace,* edited by Zoë Anglesey. Reprinted by permission.

From *Six Men* by Alistair Cooke. Copyright © 1977 by Alistair Cooke. Reprinted by permission of Alfred A. Knopf, Inc.

From *A Small Town in Germany* by John le Carré. Copyright © 1968 by Le Carré Productions, Ltd. Reprinted by permission of The Putnam Publishing Group.

From "A Small World Grows Tinier" by William D. Marbach in *Newsweek* magazine, November 30, 1987 issue. Copyright © 1987 by Newsweek, Inc. Reprinted by permission of Newsweek, Inc.

From "Song" by William Carlos Williams in *The Collected Poems of William Carlos Williams, Vol. II (1939-1962).* copyright © 1944 by William Carlos Williams. Reprinted by permission of New Directions Publishing Corporation and Carcenet Press, Ltd.

From "Sonny's Blues" in *Going to Meet the Man* by James Baldwin. Copyright © 1957 by James Baldwin. Reprinted by permission of Doubleday, a division of Bantam, Doubleday, Dell Publishing Group, Inc.

From "A State for All Seasons" in *America from the Road* edited by Carroll C. Calkins. Copyright © 1982 by the Reader's Digest Association, Inc. Reprinted by permission of the Reader's Digest Association, Inc.

From "Strike Out Little League" by Robin Roberts in *Newsweek*, July 21, 1975. Reprinted by permission.

"Symptoms of Love" in *Collected Poems by Robert Graves*. Copyright © 1958, 1965 by Robert Graves. Reprinted by permission of Oxford University Press, and A. P. Watt, Ltd.

From *Testament of Youth* by Vera Brittain. Copyright © 1970 by Literary Executors of Vera Brittain. Reprinted by permission of Viking Penguin, Inc. and Victor Gollancz, Ltd.

"That Dark Other Mountain" in *Robert Francis: Collected Poems, 1936-1976*. Copyright © 1944, 1972 by Robert Francis. Reprinted by permission of the University of Massachusetts Press.

"La Tierra Recobrada" ("The Earth Recovered") by Vidaluz Meneses, translated by Zoë Anglesey from *IXOK AMAR GO: Central American Women's Poetry for Peace*, edited by Zoë Anglesey. Reprinted by permission.

"Time" from *Collected Poems by Mary Ursula Bethell*. Copyright © 1985 by The Estate of Mary Ursula Bethell. Reprinted by permission of Oxford University Press.

From *Tracks* by Louise Erdrich. Copyright © 1988 by Louise Erdrich. Reprinted by permission of Henry Holt and Company, Inc.

From *Travels with Charley* by John Steinbeck. Copyright © 1962 by John Steinbeck. Copyright © 1961, 1962 by Curtis Publishing Co. Reprinted by permission of Viking Penguin, a division of Penguin Books USA, Inc.

"University Curriculum:" in "Fables for Love" *(Poems New and Selected)* by Bill Turner. Copyright © 1962 by Bill Turner. Reprinted by permission of the author.

From "Will Diversity = Opportunity + Advancement for Blacks?" by Sheryl Hilliard Tucker and Kevin D. Thompson in *Black Enterprise*, November 1990, p. 52 and 54. Copyright © November 1990 by Earl G. Graves Publishing Co, Inc. Reprinted by permission.

From *The Way Things Work: An Illustrated Encyclopedia* translated by C. van Amerongen. Copyright © 1967 by George Allen & Unwin, Ltd. Reprinted by permission of Unwin Hyman, Ltd.

From *West with the Night* by Beryl Markham. Copyright © 1942, 1983 by Beryl Markham. Reprinted by permission of North Point Press.

"When You Are Old" in *The Collected Poems of W. B. Yeats* by W. B. Yeats. Copyright © 1903, 1956 by The Macmillan Company. Copyright © 1940 by Georgie Yeats.

From *Who Pushed Humpty Dumpty?* by Donald Barr. Copyright © 1958, 1971 by Donald Barr. Reprinted by permission of Atheneum, an imprint of Macmillan Publishing Company.

From *Wilma* by Wilma Rudolph. Copyright © 1977 by Bud Greenspan. Reprinted by permission of New American Library, a division of Penguin Books USA Inc.

"Word" in *Stephen Spender Selected Poems* by Stephen Spender. Copyright © 1942, 1964 by Stephen Spender. Reprinted by permission of Pantheon Books, a division of Random House, Inc., and Faber & Faber, Ltd.

"Written in the Sunset" from Kenneth Rexroth: *Women Poets of China*. Copyright © 1973 by Kenneth Rexroth and Ling Chung. Reprinted by permission of New Directions Publishing Corporation.

Definitions for the words listed in Dictionary Plus are based on *The American Heritage Electronic Dictionary*, copyright © 1990, but some have been abbreviated, augmented, or otherwise adapted for instructional purposes. The pronunciation key is from *The American Heritage Dictionary, Second College Edition*, copyright © 1985.

Credits

Book design and production: Textart, Inc.

Cover photograph: Tony Craddock/Tony Stone Worldwide

Unit opener photography: Ken Karp

Photo research: Photosearch, Inc.

Technical art: Network Graphics

Logo illustration: Mark Kaplan

Calligraphy: Jon Valk

Photographs

vii Ellis Herwig/Stock, Boston viii Joseph Nettis/Photo Researchers ix Herbert Eisenberg/Shostal x Richard Pasley/Stock, Boston xi Timothy Eagan/Woodfin Camp xiii Carlos Vergaza/Nawrocki Stock Photo 9 Michal Heron 10 D. Brewster/Bruce Coleman Inc. 14 J. C. Carton/Bruce Coleman Inc. 20 David Maenza/The Image Bank 26 David Madison/Bruce Coleman Inc. 30 Peter Menzel/Stock, Boston 32 Charles Gupton/Stock, Boston 40 Tom McHugh/Photo Researchers 42 Y. Arthus-Bertrand/Peter Arnold 47 John Spragens, Jr./Photo Researchers 50 Susan Van Etten/The Picture Cube 56 Sheryl McNee/TSW–Click, Chicago 59 Alexander Lowry/Photo Researchers 66 Peter Menzel/Stock, Boston 70 Culver Pictures 78 William Meyer/TSW–Click, Chicago 91 Robert Daemmrich/TSW–Click, Chicago 100 Culver Pictures 102 John Chard/TSW–Click, Chicago 104 Richard Hutchings 109 Will McIntyre/Photo Researchers 113 Timothy Eagan/Woodfin Camp 116(l) Ray Reiss/Nawrocki Stock Photo 116(r) Ray Manley/Shostal 117 Private Collection 118(b) Culver Pictures 118(t) Superstock 119 Steve Vidler/Nawrocki Stock Photo 126 George Holton/Photo Researchers 130 Joe Collins/Photo Researchers 136 Gianni Tortoli/Photo Researchers 139 D.E. Cox/TSW-Click, Chicago 141(b) David Ellis/The Picture Cube 141(t) Phil Ellis/The Picture Cube 150 UPI/Bettmann Newsphotos 151(b) Tom McHugh/Photo Researchers 151(t) Culver Pictures 153(l) Christiana Dittman/Rainbow 154(r) Ellis Herwig/Stock, Boston 155 The Bettmann Archive 156(b) Bill Barley/Shostal 156(t) Lawrence Migdal/Stock, Boston 157 Norman Owen Tomalin/Bruce Coleman Inc. 160 Leonore Weber/Taurus 161 AP/Wide World Photos 172 The Bettmann Archive 187 Eric Lessing/Magnum Photos 189(l) Bob Daemmrich/Stock, Boston 189(r) © 1989 Martha Swope 190(l) Hank Morgan/Rainbow 191(l) James H. Carmichael/The Image Bank 191(r) E. R. Degginger/Bruce Coleman Inc. 192(b) The Bettmann Archive 192(t) Dan McCoy/Rainbow 200 B.J. Spenceley/Bruce Coleman 208 Schnepps/The Image Bank 215 Michael Sulas/The Image Bank 217 Frank Whitny/The Image Bank 224 Vernon Ezell/Nawrocki Stock Photo 225(l) Jewele Craig/Shostal 225(r) Culver Pictures 226(l) Malak/Shostal 226(m) © 1989 by the New York Times Company. Reprinted by permission. 226(r) Joseph Nettis/Photo Researchers 227(t) Paolo Koch/Photo Researchers 228 David Frazier/Photo Researchers 229(b) The Bettmann Archive 232 Martin Rogers/Stock, Boston 236 Cary Wolinsky/Stock, Boston 243 Richard Pasley/Stock, Boston 247 Jeffrey M. Hamilton/Stock, Boston 250 Shostal 255 David Madison/Bruce Coleman 259 Rob Nelson/Stock, Boston 267 Stacy Pick/Stock, Boston 268 Eric Carle/Shostal 269 D. C. Lowe/TSW-Click, Chicago 270(l) Private Collection 270(r) Bob Daemmrich/Stock, Boston 271(b) Dean Krakel II/Photo

Researchers **271**(t) Private Collection **273** D.P. Hershkowitz/Bruce Coleman **274**(b) Dean Krakel II/Photo Researchers **274**(t) Roy W. Hankey/Photo Researchers Inc. **277**(b) Culver Pictures **277**(t) Linda Barlett/Photo Researchers **280** Joan Menschenfreund/Taurus Photos **283** Peter Runyon/The Image Bank **295** Larry Gatz/ The Image Bank **302** Peter Turner/The Image Bank **307** Janeart Ltd./The Image Bank **318** Syd Greenberg/ Photo Researchers **320** Felice Frankel **322**(t) Daniel Zirinsky/Photo Researchers **324** Lara Hartley/Nawrocki Stock Photo **326**(b) Cary Wolinsky/Stock, Boston **326**(t) Peter Southwick/Stock, Boston **328**(b) Herbert Eisenberg/Shostal **328**(t) Deborah Kahn/Stock, Boston **336** Timothy Eagen/Woodfin Camp **340** Grant Heilman Photography **348** The Bettmann Archive **359** Culver Pictures **361** Martha Swope **369**(b) Adam Woolfitt/Woodfin Camp **369**(t) Susan McCartney/Photo Researchers **370** Culver Pictures **371**(t) Richard Hutchings/Photo Researchers **371**(bl) UPI/Bettmann Newsphotos **372**(br) Hank Morgan/Rainbow **372**(t) 1988 Guido, reprinted courtesy of the artist **374**(bl) John Ficara/Woodfin Camp **374**(br) Culver Pictures **374**(t) Museum of Science, Boston **375** Richard Pasley/Stock, Boston **378** Superstock **380** The Bettmann Archive **387** Dan McCoy/Rainbow **393** Gregory Heisler/The Image Bank **394** Wright State University **398** University of California at Berkeley **406** AT&T Bell Labs/Peter Arnold **413** Erwin & Peggy Bauer/ Bruce Coleman Inc. **418** Culver Pictures **431** Culver Pictures **432** Tony Angermeyer/Photo Researchers **433** Bob Daemmrich/the Image Works **521** John Ebeling/Bruce Coleman Inc. **526** The Los Angeles Museum of Natural History **527** Bruce Robert/Photo Researches **579** Peter Kaplan/Photo Researchers **590** Culver Pictures **599** Peter Tenzer/Wheeler Pictures **611**(b) Edward Lettau/Photo Researchers **611**(t) Comstock Inc. **612** Manley Photo/Shostal **613**(t) Ibid. **614**(l) Private Collection **614**(m) Superstock **614**(r) Chuck O'Rear/Woodfin Camp **618** The Bettmann Archive **626** Keystone View/F.P.G. **640** UPI/Bettmann Newsphotos **655** The Bettmann Archive **661** Culver Pictures **667** Acme/Photo Researchers **669** The Bettmann Archive **681** Ken Cohen/Photoworks/F.P.G. **698** The Bettmann Archive **700** Culver Pictures **701** Momatiuk/Eastcott/ Woodfin Camp **702**(bl) Carlos Vergaza/Nawrocki Stock Photo **702**(r) Harlee Little **702**(tl) Bill Barley/Shostal **703** Courtesy of Columbia University **720** Robert Llewellyn **723** Purdue University **728** The Bettmann Archive **732** Jerry Cooke/Photo Researchers **736** The Library of Congress **746** Robert Phillips/The Image Bank **747** Gary Gladstone/The Image Bank **749**(b) Bill Weems/Woodfin Camp **749**(t) Kevin Galvin/Bruce Coleman Inc.

Fine Art

xii "St. Mark's Square, Venice," Rennaissance painting. Coll: Conde Museum, Chantilly, France. Photo: Giraudon/Art Resource **18** Art adapted from article entitled "Teaching Word Englishes" by Braj. B. Kachru in ERIC/CLL News Bulletin, Sept. 1988. **37** *Vanity Fair* cover, 1930's of painting by Frances Perkins. Photo: Culver Pictures **74** Prehistoric cave painting of bison from the caves at Altamira, Spain. Photo: Art Resource **83** Culver Pictures **94** Culver Pictures **111** *Don Quixote* by Honoré Daumier, oil on canvas. Coll: The National Gallery, Washington, D.C. **111** *Sinbad the Sailor* by Paul Klee, Hinz Allschwell, Basel **154** *Italian Family at Ellis Island, New York* by Lewis Hine, photograph, 1905. Photo: The Bettmann Archive **166** Culver Pictures **180** Culver Pictures **190**(r) Ivory tablet sundial, 16th century. Coll: Science Museum, London. Photo: The Bridgeman Art Library/Art Resource **193**(l) "Jacob's Staff," woodcut. Photo: The Bettmann Archive **193**(r) *Numbers in Color* by Jasper Johns, encaustic and newspaper on canvas, 1959. Coll: Albright-Knox Art Gallery, Buffalo, N.Y., Gift of Seymour H. Knox, 1959. **206** Jewish omer calendar, Italian, cloisonne enamel. Coll: The Jewish Museum, New York. Photo: Art Resource. **223** *Whaleboat Comes to Grief* (detail) after a painting by Ambrose Garnery, lithograph, mid-19th century. Coll: The Shelburne Museum/Shelburne, Vt. **229**(t) "The Money Changer" (detail) from *Codice di Sphere* by Marco del'Avogaro. Coll: Bibliotéca Estense, Modena. Photo: Scala/Art Resource **271**(b) Culver Pictures **272**(b) *Portrait of the Duke of Osuna with his Children* by Francisco de Goya, oil on canvas, 1788. Coll: The Prado Museum, Madrid. Photo: Scala/Art Resource **272**(t) *Generations* by Jacob Lawrence, gouache on paper, 1967. Photo: Chris Eden **275** The Bettmann Archive **276** *Dinner Quilt* by Faith Ringgold, 1986. Coll: Lynnh Plotkin, Courtesy of Bernice Steinbaum Gallery, N.Y. **321** *Tamalada* by Carmen Lomas Garza, gouache on paper, © 1987. Photo: Wolfgang Pidze **322**(bl) Culver Pictures **322**(br) United Press Syndicate, reprinted by permission **323** Nawrocki Stock Photo **325** Drawing by E. Koren. © 1971 *The New Yorker* Magazine, Inc. **327** "Clock Sculpture" by Arman, 20th century. Photo: Mark Antman/The Image Works **523** Renaissance print shop, woodcut, 1520. Photo: The Bettmann Archive **524** *Samuel Johnson* by Sir Joshua Reynolds, oil on canvas, 1769. Coll: The Tate Gallery, London **530**(l) *God Separating Land from Sea* by Michelangelo, fresco, detail from the ceiling of the Sistine Chapel, St. Peter's Rome. Photo: Scala/Art Resource **530**(r) "St. Mark's Square, Venice," Rennaissance painting. Coll: Condé Museum, Chantilly, France. Photo: Giraudon/Art Resource **531**(l) S. Fisher Verlag, Berlin, 1930. Coll: Max Polster Archive **531**(r) *Elizabeth I* by Ditchley, oil on canvas. Photo: Superstock **534** Historical Pictures Service Chicago. **540** *Sir Thomas More* by Hans Holbein, oil on canvas. Coll: The Frick Collection, New York **543** Culver Pictures **545** *Voyages* by Theodore de Bry, 1590. Coll: Rare Book Division, New York Public Library **548** Historical Pictures Service Chicago **560** The Bettmann Archive **568** The Bettmann Archive **575** The Bettmann Archive **583** The Bettmann Archive **587** Historical Pictures Service Chicago **596** *Story of St. Francis* by Giotto. Coll: Church of St. Francis, Assisi, Italy. Photo: Scala/Art Resource **610** The Bettmann Archive **613** *Old Man and his Grandson* by Domenico Bigordi Ghirlandaio, oil and tempera on wood, late 15th century. Coll: The Louvre Museum, Paris, Photo: Giraudon/Art Resource **615** Georgia O'Keeffe and her sculpture *Abstraction*, 20th century. Photo: Rich Browne/Stock Boston **629** The Bettmann Archive **674** *Nicholas* by Andrew Wyeth, oil, 1955. Coll: Nicholas Wyeth, New York. Photo: Ken Cohen **687** Culver Pictures **699** The Bettmann Archive **730** Historical Pictures Service

Celebrating Diversity

Photographs

A1-A2 (inset) © Joe Viesti/Viesti Associates **A1-A2** (background), **A5** © Barry Hennings/Photo Researchers **A2, A6** (insets) © Alfred Geschedt/The Image Bank **A4** © Michael Quackenbush/ The Image Bank **A3-A4** The Bettmann Archive **B1-B2, B3, B4, B5** © Jeff Apoian/Nawrocki Stock Photo **B2** (inset) Courtesy the National Museum of the American Indian, Smithsonain Institution **B4** Courtesy Peabody Museum, Harvard University **B6** © C. Pinson/Photo Researchers **C1-C2** UPI/Bettmann Newsphotos **C1** Associated Press **C3-C4** AP/Wide World Photos **C4** UPI/Bettmann Newsphotos **C5-C6** UPI/Bettmann **C5** AP/Wide World Photos **D12** © Ted Horowitz/The Stock Market **D1-D2** © Photo Researchers **D3**(t) © Tim Davis/Photo Researchers **D3** © Henley & Savage/The Stock Market

D4 © Stan Pantovic/Photo Researchers D5-D6 © Grapes/ Michaud/Photo Researchers E1 Courtesy The University of Florida E2 © Carol Fields/Superstock E3 Courtesy the Belo Estate E4 © Grant Heilman/Grant Heilman Photography E5 © David Lissey/The Photo File E6 The Bettmann Archive F1-F2 © Kenneth L. Miller/ Uniphoto Picture Agency F3 © Felicia Martinez/PhotoEdit F4 © Mark E. Gibson/The Stock Market F5 © Phil Conklin/Uniphoto Picture Agency F5-F6 © Obremski/The Image Bank G1 © NASA/Science Source/Photo Researchers G3-G4 © Don Carroll/The Image Bank G4 © Abe Frajndlich/Sygma G6 The Granger Collection, New York G5-G6 © Cliff Feulner/The Image Bank H1-H2 Courtesy Frank Driggs Collection H1 UPI/Bettmann H3-H4 Courtesy Frank Driggs Collection H3 © Van Bucher/ Photo Researchers H4 Courtesy The Metropolitan Museum of Art, Gift of The James Van DerZee Institute, 1970. (1970.539.64) H5-H6 Courtesy Frank Driggs Collection I1-I2 © Tony Stone Worldwide I3 © William Roy/The Stock Market I4 © Ted Levin/ Earth Scenes I5-I6 © Paul Steel/The Stock Market J1 © Spencer Grant/Photo Researchers J2(t) © Eunice Harris/Photo Researchers J2(b) Courtesy Brown University J4(tl) © John Foraste/Brown University J4(bl) © Allen Green/Photo Researchers J4(r) © Gabe Palmer/Mugshots J5-J6 © John Foraste/Brown University

Fine Art
B1 Native American (Chippewa) beaded buckskin moccasins. Coll: Texas Memorial Museum, Austin. Photo: © Bob Daemmrich B3-B4 Native American (Southeast Ojibway) pouch. Coll. Peabody Museum, Harvard University. Photo: Hillel Burger E1, E3, E4, E6 (details) Appliqué quilt by Sarah Ann Wilson, ca. 1854. Photo: Courtesy America Hurrah antiques, NYC G2 Hindu cosmogram, from an ancient Hindu ceramic. Photo: The Granger Collection, New York.

Revising Checklist

Focus *(pages 66–69)*	• Does the topic sentence or the thesis statement clearly indicate the topic and its focusing idea? • Does each sentence develop and support the topic sentence or the thesis statement? What, if anything, might be cut? • Is the writing clearly organized? What, if anything, might be moved? • Is there enough support for the topic sentence or the thesis statement? What, if anything, might be added? • Are there clear connections between sentences and paragraphs? • Does each paragraph build toward a closing sentence? • Does the conclusion create a sense of closure? Does it echo the topic and its focusing idea?
Sentence Structure *(pages 71–86)*	• Are sentences combined effectively? • Are combined sentence parts parallel in structure? • Are all sentences as concise as possible? • Are all sentences clear and coherent? • Do the most important ideas receive emphasis? • Are the sentences varied in their beginnings, structure, and lengths?
Style and Tone *(pages 87–96)*	• Is the choice of words accurate, effective, and appropriate? • Is figurative language used effectively? • Is the level of formality appropriate? • Is the tone consistent?

Proofreading Checklist

- Have I eliminated **fragments** and **run–ons?**
- Have I checked **conjunctions** for effectiveness and clarity?
- Have I used **parallel structure** for items in a series?
- Have I used correct and consistent **verb tense?**
- Have I made all **subjects and verbs agree?**
- Have I used pronouns with **clear antecedents?** Do they agree?
- Have I eliminated misplaced **modifiers** and used correct forms?
- Have I used correct **capitalization?**
- Have I used correct **punctuation?**
- Have I handled **quotation marks** correctly?
- Have I checked all **word usage?**
- Have I used **apostrophes** correctly?
- Have I used **underlining** correctly?
- Have I correctly used **numerals** or spelled out **numbers?**
- Have I **spelled** all words correctly?